COGNITIVE DEVELOPMENT

COGNITIVE DEVELOPMENT

Critical Concepts in Psychology

Edited by Usha Goswami

Volume IV
The Development of Literacy and Numeracy,
and Aspects of Atypical Development
(Dyslexia, Dyscalculia and Autism)

Routledge
Taylor & Francis Group
LONDON AND NEW YORK

First published 2007
by Routledge
2 Park Square, Milton Park, Abingdon, Oxon, OX14 4RN

Simultaneously published in the USA and Canada
by Routledge
270 Madison Avenue, New York, NY 10016

Routledge is an imprint of the Taylor & Francis Group, an informa business

Typeset in 10/12pt Times by Graphicraft Limited, Hong Kong
Printed and bound in Great Britain by
TJI Digital, Padstow, Cornwall

British Library Cataloguing in Publication Data
A catalogue record for this book is available from the British Library

Library of Congress Cataloging in Publication Data
A catalog record for this book has been requested

ISBN10: 0-415-36063-3 (Set)
ISBN10: 0-415-36067-6 (Volume IV)

ISBN13: 978-0-415-36063-0 (Set)
ISBN13: 978-0-415-36067-8 (Volume IV)

Publisher's Note

References within each chapter are as they appear in the original complete work

CONTENTS

CONTENTS

CONTENTS

ACKNOWLEDGEMENTS

The publishers would like to thank the following for permission to reprint their material:

Macmillan Publishers for permission to reprint L. Bradley and P. E. Bryant, 'Categorizing sounds and learning to read – a causal connection', *Nature*, 301, pp. 419–420, © 1983, Macmillan Publishers Limited.

Cambridge University Press and Linnea C. Ehri for permission to reprint Linnea C. Ehri and Lee S. Wilce, 'The influence of orthography on readers' conceptualization of the phonemic structure of words', *Applied Psycholinguistics*, 1, pp. 371–385, © 1980 Cambridge University Press.

Reprinted from the *Journal of Experimental Child Psychology*, 42, Usha Goswami, 'Children's use of analogy in learning to read: a developmental study', pp. 73–83, © 1986, with permission from Elsevier.

Reprinted from the *Journal of Experimental Child Psychology*, 18, Isabelle Y. Liberman, Donald Shankweiler, F. William Fischer and Bonnie Carter, 'Explicit syllable and phoneme segmentation in the young child', pp. 201–212, © 1974, with permission from Elsevier.

Blackwell Publishing for permission to reprint Ingvar Lundberg, Åke Olofsson and Stig Wall, 'Reading and spelling skills in the first school years predicted from phonemic awareness skills in kindergarten', *Scandinavian Journal of Psychology*, 21 (Oxford: Blackwell, 1980), pp. 159–173.

Reprinted from *Cognition*, 7, José Morais, Luz Cary, Jésus Alegria and Paul Bertelson, 'Does awareness of speech as a sequence of phones arise spontaneously?', pp. 323–331, © 1979, with permission of Elsevier.

The American Psychological Association and Joanna Williams for permission to reprint Joanna P. Williams, 'Teaching decoding with an emphasis on phoneme analysis and phoneme blending', *Journal of Educational Psychology*, 72, pp. 1–15, © 1980 by the American Psychological Association.

ACKNOWLEDGEMENTS

The International Reading Association and J. Richard Gentry for permission to reprint J. Richard Gentry, 'An analysis of developmental spelling in *GNYS AT WRK*', *The Reading Teacher*, 36, 1982, pp. 192–200.

The British Psychological Society for permission to reprint Jane Oakhill, 'Constructive processes in skilled and less skilled comprehenders' memory for sentences', © *British Journal of Psychology*, 73, 1982, pp. 13–20.

The International Reading Association and Annemarie Sullivan Palincsar for permission to reprint Annemarie Sullivan Palincsar and Ann L. Brown, 'Interactive teaching to promote independent learning from text', *The Reading Teacher*, 39, 1986, pp. 771–777.

The British Psychological Society for permission to reprint Terezinha Nunes Carraher, David William Carraher and Analúcia Dias Schliemann, 'Mathematics in the streets and in schools', © *British Journal of Developmental Psychology*, 3, 1985, pp. 21–29.

The American Association for the Advancement of Science for permission to reprint Prentice Starkey & Robert G. Cooper, Jr., 'Perception of numbers by human infants', *Science*, 210, pp. 1033–1035, © 1980 AAAS.

Blackwell Publishing for permission to reprint Sue Ellen Antell and Daniel P. Keating, 'Perception of numerical invariance in neonates', *Child Development*, 54 (Oxford: Blackwell, 1983), pp. 695–701.

Reprinted from *Cognitive Development*, 3, Olivier Frydman and Peter Bryant, 'Sharing and the understanding of number equivalence by young children', pp. 323–339, © 1988, with permission from Elsevier.

Blackwell Publishing for permission to reprint Geoffrey B. Saxe, 'A developmental analysis of notational counting', *Child Development*, 48 (Oxford: Blackwell, 1977), pp. 1512–1520.

Reprinted from *Cognition*, 13, Rochel Gelman and Elizabeth Meck, 'Preschoolers' counting: principles before skill', pp. 343–360, © 1983, with permission from Elsevier.

Blackwell Publishing for permission to reprint Irene T. Miura, Chungsoon C. Kim, Chih-Mei Chang and Yukari Okamoto, 'Effects of language characteristics on children's cognitive representation of number: cross-national comparisons', *Child Development*, 59 (Oxford: Blackwell, 1988), pp. 1445–1450.

Macmillan Publishers for permission to reprint Karen Wynn, 'Addition and subtraction by human infants', *Nature*, 358, pp. 749–750, © 1992 Macmillan Publishers Limited.

Cambridge University Press and Lorna Wing for permission to reprint Lorna Wing, 'Asperger's syndrome: a clinical account', *Psychological Medicine*, 11, pp. 115–129, © 1981 Cambridge University Press.

Blackwell Publishing for permission to reprint Susan Folstein and Michael Rutter, 'Infantile autism: a genetic study of 21 twin pairs', *Journal of Child Psycholology and Psychiatry*, 18 (Oxford: Blackwell, 1977), pp. 297–321.

Blackwell Publishing for permission to reprint Amitta Shah and Uta Frith (1993), 'Why do autistic individuals show superior performance on the block design task?', *Journal of Child Psychology and Psychiatry*, 34 (Oxford: Blackwell, 1993), pp. 1351–1364.

Blackwell Publishing for permission to reprint Francesca G. E. Happé, 'Studying weak central coherence at low levels: children with autism do not succumb to visual illusions. A research note', *Journal of Child Psychology and Psychiatry*, 37 (Oxford: Blackwell, 1996), pp. 873–877.

Springer Science & Business Media and Sally Ozonoff for permission to reprint Sally Ozonoff and Jenise Jensen, 'Brief report: specific executive function profiles in three neurodevelopmental disorders', *Journal of Autism and Developmental Disorders*, 29, 1999, pp. 171–177.

Macmillan Publishers for permission to reprint L. Bradley and P. E. Bryant, 'Difficulties in auditory organisation as a possible cause of reading backwardness', *Nature*, 271, 1978, pp. 746–747, © Macmillan Publishers Limited.

The British Psychological Society for permission to reprint B. Rodgers, 'The identification and prevalence of specific reading retardation', © *British Journal of Educational Psychology*, 53, 1983, pp. 369–373.

Blackwell Publishing for permission to reprint Hollis S. Scarborough, 'Very early language deficits in dyslexic children', *Child Development*, 61 (Oxford: Blackwell, 1990), pp. 1728–1743.

Reprinted from the *Journal of Experimental Child Psychology*, 29, Margaret J. Snowling, 'The development of grapheme–phoneme correspondence in normal and dyslexic readers', pp. 294–305, © 1980, with permission from Elsevier.

The American Psychological Association and Maggie Bruck for permission to reprint Maggie Bruck, 'Persistence of dyslexics' phonological awareness deficits', *Developmental Psychology*, 28, pp. 874–886, © 1992 by the American Psychological Association.

Blackwell Publishing for permission to reprint Keith E. Stanovich, 'Does dyslexia exist?', *Journal of Child Psychology and Psychiatry*, 35 (Oxford: Blackwell, 1994), pp. 579–595.

Lippincott Williams & Wilkins for permission to reprint Bruce F. Pennington and Shelley D. Smith, 'Genetic analysis of dyslexia and other complex behavioral phenotypes', *Current Opinion in Pediatrics*, 9, pp. 636–641. Copyright © 1997 Lippincott Williams & Wilkins – All Rights Reserved.

Cortex for permission to reprint Ruth S. Shalev, Raaya Weirtman and Naomi Amir, 'Developmental dyscalculia', *Cortex*, 24, 1988, pp. 555–561.

Mac Keith Press for permission to reprint Neil Gordon, 'Children with developmental dyscalculia', *Developmental Medicine and Child Neurology*, 34, 1992, pp. 459–463.

Disclaimer

INTRODUCTION

Over the course of time, human beings have invented two symbolic systems that have transformed culture and society. These are the number system and writing systems such as the alphabetic system. Of course, not all cultures use Arabic numerals, and not all cultures use alphabets (some writing systems are based on characters or logographs). Nevertheless, the cultural invention of these systems was possible originally because of certain aspects of human cognition. For example, cognitive skills such as the ability to sort objects into sets and to recognise which set was more numerous underpinned mathematical development. Skills linked to spoken language processing underpinned reading development. It is unreasonable to expect each child to reinvent or intuitively understand the symbol systems that we now take for granted. Children have to be taught the alphabetic and counting systems and also how to use them. Understanding the cognitive developments important for language and number, as considered in the readings selected here, can also provide insights about how best to teach them.

The role of brain development in the acquisition of literacy and numeracy is receiving increasing attention. It has been demonstrated that the human brain has dedicated neural circuits for recognising numerosity, and this has led researchers to propose that human infants should have some innate knowledge of number. For reading, it has been shown that the human brain is specialised for language rather than for literacy, but that aspects of the development of the language system are critical for explaining literacy acquisition. In each case, these brain-based explanations have led to better understanding of atypical development, as in dyslexia and dyscalculia. One of the most puzzling forms of atypical cognitive development is childhood autism. Children with autism display a classic 'triad' of impairments, namely atypical social development, atypical language development, and repetitive behaviour/obsessive interests. Theoretical understanding of the basis of these impairments has been hampered by the high degree of learning difficulties and language delay found in children with autism spectrum disorders. As in dyslexia and dyscalculia, however, brain-based theories are turning out to be very helpful.

A landmark paper by Bradley and Bryant (1983) in reading research begins this volume. Bradley and Bryant were among the first researchers to demonstrate the important role of children's awareness of the constituent sounds in words (phonological awareness) for reading acquisition. Phonological awareness skills (rhyme and alliteration) were measured in 400 4- and 5-year-old children, and a causal relationship with their progress in reading and spelling three years later was demonstrated via a training design. The reading by Ehri and Wilce (1980) demonstrated the developmental difficulty of measuring phonological awareness independently of spelling knowledge once children can read. Ehri and Wilce showed that 9-year-olds systematically counted more sounds in words like 'pitch' than in words like 'rich', even though both words have the same number of sounds. The reading by Goswami (1986) introduced the notion that more than one strategy may be useful for reading some alphabetic orthographies. For orthographies like English, which are inconsistent in terms of spelling–sound relations, children are helped by using 'analogies' between letter patterns in words (e.g. using 'beak' as a basis for an analogy to 'peak'). The reading by Liberman and colleagues (1974) is included because it was a classic demonstration of how to measure children's phonological awareness at the syllable and phoneme levels. Liberman et al.'s tasks have now been used in many different languages. Phonological awareness predicts reading acquisition in every language in the world so far studied, and the classic reading by Lundberg et al. (1980) provides one example (for Danish).

Once the brain can read, language skills such as phonological awareness change in fundamental ways. The reading by Morais et al. (1979) was one of the first studies to make this point. Morais et al. demonstrated that adults who have never learned to read have poor awareness of speech as a sequence of phones. *Phoneme* awareness is hence dependent on being taught to read, and not a simple consequence of general cognitive growth. The readings by Williams (1980) and by Gentry (1982) illustrate how basic research in cognitive development can be applied to schooling. Williams describes a programme for teaching reading based on training phonological awareness. Gentry describes how teachers can develop spelling skills by understanding how spelling develops. Once decoding is acquired, reading comprehension and learning from text become critical to educational progress. Oakhill (1982) shows that other cognitive skills, such as the ability to construct memory representations, play an important role in reading comprehension. Palincsar and Brown (1986) demonstrate how such skills can be taught directly to children by their teachers.

Another aspect of cognitive development which is necessary for educational progress is mathematical development. Much of school learning – for example, understanding aspects of the physical and biological sciences – depends on mathematics. The reading by Carraher and her colleagues (1985) shows that children can often use mathematics very competently in their everyday worlds outside the classroom, while displaying a marked lack of competence in school. Brazilian children who worked as street vendors showed impressive skills in mental calculation when selling peanuts and coconut milk, but could not solve analogous sums using pencil and paper. In formal tasks they attempted to use school-taught routines, and made frequent errors. Ideally, teaching should begin from the understandings that children have already developed outside school, building on prior cognitive development.

The idea that human infants have innate knowledge about number is very exciting in this respect, as it suggests that number knowledge might be quite well-developed before children go to school. The reading by Starkey and Cooper (1980) is an early example of evidence for this idea. Using a habituation paradigm, Starkey and Cooper apparently demonstrated that infants aged 22 weeks could discriminate, represent and remember small numbers of items (two and three). The reading by Antell and Keating (1983) presents a similar study with neonates. However, it has become clear that perceptual aspects of the displays used in these studies, such as contour length and surface area, varied as well as the number of items. The infants could well have been making discriminations based on the total 'amount of stuff' in the displays. We now think that knowledge about number develops over time.

The reading by Frydman and Bryant (1988) is an example of a study aimed at discovering the precursor cognitive skills that may be important for understanding number. One such skill is one-to-one correspondence (see Piaget, 1952). In order to count correctly, each object in a set must be counted only once, and given only one number label. One-to-one correspondence is also important for understanding the relations between sets: all sets with the same number are qualitatively equivalent. Frydman and Bryant investigated 4- and 5-year-old children's understanding of this cardinal property of number by using a sharing task. The other crucial property of number is ordinal, and this is reflected by the count sequence. Numbers come in an ordered scale of magnitude, and to count correctly children need to understand that the order of numbers represents an order of increasing magnitude. Piaget (1952) suggested that children first acquire the count sequence as a linguistic routine, and have no understanding of its ordinal properties. The reading by Saxe (1979) provides an example of how to investigate children's acquisition of counting between the ages of 3 and 7. The reading by Gelman and Meck (1983) provides a different example with 3- to 5-year-olds, and the two sets of researchers reach different conclusions regarding children's understanding of the principles underlying counting. This debate is still current (see Bryant & Nunes, 2002).

The reading by Miura and her colleagues (1988) explores the potential effects of language on children's cognitive representations of number. Miura *et al.* make the important point that some languages, such as Korean

3

and Chinese, use transparent labels for numbers (for example, 14 is ten-four). They demonstrate via cross-language comparisons that language facilitates number representations in Asian groups. Finally, the notion that infants might have an innate understanding of number has also remained current. The reading by Wynn (1992), exploring addition and subtraction by 5-month-old infants, played a major role in extending this debate.

Turning to atypical development, the reading by Kanner (1943) can be credited with defining the syndrome of autism, along with a paper by Asperger (1944) published in German. These studies launched the intensive modern enquiry into autism spectrum disorders, and an influential figure in introducing the German literature to the English-speaking world was Wing. Wing's (1981) paper on Asperger's syndrome is included here. There has been debate as to whether autism and Asperger's syndrome are distinct conditions, but our current understanding is that there is a spectrum of severity. Autism spectrum disorders (ASD) have a genetic basis, as revealed by twin studies. The first twin study in English was the reading by Folstein and Rutter (1977). As well as demonstrating high heritability, it showed that twins with identical genes who were discordant for autism generally had severe language impairments linked to the social use of language. One theory is that the problems shown by children with ASD in social communication and language development are explained by a deficit in their ability to identify another person's emotions and thoughts, and thus to understand their behaviour. This theory was developed by Baron-Cohen and his colleagues (see reading 66 in Volume II), who argued that children with ASD had difficulties in developing a 'theory of mind'. Other cognitive-level explanations include information-processing deficits (see reading by Shah and Frith (1993)), and weak 'central coherence' (see reading by Happé (1996)). At one time, an explanation based on deficits in executive functions was also popular (see reading by Ozonoff and Jensen (1999); see also Volume III, readings 82, 83 and 84). Currently the dominant view is that ASD is linked to aspects of brain development, but precisely which aspects is the subject of intense debate.

Atypical development of reading in children is called dyslexia, and is usually diagnosed when reading is significantly poorer than would be expected on the basis of the child's IQ and educational experiences. Earlier readings in this volume documented the importance of phonological skills for successful reading development, and the readings on dyslexia show that a critical developmental aspect is impaired phonological awareness. The classic study by Bradley and Bryant (1978) revealed significant difficulties in recognising rhyme and alliteration, and utilised the important research design of the reading level match. The dyslexic children showed significantly poorer performance in the auditory tasks even when compared to typically-developing children who were *younger* than them, but who could read the same number of words. The dyslexic children appeared to have a specific cognitive deficit that was unrelated to IQ. The question of whether dyslexia is a distinct developmental syndrome or simply the lower end of the normal continuum of under-over-achievement is ongoing. The reading by Rodgers (1983) is a classic paper in this debate. Certainly, the phonological difficulties displayed by children with reading difficulties can be tracked from early in development, as revealed in the reading by Scarborough (1990). These specifically phonological difficulties can be revealed at all ages (see reading by Snowling (1980)), and they persist into adulthood (see reading by Bruck (1992)). Nevertheless, the debate concerning whether dyslexia exists as a distinct developmental syndrome has not gone away (see reading by Stanovich (1994)), even though it is highly heritable. Heritability is addressed in the reading by Pennington and Smith (1997). The final two readings concern developmental dyscalculia, which is under-studied relative to dyslexia. Dyscalculia is also conceptualised as a specific cognitive deficit, comprising an unexpected difficulty in number processing despite normal IQ. An early attempt to explain dyscalculia in terms of neurological development is given as the final reading (Gordon (1992)). As in all areas of cognitive development included in these volumes, more recent papers from the last decade are available electronically. The student is encouraged to consult the many excellent online search engines to discover these papers and track ongoing developments in the field.

References

Bryant, P. and Nunes, N. (2002). Children's understanding of mathematics. In U. Goswami (ed.), *Blackwell Handbook of Childhood Cognitive Development*, pp. 412–440. Oxford: Blackwell.

Piaget, J. (1952). *The Child's Conception of Number*. London: Routledge & Kegan Paul.

CATEGORIZING SOUNDS AND LEARNING TO READ—A CAUSAL CONNECTION

L. Bradley and P. E. Bryant

Source: *Nature*, 301, 1983: 419–420.

Children who are backward in reading are strikingly insensitive to rhyme and alliteration.[1] They are at a disadvantage when categorizing words on the basis of common sounds even in comparison with younger children who read no better than they do. Categorizing words in this way involves attending to their constituent sounds, and so does learning to use the alphabet in reading and spelling. Thus the experiences which a child has with rhyme before he goes to school might have a considerable effect on his success later on in learning to read and to write. We now report the results of a large scale project which support this hypothesis.

Our study combined two different methods. The first was longitudinal. We measured 403 children's skills at sound categorization before they had started to read, and related these to their progress in reading and spelling over the next 4 yr: at the end of this time the size of our group was 368. The second was intensive training in sound categorization or other forms of categorization given to a subsample of our larger group. We used both methods because we reasoned that neither on its own is a sufficient test of a causal hypothesis and that the strengths and weaknesses of the two are complementary. Properly controlled training studies demonstrate cause–effect relationships, but these could be arbitrary; one cannot be sure that such relationships exist in real life. On the other hand longitudinal studies which control for other variables such as intelligence do demonstrate genuine relationships; but it is not certain that these are causal. For example simply to show that children's skills at categorizing sounds predict their success in reading later on would not exclude the possibility that both are determined by some unknown *tertium quid*. Thus the strength of each method makes up for the weakness of the other. Together they can isolate existing relationships and establish whether these are causal.

This combination of methods has not been used in studies of reading or, as far as we can establish, in developmental research in general.

Initially we tested 118 4-yr-olds and 285 5-yr-old children (Table 1) on categorizing sounds. None of the children could read (that is, were able to read any word in the Schonell reading test). Our method, as before[2] was to say three or four words per trial, all but one of which shared a common phoneme (Table 2): the child had to detect the odd word. There were 30 trials. In such a task the child must remember the words as well as categorize their sounds. To control for this we also gave them 30 memory trials: the child heard the same words and had to recall them straightaway. In addition we tested verbal intelligence (EPVT).

At the end of the project (as well as at other times) we gave the children standardized tests of reading and spelling, and we also tested their IQ (WISC/R) to exclude the effects of intellectual differences. To check that our results were specific to reading and spelling and not to educational achievement in general we also included a standardized mathematical test (MATB-NFER), which we administered to 263 of our total sample of 368.

There were high correlations between the initial sound categorization scores and the children's reading and spelling over 3 yr later (Table 3). Stepwise multiple regressions established that these relationships remained strong even when the influence of intellectual level at the time of the initial and the final tests and of differences in memory were removed (Table 3). In every case

Table 1 Details of sample.

	Children initially tested at age 4 yr	Children initially tested at age 5 yr
N at end of project	104	264
Initial tests		
Mean age (months)	58.62	65.52
Mean EPVT	110.62	109.39
Final tests		
Mean age (months)	101.85	101.42
Mean IQ (WISC)	113.38	106.79
Mean reading age (months		
Schonell	103.13	100.03
Neale	105.13	101.30
Mean spelling age (months)		
Schonell	97.27	93.94

Table 2 Examples of words used in initial sound categorization tests and mean scores on these tests.

Sounds in common	4-yr group				5-yr group			
	Words given to children			Mean correct (out of 10)	Words given to children			Mean correct (out of 10)
First sound	*hill*	pig	pin	5.69 (1.90)	bun	bus	*rug*	5.36 (2.29)
	bus	bun	*rug*		*pip*	*hill*	pig	
Middle sound	cot	pot	*hat*	7.53 (1.96)	cot	*hat*	pot	6.89 (2.35)
	pin	bun	gun		*pin*	bun	gun	
End sound	pin	win	*sit*	7.42 (2.09)	win	*sit*	*fin*	6.67 (2.33)
	doll	hop	top		hop	top	pop	

Standard deviations given in parentheses.

Table 3 Correlations between initial sound categorization and final reading and spelling levels.

Correlations between initial scores and final scores

	Sound categorization		Initial scores: EPVT		Memory	
Final scores	4	5	4	5	4	5
Reading: Schonell	0.57	0.44	0.52	0.39	0.40	0.22
Reading: Neale	0.53	0.48	0.52	0.44	0.40	0.25
Spelling: Schonell	0.48	0.44	0.33	0.31	0.33	0.20

Multiple regressions testing relationship of initial sound categorization to final reading and spelling levels

	Schonell reading		Neale reading		Schonell spelling	
	4	5	4	5	4	5
% Of total variance accounted for by all variables	47.98	29.88	47.55	34.52	33.59	24.77
% Of total variance accounted for by sound categorization*	9.84†	4.06†	6.24†	4.56†	8.09†	5.59†

* IQ, EPVT, final CA and memory controlled.
† $P < 0.001$.

categorizing sound accounted for a significant proportion of the variance in reading and spelling with these other factors controlled.

So a definite relationship does exist between a child's skill in categorizing sounds and his eventual success in reading and spelling. The design of the project, for the reasons just given, included a training study as a check that any such relationship is a causal one. 65 children were selected from our sample and divided into four groups closely matched for age, verbal intelligence and their original scores on sound categorization. These children were drawn from those with lower scores on sound categorization (at least two standard deviations below the mean); they could not read when the training began. Starting in the second year of the project two of the groups (I and II) received intensive training in categorizing sounds. The training involved 40 individual sessions which were spread over 2 yr. With the help of coloured pictures of familiar objects the children were taught that the same word shared common beginning (hen, hat), middle (hen, pet) and end (hen, man) sounds with other words and thus could be categorized in different ways. Group I received this training only, but group II in addition was taught, with the help of plastic letters, how each common sound was represented by a letter of the alphabet (see ref. 2 for further details of this method). The other two groups were controls. Group III was also taught over the same period in as many sessions and with the same pictures how to categorize but here the categories were conceptual ones; the children were taught that the same word could be classified in several different ways (for example, hen, bat (animals); hen, pig (farm animals)). Group IV received no training at all.

The training had a considerable effect which was specific to reading and spelling (Table 4). At the end of the project group I (trained on sound categorization only) was ahead of group III (trained on conceptual categorization only) by 3–4 months in standardized tests of reading and spelling. This suggests a causal relationship between sound categorization and reading and spelling. Group II (trained with alphabetic letters as well as on sound categorization) succeeded even better than group I (trained on sound categorization only) in reading and particularly in spelling. This suggests that training in sound categorization is more effective when it also involves an explicit connection with the alphabet. That the relationship is specific to these two skills is shown by the mathematics results where the differences were a great deal smaller.

Analyses of covariance, in which the covariates were the childrens's final IQ scores and their age at the time of the final reading and spelling tests, established that the group differences were significant in the case of reading (Schonell: $F = 5.23$; d.f.3,58; $P < 0.003$. Neale: $F = 7.80$; d.f.3,58; $P < 0.001$) and of spelling ($F = 12.18$; d.f.3,58; $P < 0.001$)) but not in the case of mathematics ($F = 1.64$; d.f.3,39; P, not significant). Post tests (Tukey's HSD) showed that group II was significantly better than both control groups (groups III and IV) in Schonell and in Neale reading ($P < 0.05$) and in Schonell spelling ($P < 0.01$). There was no significant difference between groups I and II (the two groups trained in sound categorization) in the two reading tests but group II did surpass group I in spelling ($P < 0.05$). Although reading and spelling scores in group I were always ahead of those of group III this difference did not reach significance in the post tests. But the consistent 3-4-month superiority of group I over group III does strongly suggest that training in sound categorization affects progress in reading and spelling. Group I was significantly better than group IV (the untrained control group) in the two reading tests and in the spelling test ($P < 0.05$). On the other hand there were no significant differences at all between the two control groups (III and IV).

Put together our longitudinal and training results provide strong support for the hypothesis that the awareness of rhyme and alliteration which children acquire before they go to school, possibly as a result of their experiences at home, has a powerful influence on their eventual success in learning to read and to spell. Although others have suggested a link between phono logical awareness and reading[3-5] our study is the first adequate empirical evidence

Table 4 Training study: details of groups and mean final reading, spelling and mathematics levels.

| | | Mean scores | | | |
| | | Experimental groups | | Control groups | |
	Groups	I	II	III	IV
	N	13	13	26	13
Aptitude tests					
Initial EPVT		103.00	103.00	102.34	102.69
Final IQ (WISC/R)		97.15	101.23	102.96	100.15
Final educational tests					
Schonell: reading age (months)		92.23	96.96	88.48	84.46
Neale: reading age (months)		93.47	99.77	89.09	85.70
Schonell: spelling age (months)		85.97	98.81	81.76	75.15
	N	9	8	20	7
Maths MATB (ratio score)		91.27	91.09	87.99	84.13

Reading, spelling and mathematics mean scores are adjusted for two covariates: age and IQ.

that the link is causal. Our results also show how specific experiences which a child has before he goes to school may affect his progress once he gets there.

We thank Morag Maclean for help with gathering and analysing the data, the Oxford Education Authority and the schools for their co-operation, and the SSRC for supporting our research.

References

1. Bradley, L. & Bryant, P. E. *Nature* **271**, 746–747 (1978).
2. Bradley, L. *Assessing Reading Difficulties* (Macmillan, London, 1980).
3. Goldstein, D. M. *J. educ. Psychol.* **68**, 680–688 (1976).
4. Liberman, I. *et al.* in *Toward a Psychology of Reading* (eds Reber, A. & Scarborough, D.) (L. Erlbaum Association, Hillsdale, New Jersey, 1977).
5. Lunderg, I., Olofsson, A. & Wall, S., *Scand. J. Psychol* **21**, 159–173 (1980).

THE INFLUENCE OF ORTHOGRAPHY ON READERS' CONCEPTUALIZATION OF THE PHONEMIC STRUCTURE OF WORDS

Linnea C. Ehri and Lee S. Wilce[1]

Source: *Applied Psycholinguistics*, 1, 1980: 371–385.

Abstract

This study was designed to determine whether children's conceptualization of the component sounds in words is influenced by their knowledge of the words' spellings. For example, the spelling of *pitch* may lead learners to discover the phonetic element [t] in its pronunciation and to conceptualize this as a separate phoneme, whereas the spelling of *rich* should not. Positive results were obtained in a phonemic segmentation task with real and made-up words taught to fourth graders. Findings are interpreted to show that phonemic segmentation skill may be a consequence of as much as a prerequisite to learning to read words. Results are consistent with a theory of printed word learning in which visual spellings are retained in memory through a sound symbolization process.

An issue receiving much attention from reading acquisition researchers is the relationship between phonemic awareness and learning to read words printed in alphabetic orthography. Results of several studies have indicated a positive relationship (Fox & Routh, 1975, 1976; Golinkoff, 1978; Liberman, 1973; Liberman, Liberman, Mattingly, & Shankweiler, 1980; Liberman, Shankweiler, Liberman, Fowler, & Fischer, 1977; Rosner, 1974).

However, because most of these studies are correlational, it remains unclear to what extent phonemic segmentation stands as a prerequisite to, a facilitator of, or a consequence of learning to read words (Ehri, 1979). The present study was designed to examine whether the spellings of words influence how readers conceptualize their phonemic structure. Investigation of this relationship was considered important, because the favored interpretation is that phonological segmentation is a prerequisite, not a consequence. This view predominates, possibly because researchers tend to consider auditory-vocal language the primary form of language and writing a secondary form merely reflecting speech. The aim of the present study was to determine whether in some instances writing might influence how speech is analyzed.

Two previous correlational studies lend some support to the idea that phonological segmentation is a consequence of learning to read. Morais, Cary, Alegria, and Bertelson (1979) gave the task of adding and deleting phones at the beginning of non-words to literate and illiterate adults in Portugal. The literates had acquired rudimentary reading skills at age 15 or older. They were similar in environment and childhood experiences to the illiterates. Whereas the literates were successful in the task (mean correct 72%), the illiterates were not (mean correct 19%). Barton, Miller, and Macken (1980) taught preliterate preschoolers to segment singleton initial consonants in words (e.g., *m*ouse, *b*ear) and then examined how they analyzed the initial consonant clusters /tr/ and /sw/. They found that whereas nonreaders regarded the clusters as single units, children having some reading ability segmented the clusters into phonemes. These findings suggest that knowing how to read is an important contributor to phonemic segmentation skill. The primary purpose of the present study was to be more specific about the source of this contribution, to determine whether knowledge of the spellings of particular words influences how they are segmented into phonemes.

Another purpose was to test a hypothesis derived from a theory of printed word learning proposed by Ehri in which phonological awareness is regarded as central to the process of storing the orthographic representations of words in lexical memory (Ehri, 1978, 1980a, 1980b). The theory was developed in order to explain how children learn to read and spell words. According to this theory, the major task facing beginning readers is learning how to incorporate printed language into their existing knowledge of spoken language. In English the primary unit of printed language is the *word*, so it is at a lexical level that the most important learning takes place. The lexicon is viewed as consisting of abstract word units having several different identities: *phonological* identities (how words sound and are articulated), *syntactic* identities (grammatical roles in sentences), and *semantic* identities (meanings). In the course of learning to read, another identity is added to the lexicon: an *orthographic* image of the word. This image is integrated with the other identities to form a unit in lexical memory.[2] La Berge and Samuels (1974) refer to this process as unitization. Orthographic and phonological identities are unitized when letters are processed as symbols for sounds. Orthographic, syntactic, and semantic identities are unitized when printed words are read and given meaningful interpretations in sentence contexts. As a result of these experiences, orthographic images are established in lexical memory as symbols for meanings as well as sounds. Several studies have yielded evidence for one or another of these claims (Ehri, 1980a, 1980b; Ehri & Roberts, 1979; Ehri & Wilce, 1979, 1980).

The focus of the present study was upon the print-sound symbolization process. According to the theory, orthographic images are stored not as rote-memorized visual figures but as sequences of letters bearing systematic relationships to acoustic and/or articulatory segments detected in the word's phonological identity. The first few times a printed word is seen, its component letters either singly or in combination are recognized and processed as symbols for component sounds within that word, the letter sequence enters memory, and it becomes a visual symbol for the sound structure of the word. To the extent that letters are grounded in sound, clear orthographic representations are formed which can be used for reading printed words accurately and rapidly and also for producing correct spellings.

In our previous studies, we have found that the sound-symbolizing function of letters is an important factor influencing subjects' memory for spellings as well as their memory for unfamiliar sounds (Ehri, 1980a; Ehri & Wilce, 1979). The present study was designed to investigate the impact of the sound-symbolizing function of letters upon learners' conceptualization of the phonemes that constitute words. We reasoned that if, when printed words are stored, letters are interpreted as symbols for sounds, then we ought to see some *variations* evident in learners' conceptualizations of the phonemic structure of words, depending upon how the words are spelled and which sounds are represented by letters. For example, readers who learn the printed word *pitch* will be led to think it has four phonemes, whereas in learning *rich* they will be led to think it has only three phonemes. In both words, a phonetic element corresponding to the extra letter *t* is present in articulation. Whether or not readers *discover* the element and think of it as a separate phoneme may depend upon whether a separate letter signaling the phoneme is included in the spelling. If it is there, then they may conceptualize the extra phoneme. If the spelling says the sound is not there, then the element may not be detected and represented in memory.

Experiment 1 was designed to test the relationship between spelling knowledge and phonemic segmentation. Seven pairs of words were selected so that each pair shared the same target phoneme, yet the spelling of one member symbolized an extra phonetic element adjacent to the phoneme while the spelling of the other member symbolized only the phoneme. These word pairs, their shared phonemes, and the extra phonetic elements are listed in Table 1. A phonemic segmentation task was used to reveal how children conceptualized the phonological structure of these words. A spelling

Table 1 List of extra-letter and control word pairs, phonetic description, frequency that extra phonemes were detected (Phonemic Segmentation Task), and frequency of correct word spellings (Maximum = 24 subjects per word).

Word pairs		Sound structure		Phoneme detection		Spellings	
Extra		*Shared*	*Extra phonetic*	*Extra*		*Extra*	
Letter	*Control*	*Phoneme*	*Element*	*Letter*	*Control*	*Letter*	*Control*
ca*t*ch	much	/č/	[t] alveolar tap	15	1	19	24
pi*t*ch	rich	/č/	[t] alveolar tap	13	3	18	24
ba*d*ge	page	/j/	[d] alveolar tap	13	0	17	24
can *y*ou	menu	/u/	[y] glide	19	0	24	20
ne*w*	do	/u/	[w] glide	18	0	24	24
o*w*n	old	/o/	[w] glide	12	0	19	24
com*b*	home	/m/	[b] bilabial stop	6	0	20	24
			Means	13.7	0.6	20.1	23.4

task was employed to determine whether children knew the words' orthographic identities. Based upon our theory, it was expected that, among children who knew the spellings, extra segments would be detected in words whose orthographic identities included letters symbolizing those segments but omitted in words lacking extra letter symbols.

A linguistic analysis of the phonemic structure of word pairs in Table 1 would regard the shared phonemes as identical (Bloch & Trager, 1942). Phonetic elements such as the tap of the alveolar ridge symbolized by the extra letters *t* and *d*, the final bilabial stop symbolized by *b*, and the lip-rounding glide following the vowel and symbolized by *w*, would be regarded not as separate but rather as part of adjacent phonemes (i.e., part of /č/ in pi*t*ch and ri*ch*, part of /j/ in ba*d*ge and pa*ge*, part of /m/ in com*b* and ho*me*, part of /o/ in o*w*n and o*ld*, respectively). From this linguistic view, opposite predictions can be derived. Subjects should divide words into phonemes according to their spoken forms, and they should disregard the extra phonetic elements symbolized in spellings. Furthermore, whether or not subjects know the spellings of words should have little bearing on their segmentation performances.

Experiment 1

Subjects. The subjects were 24 native English speaking fourth graders (11 males, 13 females), mean age 115 months (*SD* = 3.58), drawn from a middle-class elementary classroom in northern California. Participants were those (out of 30) whose parents returned permission forms. All subjects were able to decode words at least through the fourth grade level on Calfee and Calfee's Interactive Reading Assessment System vocabulary test (1977).

Materials. Target and control words selected to study the relationship between spellings and phoneme awareness are listed in Table 1. One other word, *empty*, was included but not reported because its ambiguous phonemic structure could be represented either with or without the phoneme /p/ and because it lacked a control word mate.

Filler words were mixed in with the target words in the segmentation task to obscure the presence of any pattern and to prevent the formation of a response set. Fillers were: *up, soft, all, milk, skunk, glad, on, must.*

Words were presented in the same order to all subjects in both tasks. Pair members were always separated by 12 items in the segmentation task and 7 items in the spelling task. Four of the extra-letter words were presented before their control mates, three followed their control mates. Words with identical extra phonetic segments across pairs were always separated by at least one dissimilar word.

Procedures. Children were tested individually. First they segmented words phonemically; then they spelled them. Prior to the segmentation task, they practiced analyzing the following sounds into phonemic segments: *ă, as, has; ip, sip, stip, strip; oy, boy, boyk; en, end, rend, frend.* The child was told: "Now we're going to play a game with word sounds. First I'll say a word. Then I want you to repeat it." The child was shown how to take out a counter for each sound as he or she said it, and given the instructions, "Say the word slowly so that I can hear each sound by itself." Counters (poker chips) were lined up in a row. If the child was unsuccessful, the experimenter modeled the behavior and had the child copy her. All subjects learned to segment the practice sounds correctly. Following this, they were given 23 words (2 to 5 phonemes in length) to segment. The experimenter said, "Now I'm going to give you some more words to divide into sounds. You'll do these by yourself so that we can see if you've learned how to do it. This time I'll put each word into a sentence; then I'll say the word. Then you'll repeat the word and show me all the different sounds by putting down a counter as you say each sound." After each segmentation, the experimenter asked whether he or she could find any more sounds until the subject said no. After the segmentation task, subjects wrote out the target words. Each word was pronounced and read in a meaningful sentence by the experimenter. After children wrote each word, they were asked if it looked right. If their response was no, they were told they could write the word again. When multiple spellings were produced, children were asked to underline the one they preferred. This checking procedure was used to ensure that subjects' knowledge of word spellings was being tapped in our task. Previously written words were covered up as the task proceeded.

Results

Responses in the segmentation task were scored as correct if a counter was supplied for each phoneme and if a sound appropriate for that phoneme was pronounced as the child positioned that counter in the row of counters. Disregarding whether extra-letter phonemes were included or omitted, the mean for the seven control words was 6.3 correct ($SD = 1.0$); the mean for the seven extra-letter words was 6.3 correct ($SD = 1.0$).

To assess the influence of orthography in this task, the number of times the extra sound was detected in the segmentations of target words was counted and compared within word pairs. As is evident in Table 1, sounds were discovered frequently in words whose spellings included a letter for that sound but were almost never detected in words whose pronunciations were parallel but whose spellings lacked the letter.

Children were able to spell most of the phoneme target words. However, there were some misspellings. To determine whether subjects were less likely to detect an extra segment if they did not know that the extra letter was present in the word's spelling, the number of these cases was counted. There were 21 misspellings in which the extra letter was omitted. In 90% of these, the extra sound was also not detected in the segmentation task. This suggests that it is when children acquire orthographic symbols that they become aware of additional phonemes in the pronunciations of words.

From Table 1, it is clear that not all letters were equally likely to persuade subjects of the existence of an additional sound in the word. For example, the letter *b* at the end of *comb* was not often regarded as symbolizing a sound even though it was spelled correctly.

It was evident from subjects' comments in the phoneme task that their knowledge of spellings was influencing their segmentations. (Spellings were not visible during this task.) In segmenting *home*, two children commented that the *e* was silent. Upon encountering /ĕ/ three children pointed out that there are two letters but only one sound. Two children remarked about their uncertainty whether you could really hear the *b* in *comb*, the *t* in *pitch*, or the *d* in *badge*. However, it was not the case that spellings were the sole basis for segmentations. Only two subjects allocated chips for any silent *e*'s, and only three subjects did so for *c* and *h* separately. Most of the children (88%) ignored truly silent letters, and most (88%) created only one sound in segmenting words spelled with consonant digraphs such as *ch*. This indicates that not simply the occurrence of letters in spellings but rather their sound-symbolizing function was the critical factor.

Discussion

These results are consistent with the hypothesis that children's conceptualization of the phonemic segments in words is influenced by their knowledge of the orthographic forms of the words. However, results fall short of showing cause because they demonstrate only that a correlation exists between orthographic knowledge and phonemic conceptualization. Which caused which is thus not clear. Another limitation of this study was that some of the experimental and control word pairs were similar but not identical in pronunciation. A second experiment was conducted to investigate whether phoneme conceptualization can be shaped by experiences with the printed forms of words, specifically whether, for identically pronounced words, the way readers conceptualize their sound structure depends upon which sounds they see symbolized in the words' spellings.

Experiment 2

Subjects. Middle-class, northern California native English speaking fourth graders were selected (10 males, 14 females), mean age 116 months ($SD = 5.53$), for this study. All subjects were able to decode words at least through the fourth grade level on Calfee and Calfee's Interactive Reading Assessment System vocabulary test (1977).

Materials. Five nonsense words, each with two spellings were created as names for pictures of animals (i.e., elephant, duck, cow, snake, pig). The picture-name pairs remained constant across subjects. One spelling included an extra letter that corresponded to a potential sound in the word. The other spelling lacked this extra letter. Pronunciations were identical for pair members. The pairs (extra letters italicized) were: ban*y*u–banu; dro*w*l–drol; sim*p*ty–simty; ta*d*ge–taj; zi*t*ch–zich.

Procedures. Subjects were matched on the basis of similar printed word reading scores on a list of 84 words taken from Calfee and Calfee's Interactive Reading Assessment System (1977). One member of each pair learned the set of names spelled with the extra letter, the other member learned the control set. Procedures were identical for the two groups. Children were tested individually. On one day, they were given the Calfee word recognition test. On a subsequent day, they completed three tasks ordered as follows: word learning, phonemic segmentation, spelling.

In the word learning task, the experimenter said, "I'm going to show you some pictures of animals. I've made up a name for each animal. I want you to try to read each name. Also try to remember the names because later on I'm going to show you the pictures alone and see if you remember each animal's name." Items were presented on cards in a different, randomly determined order on each trial. Presentation of items was self-paced. Children practiced reading the five names printed beneath pictures for a minimum of three trials or until they pronounced all the words perfectly on one trial. Then they were shown the names alone and asked to recall the associated animals to a criterion of one perfect trial. Then they were shown the animal pictures in random order and tried to recall the names. They were given three trials to recall the names, and more if necessary to achieve one perfect trial. Subjects were allowed about 5 seconds to respond. Any incorrect responses were corrected by the experimenter, and the child repeated the correct name.

The phonemic segmentation task was conducted much like that in Experiment 1. First the experimenter demonstrated phonemic segmentation with an example and had children practice on the following sounds to a criterion of one perfect segmentation: ă, as, has; ti, tin, stin, stindy. Children repeated each sound, then divided it into segments by lining up counters (poker chips) to identify each phoneme as they pronounced it. Then they were reminded of the animals, shown each picture but not the print, and asked to segment its name, which was pronounced by the experimenter. The instructions were: "Remember the animals' names that you saw with the pictures before? Now I want you to divide the animals' names into sounds just as you did with the other words. Show me all the different sounds. Put down a counter for each sound as you say it." After each response, they were asked whether they could find any more sounds until they said no. Presentation order was random.

After this, their memory for the orthographic forms of the names was checked by having them write out the spellings. They were told: "Remember the animals' names that were printed below their pictures? This time you'll see just the pictures, and I want you to write out the names for me after I say them." After each response, children were asked, "Does it look like the name you saw before?" If they said no, they were encouraged to rewrite the word. Prior spellings were covered up as the task proceeded. Presentation order was random.

Results

Before results of the phonemic segmentation task are presented, it is necessary to consider the adequacy of subjects' preparation for this task. To verify that pairs of experimental and control subjects were equivalent in their word reading ability, a matched-pair t-test was conducted on their printed word recognition scores on the Calfee test. The mean number of correctly read words was 64.2 for the extra-letter group and 64.4 for the control group ($SD = 11.7$), $t(11) = 0.22$, $p > .05$ (two-tailed).

Nevertheless, the extra-letter subjects took significantly fewer trials than the control subjects in learning to read the animal names to a criterion of one perfect trial: $\overline{X}$ = 2.3 vs. 3.5 trials (SD = 1.4), $t(11)$ = 2.88, $p < .05$ (two-tailed). In order to account for this difference, the types of errors made by the two groups in pronouncing the words during the learning trials were compared. For three words, the presence of extra letters appeared to reduce the frequency of mispronunciations. Children who learned to read *banu* omitted the /y/ phoneme 14 times in their pronunciations, whereas this omission occurred only four times with *banyu*. The /č/ sound in *zich* was erroneously pronounced /k/ or /θ/ four times while this error never occurred with *zitch*. With *taj*, mispronunciations of the vowel occurred seven times and mispronunciations of the /j/ two times, whereas only three vowel errors occurred with *tadge*, a form in which *dg* functions as a marker to shorten the preceding vowel, according to Venezky (1970). These results suggest that extra letters in word spellings may reduce the time needed to learn printed words, either because they help learners decode the words more accurately or because they improve learners' memories for correct pronunciations. One exception to this generalization did occur, indicating that extra letters may not always serve this function. The presence of an extra *w* in *drowl* (a rhyme of *bowl*) prompted more vowel mispronunciations (rhymes of *towel* and fool) than *drol* (7 vs. 2 errors).

Despite some initial decoding inaccuracies, all subjects in both groups were able to reach criterion in learning the nonsense names. That they had stored the words in memory was apparent from performance on the spelling task where the mean numbers spelled correctly (maximum = 5) were high and equivalent: $\overline{X}$ = 4.2 for the extra-letter group, 4.5 for the control group, SD = 0.96, $t(11)$ = 1.75, $p > .05$ (two-tailed). Among the spellings produced, the extra letter was included in 89% of the extra-letter subjects' productions and was omitted in 93% of the control subjects' spellings. These data confirm that most of the orthographic forms were successfully stored in memory and available for use in the segmentation task.

To determine whether experimental and control groups were equally successful in segmenting words into all but the extra-letter phonemes, accuracy scores were compared for pairs of subjects in the segmentation task. A matched-pair *t*-test confirmed the absence of any difference between the groups: $t(11)$ = 0.56, $p > .05$ (two-tailed). The mean number of words correctly segmented (maximum of 5) was 4.58 for experimentals and 4.42 for controls, SD = 0.66.

Of primary interest was whether experimental subjects detected more of the extra-letter segments than control subjects in the five nonsense names. Results offered unanimous support for the hypothesis. Phonetic elements symbolized by extra letters were distinguished as separate phonemes almost exclusively by subjects who learned these spellings. Whereas every extra-letter subject included between 2 and 5 extra-letter sounds in his or her

21

segmentations ($\overline{X}$ = 2.9, SD = 1.08), all but two control subjects found no extra sounds, the two exceptions finding only one apiece out of 5 maximum. A matched-pair t-test was highly significant: $t(11)$ = 7.83, p < .01 (two-tailed). These findings indicate that the visual forms of words acquired from reading experiences serve to shape learners' conceptualizations of the phoneme segments in those words.

Inspection of segmentations revealed that some words were more likely to provoke extra-letter segments than others. The percentage of subjects out of 12 who detected an extra segment in each of the following words was: ta*d*ge (83%), zi*t*ch (83%), sim*p*ty (58%), ban*y*u (33%), drowl (33%). These proportions differ somewhat from those observed in Experiment 1 with parallel word forms: ba*d*ge (54%), pi*t*ch (54%), em*p*ty (50%), can *y*ou (79%), own (50%). Two differences between the experiments might account for some of the variation. Subjects in Experiment 1 were less accurate in their spellings than subjects in Experiment 2. Also, they had not been exposed to the spellings just prior to the segmentation task. Although individual spellings and individual subjects may introduce variability into the process by which spellings influence sound segmentation, present data nevertheless confirm that the process does operate.

Discussion

Our hypotheses were supported in the two experiments. Whereas the first study was correlational, the second was manipulative, hence permitting a causal inference. Based upon the finding in Experiment 2 that extra phonemes were detected frequently by subjects who saw the phonemes symbolized in spellings but almost never by subjects who saw spellings without these letters, we conclude that readers' conceptualization of the phonemic structure of words is influenced by their knowledge of word spellings. Although the influence of orthography was clear-cut in the sense that extra segments were rarely found if the spellings did not symbolize them, its impact fell short of maximum in that extra segments suggested by spellings were not detected in every case. Two possible reasons can be identified. One, the word learning treatment in Experiment 2 (i.e., reading the words) was weak. Subjects' attention was not directed to letter-sound relations, and they did not practice sounding out and spelling words. These latter exercises might have enhanced the phenomenon. Two, there are known to be marked individual differences in phonemic awareness (Calfee, Lindamood, & Lindamood, 1973). Also, there may be individual differences in the extent to which subjects notice letter-sound relationships in reading unfamiliar words. The fact that orthographic effects were evident but not pervasive suggests that the process does operate along with other processes yet to be understood.

The importance of phonological awareness as a prerequisite in learning to read words has been recognized by several researchers (Ehri, 1979; Fox

& Routh, 1975, 1976; Gleitmen & Rozin, 1973, 1977; Goldstein, 1976; Golinkoff, 1978; Liberman, 1973; Liberman, Shankweiler, Liberman, Fowler, & Fischer, 1977; Rosner, 1974; Rozin & Gleitman, 1977). The present study extends these findings by showing that phonemic awareness is also a consequence of printed word learning. This contributes important evidence to Ehri's theory of printed word learning, which characterizes the relationship as a two-way interactive process.[3] Readers need to be able to analyze words into sounds so as to recognize what segments there are to be symbolized in print. Likewise, when they look at the printed forms of words, they need to be able to justify the presence of letters by finding sounds in the word for them to symbolize. This reciprocal processing of letter-sound relationships is thought to be necessary in order for letters to be retained in memory as orthographic images. Present findings contribute support to this picture by indicating that orthography does leave its mark on the reader's conceptualization of the sound structure of words, very possibly in the way portrayed by the theory.

Results of the present studies failed to support predictions derived from a linguistic view of phonemic segmentation performance. Whereas subjects were expected to divide words into phonemic segments, they were found to divide them sometimes into phonetic segments. Whereas subjects were not expected to be influenced by spellings, they were found to detect or ignore phonetic segments according to whether these segments were symbolized by separate letters in the words' spellings. There are a couple of ways to reconcile results with linguistic theory. One is to regard the segmentation task as reflecting children's phonetic conceptualization rather than their phonemic conceptualization of words. However, this fails to explain the inconsistencies across parallel words (e.g., *rich-pitch*). To handle this, one can note that, since no two utterances are ever physically the same, a phonetic analysis of speech involves not one but a potentially infinite number of descriptions, depending upon how much detail is included. Any actual phonetic description captures and represents only those differences regarded as important. What children are doing in a segmentation task is indicating which sound segments they consider to be the important ones in words. One source of information about importance is orthography. Having to process and remember the spellings of words shapes children's conceptualization of their phonetic structure. The amount of phonetic detail included in this conceptualization is determined in part by the amount of detail symbolized in spellings. This source admittedly creates inconsistencies across words having the same phones because of the vagaries of printed language, yet the strategy of allowing letter symbols to dictate which sounds are "there" is probably maximally adaptive for children struggling to make sense of and remember English word spellings. This interpretation of results is compatible with linguistic theory as well as our theory of printed word learning.

To what extent word learning processes explored in the present study explain how all letters get stored in lexical memory is unclear. In the present study, letters having potential correlates in sound were examined. Truly silent letters represent another class of letters to be explained. One way to remember silent letters might be to create and store in memory special spelling pronunciations in which these letters function as symbols for sounds (e.g., *discipline*, stored as *dis-ki-plin*, Blumberg & Block, 1975). Other ways might be to recognize their functional role as markers affecting the sounds of other letters (e.g., silent *e*'s, double consonants), or as members of spelling patterns (*ghost*, ta*l*k, *light*, *cough*, a*ch*e), or as visual figures occupying space in the orthographic image but lacking any sound function (bus*i*ness, is*l*and, cas*t*le, da*h*lia, hemorr*h*age, We*d*nesday, answer, Linco*l*n). Investigation of this question is presently under way.

Included in Experiment 1 but not reported in the present paper was a syllable segmentation task. Subjects were given several words to divide into syllables and then spell. The words chosen contained an extra syllable in print that is not usually included in the pronunciation (e.g., inter*e*sting, diff*e*rent, *comfortable*–pronounced *comfterbul*). Results indicated that subjects were more likely to include the extra segments if they knew the correct spellings of the words. However, some features of the design of this study left doubt that knowledge of spellings was the factor accounting for the way subjects conceptualized the syllabic structure of the words. This topic awaits further investigation.

Other researchers have identified changes effected by orthography on readers' awareness of sounds in words. Studies of preschoolers' invented spellings (Read, 1971, 1973) reveal that children may classify sounds in unconventional ways until they learn more about standard letter-sound relations and word spellings. For example, prereaders may treat the affrication at the beginnings of words such as *train* and *chair* as the same single sound /č/ (spelled with an *h*), whereas beginning readers regard the initial sound in *train* as more like *teddy* than *chair*, and they analyze *ir* as two sounds rather than one (Barton, Miller, & Macken, 1980). Other shifts occurring in the conceptualization of sounds that may be provoked by experience with print are alveolar flaps perceived by the prereader inconsistently as *d* or *t* (*dirty* spelled *derdy*), preconsonantal nasals that may not be distinguished as separate sound segments (*sink* spelled *sic*) prior to contact with conventional spellings, verb inflections perceived phonetically at the outset (*walkt*) but shifting to a morphophonemic basis (*walked*) with print experience.

Present findings run contrary to the belief of many linguists that written language is a passive recipient of speech rather than a formative agent. For example, Bloomfied (1933, 21) declared that

> writing is not language, but merely a way of recording language by means of visible marks. . . . A language is the same no matter what

system of writing may be used to record it, just as a person is the same no matter how you take his picture.... In order to study writing, we must know something about language, but the reverse is not true.[4]

However, not all linguists agree. A case for the centrality of orthography in phonological theory is developed by Skousen (1979), who cites differences between literate adult and preliterate child perceptions about the phonological structure of words. He argues that some of the phonemic analyses performed by linguists arise solely from orthographic considerations, for example, whether the alveolar flap in words such as *ladder, latter, pedal, petal, pretty, powder* is interpreted as /t/ or /d/, the analysis of preconsonantal nasals as separate phonemes rather than nasalized vowels as in *sink* and *bank*. Moskowitz (1973) has suggested that orthography accounts for knowledge of vowel shift alternations in speech. Kerek (1976) has proposed that word spellings provide an alternative, psychologically compelling model for sound that competes with and may replace spoken pronunciations when the two differ. Ingram (1975) has proposed that written language influences syntactic development.

Present findings raise various issues suggesting directions for future research. The possibility that acquisition of spellings may alter knowledge about pronunciations points out one way that black dialect-speaking children may learn standard English, by learning to read. For example, seeing spellings may teach them about the presence of consonants deleted at the ends of words in their speech (Labov, 1967). Some correlational evidence in support of this is offered by Desberg, Elliott, and Marsh (1980). The impact of print upon pronunciations may not be limited to nonstandard dialect speakers. It may be that the process of learning to read and spell words teaches all readers a new literary English dialect reflecting the visible phonology and syntax characterizing printed forms (Gleason, 1961). Goodman and Buck (1973) reported that children may orally read a story in perfect standard English, yet immediately retell the story in a nonstandard dialect. This suggests that a child's phonological knowledge about words may become quite complex as he or she learns to read, particularly if the child is bidialectic. In considering the possible impact of orthography on phonology, one becomes aware that the idea of one fixed phonological representation for each word may be inadequate, that more likely there are multiple phonological representations stored together in memory. Which representation is tapped in any task may vary depending upon how the task is structured. A phonemic segmentation task that requires subjects to divide a continuous flow of sound into discrete units and to represent sound spatially with counters may be particularly susceptible to the influence of visible phonological representations (i.e., spellings). Clearly more research is needed to explore the various aspects of phonological knowledge and how they are related to task constraints, to spellings, and to printed word learning processes.

Notes

1 This investigation was supported by grants from the National Institute of Education (NIE-G-77-0009) and the National Institute of Child Health and Human Development (HD 12903-01). The authors would like to extend thanks to Professors Jarvis Bastian and Carol Wall for their helpful ideas offered during conversations about this work. Also, appreciation is expressed to the Davis Unified School district for its cooperation.

2 In previous papers, this process has been referred to as amalgamation. In the present paper, amalgamation is replaced by two concepts: the idea of symbolization to describe how letters enter memory as sound symbols, and the idea of unitization to describe how the various identities of words are stored together in lexical memory. This shift in terms was adopted to avoid implying that the separate identities of words are lost in memory during learning and also to discuss the process in more conventional terms.

3 As Professor John Downing pointed out at a conference on Metalinguistic Awareness and Learning to Read at the University of Victoria, 1979, adoption of an interactive view happily avoids the chicken-egg question of whether phonemic segmentation is a prerequisite or consequence of learning to read.

4 We are grateful to Takao Suzuki for this quotation.

References

Barton, D., Miller, R., & Macken, M. A. Do children treat clusters as one unit or two? Stanford University Department of Linguistics: *Papers and reports on child language development*, Stanford University, 1980, *18*, 105–137.

Bloch, B., & Trager, G. L. *Outline of linguistic analysis*. Baltimore: Linguistic Society of America, 1942.

Bloomfield, L. *Language*. London: George Allen and Unwin, 1933.

Blumberg, P., & Block, K. K. The effects of attempting spelling before feedback on spelling acquisition and retention. Paper presented at the annual meeting of the American Educational Research Association, Washington, D.C., 1975.

Calfee, R. C., & Calfee, K. H. Interactive reading assessment system (IRAS). Unpublished manuscript, Stanford University, 1977.

Calfec, R. C., Lindamood, P., and Lindamood, C. Acoustic-phonetic skills and reading—Kindergarten through twelfth grade. *Journal of Education Psychology*, 1973, *64*, 293–298.

Desberg, P., Elliott, D., & Marsh, G. American black English and spelling. In U. Frith (Ed.), *Cognitive processes in spelling*. London: Academic Press, 1980.

Ehri, L. C. Beginning reading from a psycholinguistic perspective: Amalgamation of word identities. In F. B. Murray (Ed.), *The development of the reading process*. International Reading Association Monograph (No. 3). Newark, Del.: International Reading Association, 1978.

Linguistic insight: Threshold of reading acquisition. In T. G. Waller and G. E. MacKinnon (Eds.), *Reading research: Advances in theory and practice, Volume 1*. New York: Academic Press, 1979.

The development of orthographic images. In U. Frith (Ed.), *Cognitive processes in spelling*. London: Academic Press, 1980a.

The role of orthographic images in learning printed words. In J. Kavanagh and R. Venezky (Eds.), *Orthography, reading and dyslexia*. Baltimore: University Park Press, 1980b.

Ehri, L. C., & Roberts, K. T. Do beginners learn printed words better in context or in isolation? *Child Development*, 1979, *50*, 675–685.

Ehri, L. C., & Wilce, L. S. The mnemonic value of orthography among beginning readers. *Journal of Educational Psychology*, 1979, *71*, 26–40.

Do beginners learn to read function words better in sentences or in lists? *Reading Research Quarterly*, 1980, *15*, 451–476.

Fox, B., & Routh, D. K. Analyzing spoken language into words, syllables, and phonemes: A developmental study. *Journal of Psycholinguistic Research*, 1975, *4*, 331–342.

Phonemic analysis and synthesis as word-attack skills. *Journal of Educational Psychology*. 1976, *68*, 70–74.

Gleason, H. A. *An introduction to descriptive linguistics*. New York: Holt, Rinehart & Winston, 1961.

Gleitman, L. R., & Rozin, P. Teaching reading by use of a syllabary. *Reading Research Quarterly*, 1973, *8*, 447–483.

The structure and acquisition of reading I: Relations between orthographies and the structure of language. In A. S. Reber and D. L. Scarborough (Eds.), *Toward a psychology of reading*. Hillsdale, N.J.: Lawrence Erlbaum Associates, 1977.

Goldstein, D. M. Cognitive-linguistic functioning and learning to read in preschoolers. *Journal of Educational Psychology*, 1976, *68*, 680–688.

Golinkoff, R. M. Critique: Phonemic awareness skills and reading achievement. In F. B. Murray and J. J. Pikulski (Eds.), *The acquisition of reading: Cognitive, linguistic and perceptual prerequisites*. Baltimore: University Park Press, 1978.

Goodman, K. S., & Buck, C. Dialect barriers to reading comprehension revisited. *The Reading Teacher*, 1973, *27*, 6–12.

Ingram, D. If and when transformations are acquired by children. In M. P. Dato (Ed.), *Developmental psycholinguistics: Theory and applications*. Washington, D.C.: Georgetown University Press, 1975.

Kerek, A. The phonological relevance of spelling pronunciation. *Visible Language*, 1976, *10*, 323–338.

Labov, W. Some sources of reading problems for Negro speakers of nonstandard English. In A. Frazier (Ed.), *New directions in elementary English*. Champaign. Ill.: National Council of Teachers of English, 1967, 140–167.

La Berge, D., & Samuels, S. J. Toward a theory of automatic information processing in reading. *Cognitive Psychology*, 1974, *6*, 293–323.

Liberman, I. Y. Segmentation of the spoken word and reading acquisition. *Bulletin of the Orton Society*, 1973, *23*, 65–77.

Liberman, I. Y., Liberman, A. M., Mattingly, L. G., & Shankweiler, D. Orthography and the beginning reader. In J. Kavanagh and R. Venezky (Eds.). *Orthography, reading and dyslexia*. Baltimore: University Park Press, 1980.

Liberman, I. Y., Shankweiler, D., Liberman. A. M., Fowler, C., & Fischer, F. W. Phonetic segmentation and recoding in the beginning reader. In A. S. Reber and

D. L. Scarborough (Eds.), *Toward a psychology of reading*. Hillsdale, N.J.: Lawrence Erlbaum Associates, 1977.

Morais, J., Cary, L., Alegria, J., & Bertelson, P. Does awareness of speech as a sequence of phones arise spontaneously? *Cognition*, 1979, *7*, 323–331.

Moskowitz, B. A. On the status of vowel shift in English. In T. E. Moore (Ed.), *Cognitive development and the acquisition of language*. New York: Academic Press, 1973.

Read, C. Pre-school children's knowledge of English phonology. *Harvard Educational Review*, 1971, *41*, 1–34.

Children's judgments of phonetic similarities in relation to English spelling. *Language learning*, 1973, *23*, 17–38.

Rosner, J. Auditory analysis training with prereaders. *Reading Teacher*, 1974, *27*, 379–384.

Rozin, P., & Gleitman, L. R. The structure and acquisition of reading II: The reading process and the acquisition of the alphabetic principle. In A. S. Reber and D. L. Scarborough (Eds.), *Toward a psychology of reading*. Hillsdale, N.J.: Lawrence Erlbaum Associates, 1977.

Skousen, R. English spelling and phonological representation. Paper presented at the annual meeting of the Linguistic Society of America, Los Angeles, December, 1979.

Venezky, R. *The structure of English orthography*. The Hague: Mouton, 1970.

100

CHILDREN'S USE OF ANALOGY IN LEARNING TO READ: A DEVELOPMENTAL STUDY

Usha Goswami

Source: *Journal of Experimental Child Psychology*, 42, 1986: 73–83.

If children are able to make analogies between the spelling patterns in words, this would have important consequences for theories of reading development, as a child who knew a word like *beak* could use analogy to read new words like *peak* and *bean*. A study is reported which compared the ability of children at three different reading levels to use analogy in reading both real and nonsense words. The results showed that even very young children can successfully use analogy to decode new words. This finding suggests that analogy has a role to play in the initial stages of reading acquisition.

Given current interest in the role of analogy in skilled reading (Glushko, 1979, 1981; Kay & Marcel, 1981; Norris & Brown, 1985; Patterson & Morton, 1985), a question which has received little attention is children's ability to make analogies between the spelling patterns in words. We do not know whether beginning readers can use the spelling–sound correspondence of one word (e.g., *beak*) to work out the pronunciation of similar words (e.g., *bean* and *peak*). Analogy would be a useful alternative strategy to word-specific learning (Gough & Hillinger, 1980) and phonics (letter-by-letter decoding). While some studies have examined children's ability to use analogies in reading (Baron, 1977, 1979; Marsh, Desberg, & Cooper, 1977; Marsh, Friedman, Desberg, & Saterdahl, 1981), the developmental picture remains unclear.

The work of Marsh *et al.* suggests that analogy is used only in the final stages of reading development. The claim is that analogy is not used spontaneously until after the stage of concrete operations (Marsh & Desberg, 1983). This claim is based on two studies. Marsh *et al.* (1977) asked children aged 10 and 16 years to read nonsense words which were analogs of irregular real words. An example is *puscle*, which is analogous to *muscle*. The words were chosen so that a pronunciation based on analogy ("pussle") would differ from one based on rules ("puskle"), enabling a pure measure of analogy to be obtained. It was found that 10-year-olds made analogies 39% of the time, compared to 46% for the 16-year-olds. However, the apparent developmental increase is difficult to interpret, since Marsh *et al.* did not check that the younger children could read the irregular words assumed to provide the base for the analogies. The developmental increase could thus be an artifact arising from the younger children knowing or remembering fewer base words.

Marsh *et al.* (1981) attempted to solve this problem by presenting a list of the real word analogs for the children to read before giving the nonsense words. This time the children (aged 7 and 9 years) were told that the nonsense words were analogs of the real words. Performance improved dramatically: 78% of responses were analogies at 7 years and 92% at 9 years. Children are thus able to use analogy to read nonsense words when told that it would be a useful strategy. However, the use of nonsense words may encourage unusual strategies not utilized in reading normal words. Furthermore, the developmental increase could still be artifactual, as the younger children could be worse at recalling the spelling patterns of the analogical real words at the time of reading the nonsense words. Thus, on the basis of these two studies, the role of analogy in normal reading development remains uncertain.

Baron (1977) suggested that younger children can make analogies in reading. He taught kindergarteners words and sounds such as *b*, *at*, *bat*, *ed*, *red*; and tested transfer to new words such as *bed*, *rat*, *bad*, and *bet*. Children's performance on words such as *bed* and *rat* was around 90%, compared to 15% for *bad* and *bet*. Baron argues that this was because children can use analogy to decode *bed* and *rat*, whereas *bad* and *bet* depend on "component correspondences" or letter-by-letter decoding. However, this cannot be the sole explanation, as *bad* can also be read by analogy (to *bat*). Second, children are taught about the units in the "analogous" words (e.g., *at* and *ed*), but are not taught about the units in the "correspondence" words (e.g., *ad* and *et*). This alone may account for the superior performance on the analogous words at transfer. Thus while the study is suggestive of young children's ability to use analogies in reading, the results are inconclusive. Also, as only one age group was used, the study does not contribute to the developmental question.

In a later study, Baron (1979) measured analogy by comparing children's performance on lists of real words and nonsense words (*cut-lut*). Like Marsh *et al.* (1981), he finds that 7- and 9-year-old children can use analogies to read nonsense words and can be trained to do so if originally reluctant (Experiment 3). However, the importance of analogy in decoding real words is impossible to assess, as only nonsense words are used to measure analogical responses. Also, since Baron did not make systematic age comparisons, the developmental question remains unanswered.

It is clear that a study is required which (a) does not rely solely on nonsense words, (b) compares the reading behavior of children of different reading levels on the same words, (c) controls for the accessibility of the analogous base words, and (d) does not explicitly instruct the children to use analogy. Such a study is attempted here. Children aged from 5 to 8 years played a word game in which they had to read words and nonsense words which were either analogous or nonanalogous to "clue" words such as *beak*. The clue word was present throughout each session to control for availability, although no instruction about how to use the clue word was given. To eliminate the problem of differential initial knowledge of the words, pretest scores were compared to post-test scores.

The study also asked whether analogies can be made between the beginnings of words (*beak–bean*) as well as between the ends of words (*beak–peak*), an issue which has so far attracted little attention. Given the work of Treiman (1983, 1985), which shows that the natural parsing units in words are the onset and rime, it was expected that analogies would be made more frequently on the basis of the ends of words (rimes) than on the basis of the beginnings.

Method

Subjects

The subjects were drawn from the infant classes of local primary schools (equivalent to kindergarten, first grade, and second grade). The children were divided into three groups based on performance on the Schonell Graded Word Reading Test (Schonell & Goodacre, 1971). The youngest group (Group 1) did not score on the test, and were not yet reading. Ages, reading levels, and verbal intelligence scores for the groups are detailed in Table 1.

Table 1 Subject Groups: Age, Reading Age, and Verbal Intelligence.

Group	N	Chronological age		Reading age		BPVS[a]	
		M	SD	M	SD	M	SD
1	18	5;4	3.1	6;0	0.0	104.7	15.1
2	18	6;10	8.9	6;10	1.1	96.8	13.3
3	17	7;1	8.7	7;4	3.2	100.6	12.7

[a] British version of the Peabody Picture Vocabulary Test (Dunn, Dunn, & Whetton, 1982).

Design

The children were first pretested on all the words and nonsense words being used (presented for reading in randomized lists interspersed with filler words and nonsense words as appropriate). They were then seen six times in six different sessions, each session representing a different condition. In each session they were shown a written clue word (e.g., *beak*), and asked to read seven test words, which were either analogous or nonanalogous to the clue word. The test words were either real words or nonsense words, the nonsense words being derived from the real words by changing one letter, so that the orthographic sequence required for the analogy remained intact. Two clue words and their associated test words were given during each session.

There were three types of test words: (1) Target words (two given), which shared the same orthographic sequence as the clue words at either the beginning (e.g., *beak–bean* or *beak–beal*), or the end (*beak–peak* or *beak–neak*); (2) Common Letter words (two given), which also had three letters in common with the clue words, but for which the shared letters were not in sequence (e.g., *beak–bask* and *beak–bawk*); and (3) Control words (three given), which were the Target and Common Letter words for a different clue word from the one to which they acted as controls (e.g., *beak–rain, tail, real,* or *beak–rait, kail, roal*). The words were printed in black type half an inch high on 4 × 6-in. white cards. The Common Letter words were matched as closely as possible in frequency to the Target words using the Carroll, Davies, and Richman (1971) norms. There were six sets of words and the nonsense words. All the words used are given in Table 2.

The children played the word game in three conditions: Beginning, where the Target words were analogous to the clue word at the beginning;

Table 2 Full List of Words and Nonsense Words Used.

Clue word	Beginning	End	Control 1
beak	bean (beal)	peak (neak)	lake (pake)
	bead (beap)	weak (feak)	bask (bawk)
hark	harp (harf)	lark (sark)	hawk (howk)
	harm (harn)	bark (tark)	hair (haik)
rail	rain (rait)	tail (kail)	real (roal)
	raid (raim)	hail (bail)	lain (laik)
seen	seed (seel)	queen (peen)	nest (nase)
	seem (seet)	green (reen)	nose (seng)
coat	coach (coad)	float (poat)	cast (cait)
	coast (coan)	boat (roat)	cost (cort)
skin	skip (skib)	chin (hin)	silk (soik)
	skim (skif)	pin (lin)	pink (tink)

Note: Nonsense words in parentheses.

32

End, where the Target words were analogous to the clue word at the end; and No Clue, where no clue word was presented. On the No Clue condition the child received all four Target words in a given set plus the three Control words. An example using a different set of words was given before each condition.

The three conditions were given once for real words and once for nonsense words. There was full counterbalancing of order of conditions, words per condition, and real vs nonsense words, using a Latin square design. If the children can make analogies from the clue words to the test words, they should score more highly on the Target words than on the Common Letter and Control words in the Beginning and End conditions, but not in the No Clue condition.

Results

The results for the children who could read (Groups 2 and 3) were analyzed separately from the results of the nonreaders, as the scores for the nonreading group (Group 1) were not normally distributed, and so did not lend themselves to parametric analysis. The results for Groups 2 and 3 are reported first.

Groups 2 and 3

A comparison of the mean number of words and nonsense words read correctly on the experimental sessions ($T2$) compared to the pretest sessions ($T1$) is given in Table 3.

As the table shows, the increase from $T1$ to $T2$ in the number of words read correctly is of a much greater magnitude for the Target words than for the Common Letter and Control words in the two experimental conditions, but not in the No Clue condition. This effect occurs both for words and for nonsense words, and seems to be equally strong at both reading levels.

In order to see whether our predictions had been confirmed in the way suggested above, and to check that this pattern of results held for nonsense words as well as real words, a $3 \times 2 \times 2 \times 3 \times 2 \times 3$ (Order group × Reading Level × Meaning (words vs nonsense words) × Condition × Test × Word Type) analysis of variance was performed, with repeated measures on Meaning, Condition, Test, and Word Type. This showed a significant interaction between Condition, Test, and Word Type ($F(4, 116) = 5.26$, $p < .001$).

Post hoc tests (Newman–Keuls) showed that the interaction was due to the improvement on the Target words for the Beginning and End conditions being significantly greater than the improvement on the Common Letter and Control words ($p < .05$). There was no significant improvement in the No Clue condition. Although the Control words tended to be easier than

33

Table 3 Mean Number of Words and Nonsense Words Read Correctly by Wordtype: Groups 2 and 3.

Condition	Test	Target	Common Letter	Control
		Group 2		
Words				
Beginning	T1	0.28 (0.57)	0.33 (0.49)	0.89 (1.18)
	T2	2.22 (1.48)	1.06 (1.00)	1.39 (1.24)
End	T1	0.94 (0.94)	0.56 (0.86)	0.72 (0.83)
	T2	3.00 (1.28)	0.78 (0.88)	1.22 (1.31)
No Clue[a]	T1	0.44 (0.92)	0.67 (0.69)	0.56 (0.62)
	T2	0.72 (0.89)	1.00 (1.00)	1.33 (1.14)
Nonsense words				
Beginning	T1	0.50 (0.79)	0.17 (0.38)	0.33 (0.69)
	T2	1.61 (1.33)	0.56 (0.70)	1.00 (0.97)
End	T1	0.44 (0.78)	0.06 (0.24)	0.44 (0.92)
	T2	3.00 (1.14)	0.33 (0.60)	0.50 (0.99)
No Clue[a]	T1	0.22 (0.43)	0.44 (0.86)	0.44 (0.98)
	T2	0.72 (1.13)	0.61 (0.78)	1.11 (1.08)
		Group 3		
Words				
Beginning	T1	1.06 (0.83)	1.12 (0.70)	2.00 (2.06)
	T2	2.71 (1.26)	1.76 (0.90)	2.18 (2.21)
End	T1	1.47 (1.07)	1.41 (1.06)	1.88 (1.66)
	T2	3.65 (0.86)	1.35 (1.22)	3.06 (1.71)
No Clue[a]	T1	1.41 (1.06)	1.76 (1.38)	1.88 (1.62)
	T2	1.76 (1.38)	2.18 (0.95)	2.41 (1.50)
Nonsense words				
Beginning	T1	0.82 (0.95)	0.24 (0.56)	0.88 (0.92)
	T2	2.18 (1.29)	0.86 (1.29)	1.18 (1.38)
End	T1	0.76 (0.79)	0.59 (0.62)	0.71 (1.05)
	T2	3.06 (1.19)	0.71 (1.10)	1.35 (0.93)
No Clue[a]	T1	0.76 (0.87)	0.59 (1.11)	0.71 (1.30)
	T2	1.06 (1.14)	1.18 (1.13)	1.82 (1.38)

Note: Maximum score = 6 (Target and Common Letter raw scores were multiplied by $^3/_2$ to bring them into line with Control scores). Standard deviations are in parentheses.
[a] In the case of the No Clue condition, the Target figures refer to the Target Beginning words, and the Common Letter figures to the Target End words.

the Common Letter words, this did not interfere with the highly significant improvement on the Target words in the Beginning and End conditions. This result shows that children can make analogies from clue words in reading.

Table 3 indicates that it is easier to make analogies between the ends of words than between the beginnings of words. Newman–Keuls post hoc tests confirmed that the number of analogies made between the ends of words was significantly greater than the number of analogies made between the beginnings of words, for both real words and nonsense words ($p < .01$).

A significant interaction was also found between Meaning, Condition, Test, and Word Type ($F(4, 116) = 2.10$, $p < .05$). Newman–Keuls tests showed that the interaction was due to nonsense Control words occasionally being read as well as (real) Control words, even though in general words were read better than nonsense words ($p < .05$). Examination of the Target word scores in the Beginning and End conditions showed that significantly more Target words were read at experimental test than at pretest for both words and nonsense words (p's $< .01$). So as many analogies are made between the beginnings and ends of nonsense words as real words.

The ANOVA also showed that these effects were independent of reading level. If children at a later stage of reading development are better at using analogy than children at an earlier stage of reading development, an interaction between Condition, Test, Word Type, and Reading Level, or between Meaning, Condition, Test, Word Type, and Reading Level would be predicted. Neither of these interactions approached significance ($F(4, 92) = 0.48$, and $F(4, 92) = 1.06$, respectively). The lack of an interaction with reading level is striking, as it shows that the ability to make analogies in reading is not related to reading level, at least in the initial stages of reading examined here. This finding is inconsistent with the developmental theory of analogy put forward by Marsh and Desberg (1983). Younger readers are as capable of using analogy as older readers.

In order to examine this result further, Pearson product–moment correlations were calculated between the number of analogies made and both reading level and age. Analogy use was calculated by subtracting Target word scores on the No Clue condition from Target word scores on the Beginning and End conditions, giving two measures of analogy use, AnlogB and AnlogE. None of the correlations approached significance. Correlations of AnlogB with reading level and age were $r(33) = -.05$ and $r(33) = -.03$, respectively, while correlations of AnlogE with reading level and age were $r(33) = -.14$ for both.

It can be concluded that children at both reading levels made analogies between both the beginnings and ends of words, for both real words and nonsense words, although they found analogies between the ends of words easier. We now turn to the results of the nonreaders (Group 1).

The results for the nonreading group

The mean number of words read correctly by the nonreaders is given in Table 4. Pretest scores were always zero, and so only the scores on the experimental test sessions are presented. These have been added across words and nonsense words, as scores were roughly equivalent for both word types.

Table 4 Mean Number of Words and Nonsense Words Read Correctly by Word Type for Group 1.

| Condition | Test | Word type | | |
		Target	Common Letter	Control
Beginning	T2	0.11 (0.32)	0.00 (0.00)	0.00 (0.00)
End	T2	0.89 (1.37)	0.00 (0.00)	0.05 (0.24)
No Clue	T2	0.00 (0.00)	0.05 (0.24)	0.00 (0.00)

Note: Maximum score = 12. Standard deviations in parentheses.

Most of the scores are zeros, but where analogies can be made (for Target words on the Beginning and End condition), some of the children did occasionally give the correct response. This seems to be true mainly of the End condition, where on average the children read one word correctly. As it was previously found that analogies between the ends of words were easiest, this result seems to be in line with the performance of the older children.

To see whether the performance of the nonreaders differed significantly from chance, a Friedman two-way analysis of variance by ranks was carried out on each condition, comparing Target words scores to Control word scores. The Beginning and No Clue conditions showed no significant effects ($\chi r^2(2, N = 18) = 0.25$ and 0.08, respectively). However, scores in the End condition were significantly different from chance ($\chi r^2(2, N = 18) = 9.03, p < .001$). Post hoc testing with the Wilcoxon matched pairs signed ranks test showed that significance was caused by the scores for the Target words being significantly different from the scores for the Common Letter and Control words ($T = 0, N = 8, p < .01$, for both). It seems that even children who are not yet reading are capable of making analogies between the ends of words.

Discussion

The demonstration that young children make analogies in reading when given clue words suggests that analogy may play an important role in reading development. Analogy cannot be the developmentally sophisticated strategy suggested by Marsh and Desberg (1983), as in the early stages of reading analogies are made irrespective of reading level, with even non-readers making analogies occasionally between the ends of words. It is clear from the older children that when memory/content of the visual lexicon is controlled by keeping the clue word present, no developmental increase in the use of analogy is found.

The finding that analogies between the ends of words were easier than between the beginnings of words is in accordance with the work of Treiman

(1983, 1985), who has shown that the natural parsing units in words are the onset and rime (e.g., *b* + *eak*). However, a strong version of Treiman's theory would not predict analogies between the beginnings of words at all. The finding that young children can and do use analogies between the beginnings of words in reading suggests that current notions of orthographic parsing must be extended. However, the relative strength of the beginning and end effects should be tested across as well as between stimuli (e.g., *beak–bean, mean–bean*). This was not done in the current study because of the large number of extra clue words required, which would have considerably complicated the design.

The beginning and end effects are also relevant to current analogical theories of skilled reading. Glushko (1979) suggests that analogy may work either via the comparison of similar terminal vowel–consonant segments between words, or via the "contribution of neighbors in all positions" (p. 684). He assumes that the former is most influential in determining pronunciation, citing "the salience of rhyme for adults, and the primacy with which this phonological judgment develops in children" (Glushko, 1981, p. 69). While analogies between the ends of words do seem to come first (shown by the nonreaders), and are easier to make, the beginning effect shows that an analogy model based solely on terminal vowel consonant orthography is too simple. However, analogy does not depend on the number of shared letters between words either, as no improvement was found for the Common Letter words. This suggests that lexical analogies are dependent on intact orthographic sequences at both the beginnings and ends of words.

The finding that analogies are made in certain ways means that the results are also compatible with models of reading which postulate large-unit rules (e.g., Patterson & Morton, 1985), or a combination of rules and analogy, analogies being used to apply rules (Baron, 1979). Such models differ in whether or not they postulate separate lexical and rule-based systems. If independence of the lexical and nonlexical systems is assumed, then the models cannot explain lexical effects in nonsense word pronunciation (e.g., Kay & Marcel, 1981). If the specification of independence is relaxed, a clear distinction between analogy theories and rule-based theories cannot be made.

However, rule-based theories seldom specify how spelling–sound rules are extracted or compiled. An alternative possibility to Baron's suggestion that analogies are used to apply rules, and one also compatible with the results presented here, is that analogies are used to extract rules. For example, it could be that the kind of comparison involved in making a specific analogy like *beak–peak* helps children to realize that words which rhyme tend to have the same spelling pattern at the end. This could then lead to the formation of general "rules" such as -*eak* says "eak." The idea that analogies help in rule extraction would perhaps be a better characterization of our results, as all the words used were new to the children, and so prestored rules were probably not available. By this account, using analogies would be helpful in acquiring the alphabetic principle.

Analogy is thus a useful strategy for reading single words, and seems to be available at all reading levels. We have found no development in the ability to use analogy when the basis for the analogy is provided. Instead, it can be argued that what develops is the number of words in a child's mental lexicon from which analogies can be made.

Note

This research was carried out with the assistance of a training award from the Medical Research Council of Great Britain and forms part of a doctoral thesis supervised by Professor Peter Bryant. I thank the staff and pupils of Botley County Primary School, Oxford, for their extremely kind cooperation and assistance, and Peter Bryant for his help and encouragement. Jerry Broad was very helpful in assembling the materials. I am grateful to Rebecca Treiman and three anonymous reviewers for comments on earlier drafts of this paper.

References

Baron, J. (1977). Mechanisms for pronouncing printed words: Use and acquisition. In D. LaBerge & S. J. Samuels (Eds.), *Basic processes in reading: Perception and comprehension* (pp. 175–216). Hillsdale, NJ: Erlbaum.

Baron, J. (1979). Orthographic and word specific mechanisms in children's reading of words. *Child Development*, **50**, 60–72.

Carroll, J. B., Davies, P., & Richman, B. (1971). *The word frequency book*. New York: Houghton Mifflin.

Dunn, L. M., Dunn, L. M., & Whetton, C. (1982). British Picture Vocabulary Scale. Berks., England: NFER-Nelson.

Glushko, R. J. (1979). The organization and activation of orthographic knowledge in reading aloud. *Journal of Experimental Psychology: Human Perception and Performance*, **5**, 674–691.

Glushko, R. J. (1981). Principles for pronouncing print: The psychology of phonography. In A. M. Lesgold & C. A. Perfetti (Eds.), *Interactive processes in reading* (pp. 61–84). Hillsdale, NJ: Erlbaum.

Gough, P. B., & Hillinger, M. L. (1980). Learning to read: An unnatural act. *Bulletin of the Orton Society*, **30**, 179–196.

Kay, J., & Marcel, A. (1981). One process, not two, in reading aloud: Lexical analogies do the work of non-lexical rules. *Quarterly Journal of Psychology*, **33**, 397–413.

Marsh, G., & Desberg, P. (1983). The development of strategies in the acquisition of symbolic skills. In D. R. Rogers & J. A. Sloboda (Eds.), *The acquisition of symbolic skills* (pp. 149–154) New York: Plenum.

Marsh, G., Desberg, P., & Cooper, J. (1977). Developmental strategies in reading. *Journal of Reading Behaviour*, **9**, 391–394.

Marsh, G., Friedman, M. P., Desberg, P., & Saterdahl, K. (1981). Comparison of reading and spelling strategies in normal and reading disabled children. In

M. P. Friedman, J. P. Das, & N. O'Connor (Eds.), *Intelligence and learning* (pp. 363–367). New York: Plenum.

Norris, D. G., & Brown, G. (1985). Race models and analogy theories: a dead heat? Reply to Seidenberg. *Cognition*, **20**, 155–168.

Patterson, K., & Morton, J. (1985). From orthograpy to phonology: An attempt at an old interpretation. In K. Patterson, J. C. Marshall, & M. Coltheart (Eds.), *Surface dyslexia*. London: Erlbaum.

Schonell, F., & Goodacre, E. (1971). *The psychology and teaching of Reading* (5th ed.). London & Edinburgh: Oliver & Boyd.

Treiman, R. (1983). The structure of spoken syllables: Evidence from novel word games. *Cognition*, **15**, 49–74.

Treiman, R. (1985). Onsets and rimes as units of spoken syllables: Evidence from children. *Journal of Experimental Psychology*, **39**, 161–181.

101

EXPLICIT SYLLABLE AND PHONEME SEGMENTATION IN THE YOUNG CHILD[1]

*Isabelle Y. Liberman, Donald Shankweiler,
F. William Fischer and Bonnie Carter*

Source: *Journal of Experimental Child Psychology*, 18, 1974: 201–212.

To write a language, one must first abstract the unit to be used from the acoustic stream of speech. Writing systems based on the meaningless units, syllables and phonemes, were late developments in the history of written language. The alphabetic system, which requires abstraction of the phonemic unit of speech, was the last to appear, evolved from a syllabary and, unlike the other systems, was apparently invented only once. It might therefore be supposed that phoneme segmentation is particularly difficult and more difficult, indeed, than syllable segmentation. Speech research suggests reasons why this may be so. The present study provides direct evidence of a similar developmental ordering of syllable and phoneme segmentation abilities in the young child. By means of a task which required preschool, kindergarten, and first-grade children to tap out the number of segments in spoken utterances, it was found that, though ability in both syllable and phoneme segmentation increased with grade level, analysis into phonemes was significantly harder and perfected later than analysis into syllables. The relative difficulties of the different units of segmentation are discussed in relation to reading acquisition.

To write a language, one must decide which of its several kinds and sizes of segments should be represented. The choice of kind arises from the fact that all languages have a dual structure, comprising segments that have meaning and segments that do not. Each kind of segment offers, in turn, its own set of options in size; meaningful segments can, for example, be as long as sentences or as short as words (or morphemes). Among the meaningless segments, the most likely candidates for a writing system are syllables and phonemes, the latter of which are the shortest (and least numerous) segments of all.

In the historical development of writing (Diringer, 1948; Gelb, 1963), systems that used meaningful units came first. Some were historically related; others are supposed to have developed independently. Something like the word was the segment most commonly represented, at least in those systems that have a transparent relation to speech. One thinks of Chinese writing (and the kanji part of Japanese) as a present-day approximation to this method, in which the segment represented is the word.

Writing with meaningless units is a more recent development. As with the older system, this more recent one may have developed independently several times. Among writing systems that use the meaningless kind of segment, the segment size that was represented in all the carliest examples was, at least approximately, that of the syllable. An alphabet, representing segments of phonemic size, was developed later. It is clear, moreover, that the alphabet developed historically out of a syllabary and, furthermore, that this important development occurred just once.

If a writer is to represent a segment of whatever kind or size, he must first have succeeded in explicitly abstracting it from the acoustic stream of speech. We are tempted to suppose, then, that the historical development of writing might reflect the ease (or difficulty) with which explicit segmentation can be carried out. Yielding to that temptation, we should conclude that in order of increasing difficulty there is the word, the syllable, and, hardest of all, the phoneme. More to the point of this paper, we should suppose that for the child there might be the same order of difficulty and, correspondingly, the same order of appearance in development.

In a review of the literature on the development of segmentation, Gibson and Levin (in press) conclude that meaningful units are, in fact, the first segments abstracted by the child and take priority in his analysis of speech, but our concern in this paper is more pointedly with the meaningless kind of segment. What of the syllables and phonemes, then? We have suggested elsewhere (Liberman, 1971, 1973; Shankweiler & Liberman, 1972), and Gibson and Levin concur, that segmentation into phonemes may be quite difficult for the young child and more difficult, in any event, than segmentation into syllables. However, the evidence for this conclusion has nowhere been very direct. Rather, inferences have been made from informal observation of some of the problems in rhyming and in abstracting initial and final consonants from spoken words which children have in the early stages of reading acquisition (Monroe, 1932; Savin, 1972). Reports of attempts to train prereading children also suggest that phoneme analysis may be relatively difficult (Calfee, Chapman & Venesky, 1972; Elkonin, 1973; Gleitman & Rozin, 1973; Savin, 1972).

The purpose of the experiment to be reported here is to obtain evidence that bears more specifically on this matter of explicit syllable and phoneme segmentation in the young child. Before describing the experiments, however, we should, by way of further introduction, say more about explicit segmentation. In particular, we should note how it differs from ordinary speech perception and also consider what is known about speech that might be relevant to our understanding of the problems that face the child when he goes about the segmentation task.

It must be emphasized that the difficulty a child might have in explicit segmentation is not necessarily related to his problems, if any, with ordinary speech perception. Thus, young children might, in the ordinary course of speaking and listening, readily distinguish (or identify) words like *bad* and *bat* that differ in only one phonemic segment. Indeed, there is evidence now that infants at one month of age discriminate *ba* from *pa* (and *da* from *ta*); moreover, they make this discrimination categorically, just as adults do, when the physical difference between the phonemes is very small (only 20 msec in the onset of the two parts of the acoustic pattern) (Eimas, Siqueland, Jusczyk & Vigorito, 1971). But it does not follow from the fact that a child can easily distinguish *bad* from *bat* that he can therefore respond analytically to the phonemic structure that underlies the distinction —that is, that he can demonstrate an explicit understanding of the fact that each of these utterances consists of three segments and that the difference lies wholly in the third.

What, then, is known about speech that might lead us to expect that a child who readily perceives speech might nevertheless find explicit segmentation into phonemes more difficult than explicit segmentation into syllables? If the acoustic structure of speech bore a simple one-to-one relation to the phonemic structure, just as the letters do (at least in the orthographically regular case), it would indeed be hard to see why phonemic analysis should pose special problems. That is, if there were in the word *bat* three acoustic segments, one for each of the three phonemes, then the segmentation of the word that is represented in its spelling would presumably be readily apparent.

However, as extensive research in speech perception has shown (Fant, 1962; Liberman, Cooper, Shankweiler & Studdert-Kennedy, 1967), the segmentation of the acoustic signal does not correspond directly or in any easily determined way to the segmentation at the phonemic level. Moreover, this lack of correspondence does not arise merely because the sounds of the phonemes are superficially linked together, as are the letters of the alphabet in cursive writing or as may be implied by the reading teacher who urges the child to blend b-a-t (buhatuh) into the appropriate monosyllabic word *bat*. Instead, the phonemic segments are encoded at the acoustic level into larger units of approximately syllabic size. In *bat*, for example, the initial and final consonants are, in the conversion to sound, folded into the medial vowel, with the result that information about successive segments is transmitted more or less simultaneously on the same parts of the sound (Liberman, 1970). In exactly that sense, the syllable *bat*, which has three phonemic segments, has but one acoustic segment. There is, then, no acoustic criterion by which one can segment the sound into its constituent phonemes. To recover the phonemes from the sound into which they are so complexly encoded requires a decoder which segments the continuous acoustic signal according to linguistic rules. Though we can only guess how such a decoder might work, we know that it functions quite automatically for all speaker–hearers of a language, even very young children (Liberman *et al.*, 1967; Liberman, 1974). In perceiving a spoken message, therefore, the listener need not be explicit about its phonemic structure—no more explicit, indeed, than he need be about its syntax.

If it is now apparent why explicit segmentation into phonemes might be difficult, it is still reasonable to ask why syllables should be easier. A plausible answer is not hard to find. As we noted earlier, the consonant segments of the phonemic message are typically folded, at the acoustic level, into the vowel, with the result that there is no acoustic criterion by which the phonemic segments are dependably marked. However, every syllable that is formed in this way contains a vocalic nucleus and, hence, a peak of acoustic energy. These energy peaks provide audible cues that correspond very simply, if somewhat imperfectly, to the syllable centers (Fletcher, 1929). Though such direct auditory cues could not in themselves help a listener to define exact syllable boundaries, they ought to make it easy for him to discover how many syllables there are and, in that sense, to do explicit syllable segmentation.

As we have said, there has been no direct test of the assumption that young children do, in fact, find it difficult to segment words explicitly into phonemes and that this abililty comes later and is more difficult than syllable segmentation. The present experiment was undertaken to provide such a test. The question posed was how well children in nursery school, kindergarten, and first grade can identify the number of phonemic segments in spoken utterances and how this compares with their ability to deal similarly with syllables.

Method

Subjects

The subjects were 135 white middle-class boys and girls from a public preschool program in the suburban town of Manchester, CT and from the elementary school in the adjoining town of Andover, CT. They included 46 preschoolers (mean CA = 59 months, SD = 5.40), 49 kindergarteners (mean CA = 70 months, SD = 4.10), and 40 first graders (mean CA = 83 months, SD = 5.50). All available children at the appropriate grade levels in the participating schools were used, with the following exceptions: among the nursery school children, four with speech and hearing problems, 12 who refused to enter into the testing situation at all, and five who were so inattentive and distractible that demonstration trials could not be carried out; among the kindergarteners, one who had returned to kindergarten after several months in first grade and one whose protocol was spoiled by equivocal responses. No first graders were excluded.

Alphabetized class registers at each grade level were used to alternate the children between the two experimental groups, the one requiring phoneme segmentation (Group P) and the other, syllable segmentation (Group S). Equalization of the numbers of children assigned to each type of task was complicated at the preschool level by the sporadic lack of participation of individual children. The final composition of the experimental groups was as follows: at the nursery school level, 20 in Group P and 26 in Group S; kindergarteners, 24 in Group P and 25 in Group S; first graders, 20 in each group.

The level of intelligence of all the subjects was assessed by the Goodenough Draw-A-Person Test (DAP). When computed across tasks, the mean DAP IQ was 110.06 (SD = 18.20) for the syllable group and 109.19 (SD = 15.73) for the phoneme group. Across grade levels, the mean IQ was 112.11 (SD = 17.04) for the preschoolers, 108.90 (SD = 17.92) for the kindergarteners, and 107.73 (SD = 15.90) for the first graders. Two-way analyses of variance performed on the DAP IQ scores revealed no significant differences in IQ, either across tasks or across grade levels. In addition, the mean chronological ages of the two task groups were also found to be not significantly different. The mean age in months of the syllable group was 69.41 (SD = 11.25), and of the phoneme group, 69.58 (SD = 11.18). Therefore, any performance differences in the two types of segmentation can reasonably be taken to be due to differences in the difficulty of the two tasks.

Procedure

Under the guise of a "tapping game," the child was required to repeat a word or sound spoken by the examiner and to indicate, by tapping a small wooden dowel on the table, the number (from one to three) of segments (phonemes in Group P and syllables in Group S) in the stimulus items. The test items in both the syllable and phoneme tasks were presented by the examiner (and repeated by the child) in a natural speaking manner. Instructions were the same for all three grade levels. Procedure for the two experimental groups followed an identical format, differing only with respect to the test items used for the two tasks. Four sets of training trials containing three items each were given. During training each set of three items was first demonstrated in an order of increasing complexity (from one to three segments). When the child was able to repeat and tap each item in the triad set correctly, as demonstrated in the initial order of presentation, the items of the triad were presented individually in scrambled order without prior demonstration, and the child's tapping was corrected as needed. The test trials, which followed the four sets of training trials, consisted of 42 randomly assorted individual items of one, two, or three segments that were presented without prior demonstration and were corrected by the examiner, as needed, immediately after the child's response. Testing was continued through all 42 items or until the child reached criterion of tapping six consecutive items correctly without demonstration. Each child was tested individually by the same examiner in a single session during either late May or early June.

Stimulus materials

The training trials for the phoneme task included the following four triads: (1) /u/ (as in m*oo*), boo, boot; (2) /æ/ (as in c*a*t), as, has; (3) /o/ (as in g*o*), toe, tall; (4) /I/ (as in b*i*t), ma, cut.

For the syllable task, the four training triads were: (1) but, butter, butterfly; (2) tell, telling, telephone; (3) doll, dolly, lollipop; (4) top, water, elephant.

It will be noted that, in the items used for training trials of both experimental groups, the first two triads were formed by adding a segment to the previous item, while in the third triad the final item varied from this rule. In the fourth triad, all three items varied in linguistic content so as better to prepare the child for the random distribution of linguistic elements in the subsequent test trials.

As can be seen in Tables 1 and 2, both experimental test lists contained an equal number of randomly distributed one-, two-, and three-segment items. These were presented in the same order to all children in each experimental group. The items had been checked against word recognition and vocabulary tests to ensure that they were reasonably appropriate for the vocabulary level of the children. In addition, a pilot study carried out in a day-care center had confirmed the suitability of both the vocabulary level and the test procedure for children aged 3–6 years. No further control of linguistic content was attempted in the Group S items, except that the stress in the two- and three-segment items was always on the first syllable. In the Group P list, an effort was made to include as many real words, rather than nonsense words, as possible. Of necessity, the one-segment items, which consisted of 14 different vowel sounds, usually formed nonwords. The two-segment items in Group P were constructed by adding a consonant in the initial position to six of the vowels and in the final position to the remaining eight

Table 1 Test List for the Phoneme Segmentation Task.

1. is	22. pa
2. /ɛ/ (as in b*e*t)	23. mat
3. my	24. /ʌ/ (as in b*u*t)
4. toy	25. so
5. /æ/ (as in b*a*t)	26. /ai/ (as in b*i*te)
6. /i/ (as in b*ee*t)	27. up
7. soap	28. /au/ (as in b*ou*t)
8. /I/ (as in b*i*t)	29. /ʊ/ (as in b*u*ll)
9. his	30. toys
10. pout	31. cake
11. mine	32. cool
12. caw	33. /e/ (as in bait)
13. out	34. Ed
14. red	35. cup
15. /ɔ/ (as in b*ou*ght)	36. at
16. cough	37. book
17. pot	38. /ʊk/ (as in b*oo*k)
18. /u/ (as in b*oo*t)	39. lay
19. heat	40. coo
20. he	41. /o/ (as in b*oa*t)
21. /a/ (as in h*o*t)	42. oy (as in b*oy*)

Table 2 Test List for the Syllable Segmentation Task.

1. popsicle	22. wind
2. dinner	23. nobody
3. penny	24. wagon
4. house	25. cucumber
5. valentine	26. apple
6. open	27. funny
7. box	28. boat
8. cook	29. father
9. birthday	30. holiday
10. president	31. yellow
11. bicycle	32. cake
12. typewriter	33. fix
13. green	34. bread
14. gasoline	35. overshoe
15. chicken	36. pocketbook
16. letter	37. shoe
17. jump	38. pencil
18. morning	39. Superman
19. dog	40. rude
20. monkey	41. grass
21. anything	42. fingernail

vowels. All of the three-segment items in Group P, with one exception, were constructed by the addition of one consonant to a two-segment item in the list.

Results

Two measures were used to compare the performances of the children in the syllable and phoneme segmentation tasks: trials to criterion and mean errors to pass or fail. The first measure consisted of the number of trials taken by each child to reach a criterion level of six consecutive correct test trials without demonstration by the examiner. It was apparent from this measure that the test items were more readily segmented into syllables than into phonemes. In the first place, the number of children who were able to reach criterion was markedly greater in the syllable segmentation group, whatever the grade level. At the nursery school level, none of the children could segment by phonemes, while nearly half (46%) could segment by syllables. Ability to perform phoneme segmentation was demonstrated by only 17% of the children at the kindergarten level; by contrast, almost half (48%) of the children at that level could segment syllabically. Even at the end of first grade, only 70% succeeded in phoneme segmentation, while 90% were successful in the syllable task.

The relatively greater difficulty of phoneme segmentation was indicated not only by the fact that fewer children reached criterion level with the phoneme task than with the syllables, but also by the fact that those children who did reach criterion on the phoneme task took a greater number of trials to do so. The mean number of trials taken to reach criterion by the successful children in the syllable group was 25.7 at the nursery school level, 12.1 for the kindergarteners, and 9.8 for the first graders. In contrast, in the phoneme group, no nursery school child reached criterion, while the mean number of trials for those who did in the kindergarten group was 26.0 and for the first graders, 25.6.

The contrast in difficulty between the two tasks is also seen in the proportion of children who achieved criterion in six trials (which under the procedures of the experiment was the minimum possible number). For the children who worked at the syllable task, the percentage who reached criterion in the minimum time increased steadily over the three age levels. It was 7% for the preschoolers, 16% for the kindergarteners, and 50% for the first graders. In striking contrast to this, we find that in the phoneme groups no child at any grade level attained the criterion in the minimum time.

In addition to the trials-to-criterion measure which has been discussed up to this point, the data have also been analyzed in terms of mean errors. Mean errors to passing or failing a criterion of six consecutive correct trials without demonstration are plotted by task and grade in Fig. 1. Errors on both the syllable and phoneme tasks decreased monotonically at successive

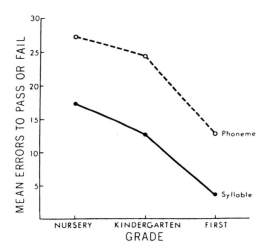

Figure 1 Mean errors to passing or failing a criterion of six consecutive correct trials in the phoneme and syllable segmentation tasks for nursery school, kindergarten, and first-grade groups.

grade levels, but the greater difficulty of phoneme segmentation at every level was again clearly demonstrated. A two-way analysis of variance was carried out in order to assess the contribution of the variables of task and grade. The effect of task was highly significant [$F(1,129) = 42.86$, $p < .001$]. The same high level of significance was also found for the effect of grade [$F(2,129) = 29.05$, $p < .001$]. As the figure shows, there is no interaction between task and grade ($F < 1$).

Discussion

It was found that the explicit analysis of spoken utterances into phonemes is significantly more difficult for the young child than analysis into syllables, and it develops later. Far fewer children in the group which received the phoneme segmentation task were able to reach criterion level; those who did made a larger number of errors, required a greater number of trials, and none reached criterion in the minimum time. Indeed, all the children in the nursery school group failed in performance of phoneme segmentation according to the criterion adopted in this study. Although it was found that syllabic segmentation was easier for young children than phoneme segmentation, it would be a mistake to suppose that syllable structure is completely transparent to the child. Sharp age trends, which are essentially parallel, were observed for both tasks.

It may be that analysis of language, even of the most elementary sort, requires instruction. It is noteworthy in this regard that a steep increase in the ability to indicate segmentation of both phonemes and syllables occurred during the first school year. We cannot judge from this experiment to what degree these measured increases represent maturational changes and to what extent they may reflect the effects of intensive instruction in reading and writing during the first grade. Whatever the effects of instruction, the findings strongly suggest that a greater level of intellectual maturity is necessary to achieve the ability to analyze words into phonemes than into syllables. In any case, the possibility that changes with age are relatively independent of instruction could be tested by a developmental study in a language community such as the Chinese, where the orthographic unit is the word and where reading instruction does not demand the kind of phonemic analysis needed in an alphabetic system.

We (and others) have noted elsewhere that the need to do explicit segmentation may be one of the important differences between speaking and listening, on the one hand, and reading and writing, on the other (Elkonin, 1973; Gleitman & Rozin, 1973; Liberman, 1971; Mattingly, 1972; Savin, 1972; Shankweiler & Liberman, 1972). If this is so, it might account for the fact that many children who readily acquire the capacity to speak and understand English do not so readily learn to read and write it. Consider in this connection, what we know of the performance of children who are resistant to early reading instruction. There is considerable agreement among investigators that these children typically show no significant difficulty in the visual identification of letters as such (Doehring, 1968; Kolers, 1972; Liberman, Shankweiler, Orlando, Harris & Berti, 1971; Shankweiler, 1964; Vernon, 1960). Moreover, these children can learn fairly quickly to approximate the letter-to-phoneme correspondence of the individual written letters (Vernon, 1960). That is, if they are asked to give the "sound" of the individual letter, they will say /b ʌ/ for a *b*, /æ/ for an *a*, and /t ʌ/ for a *t*. But if they are then shown the whole printed word *bat* and asked to read it, they may give any one of a variety of incorrect responses which indicate they cannot make appropriate use of this information. Pressed to try to "sound it out" or otherwise to use what they know about the letter-to-phoneme correspondences, they are likely to produce *buhatuh*. At that point, they are usually urged by the teacher to "say it faster, put the sounds together" or, in the phrase commonly used, "blend it." But, no matter how fast they produce these syllables or how diligently they try to put them together, they still may produce the nonsense word *buhatuh*, containing three syllables and five phonemic segments and not the word *bat*, which has three phonemes encoded into a single syllable. They cannot map the printed word *bat*, which has three segments, onto the spoken word *bat*, though it is already part of their lexicon, unless they are explicitly aware that the spoken word consists of three segments.

In any event, since explicit phoneme segmentation is harder for the young child and develops later than syllable segmentation, one would expect that

49

syllable-based writing systems would be easier to learn to read than those based on an alphabet. We may thus have an explanation for the assertion (Makita, 1968) that the Japanese kana, roughly a syllabary, is readily mastered by first-grade children. One might further expect that an orthography which represents each word with a different character (as is the case in Chinese logographs or in the closely related Japanese kanji) would also not cause the difficulties in initial learning that arise in mastering the alphabetic system. Indirect evidence of the special burden imposed by an alphabetic script can be found in the relative ease with which reading-disabled children learn kanji-like representations of language while being unable to break the alphabetic cipher (Rozin, Poritsky & Sotsky, 1971).

It would, of course, be of primary interest to learn in future research whether first-grade children who do not acquire phoneme segmentation are, in fact, deficient in reading and writing as well. If it should be found that explicit segmentation of this kind is an important factor in reading disability, we should think, as Elkonin (1973) does, that it would be possible (and desirable) to develop this ability by appropriate training methods.

Note

1 The authors are grateful to A. M. Liberman and David Zeaman for their critical reading of the manuscript and many helpful suggestions.

References

CALFEE, R., CHAPMAN, R., & VENEZKY, R. How a child needs to think to learn to read. In L. W. Gregg (Ed.), *Cognition in learning and memory*. New York: Wiley, 1972. Pp. 139–182.

DIRINGER, D. *The alphabet*. New York: Philosophical Library, 1948.

DOEHRING, D. G. *Patterns of impairment in specific reading disability*. Bloomington, IN: Indiana University Press, 1968.

EIMAS, P. D., SIQUELAND, E. R., JUSCZYK, P., & VIGORITO, J. Speech perception in infants. *Science*, 1971, **171**, 303–306.

ELKONIN, D. B. U. S. S. R. In J. Downing (Ed.), *Comparative reading*. New York: Macmillan, 1973. Pp. 551–579.

FANT, C. G. M. Descriptive analysis of the acoustic aspects of speech. *Logos*, 1962, **5**, 3–17.

FLETCHER, H. *Speech and hearing*. New York: Van Nostrand, 1929.

GELB, I. J. *A study of writing*. Chicago: University of Chicago Press, 1963.

GIBSON, E. J., & LEVIN, H. *The psychology of reading*. Cambridge, MA: M.I.T. Press, in press.

GLEITMAN, L. R., & ROZIN, P. Teaching reading by use of a syllabary. *Reading Research Quarterly*, 1973, **8**, 447–483.

KOLERS, P. Experiments in reading. *Scientific American*, 1972, **227**(13), 84–91.

LIBERMAN, A. M. The grammars of speech and language. *Cognitive Psychology*, 1970, **1**, 301–323.

LIBERMAN, A. M. The specialization of the language hemisphere. In F. O. Schmitt & F. G. Worden (Eds.), *The neurosciences: Third study program.* Cambridge, MA: M.I.T. Press, 1973. Pp. 43–56.

LIBERMAN, A. M., COOPER, F. S., SHANKWEILER, D., & STUDDERT-KENNEDY, M. Perception of the speech code. *Psychological Review,* 1967, **74**, 431–461.

LIBERMAN, I. Y. Basic research in speech and lateralization of language: Some implications for reading disability. *Bulletin of the Orton Society,* 1971, **21**, 71–87.

LIBERMAN, I. Y. Segmentation of the spoken word and reading acquisition. *Bulletin of the Orton Society,* **23**, 65–77.

LIBERMAN, I. Y., SHANKWEILER, D., ORLANDO, C., HARRIS, K. S., & BERTI, F. B. Letter confusions and reversals of sequence in the beginning reader: Implications for Orton's theory of developmental dyslexia. *Cortex,* 1971, **7**, 127–142.

MAKITA, K. Rarity of reading disability in Japanese children. *American Journal of Orthopsychiatry,* 1968, **38**, 599–614.

MATTINGLY, I. G. Reading, the linguistic process and linguistic awareness. In J. F. Kavanagh & I. G. Mattingly (Eds.), *Language by ear and by eye: The relationships between speech and reading.* Cambridge, MA: M.I.T. Press, 1972. Pp. 133–147.

MONROE, M. *Children who cannot read.* Chicago: University of Chicago Press, 1932.

ROZIN, P., PORITSKY, S., & SOTSKY, R. American children with reading problems can easily learn to read English represented by Chinese characters. *Science,* 1971, **171**, 1264–1267.

SAVIN, H. What the child knows about speech when he starts to learn to read. In J. F. Kavanagh & I. G. Mattingly (Eds.), *Language by ear and eye: The relationships between speech and reading.* Cambridge, MA: M.I.T. Press, 1972. Pp. 319–326.

SHANKWEILER, D. Developmental dyslexia: A critique and review of recent evidence. *Cortex,* 1964, 1, 53–62.

SHANKWEILER, D., & LIBERMAN, I. Y. Misreading: A search for causes. In J. F. KAVANAGH & I. G. MATTINGLY (Eds.), *Language by ear and by eye: The relationships between speech and reading.* Cambridge, MA: M.I.T. Press, 1972. Pp. 293–317.

VERNON, M. D. *Backwardness in reading.* Cambridge, England: Cambridge, University Press, 1960.

102

READING AND SPELLING SKILLS IN THE FIRST SCHOOL YEARS PREDICTED FROM PHONEMIC AWARENESS SKILLS IN KINDERGARTEN

Ingvar Lundberg, Åke Olofsson and Stig Wall

Source: *Scandinavian Journal of Psychology*, 21, 1980: 159–173.

A series of metalinguistic tasks, including segmentation and synthesis of words, were given to 143 children in kindergarten. The children were followed up in school where reading and writing achievement was assessed with several tests and ratings. A causal model was postulated concering the relationships between general abilities, metalinguistic competence, and reading and spelling skills. The quantitative implications of the model were worked out by path analysis, which revealed an orderly and interpretable picture. The most invariant and important determinant of basic reading and spelling skills was the analysis of simple words. Failure and success in school could be predicted with high accuracy on the basis of pre-school data. Over 70% of the children were classified correctly in the extreme quartiles as to their future school achievement. The methodological advantage of applying path analysis instead of conventional multiple regression analysis on the present problem was discussed.

A considerable amount of research has been directed to measure, predict and define readiness for reading and potential problems in learning to read (e.g. de Hirsh, Jansky & Langford, 1966; Dykstra, 1967; Eaves, Kendall & Crichton, 1974; Feshbach, Adelman & Fuller, 1974; Haring & Ridgway, 1967; Keogh & Smith, 1970; Pate & Webb, 1970; Stevenson, Parker,

Wilkinson, Hegion & Fish, 1976). Although, a large variety of measures have been examined and some of the standardized tests of readiness, intelligence, and achievement and several teacher's rating scales have proved quite useful as predictors, they have provided little information about the component skills which form the basis for learning how to read.

Actually, one of the best single predictors of later reading achievement has turned out to be knowledge of the printed alphabet before entering school (e.g. Calfee, 1977). However, since the causal direction of such findings is obscure, pedagogical guidelines are not provided. A better understanding of the cognitive skills which contribute to success in reading could lead to the design of more effective preschool intervention programs and to more powerful methods for assisting children who may need extra help in school.

In recent years the concept of linguistic awareness (Mattingly, 1972) has stimulated a considerable amount of research effort (see reviews in Sinclair, Jarvella & Levelt, 1978) and provided a promising approach to understanding the reading process. To a preschool child it is in no way apparent that the language consists of words, that words vary in length, that words are built up by parts etc. A most crucial aspect of linguistic awareness or metalinguistic competence is the *attention shift* from content to form, the ability to make language forms opaque (Lundberg, 1978). This seems to be a special kind of language performance, less easily and less universally acquired than normal speaking and listening. "Synthesis of an utterance is one thing; the awareness of the process of synthesis quite another" (Mattingly, 1972, p. 140). Similarly, the ability to hear the difference between different sounds such as in "pan" and "ban" is in fact far from sufficient to enable a child to succeed on tasks such as identifying words starting with a given sound.

The development of the word concept in preschool children was investigated by Lundberg & Tornéus (1978). A substantial proportion of children in the 7-year-old group seemed to have a poorly developed word concept and lacked a proper understanding of the basic relationship between spoken and written words. The serious educational consequences of starting to learn reading without necessary metalinguistic skills were discussed. Also Downing (1979) pointed out the risk of entering reading instruction in a state of cognitive confusion as far as metalinguistic concepts are concerned.

More direct data on the relationship between metalinguistic skills and reading achievement have been reported in a number of recent studies (see reviews in Lundberg, 1978, and Golinkoff, 1978). Calfee, Lindamood, & Lindamood (1973) found that more than 50% of the total variance in a reading-spelling score at all grade levels could be predicted from performance on the Lindamood Auditory Conceptualization Test, an instrument which essentially taps phonemic segmentation skills. In an unpublished study by Calfee (1972) cited in Calfee (1977) later reading achievement could be predicted with fairly good precision from phonetic segmentation skills as measured in kindergarten. Liberman, Shankweiler, Fisher & Carter (1974) had their children tap on a table for each segment in one-, two-, and three-syllabic words and found a steady improvement with age. The first graders in their study were given the Wide Range Achievement. Test several months later. Liberman (1973) reported some of the results. Half of the children in the lowest third of the class in reading had failed the phoneme segmentation task but none of the children in the top third failed that task. Finally, Goldstein (1976) found that word analysis and synthesis skills accounted for 56% of the variance on a task of reading isolated words.

In summary, the relationship between the ability to segment and synthesize spoken words and reading achievement seems to be a well established fact. However, the direction of causality remains somewhat unclear. An increase in metalinguistic competence may be the result of early reading instruction. "It may be difficult to make a clear case for the necessity of phonemic skills *prior* to reading instruction" (Golinkoff, 1978, p. 30). Linguistic awareness might, alternatively, be a manifestation of some general cognitive development, where the capacity for detachment around six to seven makes way for metalinguistic reflections. A clarification of this issue seems important from a theoretical as well as from a practical point of view.

The purpose of the present study is to further elucidate the relation between certain metalinguistic skills in kindergarten and later achievement in reading and spelling. The study differs from previous ones in several ways. First, the metalinguistic skills, measured in kindergarten, include a broader set of aspects. The number of subjects was greater than in most earlier studies and they were followed up in school for a longer period of time. Most previous studies have not explicitly controlled for differences between subjects in IQ. Such control was included here.

In the attempt to clarify the causal direction the late school start in Sweden presents an advantage, since normal or gifted non-readers are found among the 6- to 7-year-olds. This age is often assumed to be of critical importance in the mental development. The metalinguistic skills may now develop in the general context of decentering and concrete operations.

The criterion also included several measures—achievement tests on reading and spelling, as well as teacher's ratings. Finally, more relevant statistical methods were applied, e.g. path analysis in order to account for the causal link pattern. Before methods and procedures are presented a few general remarks will be given concering the need for a multivariate approach to our problem. A model is also presented where the causal network is specified.

Towards a model for predicting reading and spelling ability—a multivariate approach

Information about the relative importance of various determinants of reading and spelling ability has practical relevance only if it can add to our knowledge of the causal structure behind the actual learning process. The interpretation, in action-oriented terms, of the analysis is impossible without some basic theoretical assumptions about the levels on which different factors operate and about their degree of logical priority in relation to the criterion variable, e.g. reading ability. "Explained" variation does not necessarily permit causal interpretations and may, at least partially, be an artifact. The validity of any causal inference thus rests heavily on the accomplishment of a "dialogue" between prior theoretical knowledge and a systematic treatment of empirical findings.

For intervention purposes, quantitative estimates are needed of the possible effect of changes in factors conceived of as determinants. With regard to the present problem we may, for instance, ask how much of the achievements in reading and spelling are directly "explained" by metalinguistic skills (and which of them) as compared with general qualifications. We may also ask how much of the general ability that is mediated via metalinguistic skills and how much that "directly" explain later achievements.

A non-experimental study like the present one certainly involves confounding among potential predictors. Confounding may result from multicollinearity, i.e. the explanatory variables intercorrelate and substitute for each other in the statistical sense thereby making it difficult to assess their relative importance. This is partly a statistical problem that multivariate methods handle more or less efficiently (Blalock, 1963; Sonquist, 1969) but to a large extent also a validity problem. Variables should be chosen to represent conceptual components in a postulated model rather than what is the case in the opposite common phenomenon—a variable revealed as "important" by the analytical tool—what concept does it represent, the way it has been measured?

Path analysis is an analytical tool that permits a causal interpretation of a postulated model. It does not purport to demonstrate causality, it merely works out the logical and quantitative implications of the model assumptions. Originally introduced by Wright (1934) and Tukey (1954) and then more formally described by others (Duncan, 1966; Land, 1969) it is a technique which has found increasing use in the social science studies with a systems theory approach.

In the postulated model the variables are ordered into a causal sequence, and the structure of the interrelationships is specified. The system can be determined by sets of regression equations if the following assumptions are made: *Recursivity* (a variable may not, at the same time, be cause and effect; a longitudinal design may avoid this problem), *additivity* (interaction effects, if present, should be built into the model), *Linearity* (dependent variables are related to their postulated determinants by linear equations) and *metric* data qualities (categorical variables may be incorporated by means of dummy variables).

The estimation procedure in path analysis is similar to that of multiple regression analysis, using ordinary least squares estimation procedures. To ensure comparability the (path) regression coefficients are usually standardized, i.e. the analysis is undertaken on variables scaled to zero means and unit standard deviations. The standardized beta coefficients are called path coefficients and measure the expected change in standard units of the dependent variable, that results from one standard unit changes in a determinant. Path analysis permits a more adequate interpretation of the impact of a determinant since it takes into account also the operation of spurious effects.

Instead of giving a formal description of path analysis here, we will refer to Land (1969) for a detailed presentation of the method. The specific application of the method with regard to our present problem will be further clarified in the Results section.

An outline of the simple model that guided the present investigation is presented in Fig 1. The main determinant of reading and spelling ability in school is assumed to be a set of metalinguistic skills measured in kindergarten which included analysis as well as synthesis of phonemes and syllables. Necessary prerequistes for these skills to develop are assumed to be general intelligence and more specific ability to analyse and decenter in nonverbal tasks. The latter factors may also directly influence the reading and spelling ability.

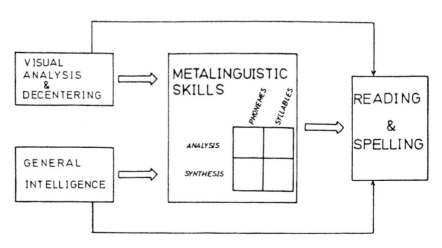

Figure 1 A simplified model of the postulated causal relationships. The thin arrows designate weaker causal links.

Method

Subjects

The kindergarten part of the investigation took place in May 1977 and included 200 children born in 1970. The institutions were scattered over the whole city of Umeå (77000 inh.). No socio-economic bias could be discerned in any place. One year later, at the end of grade 1 in school, data from 143 children (73 girls and 70 boys) from the original sample was obtained. Some six additional months later, in the first semester of grade 2, 133 children remained for the last measurement reported here. There seemed to have been a fairly representative group of Umeå children in the study. The results from several achievement tests and teacher's ratings were compared with corresponding results from a much larger group of Umeå children in the same cohort. No significant mean differences were detected. Likewise, the mean of the Ravens Coloured Matrices corresponded closely to the mean of a large group of Danish children studied in a coordinated project.

The kindergarten study

The battery of tasks in this part of the investigation included four different kinds of synthesis tasks, four segmentation tasks, one rhyming task, two tasks on perceptual decentration and finally a screening test for reading ability. The tests were administered individually at two different occasions with an interval of 2–4 days. Each session lasted for about half an hour. The child was seated at a table in a quiet area facing the experimenter.

Word synthesis

The synthesis tasks varied on two dimensions with two levels of each: without and with memory load, unit size: phoneme and syllable.

Synthesis of syllables, concretely represented (SYNSYLC). Each syllable of a given word was attached to a peg, which was inserted into a board to provide the child with a concrete representation. This was a way of avoiding memory problems and thus study the synthesizing more purely, When the child could recall the syllables perfectly from left to right on the peg board, he was requested to figure out with guidance from the syllables the content of a picture, turned upside down. A successful synthesis of the syllables yield the correct word, which was confirmed by turning the picture up. Four pictures corresponding to four three-syllabic words were used.

Synthesis of phonemes, concretely represented (SYNPHONC). The task was essentially the same as the former one, execpt for the change of unit. It was necessary for the experimenter to employ a minimum duration "schwa" vowel after stop consonants, since they cannot be pronounced otherwise. The material consisted of four CVC-words, two VCC-words and two CCV-words. The tasks of syllable synthesis and phoneme synthesis were mixed to a total test of 12 items with a reliablitity (KR 20) of 0.93.

Direct auditory synthesis of syllables (SYNSYLD). The child was play-fully introduced to a strange man on the tape recorder, who was talking in a funny way. The experimenter asked for help in understanding what the man intended to say with his slow and monotonous voice. Isolated syllables were pronounced with a pause of 1.5 sec between successive syllables of a given word. This was repeated twice with an interval of 3 sec. The total task consisted of four words (three-syllabic). HiFi-equipment was used at the recording as well as at the presentation of the voice.

Direct auditory synthesis of phonemes (SYNPHOND). Now the voice read three phonemes (with necessary "schwas") instead of syllables. The material consisted of four CVC-words, two VVC-words and two CCV-words. Half of the words were nonsense-words, a measure taken to encourage pure synthesizing and prevent wild guessing. The child was properly prewarned that the funny man sometimes meant to say words neither the child nor the experimenter even had heard before (KR 20 = 0.83).

Word analysis

Here two tasks directly corresponded to the synthesis tasks with concrete representations. In addition tasks were used which required more active mental manipulation such as position analysis and reversal. Finally a rhyming task was given. Although it probably demands some kind of analysis the character of the cognitive load is different from the rest of the tasks in this category.

Segmentation into syllables, concretely represented (ANSYLC). The task corresponds to SYNSYLC. Now, however, the child and the experimenter have changed roles. With departure from an unambiguous picture the child presented a given word to the experimenter by dividing it into its component syllables, one syllable for each peg. Synchronously with the pronunciation the pegs were inserted into the board. The experimenter was supposed to figure out, with guidance from the isolated syllables, what word the picture represented. The material consisted of four common three-syllabic words (KR 20 = 0.83).

Segmentation into phonemes, concretely represented (ANPHONC). The same procedure as in the former task was used, but the word material was analogous to that used in the phoneme synthesis task, i.e. four CVC, two VCC and two CCV, all necessarily meaningful and represented by pictures (KR 20 = 0.86).

Analysis of phoneme position (ANPHONPOS). The child was instructed to repeat and pay special attention to a certain sound, e.g. /s/ and listen carefully if a given word started with, ended with or included the critical sound in the middle. In all, 12 three-phoneme words were presented. Each of four critical sounds (phonemes) appeared in all three positions (KR 20 = 0.90).

Reversals of phonemes (ANPHONREV). The child was very carefully instructed how some words could be turned around and pronounced backwards. A few simple two-phoneme words clarified the task to the child. The test included three two-phoneme words and three three-phoneme words. All of them yielded a new meaningful Swedish word when completely reversed (KR 20 = 0.94).

Rhyme production (RHYME). The experimenter explained carefully with examples what a rhyme is like. The child was then required to produce a rhyming word to each of a set of eight simple Swedish words with several rhyming possibilities. As correct answers were accepted even constructed nonsense-words if they fulfilled conventional rhyming criteria (KR 20 = 0.82).

Non-linguistic decentration tests

The word analysis and synthesis tasks described above, all demand from the child a shift of attention from meaning to form. Perhaps, this is a general cognitive function, not exclusively limited to linguistic material presented in the auditory mode. To control for the specificity of the attention shift, two visual non-linguistic tasks were designed that in some respects simulated the cognitive demands of the linguistic tasks.

Target Identification Test (TIT). The child was presented with an outline drawing (21 cm × 30 cm) depicting a lively scenery, full of rather large and clear details. Beside the drawing was also shown a target figure on a transparent sheet, i.e. a geometrical shape with no intrinsic meaning. The target was actually also embedded as a part of the drawing, for example a part of a meaningful object seen in depth, such as a roof (see Fig. 2), or the empty space between objects in different depth positions.

In a practice trial the experimenter demonstrated how a target was constructed. The task was to detect exactly where in the drawing the target was embedded and then put the transparent sheet in the correct position over the drawing. To manage this task the child had to decenter his attention from the meaning or content of the picture to the formal relations between the lines and thus disregard the depth interpretation. If the child did not solve the task within 20 sec, a masking frame was placed on the drawing around the critical part which restricted the search area to 1/4 of the original drawing. If the child now did not come to a solution within 20 sec, he was allowed to use the transparent sheet and slide it over the drawing until the target coincided with the critical part. Thus, almost every child experienced success with the task. Seven drawings were employed in the test. For correct reaction within the first unmasked 20-sec-period two points were recorded.

Figure 2 A sample item from the Target Identification Test (TIT).

One point was given for correct answer within the second, masked period (KR 20 = 0.53).

Picture Integration Test (PIT). This task was taken from Elkind (1964). Here the child was required to pay attention to two, independent, meaningful aspects of the same object. The parallell to reading is apparent; a word has a phonological structure as well as a semantic interpretation. Both aspects must be processed almost simultaneously. Now the child was presented with a drawing consisting of parts (e.g. fruits which together constituted a whole configuration, e.g. a man). The experimenter simply asked the child what the drawing looked like. If the child answered with only one of the two possible interpretations he was further prompted after a delay of 10 sec. The maximum total exposure time was 20 sec for each picture. The same six pictures were used as were described in Elkind, Koegler & Go (1964). When part- as well as whole-answers were given, two points were recorded. Incomplete answers (either part or whole) despite prompting yielded one point. Thus, the range of total points was between 6 and 12 (KR 20 = 0.76).

Preschool reading test (PREAD)

The test was designed as a very quick and rather crude screening device organized in four hierarchical steps. At the first level five simple CVC-words were presented in typewritten lower case. Those children who succeeded to read the words went on to the next step which included three simple three-word sentences. The third step was an 11-word long sentence with a relative clause. All words were of high frequency and not longer than two syllables. The fourth step, finally, consisted of a rather complicated sentence with several multi-syllabic words of low frequency. The reading level was then assessed with scores from 0 to 4, where 0 designated failure already on the first step and 4 success on all items.

The school study

The school data were obtained within a separate and more comprehensive Nordic research cooperation, the so-called Bergen study, where a much larger group of children are followed during the first three school years. Most of our preschool children also participate in the Bergen study. So far data have been obtained at the end of grade 1 and at the beginning of grade 2.

First grade data

In the present study we only consider ability measures and aspects directly related to reading and writing. Measures of socio-emotional factors are thus excluded from the present analysis.

Silent word reading 1 (OS 400 I). The test, originally designed in Denmark by Soegaard & Bording Petersen (1974) and widely used there, consists of 400 words presented in columns. To the right of each word four alternative pictures are given, one of which is the correct representation of the word. Reading performance is expressed as the number of correct responses during a period of 15 min. One aspect of reliability is expressed by the correlation of the results after 10 min and after 15 min ($r = 0.89$). The Swedish version of the test includes only minor changes due to language differences.

Spelling I. To make inter-nordic comparisons possible a common pool of 25 words was selected from the beginner-readers used in the four

61

communities involved in the study. The Swedish version also included five additonal "local" words. Each of the 30 words formed part of a sentence which was read to the children with the instruction to write the target word on an answer sheet. The distribution of the number of correct spellings turned out to be exceptionally skewed in Sweden (a great number of children spelled all words correctly). Since the main objective was screening of poor spellers the skewness was quite acceptable in the Bergen study.

Raven's progressive matrices (RAVEN). Set A and B of the standard matrices were used (Raven, 1960). The test is an easily administrated, nonverbal way of assessing intellectual ability. A re-test reliability of $r = 0.88$ was reported by Raven (1960).

Teachers' ratings of reading ability (RATEREAD). The classroom teacher rated the children on a 3-point scale, where 1 designated low, 2 normal and 3 superior reading ability. The teachers based their ratings on eight months of experience with the children in school.

Teachers' ratings of spelling and writing ability (RATESPELL). Also in this case a three-point scale was used.

Teachers' ratings of language comprehension (LANGCOMPR). The classroom teacher was carefully instructed to use a 5-point scale for rating four different aspects or dimensions of the child's comprehension of oral language, namely (1) vocabulary, (2) the ability to follow instructions, (3) comprehension in ordinary conversation, and (4) memory for oral information. The children were observed with extra care for a period of two or three weeks before the ratings were delivered. The sum score of all ratings were used in the present data analysis.

Teachers' ratings of language production (LANGPROD). This rating domain included the following five aspects: (1) active vocabulary, (2) syntactical ability, (3) access to proper words, (4) expressive ability to tell about own experiences, (5) expressive ability to talk about a specified subject. Also here the sum score was used in the data analysis.

Second grade data

At the beginning of grade two, some six months later, 133 children with preschool data were available for retesting.

OS 400 II. The silent word reading test was used again without changes.

Spelling II. With regard to the marked skewness obtained already in the first testing it seemed now justified to use another spelling test with a more adequate level of difficulty. A widely used and well standardized Swedish battery of reading and writing tests, DLS (Björkqvist & Järpsten, 1975) offered a useful alternative. It contains a spelling test for the second grade consisting of 28 target words presented in sentence contexts as the former test.

RAVEN II. The same set of matrices as before was used.

Results

Intercorrelations among all tasks are presented in Table 1. Several rather impressive simple correlations (0.50–0.60) can be discerned between preschool tasks and later achievements in reading and writing. However, the matrix as it stands contains an overwhelming amount of information and cannot be processed efficiently by eye inspection. If one attempts to assess the relative importance of various potential determinants, a bivariate descriptive approach runs a considerable risk of being a rather meaningless exercise.

As was stated in the introduction, the multivariate nature of our problem can instead be handled by a path analysis where the various components in the associations between dependent and independent variables are determined aiming at a reduction of the apparent confusion in the intercorrelation matrix. With departure from the model presented in Fig. 1 we will now give a more detailed presentation of the method by using OS 400 I (the first reading test) as the criterion variable.

The estimated linear relationship between reading ability as measured by the OS 400 test (O) in the first school year and its postulated determinants the sum of Raven scores from two occasions (R), Sex (S), Picture Integration (P), Reversals of phonemes (A_4), and Rhyme (Rh) is given in eq. (1) with all scores expressed in standardized form. (Only variables reaching a 10% level of significance have been included.)

$$\hat{O} = p_{OR}R + p_{OS}S + p_{OP}P + p_{OA_4}A_4 + p_{ORh}Rh \tag{1}$$

The general structure is presented in Fig. 3, where all relevant measures are included.

p_{OR} (= −0.20) is the path coefficient expressing the direct effect of general abilities (as measured by the Raven tests) on reading ability. It measures the fraction of the standard deviation of O (20% of 67.2) for which R is directly responsible.

We can see that the single most powerful predictor of reading ability is A_4 (ANPHONREV) with a path coefficient of 0.56. A_4 in its turn, as postulated by the model, is strongly determined by general abilities ($p_{A_4R} = 0.47$). Thus, the direct effect of general abilities on reading is (perhaps surprisingly) −0.20, while the indirect effect is 0.47 × 0.56 = 0.26, as mediated by ANPHONREV.

Since all variables are scaled to zero means and unit variances, path coefficients are directly comparable. We also get

$$r_{OR} = \Sigma OR/n = p_{OR} + p_{OS}r_{RS} + p_{OR}r_{RP} + p_{OA_4}r_{RA_4}$$

$$+ p_{ORh}r_{RRh} = \sum_j p_{O_j}r_{Rj} \tag{2}$$

Table 1 Intercorrelations among all variables involved in the investigation.

	SYNSYLC	SYNPHONC	SYNSYLD	SYNPHOND	ANSYLC	ANPHONC	ANPHONPOS	ANPHONREV	RHYME	TIT	PIT	PREAD	OS 400 I	SPELLING I	RAVEN I	RATEREAD	RATESPELL	LANGCOMPR	LANGPROD	OS 400 II	SPELLING II	RAVEN II
SYNSYLC																						
SYNPHONC	.58																					
SYNSYLD	.42	.48																				
SYNPHOND	.49	.79	.50																			
ANSYLC	.18	.02	.04	.04																		
ANPHONC	.54	.77	.40	.68	.03																	
ANPHONPOS	.63	.78	.42	.69	.09	.86																
ANPHONREV	.49	.75	.45	.69	.16	.64	.69															
RHYME	.18	.21	.11	.13	.24	.18	.15	.16														
TIT	.17	.30	.11	.23	.07	.27	.26	.26	.10													
PIT	.33	.23	.25	.26	.13	.20	.33	.26	.19	.21												
PREAD	.46	.72	.44	.64	.18	.58	.61	.78	.13	.23	.29											
OS 400 I	.33	.50	.24	.45	.13	.47	.46	.55	.24	.19	.27	.65										
SPELLING I	.40	.46	.24	.39	.06	.48	.51	.37	.29	.21	.19	.41	.46									
RAVEN I	.34	.27	.20	.26	.26	.28	.31	.44	.24	.35	.27	.30	.19	.26								
RATEREAD	.34	.59	.35	.62	.07	.59	.56	.65	.11	.22	.17	.65	.63	.47	.26							
RATESPELL	.31	.47	.24	.48	.14	.48	.43	.54	.19	.18	.54	.55	.45	.49	.34	.73						
LANGCOMPR	.43	.44	.23	.45	.24	.48	.48	.58	.07	.25	.32	.51	.39	.36	.43	.61	.67					
LANGPROD	.47	.46	.25	.49	.32	.44	.50	.48	.15	.30	.33	.43	.29	.34	.39	.54	.56	.74				
OS 400 II	.26	.45	.16	.41	.17	.42	.44	.50	.21	.19	.24	.62	.81	.47	.21	.54	.40	.44	.39			
SPELLING II	.41	.54	.25	.46	.22	.49	.54	.58	.14	.17	.34	.63	.58	.48	.36	.58	.57	.59	.53	.61		
RAVEN II	.32	.29	.24	.29	.24	.28	.32	.44	.18	.46	.36	.31	.12	.16	.77	.28	.29	.47	.15	.44	.36	

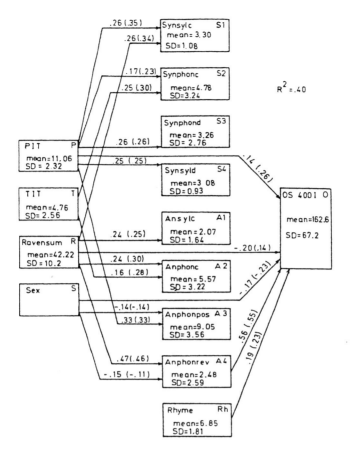

Figure 3 The results of the path analysis with the reading test in grade 1 (OS 400 I) as the last dependent variable. Above each arrow the path coefficient and within parenthesis the product moment correlation are given.

where the sum is taken over all variables from which a path leads directly to O. This is called the *path theorem* through which path analysis offers the possibility of decomposing the total association, measured by the correlation coefficient, between an independent and a dependent variable.

Apart from the *direct* effects, the remaining components represent *indirect* causal effects, where the effect is mediated via an intervening variable (e.g. ANPHONREV) and *spurious* effects which are due to joint effects of common causes (e.g. if X would cause both R and O) or the correlation between R and S and between R and P, since both S and P are causally related to O).

Since there is a postulated causal relationship between R and A_4, r_{RA_4}

$$r_{RA_4} = p_{A_4R} + p_{A_4}s^r{}_{RS} \qquad (3)$$

65

Thus, according to (2) we get

$$r_{OR} = p_{OR} + p_{OS}r_{RS} + p_{OP}r_{RP} + p_{OA_1}p_{A_1R} + p_{OA_1}p_{A_1}sr_{RS} + p_{ORh}r_{RRh} \qquad (4)$$

$$0.14 = -0.20 + (-0.17 \times 0.08) + (0.14 \times 0.36) + (0.56 \times 0.47) +$$
$$(0.56 \times (-0.15 \times 0.08)) + (0.19 \times 0.21)$$

Now we are in the position to determine the components in the association between dependent and independent variables. The results of the present analysis with OS 400 I as the starting point is summarized in Table 2.

The most powerful determinant of reading achievement in grade 1 is the ability in kindergarten to analyze phonemes and reverse their order.

OS 400 II

The level of achievement on the second silent reading test given in grade 2 (OS 400 II) must in part be determined by the initial level of reading ability in grade 1 (as measured by OS 400 I). However, an analysis where OS 400 II was located after OS 400 I in the causal chain, yielded no significant path coefficients apart from the natural link between the two reading tests ($p = 0.73$, $r = 0.81$). So in order to evaluate possible direct influences on OS 400 II from the set of metalinguistic skills and the rest of the independent variables, OS 400 II vas postulated to occupy the same position in the causal chain as OS 400 I did. The outcome of this analysis is presented in Fig. 4. The determination power of ANPHONREV and PHYME is retained, while all other factors of importance to OS 400 I now are insignificant. The total amount of explained variance R^2 has decreased from 40 to 30%.

Teachers' rating of reading achievement

(RATEREAD) The third criterion measure of reading was RATEREAD. Fig. 5 shows how this dependent variable is determined. ANPHONREV is still the most important factor. But a complete assessment of reading should certainly also include other aspects of phonemic skills. Thus, the significance of SYNPHOND and ANPHONC is not surprising.

Reading—a summary measure

The unweighted sum of z-values of the three measures of reading (OS 400 I, OS 400 II, and RATEREAD) formed an overall index of reading achievement. On this general level the importance of ANPHONREV is still very convincing (Fig. 6). A neat synthesis balance is provided by SYNPHOND. And the relevant unit seems to be the phoneme.

Table 2 The components in the association between dependent and independent variables $\sqrt{(1 - R^2)}$ is interpreted as the combined influence of extraneous sources.

Dependent variable	Independent variable	Total association	Causal effects Direct	Causal effects Indirect	Spurious effects	R^2	$\sqrt{(1 - R^2)}$
OS 400 I	RAVENSUM	.14	-.20	.26	-.08		
	SEX	-.23	-.17	-.08	.02		
	PIT	.26	.14		.12		
	ANPHONREV	.55	.56		-.01	.39	
	RHYME	.23	.19		.04		.78
SYNSYLC	RAVENSUM	.34	.26		.08		
	PIT	.35	.26		.09	.18	.91
SYNPHONC	PIT	.23	.17		.06		
	TIT	.30	.25		.05	.13	.93
SYNPHOND	PIT	.26	.26		0	.07	.96
SYNSYLD	PIT	.25	.25		0	.07	.96
ANSYLC	RAVENSUM	.25	.24		.01	.07	.96
ANPHONC	RAVENSUM	.30	.24		.06		
	TIT	.28	.16		.12	.14	.93
ANPHONPOS	SEX	-.14	-.14		0		
	PIT	.33	.33		0	.13	.93
ANPHONREV	RAVENSUM	.46	.47		-.01	.24	
	SEX	-.11	-.15		.04		.87

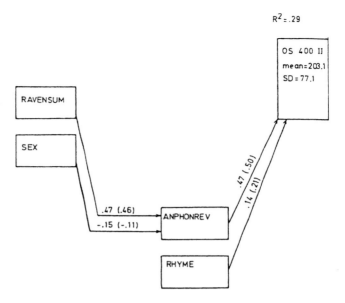

Figure 4 The results of the path analysis with the reading test in grade 2 (OS 400 II) as the last independent variable. Nonsignificant factors have been omitted and designated with a dot.

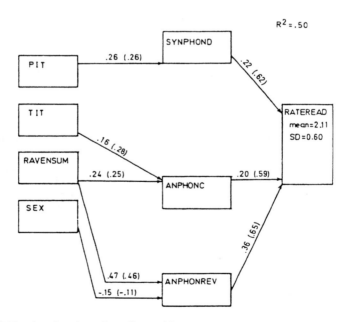

Figure 5 Teachers' rating of reading achievement (RATEREAD).

68

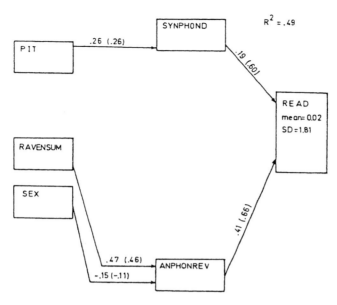

Figure 6 Reading—a summary index (READ).

Spelling I

Unfortunately the first spelling tests showed a markedly skewed distribution of scores. Originally it was constructed as a common Nordic spelling test for the first grade with a common set of words selected from the different beginner readers in the three countries. The Swedish version of the test turned out to be too easy to discriminate among normal levels of spelling ability. The original purpose, however, to aid in the selection of under-achievers, was well fulfilled. But it was considered inappropriate to include the test in the present set of path analyses.

Spelling II

The distribution of scores on the second-grade spelling test showed a more normal distribution. In Fig. 7 we can discern six significant antecedent factors directly related to spelling. Among the metalinguistic skills ANPHONREV is still the strongest. For the first time we obtained a significant contribution from a syllable task, ANSYLC. The minor effect of sex refers to the slight superiority of girls over boys.

Teachers' rating of writing

(RATEWRITE) The picture seems fairly simple and reasonable. The ability to analyse and manipulate phonemes is the most important factor in writing.

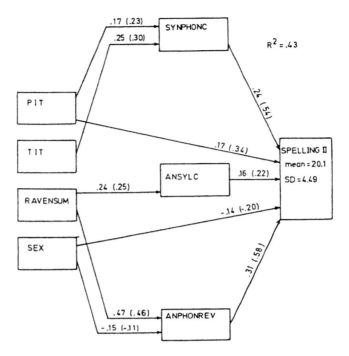

Figure 7 The spelling test given in grade 2 (SPELLING II).

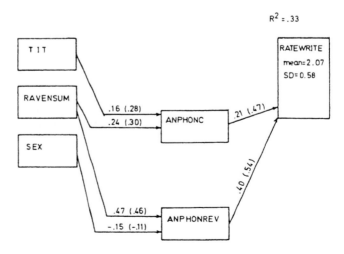

Figure 8 Teachers' rating of writing achievement (RATEWRITE).

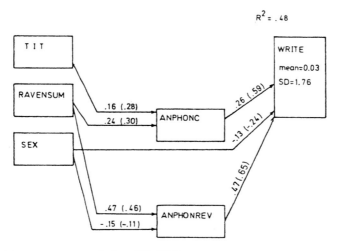

Figure 9 Writing—a summary index (WRITE).

Writing—a summary measure

As in the case of reading we formed a more general index by taking the unweighted sum of z-scores of SPELLING I, SPELLING II, and RATEWRITE. The picture is again clear and pure. Apart from a small but significant sex factor the necessary prerequisites for writing are ANPHONREV and ANPHONC. The corresponding general index of reading, however, seems to require synthesis as well.

Language abilities

The validity of the involved variables is demonstrated in Figs. 10 and 11 where a conspicuous and interpretable difference is obtained between language comprehension and language production. We can see how synthesis skills determine language production, while analysis skills are more important in understanding language. This seems straightforward enough, maybe even too simple. Anyway, the teachers seem to keep the two aspects of linguistic competence apart. And there are apparently basic distinctions within the set of metalinguistic skills.

Basics

The generalized READ and WRITE measures were combined by linear summation to an even more generalized index of basic skills in the first school years. As is shown in Fig. 12 the most powerful determinants were ANPHONC and ANPHONREV. More than half of the variance in Basics is explained by the set of antecedent variables.

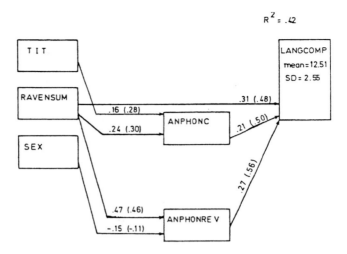

Figure 10 Teachers' rating of language comprehension (LANGCOMP).

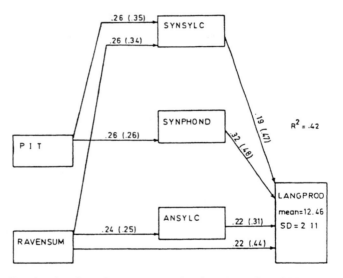

Figure 11 Teachers' rating of language production (LANGPROD).

Reading before the school start

(PREAD) The analyses presented so far have included the children who obtained PREAD > 0, i.e. they showed some simple reading skill already before they started school. Since the PREAD variable may simultaneously be both cause and effect (i.e. the recursivity assumption is invalidated) it cannot easily be located in a path model.

72

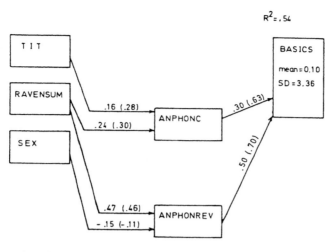

Figure 12 Basic skills in reading and writing—a summary index (BASICS).

One way out of this is to perform a separate analysis of the data for the group with PREAD = 0 and see if the metalinguistic factors still directly influence reading and writing achievement in school. Fig. 13 presents the results for the nonreaders. Due to reduced reliablility for this comparatively small group (*N* = 51) the picture is perhaps more barren now with reduced number of significant arrows. However, the general structure still holds and

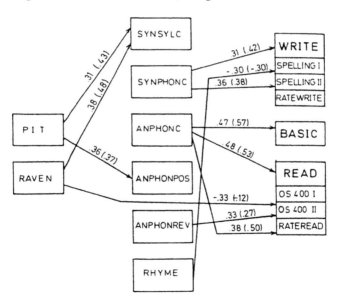

Figure 13 Determinants of basics in the subgroup of nonreaders. PREAD = 0.

the importance of metalinguistic factors for later school performance cannot be denied for this group of complete nonreaders in kindergarten.

How accurate is the prediction?

The predictive power of the independent variables is usually expressed as the proportion of the variance in the criterion that is explained by the set of independent variables, i.e. the squared multiple correlation coefficient R^2 presented in each figure.

A more precise way of expressing the predictive power is to calculate the expected scores on the criterion variable and compare these with the scores actually obtained. The expected scores are determined from the multiple regression equation. Then we can answer practical questions like for example "what is the actual fate in school of those children which on the basis of preschool data were predicted to obtain achievement scores in the lowest quartile in school?" A valid and efficient detection procedure with small risk of committing false positives or negatives is of special importance within a prevention context.

Table 3 and Fig. 14 present the results of a closer analysis of the predictive validity of the preschool battery with reference to basic skills in school.

Table 3 Predictive classification of children in different achievement groups according to the multiple regression equation.

	Observed achievement level (basics) in school			
Predicted category	Lower quartile	Average	Upper quartile	Total
Upper quartile	1	8	21	30
Average 25–75 %	7	42	9	58
Lower quartile	24	8	0	32
Total				120

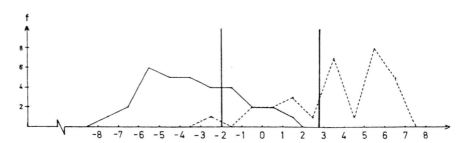

Figure 14 Frequency distributions of obtained z-scores in BASICS for the two groups predicted to fall in the extreme quartiles. The quartile limits are marked with solid vertical lines.

A predicted score on the basic index was obtained for each child by using the regression equation implied in the trimmed path model. The predicted score was compared with the score actually obtained in school. The lower and upper quartiles define the critical limits. Thus the accuracy issue under concern is to what extent children actually appear in the predicted extreme categories.

Table 3 summarizes the predictive success. Most of the children predicted to fall in the lowest quartile in school in fact also obtain a position within that category. Only a few achieve at an average level and none appear in the top quartile. Likewise the prediction of success in school is quite powerful. Only one child happens to fall in the opposite category.

Fig. 14 gives a more detailed account. We can see how small the overlap is between the frequency distributions of the extreme categories. Most of the observed scores fall on the right side of the critical limit.

Discussion

The present results strongly suggest that the achievement levels in reading and spelling of children in the first school years can be validly predicted from an assessment of their phonemic awareness skills at a time well before formal reading instruction has commenced.

One possible use of results like these is to identify highrisk children in kindergarten and pay attention to their specific needs in the hope of preventing later failures in school. However, great caution is advisable, since the prediction is after all not perfect; a few children will be mistakenly identified as problem cases and a few real problems will be missed. Long-term labelling and special placement could in fact be more harmful than positive interventions. With this precaution in mind, some constructive intervention approaches could nevertheless be discussed.

In contrast to many prediction studies the detection procedure of the present investigation is based on a theoretical effort to identify some particular skills of fundamental significance in learning to read. This strategy in combination with the application of path analysis has probably yielded more than predictive power. It has also clarified the complicated network of interrelated factors and provided some straightforward guidelines for intervention. The high predictive accuracy was largely accounted for by a small number of tasks that consistently yielded high path coefficients. The most powerful determinants of reading and writing skills turned out to be ANPHONC and ANPHONREV, i.e. the analytic ability to manipulate phonemes. These factors also dominated in the subgroup of children which did not show any sign of reading ability in kindergarten. The implication of this finding could be an intervention approach that focused on stimulating, in playful contexts, the development of such phonemic skills in kindergarten without necessarily pointing out risk children or taking any long-term labeling measures. To increase the general awareness of the importance of such stimulation in responsible teachers is probably wiser than evolving remedial and preventing measures within a labeling context.

Although the investigation carries specific educational implications and the predictive power is of encouraging strength, we need to await the final verdict of cross-validation. Our continued longitudinal follow-up of the children's performance in later grades will also provide additional information of importance to our concern.

The application of path analysis in the present case finally deserves some evaluative comments. The causal model, as hypothesized, specified the logical ordering among the variables, the quantitative implications of which were worked out by the statistical analysis or deduced from the path analysis. In this way path analysis forced us to be explicit and systematic when post-ulating our model in contrast to a conventional multiple regression analysis which is rather based on a model of "ignorance". The present field of inquiry is certainly developed enough to justify a more explicit approach.

This research was supported by a grant from the Swedish Council for Research in the Humanities and Social Sciences.

References

Björkquist, L. M. & Järpsten, B. (1975). *Manual till diagnostiska läs- och skrivprov för årskurs 2*. Stockholm: Psykologiförlaget.

Blalock, H. M. (1963). Correlated independent variables: the problem of multicollinearity. *Amer. J. Sociol. 42*, 233–237.

Calfee, R. C. (1972). Diagnostic evaluation of visual, auditory, and general language factors in pre-readers. Paper presented at the APA meeting in Hawaii, Sept. 1972.

Calfee, R. C. (1977). Assessment of independent reading skills. In A. S. Reber & D. Scarborough (Eds.), *Toward a psychology of reading*. New York: Halsted Press.

Calfee, R. C., Lindamood, P. & Lindamood, C. (1973). Acoustic-phonetic skills and reading—Kindergarten through twelfth grade. *J. Educ. Psychol. 64*, 293–298.

de Hirsch, K., Jansky, J. & Langford, W. S. (1966). *Predicting reading failure*. New York: Harper and Row.

Downing, J. (1979). *Reading and reasoning*. Bath: Chambers.

Duncan, O. D. (1966). Path analysis: Sociological examples. *Amer. J. Sociol. 72*, 1–16.

Dykstra, R. (1967). The use of reading readiness tests for prediction and diagnosis: a critique. In T. C. Barrett (Ed.), *The evaluation of children's reading achievement*. Newark, Del.: International Reading Association.

Elkind, D., Koegler, R. R. & Go, E. (1964). Studies in perceptual development. II. Part-whole perception. *Child Dev. 35*, 81–90.

Eaves, L. C., Kendall, D. C. & Crichton, J. U. (1974). The early identification of learning disabilities: a follow-up report. *J. Learn. Disabil. 7*, 632–638.

Feshbach, S., Adelman, H. & Fuller, W. (1975). The prediction of reading and related academic problems. Paper presented at the meeting of the Society for Research in Child Development, Denver, April 1975.

Goldstein, D. M. (1976). Cognitive-linguistic functioning and learning to read in preschoolers. *J. Educ. Psychol.* 68, 680–688.

Golinkoff, R. M. (1978). Phonemic awareness skills and reading achievement. In F. B. Murray & J. J. Pikulski (Eds.), *The acquisition of reading.* Baltimore: Univ. Park Press.

Haring, N. C. & Ridgway, R. W. (1976). Early identification of children with learning desabilities. *Except. Children 33*, 387–395.

Keogh, B. K. & Smith, C. E. (1967). Visual-motor ability for school prediction: a seven-year study. *Percept. Mot. Skills, 25*, 101–110.

Land, K. C. (1969). Principles of path analysis. In E. F. Borgatta (Ed.), *Sociological methodology.* San Francisco: Jossey Bass.

Liberman, I. Y. (1973). Segmentation of the spoken word and reading acquisition. Paper presented at the Society for Research in Child Development, Philadelphia, 1973.

Liberman, I. Y., Shankweiler, D., Fischer, F. W. & Carter, C. (1974). Explicit syllable and phoneme segmentation in the young child. *J. Exp. Child Psychol. 18*, 201–212.

Lundberg, I. (1978). Aspects of linguistic awareness related to reading. In A. Sinclair, R. J. Jarvella & W. J. M. Levelt (Eds.), *The child's conception of language.* Berlin: Springer-Verlag.

Lundberg, I. & Tornéus, M. (1978). Nonreaders' awareness of the basic relationship between spoken and written words. *J. Exp. Child Psychol. 25*, 404–412.

Mattingly, I. G. (1972). Reading, the linguistic process and linguistic awareness. In J. F. Kavanagh & I. G. Mattingly (Eds.), *Language by ear and by eye.* Cambridge, Mass.: MIT Press.

Pate, J. E. & Webb, W. W. Predicting failure in the primary grades. *Educ. Psychol. Meas. 30*, 459–462.

Raven, J. C. (1960). *Guide to the standard progressive matrices. Sets A, B, C, D, and E.* London: Lewis.

Sinclair, A., Jarvella, R. J. & Levelt, W. J. M. (1978). *The child's conception of language.* Berlin: Springer-Verlag.

Soegaard, A. & Bording Petersen, S. P. (1974). *OS 400 Ordstillelæsingsprøve.* Copenhagen: Dansk Psykologisk Forlag.

Sonquist, J. A. (1969). Finding variables that work. *Public Opinion Quarterly 33*, 83–95.

Stevenson, H. W., Parker, T., Wilkinson, A., Hegion, A. & Fish, E. (1976). Longitudinal study of individual differences in cognitive development and scholastic achievement. *J. Educ. Psychol. 68*, 377–400.

Tukey, J. W. (1954). Causation, regression, and path analysis. In O. Hempthorne, T. A. Bancroft, I. W. Gowen & J. D. Lush (Eds.), *Statistics and mathematics in biology.* Ames, Iowa: Iowa State College Press.

Wright, S. (1934). The method of path coefficients. *Annals of mathematical statistics 5*, 161–215.

DOES AWARENESS OF SPEECH AS A SEQUENCE OF PHONES ARISE SPONTANEOUSLY?

José Morais, Luz Cary, Jésus Alegria and Paul Bertelson

Source: *Cognition*, 7, 1979: 323–331.

Abstract

It was found that illiterate adults could neither delete nor add a phone at the beginning of a non-word; but these tasks were rather easily performed by people with similar environment and childhood experiences, who learned to read rudimentarily as adults. Awareness of speech as a sequence of phones is thus not attained spontaneously in the course of general cognitive growth, but demands some specific training, which, for most persons, is probably provided by learning to read in the alphabetic system.

Introduction

Alphabetic writing in first approximation represents speech at the level of units such as phone and phoneme.[1] Both spelling and reading in an alphabetic system imply, in addition to the ability to perceive minimal phonetic distinctions, an explicit knowledge of the phonetic structure of speech. For example, the reader/writer must not only be able to distinguish between *cat* and *bat*, but must also know that *cat* and *bat* consist of three units and differ only in the first.

An important question is how this knowledge is attained. In normal communication, people pay attention to meaning, not to the structural characteristics of the speech they hear and produce. However, conscious reflection on language and therefore explicit knowledge of the linguistic structures do occur. Awareness of speech as a sequence of phones, for instance, might appear spontaneously at some age, as a normal outcome of cognitive growth, through maturation and/or linguistic experience. Alternatively, it may require some specific training, which for most children is usually provided by reading instruction itself. The question is important not only from a theoretical point of view but also from a practical one: under the cognitive growth hypothesis, failures in learning to read can best be avoided by adjusting the age at which reading instruction is started to individual rates of development, while under the specific training hypothesis the solution should be sought in the improvement of educational practices.

That the ability to manipulate phones is related to success in learning to read has been largely documented. For instance, Savin (1972) signaled that children who failed to learn to read by the end of the first grade were generally unable to learn Pig Latin. This "secret language" requires the shifting of the initial consonant cluster of each word to the end of the word and the addition of the sound [ei]. This fact, however, may reflect either a delay in the spontaneous acquisition of the ability to analyse speech into phones or the inability to make abstract inferences about the sound system of language from its alphabetic representation.

Some observations on the linguistic behavior of preschool children would suggest that insight into the phonetic structure of language may be possible before formal learning to read and write. Read (1978) could elicit phonetically correct judgments of similarity for vowels in kindergarteners. Slobin's (1978) daughter engaged in rhyming play and noticed sound similarities in her own speech at 3;1: "eggs are beggs; more-bore". Preschool children apply the plural inflection to new words and appreciate the pronunciation of a sound in a word. However, the conscious manipulation of a particular phone or class of phones (like vowels, which are important in rhyme) does not necessarily imply awareness of speech as a sequence of phones. Phones that can be uttered in isolation may be more accessible, i.e., brought more easily to our awareness, than highly encoded ones. Awareness of such phones may be an example of awareness of a linguistic performance, rather than of a linguistic structure. The problem we consider here is how awareness of the phonetic structure, not of this or that phone, is attained.

The few studies in which the development of the ability to make an explicit analysis of utterances into phones has been investigated do not permit one to choose between the cognitive growth and the specific training hypotheses. In one of those studies (Zhurova, 1973), children were shown dolls with colored jackets and told, for instance, "the boy with the yellow jacket is Yan, the boy with the green jacket is Gan, the boy with the white jacket is Whan", etc. . . . Then, they were tested for the retention of names and questioned about other dolls with colored jackets that had not been shown before (pink, violet, etc . . .). The rule for new jackets was used successfully by 12%, 39% and 100% of the children in the 4 to 5, 5 to 6 and 6 to 7 years age groups. In another study (Liberman, Shankweiler, Fischer and Carter, 1974), children were asked to play a tapping game, in which segments of a word spoken by the experimenter had to be indicated by the number of taps. The segments were either syllables or phones. The authors found that none of the nursery school children (mean age: 4 years 10 months) could segment by phone (i.e., reach a criterion of six consecutive errorless trials) while 46% could segment by syllable. The percentage of children who were able to segment by phone increased in the other groups: 17% of the kindergarteners (mean age: 5 years 10 months) and 70% of the first graders (mean age: 6 years 11 months).

In both the Russian and the American studies the most dramatic progress in segmentation performance occurred between ages 5 and 6. As the Haskins workers pointed out, this increase "might result from the reading instruction that typically begins between ages five and six. Alternatively it might be a manifestation of cognitive growth not specifically dependent on training" (Shankweiler and Liberman, 1976). A test of the issue, they suggested, would be provided by a developmental study of segmentation skills in children learning to read in a logographic system, such as Chinese, which does not demand explicit phonetic analysis. However, such a study, they pointed out later (Liberman, Shankweiler, Liberman, Fowler and Fischer, 1977), can no longer be carried out in China, because children now learn to read alphabetic text before they start studying the logographic characters.

Fortunately, testing readers of non-alphabetic systems is not the only possibility. In communities where the writing system is alphabetic, there remains a minority of adults who either have never been taught to read or have dropped out of school at a very early stage. Illiterate people should be unable to perform tasks requiring conscious phonetic analysis, if the improvement observed between ages 5 and 6 is related to reading instruction. On the contrary, if the improvement is the result of some cognitive growth process, independent of reading, they would, of course, succeed.

Method

The present experiment was run in a poor agricultural area of Portugal (Mira de Aire, district of Leiria). Subjects were all of peasant origin, but most were now working in the textile industry. Thirty illiterate people (*I* subjects) and 30 people who learned to read beyond the usual age (*R* subjects) were tested. *I* subjects, 6 males and 24 females, were aged 38 to 60 and *R* subjects, 13 males and 17 females, were aged 26 to 60. Among *I* subjects, twenty had never received any instruction at all, four had been taught by their children to identify letters, and six had been in school for 1 to 6 months in childhood (some of them could "draw" their names). *R* subjects had attended classes for illiterate people organized by the government, by the Army or by industry. All were at that time 15 years old or more. Twenty-two, as a result, had received some kind of certificate and eight had failed to obtain any.

Two tasks were administered. In the "deletion" task, the subject had to delete the first phone from an utterance provided by the experimenter. In the "addition" task, he had to introduce an additional phone at the beginning of the utterance. Half the subjects in each group worked with one of the two tasks. For each task, five subjects worked with the phone [p], five with the phone [ʃ], and five with the phone [m]; three different groups of consonants (plosives, fricatives and nasals) were thus represented in the experiment. The test consisted of 15 introductory trials to illustrate the rule, and 20 experimental trials. The subjects were told that their task was to add (delete) one "sound" to the utterances produced by the experimenter. In the introductory trials, these utterances were non-words which became words by adding (deleting) the phone assigned to the subject. For instance "alhaço" became "palhaço" (clown) and "purso" became "urso" (bear). A correction procedure was used at that stage: when the subject failed to produce the correct response, the experimenter provided it. The experimental trials were of two types: in *W* trials, the experimenter uttered a word which, by the transformation rule, would become another word, for instance "uva" (grape) became "chuva" (rain), and vice-versa; in *NW* trials, the experimenter uttered a non-word which would become another non-word, for instance "osa" became "posa", "chosa" or "mosa" depending on phone condition. In both types of experimental trials, no information was provided after the subject's response. The subject had been told beforehand that on some experimental trials the correct response might be a non-word. All the words were of current use and, in all probability, were known by the subjects.

Results

In interpreting the results account must be taken of the fact that only *NW* trials provide unambiguous information regarding segmentation and fusion abilities. In *W* trials, the correct response might be found by searching the lexicon for a similarly sounding word. *W* trials yielded in fact better performances than *NW* ones. On *NW* trials, *I* subjects gave a very poor performance and *R* subjects quite a good one: mean correct responses were respectively 19% and 72%. The pattern of results is nearly identical for the two tasks (Table 1).

Fifty percent of *I* subjects failed on all *NW* trials, while no *R* subject did. More than 50% of *R* subjects and only one of the *I* subjects gave 8 correct responses or more on the 10 *NW* trials (Figure 1).

I subjects failed whatever the target phone: mean correct responses on *NW* trials were 17%, 19% and 20%, for [p], [ʃ] and [m] respectively. *I* subjects who had been in school for some time in childhood or who had been taught the names of letters ($n = 10$) performed somewhat better on *NW* trials (30%) than the remaining subjects (13%). The difference approached significance at $p < 0.05$ by a one-tailed t test ($t = 1.696$; df = 28).

Within the *R* group, the mean percentage of correct responses on *NW* trials was 55% for the 8 subjects without a course certificate and 79% for the

Table 1 Mean percentages of correct responses for each type of trial, task, and group of subjects. In parentheses, the percentage of subjects who attained 100% of correct responses.

		Task			
		Addition		*Deletion*	
	Trials	W	NW	W	NW
Subjects	*I*	46 (13)	19 (0)	26 (7)	19 (0)
	R	91 (33)	71 (13)	87 (47)	73 (27)

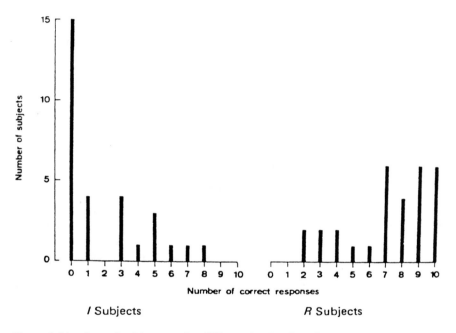

Figure 1 Number of subjects at the different levels of performance in the *I* and *R* groups (for *NW* trials only).

other 22. The difference is significant at $p < 0.025$ ($t = 2.41$; df = 28). On the other hand, *R* subjects who learned to read before age 25 ($n = 10$) did not perform significantly better than those who learned beyond that age (75% and 71% respectively; $t = 0.384$; df = 28).

The analysis of errors on *NW* trials revealed that only 19% of the incorrect responses made by *I* subjects involved the correct deletion or addition of the required phone plus some other transformation, while these kinds of responses represented 56% of the *R* subject's errors.[2] A tendency to produce

Table 2 Frequent errors in *NW* trials for each combination of group, task and phone. The first item is the stimulus and the second the response. The first number inside the brackets indicates the number of occurrences of the response; the second number indicates the total number of errors in the trial.

	[p]	*[ʃ]*	*[m]*
Deletion task			
I Subjects	Puada - Ada (2/5)	Chuada - Ada (2/5)	*Muada - Amuada* (3/5)
	Pobli - Pobre (2/4)		*Mobli - Móvel* (3/5)
	Pecli - Pé (3/4)		
		Chube - Chuva (2/4)	
		Chimá - Má (3/5)	Mimá - Má (3/5)
			Mosa - Mosa (2/5)
		Chigó - Ó (3/5)	*Migó - Amigo* (3/5)
			Maçuto - Maçuto (2/5)
		Chabatá - Batata (2/5)	Mabatá - Batata (3/5)
R Subjects	Puada - Ada (2/2)	Chuada - Ada (2/3)	
		Chobli - Bli (2/2)	
		Chimá - Má (3/3)	
		Chigó - Gó (3/4)	
		Chabatá - Tá (2/3)	
Addition task			
I Subjects	*Imá - Irmã* (2/5)		
	Abatá - Batata (2/5)		
R Subjects			Imá - Mãe (2/4)
	Açuto - Poço (2/3)	Açuto - Chuto (2/4)	

words in response to non-words was present in both *I* and *R* groups and accounted for, respectively, 46% and 32% of the errors; however, the proportion of wrong responses that both were words and involved the required phone[3] was much smaller in group *I* (6%) than in group *R* (28%). The great majority of errors made by *I* subjects can thus be linked to lack of awareness of phonetic structure, while an important portion of the errors made by *R* subjects were apparently due to some other cause.

Table 2 shows the errors that occurred twice or more (over a maximum of five) in *NW* trials for each combination of group, task and phone. It should be noticed that the most frequent errors were generally words (except *bli*, *go* and the repetitions *mosa* and *maçuto*). The items in italics are those for which the phone to be deleted (or added) has not been deleted (or added). It should be noticed that this more frequent type of error was made by the subjects of group *I*, not by those of group *R*.

Discussion

Illiterate adults were unable to delete or add a phone at the beginning of a non-word, while adults from the same environment who learned to read in youth or as adults had little difficulty. It is interesting to note that the performance of the *I* subjects was slightly inferior to that of Belgian first graders aged 6 years who were tested in the third month of the school year with similar tasks (18% correct responses for deletion, 29% for addition). The performance of the *R* subjects was at about the same level as that of Belgian second graders aged 7 years and tested in the fourth month of the school year (73% correct responses for deletion and 79% for addition) (Alegria and Morais, 1979).

The extremely poor performance of the *I* subjects cannot be explained in terms of some general inability to manipulate speech segments or to understand an inductive instruction. Cary and Morais (1979) have tested a group of 12 illiterates, from the same origin as those of the present experiment, with a more complex task which consisted in reversing the order of either phones or syllables (for instance, *cha* for *ach*, or *chave* for *vechá*, respectively) after inductive training. In the reversing phones condition the mean percentage of correct responses was 9% (ranging from 0% to 20%), while in the reversing syllables condition it was much higher: 48% (ranging from 13% to 93%).

The present results clearly indicate that the ability to deal explicitly with the phonetic units of speech is not acquired spontaneously. Learning to read, whether in childhood or as an adult, evidently allows the ability to manifest itself. Thus, it is not right to say that awareness of the phonetic structure of speech is a precondition for starting learning to read and write. The precondition for the acquisition of these skills is not phonetic awareness as such but the cognitive capacity for "becoming aware" during the first stages of the learning process. Of course, the present results do not mean that cognitive growth plays no part in the development of phonetic awareness. Specific training may not be effectual before some critical developmental stage. If awareness depends on instruction, it does not follow it necessarily. Successful instruction, on the other hand, depends on awareness. There is a reciprocal relationship between learning to read and the developmental changes in phonetic awareness.

Two important questions should now be examined. The first is to what extent phonetic awareness can be provoked by other stimulating experiences. Although for most children learning to read constitutes the exercise that renders the analysis of speech into its phonetic elements imperative, it is not necessarily unique to that function, and other kinds of training might presumably achieve the same effect.

The second question is to what extent the procedures used in recognizing and producing speech can be affected by awareness of speech as a sequence of phones. The fact that illiterates are not aware of the phonetic structure of speech does not imply, of course, that they do not use segmenting routines at this level when they listen to speech. But that fact should remind us of the risk we may incur in studying the mechanisms of speech perception through tasks that require conscious, explicit segmentation. Under the pressure of modern developments in linguistics and phonetics some psychologists were led to consider the so-called "psychological reality" of, for example, transformational grammars, or phones and phonemes. It is not always clear whether this kind of inquiry concerns implicit (tacit) or explicit knowledge (cf., a discussion of this point by Seuren, 1978). If the question concerns how we perceive speech, by first segmenting it either in phones (phonemes) or in syllables – the question apparently considered by Savin and Bever (1970) and other authors – then it refers to tacit knowledge. The present results with illiterates are irrelevant to this question, but they urge us to distinguish between the prevalence of such or such a unit in segmenting routines at an unconscious level and the ease of access to the same units at a conscious, metalinguistic level.

Notes

1 While the term phone is generally used to indicate the more elementary units of speech that are perceptibly different, there is a considerable disagreement in the literature about the definition of phoneme. In the traditional perspective, the phoneme is any collection of phones whose differences are irrelevant to meaning distinctions; in the generative-transformational perspective, the phoneme is an abstract representation that depends on morphemic information and relates to pronunciation through a set of rules. For a discussion of the distinction between phone and phoneme, from the latter point of view, in relation to the alphabetic system, see Gleitman and Rozin (1977). In the present text we shall refer to analysis into phones rather than into phonemes, because the experimental task simply required our subjects to manipulate different sounds without regard for meaning.
2 An example is the response *pili* instead of *pécli*.
3 An example is the word *poda* instead of the non-word *posa*.

References

Alegria, J. and Morais, J. (1979). Le développement de l'habileté d'analyse phonétique consciente de la parole et l'apprentissage de la lecture. *Archives de Psychologie*, in press.

Cary, L. and Morais, J. (1979). A aprendizagem da leitura e a consciência da estrutura fonética da fala. *Revista Portuguesa de Psicologia*, in press.

Gleitman, L. R. and Rozin, P. (1977). The structure and acquisition of reading. I: Relations between orthographies and the structure of language. In A. S. Reber and D. L. Scarborough (Eds.), *Toward a Psychology of Reading*. Hillsdale, Lawrence Erlbaum Associates.

Liberman, I. Y., Shankweiler, D., Fischer, F. W. and Carter, B. (1974). Reading and the awareness of linguistic segments. *J. Exper. Child Psychol.*, *18*, 201–212.

Liberman, I. Y., Shankweiler, D., Liberman, A. M., Fowler, C. and Fischer, F. W. (1977). Phonetic segmentation and recoding in the beginning reader. In A. S. Reber and D. L. Scarborough (Eds.), *Toward a Psychology of Reading*. Hillsdale, Lawrence Erlbaum Associates.

Read, C. (1978). Children's awareness of language, with emphasis on sound systems. In A. Sinclair, R. J. Jarvella and W. J. M. Levelt (Eds.), *The Child's conception of language*. Berlin, Springer-Verlag.

Savin, H. B. (1972). What the child knows about speech when he starts to learn to read. In J. F. Kavanagh and I. G. Mattingly (Eds.), *Language by ear and by eye*. Cambridge, Mass., MIT Press.

Savin, H. B. and Bever, T. G. (1970). The non-perceptual reality of the phoneme. *J. Verb. Learn. Verb. Behav.*, 9, 295–302.

Seuren, P. (1978). Grammar as an underground process. In A. Sinclair, R. J. Jarvella and W. J. M. Levelt (Eds.), *The Child's conception of language*. Berlin, Springer-Verlag.

Shankweiler, D. and Liberman, I. Y. (1976). Exploring the relations between reading and speech. In R. Knights and D. J. Bakker (Eds.), *The neuropsychology of learning disorders: Theoretical approaches*. Baltimore, University Park Press.

Slobin, D. I. (1978). A case study of early language awareness. In A. Sinclair, R. J. Jarvella and W. J. M. Levelt (Eds.), *The Child's conception of language*. Berlin, Springer-Verlag.

Zhurova, L. Y. (1973). The development of analysis of words into their sounds by preschool children. In C. A. Ferguson and D. I. Slobin (Eds.), *Studies of child language development*. New York, Holt, Rinehart and Winston, Inc.

104

TEACHING DECODING WITH AN EMPHASIS ON PHONEME ANALYSIS AND PHONEME BLENDING

Joanna P. Williams

Source: *Journal of Educational Psychology*, 72, 1980: 1–15.

This article describes a project that integrated basic educational research, the development of an instructional program, and its evaluation in a classroom setting. The program, called *The ABDs of Reading*, provided explicit training in phoneme analysis and phoneme blending, letter-sound correspondences, and decoding. Recent research indicating the importance of phoneme skills in beginning reading provided a rationale for the program. The results of 2 years of program evaluation in New York City classrooms for learning-disabled children indicated that the program successfully teaches general decoding strategies. That is, instructed children were able to decode novel combinations of letters that were not presented in training. No extensive teacher-training, teacher-aides, or other unusual classroom support was required.

The purpose of this article is to describe an instructional program that teaches basic decoding skills to learning-disabled children, to present the rationale for its development, and to present results of field trials designed to evaluate its effectiveness. The project was undertaken primarily to develop and evaluate curriculum materials. The work that was done addresses questions of current research interest and describes a process whereby basic educational research can be translated into usable school materials.

The program was developed to serve as a supplement to whatever reading program is being used in the classroom. In the work to be reported here, it was used in remedial instruction. The program's instructional sequence represents the outcome of a task analysis (Gagné, 1974; Glaser, 1977). In the first part of the program, children learned to analyze syllables and short words into phonemes and then to blend phonemes into syllables and words. Letters were introduced only after proficiency in these tasks was reached, first in the context of individual letter-phoneme correspondences. Then, decoding was taught. The name of the program, The ABDs of Reading, refers to the skills taught: analysis, blending, and decoding.

Children who successfully complete the program are able to decode regularly spelled one-syllable and multisyllable words and nonsense combinations, with and without consonant clusters, whether or not they have previously seen that particular combination of letters. Given mastery of these skills, it is expected that children will be able to succeed in any one of a number of recently developed comprehensive reading programs. Most of these programs are not geared specifically to the learning-disabled child and do not provide the necessary in-depth instruction at the very beginning stages of decoding; rather, they often assume that pupils will master these basic skills fairly easily.

One of the goals was to develop a product that would be cost effective and usable in the normal school situation. The materials are appropriate for the small-group instruction that typically goes on in the classroom, and no teacher aide is required. Moreover, the program does not require extensive teacher training to be used effectively, nor does it require any advance lesson preparation on the part of the teacher.

Program rationale

Learning-disabled children exhibit a substantial discrepancy between their estimated abilities and their school achievement, a discrepancy that is not due to mental retardation, educational or cultural deprivation, emotional disturbance, or sensory loss (Myers & Hammill, 1969). Although such children may have normal or even above-normal intelligence, they do not perform well in an ordinary school setting. The learning-disabled population is heterogeneous, but one of the problems common to a great many of these children is difficulty in learning to read.

Underlying the field of special education is a basic assumption, often implicit but almost always present, that the educational treatment most effective for handicapped populations is in some way different from that appropriate for the general population, so that the education is indeed "special." Although there have been many attempts to identify types of learning-disabled children and to specify an educational treatment most appropriate for each type, there have as yet been no successes. Nor has there been success in determining a preferred educational treatment for learning-disabled children as contrasted with nondisabled children. According to

Cronbach and Snow (1977), it is never easy to find instances of disordinal interaction. Although this conclusion may change in the future, it appears that an approach to curriculum development based on this model cannot be justified at present.

One fact, however, is clear: Learning-disabled children do have trouble learning, and children who have trouble learning, whether learning disabled or not, are likely to do better with a structured approach in which there is a sequence of specific tasks for which the child is given explicit instruction, opportunity for extensive practice, immediate feedback, minimal chance of failure, a setting in which the child is well-motivated and at ease, and so forth (Bateman, in press; Williams, Note 1). The ABDs of Reading takes the approach that slow learners in general, including those specifically designated as learning disabled, that is, those who manifest the same large variety of reading problems that other slow learners do (Vellutino, 1977), will profit from instruction that is organized according to the above principles.

Relevant literature

Decoding, the central task of the beginning reader of any language based on the alphabetic code, involves as component skills the ability to isolate the phonemes that make up a word and the ability to blend individual phonemes into whole words. Over the last few years, there has been a great deal of emphasis on these skills, and it has been noted that they are often difficult to learn (Gleitman & Rozin, 1973; Venezky, Calfee, & Chapman, 1969; Vernon, 1957).

Liberman, Shankweiler, Fischer, and Carter (1974) suggested a reason for the difficulty. Phonemes are not differentiated acoustically; the cues for recognizing the phonemes in a word occur simultaneously as well as sequentially (Liberman, Cooper, Shankweiler, & Studdert-Kennedy, 1967). Thus, the three phonemes in "pat" are not actually segments of the spoken word; blending is an abstraction. Phoneme analysis and phoneme blending have recently been called skills of "linguistic awareness" (Mattingly, 1972), "phoneme awareness" (Golinkoff, 1978), and "linguistic insight" (Ehri, 1979), on the grounds that they involve an awareness of the abstract units of which speech is composed.

There is a good deal of evidence that proficiency in these skills is important in the initial reading task. Much of the evidence is correlational and thus merely suggestive. Chall, Roswell, and Blumenthal (1963) found that blending ability in Grade 1 is highly related to later reading achievement, and the ability to blend phonemes into nonsense syllables is related to silent-reading achievement (Balmuth, 1972). Calfee, Lindamood, and Lindamood (1973), in a study of children from kindergarten through Grade 12, found that a test requiring the manipulation of phonemes predicted more than half the variance in reading achievement. Liberman et al. (1974) trained children in preschool, kindergarten, and first grade to tap out the number of segments in one- to three-syllable words. Performance improved as grade level increased, and syllable segmentation (analysis) was always easier than phoneme segmentation. The first graders' scores on the tapping task were related to their second-grade reading achievement. Other studies (e.g., Helfgott, 1976) have corroborated these findings.

Rosner and Simon (1971) found significant correlations between a task requiring deletion of syllables and phonemes ("say *mat* without the *m*") and performance on the language arts subtests of the Stanford Achievement Test at all grade levels from kindergarten to the sixth grade. Controlling for IQ, the correlations remained significant except at the sixth-grade level. Fox and Routh (1975), using an elaborate guided procedure designed to reduce as much as possible extraneous cognitive requirements in the task, found that even 3- and 4-year-olds were able to do some phoneme analysis. Proficiency increased markedly from ages 3 to 6. Phoneme analysis correlated significantly with reading achievement, whereas syllable analysis did not. Goldstein (1976) found that for a sample of middle-class 4-year-olds, a test of analysis and synthesis (including both syllable and phoneme items) predicted—independent of IQ and after several weeks of reading instruction—achievement on two tests: reading single words and reading words in a story context.

It has also been shown that children do not necessarily demonstrate phonemic analysis and synthesis skills when they do demonstrate other related skills. For example, Liberman (1973) found that some of her reading-disabled subjects could discriminate between phonemes and, when shown a letter, could provide the correct phoneme but could not segment. Wallach, Wallach, Dozier, and Kaplan (1977) also showed that nonreading lower socioeconomic status kindergarteners were successful on a phoneme-discrimination task but not on a phoneme-analysis task.

More important are several studies that show that training in auditory analysis and blending skills may have positive effects on reading. Work by Russian psychologists, including Zhurova (1963) and Elkonin (1963, 1973), emphasizes the importance of these skills. Elkonin (1963, 1973) developed a training procedure that included a visual model that made the analysis task more concrete. The model involved diagrams, in which a series of connected squares represented a word, each square represented a phoneme, and discs were used to count off the phonemes. The discs were gradually replaced during the course of instruction with the appropriate letters. According to Elkonin (1973), prereaders using this method mastered phonemic analysis relatively quickly, and this was followed by "improvements in various aspects on learning literacy" (p. 219). Unfortunately, little specific data are provided in the reports by Elkonin.

Rosner (1974) developed an extensive and carefully sequenced training program that focused on the skills of adding, omitting, substituting, and rearranging phonemes. Four- and 5-year-olds improved after several months of instruction in their ability to deal with syllables and with the initial phonemes in words. In another study, Rosner (Note 2) trained nonreading first graders in auditory analysis over the course of many sessions; their posttest scores on phoneme skills were significantly higher than those of the control group. This study is important because it succeeded in demonstrating transfer to reading: After training, the experimental group was able to read a significantly greater number of words, including words that had not been used in training, than was the control group. Wallach and Wallach (1976) developed a beginning reading program that incorporated auditory analysis training. This program was designed to be administered in a one-to-one tutorial setting. Low-readiness first graders who received this program performed significantly better than control subjects on several reading measures, including standardized tests and report-card grades.

It should be emphasized that the research discussed above identifies specific auditory tasks that are themselves components of the decoding task; it is these tasks that seem promising as training tasks. It is not likely that training of auditory skills in general will lead to better reading achievement. There is ample evidence that many auditory tasks (discrimination, memory, etc.) are correlated with reading readiness or first- and second-grade reading achievement (e.g., Dykstra, 1966; Flynn & Byrne, 1970; Harrington & Durrell, 1955). Moreover, it has been argued (Zigmond, 1969) that many types of auditory deficits are highly characteristic of learning-disabled children. But there is no evidence to suggest that training on these tasks will lead to improved performance in reading. The previously popular visual-perceptual training programs (e.g., Frostig & Horne, 1964) were based to a considerable extent on the correlations found between visual-perceptual skills and reading achievement, but the tasks that were used in training were not necessarily actual components of the reading task. It is widely acknowledged now that these programs are failures (Bateman, in press; Vellutino, 1977; Williams, 1977).

Description of program

A short introductory section of the program teaches the child the concept of analysis, that is, that words can be broken down into parts. The child learned to analyze at the level of the syllable, that is, he/she could tell what syllable occupied the initial, medial, and final positions in a three-syllable word. In addition to demonstrating the concept of analysis, there was a second reason for beginning the program with this very simple material. As the child learns to identify the syllables, he/she also learns to represent them visually with wooden squares (cf. Elkonin, 1963, 1973). This visual representation is introduced on a simple task and is thus accomplished easily.

91

Then, phoneme analysis was taught. The squares now represented phonemes and aided in focusing on the number and the order of sounds. Combinations of two phonemes were presented first, followed by combinations of three phonemes. All of this auditory analysis and sequencing practice was done with nine phonemes (seven consonants and two vowels) chosen on the basis of the following factors: (a) avoidance of auditory confusability, (b) avoidance of visual confusability, (c) ease of blendability of the phonemes in combination, (d) productivity of phonemes in creating real-word trigrams, (e) ability of children to produce sounds, (f) ease of learning grapheme-phoneme associations, and (g) regularity of phonemes in spelling patterns (with the first and fourth factors being considered most important).

The next section of the program presented blending of the same two-phoneme and three-phoneme units, which were all consonant-vowel-consonant (CVC) units. The CVCs were broken at different points. Initially, only the last phoneme was separated from the rest of the word. Next, only the first phoneme was separated from the rest of the word, and later all three phonemes were presented separately.

After this basic instructional sequence on auditory analysis and synthesis, letters were introduced, and the letter-sound correspondences for the nine phonemes were taught. The next section pulls together the auditory skills and the letter-phoneme correspondences that the child had been practicing in isolation. Again using wooden squares, which now had letters on them, the child learned to decode bigrams and trigrams made up of the same nine phonemes. He/she received extensive practice in the manipulation of these letters so that he/she could decode (read) and construct from letter squares (spell) all the possible CVC combinations. Through this extensive practice with limited content, the child learned to attend to the details required for accurate decoding, and he/she also learned the fundamental processes and strategies that would enable him/her to apply decoding skills to other content.

In the next section of the program, six additional letter-sound correspondences (five consonants and one vowel) were introduced. Then these were used in trigram decoding. Following this, all 15 letters were combined and recombined for additional decoding practice.

The final section of the program introduced, one by one, more complex units for decoding. First, CCVC patterns were decoded, followed by CVCC patterns, and then CCVCC patterns. Finally, two-syllable words made up of the same basic patterns were presented.

The instruction was organized into 12 units composed of 41 objectives. Each unit began with a story, to be read by the teacher, that incorporated a demonstration of the skills to be mastered in the unit. Following this story, a teaching procedure was presented for each objective. This consisted of a complete and explicit script for the teacher, along with as many appropriate examples as would be needed. The instruction always followed the same format. First, the teacher demonstrated the task. Then he or she called on an individual pupil, provided another example, and had the child copy him/her. Then he/she presented another example that a child had to do independently. Errors were corrected by the teacher, who provided the proper response and then had the child repeat it immediately afterward. Each unit also contained games and worksheets to provide opportunity for extensive practice of skills in a variety of contexts.

This was a decoding program, not a complete reading program. But it was important that pupils be able to apply their decoding skills in the context of actual reading. To ensure this, the teacher provided a meaningful context for words immediately after they had been decoded (or blended, earlier in the program) and used the word in a sentence or identified it as a nonsense word. In addition, simple comprehension activities were provided throughout the program. (See Williams, in press, for a more extensive description of the program.)

Evaluation

During the first stages of development, portions of the program were administered to small groups of children or to one child at a time, both by staff members and by classroom teachers. These sessions, observed by other staff members, served as the basis for development and revision of the materials. The complete program was evaluated in the field twice.

Year 1

The children were pupils in Health Conservation (HC-30) classrooms, which are administered by the New York City Board of Education's Bureau for the Education of the Physically Handicapped. All children in these classrooms were considered learning disabled.[1] Any emotional overlay to their disabilities was slight, since children with more severe emotional disturbances were placed in other classes. Children were assigned to these (or other) special classrooms when they performed unsuccessfully in a regular classroom setting and only after psychological and neurological assessment. All classrooms were in Title I Manhattan schools in central and north Harlem and on the Lower East Side. The ages of the children ranged from 7 to 12.

The main focus of the work for the first year was on formative questions; the primary interest was in making further refinements to the program on the basis of observation of actual teachers using the program in their normal classroom setting. Because of this orientation, teachers were invited who had been recommended as competent and cooperative. A half-day session at Teachers College was held to introduce the teachers to the materials and to describe the plans. In November 1975, all 157 pupils in 21 classrooms in eight schools were pretested. There were 11 children who related so poorly to the test situation that the test was not completed; there were 146 complete pretests administered. The pretest assessed competence in the specific skills covered in the program: auditory analysis and blending of both syllables and phonemes, letter-sound correspondences, and decoding. Test–retest reliability, based on a sample of 20, was .86. Table 1 presents the mean number of correct responses for all subjects.

On the basis of the pretest scores, those children who were likely to profit from the program were selected. The focus was on choosing the

Table 1 Mean Scores for All Children Initially Tested in Year 1.

Subtest	Maximum score	M number correct	SD
Syllable Analysis			
Compound words	2	1.82	.54
Two-syllable words	2	1.79	.59
Three-syllable words	2	1.39	.83
Syllable Blending			
Compound words	2	1.91	.48
Two-syllable words	2	1.90	.44
Three-syllable words	2	1.78	.58
Letter-Sound Correspondences			
Choosing letter when phoneme is presented	15	13.08	2.73
Saying phoneme when letter is presented	15	11.50	3.50
Phoneme Analysis			
Saying initial phoneme	6	4.72	1.68
Saying final phoneme	6	4.12	2.03
Saying middle phoneme	6	2.92	2.35
Saying all three phonemes	6	2.66	2.19
Phoneme Blending			
Real words			
CV-C	2	1.60	.64
C-VC	2	1.28	.80
C-V-C	2	.83	.83
Nonsense words			
CV-C	2	1.10	.84
C-VC	2	1.01	.83
C-V-C	2	.77	.81
Decoding			
Bigrams			
Real words	2	1.25	.89
Nonsense words	4	1.33	1.50
Trigrams			
Real words	6	2.54	2.08
Nonsense words	6	1.67	1.95

Note: n = 146. CVC = consonant/vowel/consonant.

(approximately) four children from each classroom who would benefit most. No specific cutoff scores were used; selection was based on a child's decoding score and his/her ability to blend and analyze on the phoneme level.

Seventeen instructional groups were formed. There were 63 children involved: 11 groups of 4 students, 4 groups of 3 students, 1 group of 2 students, and 1 group of 5 students. In consultation with the teachers, it was found that in almost every case, the same children whom the teacher had had in mind for the program had been chosen by the experimenter.

The pretest was also administered to another group of HC-30 children in comparable school districts within Manhattan. Starting with a total of 178 students in nine schools and using the same procedure that was used to select the instructional population, we formed 16 groups of 64 pupils. This was not, of course, a proper control group, but comparing these children with those who were instructed could provide us with some information about the impact of the program as well as pilot data for the second-year evaluation. There were no significant differences on any of the pretests between the instructed and the comparison subjects. (Appropriate treatment of the data would involve using each instructed group and not the individual subject as the unit of analysis. Because of the loss of data and consequent small-sized and unbalanced groups, this was not done.)

Do children who are not learning disabled and who are making "adequate" progress in regular classrooms demonstrate proficiency in the skills assessed by the pretest? To answer this question, the pretest was administered to 36 children in a regular second-grade classroom in west Harlem.

Table 2 presents means and standard deviations on the pretest for the initial 146 children from which the instructional groups were formed, the children in the instructed groups, the children in the comparison groups, and the second graders. For ease of communication, certain of the subtests have been combined. In the case of all groups, the pattern of results when the scores were broken down as in Table 1 was similar to that of the original 146 subjects. Unfortunately, the pretest data for 12 instructed children and 11 comparison children were lost. The data that are presented here include the 51 instructed children whose pretests were available for further analysis and 51 of the comparison children whose pretests were available (2 subjects in the latter group were dropped randomly in order to equate the ns in the two groups). A comparison of the pretest scores of these reduced groups indicated that in 1 out of 10 comparisons (saying the middle phoneme), the groups were significantly different, $F(1, 100) = 4.50$, $p < .05$; the mean of the comparison children was higher. The scores of the second graders were substantially higher than those of the other groups, and the scores indicate that those children did indeed exhibit ability in those skills.

Teachers were asked to use the program daily for approximately 20 minutes per session. Four teachers were observed every day. This close monitoring of the instruction is especially important when working with

Table 2 Means of Pretest Scores in Year 1.

Subtest	Maximum score	All children in instructed classes[a]	Instructed children[b]	Comparison children[b]	Second graders[c]
Syllable Analysis[d]	6	5.00 (2.65)	4.77 (2.62)	5.27 (2.70)	5.82 (2.82)
Syllable Blending[d]	6	5.59 (2.79)	5.18 (2.65)	5.16 (2.65)	6.00 (0)
Letter-Sound Correspondences					
Choosing letter when phoneme is presented	15	13.08 (2.73)	12.20 (3.05)	12.59 (2.62)	13.50 (2.14)
Saying phoneme when letter is presented	15	11.50 (3.50)	10.20 (3.57)	10.43 (3.23)	12.08 (3.58)
Phoneme Analysis (CVCs)					
Saying the initial phoneme	6	4.72 (1.68)	4.59 (1.72)	4.88 (1.41)	5.33 (1.04)
Saying final phoneme	6	4.12 (2.03)	3.27 (2.01)	3.47 (2.00)	5.08 (1.20)
Saying middle phoneme	6	2.92 (2.35)	1.67 (2.10)	2.71 (2.35)	4.67 (1.97)
Saying all three phonemes	6	2.66 (2.19)	1.41 (1.77)	1.51 (1.60)	4.22 (2.03)
Phoneme Blending[e]	12	6.59 (3.19)	4.78 (2.66)	5.66 (2.92)	9.15 (3.89)
Decoding[f]	18	6.79 (4.55)	2.96 (2.00)	2.84 (2.17)	10.75 (6.04)

Note: Numbers in parentheses are standard deviations. CVC = consonant/vowel/consonant.
[a] $n = 146$. [b] $n = 51$. [c] $n = 36$. [d] Compound words, two- and three-syllable words. [e] CV-C, C-VC, and C-V-C. [f] Bigrams and trigrams, real and nonsense.

learning-disabled children because their behavior is often extremely erratic. The other 13 classes were observed, and the teachers were interviewed once a week. Teachers were asked to work through the program exactly as it was presented, using all the games, worksheets, and so on, to provide a firm basis for evaluation and possible revision of every component. (This was not necessarily the way the program would actually be used.)

The regular reading instruction provided in these classrooms might best be described as eclectic. A wide variety of materials was used. Teachers used a different basal-reading program in almost every classroom; only one series was used by three teachers, and two other series were used by two teachers each. About 75% of the teachers also used phonics materials. (Sometimes the phonics component of the basal series and sometimes a separate phonics program was used.) No teacher dropped out of the study, and only five children dropped out of their classes—and therefore out of the program—during the year. The pretest was readministered at the end of the academic year as the posttest.

The mean length of instructional session was 29.0 minutes ($SD = 9.0$). Overall, approximately 26 weeks of instruction were given ($M = 25.6$, $SD = 3.7$). Only three groups were able to complete the entire program before the posttest was administered. The slowest group completed five units. The mean number of units completed was 8.1 ($SD = 2.2$).

Table 3 presents the means and standard deviations of the posttest scores. There was a significant gain from pretest to posttest on all but three subtests in the instructed group (syllable analysis, syllable blending, and saying the final phoneme), with $ts(100)$ ranging from 3.13 to 8.06. In the comparison group, there was a significant gain from pretest to posttest on four subtests (saying the final phoneme, saying all three phonemes, phoneme blending, and decoding) with $ts(100)$ ranging from 2.07 to 3.22.

Posttest scores of the instructed group were significantly higher than those of the comparison group on (a) the first–letter sound correspondences subtest, $F(1, 100) = 4.64$, $p < .05$; (b) the second letter–sound correspondences, $F(1, 100) = 15.76$, $p < .01$; (c) saying the middle phoneme, $F(1, 100) = 6.82$, $p < .05$; (d) saying all three phonemes, $F(1, 100) = 5.73$, $p < .05$; and (e) decoding, $F(1, 100) = 28.62$, $p < .01$. The difference between the groups on the phoneme-blending subtest was marginally significant, $F(1, 100) = 3.73$, $p < .10$.

The following January, the posttest was administered again to those children in the instructed and the comparison groups who were accessible, that is, the ones who had not moved out of Manhattan. (Of the 102 children, 66 remained in the same HC-30 classroom with the same teacher for the following year.) Scores for 36 subjects in each group are presented in Table 3 (scores of 2 additional subjects from the comparison group, chosen randomly, were dropped in order to equate the n). Results indicated that 6 months after the completion of the program, the scores of the instructed

Table 3 Means of Posttest Scores in Year 1.

Subtest	Maximum score	Immediate posttest		Delayed posttest	
		Instructed children[a]	Comparison children[a]	Instructed children[b]	Comparison children[b]
Syllable Analysis[c]	6	5.18 (1.29)	5.39 (1.44)	4.92 (1.30)	5.31 (1.01)
Syllable Blending[c]	6	5.65 (.82)	5.76 (1.34)	5.42 (1.25)	5.50 (.94)
Letter-Sound Correspondences					
Choosing the letter when phoneme is presented	15	14.25 (1.29)	13.59 (1.79)	14.50 (1.06)	14.36 (.93)
Saying the phoneme when letter is presented	15	13.73 (1.92)	11.63 (3.25)	13.08 (1.76)	12.58 (2.20)
Phoneme Analysis					
Saying initial phoneme	6	5.16 (1.50)	5.35 (1.16)	5.44 (1.25)	5.03 (1.32)
Saying the final phoneme	6	4.92 (1.64)	4.55 (1.72)	5.39 (1.02)	4.33 (1.82)
Saying middle phoneme	6	4.90 (1.87)	3.84 (2.12)	4.69 (1.98)	3.50 (2.36)
Saying all three phonemes	6	3.98 (2.03)	2.96 (2.27)	3.67 (2.03)	2.39 (2.10)
Phoneme Blending[d]	12	9.04 (3.01)	7.84 (3.21)	8.31 (3.19)	6.67 (3.21)
Decoding[e]	18	11.70 (5.10)	6.33 (5.03)	10.53 (4.65)	7.88 (4.62)

Note: Immediate posttest was given June 1976; delayed posttest was given January 1977. Numbers in parentheses are standard deviations. CVC = consonant/vowel/consonant.
[a] n = 51. [b] n = 36. [c] Compound words, two-and three-syllable words. [d] CV-C, C-VC, and C-V-C. [e] Bigrams and trigrams, real and nonsense.

group were still higher than those of the comparison group, but the only difference that was significant was on the saying-final-phoneme subtest, $t(70) = 1.72$, $p < .05$. The difference on the decoding subtest was marginal, $t(70) = 1.72$, $p < .10$.[2]

The primary purpose of the first year in the field was to determine which aspects of the program seemed to be effective and which ones might be improved through revision. Discussions of the classroom observations at weekly staff meetings led to a consensus that although much of the program was satisfactory as it was, there were also several ways in which it might be improved. Among the general decisions made were (a) to modify the format of the teacher's manual so that there was a minimum of explanatory material to be read, (b) to reduce greatly the amount of introductory material that dealt with analysis and blending on a syllable level (it simply was not necessary to spend much time on these skills), and (c) to provide more games because both teachers and pupils expressed a great deal of enthusiasm about them.

Observation in the classrooms led to favorable evaluation on certain important formative concerns: Teachers were able to work with the materials, and they liked to use the program. Moreover, the amount of time devoted to the program was substantially greater than what we had asked for, and all teachers rated the program favorably at the end of the year. Also, pupils were able and willing to respond to the instruction. There were no difficulties with understanding the tasks or with holding the pupils' attention.

In addition, the comparison of instructed children with noninstructed children indicated that the program was effective in improving the skills taught and that this improvement was to some extent maintained on a task administered 6 months after the completion of the instruction. It must be noted that these encouraging outcomes resulted from a field trial conducted under the most favorable conditions: competent, cooperative, volunteer teachers and a large amount of monitoring throughout the year.

Year 2

The second year in the field was devoted to summative evaluation and focused on the question of program effectiveness. Thanks to unusually generous cooperation from the New York City Bureau for the Education of the Physically Handicapped, it was possible to conduct a fairly large experiment. The Bureau identified six districts in New York City (in Brooklyn, the Bronx, and Manhattan, although not in the same districts in which we had worked the previous year). All HC-30 classrooms within those districts were assigned randomly to an instructional treatment (again, the program was a supplement to the regular classroom instruction) or to a no-treatment control, with the restriction that there would be three experimental classes to every two control classes.

Thus, the teachers involved in the experiment were not specifically chosen for participation. Rather, they represented all the teachers in the districts whose classes contained a suitable group of children. Far from being the enthusiastic volunteers of the previous year, their participation in the experiment was mandated.[3]

Using the same procedures as in Year 1, pretests were administered in October and November. Each tester tested approximately equal numbers of experimental and control classes and did not know to which group each class had been assigned. Small groups ($n = 179$) were formed on the basis of pretest scores, 24 experimental groups and 16 control groups. This time, teachers independently identified the children who would benefit from the program. These judgments were highly correlated with the decisions made on the basis of the pretest scores, $\chi^2(1) = 105.9$, $p < .0001$ (corrected for continuity).

Teachers assigned to the instructional treatment were asked to use the program three or four times per week in the way that was, in their opinion, most appropriate for their pupils. That is, they might skip certain objectives or even entire units, eliminate worksheets, games, unit pretests and post-tests, and so forth. They were asked to keep a record (on a form provided) of which activities were undertaken, how much time was spent on the program, pupils' scores on unit tests, and so on.

Monitoring consisted of a weekly visit to each classroom to collect these forms and the observation of one lesson in each class every 2 or 3 weeks. This low level of interaction with the teachers was aimed at keeping the evaluation as "hands-off" as possible without losing important information.

In late May and early June, the pretest was readministered as a posttest. Of the 179 children who began the experiment, 164 completed it. This loss of 15 subjects was due to transfers and chronic truants. The analysis this second year was based on the classroom group as the unit of analysis. The number of children in each group was stabilized at three by randomly dropping subjects from each group. Four experimental and 2 control groups were lost to the analysis at this point because each of them contained fewer than three subjects who completed the experiment. This left a total of 20 experimental groups ($n = 60$) and 14 control groups ($n = 42$).

Although permission to administer standardized tests was not obtained, permission to use information in the school records was granted. Even though children had been evaluated extensively before being placed in the HC-30 classes, it turned out to be difficult to find test scores for them. Only 42 intelligence test scores were obtained (an additional 12 verbal, not quantitative, descriptions of intelligence were available but not used). These scores were based on a wide variety of tests. The mean IQ of the children in the experimental group was 83.52 ($SD = 12.0$, $n = 21$) and was not significantly different, $t(40) = 1.01$, from the mean IQ of the control children ($M = 80.19$, $SD = 9.1$, $n = 21$). There were 47 grade-equivalent reading-achievement scores, again based on a large number of tests, that were available. The mean of the experimental group was 1.52 ($SD = .48$, $n = 22$) and was not significantly different, $t(45) = .77$, from the control group, $M = 1.35$ ($SD = .48$, $n = 25$). Mean chronological age as of September 1 for the experimental group was 9.37 years ($SD = 1.74$); this was not significantly different, $t(100) = 1.42$, from the mean for the control group, which was 9.77 ($SD = 1.22$).

The mean number of units of the program completed by the 20 experimental groups was 6.65 ($SD = 7.52$); the mean number of sessions was 58.20 ($SD = 18.32$); and the mean number of weeks spent on the program was 18.75 ($SD = 4.61$). The mean number of children per experimental group was 4.63 ($SD = 1.42$).

Although the teachers had been urged to use the program in any way they saw fit, only 3 of the 20 teachers skipped units, and no teacher skipped more than one. The first of the two worksheets developed for each objective was used 77% of the time, and the second of the two worksheets was used 70% of the time. Of the games, 77% were used (this was no higher than the percentage of worksheets, although the teachers had reported that both they and the children strongly preferred the games to the worksheets), and 91% of the unit pretests and posttests were administered.

Table 4 presents the means and standard deviations of the pretest scores. The pretest was a modified version of that used in Year 1: There was no syllable task and only one letter-sound correspondence task, and only trigrams were included in the decoding task. There were no significant differences between the experimental and the control groups on any of the subtests.

Table 4 Means of Pretest Scores in Year 2.

Subtest	Maximum score	Experimental (n = 20 × 3)	Control (n = 14 × 3)
Letter-Sound Correspondences			
Saying phoneme when letter is presented	18	10.15 (4.62)	10.55 (3.39)
Phoneme Analysis (CVCs)			
Saying initial phoneme	6	3.57 (1.81)	3.10 (1.32)
Saying final phoneme	6	2.47 (1.69)	2.55 (1.49)
Saying middle phoneme	6	1.22 (1.27)	1.05 (.97)
Saying all three phonemes	6	.75 (.96)	.69 (.90)
Phoneme Blending (CVCs)			
CV-C	6	2.48 (1.09)	2.07 (.98)
C-VC	6	2.08 (1.45)	2.40 (1.28)
C-V-C	6	1.32 (1.43)	1.29 (1.08)
Decoding Trigrams (CVCs)	18	2.37 (1.96)	2.55 (1.65)

Note: Numbers in parentheses are standard deviations. CVC = consonant/vowel/consonant.

101

Correlations were computed for various sections of the pretest across all 34 groups, and they are presented in Table 5. (Each of the sections contained 18 items except for the phoneme analysis section, which contained 24 items.) All $rs(68)$ were significant beyond the .01 level. The correlation of phoneme analysis and letter–sound correspondences, both of which required the child to produce individual phonemes as test responses, was significantly higher than any of the other correlations, which did not differ among themselves.

Table 6 presents the posttest data. The performance of the experimental groups improved significantly from pretest to posttest on every subtest, $ts(19)$ ranged from 5.31 to 9.90, $p < .0001$. The control groups also improved significantly from pretest to posttest on every subtest but one, $ts(13)$ ranged from 2.35 to 5.63, $p < .025$. Final-phoneme analysis was not significant, $t(13) = 1.26$. An analysis of covariance was performed on the posttest scores, using pretest score as the covariate. As indicated, the experimental groups

Table 5 Correlations Among Pretest Scores in Year 2.

Subtest	1	2	3	4
1. Phoneme Analysis	—	.578	.817	.627
2. Phoneme Blending		—	.528	.633
3. Letter-Sound Correspondences			—	.659
4. Decoding				—

Table 6 Means of Adjusted Posttest Scores in Year 2.

Subtest	Maximum score	Experimental	Control	F(1,31)
Letter-sound Correspondences				
Saying phoneme when letter is presented	18	14.33 (3.48)	12.18 (2.29)	3.97*
Phoneme Analysis (CVCs)				
Saying initial phoneme	6	4.79 (1.30)	4.44 (.85)	.79
Saying final phoneme	6	4.29 (1.48)	3.01 (.94)	7.79**
Saying middle phoneme	6	3.84 (1.57)	1.82 (1.14)	16.60**
Saying all three phonemes	6	2.86 (1.60)	1.25 (.81)	11.58**
Phoneme Blending (CVCs)				
CV-C	6	4.26 (1.21)	3.27 (1.13)	5.88*
C-VC	6	4.04 (1.39)	2.86 (.87)	7.71**
C-V-C	6	3.31 (1.57)	1.75 (.63)	11.90**
Decoding Trigrams (CVCs)	18	8.79 (4.18)	5.33 (2.82)	7.04**

Note: Numbers in parentheses are standard deviations. CVC = consonant/vowel/consonant.
* $p < .05$. ** $p < .01$.

scored significantly higher than the control groups on every subtest of the posttest except one phoneme-analysis subtest (saying initial phoneme).

Table 7 presents the correlations among total pretest score, total posttest score, number of units of the program completed, and number of teaching sessions for all 34 groups. A multiple regression analysis was performed on the posttest scores with the other three variables as independent variables. Pretest score was entered into the regression equation first (R^2 = .476). When number of units completed was entered next, the R^2 increased to .783. The number of sessions was entered next, and R^2 was then .799.

Thus, these three factors accounted for 80% of the variance in the posttest scores; the proportion of the explained variance that was accounted for by the linear regression on pretest scores was significant, $F(1, 32) = 29.08$, $p < .001$. The proportion increased significantly when number of units was added, $F(1, 31) = 43.87$, $p < .001$. It did not increase further when number of sessions was added into the regression equation, $F(1, 30) = 2.47$, indicating that number of sessions did not contribute significantly to the explained variance in posttest scores independent of the contribution of the other two variables. Similar analyses were performed on each subtest; in each case, the results were comparable to the results reported for the total score.

Transfer of skills

Evidence that the instructional program was effective in teaching the particular content covered in instruction was, of course, only a first step. An essential second step was to determine whether or not the children could generalize, that is, demonstrate transfer to content not included in the instruction. Were these subjects able to use their decoding strategies on novel materials?

Several laboratory studies have demonstrated transfer in young children (Carnine, 1977; Jeffrey & Samuels, 1967; Jenkins, Bausell, & Jenkins, 1972; Muller, 1972–1973; Silberman & Coulson, Note 3) in experiments designed to evaluate the effectiveness of explicit letter-sound training. In all of these it was found that explicit blending training was necessary for children to be able to decode new words. In a similar study, Fox and Routh (1976) taught

Table 7 Correlations Among Selected Variables in Year 2.

Variable	1	2	3	4
1. Total pretest score	—	.721	.349	−.403
2. Total posttest score		—	.654	−.006
3. Number of units completed			—	.262
4. Number of sessions				—

4-year-olds to decode words made up of combinations of phonemes and letterlike forms. Specific training in phoneme blending improved performance on the decoding task only for children already proficient in phoneme analysis. (IQ was not controlled in this study, unfortunately.) None of these studies looked at children whose IQs were as low as those in the present study.

There are few studies to cite that are based on actual classroom instruction because it is difficult to monitor the instruction carefully enough to be sure that there has been no direct training on the content to be used in assessing transfer. Because of the highly structured nature of this program, it was feasible to incorporate such a control in the training.

To do this, the experimental materials were modified in the following way. Certain trigram combinations of letters and/or phonemes, chosen randomly, were eliminated completely, page by page, from the games and worksheets and also from the long lists of "teachable" items in each lesson of the teacher's manual. Without complete monitoring of all lessons in all classrooms, it cannot be proved that a child never encountered those words and nonsense syllables in the course of the program, but it seems reasonable to assume that this was the case on the basis of (a) the classroom observations that were made and (b) the fact that teachers reported that they had used only the items provided.

When an experimental group reached each of two points in the program, a short test was administered individually to each child in the group. Control groups were chosen at random to provide yoked controls; that is, whenever an experimental group was tested, a control group was identified, and the children in it were given the same test.

The specific question that this procedure was designed to answer was: After being given decoding training on CVC combinations of a limited set of letters, can the child decode new combinations of the same letters?

Test 1 was administered at the end of Unit 7, that is, after the child had completed training on trigrams composed of 9 letters. The test consisted of 24 items: 12 familiar combinations of the 9 letters on which the child had had training and 12 unfamiliar combinations on which the child had *not* had training. Half of the familiar items were real words, and half were nonsense words; half of the unfamiliar items were real words, and half were nonsense words. Four randomized orders of presentation of the items were used; an equal number of subjects received each of the four orders. Test 2 was administered at the end of Unit 9, that is, after the child had completed training on trigrams composed of 15 letters. The test consisted of 24 items: 12 familiar and 12 unfamiliar combinations (half of each type were real words, and half were nonsense words) as in Test 1.

There were 28 subjects in the experimental group and 28 subjects in the control group who completed both tests; these are the data presented. An additional 32 subjects in the experimental group and 32 subjects in the control group completed Test 1 only; these data indicated the same effects as those presented here.

An analysis of variance (ANOVA) on the mean number of correct responses was done separately for each test. There were three factors: (a) group (experimental and control), (b) type of item (familiar and unfamiliar), and (c) type of word (real and nonsense). Table 8 presents the mean number correct in all conditions for each test. On Test 1, the ANOVA indicated the following:

1. The mean number of correct responses was significantly greater for the experimental group ($M = 4.61$) than for the control group ($M = 1.34$), $F(1, 54) = 98.06$, $p < .001$.
2. Performance on real words ($M = 3.30$) was significantly better than performance on nonsense words ($M = 2.64$), $F(1, 54) = 41.39$, $p < .001$.
3. Performance on familiar (trained) words ($M = 3.36$) was significantly better than performance on unfamiliar (transfer) words ($M = 2.59$), $F(1, 54) = 42.13$, $p < .001$.
4. There was no significant interaction between group and type of item, $F(1, 54) = .21$.
5. There was a significant interaction between group and type of word: There was no difference for the experimental group between real and nonsense words, but for the control group, performance on real words was better than that on nonsense words, $F(1, 54) = 18.90$, $p < .001$.
6. There was a significant interaction between type of item (degree of familiarity) and type of word: On trained items, scores for real words were higher than scores for nonsense words, and on transfer items the difference between real and nonsense words was smaller, $F(1, 54) = 9.66$, $p < .01$.
7. The interaction between type of item and type of work was seen only in the experimental group, as indicated by the significant three-way interaction, $F(1, 54) = 4.52$, $p < .05$.

On Test 2, results were similar to those on Test 1, except that there was no significant difference between familiar (trained) items ($M = 3.35$) and

Table 8 Mean Number Correct on the Transfer Test in Year 2.

	Test 1 items				Test 2 items			
	Trained		Transfer		Trained		Transfer	
Subjects	Real	Nonsense	Real	Nonsense	Real	Nonsense	Real	Nonsense
Experimental	5.18	4.86	4.25	4.14	4.96	4.75	5.00	4.64
Control	2.54	.86	1.25	.71	2.64	1.04	1.61	1.39

unfamiliar (transfer) items ($M = 3.16$), $F(1, 54) = 1.97$. The other comparisons were as follows: (a) group, $F(1, 54) = 72.14$, $p < .001$; (b) type of word, $F(1, 54) = 27.93$, $p < .001$; (c) Group × Type of Word, $F(1, 54) = 7.62$, $p < .01$; (d) Group × Type of Item, $F(1, 54) = 1.29$, ns; (e) Type of Word × Type of Item, $F(1, 54) = 10.73$, $p < .01$; and (f) the three-way interaction: $F(1, 54) = 16.19$, $p < .01$.

The relative difficulty of the familiar and unfamiliar items in the absence of specific training can be assessed by looking at the control group's performance. On Test 1, the items that had been selected as the transfer items were significantly more difficult than the items selected to be the familiar items tested. On Test 2, there were no differences between the familiar and unfamiliar items.

The pattern of results is similar on both tests. The experimental group performed significantly (and substantially) better than did the control group on the unfamiliar items as well as on the familiar items, indicating that transfer did occur and thus that the instructional program had succeeded in teaching strategies of decoding.

The experimental subjects did almost as well on nonsense material as on real words, whereas control subjects did much better on real words. This finding probably reflects the facts that (a) outside of the context of the program it is unlikely that there was much work with nonsense material, and (b) the control subjects' performance was more likely to be based on their ability to read sight words and not to use decoding strategies.

The interaction between type of item and familiarity of item, because it appeared only for the control group, is probably best ascribed to the specific features of the items chosen for the several conditions. The same pattern appeared on both tests. That the experimental group's performance on nonsense words was—on both tests, and for both familiar and unfamiliar items—almost as good as its performance on real words corroborates the conclusion that the program teaches process skills.

Discussion

This article illustrates a process of integrating basic research, the development of educational materials, and the evaluation of those materials in a classroom setting. The data indicate that children to whom the instructional program was administered performed significantly better on a test of decoding than did control children. The fact that this superiority was demonstrated not only on words that had been used in instruction but also on novel words indicates that the instructed children acquired general decoding strategies. Moreover, the program was effective without a large investment in costly teacher training, teacher aides, or other classroom support. These findings suggest that as a component of a well-planned comprehensive reading program, the ABDs of Reading shows promise for use with rather severely learning-disabled children. The results of the work reported here support the current interest in research on phonemic skills and the recommendations that these skills be emphasized in beginning reading instruction (Golinkoff, 1978; Richardson, DiBenedetto, & Bradley, 1977).

Notes

This work was supported by the Bureau of Education for the Handicapped, U.S. Office of Education.

I would like to express my appreciation to the New York City Board of Education for its generous cooperation and to all the teachers, administrators, and children who participated in the study. I am especially grateful to Dina Ehrlich and Sidney Goldstein. The following people participated in the development and/or evaluation of the program: Christine Ansell, Sallie Baldwin, Angela Foote, Marc Gold, Chet Gottfried, Barbara Higgins, Meredith Kattke, Nancy Kozak, Mary Oestereicher, Mary Stavrou, Norma Tan, and Suzanne Wiener. Nancy Kozak contributed a great deal to the organization of the program. I also want to thank John S. deCani for help with the statistical analysis.

1 It might be argued that the particular population studied here is not, strictly speaking, learning disabled because the mean IQ is well below "normal." However, given the lack of consensus as to how to define learning disabled, a common strategy has evolved. It consists simply of working with children who have been identified by the local school authorities as learning disabled. This is what was done here. The rationale presented in this article makes it unnecessary to agree that the subjects involved are in fact learning disabled by any strict definition.

2 Two teachers remarked at the time of the delayed posttest that because the children who had received the program the previous year had made such improvement, they were no longer spending much instructional time on decoding with these children. It goes without saying that achievement gains will dissipate over time in the absence of continued instruction. It was beyond the scope of the work reported here, as it is, unfortunately, beyond the scope of most evaluation projects, to ensure the use of appropriate follow-up instruction at the conclusion of the experimental program.

3 However, on informal questionnaires administered at the completion of the experiment, only two teachers expressed negative opinions about the program.

Reference notes

1. Williams, J. P. *Has the psychology of reading helped the teaching of reading?* Presidential address (Division 15) presented at the meeting of the American Psychological Association, Toronto, Canada, August–September, 1978.

2. Rosner, J. *Phonic analysis training and beginning reading skills* (Publication Series No. 19). Pittsburgh, Pa.: University of Pittsburgh, Learning Research and Development Center, 1971.

3. Silberman, H., & Coulson, J. *The use of exploratory research and individual tutoring techniques for the development of programming methods and theory* (Tech. Manual TM/895/200/000). Santa Monica, Calif.: System Development Corporation, June 1964.

References

Balmuth, M. Phoneme blending and silent reading achievement. In R. C. Aukerman (Ed.), *Some persistent questions on beginning reading.* Newark, Del.: International Reading Association, 1972.

Bateman, B. Teaching reading to learning-disabled children. In L. B. Resnick & P. A. Weaver (Eds.), *Theory and practice of early reading.* Hillsdale, N.J.: Erlbaum, in press.

Calfee, R. C., Lindamood, P., & Lindamood, C. Acoustic-phonetic skills and reading: Kindergarten through twelfth grade. *Journal of Educational Psychology,* 1973, *64,* 293–298.

Carnine, D. W. Phonics versus look-say: Transfer to new words. *The Reading Teacher,* 1977, *10,* 636–640.

Chall, J. S., Roswell, F. G., & Blumenthal, S. H. Auditory blending ability: A factor in success in beginning reading. *The Reading Teacher,* 1963, *17,* 113–118.

Cronbach, L. J., & Snow, R. E. *Aptitudes and instructional methods.* New York: Irvington, 1977.

Dykstra, R. Auditory discrimination abilities and beginning reading achievement. *Reading Research Quarterly,* 1966, *1,* 5–34.

Ehri, L. C. Linguistic insight: Threshold of reading acquisition. In T. G. Waller & G. E. MacKinnon (Eds.), *Reading research: Advances in theory and practice.* (Vol. 1). New York: Academic Press, 1979.

Elkonin, D. E. The psychology of mastering the elements of reading. In B. Simon & J. Simon (Eds.), *Educational psychology in the U.S.S.R.* London: Routledge & Kegan Paul, 1963.

Elkonin, D. B. U.S.S.R. In J. Downing (Ed.), *Comparative reading: Cross-national studies of behavior and processes in reading and writing.* New York: Macmillan, 1973.

Flynn, P. T. & Byrne, M. C. Relationship between reading and selected auditory abilities of third-grade children. *Journal of Speech and Hearing Research,* 1970, *13,* 731–740.

Fox, B., & Routh, D. K. Analyzing spoken language into words, syllables and phonemes: A developmental study. *Journal of Psycholinguistic Research,* 1975, *4,* 331–342.

Fox, B., & Routh, D. K. Phonemic analysis and synthesis as word-attack skills. *Journal of Educational Psychology,* 1976, *68,* 70–74.

Frostig, M., & Horne, D. *The Frostig program for the development of visual perception.* Chicago: Follett, 1964.

Gagné, R. M. *Essentials of learning for instruction.* Hinsdale, Ill.: Dryden Press, 1974.

Glaser, R. *Adaptive education: Individual diversity and learning.* New York: Holt, Rinehart & Winston, 1977.

Gleitman, L. R., & Rozin, P. Teaching reading by use of a syllabary. *Reading Research Quarterly,* 1973, *8,* 447–483.

Goldstein, D. M. Cognitive-linguistic functioning and learning to read in preschoolers. *Journal of Educational Psychology,* 1976, *68,* 680–688.

Golinkoff, R. M. Critique: Phonemic awareness skills and reading achievement. In F. B. Murray & J. J. Pikulski (Eds.), *The acquisition of reading: Cognitive, linguistic and perceptual prerequisites.* Baltimore, Md.: University Park Press, 1978.

Harrington, S. M. J., & Durrell, D. Mental maturity versus perception abilities in primary reading. *Journal of Educational Psychology*, 1955, *46*, 375–380.

Helfgott, J. Phonemic segmentation and blending skills of kindergarten children: Implications for beginning reading acquisition. *Contemporary Educational Psychology*, 1976, *1*, 157–169.

Jeffrey, W. E., & Samuels, S. J. The effect of method of reading training on initial learning and transfer. *Journal of Verbal Learning and Verbal Behavior*, 1967, *6*, 354–358.

Jenkins, J. R., Bausell, R. B., & Jenkins, L. M. Comparisons of letter name and letter sound training as transfer variables. *American Educational Research Journal*, 1972, *9*, 75–86.

Liberman, A. M., Cooper, F. S., Shankweiler, D., & Studdert-Kennedy, M. Perception of the speech code. *Psychological Review*, 1967, *74*, 431–461.

Liberman, I. Y. Segmentation of the spoken word and reading acquisition. *Bulletin of the Orton Society*, 1973, *25*, 65–77.

Liberman, I. Y., Shankweiler, D., Fischer, F. W., & Carter, B. Explicit syllable and phoneme segmentation in the young child. *Journal of Experimental Child Psychology*, 1974, *18*, 201–212.

Mattingly, I. G. Reading, the linguistic process and linguistic awareness. In J. F. Kavanaugh & I. G. Mattingly (Eds.), *Language by ear and by eye*. Cambridge, Mass.: MIT Press, 1972.

Muller, D. Phonic blending and transfer of letter training to word reading in children. *Journal of Reading Behavior*, 1972–1973, *5*, 212–217.

Myers, P., & Hammill, D. *Methods for learning disorders*. New York: Wiley, 1969.

Richardson, E., DiBenedetto, B., & Bradley, C. M. The relationship of sound blending to reading achievement. *Review of Educational Research*, 1977, *47*, 319–334.

Rosner, J. Auditory analysis training with prereaders. *The Reading Teacher*, 1974, *27*, 379–381.

Rosner, J., & Simon, D. P. The auditory analysis test: An initial report. *Journal of Learning Disabilities*, 1971, *4*, 384–392.

Vellutino, F. R. Alternative conceptualizations of dyslexia: Evidence in support of a verbal deficit hypothesis. *Harvard Educational Review*, 1977, *47*, 334–354.

Venezky, R. L., Calfee, R. C., & Chapman, R. S. Skills required for learning to read. *Education*, 1969, *89*, 298–302.

Vernon, M. D. *Backwardness in reading*. Cambridge, England: Cambridge University Press, 1957.

Wallach, L., Wallach, M. A., Dozier, M. G., & Kaplan, N. E. Poor children learning to read do not have trouble with auditory discrimination but do have trouble with phoneme recognition. *Journal of Educational Psychology*, 1977, *69*, 36–39.

Wallach, M. A., & Wallach, L. *Teaching all children to read*. Chicago: University of Chicago Press, 1976.

Williams, J. P. Building perceptual and cognitive strategies into a reading curriculum. In A. S. Reber & D. L. Scarborough (Eds.), *Toward a psychology of reading*. Hillsdale, N.J.: Erlbaum, 1977.

Williams, J. P. The ABD's of reading: A program for the learning-disabled. In L. B. Resnick & P. A. Weaver (Eds.), *Theory and practice in beginning reading*. Hillsdale, N.J.: Erlbaum, in press.

Zhurova, L. E. The development of analysis of words into sounds by preschool children. *Soviet Psychology and Psychiatry*, 1963, *2*, 17–27.

Zigmond, N. Auditory processes in children with learning disabilities. In L. Tarnopol (Ed.), *Learning disabilities: Introduction to educational and medical management.* Springfield, Ill.: Charles C Thomas, 1969.

105

AN ANALYSIS OF DEVELOPMENTAL SPELLING IN *GNYS AT WRK*

J. Richard Gentry

Source: *The Reading Teacher*, 36, 1982: 192–200.

Children go through five stages of development in learning to spell. Using the case study reported in GNYS AT WRK as an example, Gentry shows what's involved in each stage and what the teacher can do to help.

Teachers who understand that spelling is a complex developmental process can help students acquire spelling competency. Initially, the teacher must recognize five stages of spelling development. Once the stages are identified, the teacher can provide opportunities for children to develop cognitive strategies for dealing with English orthography, and assess the pupils' development. This article demonstrates a scheme for categorizing spelling development and shows ways to foster pupils' spelling competency. In doing so, it integrates important work by Bissex (1980), spelling researchers, and reading/language researchers over the past decade.

GNYS AT WRK, an account of a case study conducted by Glenda Bissex (1980), contributes much understanding to how children may develop reading, writing, and oral language skills. In addition, it provides an excellent data base for this focus on spelling development. Bissex traces her son Paul's written language development from his first writing as a 4 year old through productions typical of fourth graders whose reading, writing, and spelling development has progressed normally up through the ages of 9 or 10 years.

This article applies a developmental spelling classification system to the Bissex case study, revealing developmental stages that researchers (Beers and Henderson, 1977; Gentry, 1977; Henderson and Beers, 1980; Read,

1975) have discovered in children's early spelling and writing. Such pre-existing form suggests "that learning to spell is not simply a matter of memorizing words but in large measure a consequence of developing cognitive strategies for dealing with English orthography ..." (Read and Hodges, in press). Further, the article outlines the developmental process and provides suggestions for how spelling development may be nurtured in the classroom.

As children discover the intricacies of printed English, they progress through five levels of spelling, with each representing a different conceptualization of English orthography: precommunicative spelling, semiphonetic spelling, phonetic spelling, transitional spelling, and correct spelling (Gentry, 1978). A progressive differentiation of orthographic knowledge may be observed which, over time, enables the competent speller to rely on multiple strategies, including visual, phonological, and lexical or morphological information accrued not from rote memory but from extensive experience with written language (Read and Hodges, in press). The classification system applied here to the Bissex case study focuses on an analysis of spelling miscues and observation of the strategies used to spell words. Classification is based primarily on studies reported by Read (1975) and Henderson and Beers (1980).

Precommunicative stage

Developmental spelling studies (Gentry, 1977; Henderson and Beers, 1980) have identified the earliest level of spelling development as the level where a child first uses symbols from the alphabet to represent words. [Note, however, that writing development begins much earlier, with pencil or pen handling and scribbling as early as 18 months of age (Gibson and Levin, 1975).] Paul, before the formal observation of the Bissex case study began, had clearly been a precommunicative speller. Bissex provides two examples of Paul's productions at this earliest spelling level which, for Paul, appeared while he was still 4 years old. She describes the first example as a "welcome home" banner that took the following form (actual size 1 by 4 feet, 30 by 120 cm):

Bissex (1980, p. 4) reports other incidences of precommunicative spelling: "Next, he [Paul] typed strings of letters which he described as notes to his friends. Then he produced a handwritten message—large, green letters to cheer me up when I was feeling low:

These first, occasional writings spanned several months, during which time he showed an interest in handwriting." Such instances clearly document Paul's stint as a precommunicative speller. [Illustrations from *GNYS AT WRK: A Child Learns to Write and Read*, by Glenda L. Bissex, published by Harvard University Press, reprinted by permission of the publisher.]

A speller is specifically precommunicative when his/her spelling errors are characterized by the following behaviors (Bissex, 1980; Goodman, 1980; Söderbergh, 1971; Torrey, 1973).

(1) The speller demonstrates some knowledge of the alphabet through production of letter forms to represent a message.
(2) The speller demonstrates *no* knowledge of letter-sound correspondence. Spelling attempts appear to be a random stringing together of letters of the alphabet which the speller is able to produce in written form.
(3) The speller may or may not know the principle of left-to-right directionality for English spelling.
(4) The speller may include number symbols as part of the spelling of a word.
(5) The speller's level of alphabet knowledge may range from much repetition of a few known alphabetic symbols to substantial production of letters of the alphabet.
(6) The speller frequently mixes uppercase and lowercase letters indiscriminately.
(7) The speller generally shows a preference for uppercase letter forms in his/her earliest samples of writing.

The primary constraint under which the precommunicative speller operates is a lack of knowledge of letter-sound correspondence. As a result, precommunicative spelling attempts are not readable—hence the term "precommunicative." Though these initial attempts are purposeful productions representing the child's concept of words, at this stage spellings do not communicate language by mapping letters to sounds.

113

"Precommunicative" appears to be a more appropriate label for this first stage than the term "deviant," which is used in some earlier studies (Gentry, 1977; Gentry, 1978). Although precommunicative spellings deviate extensively from conventional spelling patterns, they are in no sense unnatural or uncommon, as the word "deviant" implies. Precommunicative spelling is the natural early expression of the child's initial hypotheses about how alphabetic symbols represent words.

The semiphonetic stage

The second stage of spelling development, which for Paul began at 5 years 1 month of age and lasted only a few weeks, is illustrated by productions such as: RUDF [Are you deaf?!], GABJ [garbage], BZR [buzzer], KR [car], TLEFNMBER [telephone number], PKIHER [picture], BRZ [birds], DP [dump], HAB [happy], OD [old]. These invented spellings, called semiphonetic (reported as "prephonetic" in some earlier studies), represent the child's first approximations to an alphabetic orthography.

Unlike the previous stage, semiphonetic spellings represent letter-sound correspondence. It is at this stage that a child first begins to conceptualize the alphabetic principle. The conditions of semiphonetic spelling are:

(1) The speller begins to conceptualize that letters have sounds that are used to represent the sounds in words.
(2) Letters used to represent words provide a partial (but not total) mapping of phonetic representation for the word being spelled. Semiphonetic spelling is abbreviated; one, two, or three letters may represent the whole word.
(3) A letter name strategy is very much in evidence at the semiphonetic stage. Where possible the speller represents words, sounds, or syllables with letters that match their letter names (e.g., R [are]; U [you]; LEFT [elephant]) instead of representing the vowel and consonant sounds separately.
(4) The semiphonetic speller begins to grasp the left-to-right sequential arrangement of letters in English orthography.
(5) Alphabet knowledge and mastery of letter formation become more complete during the semiphonetic stage.
(6) Word segmentation may or may not be in evidence in semiphonetic spelling.

Paul's rather short stint as a semiphonetic speller may be attributed to the intensity and quantity of writing during the first month after his fifth birthday and to his mother's intervention (e.g., suggestions for spacing between words, supplying letter-sound correspondences upon request, encouragement and obvious interest in Paul's invented spellings). Bissex reports "rapid flourishing and evolution of that development" (Bissex, 1980, p. 11) which is evident as Paul moved quickly from semiphonetic to complete phonetic spelling. The evolution of complete phonetic spelling from the earlier semiphonetic version is demonstrated as Paul switched from TLEFN [telephone] to TALAFON [telephone], KR [car] to KOR [car], BRZ [birds] to BRDE [birdie], and produced messages with fewer semiphonetic and more phonetic spellings, such as the message Paul typed at 5 years 2 months:

EFUKANOPNKAZIWILGEVUAKNOPENR

[If you can open cans I will give you a can opener] (underlined words are phonetic spellings) (p. 11).

The phonetic stage

Paul enjoyed spurts as a prolific phonetic speller from 5 years 1 month through around 5 years 8 months to 6 years 1 month, writing in a wide variety of forms: signs, lists, notes, letters, labels and captions, stories, greeting cards, game boards, directions, and statements (Bissex, 1980, p. 15). Examples of his phonetic spelling include: IFU LEV AT THRD STRET IWEL KOM TO YOR HAWS THE ED [If you live at Third Street I will come to your house. The End] (p. 13), and PAULZ RABR SAF RABRZ KANT GT EN [Paul's robber safe. Robbers can't get in] (p. 23).

The phonetic stage has been well documented in the literature (Beers, 1974; Gentry, 1977, 1978, 1981; Gentry and Henderson, 1978; Henderson and Beers, 1980; Read, 1971, 1975, 1980; Zutell, 1975, 1978). Read's (1975) very complete documentation reports children's phonetic spellings of 80 phonetypes, some reflecting obscure details of phonetic form. Children's phonetic spelling is the ingenious and sytematic invention of an orthographic system that completely represents the entire sound structure of the word being spelled. Though some of the inventive speller's letter choices do not conform to conventional English spelling for some sounds, the choices are systematic and perceptually correct. Phonetic spellings (which are quite readable) adhere to the following conditions:

(1) For the first time the child is able to provide a total mapping of letter-sound correspondence; all of the surface sound features of the words being spelled are represented in the spelling.
(2) Children systematically develop particular spellings for certain details of phonetic form; namely, tense vowels, lax vowels, preconsonantal nasals, syllabic sonorants, -ed endings, retroflex vowels, affricates, and intervocalic flaps (Gentry, 1978; Read, 1975).
(3) Letters are assigned strictly on the basis of sound, without regard for acceptable English letter sequence or other conventions of English orthography.

(4) Word segmentation and spatial orientation are generally, but not always, in evidence during the phonetic stage.

Bissex reports examples of Paul articulating an awareness of English orthography that was developing through the mental exercise employed each time he wrote. "'With letters there's two ways of spelling some words,' he said, pointing out that 'cat' could be spelled K-A-T or C-A-T and 'baby' B-A-B-Y or B-A-B-E" (p. 10). This cognitive awareness of English ortho-graphy becomes markedly more developed in children who are allowed to invent their own spellings during their progression through the phonetic stage. As they become more and more aware of the conventions of English spelling, they emerge into the fourth stage.

Bissex correctly predicted Paul's move into "the next phase of his spelling development," the transitional stage (p. 15).

> While writing the song book, Paul observed, "You spell 'book' B-O-O-K. To write 'look' you just change one letter—take away the B and add an L." This mental spelling and word transforming continued after his writing spurt temporarily petered out: "If you took the L out of 'glass' and pushed it all together, you'd have 'gas,'" he mused while lying in bed. Such manipulation was the form that the next phase of his spelling development took. The following week (5:3) he mentally removed the L from "please," (or "peas" or "pees"), and after we had some conversation about Daedalus and Icarus, observed that "if you put an L in front of Icarus, you get 'licorice.'" And "If you take the T and R off of 'trike' and put a B in front, you have 'bike.'"

The transitional stage

Most of Paul's mental rehearsal and hypothesizing about words were unrecorded. It took place, however, whenever he wrote and, as Bissex reports, sometimes when he was not writing. This kind of mental activity allowed Paul to make the discoveries necessary for moving into the tran-sitional stage of spelling development. After 6 years 1 month, his spelling looked different from the previous phonetic spelling. A weather forecast from Newspaper # 1 said: THES AFTERNEWN IT'S GOING TO RAIN. IT'S GOING TO BE FAIR TOMORO. A news item in Newspaper # 4 read: FAKTARE'S [factories] CAN NO LONGER OFORD MAKING PLAY DOW [dough] (p. 46).

Paul was a transitional speller throughout most of his first and second grade years.

The transition stage, during which time great integration and differentia-tion of orthographic forms take place, marks a major move toward standard

English orthography. During this stage, the speller begins to assimilate the conventional alternatives for representing sounds. The speller undergoes a transition from great reliance on phonology or sound for representing words in the printed form to much greater reliance on visual and morphological representations. During this stage, instruction in reading and spelling facilitates the move toward spelling competency, but the changes affecting the speller's conceptualization of orthography are too complex to be explained by a simple visual memorization of spelling patterns (Chomsky and Halle, 1968; Henderson and Beers, 1980; Read and Hodges, in press).

Transitional spelling exhibits the following characteristics:

(1) Transitional spellers adhere to basic conventions of English orthography: vowels appear in every syllable (e.g., EGUL instead of the phonetic EGL [eagle]; nasals are represented before consonants (e.g., BANGK instead of the phonetic BAK [bank]); both vowels and consonants are employed instead of a letter name strategy (e.g., EL rather than L for the first syllable of ELEFANT [elephant]); a vowel is represented before syllabic *r* even though it is not heard or felt as a separate sound (e.g., MONSTUR instead of the phonetic MOSTR [monster]); common English letter sequences are used in spelling (e.g., YOUNITED [united], STINGKS [stinks]; especially liberal use of vowel digraphs like *ai, ea, ay, ee,* and *ow* appears; silent *e* pattern becomes fixed as an alternative for spelling long vowel sounds (e.g., TIPE in place of the phonetic TIP [type]; inflectional endings like *s, 's, ing,* and *est* are spelled conventionally.

(2) Transitional spellers present the first evidence of a new visual strategy; the child moves from phonological to morphological and visual spelling (e.g., EIGHTEE instead of the phonetic ATE [eighty]).

(3) Due to the child's new visual strategy, transitional spellers may include all appropriate letters, but they may reverse some letters (e.g., TAOD [toad], HUOSE [house], OPNE [open]. Bissex (p. 44) attributes this phenomenon to interference. The new visual strategy, though in use, is not yet integrated to the point that the speller recognizes what "looks right."

(4) Transitional spellers have not fully developed the use of factors identified by researchers that contribute to spelling competency: graphemic environment of the unit, position in the word, stress, morpheme boundaries, and phonological influences (Bissex, 1980; Gibson and Levin, 1975; Venezky, 1970).

(5) Transitional spellers differentiate alternate spellings for the same sound. A long *a* sound, for example, may be spelled the following ways by a transitional speller: EIGHTE [eighty], ABUL [able], LASEE [lazy], RANE [rain], and SAIL [sale]. However, as indicated above in conditon

number 4, the conditions governing particular alternatives for representing a sound are only partially understood at the transitional stage.

(6) Transitional spellers generally use learned words (correctly spelled words) in greater abundance in their writing.

Thus far, this analysis of developmental spelling has focused on information obtained from misspelled words. Early in development, semiphonetic and even some precommunicative spellers may have "learned" or "automatic" spellings for certain words like C-A-T or their names. These correct spellings offer no clues to the speller's notion of how English orthography works and are interspersed with developmental forms in varying degrees. For example, correct forms may account for from 0 to 50% or more of the words in semiphonetic writing, depending largely upon the writer's exposure to reading and the amount and type of instructional intervention experienced. Developmental spelling levels may be determined only by observing spelling miscues, not by observation of words spelled correctly. As in reading miscue analysis, the miscues are "the windows into the mind" (Goodman, 1979, p. 3) that allow the observer to determine the speller's level of development. Beyond the transitional stage, the child reaches a stage where miscues are relatively infrequent.

The correct stage

Correct spelling, though easily identified, may exist at different levels. Instructionally, a second grader is a "correct speller" after mastering a certain corpus of words that has been designated as "second grade level." Likewise, a sixth grade level speller has mastered the designated sixth grade level corpus. "Correct spelling" is usually viewed from the instructional scheme rather than the developmental scheme because developmental spelling research beyond the ages of 8 or 9 is limited to a few research studies (Juola et al., 1978; Marsh et al., 1980; Templeton, 1979).

It may be that the major cognitive changes necessary for spelling competency are accomplished by the end of the transitional stage and that further growth is an extension of existing strategies. Research suggests that formal spelling instruction facilitates spelling growth once the child gets into the transitional stage (Allen and Ager, 1965). In addition to formal instruction, the child continues to learn from being attentive and interested in spelling through writing experiences. Beyond the transitional stage, frequent writing experiences with some formal instruction enables children to attain spelling competency over a period of time (usually 5 or 6 years).

Developmentally, Paul was a "correct" speller by the time he was 8 years old. At that time he knew the English orthographic system and its basic rules. (At 8, Paul's spelling achievement was superior to the average development for children his age.) Further experience with words would result in finer discrimination and an extension of orthographic knowledge, but Paul had entered the correct stage, where the basis of his knowledge of English orthography was firmly set. His spelling matched well the characteristics of the developmentally correct speller:

(1) The speller's knowledge of the English orthographic system and its basic rules is firmly established.
(2) The correct speller extends his/her knowledge of word environmental constraints (i.e., graphemic environment in the word, position in word, and stress).
(3) The correct speller shows an extended knowledge of word structure including accurate spelling of prefixes, suffixes, contractions, and compound words, and ability to distinguish homonyms.
(4) The correct speller demonstrates growing accuracy in using silent consonants and in doubling consonants appropriately.
(5) The correct speller is able to think of alternative spellings and employ visual identification of misspelled words as a correction strategy. He/she recognizes when "words don't look right."
(6) The correct speller continues to master uncommon alternative patterns (e.g., *ie* and *ei*) and words with irregular spellings.
(7) The correct speller masters Latinate forms and other morphological stuctures.
(8) The child accumulates a large corpus of learned words.

The developmental spelling scheme presented here has progressed through precommunicative, semiphonetic, phonetic, transitional, to correct spelling. Change from one spelling stage to the next is more or less gradual; samples of more than one stage may co-exist in a particular sample of writing as the child moves from one stage to the next.

Development, however, is continuous. Children do not fluctuate between stages, passing from phonetic back into semiphonetic spelling or from transitional back to phonetic (Gentry, 1977). As spelling develops, children draw increasingly from alternative strategies—phonological, visual, and morphological. Development proceeds from simple to more complex, from concrete to more abstract form, toward differentiation and integration. Teachers can nurture this process in the classroom by providing opportunities for children to develop cognitive strategies for dealing with English orthography.

Fostering spelling competency in the classroom

The following guidelines enable primary teachers to help children acquire foundations for spelling competency.

(1) Provide purposeful writing experiences in the classroom. Purposeful writing is the key to cognitive growth in spelling. As pupils hypothesize and mentally rehearse printed representations for words, they engage in the cognitive activity needed for developmental growth. This activity is most frequent and natural when children write for a purpose, that is, enjoy a meaningful experience of sharing information in print. This occurs whenever children write stories, songs, lists, plans, messages, recipes, letters, and signs. It occurs when writing is both functional and fun.

(2) Have pupils write frequently. Pupils should add something new to their creative writing folders each week. Writing (integrated with all aspects of the curriculum and with all classroom activity), should be a natural part of the daily classroom routine. As in learning any complex cognitive process, practice and frequency of occurrence are important. Frequent application of spelling knowledge while writing moves spelling forward developmentally.

(3) De-emphasize correctness, writing mechanics, and memorization. The primary school teacher's main job is to set the foundations for spelling growth. When frequent purposeful writing in the classroom takes precedence, focus on correctness, mechanics, and memorization must be secondary. Early overemphasis on mechanical aspects of spelling inhibits natural developmental spelling competency and growth. This is not to suggest eliminating mechanics altogether. Proofreading and editing should begin early. Handwriting should be taught. Models of correct writing, patterns of written form, and teacher edited and typed versions of children's work should be a part of the classroom. The core of this activity, however, should be children's purposeful writing. Teacher expectations for correctness should be adjusted to fit the pupils' level of development.

(4) Help pupils develop spelling consciousness. An environment of frequent purposeful writing provides numerous opportunities for teachers to help students discover more about spelling words. In responding to children's writing, teachers build pupil interest in words, make word study fun, answer questions, and teach skills. Pupils become conscious of English spelling without being overwhelmed by its complexity.

(5) Observe and assess pupil progress. Guidelines 1 through 4 suggest ways the teacher may teach spelling as a cognitive activity. Knowing how to intervene and what instructional skills to address hinge upon teacher knowledge of the developmental process, teacher observation, and assessment. Teachers may begin by applying stage descriptions (provided in this article) to samples of the child's writing to determine the child's developmental level. Level of development and observation provide clues for instruction. For precommunicative and semiphonetic spellers, instruction may focus on alphabet knowledge, directionality of print and its spatial orientation, children's concept of words, matching oral

language to print, and representing sounds with letters. Phonetic spellers are ready for introduction to the conventions of English orthography: word families, spelling patterns, phonics, and word structure. Word study is extended for the transitional speller, who is ready for a spelling textbook and formal spelling instruction. Even after formal spelling instruction begins, the pupil must maintain a vigorous program of independent writing. All writing is collected in a writing folder which becomes the focal point for assessment. The teacher analyzes the writing samples, noting changes in spelling strategies, application of skills taught, and general progress toward spelling competency.

In summary, learning to spell must be treated as a complex developmental process that begins at the preschool and primary school levels. As teachers observe spelling skills unfold, they must engage pupils in the kinds of cognitive activity that lead to spelling competency.

References

Allen, D., and J. Ager. "A Factor Analytic Study of the Ability to Spell." *Educational and Psychological Measurement*, vol. 25 (1965), pp. 153–61.

Beers, James W. "First and Second Grade Children's Developing Orghographic Concepts of Tense and Lax Vowels." Doctoral dissertation, University of Virginia, Charlottesville, 1974.

Beers, James W., and Edmund H. Henderson. "A Study of Developing Orthographic Concepts among First Grade Children." *Research in the Teaching of English*, vol. 11 (Fall 1977), pp. 133–48.

Bissex, Glenda L. *GNYS AT WRK: A Child Learns to Write and Read*. Cambridge, Mass.: Harvard University Press, 1980.

Chomsky, Noam, and Morris Halle. *The Sound Pattern of English*. New York, N.Y.: Harper and Row, 1968.

Gentry, J. Richard. "A Study of the Orthographic Strategies of Beginning Readers." Doctoral dissertation, University of Virginia, Charlottesville, 1977.

Gentry, J. Richard. "Early Spelling Strategies." *The Elementary School Journal*, vol. 79 (November 1978), pp. 88–92.

Gentry, J. Richard. "Learning to Spell Developmentally." *The Reading Teacher*, vol. 34 (January 1981), pp. 378–81.

Gentry, J. Richard, and Edmund H. Henderson. "Three Steps to Teaching Beginning Readers to Spell." *The Reading Teacher*, vol. 31 (March 1978), pp. 632–37.

Gibson, Eleanor, and Harry Levin. *The Psychology of Reading*. Cambridge, Mass.: The MIT Press, 1975.

Goodman, Kenneth S., ed. *Miscue Analysis: Applications to Reading Instruction*. Urbana, Ill.: National Council of Teachers of English, 1979.

Goodman, Yetta M. "The Roots of Literacy." In *Claremont Reading Conference: Forty-fourth Yearbook*, edited by Malcolm P. Douglas. Claremont, Calif.: Claremont Reading Conference, 1980.

Henderson, Edmund, and James W. Beers. *Developmental and Cognitive Aspects of Learning to Spell*. Newark, Del.: International Reading Association, 1980.

Juola, J. F., M. Schadler, R. J. Chalot, and M. W. McCaughey. "The Development of Visual Information Processing Skills Related to Reading." *Journal of Experimental Child Psychology*, vol. 25 (1978), pp. 459–76.

Marsh, G., M. Friedman, V. Welch, and P. Desberg. "The Development of Strategies in Spelling." In *Cognitive Processes in Spelling*, edited by Uta Frith. London, England: Academic Press, 1980.

Read, Charles. "Preschool Children's Knowledge of English Phonology." *Harvard Educational Review*, vol. 41 (1971), pp. 1–34.

Read, Charles. *Children's Categorizations of Speech Sounds in English*. Urbana, Ill.: National council of Teachers of English, 1975.

Read, Charles. "Creative Spelling by Young Children." In *Standards and Dialects in English*, edited by T. Shopen and J. M. Williams, Cambridge, Mass.: Winthrop Publishers, 1980.

Read, Charles, and Richard E. Hodges. "Spelling." In *Encyclopedia of Educational Research*, 5th ed. New York, N.Y.: Macmillan, in press.

Söderbergh, R. *Reading in Early Childhood*. Stockholm, Sweden: Almqvist and Wiksell, 1971.

Templeton, Shane. "Spelling First, Sound Later: The Relationship between Orthography and Higher Order Phonological Knowledge in Older Students." *Research in the Teaching of English*, vol. 13(1979), pp. 255–64.

Torrey, Jane. "Learning to Read without a Teacher: A Case Study." In *Psycholinguistics and Reading*, edited by Frank Smith. New York, N.Y.: Holt, Rinehart, and Winston, 1973.

Venezky, Richard. *The Structure of English Orthography*. The Hague, Netherlands: Mouton, 1970.

Zutell, Jerry B., Jr. "Spelling Strategies of Primary School No. 1 Children and Their Relationship to the Piagetian Concept of Decentration." Doctoral dissertation, University of Virginia, Charlottesville, 1975.

Zutell, Jerry B., Jr. "Some Psycholinguistic Perspectives on Children's Spelling." *Language Arts*, vol. 55 (1978), pp. 844–50.

CONSTRUCTIVE PROCESSES IN SKILLED AND LESS SKILLED COMPREHENDERS' MEMORY FOR SENTENCES

Jane Oakhill

Source: *British Journal of Psychology*, 73, 1982: 13–20.

An experiment was carried out to investigate seven–eight-year-old children's memory for aurally presented sentences. A recognition-memory task was used to probe constructive memory processes in two groups differentiated by their ability at comprehending printed text. The recognition errors of both groups indicated that they constructed meanings implied by the original input sentences, whilst demonstrating poor memory for the syntactic form of the sentences. The tendency to construct meanings implied by the original input sentences was greater in children who scored higher on tests of reading comprehension of text. These results indicate that constructive memory processes are related to comprehension ability in young readers.

Studies of adults have shown that they spontaneously make inferences and integrate information from separate sentences in a text, rapidly forgetting the syntax of the original sentences once the meaning has been extracted. The effects of these constructive processes can be detected in terms of memory for sentences or for passages of prose (e.g. Bartlett, 1932; Johnson-Laird & Stevenson, 1970; Bransford & Franks, 1971; Bransford *et al.*, 1972). Similar studies suggest that children also make use of constructive memory when processing text (e.g. Paris & Carter, 1973; Paris & Mahoney, 1974).

The purpose of the present experiment was to examine the relation between children's reading comprehension and their use of constructive memory representations. Children who have adequate ability at reading aloud and at comprehending single printed words may, nevertheless, fail to understand or to remember a text fully because they do not construct an adequate representation of it in the first place. This potential source of comprehension differences was investigated by comparing groups who are average or above in reading skill, as measured by ability to read aloud and to comprehend isolated printed words, but who differ in text comprehension ability, as measured by a standardized reading test.

In the studies by Paris and his associates, children were read a series of short stories, and then presented with a recognition test which included original sentences, as well as new sentences, half of which could be validly inferred from the originally presented story and half of which could not. These recognition foils were labelled true and false inferences, respectively. If children actively construct a meaning representation of the stories, whilst failing to maintain the exact syntactic form, then they should accept or reject recognition items as old or new on the basis of their semantic congruence with the original stories, rather than their syntactic similarity. Paris and his associates have found this to be the case in children as young as seven years. However, the validity of the experimental procedure on which these studies are based is questionable. In the Paris & Carter (1973) study, children were read seven three-sentence stories such as:

(*a*) The bird is inside the cage.
(*b*) The cage is under the table.
(*c*) The bird is yellow.

The recognition items for this story included (*a*) as the true premise sentence, together with 'a slightly altered false premise', (*d*) The cage is over the table, 'a permissible true inference', (*e*) The bird is under the table, and 'an invalid false inference', (*f*) The bird is on top of the table. As Posnansky & Liben (1977) have argued, the recognition foils in the test allowed children to discriminate new items not only on the basis of judgements of semantic consistency, but also because they contained new words. Whereas the true inference includes a relational term (*under*), which occurred in the original story, the two false inferences use relational terms (*over* and *on top of*) which did not occur in the original story. This lexical distinction between true and false inferences is present in the test items of all seven stories used by Paris & Carter (1973). Thus, the false inferences can be rejected not only because they are inconsistent with the meaning of the original stories, but also because they introduce new lexical information. Posnansky & Liben (1977) corrected this defect and found little evidence of semantic integration in young children.

In the present study, the items presented in the recognition test were designed to overcome these problems. They included two of the orginal premises and two additional false sentences for each story. The two false sentences were a semantically congruent sentence, which could be inferred from information in the original story, and an incongruent sentence, which could not. Neither incorporated any vocabulary items which were not in the original stories.

If children recognized 'true inferences' in the previous studies only on the basis of surface vocabulary information, then there should be no difference in error rates between the semantically congruent and incongruent recognition foils in the present study. If the differences in error rates found between true and false inferences were due to the differential semantic compatibility of these items with the original stories, then differences in error rates would be predicted even when, as in the present study, vocabulary items are held constant.

It was proposed earlier that, during normal language understanding, the comprehender is likely to infer additional relations from a text and that this enables the construction of an integrated semantic representation, which is more abstract than the sentences actually presented. If skilled comprehenders differ from the less skilled because they are more likely to build such integrated representations, then they would be expected to make a higher proportion of errors in recognizing semantically congruent recognition foils, whilst making similar numbers of recognition errors on the original sentences and semantically incongruent foils. Comprehension level, therefore, whilst not constituting a significant main effect, was expected to interact with the semantic acceptability of the recognition foils.

In the present study, stories were read aloud to the subjects so that the input time was approximately equal for all subjects. If the predicted effects are evident with aural presentation, this will also demonstrate that the effects are due to differences in language comprehension ability and are not specific to reading tasks.

Method

Subjects

One hundred and sixty-eight children (aged seven–eight years) attending two Brighton primary schools were screened initially, using an adapted form of the Gates–McGinitie Primary Two vocabularly test, in which the few American English items were replaced (e.g. 'trash' became 'rubbish'). The test involves matching a series of pictures with a choice of four printed words per picture, and was administered to each class to provide a general indication of each child's sight recognition and vocabulary ability. On the basis of this test and teachers' judgements, 71 average to good readers were selected and then individually tested, using the Neale Analysis of Reading Ability (form C). This test provides age-related measures both of children's

125

ability to read aloud words in context and of their comprehension of short passages. Twenty-eight children were selected to participate in the experiment. They were matched on reading aloud skill (Neal Accuracy score) and on skill at comprehending isolated printed words (Gates–McGinitie score); they differed in ability to comprehend text (Neale comprehension score). Fourteen less skilled comprehenders were chosen, according to the following criteria: (a) their Neale Accuracy age was above their chronological age, (b) their Neale Comprehension age was at least 0.5 years below their reading accuracy age. A group of skilled comprehenders was chosen who were matched with the less skilled group for sex (three males and eleven females in each group), mean chronological age and Neale Accuracy age. The matching on Neale Accuracy scores was based on the regressed scores of the two groups, which takes into account the possibility that the two comprehension skill groups were selected from populations which differ in reading aloud ability. If this were the case, the groups might be found to differ in their reading aloud scores if retested, due to regression toward the mean scores of the populations from which they were derived (McNemar, 1962). Adopting the most unfavourable assumption (that the mean Accuracy age score of the population from which the poor comprehenders were drawn is equal to their Comprehension age score, 7.25 years, and similarly that the mean Accuracy age score of the population from which the good comprehenders were drawn is equal to their Comprehension age score, 9.19 years), regressed Accuracy scores were calculated for all children. Given that the reliability of the Neale Accuracy score is 0.98 (Neale, 1966), the means of the samples of regressed scores were 8.66 years (poor comprehenders) and 8.62 years (good comprehenders), and these did not differ significantly, $t = 0.13$, d.f. $= 24$. Hence, even when regression is taken into account, the two groups are matched on Neale Accuracy scores. Their comprehension scores, however, did differ significantly, $t = 6.88$, d.f. $= 24$, $P < 0.001$. The skilled group was also selected so that their scores on the Gates–McGinitie Primary Two vocabulary test did not differ significantly from those of the less skilled group, $t = 0.76$, d.f. $= 24$, an indication that their reading aloud ability carried over to word–picture matching tasks and was not purely a decoding skill, which did not entail knowledge of word meanings.

The subject characteristics of the two groups of 13 whose data were used are shown in Table 1; one female subject was excluded from each group (see results section for explanation).

Materials

Eight stories, each three sentences long, were written, using a suitable vocabulary. The words used in the stories were checked for comprehensibility by asking 10 independent subjects of approximately the same age and ability to describe the meanings of the words used. Any word which did not

Table 1 Mean and standard deviation of subject characteristics.

Characteristic: Group	Chronological age (years)	Accuracy age (years)	Comprehension age (years)	Gates–McGinitie (score/48)
Less skilled (*n* = 13)	7.72 (0.25)	8.66 (0.66)	7.25 (0.27)	37.08 (3.75)
Skilled (*n* = 13)	7.67 (0.34)	8.62 (0.76)	9.19 (0.98)	38.31 (4.48)

produce 100 per cent correct response was replaced and the new word retested. Each story was composed of two event and one stative sentence, the two event sentences having the same subject. Animacy/inanimacy of the subject was counterbalanced within event sentences and across all story sentences. An example of the stories used was:

The car crashed into the bus. (event)
The bus was near the crossroads. (stative)
The car skidded on the ice. (event)

The recognition set for each story consisted of two new sentences. One of these was semantically congruent and the other incongruent with the original story, but both were composed entirely from the original vocabulary items. These sentences were presented together with two of the original sentences from each story. For example, the following four sentences were the test sentences for the sample story above:

The car crashed into the bus. (original sentence)
The bus was near the crossroads. (original sentence)
The car was near the crossroads. (semantically congruent foil)
The bus skidded on the ice. (semantically incongruent foil)

The recognition sentences were drawn equally from the first and second or second and third positions in the original stories so as to include one stative and one event sentence for each story. The two recognition foils were also composed from the original story sentences so that there was one stative and one event sentence foil for each story. A full list of the stories and recognition sentences used is presented in the Appendix.

Design

Each subject received the same eight stories and the same recognition sentences. The stories were presented in a different random order for each subject. The set of recognition sentences for a story were presented together (in a block). The order of these sets, and the order of the sentences within them, was randomized.

Procedure

Children were already familiar with the experimenter from the preceding test sessions. They were seen individually in a quiet room. They were told that the experimenter was interested in how well children remember things, and that they would be read some 'short stories' which they were to try to remember and on which they would later be questioned. The eight stories were read aloud slowly to the children, with a pause between each sentence and a final longer pause to indicate that the story was complete. They then completed a three-minute card sorting task, before being read the 32 recognition sentences, to which they were instructed to say 'yes' if they thought they had heard exactly the same sentence before, in the stories, and 'no' if they had not heard it before. The children's responses were noted at the time of testing.

Results

The mean errors on the recognition test were tabulated for each sentence type for the two comprehension groups and are shown in Fig. 1. The pattern of error rates was similar for both groups but there were differences in relative magnitude between the groups.

One female subject (a skilled comprehender) was excluded from the analysis because she did not make any 'yes' responses. In order that the remaining groups were still balanced for sex and matched on their defining characteristics, the youngest female subject was also excluded from the less skilled group.

Two 2×2 analyses of variance were computed on the error data for the false recognition sentences, one in which subjects were treated as a random factor collapsing across stories and the other collapsing across subjects and treating stories as a random factor. The resulting F ratios are referred to as 'F_1' and 'F_2' respectively. There was a significant main effect of recognition sentence type, more errors being made on semantically congruent than on incongruent items, $F_1 = 53.25$, d.f. $= 1,24$, $P < 0.001$; $F_2 = 50.17$, d.f. $= 1,24$, $P < 0.001$. The interaction between comprehension level and recognition sentence type was also significant, $F_1 = 7.78$, d.f. $= 1,24$, $P < 0.025$, $F_2 = 7.34$, d.f. $= 1,14$, $P < 0.025$: as predicted, skilled comprehenders made more errors than less skilled comprehenders on semantically congruent new items whereas, on the semantically incongruent new items, skilled comprehenders made fewer errors. The main effect of comprehension level was not significant, both Fs < 1.

Although the mean error rate for original sentences was slightly higher for the less skilled group, the difference was not significant, either by subjects, $t = 1.27$, d.f. $= 24$, or by materials, $t = 1.65$, d.f. $= 14$.

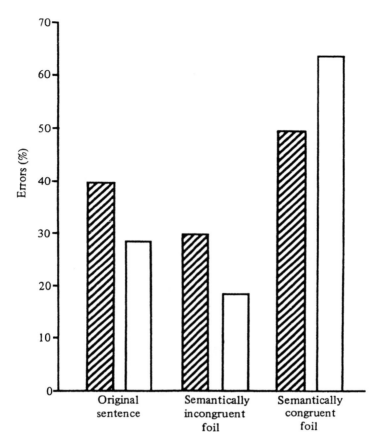

Figure 1 Percentage recognition errors for skilled and less skilled comprehenders as a function of recognition sentence type. □, skilled comprehender; ▨, less skilled comprehender.

Discussion

The experiment confirmed that skilled comprehenders are more likely than less skilled comprehenders to form constructive memory representations from sets of related sentences. In both groups, the mean recognition error for semantically congruent test items was greater than 50 per cent. The finding that both skilled and less skilled comprehenders made significantly more errors on the semantically congruent foils than on semantically incongruent foils indicates that their errors were due to confusions with true premise information at a semantic, rather than at a surface-structure lexical, level. The higher error rates of skilled comprehenders on semantically congruent foils, compared to less skilled comprehenders, indicates that they were more involved in the active construction of meanings than were the less skilled group.

An alternative view is that comprehension may be directly linked to the false recognition of semantically congruent sentences because the skilled comprehenders have a superior general knowledge of situations such as those presented in the stories, and therefore have access to a wider range of schemata with which to interpret discourse. However, if major qualitative differences in children's story schemata were responsible for the results obtained in this study, then less skilled comprehenders might be expected to produce much lower error rates on the semantically congruent false items than they did. Less skilled comprehenders made a high proportion of errors on semantically congruent false items themselves. This pattern of results appears to be more consistent with the first view, that reading comprehension ability is related to constructive memory processes: a relation not necessarily dependent on the availability of general knowledge about the situations presented.

This experiment does not directly address the problem of the locus of integrative processes: these may occur during the initial reading or at the presentation of recognition items. The time at which integration occurs may be reflected in the observed differences in group error patterns, i.e. less skilled comprehenders may experience greater difficulty in remembering the recognition sentences and relating them to the original stories. However, since there was no overall difference in recognition errors between the groups, this hypothesis seems implausible. It was also found that the groups did not differ in errors for the original sentences. This result rules out the suggestion that the skilled comprehender's propensity to recognize congruent foils as 'old' can be attributed to their superior ability to retain the original sentences, making inferences to relate them to the recognition items in an *ex post facto* manner.

It would seem that the subject who rejected all of the recognition items either did not fully understand the task, or adopted a very high acceptance threshold, rather than that her performance was a true reflection of her memory ability, since the same subject had previously demonstrated text recall within the normal range.

Given that less skilled comprehenders make relatively less use of constructive processes in remembering text, the question arises as to what could be done to improve comprehension in this group. As has already been discussed, the less skilled group do seem to be able to integrate information, so it is reasonable to suppose that they would be able to make greater use of this ability, if they were more aware of its utility. They might be encouraged to become so by training them in selection of pictures or summary statements which represent integrated versions of the original material and by encouraging discussion of the greater suitability of some models of the information than others.

In summary, it appears that, even when the ability to read aloud and to comprehend isolated words is adequate, some young readers may still have problems remembering and understanding texts. That this occurs for aurally presented materials shows that the problem is not specific to reading. The present experiment demonstrated that these problems are not due to a straightforward inability to recall sentences but appear, rather, to be linked to a reduced level of constructive memory processing by the less skilled comprehenders.

Acknowledgements

This research was supported by a postgraduate studentship from the Social Science Research Council (GB). The author would like to thank Phil Johnson-Laird and Max Coltheart for their comments on earlier drafts of the paper.

References

Bartlett, F. C. (1932). *Remembering*. Cambridge: Cambridge University Press.
Bransford, J. D., Barclay, J. R. & Franks, J. J. (1972). Sentence memory: A constructive versus interpretive approach. *Cognitive Psychology*, **3**, 193–209.
Bransford, J. D. & Franks, J. J. (1971). The abstraction of linguistic ideas. *Cognitive Psychology*, **2**, 331–350.
Johnson-Laird, P. N. & Stevenson, R. (1970). Memory for syntax. *Nature, London*, **227**, 412.
McNemar, Q. (1962). *Psychological Statistics*, 3rd ed. New York: Wiley.
Neale, M. D. (1966). *The Neale Analysis of Reading Ability. Manual of Directions and Norms*, 2nd ed. London: Macmillan Education.
Paris, S. G. & Carter, A. Y. (1973). Semantic and constructive aspects of sentence memory in children. *Developmental Psychology*, **9**, 109–113.
Paris, S. G. & Mahoney, G. J. (1974). Cognitive integration in children's memory for sentences and pictures. *Child Development*, **45**, 633–642.
Posnansky, C. J. & Liben, L. S. (1977). Inferences on inference: A developmental investigation. Paper presented at the Society for Research in Child Development, New Orleans.

Appendix
Materials used in the experiment

Stories

(1)
The plane flew over the house.
The house was in Crawley.
The plane landed in a field.

131

(2)
The soldier aimed at the target.
The target was a tree.
The soldier hit a wall.
(3)
The car crashed into the bus.
The bus was near the crossroads.
The car skidded on the ice.
(4)
The man sat down behind the lady.
The lady was on the train.
The man looked out of the window.
(5)
The girl chased the boy.
The boy was in the playground.
The girl ran away into the school
(6)
The bottle fell onto the jar.
The jar was in the kitchen.
The bottle broke into pieces.
(7)
The boat left the harbour.
The harbour was at Newhaven.
The boat sailed to Brighton.
(8)
The mouse ate the food.
The food was bread.
The mouse looked for some cheese.

Recognition sentences

(for each set, the first two items are original sentences, the third a semantically congruent foil and the fourth a semantically incongruent foil.)

(1)
The plane flew over the house.
The house was in Crawley.
The plane flew over Crawley.
The house was in a field.
(2)
The soldier aimed at the target.
The target was a tree.
The soldier aimed at a tree.
The target was a wall.
(3)
The car crashed into the bus.
The bus was near the crossroads.
The car was near the crossroads.
The bus skidded on the ice.

(4)
The man sat down behind the lady.
The lady was on the train.
The man was on the train.
The lady looked out of the window.
(5)
The boy was in the playground.
The girl ran away into the school.
The girl was in the playground.
The boy ran away into the school.
(6)
The jar was in the kitchen.
The bottle broke into pieces.
The bottle was in the kitchen.
The jar broke into pieces.
(7)
The harbour was at Newhaven.
The boat sailed to Brighton.
The boat left Newhaven.
The harbour was at Brighton.
(8)
The food was bread.
The mouse looked for some cheese.
The mouse ate the bread.
The food was some cheese.

107

INTERACTIVE TEACHING TO PROMOTE INDEPENDENT LEARNING FROM TEXT

Annemarie Sullivan Palincsar and Ann L. Brown

Source: *The Reading Teacher*, 39, 1986: 771–777.

The authors describe reciprocal teaching, a strategy that promotes both comprehension of text and comprehension monitoring

Student 1: My question is, what does the aquanaut need when he goes under water?

Student 2: A watch.

Student 3: Flippers.

Student 4: A belt.

Student 1: Those are all good answers.

Teacher: Nice job! I have a question too. Why does the aquanaut wear a belt? What is so special about it?

Student 3: It's a heavy belt and keeps him from floating up to the top again.

Teacher: Good for you.

Student 1: For my summary now: This paragraph was about what aquanauts need to take when they go under the water.

Student 5: And also about why they need those things.

Student 3: I think we need to clarify gear.

Student 6: That's the special things they need.

Teacher: Another word for gear in this story might be equipment, the equipment that makes it easier for the aquanauts to do their job.

Student 1: I don't think I have a prediction to make.

Teacher: Well, in the story they tell us that there are "many strange and wonderful creatures" that the aquanauts see as they do their work. My prediction is that they'll describe some of these creatures. What are some of the strange creatures you already know about that live in the ocean?

Student 6: Octopuses.

Student 3: Whales?

Student 5: Sharks!

Teacher: Let's listen and find out. Who'll be our teacher?

Instructing students to read for meaning

The dialogue presented above captures a bit of conversation a teacher and her group of first grade students recently had concerning a passage about aquanauts which the teacher was reading aloud. This article will suggest how a teacher might stimulate such discussion about text, what the purpose of such conversation is, and what the benefits of engaging in such dialogue are. Finally, we will address a number of questions teachers have asked about the instructional procedure we will describe.

The teacher and students above are engaged in an activity we call *reciprocal teaching*. In reciprocal teaching, the adult and students take turns assuming the role of teacher. The "teacher" is responsible for leading a dialogue about a passage which the students are reading silently or with the assistance of the adult. Anyone who has struggled to make conversation will appreciate that dialogue flows more smoothly when the participants share similar goals. The participants in reciprocal teaching share four goals: *predicting, question generating, summarizing, and clarifying*.

Teachers will recognize that each of these goals represents a strategy that promotes both comprehension of text and comprehension monitoring. When students make *predictions*, they hypothesize what the author will discuss next in the text. To do this successfully, they must activate the relevant background knowledge that they already possess. In the illustration above, the students have contemplated what they already know about creatures that live in the ocean and have anticipated some specific ocean life that they will read about. They now have a purpose for reading—to confirm or disprove their hypotheses. Furthermore, the opportunity has been created for the students to link the new knowledge they will encounter in the text with the knowledge they already possess. The predicting strategy also facilitates use of text structure. Students learn that headings, subheadings, and questions embedded in text are useful means of anticipating what might occur next.

Question generating gives the students an opportunity to identify the kind of information that provides the substance for a good question, to frame that question, and then engage in self-testing. The students become much more involved in the reading activity and in the text when they are posing and answering the questions and not merely responding to teacher or text questions.

Summarizing is an excellent tool for integrating the information presented in the text. In the example above, the students jointly identified the most important content of the paragraph. As they proceed through the passage, the teacher will guide them in integrating the content across paragraphs and sections of the passage.

Clarifying is particularly important with students who have a history of comprehension difficulty. Such students can be thought of as making a habit of not understanding what they read. These students very likely believe that the purpose of reading is saying the words correctly; they may not be particularly uncomfortable with the fact that the words and, in fact, the passage are not making much sense. When students are asked to clarify, their attention is called to the fact that there may be many reasons why text is difficult to understand, e.g., unfamiliar vocabulary, unclear referent words, new and perhaps complicated concepts. They are taught to be alert to the effects of such impediments on comprehension and to take the necessary measures to restore meaning, e.g., reread, ask for help.

Now, it is important to call the reader's attention to the fact that the dialogue above did not occur the first day that the teacher and students began reciprocal teaching. In fact, this dialogue occurred on the 10th day. What we wish to discuss is how the teacher went about working with her students so that by day 10 they are enjoying a spontaneous, informed, and informative discussion. The components might be described as the following: explanation, instruction, modeling, guided practice, praise, and teacher judgment.

When instruction first begins, the teacher explains what strategies the students will be learning, why they are learning these particular activities, in what situations such strategies will be helpful, and how they will go about learning the strategies (i.e., turn taking as teacher). This explanation, which is reviewed regularly, is followed by instruction on the four strategies. This instruction is for the purpose of defining each of the strategies, teaching the students rules that will help them learn the strategies, and ensuring that the students have minimal competency with each of the strategies, before they engage in the dialogue.

For the purpose of illustration, we will highlight the instruction students receive regarding questioning. After a brief discussion about the role that questions play in our lives, particularly our school lives, the students are asked to generate information seeking questions about everyday events, e.g., "If you are interested in knowing what time the afternoon movie begins, you call the theatre and ask: _____." Such an activity allows the teacher to ascertain that her students do indeed know how to phrase a question. The students are then given simple sentences about which they are to ask a question and are supplied words they might use to begin their questions. The question words are then faded out and the sentences become longer.

Keep in mind that these activities are only for the purpose of exposing the students to the strategies; the teachers with whom we have worked spend but one day introducing each strategy. After this brief instruction, the group begins the dialogue and it is at this point that the major component becomes modeling. For the initial days of reciprocal teaching, the adult teacher leads the dialogue, modeling how she employs the four strategies while reading. At this point, the students are encouraged to comment on the teacher's summaries, add their own predictions and clarifications, and respond to the teacher generated questions.

As the days of instruction proceed, more responsibility for initiating and sustaining the dialogue is transferred to the students. It is this transfer of responsibility for leading the dialogue that we are describing when we speak of guided practice. The teacher is now monitoring the success with which the students are employing the strategies, praising their attempts, and providing further modeling and instruction as teacher judgement indicates.

To return to the dialogue above, while the students are playing the principal role in this discussion, the teacher maintains a critical role as well. After Student 1 asks his question, which requires the recall of specific pieces of information in the text, the teacher praises the group and models a question that requires the students to reason about the information; when the student teacher is unable to generate a prediction, the adult teacher provides instruction about a clue the text has provided and then provides the opportunity for the students to do their own predicting.

The hallmark of this form of instruction is its interactive nature. There is ongoing interplay among the teacher and students as they work toward the goal of understanding the text. Such instruction has been called scaffolded instruction (Wood, Bruner, and Ross, 1976). The metaphor is quite appropriate, as a scaffold is a support that is adjustable and temporary. The teacher supports each student in the acquisition and mastery of the strategies through the use of explanation, instruction, and modeling, but the support is temporary and the student is challenged to use the strategy independently as he or she displays increased competence with comprehension.

Evaluating reciprocal teaching

For the past 5 years, we have been evaluating the effectiveness of reciprocal teaching. The research has been developmental in nature and has sprung not only from the questions that we have raised regarding reciprocal teaching but also from the questions that educators have posed. For this reason, perhaps the most effective manner in which we might present the research findings is by addressing the questions that motivated the research.

● What effect does reciprocal teaching have on the reading comprehension ability of poor comprehenders?

For the purpose of our research, poor comprehenders have been defined as students who are able to decode grade level material with a fair degree of fluency but whose comprehension of that text is not commensurate with their decoding ability. For example, the typical junior high student with whom we have worked was decoding seventh grade material at a rate of at least 100 words per minute correct, with fewer than 2 error words per minute; however, on standardized measures of comprehension, they were performing 2 years below grade level, and on criterion referenced measures of comprehension they averaged 45% accuracy.

Our initial investigations were conducted by adult tutors working with students in pairs and volunteer Chapter 1 teachers working with groups of about five students (Brown and Palincsar, 1982; Palincsar and Brown, 1984). These teachers engaged in reciprocal teaching for 20 consecutive school days using passages from basal readers. Several measures were taken to assess the effectiveness of the instruction:

(1) Quantitative and qualitative analyses of the transcripts showed substantial changes in the dialogue during the 20 instructional days. For example, students asked many more main idea questions over the course of time and functioned more independently of the teacher as time passed.

(2) The changes in the dialogue were also reflected on other direct measures of comprehension. Daily, the students read independently a passage of about 450 words and answered 10 comprehension questions from recall. The students completed five of these assessments prior to the first day of instruction and one each day after the 30 minute reciprocal teaching session. All but one of the experimental students achieved criterion performance, which we had defined as 70% accuracy on the comprehension measures for 4 out of 5 consecutive days. This is in contrast to the control students, who completed an equivalent number of assessments but showed no improvement.

(3) The students were also given measures to evaluate their ability to write summaries of text, generate written questions about text, and detect incongruities in text. The experimental children were indeed able to transfer the skills they had learned to these similar but distinct activities.

(4) Finally, generalization probes administered in the social studies and science classes these students attended indicated that they were able to apply independently the newly acquired skills, as their percentile rankings in these classes jumped from the 20th percentile and below to the 50th percentile and higher.

● Can reciprocal teaching be implemented in settings where there are larger and more heterogenous groups of students?

To investigate this question, we implemented the reciprocal teaching procedure with six middle school remedial reading teachers in an inner-city district (Brown and Palincsar, in press; Palincsar, 1984; Palincsar and Brown, 1985a, 1985b). For each teacher we identified the two classes that come closest to the description of the students we described above, i.e., adequate decoders but poor comprehenders. One class served as the control group and received individualized basic skill instruction, while the second class received 20 days of reciprocal teaching. The number of students in the experimental groups ranged from 8 to 18.

In this study 71% of the experimental students achieved criterion performance, in contrast to 19% of the control students. Despite the larger number of students and the teachers' concerns that the management of such large groups would be problematic, the students did extremely well and the teachers observed that they had fewer behavior problems than in their control groups, as the students involved in reciprocal teaching enjoyed it, particularly the opportunity to assume the role of teacher.

As an alternative to whole group instruction, we investigated the use of peer tutoring in small group reciprocal teaching. Three seventh grade teachers trained four of their best students (who were averaging 72% on the daily assessments prior to instruction) in the reciprocal teaching procedure. After 10 days of instruction, the tutors were assigned two tutees who were achieving a mean of 49% on the assessments before instruction. After 20 days of instruction, the tutees were achieving 78% accuracy while the tutors were achieving 87% accuracy with the comprehension measures. It is important to note that the teachers in each of these classrooms monitored the performance of the tutors quite closely, dividing their time among the peer groups each day, providing the tutors evaluative information, suggesting how they might improve their instruction, and assisting when students were experiencing particular difficulty.

● How can reciprocal teaching be incorporated in content area instruction?

Our interest in teaching students how to learn from text across the curriculum motivated a further study with the students who had served as control children in the large group study reported above (Brown and Palincsar, in press). Reciprocal teaching, again for a 20 day period was given with the following modifications.

The material with which the students worked were science texts that were not currently being used in the school but were available to all students. Each day the students were assigned segments of text to read. Given the heading of each segment, the students were to write two statements indicating what they thought they would learn in this portion of the text. In a discussion, the teacher elicited from the group and compared the predictions they had made. The students then read one segment (generally four paragraphs). They wrote two questions and a summary reflecting the information in that segment. Finally, they noted, in writing, any information which required clarification.

The classes then discussed their questions, summaries, and clarifications. To approximate the way in which students are tested in school, we assessed these students by giving weekly science tests which covered the material they had worked on during the week. When we had pretested them on their comprehension and recall of science text, they averaged 36% accuracy; by the 4th week, the students were generally scoring 20% higher on these weekly tests.

● What's the difference between reciprocal teaching and skill instruction?

There was a time not long ago in reading education when successful reading was thought to be the execution of a series of component subskills. This orientation suggested that our instruction be directed at the mastery of such skills as finding the main idea, identifying the sequence of events in a story, and using context clues.

We know now that it is possible for students to master such skills and still not be successful readers. In reciprocal teaching the acquisition of the strategies is not the ultimate goal of instruction. The strategies are but a means to an end; they provide the vehicle for teaching students to read for meaning and to monitor their reading to ensure that they are understanding.

● Can reciprocal teaching be used to teach narrative text?

In our research we have employed expository or informational text almost exclusively; yet the story structure found in narrative text lends itself quite well to reciprocal teaching. The discussion now becomes focused on the characters in the story; summaries can be attentive to the problem posed in the story; predictions can be directed at speculating what the solutions might be. In short, the dialogue is guided by using the strategies as well as the structure of the text.

● Can reciprocal teaching be used with nonreaders?

Interest in exploring how very young children and students who are not yet decoding might engage in comprehension activities leads us to the series of studies we are presently conducting (Brown and Palincsar, in press; Palincsar, in press). First grade teachers are working with groups of six students. In each group there are two students of above average ability and four students who are experiencing academic difficulty as determined by teacher observation and performance on standardized measures of listening and reading comprehension.

The reciprocal teaching procedure is the same with the exception that the teachers read the text aloud. Our work to date suggests that this is a reasonable form of instruction. The first grade students become involved willingly in the dialogue and the more capable students serve as catalysts in the discussion. Assessments, which are being conducted orally as well, indicate that the students' ability to learn from text has improved and, very importantly, the classroom teachers report that their reciprocal teaching students are spontaneously engaging in discussion using the four strategies during their reading group instruction as well.

Summary

The purpose of this article was to describe one means by which teachers can provide instruction in learning from text. The procedure, reciprocal teaching, is best characterized as a dialogue in which the students and teacher work together to comprehend text. The dialogue is structured by the use of four comprehension fostering and comprehension monitoring strategies: predicting, questioning, summarizing, and clarifying. The teacher balances the use of explanation, instruction, and modeling with guided practice, so that there is a gradual transfer of responsibility for sustaining the dialogue, thus ensuring that the students can independently apply the strategies and independently learn from text.

Reciprocal teaching has been effectively implemented by teachers working in both small and large group settings, in a peer tutoring situation, in content area instruction, and most recently in listening comprehension instruction.

References

Brown, Ann L., and Annemarie Sullivan Palincsar. "Inducing Strategic Learning from Texts by Means of informed, Self-control Training." *Topics in Learning and Learning Disabilities*, vol. 2 (April 1982), pp. 1–17.

Brown, Ann L., and Annemarie Sullivan Palincsar. "Reciprocal Teaching of Comprehension Strategies. A Natural History of One Program for Enhancing Learning." In *Intelligence and Cognition in Special Children: Comparative Studies of Giftedness. Mental Retardation and Learning Disabilities*, edited by John Borkowski and Jeanne D. Day. New York, N.Y.: Ablex, in press.

Palincsar, Annemarie Sullivan. "The Quest for Meaning from Expository Text: A Teacher Guided Journey." In *Comprehension Instruction: Perspectives and Suggestions*, edited by Gerald Duffy, Laura Roehler, and Jana Mason. New York, N.Y.: Longman, 1984.

Palincsar, Annemarie Sullivan. "The Role of Dialogue in Scaffolded Instruction." *Educational Psychologist*, in press.

Palincsar, Annemarie Sullivan, and Ann L. Brown. "A Means to a Meaningful End." In *Research Foundations for a Literate America*, edited by Richard Anderson, Jean Osborn, and Paul Wilson. New York, N.Y.: D. C. Heath, 1985a.

Palincsar, Annemarie Sullivan, and Ann L. Brown. "Reciprocal Teaching: Activities to Promote 'Read(ing) with Your Mind.'" In *Reading, Thinking, and Concept Development: Interactive Strategies for the Class*, edited by Eric J. Cooper. New York, N.Y.: The College Board, 1985b.

Palincsar, Annemarie S., and Ann L. Brown. "Reciprocal Teaching of Comprehension-Fostering and Comprehension-Monitoring Activities." *Cognition and Instruction*, vol. 2 (Spring 1984), pp. 117–75.

Wood, David, Jerome Bruner, and Gail Ross. "The Role of Tutoring in Problem Solving." *Journal of Child Psychology and Psychiatry*, vol. 17 (September 1976), pp. 89–100.

108

MATHEMATICS IN
THE STREETS AND IN SCHOOLS

Terezinha Nunes Carraher, David William Carraher
and Analúcia Dias Schliemann

Source: *British Journal of Developmental Psychology*, 3, 1985: 21–29.

An analysis of everyday use of mathematics by working youngsters in commercial transactions in Recife, Brazil, revealed
computational strategies different from those taught in schools.
Performance on mathematical problems embedded in real-life
contexts was superior to that on school-type word problems and context-free computational problems involving the
same numbers and operations. Implications for education are
examined.

There are reasons for thinking that there may be a difference between solving mathematical problems using algorithms learned in school and solving
them in familiar contexts out of school. Reed & Lave (1981) have shown
that people who have not been to school often solve such problems in
different ways from people who have. This certainly suggests that there are
informal ways of doing mathematical calculations which have little to do
with the procedures taught in school.

Reed & Lave's study with Liberian adults showed differences between
people who had and who had not been to school. However, it is quite
possible that the same differences between informal and school-based
routines could exist within people. In other words it might be the case that
the same person could solve problems sometimes in formal and at other
times in informal ways. This seems particularly likely with children who
often have to do mathematical calculations in informal circumstances
outside school at the same time as their knowledge of the algorithms which
they have to learn at school is imperfect and their use of them ineffective.

We already know that children often obtain absurd results such as finding a remainder which is larger than the minuend when they try to apply routines for computations which they learn at school (Carraher & Schliemann, in press). There is also some evidence that informal procedures learned outside school are often extremely effective. Gay & Cole (1976) for example showed that unschooled Kpelle traders estimated quantities of rice far better than educated Americans managed to. So it seems quite possible that children might have difficulty with routines learned at school and yet at the same time be able to solve the mathematical problems for which these routines were devised in other more effective ways. One way to test this idea is to look at children who have to make frequent and quite complex calculations outside school. The children who sell things in street markets in Brazil form one such group (Carraher et al., 1982).

The cultural context

The study was conducted in Recife, a city of approximately 1.5 million people on the north-eastern coast of Brazil. Like several other large Brazilian cities, Recife receives a very large number of migrant workers from the rural areas who must adapt to a new way of living in a metropolitan region. In an anthropological study of migrant workers in São Paulo, Brazil, Berlinck (1977) identified four pressing needs in this adaptation process: finding a home, acquiring work papers, getting a job, and providing for immediate survival (whereas in rural areas the family often obtains food through its own work). During the initial adaptation phase, survival depends mostly upon resources brought by the migrants or received through begging. A large portion of migrants later become unspecialized manual workers, either maintaining a regular job or working in what is known as the informal sector of the economy (Cavalcanti, 1978). The informal sector can be characterized as an unofficial part of the economy which consists of relatively unskilled jobs not regulated by government organs thereby producing income not susceptible to taxation while at the same time not affording job security or workers' rights such as health insurance. The income generated thereby is thus intermittent and variable. The dimensions of a business enterprise in the informal sector are determined by the family's work capability. Low educational and professional qualification levels are characteristic of the rather sizable population which depends upon the informal sector. In Recife, approximately 30 per cent of the workforce is engaged in the informal sector as its main activity and 18 per cent as a secondary activity (Cavalcanti, 1978). The importance of such sources of income for families in Brazil's lower socio-economic strata can be easily understood by noting that the income of an unspecialized labourer's family is increased by 56 per cent through his wife's and children's activities in the informal sector in São Paulo (Berlinck, 1977).

In Fortaleza it represents fully 60 per cent of the lower class[1] family's income (Cavalcanti & Duarte, 1980a).

Several types of occupations—domestic work, street-vending, shoe-repairing and other types of small repairs which are carried out without a fixed commercial address—are grouped as part of the informal sector of the economy. The occupation considered in the present study—that of street-vendors—represents the principal occupation of 10 per cent of the economically active population of Salvador (Cavalcanti & Duarte, 1980b) and Fortaleza (Cavalcanti & Duarte, 1980a). Although no specific data regarding street-vendors were obtained for Recife, data from Salvador and Fortaleza serve as close approximations since these cities are, like Recife, State capitals from the same geographical region.

It is fairly common in Brazil for sons and daughters of street-vendors to help out their parents in their businesses. From about the age of 8 or 9 the children will often enact some of the transactions for the parents when they are busy with another customer or away on some errand. Pre-adolescents and teenagers may even develop their own 'business', selling snack foods such as roasted peanuts, pop-corn, coconut milk or corn on the cob. In Fortaleza and Salvador, where data are available, 2.2 and 1.4 per cent, respectively, of the population actively engaged in the informal sector as street-vendors were aged 14 or less while 8.2 and 7.5 per cent, respectively, were aged 15–19 years (Cavalcanti & Duarte, 1980a,b).

In their work these children and adolescents have to solve a large number of mathematical problems, usually without recourse to paper and pencil. Problems may involve multiplication (one coconut cost x; four coconuts, $4x$), addition (4 coconuts and 12 lemons cost $x + y$), and subtraction (Cr$ 500—i.e. 500 cruzeiros—minus the purchase price will give the change due). Division is much less frequently used but appears in some contexts in which the price is set with respect to a measuring unit (such as 1 kg) and the customer wants a fraction of that unit: for example, when the particular item chosen weighs 1.2 kg. The use of tables listing prices by number of items (one egg—12 cruzeiros; two eggs—24, etc.) is observed occasionally in natural settings but was not observed among the children who took part in the study. Pencil and paper were also not used by these children, although they may occasionally be used by adult vendors when adding long lists of items.

Method

Subjects

The children in this study were four boys and one girl aged 9–15 years with a mean age of 11.2 and ranging in level of schooling from first to eighth grade. One of them had only one year of schooling; two had three years of schooling; one, four years; and one, eight years. All were from very poor backgrounds. Four of the subjects were attending school at the time and one had been out of school for two years. Four of these subjects had received formal instruction on mathematical operations and word problems. The subject who attended first grade and dropped out of school was unlikely to have learned multiplication and division in school since these operations are usually initiated in second or third grade in public schools in Recife.

Procedure

The children were found by the interviewers on street corners or at markets where they worked alone or with their families. Interviewers chose subjects who seemed to be in the desired age range—school children or young adolescents—obtaining information about their age and level of schooling along with information on the prices of their merchandise. Test items in this situation were presented in the course of a normal sales transaction in which the researcher posed as a customer. Purchases were sometimes carried out. In other cases the 'customer' asked the vendor to perform calculations on possible purchases. At the end of the informal test, the children were asked to take part in a formal test which was given on a separate occasion, no more than a week later, by the same interviewer. Subjects answered a total of 99 questions on the formal test and 63 questions on the informal test. Since the items of the formal test were based upon questions of the informal test, order of testing was fixed for all subjects.

(1) *The informal test.* The informal test was carried out in Portuguese in the subject's natural working situation, that is, at street corners or an open market. Testers posed to the subject successive questions about potential or actual purchases and obtained verbal responses. Responses were either tape-recorded or written down, along with comments, by an observer. After obtaining an answer for the item, testers questioned the subject about his or her method for solving the problem.

The method can be described as a hybrid between the Piagetian clinical method and participant observation. The interviewer was not merely an interviewer; he was also a customer—a questioning customer who wanted the vendor to tell him how he or she performed their computations.

An example is presented below taken from the informal test with M., a coconut vendor aged 12, third grader, where the interviewer is referred to as 'customer':

Customer: How much is one coconut?
M: 35.
Customer: I'd like ten. How much is that?

M: (Pause) Three will be 105; with three more, that will be 210. (Pause) I need four more. That is . . .[2] (pause) 315 . . . I think it is 350.

This problem can be mathematically represented in several ways: 35×10 is a good representation of the *question* posed by the interviewer. The subject's answer is better represented by $105 + 105 + 105 + 105 + 35$, which implies that 35×10 was solved by the subject as $(3 \times 35) + (3 \times 35) + (3 \times 35) + 35$. The subject can be said to have solved the following subitems in the above situation:

(*a*) 35×10;
(*b*) 35×3 (which may have already been known);
(*c*) $105 + 105$;
(*d*) $210 + 105$;
(*e*) $315 + 35$;
(*f*) $3 + 3 + 3 + 1$.

When one represents in a formal mathematical fashion the problems which were solved by the subject, one is in fact attempting to represent the subject's mathematical competence. M. proved to be competent in finding out how much 35×10 is, even though he used a routine not taught in third grade, since in Brazil third-graders learn to multiply any number by ten simply by placing a zero to the right of that number. Thus, we considered that the subject solved the test item (35×10) and a whole series of sub-items (*b* to *f*) successfully in this process. However, in the process of scoring, only *one* test item (35×10) was considered as having been presented and, therefore, correctly solved.

(2) *The formal test.*   After subjects were interviewed in the natural situation, they were asked to participate in the formal part of the study and a second interview was scheduled at the same place or at the subject's house.

The items for the formal test were prepared for each subject on the basis of problems solved by him or her during the informal test. Each problem solved in the informal test was mathematically represented according to the subject's problem-solving routine.

From all the mathematical problems *successfully solved* by each subject (regardless of whether they constituted a test item or not), a sample was chosen for inclusion in the subject's formal test. This sample was presented in the formal test either as a mathematical operation dictated to the subject (e.g. $105 + 105$) or as a word problem e.g. Mary bought x bananas; each banana cost y; how much did she pay altogether?). In either case, *each subject solved problems employing the same numbers involved in his or her own informal test.* Thus quantities used varied from one subject to the other.

Two variations were introduced in the formal test, according to methodological suggestions contained in Reed & Lave (1981). First, some of the items presented in the formal test were the inverse of problems solved in the informal test (e.g. 500 – 385 may be presented as 385 + 115 in the formal test). Second, some of the items in the informal test used a decimal value which differed from the one used in the formal test (e.g. 40 *cruzeiros* may have appeared as 40 *centavos* or 35 may have been presented as 3500 in the formal test—the principal Brazilian unit of currency is the *cruzeiro*; each *cruzeiro* is worth one hundred *centavos*).

In order to make the formal test situation more similar to the school setting, subjects were given paper and pencil at the testing and were encouraged to use these. When problems were nonetheless solved without recourse to writing, subjects were asked to write down their answers. Only one subject refused to do so, claiming that he did not know how to write. It will be recalled, however, that the school-type situation was not represented solely by the introduction of pencil and paper but also by the very use of formal mathematical problems without context and by word problems referring to imaginary situations.

In the formal test the children were given a total of 38 mathematical operations and 61 word problems. Word problems were rather concrete and each involved only one mathematical operation.

Results and discussion

The analysis of the results from the informal test required an initial definition of what would be considered a test item in that situation. While, in the formal test, items were defined prior to testing, in the informal test problems were generated in the natural setting and items were identified *a posteriori*. In order to avoid a biased increase in the number of items solved in the informal test, the definition of an item was based upon *questions* posed by the customer/tester. This probably constitutes a conservative estimate of the number of problems solved, since subjects often solved a number of intermediary steps in the course of searching for the solution to the question they had been asked. Thus the same defining criterion was applied in both testing situations in the identification of items even though items were defined prior to testing in one case and after testing in the other. In both testing situations, the subject's oral response was the one taken into account even though in the formal test written responses were also available.

Context-embedded problems were much more easily solved than ones without a context. Table 1 shows that 98.2 per cent of the 63 problems presented in the informal test were correctly solved. In the formal test word problems (which provide some descriptive context for the subject), the rate of correct responses was 73.7 per cent, which should be contrasted with a 36.8 per cent rate of correct responses for mathematical operations with no context.

Table 1 Results according to testing conditions.

| | Informal test | | Formal test | | | |
| | | | Mathematical operations | | Word problems | |
Subject	Score[a]	Number of items	Score	No. items	Score	No. items
M	10	18	2.5	8	10	11
P	8.9	19	3.7	8	6.9	16
Pi	10	12	5.0	6	10	11
MD	10	7	1.0	10	3.3	12
S	10	7	8.3	6	7.3	11
Totals		63		38		61

[a] Each subject's score is the percentage of correct items divided by 10.

The frequency of correct answers for each subject was converted to scores from 1 to 10 reflecting the percentage of correct responses. A Friedman two-way analysis of variance of score ranks compared the scores of each subject in the three types of testing conditions. The scores differ significantly across conditions ($\chi^2 r = 6.4$, $P = 0.039$). Mann–Whitney Us were also calculated comparing the three types of testing situations. Subjects performed significantly better on the informal test than on the formal test involving context-free operations ($U = 0$, $P < 0.05$). The difference between the informal test and the word problems was not significant ($U = 6$, $P > 0.05$).

It could be argued that errors observed in the formal test were related to the transformations that had been performed upon the informal test problems in order to construct the formal test. An evaluation of this hypothesis was obtained by separating items which had been changed either by inverting the operation or changing the decimal point from items which remained identical to their informal test equivalents. The percentage of correct responses in these two groups of items did not differ significantly; the rate of correct responses in transformed items was slightly higher than that obtained for items identical to informal test items. Thus the transformations performed upon informal test items in designing formal test items cannot explain the discrepancy of performance in these situations.

A second possible interpretation of these results is that the children interviewed in this study were 'concrete' in their thinking and, thus, concrete situations would help them in the discovery of a solution. In the natural situation, they solved problems about the sale of lemons, coconuts, etc., when the actual items in question were physically present. However, the presence of concrete instances can be understood as a facilitating factor if the instance somehow allows the problem-solver to abstract from the concrete example to a more general situation. There is nothing in the nature of coconuts that makes it relatively easier to discover that three coconuts (at Cr$ 35.00 each) cost Cr$ 105.00. The presence of the groceries does not simplify the arithmetic of the problem. Moreover, computation in the natural situation of the informal test was in all cases carried out mentally, without recourse to external memory aids for partial results or intermediary steps. One can hardly argue that mental computation would be an ability characteristic of concrete thinkers.

The results seem to be in conflict with the implicit pedagogical assumption of mathematical educators according to which children ought first to learn mathematical operations and only later to apply them to verbal and real-life problems. Real-life and word problems may provide the 'daily human sense' (Donaldson, 1978) which will guide children to find a correct solution intuitively without requiring an extra step—namely, the translation of word problems into algebraic expressions. This interpretation is consistent with data obtained by others in the area of logic, such as Wason & Shapiro (1971), Johnson-Laird *et al.* (1972) and Lunzer *et al.* (1972).

How is it possible that children capable of solving a computational problem in the natural situation will fail to solve the same problem when it is taken out of its context? In the present case, a qualitative analysis of the protocols suggested that the problem-solving routines used may have been different in the two situations. In the natural situations children tended to reason by using what can be termed a 'convenient group' while in the formal test school-taught routines were more frequently, although not exclusively, observed. Five examples are given below, which demonstrate the children's ability to deal with quantities and their lack of expertise in manipulating symbols. The examples were chosen for representing clear explanations of the procedures used in both settings. In each of the five examples below the performance described in the informal test contrasts strongly with the same child's performance in the formal test when solving the same item.

(1) **First example (M, 12 years)**
   Informal test
   Customer: I'm going to take four coconuts. How much is that?
   Child: Three will be 105, plus 30, that's 135 . . . one coconut
               is 35 . . . that is . . . 140!
   Formal test
   Child resolves the item 35 × 4 explaining out loud:
   4 times 5 is 20, carry the 2; 2 plus 3 is 5, times 4 is 20.
   Answer written: 200.

(2) **Second example (MD, 9 years)**
   Informal test
   Customer: OK, I'll take three coconuts (at the price of Cr$ 40.00
               each). How much is that?

150

Child: (Without gestures, calculates out loud) 40, 80, 120.

Formal test

Child solves the item 40 × 3 and obtains 70. She then explains the procedure 'Lower the zero; 4 and 3 is 7'.

(3) Third example (MD, 9 years)

Informal test

Customer: I'll take 12 lemons (one lemon is Cr$ 5.00).

Child: 10, 20, 30, 40, 50, 60 (while separating out two lemons at a time).

Formal test

Child has just solved the item 40 × 3. In solving 12 × 5 she proceeds by lowering first the 2, then the 5 and the 1, obtaining 152. She explains this procedure to the (surprised) examiner when she is finished.

(4) Fourth example (S, 11 years)

Informal test

Customer: What would I have to pay for six kilos? (of watermelon at Cr$50.00 per kg).

Child: [Without any appreciable pause] 300.

Customer: Let me see. How did you get that so fast?

Child: Counting one by one. Two kilos, 100. 200. 300.

Formal test

Test item: A fisherman caught 50 fish. The second one caught five times the amount of fish the first fisherman had caught. How many fish did the lucky fisherman catch?

Child: (Writes down 50 × 6 and 360 as the result; then answers) 36.

Examiner repeats the problems and child does the computation again, writing down 860 as result. His oral response is 86.

Examiner: How did you calculate that?

Child: I did it like this. Six times six is 36. Then I put it there.

Examiner: Where did you put it? (Child had not written down the number to be carried.)

Child: (Points to the digit 5 in 50). That makes 86 [apparently adding 3 and 5 and placing this sum in the result].

Examiner: How many did the first fisherman catch?

Child: 50.

A final example follows, with suggested interpretations enclosed in parentheses.

(5) Fifth example

Informal test

Customer: I'll take two coconuts (at Cr$ 40.00 each. Pays with a
             Cr$ 500.00 bill). What do I get back?
Child: (Before reaching for customer's change) 80, 90, 100.
             420.

Formal test

Test item: 420 + 80.

The child writes 420 plus 80 and claims that 130 is the result. [The
procedure used was not explained but it seems that the child
applied a step of a multiplication routine to an addition problem
by successively adding 8 to 2 and then to 4, carrying the 1; that is,
8 + 2 = 10, carry the one, 1 + 4 + 8 = 13. The zeros in 420 and 80
were not written. Reaction times were obtained from tape record-
ings and the whole process took 53 seconds.]

Examiner: How did you do this one, 420 plus 80?
Child: Plus?
Examiner: Plus 80.
Child: 100, 200.
Examiner: (After a 5 second pause, interrupts the child's response
             treating it as final) Hum, OK.
Child: Wait a minute. That was wrong. 500. [The child had
             apparently added 80 and 20, obtaining one hundred,
             and then started adding the hundreds. The experi-
             menter interpreted 200 as the final answer after a
             brief pause but the child completed the computation
             and gave the correct answer when solving the
             addition problem by a manipulation-with-quantities
             approach.]

In the informal test, children rely upon mental calculations which are
closely linked to the quantities that are being dealt with. The preferred
strategy for multiplication problems seems to consist in chaining successive additions. In the first example, as the addition became more difficult,
the subject decomposed a quantity into tens and units—to add 35 to 105,
M. first added 30 and later included 5 in the result.

In the formal test, where paper and pencil were used in all the above
examples, the children try to follow, without success, school-prescribed
routines. Mistakes often occur as a result of confusing addition routines
with multiplication routines, as is clearly the case in examples (1) and (5).
Moreover, in all the cases, there is no evidence, once the numbers are
written down, that the children try to relate the obtained results to the
problem at hand in order to assess the adequacy of their answers.

Summarizing briefly, the combination of the clinical method of questioning with participant observation used in this project seemed particularly
helpful when exploring mathematical thinking and thinking in daily life.

The results support the thesis proposed by Luria (1976) and by Donaldson (1978) that thinking sustained by daily human sense can be—in the same subject—at a higher level than thinking out of context. They also raise doubts about the pedagogical practice of teaching mathematical operations in a disembedded form before applying them to word problems.

Our results are also in agreement with data reported by Lave *et al.* (1984), who showed that problem solving in the supermarket was significantly superior to problem solving with paper and pencil. It appears that daily problem solving may be accomplished by routines different from those taught in schools. In the present study, daily problem solving tended to be accomplished by strategies involving the mental manipulation of quantities while in the school-type situation the manipulation of symbols carried the burden of computation, thereby making the operations 'in a very real sense divorced from reality' (see Reed & Lave, 1981, p. 442). In many cases attempts to follow school-prescribed routines seemed in fact to interfere with problem solving (see also Carraher & Schliemann, in press).

Are we to conclude that schools ought to allow children simply to develop their own computational routines without trying to impose the conventional systems developed in the culture? We do not believe that our results lead to this conclusion. Mental computation has limitations which can be overcome through written computation. One is the inherent limitation placed on multiplying through successive chunking, that is, on multiplying through repeated chunked additions—a procedure which becomes grossly inefficient when large numbers are involved.

The sort of mathematics taught in schools has the potential to serve as an 'amplifier of thought processes', in the sense in which Bruner (1972) has referred to both mathematics and logic. As such, we do not dispute whether 'school maths' routines can offer richer and more powerful alternatives to maths routines which emerge in non-school settings. The major question appears to centre on the proper pedagogical point of departure, i.e. where to start. We suggest that educators should question the practice of treating mathematical systems as formal subjects from the outset and should instead seek ways of introducing these systems in contexts which allow them to be sustained by human daily sense.

Acknowledgements

The research conducted received support from the Conselho Nacional de Desenvolvimento Científico e Tecnológico, Brasília, and from the British Council.

The authors thank Peter Bryant for his helpful comments on the present report.

Notes

1 In the present report the term 'class' is employed loosely, without a clear distinction from the expression 'socio-economic stratum'.
2 (. . .) is used here to mark ascending intonation suggestive of the interruption, and not completion, of a statement.

References

Berlinck, M. T. (1977). *Marginalidade Social e Relações de Classe em São Paulo.* Petrópolis, RJ, brazil: Vozes.

Bruner, J. (1972). *Relevance of Education.* London: Penguin.

Carraher, T., Carraher, D. & Schliemann, A. (1982). Na vida dez, na escola zero: Os contextos culturais da aprendizagem da matemática. *Cadernos de Pesquisa,* **42,** 79–86. (São Paulo, Brazil, special UNESCO issue for Latin America.)

Carraher, T. & Schliemann, A. (in press). Computation routines prescribed by schools: Help or hindrance? *Journal for Research in Mathematics Education.*

Cavalcanti, C. (1978). *Viabilidade do Setor Informal. A Demanda de Pequenos Serviços no Grande Recife.* Recife, PE, Brazil: Instituto Joaquim Nabuco de Pesquisas Sociais.

Cavalcanti, C. & Duarte, R. (1980a). *A Procura de Espaço na Economia Urbana: O Setor Informal de Fortaleza.* Recife, PE, Brazil: SUDENE/FUNDAJ.

Cavalcanti, C. & Duarte, R. (1980b). *O Setor Informal de Salvador: Dimensões, Natureza, Significação.* Recife, PE, Brazil: SUDENE/FUNDAJ.

Donaldson, M. (1978). *Children's Minds.* New York: Norton.

Gay, J. & Cole, M. (1976). *The New Mathematics and an Old Culture: A Study of Learning among the Kpelle of Liberia.* New York: Holt, Rinehart & Winston.

Johnson-Laird, P. N., Legrenzi, P. & Sonino Legrenzi, M. (1972). Reasoning and a sense of reality. *British Journal of Psychology,* **63,** 395–400.

Lave, J., Murtaugh, M. & de La Rocha, O. (1984). The dialectical construction of arithmetic practice. In B. Rogoff & J. Lave (eds), *Everyday Cognition: Its Development in Social Context,* pp. 67–94. Cambridge, MA: Harvard University Press.

Lunzer, E. A., Harrison, C. & Davey, M. (1972). The four-card problem and the development of formal reasoning. *Quarterly Journal of Experimental Psychology,* **24,** 326–339.

Luria, A. R. (1976). *Cognitive Development: Its Cultural and Social Foundations.* Cambridge, MA: Harvard University Press.

Reed, H. J. & Lave, J. (1981). Arithmetic as a tool for investigating relations between culture and cognition. In R. W. Casson (ed.), *Language, Culture and Cognition: Anthropological Perspectives.* New York: Macmillan.

Wason, P. C. & Shapiro, D. (1971). Natural and contrived experience in a reasoning problem. *Quarterly Journal of Experimental Psychology,* **23,** 63–71.

109

PERCEPTION OF NUMBERS
BY HUMAN INFANTS

Prentice Starkey and Robert G. Cooper, Jr.

Source: *Science*, 210, 1980: 1033–1035.

Abstract

Infants are capable of discriminating, representing, and remembering particular small numbers of items. A perceptual enumeration process called subitizing, present in 2-year-olds, probably underlies this capacity. This finding indicates that some number capacity is present before the onset of verbal counting, and it suggests that verbal counting may have precursors present during infancy.

One view of cognitive developmental psychology is that the earliest phases of development must be characterized in terms of capacities as well as incapacities in order to understand the courses (both normal and abnormal) of later development (*1*). Much of the theoretical and empirical research on numerical development has, in the last decade, focused on very young children; we now know that 2- to 4-year-olds understand some basic number concepts (*2*). The presence of numerical abilities in very young children led to the question of the precursors of these abilities, which in turn led us to investigate whether infants have any basic numerical abilities. Our research was motivated by the belief that the ability to represent the numerical value of a set of items may be necessary for the development of an understanding of number. Two-year-olds use a rapid perceptual process (called subitizing) to distinguish among arrays containing fewer than four items (*3*). In this report, we present evidence that 22-week-old infants can also discriminate exact numbers of items. This raises the possibility that the young child's verbal counting abilities grow in part from the infant's numerical ability.

The focus of our study was to demonstrate skills for perceiving and representing specific small numbers of items. This focus differs from that of experiments demonstrating the ability of infants to discriminate stimulus arrays that greatly differ in number (such as 2 versus 8 versus 32 versus 128 items) (*4*). These discriminations treat numbers of items that massively exceed the range of those adults and children can subitize, since the adult subitizing range is one to four or five items (*5*). The bases of discriminations among large values are not known and may vary with different types of arrays (for example, dot size, the spatial distance separating adjacent dots, or surface area of the total array). The ability underlying these discriminations might be the same as that which allows adults to estimate the more numerous of two arrays differing substantially in number; however, such skills are clearly different from subitizing, and they cannot provide the same kind of information for later number development as the perception and representation of exact small numerical values.

Our experimental method used duration of first fixation in a standard habituation- dishabituation-of-looking procedure (*6*). The subjects were 72 normal, full-term infants with a mean age of 22 weeks (range, 16 to 30 weeks). The infants were first habituated to arrays containing a particular number of dots and were then presented a posthabituation (PH) array containing a different number of dots (Fig. 1). The small-number conditions ($2 \rightarrow 3$ and $3 \rightarrow 2$) were chosen because 2-year-olds can perceive and store the number of items of 2- and 3-dot arrays (*3*); both $2 \rightarrow 3$ and $3 \rightarrow 2$ were used because infants might prefer complexity. The large-number conditions ($4 \rightarrow 6$ and $6 \rightarrow 4$) were chosen as controls because 2-year-olds can not perceive (that is, subitize) arrays containing four or more dots (*3*). Since 4:6 maintains the same ratio as 2:3, large-number conditions to some extent control for discrimination based on physical cues such as differences in total contour.

We analyzed the data several ways, and each analysis revealed the same pattern of results: dishabituation occurred when the number of items was small but not when it was large (Table 1). We also compared looking time on the final presentation of particular habituation arrays (H1 and H2) with mean looking time on the first three PH trials. Significant dishabituation was revealed in both small-number conditions but not in the large-number conditions. The infants also discriminated among small arrays that were identical in length but not number (H1 versus PH in the $2 \rightarrow 3$ condition and H2 versus PH in $3 \rightarrow 2$) and in density but not number (H2 versus PH in $2 \rightarrow 3$ and H1 versus PH in $3 \rightarrow 2$). These discriminations did not occur in the large-number conditions.

A number of potential explanations for these findings can be ruled out. The discrimination of small arrays can not be based on the length, density, or dot positions of the PH arrays, because (i) the same value of these cues appeared in at least 50 percent of the H trials and (ii) the infants

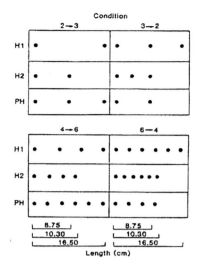

Figure 1 Representation of stimuli. Abbreviations: *H1* and *H2*, habituation arrays; *PH*, posthabituation arrays. Dots were 1 cm in diameter; luminance of the dots was 280 mL and of the 20-cm by 30-cm screen, 2.4 mL. Infants were approximately 60 cm from the screen. In each condition, the two habituation arrays contained the same number of dots but differed in length and density; the posthabituation array contained a different number of dots but the same length as one habituation array and the same density as the other. Habituation arrays were presented in random orders. In each condition (except 4 → 6), the location of each dot in the posthabituation array was identical to the location of a dot in a habituation array. The distance between any pair of adjacent dots was equal to the distance between any other pair of adjacent dots in the same array. Thus, the stimuli were constructed to avoid discrimination by dot spacing or configurational cues such as triangularity (*11*).

discriminated between small arrays that were identical in length but not number and in density but not number. Complexity preference also cannot be responsible for the results since dishabituation occurred in both small-number conditions.

It is unlikely that the infants' discrimination was based on brightness or contour-density differences between the H and PH arrays, because discrimination should also have occurred for the large-number conditions in which these differences were larger. Also, adults cannot discriminate those brightness differences, and infants are apparently no more sensitive than adults (*7*). Thus, we conclude that the change in number per se was the basis for dishabituation when the arrays had few items; dishabituation did not occur in the large-number conditions because infants can not perceive the particular absolute number of an array of more than two or three items (*8*).

LITERACY, NUMERACY AND AUTISM

Table 1 Means and standard deviations of looking times (in seconds) during habituation (H) and posthabituation (PH) trials.

Condition	Final three H trials	First three PH trials	d.f.	t	P	d.f.	t	P
2 → 3	2.09 ± 0.53	2.53 ± 1.15	17	2.08	<.06	35	3.46	<.005
3 → 2	2.03 ± 0.67	2.8 ± 1.65	17	2.77	<.02			
4 → 6	2.69 ± 0.95	2.58 ± 0.87	17	0.48	>.50	35	0.66	>.50
6 → 4	2.48 ± 0.79	2.42 ± 0.77	17	0.46	>.50			

Condition	Final H trials	First PH trials	d.f.	t	P	d.f.	t	P
2 → 3	1.93 ± 0.67	2.54 ± 1.36	17	2.46	<.03	35	3.71	<.001
3 → 2	1.70 ± 0.64	2.44 ± 1.45	17	2.71	<.02			
4 → 6	2.33 ± 0.94	2.40 ± 1.09	17	0.29	>.50	35	1.40	>.15
6 → 4	2.08 ± 0.62	2.46 ± 0.76	17	1.86	>.08			

Statistical comparisons*

* The same significance patterns were obtained for log-transformed looking times.

We think it likely that subitizing underlies the infants' performance in the small-number conditions. The basis for our position is the presence of subitizing in children (*3, 9*), the rapidity and numerical range of the enumeration process used by the infants, and the unlikelihood that infants can count verbally or that two independent processes for establishing exact small numbers would have evolved (*10*). However, even if we were to conclude that a subitizing phenomenon had been observed in infants, we would still know little about its component processes (for example, whether iteration or template-matching takes place or whether the same iteration process is used in verbal counting and in subitizing—as a primitive form of counting). Also, the component processes may change with age (infants may represent a two-object array as "a thing and a thing," whereas young children represent it as "two things"). Further work is needed on problems such as the nature of infant number abilities, the nature and early development of subitizing, its link (if any) to verbal counting, and whether subitizing serves as a psychological foundation of the number system.

References and notes

1. R. Gelman, in *Annu. Rev. Psychol.* **29**, 297 (1978).
2. —— and C. R. Gallistel. *The Child's Understanding of Number* (Harvard Univ. Press, Cambridge, Mass., 1978); D. Klahr and J. G. Wallace, *Cognitive Development. An Information Processing View* (Erlbaum, Hillsdale, N.J., 1976); J. Mehler and T. G. Bever, *Science* **158**, 141 (1967); J. Piaget, *ibid.* **162**, 976 (1968).

3. R. G. Cooper and P. Starkey, in preparation. Two-year-olds were presented linear arrays containing from one to five dots of white light. Arrays of dots were presented for 200 msec and followed by a light mask. Children were required to make a same-different judgment by comparing an array containing N dots with a spatially larger array containing N, $N + 1$, or $N - 1$ red chips. The percentage of correct judgments was significantly better than chance (50 percent) for one-, two-, and three-dot arrays; chance performance was obtained for four- and five-dot arrays. The same pattern of results was obtained in a condition in which dots were visible until the child responded "same" or "different."

4. L. B. Cohen, J. S. Deloache, W. R. Rissman, *Child Dev.* **46**, 611 (1975); R. Fantz and J. F. Fagan, *ibid.*, p. 3; D. J. Greenberg and S. Z. Blue, *ibid.*, p. 375.

5. D. Klahr, in *Visual Information Processing*, W. G. Chase, Ed. (Academic Press, New York, 1973), pp. 3–34.

6. Each trial began when the infant looked at the stimulus and ended when the infant looked away. An observer judged infant looking behavior and affective state. The observer was unaware of the experimental condition to which the infant had been assigned, of clock-measured looking times, and of the point at which the habituation criterion had been met. The habituation criterion was a 50 percent decrement in average three-trial looking time from maximum looking time averaged over three successive trials (for example; mean of trials 1, 2, and 3 versus mean of trials 2, 3, and 4).

7. B. Leskowitz. H. Taub. D. Raab, *Percept. Psychophys*, **4**, 207 (1968); D. Y. Teller, D. R. Peeples, M. Sekel, *Vision Res.* **18**, 41 (1978).

8. We have subsequently replicated these findings with older infants. Included was a control condition for possible regression to the mean in small-number conditions; infants habituated to two-dot arrays did not dishabituate to a two-dot array; the same was found for three-dot arrays. Also, infants habituated to two-dot arrays having the same densities as the four-dot arrays dishabituated to a three-dot array having the same density as the six-dot array (R. G. Cooper, P. Starkey, J. Dannemiller, in preparation). In two other experiments (P. Starkey, E. Spelke, R. Gelman, in preparation) infants discriminated three- versus four-dot arrays and two- versus three-object arrays when slides of heterogeneous arrays of common household objects rather than dots were used as stimuli. This study is important since total contour varied considerably from slide to slide.

9. M. T. H. Chi and D. Klahr, *J. Exp. Child Psychol.* **19**, 434 (1975).

10. M. H. Bickhard, *Hum. Dev.* **22**, 217 (1979).

11. A. E. Milewski, *Dev. Psychol.* **15**, 357 (1979).

12. Supported by NIMH grant MH31895-01 to R. G. C. and a NIH postdoctoral fellowship and the University of Pennsylvania Cognitive Science Program (supported by the Sloan Foundation) to P. S. We thank M. Banks for serving as consultant and J. Dannemiller for helping collect the data. We also thank R. Gelman, E. Spelke, and anonymous referees for comments on earlier drafts. Brief versions of this work were given at the meetings of the Society for Research in Child Development, American Association for the Advancement of Science, and the Jean Piaget Society, 1979.

110

PERCEPTION OF NUMERICAL INVARIANCE IN NEONATES

Sue Ellen Antell and Daniel P. Keating

Source: *Child Development*, 54, 1983: 695–701.

40 healthy, normal newborn infants were evaluated with reference to their ability to discriminate among visual stimulus arrays consisting of 2 versus 3 or 4 versus 6 black dots. Infants made this discrimination within a habituation/dishabituation paradigm for the small number sets (2 to 3 and 3 to 2) but not for the larger sets (4 to 6 and 6 to 4). We argue that this suggests the ability to abstract numerical invariance from small-set visual arrays and may be evidence for complex information processing during the first week of life.

Research into neonatal cognitive processing has traditionally consisted of the investigation of elementary processing and the elucidation of techniques whereby such mechanisms may be objectively quantified (Fantz, 1963, 1965; Friedman, 1972b). Another, more recent line of work (e.g., Brazelton, 1973) has investigated basic issues in neurological integration, organization, and state functions in very young infants. Such work has provoked a reconceptualization of infants as active, organized information processors rather than passive and disorganized sensory receptors. The research in which we are engaged takes this as its starting point and examines newborns to gain some understanding of the "rules" by which information may be processed. Gibson (1969) has argued that cognitive development consists in part of the ability to abstract the invariant features in a changing environment and, in this way, to organize experience. In this research, we attempted to extend this principle downward to examine whether the neonate enters the world with significant components of such abstraction. To investigate this possibility, we selected the numerosity problem presented to 4-month-old infants by Starkey and Cooper (1980). In that experiment, the infants were tested for their ability to abstract a small-set numerical invariance from simple stimulus arrays. The investigation of numeric competency in preschool children has revealed the presence of numeric discrimination prior to the adoption of a "mature" form of the counting system (Gelman, 1972; Gelman & Galistel, 1978). Starkey, Spelke, and Gelman (Note 1) suggest that number may represent a "natural domain of competence," and suggest that similar processes may underlie the ability of 4-month-old infants to make simple numeric discriminations. If this is indeed the case, then it is not unreasonable to suspect that even very young infants may be able to demonstrate similar abilities under well-controlled conditions.

Although it was previously assumed that visual acuity in the newborn is too poor to allow for any reliable assessment of complex visual information processing, recent research has established that acuity in the newborn is at least 20/150 (Dayton, Jones, & Aui, 1964). Harris and Macfarlane (1974) demonstrated the principle of active peripheral vision and identified the visual field of the neonate as an angle of at least 25 from the center of fixation to the periphery.

Friedman and his colleagues (Friedman, 1972a, 1972b; Friedman, Bruno, & Vietze, 1974; Friedman & Carpenter, 1971; Friedman, Nagy, & Carpenter, 1970) conducted a number of studies designed to explore in detail the habituation of visual fixation in neonates. They found, as predicted, that attention declined over trials but increased significantly when novelty was introduced. Such work demonstrated clearly that visual habituation is not attributable to generalized ocularmotor fatigue and could be used as a measure of differential response to stimulus.

Neonates thus probably do possess some primitive "memory" capacity, the ability to detect stimuli presented to the periphery and actively orient toward it, and the ability and inclination to search the environment for visually interesting stimuli, but this still fails to provide any substantive evidence of processing higher than the level of sensory systems by which information may be organized.

The research described here provides initial evidence for such organizational processes. It begins with the hypothesis that cognitive development is a continuous process, and that precursors of later abilities can be identified even in neonates when performance factors are carefully controlled. We use the habituation/recovery technique of observing infant attention as an index of complex processing. By controlling the stimuli so that dishabituation is tied to the discrimination of novelty in a previously invariant feature, we have been able to assess directly such a function in infants during the first week of life.

Method

Subjects.—Subjects for this research were 40 normal, healthy newborn infants ranging from 21 to 144 hours old (M = 53 hours) who were in residence in the newborn nursery at Sinai Hospital in Baltimore. Infants included in the study met the following minimum criteria: weight greater than 2,720 grams; Caesarean section for maternal cause only; Apgar scores at least 8/9; estimated gestational age not less than 38 weeks; no evidence of fetal distress during labor; obstetrical medication consisting of regional anesthesia only, 50 mg demerol or equivalent, or no medication; no obvious neonatal abnormality or illness; bilirubin less than 7 mg on day 1, 10 mg on day 2, and 12 mg thereafter; infants not undergoing phototherapy; no chronic or gestational illness in mother; male infants tested prior to circumcision. Consents were obtained from the parent of an additional 25 normal infants, but these additional subjects were dropped from the study for failure to attain or maintain the desired state (quiet alert) long enough for the full procedure. Infants were tested within 1 hour of the next scheduled feeding, typically in the late afternoon.

Stimuli.—The stimulus materials consisted of eight 15 × 15-cm white cards upon which were printed a discrete number (2, 3, 4, or 6) of black dots of .8 cm diameter. Each habituation array contained two stimulus cards with the same number of dots but which varied in terms of the length of the line or the density between the dots. The posthabituation array in each stimulus condition consisted of a card which contained a novel number of dots (2 to 3, 3 to 2, 4 to 6, or 6 to 4), but which maintained the line length of one of the habituation arrays and the dot density of the other (see Figure 1). During exposure, the stimulus cards were inserted into a white bracket affixed to a white foam-board screen that had been cut to fit the side of the hospital bassinet. This screen shielded the infant from all nonexperimental

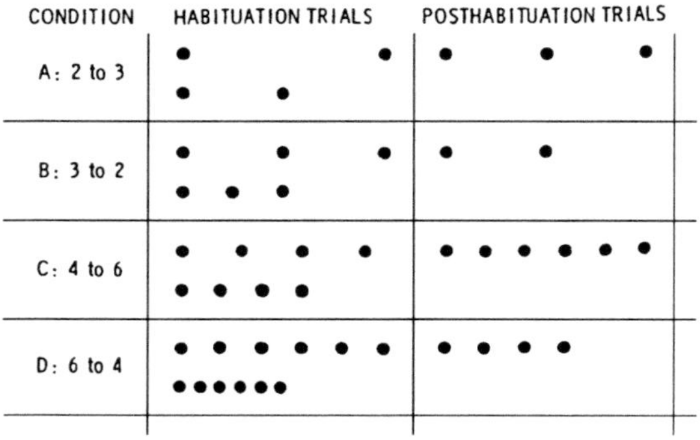

Figure 1 Simulus array for conditions 1–4.

visual stimuli as long as he or she remained visually oriented in the direction of the target.

Procedure.—After parental consents were obtained, the investigator checked the selected subjects for state. Any infant who was found spontaneously in the quiet alert state was tested immediately. Infants who were awake but crying were settled into the appropriate state prior to testing. Infants who were found to be asleep at the time of testing were gently awakened and the desired state induced if possible. Once in the quiet alert state, infants were placed on their left sides in their own hospital bassinet, at an optimal distance of approximately 17–19 cm from the screen (Haynes, White, & Held, 1965). Infants who were very active and needed restraining were swaddled; pacifiers were also used by all subjects.

Although pacifiers have been found to decrease the amount of visual scanning in young infants (Bruner, 1973), they have been found to be useful in maintaining concentration and orientation to the stimulus (Bruner, 1973; Haith, 1980; Mendelson & Haith, 1975). Additionally, nonnutritive sucking is considered by some (Bower, 1967; Bruner, 1973) to be a reliable index of visual discrimination. Infants were then manually oriented toward the screen and the first habituation target was displayed. During the procedure, the investigator stood behind the infant with her right hand lightly touching the pacifier (so that it would not be lost during testing) and her left hand resting on the infant's abdomen. This physical contact was used to maintain a quiet alert state. The investigator maintained a very light and constant pressure on all infants in all conditions, regardless of whether they appeared to be attending to the stimulus.

Each trial began when the observer (who was unaware of the experimental condition and the criterion of habituation), standing to the left of and above the infant's head (out of the line of vision), adjudged the infant to be looking at the target. A trial continued for a maximum of 40 sec, or until the observer judged the infant to be visually off target for 2 or more sec. Off-target behaviors included closing of eyes, turning head or body away from the target, crying, or falling asleep. If an infant fell asleep during the trial, the trial was concluded, but if he or she could be alerted again within the 10-sec intertrial interval, testing continued. In practice, some infants did doze slightly between trials, but would alert fully upon stimulation. Those infants ($N = 25$) who could not be again alerted were dropped from the study for failure to maintain state.

During the habituation phase, the infant received exposure alternately to two stimulus cards containing the same number of dots but varying in length of line and density between the dots. They continued receiving exposure to these same two cards until they reached a preset criterion of habituation: two consecutive trials in which there had been a minimum decrement of 8 sec from the mean looking time recorded for the first two trials. This habituation criterion is the one described by Friedman (1972a,

1972b) as having the greatest empirical utility. In terms of this research, the mean decrease in looking time was 56%, but the criterion was an absolute rather than a percentage value. After reaching criterion, the infants were exposed to the third card in the condition, which represented a test of perception of numerosity. This new card contained a novel number of dots but maintained the line length of one of the habituation arrays and the dot density of the other. Infants received two trials with the test stimulus.

Recording of time of visual fixation was accomplished manually by either of two trained research assistants with a Casio digital stopwatch with readout to .01 sec. Pearson correlation coefficients computed on looking time as recorded by the two observers during three sessions of testing for interrater reliability were .99, .995, and .995 for each of the 3 individual days and .952 over the three testing sessions (total observation time = 58.2 min; total number of trials = 126). Male and female infants were randomly assigned to each of the four stimulus conditions so that each condition cell contained five male and five female infants.

Results

The design for the experiment consisted of a 4 (condition) × 2 (gender) × 2 (habituation/posthabituation) mixed analysis of variance (ANOVA), with the first two factors between subjects and the last within subjects. The dependent variables were mean times of visual fixation for the last two habituation trials and the first two posthabituation trials, respectively. In order to obtain results more comparable with those reported by Starkey and Cooper (1980), we also compared the times obtained on the last habituation trial with those obtained on the first test trial by means of simple t tests.

Additional data analyses consisted of two 2 (condition) × 2 (gender) ANOVAs in which the dependent variables were trials to criterion and total time of visual fixation during habituation, respectively. Correlational analyses of obstetrical factors (obtained from infants' medical charts) with trials to criterion and with sum of habituation time were also conducted.

Results of the primary data analysis revealed a significant main effect for habituation/dishabituation, $F(1,32) = 31.57$, $p < .001$, indicating that overall, infants looked more during the two test trials than they did during the last two habituation trials. The crucial habituation × condition interaction was also significant, $F(3,32) = 5.81$, $p < .003$. The increase in looking time was substantial in the two small-number conditions (2 to 3 and 3 to 2, with an average increase of 102% and 67%, respectively) in contrast to the two large-number conditions (4 to 6 and 6 to 4, with an average increase of 13% and 16%, respectively). We further confirmed the interaction in an analysis of the last habituation and first posthabituation trial only, using a series of pooled-variance t tests. The obtained t's by condition were 3.88, $p < .001$

(2 to 3); 3.01, $p < .05$ (3 to 2); .82, N.S. (4 to 6); and .29, N.S. (6 to 4). The means and standard deviations of the last two and first two trials are shown in Table 1. These results form essentially the same pattern reported by Starkey and Cooper (1980) for 4-month-old infants and suggest that the ability to abstract numerical invariance in small sets is present in human newborns.

The only other significant result was the habituation × gender interaction, $F(1,32) = 4.50$, $p < .05$, indicating that change in looking time between habituation and test arrays for male infants was greater than for female infants: males had a mean looking time of 14.85 sec for the last two habituation trials and a mean of 25.42 for the two test trials across all conditions; females had a mean of 15.85 sec and 20.62 sec. This difference could not be attributed to any obvious obstetrical factors and needs to be evaluated in light of research into gender effects on habituation (Tighe & Powlison, 1978; Antell, Note 2).

The two additional ANOVAs yielded no significant main effects or interactions, indicating that neither gender nor condition had an effect upon either trials to criterion or total looking time during habituation.

Finally, the correlational analysis revealed no significant relationships between the use of anesthesia, analgesia, length of second stage, method of feeding, age of infant, or use of pitocin with either the sum of the habituation time or with the number of trials to criterion, with the exception of a just significant correlation ($r = .31$, $p < .05$) between the use of regional anesthesia and the sum of habituation time, in the direction that those infants whose mothers had received regional anesthesia had marginally longer looking times.

This result is interesting in light of research that suggests that visual information processing in infants may be affected by maternal medication (Bowes, Brackbill, Conway, & Steinschneider, 1970; Stechler, 1964). There was, however, no evidence in our data to suggest a medication effect on discrimination, but rather only on total length of looking during habituation.

Table 1 Means and Standard Deviations of Last Two Habituation and First Two Posthabituation Trials, by Condition (in Seconds).

Condition	Last Two Habituation Trials		First Two Posthabituation Trials	
	Mean	SD	Mean	SD
2 to 3	15.3	5.6	30.8	9.1
3 to 2	15.9	7.6	26.6	6.6
4 to 6	14.9	5.9	16.9	9.2
6 to 4	15.3	9.8	17.8	4.7

Discussion

Previous research using the habituation paradigm has been used to identify important parameters of newborn visual preference (Fantz, 1963, 1965; Friedman, 1972a, 1972b; Friedman, Carpenter, & Nagy, 1970; Friedman et al., 1970; Hershenson, 1964). In this research we capitalized upon those earlier findings and used the same paradigm to demonstrate the ability of neonates to detect numerical difference in arrays consisting of small numbers of discrete stimuli, an ability that breaks down when the set becomes too large. This is the same pattern of results obtained by Starkey and his colleagues with older infants (Starkey & Cooper, 1980; Starkey et al., Note 1; Starkey & Cooper, Note 3) using essentially the same methodology. In the Starkey and Cooper (1980) experiment, as well as our own, the infants were exposed to an invariant feature (numerosity) within arrays that varied two other dimensions (length and density). At test, only the numerosity varied, which suggests that infants made the discrimination by abstracting the numerical invariance and recognizing the novel numerosity as different. The fact that they could not make this discrimination in the two large-number conditions suggests that they were not merely responding to a change in contour density, and later research by Starkey et al. (Note 1), in which novel objects instead of dots were used to provide a number of changes in contour density during both habituation and test, argues even more forcefully for this conclusion. We would presume that essentially the same principle is operative in our own research, especially in view of the lack of discrimination in the large-number conditions, although further research is needed to confirm this assumption.

Although the evidence from this study supports the general notion of the ability of newborn infants to abstract invariant features in a stimulus array, the presence of additional redundant cues (such as background brightness, background area, and total target area) leaves open the possibility that the infants were abstracting an invariant other than number, despite the fact that they were apparently unable to extract any such information (including number) in the large-number conditions. While we think it implausible that it was these cues, rather than number cues, that enabled the infants to discriminate the arrays, further research is needed in which such extraneous cues are controlled before final conclusions regarding numeric competence can be drawn.

Additional evidence for an information-processing interpretation of the data comes from an evaluation of the mean looking times for the first two habituation arrays in each condition. The means obtained were 33.06, 33.698, 34.99, and 33.625 for the first two trials in the 2 to 3, 3 to 2, 4 to 6, and 6 to 4 conditions, respectively. This indicates that infants had no prior preference for any of the stimuli and so could not be discriminating merely on the basis of some "pre-wired" response mechanism (such as seems to operate in color discrimination). It further suggests some processing that requires an active organizational ability on the part of the subjects. In this paper, we have advanced the theoretical notion that newborn infants may begin this process of organization by tuning into the invariant stimulus features in the surround.

Similar techniques have been used extensively to document the ability of older (2 or more months) infants to abstract stimulus invariants from arrays that varied along a number of dimensions. Caron, Caron, and Carlson (1979) and McGurk (1972) found that infants were able to discriminate an invariant shape across changes in color, size, and orientation, and further to generalize habituation to a novel instance of the redundant property. Others have demonstrated the capacity of infants to abstract color across changes in wavelength (Bornstein, Kessen, & Weiskopf, 1976) and object rigidity across movement transformations (Gibson, Owsley, & Johnston, 1978).

Investigators have also examined the ability of infants to abstract information regarding the nature of the relations between stimulus components and have demonstrated the ability to do so across changes in shape, density, and orientation (Caron & Caron, 1980; Cornell, 1975; Milewski, 1979; Ruff, 1976; Schwartz & Day, 1979). That the foregoing process may represent a kind of primitive category construction has been posited by a number of authors (Caron & Caron, 1982; Cohen & Strauss, 1979) as an explanation of cognitive development in older infants.

It is important in this context to note that the ability to abstract invariant stimulus features and the discrimination of novelty based on such abstraction does not imply an understanding of the features by the infant or the ability at this stage to integrate the information in a meaningful way. What it does suggest is that the rules whereby information is extracted may be similar throughout infancy, and this is important for both practical and epistemological reasons to researchers in the cognitive development of infancy.

Numerosity is but one example of the kinds of information that may be accessible to neonates. Additional research needs to be done to determine the range of such abilities. Our research demonstrates that by using simple procedures that do not require the infant to deal with too much unnecessary information, evidence for such processes may be obtained.

Note

This research was partially supported by the Graduate Student Research Award from the Maryland Psychological Association to the first author. Computer time was donated by the University of Maryland Baltimore County. We thank Albert Caron and Rose Caron for their encouragement and helpful comments. We also thank Jacob Felix and Kathleen Stevens, neonatologist in charge of the newborn nurseries at Sinai Hospital of Baltimore; Cindy Ziegler, head nurse, newborn nursery; and the nursery staff for their assistance and cooperation during this project. Research assistants for the project were Lisa Schneider and Nilima Bhatt.

Reference notes

1. Starkey, P., Spelke, E., & Gelman, R. *Number competence in infants: Sensitivity to numeric invariance and numeric change.* Paper presented at the International Conference on Infant Studies, New Haven, Conn., April 1980.
2. Antell, S. *Sex differences in habituation research.* Unpublished manuscript, 1981.
3. Starkey, P., & Cooper, R. *Number development: Numerosity perception in infants.* Mimeographed. Final report, National Institute of Mental Health grant no. RO1MH31895.

References

Bornstein, M., Kessen, W., & Weiskopf, S. Color vision and hue categorization in young human infants. *Journal of Experimental Psychology: Human Perception and Performance*, 1976, **2**, 115–129.

Bower, T. G. The development of object permanence: Some studies of object constancy. *Perceptual Psychophysics*, 1967, **2**, 411–418.

Bowes, W. A., Brackbill, Y., Conway, E., & Steinschneider, A. The effects of obstetrical medication on fetus and infant. *Monographs of the Society for Research in Child Development*, 1970, **35** (4, Serial No. 137).

Brazelton, T. B. *Neonatal behavioral assessment scale.* Philadelphia: Heinemann, 1973.

Bruner, J. Pacifier produced visual buffering in human infants. *Developmental Psychobiology*, 1973, **19**, 434–439.

Caron, A., & Caron, R. Processing of relational information as an index of infant risk. In S. L. Friedman & M. Sigman (Eds.), *Preterm birth and psychological development.* New York: Academic Press, 1980.

Caron, A., & Caron, R. Cognitive development in early infancy. In T. Field, A. Huston, H. Quay, L. Troll, & G. Finley (Eds.), *Review of human development.* New York: Wiley, 1982.

Caron, A., Caron, R., & Carlson, V. Infant perception of the invariant shape of an object varying in slant. *Child Development*, 1979, **50**, 716–721.

Cohen, L., & Strauss, M. Concept acquisition in the human infant. *Child Development*, 1979, **50**, 419–424.

Cornell, E. H. Infants' visual attention to pattern arrangement and orientation. *Child Development*, 1975, **46**, 229–232.

Dayton, G., Jones, M., Aui, P. Developmental study of coordinated eye movement in the human infant. I. Visual activity in newborn humans: A study based on induced optokinetic nystagmus recorded by electrooculography. *Archives of Ophthalmology*, 1964, **71**, 865.

Fantz, R. Pattern vision in newborn infants. *Science*, 1963, **140**, 296–297.

Fantz, R. Visual perception from birth as shown by pattern selectivity. *Annals of the New York Academy of Sciences*, 1965, **118**, 793–814.

Friedman, S. Newborn visual attention to repeated exposure of redundant vs. "novel" targets. *Perception and Psychophysics*, 1972, **12**, 291–292. (a)

Friedman, S. Habituation and recovery of visual response in the alert human newborn. *Journal of Experimental Child Psychology*, 1972, **13**, 339–349. (b)

Friedman, S., Bruno, L., Vietze, P. Newborn habituation to visual stimuli: A sex difference in novelty detection. *Journal of Experimental Child Psychology*, 1974, **18**, 242–251.

Friedman, S., & Carpenter, G. Visual response decrement as a function of age of human newborn. *Child Development*, 1971, **42**, 1967–1971.

Friedman, S., Carpenter, G., & Nagy, A. Decrement and recovery of response to visual stimuli in the newborn human. *Proceedings of the American Psychological Association*, 1970, **5**, 273–274.

Friedman, S., Nagy, A., & Carpenter, G. Newborn attention: Differential response decrement to visual stimuli. *Journal of Experimental Child Psychology*, 1970, **10**, 44–51.

Gelman, R. Early number concepts. In H. W. Reese (Ed.), *Advances in child development and behavior* (Vol. 7). New York: Academic Press, 1972.

Gelman, R., & Galistel, C. R. *The child's understanding of number*. London: Harvard University Press, 1978.

Gibson, E. J. *Principles of perceptual learning and development*. New York: Appleton-Century-Crofts, 1969.

Gibson, E. J., Owsley, C. J., & Johnston, J. Perception of invariants by five-month old infants: Differentiation of two types of motion. *Developmental Psychology*, 1978, **14**, 407–415.

Haith, M. *Rules that babies look by*. Hillsdale, N.J.: Earlbaum, 1980.

Harris, P., & Macfarlane, A. The growth of the effective visual field from birth to seven weeks. *Journal of Experimental Child Psychology*, 1974, **18**, 340–348.

Haynes, H., White, B. L., & Held, R. Visual accommodation in human infants. *Science*, 1965, **148**, 528–530.

Hershenson, M. Visual discrimination in the human newborn. *Journal of Comparative and Physiological Psychology*, 1964, **56**, 270–276.

McGurk, H. Infant discrimination of orientation. *Journal of Experimental child Psychology*, 1972, **14**, 151–164.

Mendelson, M., & Haith, M. The relation between nonnutritive sucking and visual information processing in the human newborn. *Child Development*, 1975, **46**, 1025–1029.

Milewski, A. Visual discrimination and detection of configural invariance in 3-month infants. *Developmental Psychology*, 1979, **15**, 357–363.

Ruff, H. Developmental changes in the infant's attention to pattern detail. *Perceptual and Motor Skills*, 1976, **43**, 351–358.

Schwartz, M., & Day, R. Visual shape perception in early infancy. *Monographs of the Society for Research in Child Development*, 1979, **44** (7, Serial No. 182).

Starkey, P., & Cooper, R. Perception of numbers by human infants. *Science*, 1980, **210**, 1033–1034.

Stechler, G. Newborn attention as affected by medication during labor. *Science*, 1964, **144**, 315–317.

Tighe, T., & Powlison, L. Sex differences in infant habituation research: A survey and some hypotheses. *Bulletin of the Psychonomic Society*, 1978, **12**, 337–340.

111

SHARING AND THE UNDERSTANDING OF NUMBER EQUIVALENCE BY YOUNG CHILDREN

Olivier Frydman and Peter Bryant

Source: *Cognitive Development*, 3, 1988: 323–339.

Little is known about children's sharing skills and the relation of these skills to the understanding of number equivalence. In a series of three experiments, we found that 4-year-old children were able to share discontinuous quantities using temporal, one-to-one correspondence but usually did not make any connection between sharing and cardinal equivalence. Nor could they cope well with a task in which the recipients had to be given the same total number but different units had to be dealt to different recipients (single blocks to one person and doubles or triples to another). Most 5-year-olds performed correctly in this task. In a final experiment, we showed that children were much better at sharing in different units with the help of relevant color cues and also that experience with such a task improved their performance in a later one in which the color cues were removed.

The one-to-one correspondence principle is an essential component of the development of mathematical skills. No child can be said to have a real understanding of the cardinal properties of number unless he or she has understood that two sets of objects are equivalent in number when there is a reciprocal correspondence between the items in one set and the items in the other. The majority of tests devised to measure children's grasp of one-to-one correspondence has involved spatial displays; the children have had to make a quantitative comparison between two sets of objects laid alongside each other. Young children have difficulty using one-to-one correspondence in tests of this sort and their mistakes can usually be traced back to details of the spatial arrangement. The children often make their judgments on the basis of the relative length or density of the two sets, rather than by pairing individual members in the different sets (Cowan, 1987; Piaget & Szeminska, 1952).

One-to-one correspondence tests do not have to be spatial ones. Temporal tasks provide as valid and as interesting a way of looking at the understanding of the one-to-one correspondence principle as the traditional tasks which involve spatial displays. A child who has to give two people an equal amount of sweets and does so successively on a one-for-A, one-for-B basis may well be using the principle of one-to-one correspondence to do so, because sharing of this sort seems to involve a temporal matching of individual pairs in the two sets.

Informal observation suggests that sharing is a common enough activity among young children who would not fare well in tests involving spatial one-to-one correspondence. In fact, Piaget (Piaget & Szeminska, 1952) reported several instances of children failing to share a quantity between two people fairly. He argued that their mistakes were another instance of young children's difficulties with one-to-one correspondence. However, there is now other, convincing, empirical evidence that children as young as 3 years can manage quite well in formal tasks in which they have to share discontinuous quantities between two or more people and that they do so on a one-for-him, one-for-her basis which, on the surface at least, looks very like one-to-one correspondence (Desforges & Desforges, 1980; Miller, 1984; Klein & Langer, 1987). Thus, there is an apparent discrepancy between young children's difficulties with spatial tests and their apparent success with temporal ones. There are two possible explanations for this apparent conflict. One is that spatial tasks give an underestimate and the other that temporal tasks give an overestimate of the young child's understanding of one-to-one correspondence. We can look at these two possibilities in turn, beginning with the spatial tests.

Piaget (Piaget & Szeminska, 1952) was the first to look at the understanding of one-to-one correspondence, and he did so mainly with spatial tasks. He presented children with a row of items, for example, six bottles, beside which they had to build a row of glasses of the same number. He described three stages in the development of the ability to do this task: In the first, children tend to match the two rows on the basis of length, regardless of number. Later, they become able to match the rows in number but are misled by spatial transformations. If the perceptual similarity between the two rows is broken—for example, if one of them is squeezed or is spread out—the children of this stage will reckon that the rows do not have the same number of items any more. Finally, in the third stage, children become aware that the change in the perceptual appearance of the rows has no bearing on their actual numerosity. According to Piaget, the third stage is the only one which reflects an operational understanding of the one-to-one correspondence.

Despite other recent work that appears to demonstrate that preoperational children do possess several numerical skills (Starkey & Gelman, 1983; Gelman & Gallistel, 1978; Hughes, 1986), there remain insufficient empirical grounds for rejecting Piaget's claim about the initial difficulty of spatial one-to-one correspondence. Indeed, recent work by Cowan (1987) supports Piaget's contention that young children do not have a complete grasp of the one-to-one correspondence principle.

However, training involving one-to-one correspondence can lead to considerable improvement in young children's performance on number conservation tasks. Gelman (1982) tested a training procedure in which children had to assess by counting the cardinal value of equal and unequal small rows of items placed in one-to-one correspondence, before and after one of the rows was transformed. Hence, they were shown that a complete one-to-one correspondence leads to identical cardinal values whereas an incomplete one-to-one correspondence leads to different cardinal values. They could also find out that those cardinal values were not modified by the transformation of the array. Most 4- and 3-year-olds who received this training gave correct answers in subsequent number-conservation tasks, even with large sets of items. Gelman suggested that young children have some implicit knowledge of the one-to-one correspondence principle, which appears in counting and which her training procedure helped to make explicit. Thus, Piaget's suggestion is that children lack any knowledge of the one-to-one principle, whereas Gelman's is that they may have difficulty gaining access to it.

A third possibility is that the children know about one-to-one correspondence and have access to this knowledge but are distracted from using it by the spatial properties of the traditional one-to-one correspondence tests. The evident salience of the length cue, in particular, may lead them to forget about the possibilities of pairing off objects in the two sets. It is also possible that they may be confused enough to treat discontinuous quantities, for which length has no reliable bearing, as continuous quantities for which, of course, length is highly relevant.

Just as spatial tasks may give a misleadingly low estimate of children's understanding of one-to-one correspondence, sharing tasks could lead to an overestimate. The high proficiency shown by 3-year-olds in the equal distribution of discontinuous quantities in the studies by Desforges and Desforges (1980), Miller (1984), and Klein and Langer (1987) is impressive, but one should be cautious about any claim that the children's successes demonstrate an understanding of the relation between one-to-one correspondence and quantity. (In fact, none of these authors made such a claim.) The children may only be repeating a drill—a repetitive action which they have learned from others and apply without any understanding of its quantitative significance—when they share. There is no guarantee that they understand the quantitative significance of what they are doing as they share discontinuous quantities among others.

There are empirical solutions to these problems. If children have a full and explicit understanding of the quantitative significance of sharing, they should be able to infer the number of items in one shared set when they know the number in the other. This is easy to check. A failure on the part of young children to make the inference would cast doubt on their ability to understand that sharing is a way of achieving numerical equality, either because they do not understand the principle of sharing or because they have not grasped its relation to number. Another point is that children with a full and explicit understanding of the use of one-to-one correspondence should be able to adjust what they do when the quantities have to be shared in single units to one person but, say, in pairs to the other. In that case, simply repeating the same set of actions (one to him, one to her) will not work because the second recipient would end up with twice as much as the first. The child who has a proper understanding of the role of one-to-one correspondence in sharing would make twice as many actions to the recipient to whom she must deal singles as to the one to whom she hands out pairs. A failure which took the form of children giving out as many pairs to one recipient as singles to the other would suggest that they have adopted sharing as a rote, repetitive procedure which they are unable to adjust.

The interesting and apparently pervasive phenomenon of sharing among young children can only be taken as good evidence that they understand one-to-one correspondence if it can be shown that they are able to pass these two extra tests as well. We could find no evidence on these points, and so we designed three experiments to find out.

Experiment 1

Can young children share and can they connect sharing with number?

The aim was to see how well children share and if they can make inferences about number on the basis of sharing. There were two parts to the experiment: Part 1 dealt with children's ability to share sets of blocks equally and Part 2, with their ability to infer the equivalence of the cardinal values of two shared sets.

Method

Subjects.   These were 24 children (12 boys, 12 girls), some working class and others middle class, at a state nursery school in Oxford. Their ages ranged from 3 years, 11 months to 5 years, with an average of 4 years, 5 months.

Part 1: Sharing

Design. In this part of the experiment, the children simply had to share blocks in equal quantities. There were two independent variables:

1. *The number of blocks in the total set to be shared.* The set which had to be shared contained either 12 or 24 items.
2. *The number of divisors.* The child had to divide each total set among 2, 3, or 4 dolls.

The design was a repeated-measures one, so that each child was given six tasks (both set sizes divided among 2, 3, and 4 dolls).

Procedure. The experimenter spent 3 days in the classroom playing with the children so that they could become used to him. Each child was then given the arithmetic test of the Wechsler Preschool and Primary Scale of Intelligence (WPPSI). After that, the experiment itself started.

Each child was seen in two sessions. The child had to deal a set of 12 items in one session and a set of 24 in the other; half the children started with one set and the rest, with the other. The order of conditions within each session was systematically varied between children. The children were allocated to one of six order groups, and the groups represented the six possible orders (1,2,3; 1,3,2; 2,3,1; 2,1,3; 3,1,2; 3,2,1) of the three conditions.

The children were taken, one by one, to a separate room. The experimenter first asked the child to say how many dolls there were on the table (2, 3, or 4). He then gave the child a set of 12 or 24 red plastic blocks which he presented as toy sweets. The children were asked to share the sweets between the dolls and to make sure each doll was given the same number of sweets.

Part 2: Inferences about number

In a third session, the children were given two additional sharing tasks and then asked questions about the numbers of items in the shared sets. The aim was to see whether they realized that the number in each of the sets was equivalent.

The methods adopted in the sharing tasks were broadly similar to those used in Part 1. There were two differences: We corrected any mistakes that the children made while sharing at the time that they made them, and we used only one divisor (3).

We gave the children two tasks. In one, they had to divide 18 blocks between three dolls and in the other 15 blocks between three dolls. If the child made a mistake in sharing, the experimenter asked her to start again and if the child erred again in the second trial the experimenter corrected him or her when necessary. Once the sharing had been completed correctly, the experimenter lined up the blocks in front of each doll in rows of equal length and told the child, "You've done very well. Could you tell me how many sweets you gave to this doll?" If the child counted wrongly, he or she was asked to start again, and the experimenter helped with his finger. Once the child had stated the correct number, he or she was asked to say how many sweets had been given to the second doll (and then to the third, if any).

If the child started to count again, the experimenter immediately hid the set with his hand and asked, "Could you give me the answer without counting?" If the child could not, we always checked that he or she still remembered the number given to the first doll and, if necessary, had the child count again.

Results and discussion

Part 1

Table 1 presents the number of children who performed correctly in each task, that is, who shared the set of blocks into equal portions. We can see that most children did well in every task. The percentage of correct performance ranges between 71% and 100%. There is clearly no effect of the number of divisors. However, the performance is affected by the set size. Performance with 12 blocks was significantly better than with 24 blocks, $t(22) = 2.63$, $p < .01$.

The children shared in a one-to-one way in 76% of the trials, that is, they distributed the blocks one by one to one doll at a time. In the remaining 24% of the trials, the commonest pattern of performance (18 trials out of 34) was to allocate a different number of blocks at each turn. Another pattern, displayed in only 12 trials, consisted of sharing the whole set into different portions at one go. This, of course, is very far from temporal one-to-one correspondence. One of the children who adopted this tactic put the blocks of each portion on top of one another and used height to make them equal.

The use of one-to-one correspondence was much commoner in trials in which the children were correct than in those where they were not. In 83%

Table 1 Number of Children (out of 24) Correct in Each Condition.

	Number of Recipients		
Set Size	2	3	4
12	21	24	20
24	19	17	19

of the correct trials, children shared on a one-to-one basis; they did so in only 40% of the incorrect trials.

When we compared our results to those obtained by Desforges and Desforges (1980), we found that the percentage of errors was much higher in their study than in ours. The percentage of trials in which a one-to-one, correspondence-based strategy was used was also higher in our study, although this pattern was also the most frequent in their study. However, their experiment differed from ours in several ways. In most of the trials in the Desforges and Desforges experiment, the children had to deal with remainders and most errors were made in trials involving remainders. As well, there were more trials in their experiment (24 in all), and it may have been the case that the children's concentration suffered as a result.

In the Desforges and Desforges (1980) study, as well as in ours, perform-ance was lower with the larger sets. On the other hand, they found an association between the pattern of performance and the set size, whereas we failed to find any. Seventy-four percent of the trials involving 12 blocks in our study and 79% of the trials involving 24 blocks were dealt in a one-to-one manner.

Part 2

In the second part of this experiment, we tried to find out if children under-stood that the quantitative equivalence of two shared portions implies an equivalence of their cardinal values. When asked to say how many sweets they had given to the second doll, all the children started to count that doll's sweets. None of them spontaneously said that counting was unnecessary.

Once the blocks were hidden in order to prevent counting, only 10 chil-dren out of the 24 were able to give the correct answer. This result suggests that a majority of 4-year-olds are not aware of the actual relationship existing between numerical equivalence and the equivalence of quantities. Many children monitored the sharing process with great accuracy and sometimes even emphasized it verbally ("one for him and one for her, etc . . .") but still could not make the inference afterwards. However, it is worth noting that a substantial minority of these 4-year-olds (10 of 24) did make the inference and thus apparently did have a correct understanding of the numerical significance of sharing.

The size of the set made no difference: The children were either successful with both or unsuccessful with both set sizes.

Experiment 2

The first experiment showed that most young children can share effectively on a one-to-one basis, but that many of them may have little in the way of an explicit understanding of the numerical significance of sharing. However, their apparent inability to make inferences about the number of shared sets does not necessarily mean that they have no idea of the quantitative significance of sharing. They may know that sets shared on a one-to-one correspondence basis are equal and yet may not realize that this means that the same number names should be given to the two sets.

So, we are faced with two possibilities: One is that children share in a rote way but have no real idea of the significance of these repetitive actions. The other is that they do realize the quantitative significance of their actions even if they cannot express this knowledge in actual numbers.

One way of establishing if they understand the rationale for one-to-one correspondence in sharing—if, that is, sharing is more for them than just a mechanical, repetitive action—is to vary the actual quantities that have to be shared with the different recipients. Suppose that a child is given a set of bricks to share and that some of these bricks are single ones, whereas others are stuck together in pairs. Suppose, too, that the child is asked to share them so that each of two recipients ends up with the same amount but that one recipient is given the single bricks and the other, the pairs. In this case, sharing merely on the basis of repetitive actions would be quite wrong. The child would give twice as much to one recipient as to the other.

We need to know, then, if young children can see the difference between a task in which they have to share equal units with all the recipients and one in which they have to deal different-size units to different recipients. Do they realize that sharing in a simple one-to-one way works in the former but not in the latter situation? To do so, they would have to work out at some level that $1 \times 2 = 2 \times 1$ or $1 \times 3 = 3 \times 1$ (a commutativity problem) and adjust the number of units dealt to each recipient accordingly.

Method

Subjects.   The subjects were 20 children from a nursery school in Oxford and 20 first-grade children from a primary school, also in Oxford. Both schools mixed working-class and middle-class children. In the first group, the ages ranged from 3,11 to 5,1 years/months with an average of 4,6. In the second group, the ages ranged from 5,0 to 6,1 years/months with an average of 5,6.

Tasks.   There were five tasks. Three were control tasks in which the children had to share units of equal quantity, and two were experimental tasks in which they had to share units of different size with different recipients. The tasks were

   Control tasks
     Task 1 involved only single blocks (see Experiment 1).
     Task 2 involved only double blocks.
     Task 3 involved only triple blocks.

Experimental tasks
   Task 4 involved one set of 14 singles and one set of 8 doubles.
   Task 5 involved one set of 14 singles and one set of 6 triples.

The first three tasks and Task 5 involved total sets of 30 blocks. In Task 4, the total set was 32 blocks. Because the number of divisors does not seem to have any effect, only two dolls were used in each task.

Material and procedure

The material consisted of the same red plastic blocks used in Experiment 1. This time, they were presented to the child as toy pieces of chocolate "broken from chocolate bars."

We first showed the child a row of 10 blocks and demonstrated how the blocks could be taken apart or and assembled in different units (2 or 3, stuck together).

In the three control tasks, the procedure was exactly the same as in Experiment 1 except for the units that had to be shared. In Task 1, these were single bricks; therefore, the procedure was identical to that of the first experiment. In Tasks 2 and 3, the units were doubles or triples. Here, we asked the child to count how many pieces of chocolate there were in each unit.

In the experimental tasks (4 and 5), the child had to deal different units to the two recipients. Before each task started, the experimenter drew the child's attention very explicitly to the difference between the two kinds of unit to be used in the task. The experimenter showed the child that one unit consisted of a single portion of chocolate. Then, he pointed to a double (in Task 4) or to a triple (in Task 5) and asked the child to say how many portions were stuck together in that unit. Once the child had stated the correct number, the experimenter showed him or her that the chocolate bars had been broken in pieces of either one or two portions (or three).

In addition to the usual instructions, we told the child that each doll was to be given units of one kind only. We explained to the child that the singles would have to be given to one doll and the doubles (or triples) to the other, and we told the child which doll was to be given the singles and which, the doubles (or triples). We also explained that, despite this difference, both dolls should be given the same total quantity. The child was not allowed to break the doubles and the triples into separate portions but was allowed to arrange the singles as he or she wanted.

In both tasks, the child was instructed to keep sharing until told to stop and to be very certain at each step that both dolls received the same number of portions (we pointed to a single block/portion as we were saying that). We stopped the child once he or she had allocated 12 portions (i.e., 12 singles or 6 doubles or 4 triples) to one doll. Some children did not, at first, follow a one-to-one correspondence strategy and distributed several units to one doll without giving any to the other. Whenever this happened, we asked the children, after we stopped them, to give the same number of portions from the other set to the second doll (the one which had received nothing).

If the children started by taking no account of the number of portions, but simply shared units on a one-to-one correspondence basis, we stopped them and asked them to count the number of portions they had given to each recipient. We did this in order to make sure that they had understood the instructions. If, in this case, the children counted the number of units allocated instead of the actual number of portions, the experimenter then showed them that they were wrong by counting slowly in front of them the number of portions that each doll had received. The instructions were stated again, and we insisted once more on the difference between the two kinds of unit. Then, we asked the children to start sharing again and to be more careful about the number of portions they gave to each doll. Each child went through all five tasks in one session. The order in which they were given was systematically varied between children in a 5 × 5 Latin square.

Results and discussion

Table 2 presents the number of children in each age group who performed correctly in each task.

We will deal with the 4-year-olds first. Nearly all the 4-year-olds did well in the control tasks. The slightly higher rate of correct trials in the control tasks involving doubles and triples compared to the one involving singles is presumably due to the fewer allocations that these two tasks required. In contrast, the experimental tasks for which simple one-to-one correspondence sharing was inappropriate caused the children a great deal more difficulty. Only 3 children in this age group succeeded in both experimental tasks. Three other children solved only one of them correctly.

Four different strategies were adopted in the experimental tasks. Strategy 1 consisted of dealing out one set at a time by giving one recipient one set and the other recipient the rest, regardless of the numerical differences between the blocks and with no serious attempt to check how many portions were given. Strategy 2 consisted also of allocating a certain number of

Table 2 Number of Children (out of 20) Correct in the Second Experiment.

	Control Conditions			Experimental Conditions	
Age	S	D	Tr	S and D	S and Tr
Four years	16	20	20	5	4
Five years	19	20	20	15	14

S = singles; D = doubles; Tr = triples.

portions to one doll first and then to the second doll but also counting the number of portions given. Strategy 3 (simple one-to-one correspondence) involved an object-based, one-to-one correspondence, that is, the two sets were considered the same. Each doll was given one quantity at a time but no attention was paid to the difference between singles and doubles or triples. Strategy 4 (the correct one) involved a number-based, one-to-one correspondence, that is, each time one doll was given a double or a triple, the other one was given two or three single portions. Alternatively, the child could first assemble the singles into doubles or triples and then carry on a simple one-to-one distribution.

Table 3 presents the distribution of the four strategies across the 40 trials (Tasks 4 and 5 taken together). It is important to note that, apart from the 3 children who adopted Strategy 1 in both trials and one child who used the number-based strategy straightaway, all the others started by adopting Strategy 3 for at least the first of the two trials. After we had restated the instructions, 2 children switched to the number-based, one-to-one correspondence strategy and performed correctly. Another child did so for the second trial only. Two children adopted the counting strategy. Both succeeded in one trial but got lost at one stage of the counting process in the other trial and failed to reach equivalent portions.

The great majority of children in this age group, however, persevered with the same strategy. When we stopped them again after a few turns and asked them to count the number of portions already allocated to each doll, all of them counted correctly this time. Giving them a third chance to start again proved completely useless.

In this situation, children were actually facing a conflict between the outcome of the strategy which they tended to use spontaneously and the outcome of counting used as a verifying strategy. This conflict did not help the majority of them to give up the inappropriate strategy for a number-based one, despite their awareness of the numerical differences between the blocks. A lack of the numerical knowledge required cannot be considered as the source of the problem. All the children had to do was to count two or three portions each time they took a double or a triple. It seems that they have difficulty in using their numerical knowledge in this kind of task.

Table 3 Number of Trials (out of 40) in Which Different Strategies Were Used in the Second Experiment.

Age	Strategy 1	Strategy 2	Strategy 3	Strategy 4
Four years	6	4	23	7
Five years	0	0	13	27

Strat 1 = sharing the 2 sets without counting; Strat 2 = sharing the 2 sets one at a time with counting; Strat 3 = simple one-to-one correspondence; Strat 4 = the correct solution.

The fact that most of the 4-year-olds persisted in responding in a simple one-to-one way in the two experimental tasks suggests that these children do not have a good grasp of the principle of sharing or of temporal one-to-one correspondence. They seem blind to the fact that an equal number of actions to each recipient will not automatically ensure that each recipient gets the same amount as the other. For them, the number of actions rather than the amounts dealt to each recipient seem the important variable. This result, taken together with the earlier discovery of their inability to use sharing as a basis for inferences about number, suggests that, though 4-year-olds definitely share quite well, they have very little idea of the numerical or quantitative rationale of what they are doing. Sharing by this age group cannot be used as evidence that they understand the significance of one-to-one correspondence.

In marked contrast, the 5-year-old children did a great deal better in both experimental tasks. Fourteen children in this age group did well in both tasks. Eight of them adopted the number-based, one-to-one correspondence strategy straightaway. The rest started by sharing the sets on the basis of the discrete quantities but switched without hesitation to the correct pattern as soon as we pointed out the mistake. None of the children adopted Strategies 1 or 2.

We used a t-test to compare the age groups in the two experimental conditions. The scores represented the number of portions (single blocks) allocated to one doll once six doubles or four triples had been given to the other doll. Thus, a correct performance led to a score of 12. An object-based, one-to-one correspondence usually led to a score of 6 for the task involving doubles and singles and to a score of 4 for the task involving triples and singles. We added the scores obtained in the two tasks. With this procedure, it was not possible to score the performance of the 3 children who shared the blocks intuitively, and so we did not include them in the analysis. The t-test revealed a highly significant difference between the two age groups in the experimental conditions, $t(35) = 3.21$, $p < .01$.

This result suggests a major development in the understanding of the rationale behind sharing and of the principle of one-to-one correspondence at the age of around 5. However, because the experiment was carried out at the beginning of most of the 5-year-olds' third term at school, this development could have been the product of formal teaching. A comparison with 5-year-olds from a country in which school starts at 6 rather than at 5 years of age would be useful.

Experiment 3

Can 4-year-olds be helped to incorporate number with sharing?

The last experiment showed that 4-year-old children do not take into account variations in the actual quantities that they have to deal out when they are sharing. Even when they are shown that there is a conflict between the outcome of the way they share these quantities and the outcome of counting the final product, they still maintain the same sharing strategy. It seemed possible to us that they might be helped by a method which emphasizes the use of one-to-one correspondence to solve the problem.

We decided to look at this possibility by using color cues. We did this by using doubles and triples made with blocks of different colors. This manipulation might allow children to account for numerosity through color-based, one-to-one correspondence. The aim of Experiment 3 was to see whether experience with this type of one-to-one correspondence would help 4-year-old children understand how to cope with units of different quantities in a sharing task.

Method

Subjects. The children were 28 children from another state nursery school in Oxford. Their ages ranged between 3 years, 11 months and 5 years 1 month with a mean of 4 years, 6 months. The children were equally divided into an experimental and a control group.

Design. The children were seen in two sessions. The pretest was administered in the first session, the training and the posttest, in the second session. The experimental and the control group received the same treatment in the pre- and posttests but were given different forms of training in the training session.

Tasks and Material. The pretest, the training, and the posttest consisted of the same two tasks which were also exactly the same as Tasks 4 and 5 in the previous experiment (in which the children had to deal out single portions to one recipient and doubles or triples to the other). The pre- and posttests involved only red blocks. In the training, the blocks came in two different colors but the arrangement of these colors and, therefore, their significance varied between groups.

In the experimental group, the doubles were all made of one blue block and one yellow block. The triples had one blue block between two yellows or one yellow block between two blues. The sets of singles included an equal number of blue and yellow blocks.

In the control group, the sets of singles were the same as in the experimental task. The doubles and the triples were made entirely of blue blocks *or* of yellow blocks. Half the set of doubles and half the set of triples were blue blocks. The other halves were yellow blocks.

Thus, the only difference between the experimental and the control groups was in the arrangement of the colors in the larger units. The experimental group was given larger units which consisted of bricks of the two different colors, and the purpose here was to make it easier for them to realize that the larger unit consisted of two or three subunits and to relate these subunits to the single bricks of the same colors which had to be shared out to the other recipient. On the other hand, the control group did not have this cue. Some of the larger units were blue and others, yellow, but, in every case, these units were characterized by one color only.

The training that was given to both groups consisted of a fixed amount of extra experience with color cues. We did not attempt to train them to perform correctly and we ended the training at the same point for every child whether or not he or she was performing well.

Procedure. Before the experiment started, we spent two days in the nursery class playing with the children. In order to begin the experiment with a simple task, all the children were asked, right before the pretest trials, to share a set of 14 single blocks between 2 people (the experimenter and the child). If necessary, they were helped by the experimenter.

The procedure in each of the tasks was exactly the same as in Experiment 2, apart from differences in material. In the intervening color tasks, we drew the child's attention to the different colors, that is, that each block was made of a blue piece and of a yellow piece or that some blocks were made of two blue portions and some others of two yellow portions.

Results

Table 4 presents the number of children from both groups who performed correctly at the different stages of the experiment.

The results of the pretest confirm the trends observed in Experiment 2. Only 4 children adopted a number-based, one-to-one correspondence strategy. They did well in both trials. Among the remaining 24 children, 20 displayed an object-based, one-to-one correspondence strategy. Two of them did attempt to level the portions by counting but did not do it accurately. The 4 remaining children distributed the sets one after the other without any real attempt to make the parts equivalent.

Table 4 Number of Children (out of 14) Correct in the Different Tests and Conditions in the Third Experiment.

	Experimental Group		Control Group	
Test	S and D	S and Tr	S and D	S and Tr
Pretest	2	2	2	2
Intervening task	9	9	2	2
Posttest	9	9	3	3

S = singles; D = doubles; Tr = triples.

The experimental group did a great deal better in the intervening color task. The control group, on the other hand, stayed at the same level as in the pretest. Seven children in the experimental group who failed in the pretest did well in both intervening color tasks. All 7 had performed according to the object-based pattern in the pretest. In contrast, none of the children in the control group consistently took into account the differences in the units' quantities, although 2 of them showed some sporadic signs of doing so. Subjects' performance was scored in the same way as in Experiment 2 and the scores in both tasks were added. The t-test carried out on the results in the intervening color tasks reveals a highly significant difference between the two groups, $t(16) = 3.84$, $p < .01$.

This difference between the two groups was maintained in the posttest. All 7 of the children in the experimental group who, having failed in the pretest, performed well in the intervening color tasks continued to do so in the posttest where the color cue was no longer available. On the other hand, the control-group children maintained their low-level performance in the posttest. The fact that all the children who improved in the test trials still performed correctly in the posttest shows that they started taking numerosity into account.

The results were analyzed in an analysis of variance in which the main terms were Groups (experimental vs. control) and Tests (pre vs. post) with repeated measures on Tests. The scores of each child in the two tasks (doubles and triples) were added. The 4 children whose performance was correct in the pretest were not included in the statistical analyses. The results of the ANOVA reveals a highly significant test × group interaction, $F(1,26) = 8.15$, $p < .01$. Post hoc analyses (Neuman–Keuls) showed that the interaction was due to the improvement of the experimental group in the posttests being significantly greater than the improvement of the control group ($p < .01$). There was no significant difference between the two groups in the pretest.

Discussion

We have confirmed that young preschool children can share discontinuous material with great efficiency, using a form of temporal one-to-one correspondence. However, the majority of them could not use this principle to infer the equivalence of the respective cardinal values of the shared sets. Nor could most of them adjust the way that they shared when they had to deal out units of varying quantities. Although they certainly know that one brick added to another brick makes two bricks, they did not apply this knowledge to the sharing task in our second experiment.

On the other hand, 5-year-old children did cope with units of different quantities very well and, therefore, were able to incorporate numerical information with temporal one-to-one correspondence. Their success definitely suggests that they have a good grasp of the quantitative significance of temporal one-to-one correspondence and this, it should be noted, at an age before they can manage traditional tests of spatial one-to-one correspondence. These results therefore demonstrate a surprisingly early understanding of one-to-one correspondence.

There is, thus, a definite development between the ages of 4 and 5 years, but the exact nature of this development depends on the interpretation of the performance of the 4-year-old group. We can be reasonably sure that 5-year-olds understand the quantitative rationale of temporal one-to-one correspondence. Can we be as sure that 4-year-olds do not?

There seem to us to be two possible hypotheses: One is that, when 4-year-olds share, they are engaged in a meaningless (to them), rote-learned and automatic drill which they have picked up from others but which they do not really understand. They know that "one for you, one for me" is the correct way to proceed when sharing, but, if they think anything, it is that an equal number of responses must be made to each recipient.

In fact, the results of the first two experiments could suggest that this first hypothesis is true. Still, it is worth noting that, in Experiment 1, even those children who managed to make the inference had to be prompted explicitly not to count. This suggests that children do not spontaneously relate sharing to numerical equivalence, but that some may be able to do so with prompting. It is possible that the children did not keep quantitative equivalence in mind while sharing because they relied on being able to count if they had to check for equivalence. This could be tested by giving children a similar task in which counting would obviously be impossible from the beginning. In fact, Sophian (1987) has recently shown that young children do often make similar inferences about the cardinal value of one quantity compared to another on the basis of spatial one-to-one correspondence, when the items of the two sets are presented in a pairwise fashion, one pair at a time. This suggests that they may, in principle, be able to make the connection between one-to-one correspondence and number equivalence but may not do so on every occasion. It is also possible that children are aware of the quantitative equivalence between the shared sets but do not realize that quantitative equivalence implies an equivalence of the respective numbers. This would also require further investigation. As far as the results of the first two experiments are concerned, there is very little, indeed, to suggest that the first interpretation of the 4-year-olds' performance is wrong.

However, the third experiment produces a second hypothesis. The 4-year-old children's greater success in the color task in which the double (or triples) were made up of different-colored bricks suggests that they can take into account differences in the quantities to be shared and adjust what they do when they share accordingly. The considerable number of children who abandoned the simple, and inappropriate, one-to-one strategy in this task is certainly impressive and indicates that children of this age do not always blindly follow the one-for-you, one-for-me routine. An even more important result was the continuing success of these children in the post-test where the color cues were no longer available. This, surely, confirms that these children became aware of the quantitative significance of the difference between the units to be shared.

So, the second hypothesis about the 4-year-olds is that they do have a basic understanding of one-to-one correspondence but that they find it difficult to understand that a discrete quantity can be one object and also two or three sweets at the same time. By using different identifiable units in the doubles and triples, we allowed children to work out the problem according to a color based, one-to-one correspondence and this probably facilitated the incorporation of their numerical knowledge. We favor the second hypothesis and, in fact, we cannot see any way in which the first hypothesis could account for the results of the third experiment.

It is important to know more about the origins of sharing. It was quite apparent from the expertise shown by the 4-year-olds that they had been doing it for some time. One possibility is that they learn to share as a mere drill at first, but that their experiences with sharing lead them into the beginnings of a genuine understanding of one-to-one correspondence. The question is a causal one. Do children learn about one-to-one corres-pondence through sharing which they first learn as a drill? Or do they adopt sharing only as a result of some prior understanding of temporal one-to-one correspondence. The question can only be answered with the help of longitudinal research.

We also need to know more about the inferences that we looked for but failed to find in our first experiment. It seems likely that the 5-year-old group would be able to make such inferences, but we need to establish whether there is development on that front too. It would as well be interest-ing to know whether there is a connection between the difficulties experi-enced by the 4-year-old children in the first and the second experiments. One question to be asked is if our successful training procedures in the second experiment, which stopped the children sharing in a repetitive and inflexible manner, would also make it more likely that they would make the numerical inference which we were looking for in the first experiment. This would, of course, be very easy to test.

Our study establishes that the everyday activity of sharing has consider-able significance for the study of the child's growing awareness of number and quantity. We have shown through sharing that 5-year-old children do have a considerable grasp of the principle of one-to-one correspondence, at least in its temporal form, and we have demonstrated that even 4-year-old children can learn to incorporate numerical information when they share.

Note

We are extremely grateful to the head teachers, staff, and children of the Slade Nursery School, Wolvercote Nursery School, and Cutteslowe First School in Oxford for allowing us to do this research and for their helpful cooperation. We should also like to thank Cathy Sophian and Richard Cowan for helpful comments on an earlier draft of the paper and the editor and reviewer for their suggestions about the submitted paper. The first author wishes to thank the Foundation P. Wiener–M. Anspach of Brussels and the Belgian Fonds National pour la Recherche Scientifique for supporting him with training grants.

References

Cowan, R. (1987). Assessing young children's understanding of one-to-one correspondence. *British Journal of Developmental Psychology* 5, 149–153.

Desforges A., & Desforges, G. (1980). Number-based strategies of sharing in young children. *Educational Studies 6*, 97–109.

Gelman, R. (1982). Accessing one-to-one correspondence: Still another paper about conservation. *British Journal of Psychology, 73*, 209–220.

Gelman, R., & Gallistel, C. R. (1978). *The child's understanding of number*. Cambridge, MA: Harvard University Press.

Hughes, M. (1986). *Children and Number*. Oxford, England: Blackwell

Klein, A., & Langer, J. (1987, April). *Elementary numerical constructions by toddlers*. Paper presented to the biennial meeting of the SRCD at Baltimore, MD.

Miller, K. (1984). The child as the measurer of all things: Measurement procedures and the development of quantitative concepts. In C. Sophian (Ed.), *Origins of cognitive skills*. Hillsdale, NJ: Erlbaum.

Piaget, J., & Szeminska, A. (1952). *The child's conception of number*. London: Routledge & Kegan Paul.

Sophian, C. (1987). Early developments in children's understanding of number: Inferences about numerosity and one-to-one correspondence. Unpublished manuscript.

Starkey, P., & Gelman, R. (1982). The development of addition and subtraction abilities prior to formal schooling in arithmetic. In T. P. Carpenter, J. M. Moser, & T. A. Romberg (Eds.), *Addition and subtraction: A cognitive perspective*. Hillsdale, NJ: Erlbaum

112

A DEVELOPMENTAL ANALYSIS
OF NOTATIONAL COUNTING

Geoffrey B. Saxe

Source: *Child Development*, 48, 1977: 1512–1520.

The 2 studies of this report trace the child's acquisition of counting as a means to extract, compare, and reproduce number from arrays of objects. In study 1, 3-, 4-, and 7-year-olds' use of counting to compare and reproduce arrays numerically was analyzed with respect to 2 features: (1) counting accuracy, and (2) counting strategy. In study 2, 9 of the 3-year-olds who participated in study 1 were retested 12 and 18 months following their initial assessments. As predicted, in both studies there was an age-related improvement in accuracy which was interrelated with a progression from the use of prequantitative to the use of quantitative counting strategies to compare and reproduce number.

Our counting system consists of a set of ordered number names. If these names are applied in serial one-to-one correspondence to a set of objects they can be used to symbolize cardinal and ordinal values. The purpose of the present research was to study developmental changes in the way children use counting as a notational symbol system to manipulate numerical information.

In this paper, notational counting is defined in terms of three interrelated functions: first, as a means to extract (or determine) the number of an array of elements; second, as a means to compare two arrays numerically; and third, as a means to reproduce a model array numerically.

The previous research on the development of counting generally only studied its extractive function, or accuracy, to the neglect of how the child actually used counting as a means to compare and reproduce number. The accuracy studies indicate that 3- and 4-year-olds can accurately count small arrays (e.g., three and four objects) but infrequently count large arrays accurately. With age, accuracy improves for large arrays (see Gelman [1972] for an extensive review).

Although no systematic evidence exists to date, there is some indication that, at least for arrays which contain more than five objects, children's counting strategies to compare and reproduce number undergo developmental changes partially independent of their counting accuracy. For instance, Schaeffer, Eggleston, and Scott (1974) report the following experiment. They asked children to count an array (between five and seven objects) and then screened the array from the child's view. They then asked the child how many objects were underneath the screen. Although some of the young children counted the arrays accurately, they often reported a number other than that which they counted. Schaeffer *et al.* interpreted this to mean that the young children did not understand the "cardinality" rule, that is, for these children the last numeral recited did not represent the cardinal value of the array.

These findings suggest that if children are presented with tasks which require them to use counting to compare and to reproduce collections which they cannot easily estimate, a developmental sequence should be observable in their counting behavior. Young children should not use counting strategies which have quantitative significance, but with age children's counting strategies should change to quantitative ones. Moreover, children's counting strategies and counting accuracy should be partially independent developments. That is, young children, who use prequantitative strategies (i.e., do not use counting to compare or reproduce number), may sometimes count accurately, while older children, who use quantitative strategies, may sometimes miscount. It can also be expected that as children's counting strategies change from prequantitative to quantitative forms, the need for accuracy will become more apparent to the child. Therefore, it is predicted that accuracy and the transition from prequantitative to quantitative strategies should be interrelated.

In order to test these expectations, various tasks were devised to sample the way in which children used counting to compare or reproduce number. The tasks differed from one another in either the mode of reproduction (e.g., copying a model collection by drawing an equivalent number of objects as opposed to copying a model collection by placing an equivalent number of objects) or the spatial characteristics of the arrays (e.g., constructing a numerical copy near to or distant from the model collection). The diverse battery of counting tasks was used so that children's counting performance on any one task could be compared to their counting performance on other tasks.

Two studies were conducted. Study 1 reports cross-sectional findings on children's counting behavior on the tasks, and study 2 reports a follow-up study using the same counting tasks.

Study 1

Method

Subjects

Children at three age levels were interviewed: 3-1 to 3-11 (mean age = 3.7, N = nine boys and eight girls), 4-0 to 4-11 (mean age = 4-5, N = eight boys and seven girls), and 6-5 to 7-3 (mean age = 6-8, N = five boys and five girls). The children attended nursery or elementary schools in the Berkeley, California, area and were from middle-class backgrounds.

Counting tasks

Prior to the administration of the tasks, an estimate of rote counting ability was obtained by asking each child to count as far as possible. For those who could not count as far as 9, the number of objects used in the tasks was reduced to a number they could count by rote. Only three of the 3-year-olds could not count to 9.

Object placement task.—The experimenter presented a linear array of nine beads (each $^1/_4$ inch in diameter) and asked the child to "put out just the same number" from an identical set of 15 beads. As in all of the counting tasks, those children who did not spontaneously use counting received a suggestion to do so after their initial reproduction, for example, "Would counting help?"

Drawing task.—The experimenter presented a linear array of nine cardboard circles ($^3/_4$ inch in diameter) which extended about 16 inches, a pencil or crayon, and a piece of paper ($8^1/_2$ inches × 11 inches). The child was asked to "draw just the same number" of circles on the piece of paper as there were in the model array.

Remote placement task.—The experimenter presented two puppets, one on a table in front of the child, the other under the table at the child's feet. The placement was such that the child could not see both puppets at the same time. The experimenter gave the puppet on the floor nine small toy animals to "eat" and then instructed the child to give the puppet on the table "just as many" or "just the same number to eat" from an additional set of 14 small toy animals.

Comparison task.—The experimenter presented the child with two unequal linear arrays (nine horses, each 1 inch in length, and 11 pigs, each $^1/_2$ inch in length). The endpoints of the two rows were aligned in spatial correspondence. The child was questioned about the numerical relation between the two arrays, that is, "Are there just the same number of pigs and horses, or does one have more?"

Procedure

Each child performed the four tasks individually in a small interview room. A research assistant recorded verbal protocols, as well as the children's use of pointing gestures while counting as the interviewer administered the tasks. The order of the four tasks was counterbalanced.

Generally, administration of the tasks was completed in 15–20 min, but if children seemed fatigued during the interview it was terminated and resumed the following day. Although we attempted to administer every task to each child, not all of the children completed the full battery and not all of them used a counting strategy on every task, despite suggestions to do so: Four 3-year-olds, four 4-year-olds, and one 7-year-old were not scored on three of the four tasks, and one 4-year-old was not scored on two of the four tasks.

Scoring accuracy

Practically all of the 3- and 4-year-olds made pointing gestures to objects as they counted. Observing such gestures made it possible to score not only each instance that the child accurately counted an array, but also to score different forms of inaccurate counting (i.e., the absence of a one-to-one coordination between objects and the recitation of numerals). The forms of inaccurate and accurate counting were recorded and are described below:

1. *Numeral recitation without gestures.* Numbers were recited without gestural or visual reference to distinct objects.
2. *Gestural counting without numeral recitation.* Without reciting numbers, either (1) pointing gestures were made to specific objects, or (2) sweeping gestures were made across objects.
3. *Global correspondences.* Numbers were recited as the child made a continuous sweeping gesture across objects.
4. *Many-to-one correspondences.* Numbers were recited as the child made discrete pointing gestures to objects. However, the correspondences were not one to one between objects and numerals. Sometimes there were more (or fewer) gestures than objects and/or more (or fewer) numerals than gestures; or children miscounted without using gestures.
5. *Accurate counting.* Children counted accurately with or without the use of gestures.

Scoring children's counting strategies to compare and reproduce number. —Children's counting strategies were scored without reference to their counting accuracy. Strategies were scored as either prequantitative (level 1) or quantitative (level 2). At each strategy level it was also possible to score two types of prequantitative and two types of quantitative counting strategies (sublevels 1a and 1b, and sublevels 2a and 2b). For reasons described later, there were two differences in the scoring system for the comparison task: (1) it was possible to score a transitional level between the prequantitative and the quantitative level (sublevel 1bT), and (2) it was not possible to score the final sublevel (2b). The sequence of strategies scored, with behavioral examples from each task, is presented in table 1.

Each child's performance on each task was scored for counting strategy sublevel. Twenty-four task performances were scored for reliability (two protocols from each of the four tasks at each of the three age levels). There was an 87.5% agreement between the two sets of scores.

Results

The results are presented in three sections: (1) age trends in accuracy, (2) age trends in counting strategies, and (3) the pattern of relations between accuracy and strategy.

Age trends in forms of accurate and inaccurate counting.—There was a wide range in how many instances each child counted across tasks (range = six to 26 instances, median number of counts recorded per child = 11). The wide range was due both to missing data on some children and to individual differences on how many times children counted on any particular task.

Table 2 presents the percentages of inaccurate and accurate counting used in each age group. These percentages were determined by pooling all responses by form within each group and then computing the percentage of occurrence of each form of counting within each age group.[1]

Table 2 indicates that at 3 years of age, children's use of many-to-one and global correspondences predominated and accurate counting was used infrequently. At 4 years, both global and many-to-one correspondences declined in frequency and accurate counting rose sharply. At the same time, numeral recitation without gestures and gestural counting without numeral recitation were not represented. In the oldest group, accurate counting continued to increase and many-to-one correspondences were used infrequently. None of the other forms was represented.

Age trends in counting strategy sublevels.—As previously noted, sublevels 1a, 1b, 2a, and 2b were scored on the object placement task (OPT), drawing task (DT), and remote placement task (RPT), whereas sublevels 1a, 1b, 1bT, and 2a were scored on the comparison task (CT). The presence of the transitional sublevel (1bT) and the absence of the final sublevel (2b) on the comparison task were due to two factors. First, the comparison task was the only task in which spatial variables conflicted with number. This feature of the task made it possible to observe those children who were in conflict between an evaluation of number on the bases of spatial extent and the products of their counting, that is, a form between the prequantitative

Table 1

Strategies	Examples
Level 1 (Prequantitative counting). Counting is not used as a means to produce numerical comparisons or reproductions.	*Object placement task.* Subject makes a semicircle of 15 beads opposite the model. (Would counting help you?) Subject counts to 14 as she gestures back and forth over the model and copy. She makes no further modification of the model or copy.
Sublevel 1a. For reproductions, the child makes an approximate copy of the model without counting. After direct suggestion (e.g., "Would counting help?"), the child counts. For comparisons, the child counts only one collection, or both collections continuously as if they were one.	*Drawing task.* Subject draws 11 circles, filling the page. (How do you know that's right?) CAUSE THEY ARE. Subject counts the copy to 10.
	Remote placement task. Subject gives the puppet on the table all of the available ducks. (Would counting help?) Subject counts the 13 ducks on the table to 10. (Are there the same number?) YES, BECAUSE I COUNTED THEM.
	Comparison task. Subject counts horses 1–6 and continues counting the pigs 7, 8, 9, 10, 13, 14. (So, are there the same number of pigs and horses or does one have more?) SAME NUMBER.
Sublevel 1b. For reproductions, the child again makes an approximate copy of the model without counting. After direct suggestion, the child counts both collections *separately*, but counting is not used as a basis to compare these sets.	*OPT.* Subject makes a reproduction of six beads in a straight line opposite the model without matching endpoints. YOU HAVE 1, 2, 3, 4, 5, 6, 7, 8, 9, 10, 11. I HAVE 1, 2, 3, 4, 5, 6, 7. The information is not used to modify the copy.
	DT. Subject draws 12 circles, filling the page. (How do you know that's the same number?) Subject counts the copy to 7 and the model to 11. THEY'RE THE SAME NUMBER.
	RPT. Subject places the entire available set on the table. (Could you make sure it's the same number?) Subject counts the toy ducks on the table, 14. Then she counts the toy fish on the floor to 6. (Are there just as many?) YES, BECAUSE I COUNTED.
	CT. Subject counts the horses 1–8 and then counts the pigs 1–7. THEY ARE THE SAME NUMBER.

Table 1 (cont'd)

Strategies	Examples
Sublevel 1bT (Transitional). Numerical comparisons based on counting and spatial extent compete with one another. The child either modifies counting so that it conforms to spatial evaluations or fluctuates between an evaluation based upon counting and spatial extent.	*CT*. (Are there the same number or does one row have more?) SAME NUMBER. Subject counts the pigs 1–11 using one-to-one correspondences. Subject then counts the horses and appears to purposely miscount so that she ends on 11 also. THEY BOTH HAVE THE SAME.
Level 2 (Quantitative counting). Counting is used as a means to produce numerical comparisons and reproductions of arrays.	
Sublevel 2a. For reproductions, the child makes an approximate copy of the model without the use of counting and counts both collections separately. Although these numerical comparisons are based upon counting, the child uses a trial-and-error method in order to attain a numerical equivalence between model and copy.	*OPT*. Subject makes a reproduction of 15 beads and matches the endpoints with the model. (Do we have the same number?) NO. He proceeds by making a series of additions and subtractions interspersed with recounts until an equality is achieved. *DT*. Subject draws 11 circles in a random array. (How do you know that's right?) Subject counts the model and the copy. Subject then turns the paper over and redraws a copy. Then after a series of counts, erasures and recounts, she eventually reaches an equality. *RPT*. Subject places the entire available set on the table. (Could you make sure it's the same number?) Subject counts the toy fish on the floor to 10 and the toy ducks on the table to 14. Through trial-and-error process of counts, additions and subtractions, and recounts, he equalizes the model and the copy. *CT*. Subject counts pigs to 11 and the horses to 9. THERE ARE MORE PIGS.
Sublevel 2b. For reproductions, the child counts the model and then produces a numerically equivalent copy, or the child produces an approximate copy and then systematically adjusts the copy through counting to attain a numerical equivalence with the model.	*OPT*. Subject counts the model collection and then counts out the same number in the available set and places them opposite the model. *DT*. Subject counts the model array and then proceeds to draw the same number on his paper with accompanying counting. *RPT*. Subject counts the toy fish on the floor using one-to-one correspondences. She then counts out the identical number on the table using one-to-one correspondences. *CT*. Same as level 2a.

Table 2 Percentages of Accurate and Inaccurate Counting Used at Three Age Levels.

Correspondence between Numeral Recitation and Objects	Age (in Years)		
	3	4	7
Gestural counting without numeral recitation	2	0	0
Numeral recitation without gestures	1	0	0
Global correspondences	32	6	0
Many-to-one correspondences	49	31	9
Accurate counting	16	63	91

and the quantitative counting levels (sublevel 1bT). Second, the comparison task was the only one which did not require a numerical reproduction. This meant that the quantitative trial-and-error use of counting, characteristic of sublevel 2a on the reproduction tasks, would lead to a systematic solution on the comparison task. Consequently, sublevel 2a was the most advanced sublevel scored on the comparison task.

Table 3 presents the distribution of children across sublevels on each of the counting tasks. It indicates that, although the same transition from prequantitative to quantitative sublevels can be observed across each of the tasks, an earlier development tends to occur on the comparison task and a later development tends to occur on the remote placement task, as contrasted with the object placement and drawing tasks. These differences suggest that the level of maturity of children's counting strategies is related to specific task demands.

Relations between accuracy and strategies.—In order to determine whether the development of counting strategies is related to the improvement of counting accuracy, the tasks were separated into two groups, corresponding to differences previously noted in the sublevel scoring systems (reproduction tasks and comparison task). On the reproduction tasks (OPT, DT, RPT) a global sublevel score was calculated for each child by transforming sublevels into sublevel equivalent scores as follows: sublevel 1a = 1.0, sublevel 1b = 2.0, sublevel 2a = 3.0, sublevel 2b = 4.0. A global sublevel reproduction score was then calculated by determining the mean of each child's sublevel scores. The following intervals were used to define global sublevel reproduction scores: 1.0–1.49 = sublevel 1a, 1.50–2.49 = sublevel 1b, 2.50–3.49 = sublevel 2a, 3.50–4.0 = sublevel 2b. Since only one comparison task was used, a global sublevel score was not determined.

Figure 1 presents the percentage of accurate counting on the reproduction tasks and the comparison task as a function of the counting sublevels. The figure indicates that on the reproduction tasks there was a steady rise in the use of accurate counting between sublevels 1a and 2b. On the comparison task, there was also an increase in the use of accurate counting with

Table 3 Percentage Distribution of Three Age Groups across Notational Counting Sublevels.

Task and Age (Years)

Sublevel	OPT			DT			RPT			CT		
	3	4	7	3	4	7	3	4	7	3	4	7
2b	7	31	100	7	36	100	6	14	91	...	...	...
2a	0	38	0	0	21	0	0	29	9	6	38	100
1bT	...	...	...	...	...	...	...	...	...	0	31	0
1b	7	23	0	0	21	0	0	29	0	35	31	0
1a	87	8	0	93	21	0	94	29	0	59	0	0

Note: OPT = object placement task; DT = drawing task; RPT = remote placement task; CT = comparison task.

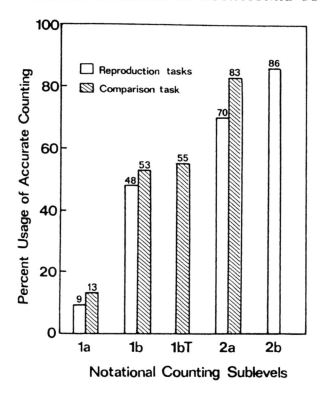

Figure 1 Percentage of usage of accurate counting as a function of counting sublevels on the comparison and reproduction tasks.

developmental sublevel. However, two differences between the trends in accuracy for the comparison task as opposed to the reproduction tasks are notable. First, as previously reported, at sublevel 1bT on the comparison task, children tended to modify their accurate counting to accommodate their spatial evaluations, and this may have contributed to the relative plateau in accurate counting between sublevels 1b and 1bT on the comparison task. Second, the high frequency in the use of accurate counting at sublevel 2a on the comparison task relative to the reproduction tasks (83% as opposed to 70% at sublevel 2a on the reproduction tasks) is probably due to the fact that sublevel 2a was the highest scorable sublevel on this task (so that all children who were assessed at sublevel 2b on the reproduction tasks were only assessed at sublevel 2a on the comparison task).

Study 2

The cross-sectional findings support the claim that children progress from the use of prequantitative to quantitative counting strategies in the

3- to 7-year age period and that this progression is interrelated with count-ing accuracy. They also lead to the hypothesis that if children are followed longitudinally, they will reflect a developmental progression through the counting sublevel sequence and that children's progress in the sublevel sequence will be interrelated with improvement of counting accuracy. In order to test these hypotheses, a subset of the children interviewed in study 1 was retested 12 and 18 months following the initial testing.

Method

Subjects

Nine of the 3-year-olds who participated in study 1 were retested in study 2. Children were selected on the basis of their availability. Two of the nine children were not available at the 18-month retest, and two additional children did not use a counting strategy on the comparison task at the 18-month retest.

Procedures

The tasks used to interview the children were identical to those used in the initial testing and included the object placement task (OPT), drawing task (DT), remote placement task (RPT), and comparison task (CT). Each child's protocol for each task was scored for both counting sublevel and accuracy.

Results

As in study 1, children's performances were analyzed separately for the comparison task and the reproduction tasks. Figure 2 presents the longi-tudinal trends for each child's counting behavior on the comparison task. In the figure, individual children are represented by connecting squares. Within the squares is a code representing the degree of counting accuracy for each child at each testing.

Figure 2 indicates that, as expected, children progressed in both count-ing sublevel and the degree of accuracy as a function of age. At the initial testing, all children used prequantitative strategies; five used sublevel 1a and three used sublevel 1b. With one exception, these children frequently counted inaccurately. At the second testing (t2), all children advanced in their count-ing strategies. Two children advanced to sublevel 1b, three to the transitional level 1bT, and three to the quantitative level (2a). Four of these children also advanced in counting accuracy, while three children remained unchanged and one child decreased in accuracy. The one child who decreased in accuracy did so apparently as a result of her progress in understanding the function of counting; that is, at t1 she counted with greater accuracy than

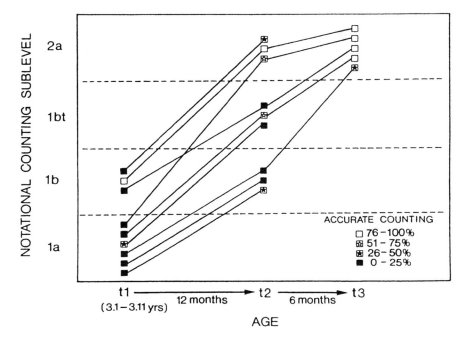

Figure 2 Longitudinal trends for nine children on the comparison task showing counting sublevels and counting accuracy at initial testing (t1) and two retests (t2, t3).

she did at t2, where she apparently miscounted in order to reconcile the products of her counting with her spatial evaluation of number. At the third testing session (t3), all children used quantitative counting strategies; all but one child consistently counted accurately.

Figure 3 presents the longitudinal trends on the reproduction tasks for each child. As in study 1, global counting sublevel scores were determined by transforming sublevel scores from each reproduction task into sublevel equivalent scores and averaging each child's scores across the tasks. The percentage of each child's use of accurate counting was determined by calculating the percentage of accurate counting across the reproduction tasks.

Figure 3 indicates that at the initial testing all children received a global score equivalent to the first prequantitative strategy sublevel (1a), and children infrequently used accurate counting. At the second testing, all children advanced in their strategies. Six advanced to sublevel 1b, three advanced to sublevel 2a, and one advanced to sublevel 2b. For most of the children there was an associated shift to greater degrees of accurate counting. At the final testing (t3), all but two of the children received global scores at the most advanced sublevel, and children usually counted accurately.

199

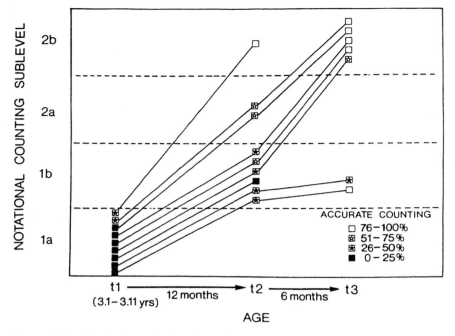

Figure 3 Longitudinal trends for nine children on the reproduction tasks showing global counting sublevels and counting accuracy at initial testing (t1) and two retests (t2, t3).

As in study 1, at the retest sessions children were only moderately consistent in their counting strategies. However, unlike study 1, no consistent trends were observed in the order of task difficulty.

Discussion

As expected, both the cross-sectional and the longitudinal findings indicate that children progress from the use of prequantitative to the use of quantitative counting strategies, and improvement in counting accuracy is interrelated with this developmental transition. That is, at the prequantitative sublevels (1a and 1b), children infrequently counted accurately. At the transitional sublevel (1bT) there was an indication that some children "purposely" miscounted as a result of trying to integrate their spatial judgments of number with the products of their counting. At the quantitative sublevels (2a and 2b), counting accuracy markedly improved.

The finding that counting accuracy and counting strategy develop in concert suggests that they are both regulated by the same underlying cognitive development. That is, as the child acquires an understanding that in order to determine the numerosity of an array the number names must be applied in a serial one-to-one correspondence to objects, two changes occur in the child's counting behavior: (1) the child's counting accuracy improves since accuracy is now motivated by an understanding of the "logic" of the counting system, and (2) the child begins to construct quantitative counting strategies to compare and reproduce number since counting is now understood to be a means to extract numerical information from arrays.

The two studies reported examined children's use of notational counting for collections which are too large for the child to easily estimate. As such, the focus was on developmental changes in how the child uses counting to manipulate numerical information which is not "concrete" or "perceptually salient." Research on children's conception of small numbers (see Gelman 1972) suggests that if a similar study were conducted with small numbers which the young child can estimate (e.g., two or three objects), a different rate of development and possibly a different developmental process would be observed in children's counting behavior.

Notes

Appreciation is extended to Allen Black, Jonas Langer, Howard Gardner, Stephen Kosslyn, and the anonymous consulting editor for commenting on drafts of this paper. Sue Britson and Linda Finkelstein both aided in data collection. The author was supported by National Institutes of Health research fellowship award 1 F32 MH 05295 during the preparation of the manuscript.

1 A similar percentage distribution of counting accuracy is obtained if the percentage of each form of inaccurate and accurate counting is computed for each child and then these percentages are averaged by form for each age group.

References

Gelman, R. The nature and development of early number concepts. In H. A. Reese (Ed.), *Advances in child development and behavior.* Vol. 7. New York: Academic Press, 1972.

Schaeffer, G.; Eggleston, V. H.; & Scott, J. L. Number development in young children. *Cognitive Psychology*, 1974, **6**, 357–379.

113

PRESCHOOLERS' COUNTING: PRINCIPLES BEFORE SKILL*

Rochel Gelman and Elizabeth Meck

Source: *Cognition*, 13, 1983: 343–359.

Abstract

Three- to 5-year-old children participated in one of 4 counting experiments. On the assumption that performance demands can mask the young child's implicit knowledge of the counting principles, 3 separate experiments assessed a child's ability to detect errors in a puppet's application of the *one-one, stable-order* and *cardinal* count principles. In a fourth experiment children counted in different conditions designed to vary performance demands. Since children in the errror-detection experiments did not have to do the counting, we predicted excellent performance even on set sizes beyond the range a young child counts accurately. That they did well on these experiments supports the view that errors in counting—at least for set sizes up to 20—reflect performance demands and not the absence of implicit knowledge of the counting principles. In the final experiment, where children did the counting themselves, set size did affect their success. So did some variations in conditions, the most difficult of which was the one where children had to count 3-dimensional objects which were under a plexiglass cover. We expected that this condition would interfere with the child's tendency to point and touch objects in order to keep separate items which have been counted from those which have not been counted.

Although preschoolers count only small sets accurately, Gelman and Gallistel (1978) propose that preschoolers' counting is governed by the *implicit* knowledge of five counting principles. These are: (1) the one-one principle—every item in a display should be tagged with one and only one unique tag; (2) the stable order principle—the tags must be ordered in the same sequence across trials; (3) the cardinal principle—the last tag used in a count sequence is the symbol for the number of items in the set; (4) the abstraction principle—any kinds of objects can be collected together for purposes of a count; and (5) the order-irrelevance principle—the objects in a set may be tagged in any sequence as long as the other counting principles are not violated. The first three of these principles define the counting procedure; the fourth determines the types of sets to which the procedure may be applied; and the fifth distinguishes counting from labelling. Gelman and Gallistel suggest that children know these principles at a very early age but have difficulty putting them into practice with larger sets.

We refer to knowledge young children have about counting as *implicit*, as opposed to explicit, for much the same reasons such a distinction is made in the psycholinguistics literature. Very young children are granted implicit knowledge of language rules well before they are said to have explicit knowledge of their grammar (e.g., Clark and Clark, 1977; Gleitman *et al.*, 1972). Explicit knowledge involves the ability to say why a given sentence is agrammatical or not. This metalinguistic ability develops around five or six years of age. Long before these young children have implicit knowledge of the language they speak because: they utter novel sentences that honor rules of the language; they self-rehearse and self-correct their sentences; they produce overgeneralizations that accord with a rule-governed knowledge of the grammar but do not accord with what the child has actually heard; and they can recognize violations of rules in the speech of others (Clark and Clark, 1977).

When we distinguish between implicit and explicit knowledge of the counting principles we mean to distinguish between the ability to verbalize or state the counting principles and the ability to demonstrate that one's behavior is systematically governed by the principles (see also Greenö *et al.*, 1982). Gelman and Gallistel offered two kinds of evidence for the young child's implicit knowledge of counting principles. First they noted the orderly count sequences observed in young children. Preschoolers do not invariably count correctly, however. There are errors and the nature of the errors served as the second source of evidence for the Gelman–Gallistel conclusion. Errors which were observed were classified as performance errors or idiosyncratic 'errors'. To show why the latter errors are especially telling, it is best to give an example. Some 2-year-old children count with what Fuson and Richards (1979) calls nonstandard and we call idiosyncratic count lists. Consider the child who says '1-2-8' when pointing to a 3-item array and '1-2-8-10' when pointing to items in a 4-item array and '10' when asked *how many* there are in the latter case. The child meets the requirements of the counting principles with an unconventional list of her own. Since Gelman (1977) first reported such a finding, parents have been coming to us with the list their child once used. Two favorite ones reported by parents are '1-2-3-4-5-6-7-h-i-j-k' (the switch in lists is most likely due to an acoustic confusion error between 8- and h) and 'red, yellow, blue' (even where the objects were all the same color).

The invention and correct use of idiosyncratic lists is hard to explain unless appeal is made to some implicit rules that guide the children's search of their environment for a list with which to count. This argument is the same one used to account for overgeneralization errors, e.g., runned, unthirsty, in a child's speech. The occurrence of such novel but lawful count sequences makes it necessary to postulate an implicit set of rules.

Gelman and Gallistel also noted that young children have a tendency to generate count sequences without prompting and self-correct the errors they make in the course of these self-generated sequences. Again, it is hard to imagine a child doing this unless the child refers its counting perform-ance to some set of internally represented principles. Yet, it has been argued (Siegler, 1979; Sternberg, 1980) that Gelman and Gallistel grant young children too great a competence when they impute principles to very young children. The experiments reported here buttress the data base for the idea that counting principles guide the counting behavior of young children.

One reason to challenge our view of preschooler's competence is that their ability to count accurately is restricted to small set sizes. Poor skill at counting set sizes larger than 5 is taken as evidence for the conclusion that many of the component counting principles have yet to be learned (e.g., Mierkiewicz and Siegler, 1981). Gelman and Gallistel maintain that children count small set sizes better than they count large set sizes because the latter present too much of a performance demand on the children. If so variations in performance demands should produce variations in success on count-ing tasks. By contrasting performance in easy tasks (error detection) and hard tasks (counting items under a plexiglass cover) we hoped to show that performance problems and not faulty principles explain many of the errors in the counting behavior of very young children.

The error detection studies

In the error detection experiments children watched a puppet count and told the experimenter whether the puppet was right or wrong. Thus children did not have to generate the counting performance, they only monitored it for conformance to the principles. When the child does the counting her-self, she must both generate and monitor the performance. Hence, an error detection task should be easier than a standard counting task.

There were three error detection experiments. One focused on the one-one principle, one on the stable-order principle, and a third on the cardinal principle. In all cases, children were asked to help teach a puppet to count by indicating whether a particular count sequence was correct. In all cases the experiment proper began only after the experimenter had spent time playing with the children in their classrooms and then taken each child individually to play with commercially bought toys in the experimental room.

The one-one study

Children who participated in this study were given three kinds of trials; correct, in-error, pseudoerror. On the two correct trials the puppet correctly counted a linear array from beginning to end. The two in-error trials were of two types, an item was *skipped* or an item was *double counted*. The two pseudoerror trials were included for purposes of comparison with a study which was being run by Mierkiewicz and Siegler (1981). On one of these trials, a puppet started counting in the middle of a linear array, then continued to the end of that row before returning to the beginning of the array for the remaining to-be-counted items. On the other trial, the puppet confronted a row of alternating red and blue chips and counted the red ones before doubling back to count the blue ones.

Subjects

The children in this study were 12 3-year-olds (median age, 3 yr. 7 mo.; range, 3 yr. 1 mo.–3 yr. 11 mo.) and 12 4-year-olds (median age, 4 yr. 5 mo.; range, 4 yr. 1 mo.–4 yr. 10 mo.). They were from one of two daycare centers or one of two nursery schools in the Greater Philadelphia area. The population served by these schools tends to be middle-class; although the children in attendance at these schools are quite heterogeneous with respect to race or ethnic background.

Procedure

To start the experiment, children were shown a row of red and blue objects and then told: "This is my friend, Mr. Horse (Lion) and he would like you to help in playing the game. Mr. Horse is going to count the things on the table but Mr. Horse is just learning how to count and sometimes he makes mistakes. Sometimes he counts in ways that are OK but sometimes he counts in ways that are not OK and that are wrong. It is your job to tell him after he finishes counting if it was OK to count the way he did or not OK. So remember you have to tell him if he counts in a way that is OK or in a way that is not OK and wrong".

Each child was given 6 trials per set size: two correct trials, two in-error trials and two pseudoerror trials. The 4-year-olds were tested on set sizes of 6, 8, 12, and 20. The 3-year-olds were tested on only set sizes 6 and 12 because we assumed that even this many trials might tax their attention span. (To catch the puppet skipping or double-counting but one item, the children had to pay close attention). The order of the six trials within a set-size block was random as was the order in which a set size was presented. The session lasted 15 minutes.

In pilot work we found that some children would declare a trial incorrect or correct before the puppet had finished that trial. When this happened in the present study the child was told to wait until the puppet finished and then the experimenter restarted that trial.

Results and discussion

Nearly all of the three- and four-year-old children detected skipping and double-counting errors in the puppet's counting on a majority of the trials in which such errors occurred. Table 1 shows that 9 of 12 three-year-olds caught the puppet's mistake on at least 3 of 4 trials, as did 10 of 12 four-year-olds. There was no effect of set size in either group.

Table 2 gives the mean percent correct answers per child as a function of age (3 years *versus* 4 years) and type of trial (correct, pseudoerror, in-error). An ANOVA on trials with set sizes of 6 and 12 (the sizes used with both age groups) showed that the rightness of the child's assessment of the puppet's counting depended on the type of trial, (F2,44 = 21.4, p < 0.001). This reflects the fact that the children made no errors on correct trials. When they erred it was when judging error trials. There was also an interaction between age and type of trial, the younger children being worse than the

Table 1 Number of children who meet the 75% criterion as a function of problem type for set sizes 6 and 12*.

Age group	Problem type in the one-one experiment		
	Correct	Pseudoerrors	Incorrect
(N = 12)			
3-years	12	11	9
4-years	12	10	10

* The 4-year-olds' trials for set sizes 8 and 20 are not included for this summary.

Table 2 Average percent correct responses on each trial type in the one-one error detection task.

Age/Set sizes	Type of trial		
	Correct	Pseudo	Error
3-yrs.—6 & 12	100	96	67
4-yrs.—6 & 12	100	96	83
4-yrs.—all	100	95	82

older at spotting errors, but not at judging correctly the other two kinds of trials ($F2,44 = 3.22$, $p < 0.05$). The ANOVA showed no main effect of age or set size. A separate ANOVA for the 4-year-olds revealed no effect of set size ($F3,33 = 1.24$, $p < 0.31$) where set sizes were 6, 8, 12 and 20. And as before, type of trial did matter ($F2,22 = 5.70$, $p < 0.01$). Otherwise, there were no reliable effects.

Further support for the conclusion that the children knew that skipping and double-counting are errors comes from their explanations. All but two 3-year-olds and one of the 4-year-olds offered at least one argument that the puppet 'missed one' or 'did it again' (double-counted). Although 10 of 12 three-year-olds and 11 of 12 four-year-olds offered an explanation on at least one of the in-error trials, they did not do so very often; explanations were *not* obtained on a majority of error trials. Comments on the pseudo-error trials, while also infrequent were usually illuminating e.g., "It's a little bit funny to count that way" or "Yes, that's OK—you count this one, the other ones (points to reds) and on the way back you count this blue one and this blue one . . ." The explanations quoted here reflect a common feature: When they did explain a trial, children could say what kind of error was made or what was peculiar about the counting (in the case of pseudo-error trials); however, none of the children articulated the one-one principle itself, i.e., that each and every object needed to be tagged once and only once with one unique tag. This is consistent with the hypothesis that explicit knowledge is relatively late to develop. (cf., the literature on meta-memory, e.g., Flavell and Wellman 1977.).

We find that 3- and 4-year-old children are able to distinguish between erroneous and correct applications of the one-one count principle. Four-year-olds are better at this than are 3-year-olds. Both groups treat a pseudo-error trial as just that, peculiar but not erroneous. Most importantly, set size has little effect, if any, on this ability. In contrast, it has a very strong effect on children's ability to do the correct count themselves (Gelman and Gallistel, 1978; Fuson and Richards, 1979; and the final study in this paper).

We were surprised at how well the children handled the pseudoerror trials. This is because Mierkiewicz and Siegler (1981), in a fairly comparable study reported that even 5-year-olds failed to recognize what we call pseudoerrors as such. There are two possible reasons for the discrepancy. First, children in the latter experiment were tested on 72 trials over-all and hence possibly paid less attention; ours received many fewer trials. Also, recall that when the child said the puppet had been correct or incorrect before waiting until the puppet finished, the trial was started again. If we had not followed this rule pseudoerror trials could have been treated as 'mistakes' simply because the child did not wait out the trial. It appears that Mierkiewicz and Siegler (1981) did not start a trial over whenever a child judged it correct or incorrect before hearing it to the end.

The fact that variations in set-size had little effect on success rates deserves comment. Children as young as these seldom count correctly set sizes even as small as 8 (e.g., Gelman and Gallistel, 1978). In the present experiment, the children did not do the counting themselves; they commented on what the puppet did. The experiment did more than investigate the ability to detect errors in the application of the one-one principle. It provided evidence that children who do not have to do the work themselves are able to recognize when a count trial is correct or not—even for sets well beyond what they themselves can count. This implies that these young children know in principle what it is to count rather large sets but they have difficulty putting their principles into practice. Of course, it is possible that children would have difficulty with larger set sizes, especially the 3-year-olds. Hence the decision to try to test all children on set size 20 in the following 2 experiments.

The stable order study

Children in this experiment were given five trials per set size, two correct ones and three during which the stable order principle was violated in one of three ways: The violations were (1) use of a list wherein the conventional order of two items was reversed, e.g., 1, 2, 4, 3, 5, 6: (2) a use of a randomly-ordered list for the set size in question e.g., 2, 1, 5, 3, 4; and (3) use of a list which skipped one or more tags in a standard count list e.g. 1, 2, 3, 5, 6, and 1, 2, 3, 4, 7, 8, 9.

Subjects

The children in this study were 12 3-, 12 4- and 12 5-year-olds. The respective medians and ranges of age were 3 yr. 7 mo. (3 yr. 1 mo.–3 yr. 11 mo.); 4 yr. 5 mo. (4 yr. 2 mo.–4 yr. 7 mo.), and 5 yr. 5 mo. (5 yr. 0 mo.–5 yr. 11 mo.). Children were drawn from the same sample as that used for the first experiment.

Procedure

The instructions were the same as those used in the first experiment. The objects were small trinkets which varied in type and color. The set sizes were 5, 7, 12, and 20, all of which were displayed in a row. The five trials (2 correct, 3 incorrect) for each set size were run in random order, and the order in which a child encountered the block of 5 trials for a set size was also randomized. In trials where number names were omitted, whether 1, 2, or 3 were dropped was randomly determined: so was the locus of omission within the sequence.

Results and discussion

The overall tendency for children to indicate when the puppet made a stable-order error in counting is shown in Table 3. Nearly all children at all ages were able to say that a correct use of the conventional list was just that. Similarly, the children did well at calling an error an error.

An analysis of variance revealed a significant effect of age ($F_{2,33} = 6.34$, $p < 0.01$), error-trial type ($F_{2,66} = 7.73$, $p < 0.001$) and age × trial type interaction ($F_{4,66} = 4.56$, $p < 0.01$). There was no reliable effect of set-size ($F_{3,99} = 2.24$, $p = 0.09$) or other interactions.

The significant effect on error trials for the type-of-trial variable means that the three-year-olds had trouble detecting jump-in-the-list errors. In this younger group, only 60% of the trials in which number names were omitted were correctly identified as error trials. In contrast, the 3-year-olds caught 80% of the trials which involved a reversal of a pair of items in the conventional count list, and 90% of the random strings of number words. We find it most interesting that the jump-in-list trials were so hard for the 3-year-olds for this is just the kind of error that occurs in young children's own lists when they are summoning them up in the course of a count (Fuson and Mierkiewicz, 1981). Of the 3 error types this can be taken as the less deviant form because the resulting lists are still ordered according to the conventional list. Hence it is possible that some of the 3-year-olds in the study had yet to accommodate fully their own counting lists to the conventional list. Still, they were able to determine whether a puppet's count was correct or not as a function of the other 2 error types.

Once again we find no effect of set size. This nonresult is consistent with the position that the young child's counting errors are due more to excess demands on processing activities than to a faulty understanding of counting principles.

The cardinal study

The instructions in this study were somewhat different owing to the nature of the principle being tested. Children were asked to indicate whether the

Table 3 Mean percent correct judgments of correct or incorrect on stable-order trials as a function of age and trial type.

Age (N = 12)	Correct order trials	Incorrect order trials
3	96	76
4	100	96
5	98	97
Mean	98	89

puppet gave the right answer when, after counting, it was asked "how many?". They were also encouraged to tell the puppet what the right answer was. Otherwise the procedure was as in the stable-order experiment. Hence there was a block of five trials per set size. Set sizes were 5, 7, 12 and 20. On two of the trials the puppet gave the correct cardinal number; on three it gave an erroneous number. The order of set-size blocks and within-block trials was randomized as before.

The error trials represented 3 deviations from the principle that the last tag in a count sequence represents the cardinal value n of a display. They were: (a) to give the nth + 1 value in response to the *how many* question; (b) to answer $a < n$, a number preceding n in the list of n tags and (c) to offer the color or some other irrelevant designation of the nth object, e.g., a boat. We have observed that some severely retarded children produce the last error. They and very young children also produce the $a < n$ error.

Subjects

Twelve 3- and twelve 4-year-olds served as subjects. Their median age and respective range of ages were: 3 yr. 7 mo. (3 yr. 2 mo.–3 yr. 10 mo.) and 4 yr. 5 mo. (4 yr. 4 mo.–4 yr. 11 mo.). They attended the same schools as those in the above experiments.

Results and discussion

The error detection task was especially easy for the children. Three-year-olds gave the right answer on an average of 85% and 96% of their error and correct trials, respectively. For 4-year-olds, the comparable figures were 99 and 100%. An analysis of variance revealed a significant effect of age. Otherwise there were no reliable effects in an analysis of age, set size and error-type.

Children in this experiment were asked if they wanted to change the puppet's answer and if so to go ahead. The 4-year-olds attempted to correct 90% of the puppet's error trials; 93% of the answers on these attempts were correct. The 3-year-olds attempted a correction on 70% of the puppet's error-trials and 94% of these corrections were right. The children in this experiment knew not only that the puppet had erred; they knew what it had done wrong and could correct the mistake. (By contrast, the nonmusical may often know that a singer has erred but not know how and not be able to sing it the way it ought to have been sung.)

The findings in these error-detection experiments support the hypothesis that children as young as three have implicit knowledge of the counting principles. That we failed to show an effect of set size in all of the studies is consistent with the Gelman and Gallistel hypothesis that knowledge of the counting principles guides the child's interaction with her environment and that it is the perfection of superior procedures that underlies the development of counting within the preschool period rather than the emergence of new or firmer principles. Wilkinson's (1981) treatment of the nature of partial knowledge provides another way of stating this hypothesis.

Wilkinson makes a distinction between what he calls the *variable* and *restrictive* application of a given domain of knowledge. Knowledge that is variable is that kind of knowledge which varies as do the performance demands of the task. In contrast, restricted knowledge may be revealed in every task but only for a limited set of stimuli. In the case of number, Wilkinson points out that the distinction will be between whether the children's knowledge is only as extensive as the set sizes on which they never err or whether the knowledge is fragile, albeit for a wide range of set sizes. In the latter case, success on a task will vary as a function of set size only when there is reason to believe that the performance demands of a task are too great. The next experiment was based on such considerations.

The plexiglass study

Young children are prone to point to, touch and/or move items as they are counted (e.g., Gelman and Gallistel, 1978; Fuson and Richards, 1979). This presumably serves their efforts to keep separate the items which they have already counted and those remaining to-be-counted. Hence, 3-dimensional items which can be touched, pointed to, and/or moved should be easier to count than 3-dimensional items which cannot be touched, etc. To find out if this was the case, we asked the same children to count the exact same set of 3-dimensional objects twice; once without a cover and once with a cover made out of plexiglass. The same children also participated in two further conditions. In both of these, the items were a heterogeneous collection of stickers on a card, i.e., the items were 2-dimensional. Since children would be able to point to and touch the items in these 2-dimensional (2D) displays, we thought that they would do better in these conditions than they would in the plexiglass one. The two 2D conditions differed with respect to the degree of spacing there was between each of the items on the cards. The items in the 2D-*near* condition touched each other. Those in the *far* condition did not.

Subjects

Eighteen 3- and 18 4-year-old children were the subjects in this experiment. Their respective median ages were 3 yr.–4 mo. (range 3 yr. 0 mo.–3 yr. 10 mo.) and 4 yr. 5 mo. (range 4 yr. 0 mo.–4 yr. 9 mo.).

Procedure

As above, we used a repeated subjects design for this experiment. Children were tested on each of the 4 main conditions with all set sizes (3, 4, 5, 7, 9,

11, 15, 19) over two sessions. (In the case of the 3-year-olds, many took 3 sessions.) The nature of the stimulus type (2D or 3D) was counterbalanced across the two sessions. The order in which the two conditions for each kind of stimulus were encountered was also counterbalanced. There were 3 trials for each set size within a condition and thus 12 trials per set size all together. Within a condition, the order of set sizes was random, with the provision that all 3 trials for a given set size within the condition were run one after the other.

We anticipated that the children in this study might find it tedious; hence, the experimenter interrupted a session with little breaks for playing with other toys or just chatting. In addition, the testing involved a 3-way conversation between the child, the experimenter and a puppet. We have found the latter manipulation very useful in cases where the child might not want to continue (e.g., Bullock and Gelman, 1977).

Stimuli for the 3D conditions were a variety of magnetized objects which are used to hold up memos on metal surfaces like a refrigerator. They varied in color, size and shape, and were approximately 4 cm high. Stimuli for the 2D conditions were colored stickers which were of about the same size and which represented a variety of colors, types, and so on. The 3D stimuli were arrayed on a large metal plate (14.5 in. in diameter) which in turn was placed on a base. Since the plate was metal, the magnetized objects stayed in place. Since the base rotated, the display could be turned around between the count trials for a given set size. And since the base stood off the ground, this could be done from beneath the display. The plexiglass cover, when in place, sat over the plate on the base.

The stimuli in the 3D conditions were arranged in a row or a crescent (for the larger set sizes). The row of stickers in the 2D conditions either touched each other (*near*) or were separated by 1.5 cm (*far*). For the 3 trials within a set size, the displays were rotated 90° or 180°.

The child's task was to count the number of objects and then, while the array was covered with a black cloth, indicate the cardinal value of that display. All sessions were video-recorded.

Each of the children's trials were scored as correct or incorrect. Following Gelman and Gallistel, a child could be scored correct if he or she used an idiosyncratic list, as long as that list was used consistently. Otherwise, to receive credit for the trial, the child had to use all 3 how-to-count principles correctly. If a trial and/or set size was not run the child received a zero for that trial (set size).

Results and discussion

The results are shown in Figures 1 and 2.

Not surprisingly, an ANOVA showed that 4-year-olds did better than the younger children and larger set sizes were harder than smaller set sizes (in

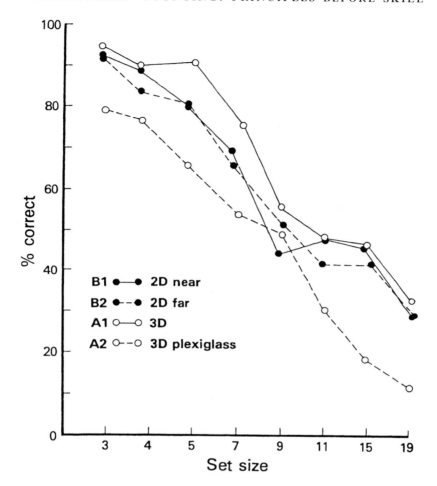

Figure 1 Percent correct counting trials as a function of set size and condition in plexiglass experiment.

both cases p < 0.001). That there was a significant interaction between set size and age (p < 0.001) reflects the fact as shown in Figure 1, that the effect of set size appears at lower values for the younger children. There was also an effect of the conditions under which the child had to count. This effect (p < 0.001) was due mainly to the difficulty children had with the plexiglass condition which was *harder* than the standard 3D condition. The difference between the two 2D conditions was not significant. It is noteworthy that the plexiglass condition was more difficult than either of the 2D conditions. Theories which maintain that children are late to apply their number knowledge to two dimensional items because they are more abstract stimuli than

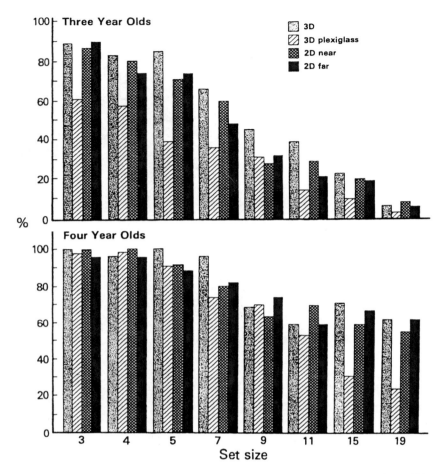

Figure 2 Percent correct counting trials as a function of age, set size and condition in plexiglass experiment.

are three dimensional ones (e.g., Gast, 1957; Klahr and Wallace, 1976) are challenged by such a finding

The ANOVA also showed an expected two-way interaction between age and set size ($p = 0.001$) and an expected three-way interaction between age, set size, and condition ($p < 0.001$). The younger children with more presumably fragile and less practiced performance skills begin making mistakes at smaller set sizes that the older, more skillful, children can handle: hence, the two-way interaction. The older, more skillful, children also can handle the smaller sets under all conditions—including even the most difficult, plexiglass one. They first begin to falter when they encounter the larger sets under the hardest partitioning conditions: hence the three-way interaction between age, set size, and counting condition.

Overview

The above findings offer strong support that children as young as 3 years know the principles that a procedure must conform to in order to be a valid counting procedure, although of course, they cannot articulate these principles. The range of set sizes to which the children know that these principles apply is much greater than the range that they can successfully count. Indeed, there is no evidence that the children recognize any upper bound on the range of set sizes to which these principles apply. The development of counting in the early years would appear to be mostly a matter of developing procedures that implement these principles and acquiring skill in the carrying out of these procedures.

We do not mean to suggest that the development of counting in children beyond the age of 2 or 3 years does not involve the emergence of any new principles. We have argued elsewhere that at least three new principles of far reaching significance emerge. The emergence of all of these principles may be induced in the course of carrying out the kinds of procedures dictated by the counting principles. We offer three examples of such development.

The counting of large sets requires a lengthy and stably ordered list of number words, and humans have difficulty forming such lists. The first consequence of this difficulty is that very few five-year-olds can count to 20 reliably and need to work hard to achieve this ability. If learning to count from 3 on up to 20 were any predictor of the difficulty of learning to count from 20 on up to a thousand, it is safe to say that very few humans would ever learn to count to a thousand. But humans never construct a list of a thousand number words by brute force—as could a computer. They invariably fasten on a generative scheme involving one or more number-generating bases (Zaslavsky, 1973; Saxe and Moylan, 1982). Such schemes permit the generation of indefinitely long lists of numerlogs[1] by the lawful combination of the relatively few numerlogs in a base set. Note, in turn, the use of a generative scheme for producing number names contains the seeds of the multiplication operation.

Another principle that preschool children seem not to understand is the principle that the list of number words is indeed unending. Their appreciation of this principle, like their appreciation of the generative principles for producing ever more numerlogs seems to depend upon experience with counting ever larger sets and the appreciation of the generative power of a base system. This principle, of course, leads on to a beginning understanding of the infinity of the numbers, a concept that preschool children seem not to have (Evans and Gelman, 1982).

Thirdly, the application of counting procedures in the course of solving subtraction can lead to the recognition that there are 'numbers' other than those that may be arrived at in the course of ordinary counting, for example, zero (Evans, 1983). Preschool children seem to recognize only those numbers that they can arrive at by a counting procedure.

The findings presented in this paper underscore the need for theories of cognitive development to distinguish between implicit principles of knowledge and skills that derive from and/or are related to these principles. It will not do to base accounts of knowledge on a requirement that skills which reflect that knowledge be executed without error. Errors due to performance demands are to be expected.

Notes

* Support for this work came from NSF grants BNS-8004885 and BNS-8140573. We thank Ellen Markman for suggesting a version of experiment 3 and C. R. Gallistel and Jim Greenö for comments on an earlier version of this manuscript.

1 Gelman and Gallistel (1978) coined the term numerlog to deal with the fact that the verbal tags used in a count need not be the number words. The latter are one kind of a set of numerlogs.

References

Bullock, M., and Gelman, R. (1977) Numerical reasoning in young children: The ordering principle. *Child Devel.*, 48, 427–434.

Clark, H. H., and Clark, E. V. (1977) *Psychology and Language: An Introduction to Psycholinguistics.* New York, Harcourt Brace Jovanovich, Inc.

Evans, D. (1983) *Understanding Infinity and Zero in the Early School Years.* Unpublished doctoral dissertation, University of Pennsylvania.

Evans, D. and Gelman, R. (1982) *Understanding Infinity: A Beginning Inquiry.* Unpublished manuscript, University of Pennsylvania.

Flavell, J. H., and Wellman, H. M. (1977) Metamemory. In R. V. Kail, Jr., and J. W. Hagen (Eds.), *Perspectives on the Development of Memory and Cognition.* Hillsdale, NJ, Erlbaum.

Fuson, K. C. and Mierkiewicz, D. B. (1980) *A Detailed Analysis of the Act of Counting.* Paper presented in April at American Educational Research Association, Boston.

Fuson, K. C., and Richards, J. (1979) *Children's Construction of the Counting Numbers: From a Spew to a Bidirectional Chain.* Northwestern University, July, 1979; unpublished manuscript.

Gast, H. (1957) Der Umgang mit Zahlen und Zahlgebilden in der frühren Kindeit. *Zeitschrift für Psychologie, 161,* 1–90.

Gelman, R. (1977) How young children reason about small numbers. In N. J. Castellan, D. B. Pisoni and G. R. Potts (eds.), *Cognitive Theory,* Vol. 2. Hillsdale, New Jersey: Erlbaum.

Gelman, R., and Gallistel, C. R. (1978) *The Child's Understanding of Number.* Cambridge, Mass., Harvard University Press.

Gleitman, L. R., Gleitman, H., and Shipley, E. F. (1972) The emergence of the child as grammarian. *Cog., 1*, 137–164.

Greenõ, J. G., Riley, M. S., and Gelman, R. (1982) *Young Children's Counting and Understanding of Principles*. Unpublished manuscript, University of Pittsburgh and University of Pennsylvania.

Klahr, D., and Wallace, J. G. (1976) *Cognitive Development, an Information Processing View*. Hillsdale, NJ, Erlbaum.

Mandler, G., and Shebo, B. J. (In press) Subitizing: An analysis of its component processes. *J. exper. Psychol.: Gen.*

Mierkiewicz, D. B., and Siegler, R. S. (1981) *Preschoolers' Ability to Recognize Counting Errors*. Presented at the Spring meeting of the Society for Research on Child Development, Boston.

Saxe, G. B., and Moylan, T. (1982) *Developing Systems for Number Representation and Arithmetic Operations among the Oksapmin*. Paper presented in March at the American Education Research Association, New York.

Siegler, R. S. (1979) What young children do know. *Contemp. Psychol., 24*, 613–615.

Sternberg, R. J. (1980) Capacity of young children. *Sci., 208*, 47–48.

Wilkinson, A. C. (1981) *Children's Partial Knowledge of Counting*. Unpublished manuscript, University of Wisconsin, Madison.

Zaslavsky, C. (1973) *Africa Counts*. Boston, Prindle, Weber and Schmidt.

114

EFFECTS OF LANGUAGE CHARACTERISTICS ON CHILDREN'S COGNITIVE REPRESENTATION OF NUMBER: CROSS-NATIONAL COMPARISONS

*Irene T. Miura, Chungsoon C. Kim, Chih-Mei Chang
and Yukari Okamoto*

Source: *Child Development*, 59, 1988: 1445–1450.

We compared the cognitive representation of number of American, Chinese, Japanese, and Korean first graders, and Korean kindergartners, to determine if there might be variations in those representations resulting from numerical language characteristics that differentiate Asian and non-Asian language groups. Children were asked to construct various numbers using base 10 blocks. Chinese, Japanese, and Korean children preferred to use a construction of tens and ones to show numbers; place value appeared to be an integral component of their representations. In contrast, English-speaking children preferred to use a collection of units, suggesting that they represent number as a grouping of counted objects. More Asian children than American children were able to construct each number in 2 ways, which suggests greater flexibility of mental number manipulation.

Cross-national comparisons of mathematics achievement have consistently shown impressive differences in favor of Asian students (Husen, 1967; Miller & Linn, 1986; Stanley, Huang, & Zu, 1986; Stevenson, Lee, & Stigler, 1986; Stigler, Lee, Lucker, & Stevenson, 1982). Attempts to explain these differences in mathematics performance have generally examined varying home and school experiences. Parental expectations for school achievement, effort attributions for academic performance (Hess *et al.*, 1986; Mordkowitz & Ginsburg, 1987; Stevenson *et al.*, 1986), and the proportion of school time allocated to mathematics instruction (Stevenson *et al.*, 1986) are some of the factors that have differentiated the experiences of Asian and American students. In addition, Lynn (1982), citing the superior performance of Japanese children on the Wechsler IQ test, has suggested innate ability to account for these differences. However, Stevenson *et al.* (1986), who examined cognitive skills in their study, did not find evidence to support the notion that variations in academic achievement were due to differences in cognitive functioning. In the present study, we examined the idea that variability in mathematics performance may be related to differences in the cognitive organization of number that is affected by numerical language characteristics that differentiate Asian from non-Asian groups.

Symbolically, through language, numbers are mentally represented and stored, and for those languages that are rooted in ancient Chinese (among them, Chinese, Japanese, and Korean), numerical names are organized so that they are congruent with the traditional base 10 numeration system. In this system, the value of a given digit in a multidigit numeral depends on the face value of the digit (0 through 9) and on its position in the numeral, with the value of each position increasing by powers of 10 from right to left. The spoken numerals in Western languages (e.g., twelve and twenty in English and four-twenty for 80 in French) may lack the elements of tens and ones that are contained in them. Also, the order of spoken and written numerals may not agree (e.g., fourteen for 14 in English and three-and-forty for 43 in German). In the Asian languages mentioned previously, 12 is read as ten-two, 14 as ten-four, 20 as two-ten(s), 43 as four-ten(s)-three, and 80 as eight-ten(s). Fourteen and 40, which are phonetically similar in English, are differentiated in Chinese, Japanese, or Korean; 14 is spoken as ten-four and 40 as four-ten(s). Plurals are tacitly understood in these Asian languages; thus, the spoken numeral corresponds exactly to the implied quantity represented in the written form. Furthermore, when character number symbols are used in place of the Arabic numerals, the correspondence between spoken and written numeral is even more precise; for example, the numeral 46 is written in character symbols as four-ten(s)-six.

The Asian spoken numeral describes precisely what is represented by the base 10 numeration system. Place value (i.e., the meaning of tens and ones in two-digit numeral) is an inherent element of those representations. Therefore, it seems reasonable to suggest that the Asian number system could assist children to develop cognitive number structures or representations that reflect the base 10 system.

In this study, we explored ways in which children symbolically represent and store number. Because symbolic representation can only be inferred from behavior, we asked children to show us numbers using a set of unit blocks and 10 blocks. In an earlier study, Miura (1987) found that English- and Japanese-speaking first graders residing in the United States differed in the cognitive representation of number. Japanese speakers were more likely than English speakers to use a construction of tens and ones to represent numbers concretely. English speakers, in contrast, preferred to use a collection of units. In the present research, Chinese, Japanese, and Korean children were tested in their respective countries. These data were compared with the findings from a comparable group of English-speaking children in the United States.

Method

Subjects

There were five groups of monolingual children in the study: one kindergarten sample from Korea and four first-grade samples from the People's Republic of China (P.R.C.), Japan, the United States, and Korea. The children in the P.R.C., Japan, and the United States were beginning first graders. In Korea, where the academic year begins in April, the children were in the middle of their first grade year. The four groups of first graders were matched as closely as possible for age, family income level, and parents' occupations and educational level. They would be considered upper middle class in their respective countries. The U.S. and Korean children attended private grammar schools where enrollment is competitive, and the course work academically rigorous. The Chinese children attended a Key school in Beijing; the curriculum in Key schools is considered to be academically challenging. The Japanese children attended a public school located in an upper-middle-class neighborhood of Tokyo.

We had intended to limit the study to first graders for three reasons. First, we wanted to select as low a grade level as possible to minimize the effects of formal mathematics instruction. Second, pilot work in the United States suggested that the task demands were too difficult for kindergartners. Finally, kindergartens are not part of the regular sequence of classes in the P.R.C., Japan, and Korea. However, we tested a sample of kindergartners in Korea using the same procedure. These children were selected from a private school in Seoul. They were also in the middle of the academic year at the time of the testing. We have included these data in the analyses.

The U.S. sample consisted of 24 children, 11 boys and 13 girls. Their ages ranged from 73 to 91 months, with a mean age of 82 months. Twenty-five children were tested in the P.R.C., 10 boys and 15 girls. The ages in the P.R.C. were given in half-year increments. These ranged from 72 to 96 months, with a mean age of 79 months. There were 24 first graders in Japan, 13 boys and 11 girls. Their ages ranged from 78 to 88 months, with a mean age of 83 months. There were 40 first graders tested in Korea, 20 boys and

220

20 girls. Ages ranged from 78 to 91 months, with a mean age of 85 months. The kindergarten sample consisted of 10 boys and 10 girls. Their ages ranged from 65 to 78 months, with a mean age of 71 months.

Procedure

Children were seen individually and were shown a set of commercially available base 10 blocks. These blocks are designed so that 10 unit blocks are equivalent to 1 ten block, a bar that is marked into 10 segments. Children were told that the blocks could be used for counting and to show (construct) numbers. The experimenter demonstrated by counting out 10 unit blocks and by lining them up to show their equivalence to 1 ten block. The relation was pointed out verbally as well. Children were then asked to read a numeral printed on a card and to show the number using the blocks. Coaching was permitted on two practice items to be sure the children knew what to do. There were 100 unit blocks and 20 ten blocks available (more than adequate for the tasks) so there would be no constraints on which blocks to use. Test items—the numerals 11, 13, 28, 30, and 42—were presented in random order. The procedure was translated into Chinese, Japanese, and Korean by native speakers who were also fluent in English. All children in the study could read the numbers correctly.

There were two trials. Children's responses on the first trial were recorded. Immediately following the first trial, they were reminded of the equivalence between 1 ten block and 10 unit blocks. Then, children were shown their first constructions and asked if they could show the number in a different way using the blocks. They were encouraged to use additional blocks from the pile if they chose simply to rearrange the blocks from their first constructions.

Responses were coded as correct if the blocks summed to the whole numeral. In a few cases, where a child made a counting error (e.g., 14, 15, 17, . . . , 28), or a correspondence error (e.g., a block not being fingered so that the final construction contained 41 instead of 42 blocks), these instances were scored as correct because the procedure was designed to examine cognitive representation rather than to assess counting accuracy. Correct constructions were categorized separately for trials 1 and 2. Categories were labeled incorporating Ross's (1986) term as follow: (a) one-to-one collection— the construction used only unit blocks (e.g., 24 unit blocks for 24); (b) canonical base 10 representation—the construction used the correct number of ten blocks and unit blocks, with no more than 9 units in the ones position (e.g., 2 ten blocks and 4 unit blocks for 24); and (c) noncanonical base 10 representation—the construction used some other correct number of ten blocks and unit blocks that allowed more than 9 units in the ones position (e.g., 1 ten block and 14 unit blocks for 24). The number of items for which two correct representations (one on each trial) were constructed was also noted.

Results

Based on our hypothesis that numerical language characteristics would affect children's cognitive representation of number, we expected to see similarities between the three Asian language groups and differences between these groups and the U.S. sample. There were no gender differences within each of the national samples; therefore, children in each country were treated as one group. Table 1 shows the percent of correct representations in each category for Trials 1 and 2. Incorrect constructions were not categorized.

Trial 1.—In Trial 1, the U.S. group preferred to use collections, but the Chinese, Japanese, and Korean first-grade groups preferred canonical representations, $\chi^2(8, N = 133) = 311.09$, $p < .001$. Korean kindergartners also showed a slight preference for using a collection to represent numbers on the first trial. The error rate on Trial 1 was very small. Nine percent of the constructions made by the U.S. children on this trial were incorrect. One percent of those made by the Chinese and Japanese children, respectively, were incorrect. The Korean children made no incorrect constructions on Trial 1.

Trial 2.—U.S. first graders were unable to make correct constructions for 66% of the numbers on the second trial. Incorrect construction rates varied for the other groups; 4% for Chinese children, 7% for Japanese children, and 1% for the Korean first graders. Korean kindergartners again made no incorrect constructions. As in Trial 1, only correct constructions were categorized for the second trial. The groups differed in the types of constructions

Table 1 Percent of Correct Representations in Each Category for the Five Groups.

	U.S. (N = 24)	P.R.C. (N = 25)	Japan (N = 24)	Korea-1 (N = 40)	Korea-K (N = 20)
Trial 1:[a]					
One-to-one collection	.91	.10	.18	.06	.59
Canonical base 10	.08	.81	.72	.83	.34
Noncanonical base 10	.01	.09	.10	.11	.07
Trial 2:[a]					
One-to-one collection	.10	.43	.59	.56	.33
Canonical base 10	.71	.16	.12	.09	.48
Noncanonical base 10	.19	.41	.29	.35	.19

Note: Only correct constructions were categorized. For example, for the U.S. group on Trial 1, 109 of 120 possible constructions were coded as correct. Of the 109 correct constructions, 91% were categorized as one-to-one collections, 8% as canonical base 10 representations, and 1% as noncanonical base 10 representations.
[a] Chi-square significant at $p < .001$.

they made on Trial 2, $\chi^2(8, N = 133) = 128.41, p < .001$. Korean kindergartners and U.S. first graders used a greater percentage of canonical constructions than the other groups did, while the Asian first graders showed a preference for using a collection of units on the second trial. All four Asian groups also used more noncanonical representations than did the U.S. group.

A procedure for post hoc multiple comparisons in sample proportions for tests of homogeneity (Marascuilo & McSweeney, 1977, pp. 141–147) was used to conduct a posteriori comparisons between the U.S. sample and all other groups. The procedure results in a multiple Z score which is associated with a s^* critical value; multiple $Z = 0$ indicates no difference between groups. The U.S. sample differed significantly from the other groups for all three categories of constructions: one-to-one collection (multiple $Z = 8.22$), canonical representation (multiple $Z = -5.06$), and noncanonical representation (multiple $Z = 6.00$), s^* critical value = 3.85, $p < .005$, for all three comparisons.

Children in the P.R.C., Japan, and Korea were able to construct the numbers correctly on both trials more often than children in the United States. All of the Korean kindergartners, 98% of Korean first graders, 76% of those in the P.R.C., and 79% of the Japanese sample were able to show all five numbers correctly in two ways. Only 13% of U.S. children were able to do so; half of the U.S. sample could not make two constructions for any of the numbers.

The incorrect constructions made by the 24 U.S. children do not appear to be related to number size. There were only 11 errors for 120 possible constructions on Trial 1. On Trial 2, there were 79 errors that were evenly distributed across the five numbers. Seventy-one percent of the errors were instances in which children either said they could not think of another way to show the number, or persisted in rearranging the blocks from the first trial to show the number in a perceptually different way.

Across the two trials, 84% of the children in the P.R.C., 67% of those in Japan, 75% of Korean first graders, and 60% of Korean kindergartners used a canonical representation to construct all five numbers, while only 8% of U.S. children did so. One-half of the U.S. children used no canonical constructions at all.

Discussion

The results from this study supported an earlier finding (Miura, 1987) which suggested that Asian-language speakers appear to represent numbers differently than English speakers. Compared to the American children, who seemed to prefer using a one-to-one collection to represent numbers, the Chinese, Japanese, and Korean first graders in this study showed an initial preference for representing numbers using a canonical construction; place value appears to be an integral component of these representations. Korean kindergarten children also preferred to use a one-to-one collection on the first trial, then switched to a canonical construction on the second trial. This tendency, or preference, on the part of kindergartners for counting out the number may reflect an earlier stage in the development of number representation.

Young children use a counting procedure to represent the numerosity or cardinal number of a set of items (Gelman & Gallistel, 1978). The mental entities (Gelman's term), or cognitive representations of number that the child manipulates in numerical reasoning tasks, are derived by counting. The kindergartners in our study were only a few months older than Gelman's oldest sample, and it seems reasonable to assume that our sample might also prefer to use a counting procedure to construct number quantities. For the Asian child, this preference is soon replaced by a canonical representation.

Like the Korean kindergartners, English speakers also preferred to use a collection of units to represent numbers. Most of the American children, however, were unable to show the number in a different way on the second trial; the majority of these incorrect constructions were due to children's persistence in rearranging the blocks that resulted in a perceptual rather than a conceptual difference. In contrast, all Korean kindergartners were able to make two constructions for the set of five numbers. Thus, the younger Asian children do not appear to be limited to a counting procedure but seem simply to prefer it initially. Sixty percent of the Korean kindergartners, but only 8% of U.S. first graders, used a canonical representation for all five numbers.

Pilot work in the United States had indicated that the procedure was too difficult for 5-year-olds, but in Korea, the kindergarten sample performed equally as well as the first graders. Most of the U.S. kindergartners we tested were not able to count consistently and accurately to 50, and thus were unable to perform our tasks. In learning the counting sequence, children must memorize a base sequence of count words, or numerical names. Higher members of the sequence are generated according to a set of rules (Gelman & Gallistel, 1978). In the traditional base 10 numeration system, the higher members of the sequence are generated by multiples of ten. In English, the numerical names for one through ten must be memorized. In addition, because the numerical names for eleven, twelve, and thirteen do not contain the elements of tens and ones that are contained in them, these, too, must be committed to memory. Fourteen through nineteen (except for fifteen) do reflect their components, but the spoken elements are reversed from their written order. The decades, 20 through 90, must also be memorized. The decade names present an added complexity because they are phonetically very similar to the teen numbers. The Asian number system, in contrast, requires the memorization of the numbers from one to ten only. Beyond that, generation of number names follows an orderly set of rules that reflect the written numeral, and the sequence of counting numbers is easily learned and practiced.

In Japan and Korea, there are also informal counting systems that are used by young children before they enter first grade. Song and Ginsburg (1987) reported that Korean kindergartners' scores on informal mathematics skills were lower than those of a comparable group of U.S. children. One explanation they gave was that the Korean children's attempts to learn a dual system of counting might affect performance on their measures during the preschool years. About half of our Korean and Japanese subjects used an informal system of counting, but this did not appear to affect their cognitive representation of number as reflected in the block constructions, nor were they hampered in counting to 42, the largest number in our procedure. These informal systems are also congruent with the base 10 system and are structurally similar to the formal counting procedure that is used in mathematics and to enumerate abstract entities. Counting alternates between the systems. In our study, the Japanese and Korean children's performance did not differ from that of their Chinese counterparts who have only one counting system.

The dual counting system, when mastered, may be very effective. Our current work examining the understanding of the place-value concept in Japan and the United States (Miura & Okamoto, 1987) shows significant differences in favor of the Japanese. A cognitive representation of number that incorporates place value may facilitate understanding of this concept, especially if the concept is reinforced by mastery in two conceptually similar number systems.

Asian-language speakers in this study were also more likely than English speakers to use noncanonical constructions, which may indicate greater facility with number quantities. In addition, only three children in the United States (13% of the total sample) were able to construct two representations for all five numbers. All of the Korean kindergartners, 98% of the Korean first graders, 76% of those in China, and 79% of the Japanese first graders were able to do so. The ability to think of more than one way to show each number suggests greater flexibility of mental number manipulation. When asked to construct the larger numbers, some of the Asian children offered that there were several ways to do so.

The differences in cognitive representation of number do not appear to be due to differential experience in using blocks to represent numbers. Blocks are not typically used in the mathematics curriculum in Asia, and an English derivative term for "block" was used with the Asian children to perform the exercises.

Differences in representation of number also do not appear to be due to specific teaching strategies or the use of an abacus. The Chinese, Japanese, and American first graders in our sample had been exposed to formal schooling for less than 4 months, and our Korean children for only half an academic year. The school curriculum in Asian countries is controlled by ministries of education, and the abacus is not introduced until the third or fourth grade in Japan and China, and the fifth or sixth grade in Korea.

Note

This research was supported in part by two San Jose State University Foundation grants to the first author. We thank the head of school, principals, teachers, and students of the five schools that participated in the study. Appreciation is extended to Dr. Jae Yeon Lee, Department of Child Study, Sook Myoung Women's University, Seoul, Korea, and to Masumi Saito, Tokyo, Japan, for their assistance with the data collection in Korea and Japan, respectively. We also wish to thank the reviewers for their helpful comments.

References

Gelman, R., & Gallistel, C. R. (1978). *The child's understanding of number.* Cambridge, MA: Harvard University Press.

Hess, R. D., Azuma, H., Kashiwagi, K., Dickson, W. P., Nagano, S., Holloway, S., Miyake, K., Price, G., Hatano, G., & McDevitt, T. (1986). Family influences on school readiness and achievement in Japan and the United States: An overview of a longitudinal study. In H. Stevenson, H. Azuma, & K. Hakuta (Eds.), *Child development and education in Japan* (pp. 147–166). New York: Freeman.

Husen, T. (1967). *International study of achievement in mathematics: A comparison of twelve countries* (Vol. 2). Stockholm, Sweden: Almqvist & Wiksell.

Lynn, R. (1982). IQ in Japan and in the United States shows a growing disparity. *Nature*, **297**, 222–223.

Marascuilo, L. A., & McSweeney, M. (1977). *Nonparametric and distribution-free methods for the social sciences.* Monterey, CA: Brooks/Cole.

Miller, M. D., & Linn, R. L. (1986, April). *Cross national achievement with differential retention rates.* Paper presented at the annual meetings of the American Educational Research Association, San Francisco.

Miura, I. T. (1987). Mathematics achievement as a function of language. *Journal of Educational Psychology*, **79**, 79–82.

Miura, I. T., & Okamoto, Y. (1987, November). *The effects of language characteristics on mathematics performance: Comparisons of US and Japanese first graders.* Paper presented at the West Coast Regional Conference of the Comparative and International Educational Society, Los Angeles.

Mordkowitz, E. R., & Ginsburg, H. P. (1987). The academic socialization of successful Asian American college students. *Quarterly News Letter of the Laboratory for Comparative Human Cognition*, **9**, 85–91.

Ross, S. H. (1986, April). *The development of children's place-value numeration concepts in grades two through five.* Paper presented at the annual meetings of the American Educational Research Association, San Francisco.

Song, M-J., & Ginsburg, H. P. (1987). The development of informal and formal mathematical thinking in Korean and U.S. children. *Child Development*, **58**, 1286–1296.

Stanley, J. C., Huang, J-f., & Zu, X-m. (1986). SATM scores of highly selected students in Shanghai tested when less than 13 years old. *College Board Review*, **140**, 10–13.

Stevenson, H. W., Lee, S-Y., & Stigler, J. W. (1986). Mathematics achievement of Chinese, Japanese, and American children. *Science*, **231**, 593–699.

Stigler, J. W., Lee, S-Y., Lucker, W., & Stevenson, H. W. (1982). Curriculum and achievement in mathematics: A study of elementary school children in Japan, Taiwan, and the United States. *Journal of Educational Psychology*, **74**, 315–322.

115

ADDITION AND SUBTRACTION
BY HUMAN INFANTS

Karen Wynn

Source: *Nature*, 358, 1992: 749–750.

Human infants can discriminate between different small numbers of items[1-4], and can determine numerical equivalence across
perceptual modalities[5,6]. This may indicate the possession of
true numerical concepts[1,4-7]. Alternatively, purely perceptual
discriminations may underlie these abilities[8,9]. This debate
addresses the nature of subitization, the ability to quantify
small numbers of items without conscious counting[10,11]. Subitization may involve the holistic recognition of canonical perceptual
patterns that do not reveal ordinal relationships between the
numbers[12], or may instead be an iterative or 'counting' process
that specifies these numerical relationships[4,13]. Here I show that
5-month-old infants can calculate the results of simple arithmetical operations on small numbers of items. This indicates
that infants possess true numerical concepts, and suggests
that humans are innately endowed with arithmetical abilities.
It also suggests that subitization is a process that encodes
ordinal information, not a pattern-recognition process yielding non-numerical percepts.

The experiments used a looking-time procedure that has become standard
in studies of infant cognition[14-17]. Thirty-two infants participated in experiment 1. They were normal, full-term infants with a mean age of 5 months
1 day (range, 4 months 19 days to 5 months 16 days). Infants were divided
randomly into two equal groups. Those in the '1 + 1' group were shown a
single item in an empty display area. A small screen then rotated up, hiding
the item from view, and the experimenter brought a second identical item
into the display area, in clear view of the infant. The experimenter placed

the second item out of the infant's sight behind the screen (Fig. 1). Thus, infants could clearly see the nature of the arithmetical operation being performed, but could not see the result of the operation. The '2–1' group were similarly shown a sequence of events depicting a subtraction of one item from two items (Fig. 1). For both groups of infants, after the above sequence of events was concluded, the screen was rotated downward to reveal either 1 or 2 items in the display case. Infants' looking time to the display was then recorded. Each infant was shown the addition or subtraction 6 times, the result alternating between 1 item and 2 items. Before these test trials, infants were presented with a display containing 1 item and a display containing 2 items and their looking time was recorded, to measure the baseline looking preferences for the two displays.

Infants look longer at unexpected events than expected ones, thus, if they are able to compute the numerical results of these arithmetical operations, they should look longer at the incorrect than at the correct results. The two groups should respond differently to results of 1 and 2 items: the '2–1' group should look longer than the '1 + 1' group when the result is 2 items than when it is 1 item, which is what is found (Table 1). Pretest trials showed that infants in the two groups did not differ from each other in their baseline looking times to 1 or 2 objects. But in the test trials, infants in the two groups differed significantly—infants in the '1 + 1' group looked longer at 1, whereas infants in the 2–1 group looked longer at 2. Thus, both groups looked longer at the incorrect than at the correct outcomes (Table 1).

Experiment 2 was a replication of experiment 1 with a smaller number of subjects (sixteen). Their mean age was 4 months 25 days (range, 4 months 18 days to 5 months 5 days). The same pattern of results was obtained; infants in each group looked longer at the incorrect outcome than at the correct outcome (Table 1).

These results show that infants know that an addition or subtraction results in a change in the number of items. But the results are consistent with two distinct hypotheses: (1) that infants are able to compute the precise results of simple additions and subtractions and (2) that infants expect an arithmetical operation to result in a numerical change, but have no expectations about either the size or the direction of the change. They may simply expect that adding an item to an item will result in some number other than 1; and that subtracting an item from 2 items will result in some number other than 2. To determine whether infants are able to compute the precise results of simple arithmetical operations, I conducted a third experiment.

Experiment 3 tested 16 infants with a mean age of 4 months 18 days (range, 4 months 4 days to 5 months 4 days). Infants were shown a '1 + 1' addition as before, except that the final number of objects revealed behind the screen was either 2 or 3. In both cases, the result is numerically different from the initial number of items. If infants are computing the exact

229

Sequence of events 1+1 = 1 or 2

1. Object placed in case   2. Screen comes up   3. Second object added   4. Hand leaves empty

Then either : possible outcome

5. Screen drops...   revealing 2 objects

or : impossible outcome

5. Screen drops ...   revealing 1 object

Sequence of events 2–1 = 1 or 2

1. Objects placed in case   2. Screen comes up   3. Empty hand enters   4. One object removed

Then either : possible outcome

5. Screen drops...   revealing 1 object

or : impossible outcome

5. Screen drops ...   revealing 2 objects

Figure 1 Sequence of events for '1 + 1' and '2 + 1' situations presented in experiments 1 and 2.

METHODS. Trials alternated between a 1-item and a 2-item result, half of the infants received the ordering (1, 2, 1, 2, 1, 2), the remainder receiving the reverse ordering. Infants sat facing the display; parents either stood out of sight behind and not touching the infant, or else gently touched the infant while facing away from the display. The experimenter was hidden behind the display, and manipulated the objects by means of a hidden trap door in the back wall of the display. A hidden observer, unaware of the infant group and of the trial ordering, timed infants' looks to the display. In all experiments, infants were excluded if they became fussy or drowsy during the experiment (16 infants), if their test preference was more than 2.5 standard deviations away from the mean for that group (1 infant), or if they had a pretest preference of more than 10 s for either number (19 infants). The choice of 10 s does not affect the pattern of results (the analyses for experiments 1 and 2 combined give the same pattern even with no cutoff).

Table 1 Looking times and preference for 2 items over 1 item.

Experiment	Trials	Group	LT(1)*	LT(2)*	P(2)*	d.f.	t	p
1	Pretest	1 + 1	20.06	20.80	0.74	30	0.649	>0.5
		2 − 1	17.99	19.61	1.62			
	Test	1 + 1	13.36	12.80	−0.53	30	2.078	<0.05
		2 − 1	10.54	13.73	3.19			
2	Pretest	1 + 1	11.12	10.62	−0.50	14	0.677	>0.5
		2 − 1	10.35	11.44	1.09			
	Test	1 + 1	12.08	9.45	−2.65	14	1.795	<0.05
		2 − 1	10.98	8.05	2.94			
1 + 2	Pretest	1 + 1	17.62	18.02	0.41	46	0.873	>0.35
		2 − 1	15.05	16.47	1.42			
	Test	1 + 1	13.01	11.89	−1.11	46	2.73	<0.005
		2 − 1	9.59	12.67	3.09			

Statistical significance was determined by between-group t-tests on infants' P(2) values. Probability values are 2-tailed for test comparisons, 1-tailed for pretest comparisons. In experiment 1, a trial concluded when an infant looked away for 2 consecutive seconds after looking at the display for at least 4 cumulative seconds, or had looked for 30 cumulative seconds. Experiment 2: same criteria, except that minimum cumulative looking time was only 2 s. The shorter mean looking times in experiment 2 are probably due to this procedural change. Times are lower in test than pretest trials because infants' looks decrease during the experiment as they become more familiar with the display. Experiment 2, 6 infants in the 1 + 1 group, 10 infants in the 2 − 1 group.

* P(2) = LT(2) − LT(1); where P(2), preference for 2; LT(1) and LT(2) are the mean looking times to 1 and 2 items (in seconds).

numerical result of the addition, they would be expected to look longer at the result of 3 items than of 2 items. This pattern was indeed observed (Table 2); infants significantly preferred 3 in the test trials, but not the pretest trials, showing that they were surprised when the addition appeared to result in 3 items. The results from the three experiments support the claim[7] that 5-month-old human infants are able to calculate the precise results of simple arithmetical operations.

There is an alternative explanation for infants' success in these experiments. Infants may be calculating the results of the addition and subtraction, not of a discrete number of items, but of a continuous amount of physical substance; infants may possess an ability to measure and operate on continuous quantities. But there are reasons to prefer the hypothesis that it is the number of items, not amount of substance, that infants are computing. It has been shown that infants are sensitive to small numerical changes[1-4], but there is no evidence of a sensitivity to small differences in amount of physical matter. Infants are predisposed to interpret the physical world as composed of discrete, individual entities when perceiving spatial layouts[14,15], and they represent the precise spatial locations and trajectories of individual objects relative to each other[16,17]. Thus, the notion of 'individual entity' plays a prominent role in infants' conceptualization and representation of the physical world, and they have abilities that allow them to track distinct entities over time and space. This, together with infants' sensitivity to small numerical differences in collections of items, lends independent support to the hypothesis that infants possess a mechanism for quantifying collections of discrete entities. The most plausible explanation for the findings presented here is that infants can compute the results of simple arithmetical operations.

In sum, infants possess true numerical concepts—they have access to the ordering of and numerical relationships between small numbers, and can manipulate these concepts in numerically meaningful ways. This in turn

Table 2 Looking times and preferences for 3 items over 2.

Condition	LT(2)*	LT(3)*	P(3)*	d.f.	t	p
Pretest	14.16	13.87	−0.29	15	−0.224	>0.5
Test	9.96	11.89	1.92	15	2.044	>0.03

Statistical significance was determined by *t*-tests comparing infants' P(3) values to the null hypothesis of no preference. Probability value for pretest comparison is 2-tailed; that for test comparison is 1-tailed. As in experiments 1 and 2, infants were excluded if they showed more than a 10-second pretest preference for one of the numbers; the pattern of results remains the same when these infants are included in the analyses. Experiment 3 used the same criterion for end-of-trial as that used in experiment 2.

  * P(3) = LT(3) − LT(2), where P(3), preference for 3; LT(3) and LT(2) are the mean looking times to 3 and 2 items (in seconds).

indicates that the mental process giving rise to these concepts yields true numerical outputs that encode numerical relationships, not holistic percepts derived from a pattern-recognition process. The existence of these arithmetical abilities so early in infancy suggests that humans innately possess the capacity to perform simple arithmetical calculations, which may provide the foundations for the development of further arithmetical knowledge[7,18].

Received 20 May: accepted 16 July 1992.

Acknowledgements

I thank E. S. Spelke and R. Baillargeon for advice and suggestions; F. Bedford, P. Bloom, M. Peterson, and R. Rosser for suggestions and comments; and H. Campbell, K. Fohr, C. Mannering, and T. Wilcox for help in the testing of infants. This was supported by the NIH (Institutional BPSG grant) and the University of Arizona (SBSRI grant).

References

1. Starkey, P. & Cooper, R. G. *Science* **210**, 1033–1035 (1980).
2. Strauss, M. S. & Curtis, L. E. *Child Dev.* **52**, 1146–1152 (1981).
3. Antell, S. & Keating, D. P. *Child Dev.* **54**, 695–701 (1983).
4. van Loosbroek, E. & Smitsman, A. W. *Devl Psychol.* **26**, 916–922 (1990).
5. Starkey, P., Spelke, E. S. & Gelman, R. *Science* **222**, 179–181 (1983).
6. Starkey, P., Spelke, E. S. & Gelman, R. *Cognition* **36**, 97–127 (1990).
7. Wynn, K. *Mind Lang.* (in the press).
8. Davis, H., Albert, M. & Barron, R. W. *Science* **228**, 1222 (1985).
9. Cooper, R. G. in *Origins of Cognitive Skills* 157–192 (ed. Sophian, C.) (Erlbaum, Hillsdale, New Jersey, 1984).
10. Chi, M. T. H. & Klahr, D. *J. exp. Child Psychol.* **19**, 434–439 (1975).
11. Silverman, I. W. & Rose, A. P. *Devl Psychol.* **16**, 539–540 (1980).
12. Mandler, G. & Shebo, B. J. *J. exp. Psychol. Gen.* **11**, 1–22 (1982).
13. Gallistel, C. R. *The Organization of Learning* 343–348 (MIT, Cambridge, Massachusetts, 1990)
14. Spelke, E. S. in *Perceptual Development in Infancy: Minnesota Symposia on Child Psychology* Vol. 20 (ed. Yonas, A.) 197–234 (Erlbaum, Hillsdale, New Jersey, 1988).
15. Spelke, E. S., *Cog. Science* **14**, 29–56 (1990).
16. Baillargeon, R. *Cognition* **38**, 13–42 (1991).
17. Baillargeon, R. & DeVos. J. *Child Dev.* **62**, 1227–1246 (1991).
18. Wynn, K. *Cog. Psychol.* **24**, 220–251 (1992).

116

AUTISTIC DISTURBANCES OF AFFECTIVE CONTACT

Leo Kanner

Source: *Nervous Child*, 2, 1943: 217–250.

> To understand and measure emotional qualities is very difficult. Psychologists and educators have been struggling with that problem for years but we are still unable to measure emotional and personality traits with the exactness with which we can measure intelligence.
>
> —ROSE ZELIGS in *Glimpses into Child Life*

Since 1938, there have come to our attention a number of children whose condition differs so markedly and uniquely from anything reported so far, that each case merits—and, I hope, will eventually receive—a detailed consideration of its fascinating peculiarities. In this place, the limitations necessarily imposed by space call for a condensed presentation of the case material. For the same reason, photographs have also been omitted. Since none of the children of this group has as yet attained an age beyond 11 years, this must be considered a preliminary report, to be enlarged upon as the patients grow older and further observation of their development is made.

Case 1. Donald T. was first seen in October, 1938, at the age of 5 years, 1 month. Before the family's arrival from their home town, the father sent a thirty-three-page typewritten history that, though filled with much obsessive detail, gave an excellent account of Donald's background. Donald was born at full term on September 8, 1933. He weighed nearly 7 pounds at birth. He was breast fed, with supplementary feeding, until the end of the eighth month; there were frequent changes of formulas. "Eating," the report said, "has always been a problem with him. He has never shown a normal appetite. Seeing children eating candy and ice cream has never been a temptation to him." Dentition proceeded satisfactorily. He walked at 13 months.

At the age of 1 year "he could hum and sing many tunes accurately." Before he was 2 years old, he had "an unusual memory for faces and names,

234

knew the names of a great number of houses" in his home town. "He was encouraged by the family in learning and reciting short poems, and even learned the Twenty-third Psalm and twenty-five questions and answers of the Presbyterian Catechism." The parents observed that "he was not learning to ask questions or to answer questions unless they pertained to rhymes or things of this nature, and often then he would ask no question except in single words." His enunciation was clear. He became interested in pictures "and very soon knew an inordinate number of the pictures in a set of *Compton's Encyclopedia.*" He knew the pictures of the presidents "and knew most of the pictures of his ancestors and kinfolks on both sides of the house." He quickly learned the whole alphabet "backward as well as forward" and to count to 100.

It was observed at an early time that he was happiest when left alone, almost never cried to go with his mother, did not seem to notice his father's homecomings, and was indifferent to visiting relatives. The father made a special point of mentioning that Donald even failed to pay the slightest attention to Santa Claus in full regalia.

> He seems to be self-satisfied. He has no apparent affection when petted. He does not observe the fact that anyone comes or goes, and never seems glad to see father or mother or any playmate. He seems almost to draw into his shell and live within himself. We once secured a most attractive little boy of the same age from an orphanage and brought him home to spend the summer with Donald, but Donald has never asked him a question nor answered a question and has never romped with him in play. He seldom comes to anyone when called but has to be picked up and carried or led wherever he ought to go.

In his second year, he "developed a mania for spinning blocks and pans and other round objects." At the same time, he had

> A dislike for self-propelling vehicles, such as Taylor-tots, tricycles, and swings. He is still fearful of tricycles and seems to have almost a horror of them when he is forced to ride, at which time he will try to hold onto the person assisting him. This summer [1937] we bought him a playground slide and on the first afternoon when other children were sliding on it he would not get about it, and when we put him up to slide down it he seemed horror struck. The next morning when nobody was present, however, he walked out, climbed the ladder, and slid down, and he has slid on it frequently since, but slides only when no other child is present to join him in sliding. . . . He was always constantly happy and busy entertaining himself, but resented being urged to play with certain things.

235

When interfered with, he had temper tantrums, during which he was destructive. He was "dreadfully fearful of being spanked or switched" but "could not associate his misconduct with his punishment."

In August, 1937, Donald was placed in a tuberculosis preventorium in order to provide for him "a change of environment." While there, he had a "disinclination to play with children and do things children his age usually take an interest in." He gained weight but developed the habit of shaking his head from side to side. He continued spinning objects and jumped up and down in ectasy as he watched them spin. He displayed

> An abstraction of mind which made him perfectly oblivious to everything about him. He appears to be always thinking and think-ing, and to get his attention almost requires one to break down a mental barrier between his inner consciousness and the outside world.

The father, whom Donald resembles physically, is a successful, meticu-lous, hard-working lawyer who has had two "breakdowns" under strain of work. He always took every ailment seriously, taking to his bed and following doctors' orders punctiliously even for the slightest cold. "When he walks down the street, he is so absorbed in thinking that he sees nothing and nobody and cannot remember anything about the walk." The mother, a college graduate, is a calm, capable woman, to whom her husband feels vastly superior. A second child, a boy, was born to them on May 22, 1938.

Donald, when examined at the Harriet Lane Home in October, 1938, was found to be in good physical condition. During the initial observation and in a two-week study by Drs. Eugenia S. Cameron and George Frankl at the Child Study Home of Maryland, the following picture was obtained:

There was a marked limitation of spontaneous activity. He wandered about smiling, making stereotyped movements with his fingers, crossing them about in the air. He shook his head from side to side, whispering or humming the same three-note tune. He spun with great pleasure anything he could seize upon to spin. He kept throwing things on the floor, seeming to delight in the sounds they made. He arranged beads, sticks, or blocks in groups of different series of colors. Whenever he finished one of these per-formances, he squealed and jumped up and down. Beyond this he showed no initiative, requiring constant instruction (from his mother) in any form of activity other than the limited ones in which he was absorbed.

Most of his actions were repetitions carried out in exactly the same way in which they had been performed originally. If he spun a block, he must always start with the same face uppermost. When he threaded buttons, he arranged them in a certain sequence that had no pattern to it but happened to be the order used by the father when he first had shown them to Donald.

There were also innumerable verbal rituals recurring all day long. When he desired to get down after his nap, he said, "Boo [his word for his mother], say 'Don, do you want to get down?'"

His mother would comply, and Don would say: "Now say 'All right.'"

The mother did, and Don got down. At mealtime, repeating something that had obviously been said to him often, he said to his mother, "Say 'Eat it or I won't give you tomatoes, but if you don't eat it I will give you tomatoes,'" or "Say 'If you drink to there, I'll laugh and I'll smile.'"

And his mother had to conform or else he squealed, cried, and strained every muscle in his neck in tension. This happened all day long about one thing or another. He seemed to have much pleasure in ejaculating words or phrases, such as "Chrysanthemum"; "Dahlia, dahlia, dahlia"; "Business"; "Trumpet vine"; "The right one is on, the left one is off"; "Through the dark clouds shining." Irrelevant utterances such as these were his ordinary mode of speech. He always seemed to be parroting what he had heard said to him at one time or another. He used the personal pronouns for the persons he was quoting, even imitating the intonation. When he wanted his mother to pull his shoe off, he said: "Pull off your shoe." When he wanted a bath, he said: "Do you want a bath?"

Words to him had a specifically literal, inflexible meaning. He seemed unable to generalize, to transfer an expression to another similar object or situation. If he did so occasionally, it was a substitution, which then "stood" definitely for the original meaning. Thus he christened each of his water color bottles by the name of one of the Dionne quintuplets—Annette for blue, Cécile for red, etc. Then, going through a series of color mixtures, he proceeded in this manner: "Annette and Cécile make purple."

The colloquial request to "put that *down*" meant to him that he was to put the thing on the floor. He had a "milk glass" and a "water glass." When he spit some milk into the "water glass," the milk thereby became "white water."

The word "yes" for a long time meant that he wanted his father to put him up on his shoulder. This had a definite origin. His father, trying to teach him to say "yes" and "no," once asked him, "Do you want me to put you on my shoulder?"

Don expressed his agreement by repeating the question literally, echolalia-like. His father said, "If you want me to, say 'Yes'; if you don't want me to, say 'No.'"

Don said "yes" when asked. But thereafter "yes" came to mean that he desired to be put up on his father's shoulder.

He paid no attention to persons around him. When taken into a room, he completely disregarded the people and instantly went for objects, preferably those that could be spun. Commands or actions that could not possibly be disregarded were resented as unwelcome intrusions. But he was never angry at the interfering *person*. He angrily shoved away the *hand* that was in his way or the *foot* that stepped on one of his blocks, at one time referring to the foot on the block as "umbrella." Once the obstacle was removed, he forgot the whole affair. He gave no heed to the presence of other children but went about his favorite pastimes, walking off from the children if they were so bold as to join him. If a child took a toy from him, he passively permitted it. He scrawled lines on the picture books the other children were coloring, retreating or putting his hands over his ears if they threatened him in anger. His mother was the only person with whom he had any contact at all, and even she spent all of her time developing ways of keeping him at play with her.

After his return home, the mother sent periodic reports about his development. He quickly learned to read fluently and to play simple tunes on the piano. He began, whenever his attention could be obtained, to respond to questions "which require yes or no for an answer." Though he occasionally began to speak of himself as "I" and of the person addressed as "you," he continued for quite some time the pattern of pronominal reversals. When, for instance, in February, 1939, he stumbled and nearly fell, he said of himself, "*You* did not fall down."

He expressed puzzlement about the inconsistencies of spelling: "bite" should be spelled "bight" to correspond to the spelling of "light." He could spend hours writing on the blackboard. His play became more imaginative and varied, though still quite ritualistic.

He was brought back for a check-up in May, 1939. His attention and concentration were improved. He was in better contact with his environment, and there were some direct reactions to people and situations. He showed disappointment when thwarted, demanded bribes promised him, gave evidence of pleasure when praised. It was possible, at the Child Study Home, to obtain with constant insistence some conformity to daily routine and some degree of proper handling of objects. But he still went on writing letters with his fingers in the air, ejaculating words—"Semicolon"; "Capital"; "Twelve, twelve"; "Slain, slain"; "I could put a little comma or semicolon"—chewing on paper, putting food on his hair, throwing books into the toilet, putting a key down the water drain, climbing onto the table and bureau, having temper tantrums, giggling and whispering autistically. He got hold of an encyclopedia and learned about fifteen words in the index and kept repeating them over and over again. His mother was helped in trying to develop his interest and participation in ordinary life situations.

The following are abstracts from letters sent subsequently by Donald's mother:

> *September, 1939.* He continues to eat and to wash and dress himself only at my insistence and with my help. He is becoming resourceful, builds things with his blocks, dramatizes stories, attempts to wash the car, waters the flowers with the hose, plays store with the

grocery supply, tries to cut out pictures with the scissors. Numbers still have a great attraction for him. While his play is definitely improving, he has never asked questions about people and shows no interest in our conversation. . . .

October, 1939 [a school principal friend of the mother's had agreed to try Donald in the first grade of her school]. The first day was very trying for them but each succeeding day he has improved very much. Don is much more independent, wants to do many things for himself. He marches in line nicely, answers when called upon, and is more biddable and obedient. He never voluntarily relates any of his experiences at school and never objects to going. . . .

November, 1939. I visited his room this morning and was amazed to see how nicely he cooperated and responded. He was very quiet and calm and listened to what the teacher was saying about half the time. He does not squeal or run around but takes his place like the other children. The teacher began writing on the board. That immediately attracted his attention. She wrote:

BETTY MAY FEED A FISH.
DON MAY FEED A FISH.
JERRY MAY FEED A FISH.

In his turn he walked up and drew a circle around his name. Then he fed a goldfish. Next, each child was given his weekly reader, and he turned to the proper page as the teacher directed and read when called upon. He also answered a question about one of the pictures. Several times, when pleased, he jumped up and down and shook his head once while answering. . . .

March, 1940. The greatest improvement I notice is his awareness of things about him. He talks very much more and asks a good many questions. Not often does he voluntarily tell me of happenings at school, but if I ask leading questions, he answers them correctly. He really enters into the games with other children. One day he enlisted the family in one game he had just learned, telling each of us just exactly what to do. He feeds himself some better and is better able to do things for himself. . . .

March, 1941. He has improved greatly, but the basic difficulties are still evident. . . .

Donald was brought for another check-up in April, 1941. An invitation to enter the office was disregarded, but he had himself led willingly. Once inside, he did not even glance at the three physicians present (two of whom he well remembered from his previous visits) but immediately made for the desk and handled papers and books. Questions at first were met with the stereotyped reply, "I don't know." He then helped himself to pencil and paper and wrote and drew pages and pages full of letters of the alphabet and a few simple designs. He arranged the letters in two or three lines, reading them in vertical rather than horizontal succession, and was very much pleased with the result. Occasionally he volunteered a statement or question: "I am going to stay for two days at the Child Study Home." Later he said: "Where is my mother?"

"Why do you want her?" he was asked.

"I want to hug her around the neck."

He used pronouns adequately and his sentences were grammatically correct.

The major part of his "conversation" consisted of questions of an obsessive nature. He was inexhaustible in bringing up variations: "How many days in a week, years in a century, hours in a day, hours in half a day, weeks in a century, centuries in half a millennium," etc., etc.; "How many pints in a gallon, how many gallons to fill four gallons?" Sometimes he asked, "How many hours in a minute, how many days in an hour?" etc. He looked thoughtful and always wanted an answer. At times he temporarily compromised by responding quickly to some other question or request but promptly returned to the same type of behavior. Many of his replies were metaphorical or otherwise peculiar. When asked to subtract 4 from 10, he answered: "I'll draw a hexagon."

He was still extremely autistic. His relation to people had developed only in so far as he addressed them when he needed or wanted to know something. He never looked at the person while talking and did not use communicative gestures. Even this type of contact ceased the moment he was told or given what he had asked for.

A letter from the mother stated in October, 1942:

> Don is still indifferent to much that is around him. His interests change often, but always he is absorbed in some kind of silly, unrelated subject. His literal-mindedness is still very marked, he wants to spell words as they sound and to pronounce letters consistently. Recently I have been able to have Don do a few chores around the place to earn picture show money. He really enjoys the movies now but not with any idea of a connected story. He remembers them in the order in which he sees them. Another of his recent hobbies is with old issues of *Time* magazine. He found a copy of the first issue of March 3, 1923, and has attempted to make a list of the dates of publication of each issue since that time. So far he has gotten to April, 1934. He has figured the number of issues in a volume and similar nonsense.

Case 2. Frederick W. was referred on May 27, 1942, at the age of 6 years, with the physician's complaint that his "adaptive behavior in a social setting is characterized by attacking as well as withdrawing behavior." His mother stated:

The child has always been self-sufficient. I could leave him alone and he'd entertain himself very happily, walking around, singing. I have never known him to cry in demanding attention. He was never interested in hide-and-seek, but he'd roll a ball back and forth, watch his father shave, hold the razor box and put the razor back in, put the lid on the soap box. He never was very good with cooperative play. He doesn't care to play with the ordinary things that other children play with, anything with wheels on. He is afraid of mechanical things; he runs from them. He used to be afraid of my egg beater, is perfectly petrified of my vacuum cleaner. Elevators are simply a terrifying experience to him. He is afraid of spinning tops.

Until the last year, he mostly ignored other people. When we had guests, he just wouldn't pay any attention. He looked curiously at small children and then would go off all alone. He acted as if people weren't there at all, even with his grandparents. About a year ago, he began showing more interest in observing them, would even go up to them. But usually people are an interference. He'll push people away from him. If people come too close to him, he'll push them away. He doesn't want me to touch him or put my arm around him, but he'll come and touch *me*.

To a certain extent, he likes to stick to the same thing. On one of the bookshelves we had three pieces in a certain arrangement. Whenever this was changed, he always rearranged it in the old pattern. He won't try new things, apparently. After watching for a long time, he does it all of a sudden. He wants to be sure he does it right.

He had said at least two words ["Daddy" and "Dora," the mother's first name] before he was 2 years old. From then on, between 2 and 3 years, he would say words that seemed to come as a surprise to himself. He'd say them once and never repeat them. One of the first words he said was "overalls." [The parents never expected him to answer any of their questions, were *once* surprised when he did give an answer—"Yes"]. At about $2^1/_2$ years, he began to sing. He sang about twenty or thirty songs, including a little French lullaby. In his fourth year, I tried to make him ask for things before he'd get them. He was stronger-willed than I was and held out longer, and he would not get it but he never gave in about it. Now he can count up to into the hundreds and can read numbers, but he is not interested in numbers as they apply to objects. He has great difficulty in

241

learning the proper use of personal pronouns. When receiving a gift, he would say of himself: "You say 'Thank you.'"

He bowls, and when he sees the pins go down, he'll jump up and down in great glee.

Frederick was born May 23, 1936, in breech presentation. The mother had "some kidney trouble" and an elective cesarean section was performed about two weeks before term. He was well after birth; feeding presented no problem. The mother recalled that he was never observed to assume an anticipatory posture when she prepared to pick him up. He sat up at 7 months, walked at about 18 months. He had occasional colds but no other illness. Attempts to have him attend nursery school were unsuccessful: "he would either be retiring and hide in a corner or would push himself into the middle of a group and be very aggressive."

The boy is an only child. The father, aged 44, a university graduate and a plant pathologist, has traveled a great deal in connection with his work. He is a patient, even-tempered man, mildly obsessive; as a child he did not talk "until late" and was delicate, supposedly "from lack of vitamin in diet allowed in Africa." The mother, aged 40, a college graduate, successively a secretary to physicians, a purchasing agent, director of secretarial studies in a girls' school, and at one time a teacher of history, is described as healthy and even-tempered.

The paternal grandfather organized medical missions in Africa, studied tropical medicine in England, became an authority on manganese mining in Brazil, was at the same time dean of a medical school and director of an art museum in an American city, and is listed in *Who's Who* under two different names. He disappeared in 1911, his whereabouts remaining obscure for twenty-five years. It was then learned that he had gone to Europe and married a novelist, without obtaining a divorce from his first wife. The family considers him "a very strong character of the genius type, who wanted to do as much good as he could."

The paternal grandmother is described as "a dyed-in-the-wool missionary if ever there was one, quite dominating and hard to get along with, at present pioneering in the South at a college for mountaineers."

The father is the second of five children. The oldest is a well known newspaper man and author of a best-seller. A married sister, "high-strung and quite precocious," is a singer. Next comes a brother who writes for adventure magazines. The youngest, a painter, writer, and radio commentator, "did not talk until he was about 6 years old," and the first words he is reported to have spoken were, "When a lion can't talk he can whistle."

The mother said of her own relatives, "Mine are very ordinary people." Her family is settled in a Wisconsin town, where her father is a banker; her mother is "mildly interested" in church work, and her three sisters, all younger than herself, are average middle-class matrons.

Frederick was admitted to the Harriet Lane Home on May 27, 1942. He appeared to be well nourished. The circumference of his head was 21 inches, of his chest 22 inches, of his abdomen 21 inches. His occiput and frontal region were markedly prominent. There was a supernumerary nipple in the left axilla. Reflexes were sluggish but present. All other findings, including laboratory examinations and X ray of his skull, were normal, except for large and ragged tonsils.

He was led into the psychiatrist's office by a nurse, who left the room immediately afterward. His facial expression was tense, somewhat apprehensive, and gave the impression of intelligence. He wandered aimlessly about for a few moments, showing no sign of awareness of the three adults present. He then sat down on the couch, ejaculating unintelligible sounds, and then abruptly lay down, wearing throughout a dreamy-like smile. When he responded to questions or commands at all, he did so by repeating them echolalia fashion. The most striking feature in his behavior was the difference in his reactions to objects and to people. Objects absorbed him easily and he showed good attention and perseverance in playing with them. He seemed to regard people as unwelcome intruders to whom he paid as little attention as they would permit. When forced to respond, he did so briefly and returned to his absorption in things. When a hand was held out before him so that he could not possibly ignore it, he played with it briefly as if it were a detached object. He blew out a match with an expression of satisfaction with the achievement, but did not look up to the person who had lit the match. When a fourth person entered the room, he retreated for a minute or two behind the bookcase, saying, "I don't want you," and waving him away, then resumed his play, paying no further attention to him or anyone else:

Test results (Grace Arthur performance scale) were difficult to evaluate because of his lack of cooperation. He did best with the Seguin form board (shortest time, 58 seconds). In the mare and foal completion test he seemed to be guided by form entirely, to the extent that it made no difference whether the pieces were right side up or not. He completed the triangle but not the rectangle. With all the form boards he showed good perseverance and concentration, working at them spontaneously and interestedly. Between tests, he wandered about the room examining various objects or fishing in the wastebasket without regard for the persons present. He made frequent sucking noises and occasionally kissed the dorsal surface of his hand. He became fascinated with the circle from the form board, rolling it on the desk and attempting, with occasional success, to catch it just before it rolled off.

Frederick was enrolled at the Devereux Schools on September 26, 1942.

Case 3. Richard M. was referred to the Johns Hopkins Hospital on February 5, 1941, at 3 years, 3 months of age, with the complaint of deafness because he did not talk and did not respond to questions. Following his admission, the interne made this observation:

The child seems quite intelligent, playing with the toys in his bed and being adequately curious about instruments used in the examination. He seems quite self-sufficient in his play. It is difficult to tell definitely whether he hears, but it seems that he does. He will obey commands, such as "Sit up" or "Lie down," even when he does not see the speaker. He does not pay attention to conversation going on around him, and although he does make noises, he says no recognizable words.

His mother brought with her copious notes that indicated obsessive preoccupation with details and a tendency to read all sorts of peculiar interpretations into the child's performances. She watched (and recorded) every gesture and every "look," trying to find their specific significance and finally deciding on a particular, sometimes very farfetched explanation. She thus accumulated an account that, though very elaborate and richly illustrated, on the whole revealed more of her own version of what had happened in each instance than it told of what had actually occurred.

Richard's father is a professor of forestry in a southern university. He is very much immersed in his work, almost entirely to the exclusion of social contacts. The mother is a college graduate. The maternal grandfather is a physician, and the rest of the family, in both branches, consists of intelligent professional people. Richard's brother, thirty-one months his junior, is described as a normal, well developed child.

Richard was born on November 17, 1937. Pregnancy and birth were normal. He sat up at 8 months and walked at 1 year. His mother began to "train" him at the age of 3 weeks, giving him a suppository every morning "so his bowels would move by the clock." The mother, in comparing her two children, recalled that while her younger child showed an active anticipatory reaction to being picked up, Richard had not shown any physiognomic or postural sign of preparedness and had failed to adjust his body to being held by her or the nurse. Nutrition and physical growth proceeded satisfactorily. Following smallpox vaccination at 12 months, he had an attack of diarrhea and fever, from which he recovered in somewhat less than a week.

In September, 1940, the mother, in commenting on Richard's failure to talk, remarked in her notes:

I can't be sure just when he stopped the imitation of word sounds. It seems that he has gone backward mentally gradually for the last two years. We have thought it was because he did not disclose what was in his head, that it was there all right. Now that he is making so many sounds, it is disconcerting because it is now evident that he can't talk. Before, I thought he could if he only would. *He gave the impression of silent wisdom to me. . . .* One puzzling and discouraging thing is the great difficulty one has in getting his attention.

244

On physical examination, Richard was found to be healthy except for large tonsils and adenoids, which were removed on February 8, 1941. His head circumference was 54½ cm. His electroencephalogram was normal.

He had himself led willingly to the psychiatrist's office and engaged at once in active play with the toys, paying no attention to the persons in the room. Occasionally, he looked up at the walls, smiled and uttered short staccato forceful sounds—"Ee! Ee! Ee!" He complied with a spoken and gestural command of his mother to take off his slippers. When the command was changed to another, this time without gestures, he repeated the original request and again took off his slippers (which had been put on again). He performed well with the unrotated form board but not with the rotated form board.

Richard was again seen at the age of 4 years, 4 months. He had grown considerably and gained weight. When started for the examination room, he screamed and made a great fuss, but once he yielded he went along willingly. He immediately proceeded to turn the lights on and off. He showed no interest in the examiner or any other person but was attracted to a small box that he threw as if it were a ball.

At 4 years, 11 months, his first move in entering the office (or any other room) was to turn the lights on and off. He climbed on a chair, and from the chair to the desk in order to reach the switch of the wall lamp. He did not communicate his wishes but went into a rage until his mother guessed and procured what he wanted. He had no contact with people, whom he definitely regarded as an interference when they talked to him or otherwise tried to gain his attention.

The mother felt that she was no longer capable of handling him, and he was placed in a foster home near Annapolis with a woman who had shown a remarkable talent for dealing with difficult children. Recently, this woman heard him say clearly his first intelligible words. They were, "Good night."

Case 4. Paul G. was referred in March, 1941, at the age of 5 years, for psychometric assessment of what was thought to be a severe intellectual defect. He had attended a private nursery school, where his incoherent speech, inability to conform, and reaction with temper outbursts to any interference created the impression of feeblemindedness.

Paul, an only child, had come to this country from England with his mother at nearly 2 years of age. The father, a mining engineer, believed to be in Australia now, had left his wife shortly before that time after several years of an unhappy marriage. The mother, supposedly a college graduate, a restless, unstable, excitable woman, gave a vague and blatantly conflicting history of the family background and the child's development. She spent much time emphasizing and illustrating her efforts to make Paul clever by teaching him to memorize poems and songs. At 3 years, he knew the words of not less than thirty-seven songs and various and sundry nursery rhymes.

He was born normally. He vomited a great deal during his first year, and feeding formulas were changed frequently with little success. He ceased vomiting when he was started on solid food. He cut his teeth, held up his head, sat up, walked, and established bowel and bladder control at the usual age. He had measles, chickenpox, and pertussis without complications. His tonsils were removed when he was 3 years old. On physical examination, phimosis was found to be the only deviation from otherwise good health.

The following features emerged from observation on his visits to the clinic, during five weeks' residence in a boarding home, and during a few days' stay in the hospital.

Paul was a slender, well built, attractive child, whose face looked intelligent and animated. He had good manual dexterity. He rarely responded to any form of address, even to the calling of his name. At one time he picked up a block from the floor on request. Once he copied a circle immediately after it had been drawn before him. Sometimes an energetic "Don't!" caused him to interrupt his activity of the moment. But usually, when spoken to, he went on with whatever he was doing as if nothing had been said. Yet one never had the feeling that he was willingly disobedient or contrary. He was obviously so remote that the remarks did not reach him. He was always vivaciously occupied with something and seemed to be highly satisfied, unless someone made a persistent attempt to interfere with his self-chosen actions. Then he first tried impatiently to get out of the way and, when this met with no success, screamed and kicked in a full-fledged tantrum.

There was a marked contrast between his relations to people and to objects. Upon entering the room, he instantly went after objects and used them correctly. He was not destructive and treated the objects with care and even affection. He picked up a pencil and scribbled on paper that he found on the table. He opened a box, took out a toy telephone, singing again and again: "He wants the telephone," and went around the room with the mouthpiece and receiver in proper position. He got hold of a pair of scissors and patiently and skilfully cut a sheet of paper into small bits, singing the phrase "Cutting paper," many times. He helped himself to a toy engine, ran around the room holding it up high and singing over and over again, "The engine is flying." While these utterances, made always with the same inflection, were clearly connected with his actions, he ejaculated others that could not be linked up with immediate situations. These are a few examples: "The people in the hotel"; "Did you hurt your leg?" "Candy is all gone, candy is empty"; "You'll fall off the bicycle and bump your head." However, some of those exclamations could be definitely traced to previous experiences. He was in the habit of saying almost every day, "Don't throw the dog off the balcony." His mother recalled that she had said those words to him about a toy dog while they were still in England. At the sight of a saucepan he would invariably exclaim, "Peten-eater." The mother remembered that this particular association had begun when he was 2 years old and she happened to drop a saucepan while reciting to him the nursery rhyme about "Peter, Peter, pumpkin eater." Reproductions of warnings of bodily injury constituted a major portion of his utterances.

None of these remarks was meant to have communicative value. There was, on his side, no affective tie to people. He behaved as if people as such did not matter or even exist. It made no difference whether one spoke to him in a friendly or a harsh way. He never looked up at people's faces. When he had any dealings with persons at all, he treated them, or rather parts of them, as if they were objects. He would use a hand to lead him. He would, in playing, butt his head against his mother as at other times he did against a pillow. He allowed his boarding mother's hands to dress him, paying not the slightest attention to *her*. When with other children, he ignored them and went after their toys.

His enunciation was clear and he had a good vocabulary. His sentence construction was satisfactory, with one significant exception. He never used the pronoun of the first person, nor did he refer to himself as Paul. All statements pertaining to himself were made in the second person, as literal repetitions of things that had been said to him before. He would express his desire for candy by saying, "*You* want candy." He would pull his hand away from a hot radiator and say "*You* get hurt." Occasionally there were parrot-like repetitions of things said to him.

Formal testing could not be carried out, but he certainly could not be regarded as feebleminded in the ordinary sense. After hearing his boarding mother say grace three times, he repeated it without a flaw and has retained it since then. He could count and name colors. He learned quickly to identify his favorite victrola records from a large stack and knew how to mount and play them.

His boarding mother reported a number of observations that indicated compulsive behavior. He often masturbated with complete abandon. He ran around in circles emitting phrases in an ecstatic-like fashion. He took a small blanket and kept shaking it, delightedly shouting, "Ee! Ee!" He could continue in this manner for a long time and showed great irritation when he was interfered with. All these and many other things were not only repetitions but recurred day after day with almost photographic sameness.

Case 5. Barbara K. was referred in February, 1942, at 8 years, 3 months of age. Her father's written note stated:

> First child, born normally October 30, 1933. She nursed very poorly and was put on bottle after about a week. She quit taking any kind of nourishment at 3 months. She was tube-fed five times daily up to 1 year of age. She began to eat then, though there was much difficulty until she was about 18 months old. Since then she has

been a good eater, likes to experiment with food, tasting, and now fond of cooking.

Ordinary vocabulary at 2 years, but always slow at putting words into sentences. Phenomenal ability to spell, read, and a good writer, but still has difficulty with verbal expression. Written language has helped the verbal. Can't get arithmetic except as a memory feat.

Repetitious as a baby, and obsessive now: holds things in hands, takes things to bed with her, repeats phrases, gets stuck on an idea, game, etc., and rides it hard, then goes to something else. She used to talk using "you" for herself and "I" for her mother or me, as if she were saying things as we would in talking to her.

Very timid, fearful of various and changing things, wind, large animals etc. Mostly passive, but passively stubborn at times. Inattentive to the point where one wonders if she hears. (She does!) No competitive spirit, no desire to please her teacher. If she knew more than any member in the class about something, she would give no hint of it, just keep quiet, maybe not even listen.

In camp last summer she was well liked, learned to swim, is graceful in water (had always appeared awkward in her motility before), overcame fear of ponies, played best with children of 5 years of age. At camp she slid into avitaminosis and malnutrition but offered almost no verbal complaints.

Barbara's father is a prominent psychiatrist. Her mother is a well educated, kindly woman. A younger brother, born in 1937, is healthy, alert, and well developed.

Barbara "shook hands" upon request (offering the left upon coming, the right upon leaving) by merely raising a limp hand in the approximate direction of the examiner's proffered hand; the motion definitely lacked the implication of greeting. During the entire interview there was no indication of any kind of affective contact. A pin prick resulted in withdrawal of her arm, a fearful glance at the pin (not the examiner), and utterance of the word "Hurt!" not addressed to anyone in particular.

She showed no interest in test performances. The concept of test, of sharing an experience or situation, seemed foreign to her. She protruded her tongue and played with her hand as one would with a toy. Attracted by a pen on the desk stand, she said: "Pen like yours at home." Then, seeing a pencil, she inquired: "May I take this home?"

When told that she might, she made no move to take it. The pencil was given to her, but she shoved it away, saying, "It's not my pencil."

She did the same thing repeatedly in regard to other objects. Several times she said, "Let's see Mother" (who was in the waiting room).

She read excellently, finishing the 10-year Binet fire story in thirty-three seconds and with no errors, but was unable to reproduce from memory anything she had read. In the Binet pictures, she saw (or at least reported) no action or relatedness between the single items, which she had no difficulty enumerating.. Her handwriting was legible. Her drawing (man, house, cat sitting on six legs, pumpkin, engine) was unimaginative and stereotyped. She used her right hand for writing, her left for everything else; she was left-footed and right-eyed.

She knew the days of the week. She began to name them: "Saturday, Sunday, Monday," then said, "You go to school" (meaning, "on Monday"), then stopped as if the performance were completed.

Throughout all these procedures, in which—often after several repetitions of the question or command—she complied almost automatically, she scribbled words spontaneously: "oranges"; "lemons"; "bananas"; "grapes"; "cherries"; "apples"; "apricots"; "tangerine"; "grapefruits"; "watermelon juice"; the words sometimes ran into each other and were obviously not meant for others to read.

She frequently interrupted whatever "conversation" there was with references to "motor transports" and "piggy-back," both of which—according to her father—had preoccupied her for quite some time. She said, for instance, "I saw motor transports"; "I saw piggy-back when I went to school."

Her mother remarked, "Appendages fascinate her, like a smoke stack or a pendulum." Her father had previously stated: "Recent interest in sexual matters, hanging about when we take a bath, and obsessive interest in toilets."

Barbara was placed at the Devereux Schools, where she is making some progress in learning to relate herself to people.

Case 6. Virginia S., born September 13, 1931, has resided at a state training school for the feebleminded since 1936, with the exception of one month in 1938, when she was paroled to a school for the deaf "for educational opportunity." Dr. Esther L. Richards, who saw her several times, clearly recognized that she was neither deaf nor feebleminded and wrote in May, 1941:

> Virginia stands out from other children [at the training school] because she is absolutely different from any of the others. She is neat and tidy, does not play with other children, and does not seem to be deaf from gross tests, but does not talk. The child will amuse herself by the hour putting picture puzzles together, sticking to them until they are done. I have seen her with a box filled with the parts of two puzzles gradually work out the pieces for each. All findings seem to be in the nature of a congenital abnormality which looks as if it were more of a personality abnormality than an organic defect.

Virginia, the younger of two siblings, was the daughter of a psychiatrist, who said of himself (in December, 1941): "I have never liked children, probably a reaction on my part to the restraint from movement (travel), the minor interruptions and commotions."

Of Virginia's mother, her husband said: "She is not by any means the mother type. Her attitude [toward a child] is more like toward a doll or pet than anything else."

Virginia's brother, Philip, five years her senior, when referred to us because of severe stuttering at 15 years of age, burst out in tears when asked how things were at home and he sobbed: "The only time my father has ever had anything to do with me was when he scolded me for doing something wrong."

His mother did not contribute even that much. He felt that all his life he had lived in "a frosty atmosphere" with two inapproachable strangers.

In August, 1938, the psychologist at the training school observed that Virginia could respond to sounds, the calling of her name, and the command, "Look!"

> She pays no attention to what is said to her but quickly comprehends whatever is expected. Her performance reflects discrimination, care, and precision.

With the nonlanguage items of the Binet and Merrill-Palmer tests, she achieved an I.Q. of 94. "Without a doubt," commented the psychologist,

> Her intelligence is superior to this. . . . She is quiet, solemn, composed. Not once have I seen her smile. She retires within herself, segregating herself from others. She seems to be in a world of her own, oblivious to all but the center of interest in the presiding situation. She is mostly self-sufficient and independent. When others encroach upon her integrity, she tolerates them with indifference. There was no manifestation of friendliness or interest in persons. On the other hand, she finds pleasure in dealing with things, about which she shows imagination and initiative. Typically, there is no display of affection. . . .
>
> *Psychologist's note, October, 1939.* Today Virginia was much more at home in the office. She remembered (after more than a year) where the toys were kept and helped herself. She could not be persuaded to participate in test procedures, would not wait for demonstrations when they were required. Quick, skilled moves. Trial and error plus insight. Very few futile moves. Immediate retesting reduced the time and error by more than half. There are times, more often than not, in which she is completely oblivious to all but her immediate focus of attention. . . .

January, 1940. Mostly she is quiet, as she has always worked and played alone. She has not resisted authority or caused any special trouble. During group activities, she soon becomes restless, squirms, and wants to leave to satisfy her curiosity about something else-where. She does make some vocal sounds, crying out if repressed or opposed too much by another child. She hums to herself, and in December I heard her hum the perfect tune of a Christmas hymn while she was pasting paper chains.

June, 1940. The school girls have said that Virginia says some words when at the cottage. They remember that she loves candy so much and says "Chocolate," "Marshmallow," also "Mama" and "Baby."

When seen on October 11, 1942, Virginia was a tall, slender, very neatly dressed 11-year-old girl. She responded when called by getting up and coming nearer, without ever looking up to the person who called her. She just stood listlessly, looking into space. Occasionally, in answer to questions, she muttered, "Mamma, baby." When a group was formed around the piano, one child playing and the others singing, Virginia sat among the children, seemingly not even noticing what went on, and gave the impression of being self-absorbed. She did not seem to notice when the children stopped singing. When the group dispersed she did not change her position and appeared not to be aware of the change of scene. She had an intelligent physiognomy, though her eyes had a blank expression.

Case 7. Herbert B. was referred on February 5, 1941, at 3 years, 2 months of age. He was thought to be seriously retarded in intellectual development. There were no physical abnormalities except for undescended testicles. His electroencephalogram was normal.

Herbert was born November 16, 1937, two weeks before term by elective cesarean section; his birth weight was $6\frac{1}{4}$ pounds. He vomited all food from birth through the third month. Then vomiting ceased almost abruptly and, except for occasional regurgitation, feeding proceeded satisfactorily. According to his mother, he was "always slow and quiet." For a time he was believed to be deaf because "he did not register any change of expression when spoken to or when in the presence of other people; also, he made no attempt to speak or to form words." He held up his head at 4 months and sat at 8 months, but did not try to walk until 2 years old, when suddenly "he began to walk without any preliminary crawling or assistance by chairs." He persistently refused to take fluid in any but an all-glass container. Once, while at a hospital, he went three days without fluid because it was offered in tin cups. He was "tremendously frightened by running water, gas burners, and many other things." He became upset by any change of an accustomed pattern: "if he notices change, he is very fussy and cries." But he himself liked to pull blinds up and down, to tear cardboard boxes into small pieces and play with them for hours, and to close and open the wings of doors.

Herbert's parents separated shortly after his birth. The father, a psychiatrist, is described as "a man of unusual intelligence, sensitive, restless, introspective, taking himself very seriously, not interested in people, mostly living within himself, at times alcoholic." The mother, a physician, speaks of herself as "energetic and outgoing, fond of people and children but having little insight into their problems, finding it a great deal easier to accept people rather than try to understand them." Herbert is the youngest of three children. The second is a normal, healthy boy. The oldest, Dorothy, born in June, 1934, after thirty-six hours of hard labor, seemed alert and responsive as an infant and said many words at 18 months, but toward the end of the second year she "did not show much progression in her play relationships or in contacts with other people." She wanted to be left alone, danced about in circles, made queer noises with her mouth, and *ignored persons completely* except for her mother, to whom she clung "in panic and general agitation." (Her father hated her ostensibly.) "Her speech was very meager and expression of ideas completely lacking. She had *difficulties with her pronouns* and would repeat 'you' and 'I' instead of using them for the proper persons." She was first declared to be feebleminded, then schizophrenic, but after the parents separated (the children remaining with their mother), she "blossomed out." She now attends school, where she makes good progress; she talks well, has an I.Q. of 108, and—though sensitive and moderately apprehensive—is interested in people and gets along reasonably well with them.

Herbert, when examined on his first visit, showed a remarkably intelligent physiognomy and good motor coordination. Within certain limits, he displayed astounding purposefulness in the pursuit of self-selected goals. Among a group of blocks, he instantly recognized those that were glued to a board and those that were detachable. He could build a tower of blocks as skilfully and as high as any child of his age or even older. He could not be diverted from his, self-chosen occupations. He was annoyed by any interference, shoving intruders away (without ever looking at them), or screaming when the shoving had no effect.

He was again seen at 4 years, 7 months, and again at 5 years, 2 months of age. He still did not speak. Both times he entered the office without paying the slightest attention to the people present. He went after the Seguin form board and instantly busied himself putting the figures into their proper spaces and taking them out again adroitly and quickly. When interfered with he whined impatiently. When one figure was stealthily removed, he immediately noticed its absence, became disturbed, but promptly forgot all about it when it was put back. At times, after he had finally quieted down following the upset caused by the removal of the form board, he jumped up and down on the couch with an ecstatic expression on his face. He did not respond to being called or to any other words addressed to him. He was completely absorbed in whatever he did. He never smiled. He sometimes uttered inarticulate sounds in a monotonous singsong manner. At one time he gently stroked his mother's leg and touched it with his lips. He very frequently brought blocks and other objects to his lips. There was an almost photographic likeness of his behavior during the two visits, with the main exception that at 4 years he showed apprehension and shrank back when a match was lighted, while at 5 years he reacted by jumping up and down ecstatically.

Case 8. Alfred L. was brought by his mother in November, 1935, at 3½ years of age with this complaint:

> He has gradually shown a marked tendency toward developing one special interest which will completely dominate his day's activities. He talks of little else while the interest exists, he frets when he is not able to indulge in it (by seeing it, coming in contact with it, drawing pictures of it), and it is difficult to get his attention because of his preoccupation. . . . There has also been the problem of an overattachment to the world of objects and failure to develop the usual amount of social awareness.

Alfred was born in May, 1932, three weeks before term. For the first two months, "the feeding formula caused considerable concern but then he gained rapidly and became an unusually large and vigorous baby." He sat up at 5 months and walked at 14.

> Language developed slowly; he seemed to have no interest in it. He seldom tells experience. He still confuses pronouns. He never asks questions in the form of questions (with the appropriate inflection). Since he talked, there has been a tendency to repeat over and over one word or statement. He almost never says a sentence without repeating it. Yesterday, when looking at a picture, he said many times, "Some cows standing in the water." We counted fifty repetitions, then he stopped after several more and then began over and over.

He had a good deal of "worrying":

> He frets when the bread is put in the oven to be made into toast, and is afraid it will get burned and be hurt. He is upset when the sun sets. He is upset because the moon does not always appear in the sky at night. He prefers to play alone; he will get down from a piece of apparatus as soon as another child

approaches. He likes to work out some project with large boxes (make a trolley, for instance) and does not want anyone to get on it or interfere.

When infantile thumb sucking was prevented by mechanical devices, he gave it up and instead put various objects into his mouth. On several occasions pebbles were found in his stools. Shortly before his second birthday, he swallowed cotton from an Easter rabbit, aspirating some of the cotton, so that tracheotomy became necessary. A few months later, he swallowed some kerosene "with no ill effects."

Alfred was an only child. His father, 30 years old at the time of his birth, "does not get along well with people, is suspicious, easily hurt, easily roused to anger, has to be dragged out to visit friends, spends his spare time reading, gardening, and fishing." He is a chemist and a law school graduate. The mother, of the same age, is a "clinical psychologist," very obsessive and excitable. The paternal grandparents died early; the father was adopted by a minister. The maternal grandfather, a psychologist, was severely obsessive, had numerous tics, was given to "repeated hand washing, protracted thinking along one line, fear of being alone, cardiac fears." The grandmother, "an excitable, explosive person, has done public speaking, published several books, is an incessant solitaire player, greatly worried over money matters." A maternal uncle frequently ran away from home and school, joined the marines, and later "made a splendid adjustment in commercial life."

The mother left her husband two months after Alfred's birth. The child has lived with his mother and maternal grandparents. "In the home is a nursery school and kindergarten (run by the mother), which creates some confusion for the child." Alfred did not see his father until he was 3 years, 4 months old, when the mother decided that "he should know his father" and "took steps to have the father come to the home to see the child."

Alfred, upon entering the office, paid no attention to the examiner. He immediately spotted a train in the toy cabinet, took it out, and connected and disconnected the cars in a slow, monotonous manner. He kept saying many times, "More train—more train—more train." He repeatedly "counted" the car windows: "One, two windows—one, two windows—one, two windows—four window, eight window, eight windows." He could not in any way be distracted from the trains. A Binet test was attempted in a room in which there were no trains. It was possible with much difficulty to pierce from time to time through his preoccupations. He finally complied in most instances in a manner that clearly indicated that he wanted to get through with the particular intrusion; this was repeated with each individual item of the task. In the end he achieved an *I.Q. of 140.*

The mother did not bring him back after this first visit because of "his continued distress when confronted with a member of the medical profession." In August, 1938, she sent upon request a written report of his development. From this report, the following passages are quoted:

> He is called a lone wolf. He prefers to play alone and avoids groups of children at play. He does not pay much attention to adults except when demanding stories. He avoids competition. He reads simple stories to himself. He is very fearful of being hurt, talks a great deal about the use of the electric chair. He is thrown into a panic when anyone accidentally covers his face.

Alfred was again referred in June, 1941. His parents had decided to live together. Prior to that the boy had been in eleven different schools. He had been kept in bed often because of colds, bronchitis, chickenpox, streptococcus infection, impetigo, and a vaguely described condition which the mother—the assurances of various pediatricians to the contrary notwithstanding—insisted was "rheumatic fever." While in the hospital, he is said to have behaved "like a manic patient." (The mother liked to call herself a psychiatrist and to make "psychiatric" diagnoses of the child.) From the mother's report, which combined obsessive enumeration of detailed instances with "explanations" trying to prove Alfred's "normalcy," the following information was gathered.

He had begun to play with children younger than himself, "using them as puppets—that's all." He had been stuffed with music, dramatics, and recitals, and had an excellent rote memory. He still was "terribly engrossed" in his play, didn't want people around, just couldn't relax:

> He had many fears, almost always connected with mechanical noise (meat grinders, vacuum cleaners, street cars, trains, etc.). Usually he winds up with an obsessed interest in the things he was afraid of. Now he is afraid of the shrillness of a dog's barking.

Alfred was extremely tense during the entire interview, and very serious-minded, to such an extent that had it not been for his juvenile voice, he might have given the impression of a worried and preoccupied little old man. At the same time, he was very restless and showed considerable pressure of talk, which had nothing personal in it but consisted of obsessive questions about windows, shades, dark rooms, especially the X-ray room. He never smiled. No change of topic could get him away from the topic of light and darkness. But in between he answered the examiner's questions, which often had to be repeated several times, and to which he sometimes responded as the result of a bargain—"You answer my question, and I'll answer yours." He was painstakingly specific in his definitions. A balloon "is made out of lined rubber and has air in it and some have gas and sometimes they go up in the air and sometimes they can hold up and when they got a hole in it they'll bust up; if people squeeze they'll bust. Isn't it right?" A tiger "is a thing, animal, striped, like a cat, can scratch, eats people up, wild, lives in the jungle sometimes and in the forests, mostly in the jungle. Isn't it right?" This question "Isn't it right?" was definitely meant to be answered; there was a serious desire to be assured that the definition was sufficiently complete.

He was often confused about the meaning of words. When shown a picture and asked, "What is this picture about?" he replied, "People are moving *about*."

He once stopped and asked, very much perplexed, why there was "The Johns Hopkins Hospital" printed on the history sheets: "Why do they have to say it?" This, to him, was a real problem of major importance, calling for a great deal of thought and discussion. Since the histories were taken at the hospital, why should it be necessary to have the name on every sheet, though the person writing on it knew where he was writing? The examiner, whom he remembered very well from his visit six years previously, was to him nothing more nor less than a person who was expected to answer his obsessive questions about darkness and light.

Case 9. Charles N. was brought by his mother on February 2, 1943, at 4½ years of age, with the chief complaint, "The thing that upsets me most is that I can't reach my baby." She introduced her report by saying: "I am trying hard not to govern my remarks by professional knowledge which has intruded in my own way of thinking by now."

As a baby, the boy was inactive, "slow and phlegmatic." He would lie in the crib, just staring. He would act almost as if hypnotized. He seemed to concentrate on doing one thing at a time. Hypothyroidism was suspected, and he was given thyroid extract, without any change of the general condition.

> His enjoyment and appreciation of music encouraged me to play records. When he was 1½ years old, he could discriminate between eighteen symphonies. He recognized the composer as soon as the first movement started. He would say "Beethoven." At about the same age, he began to spin toys and lids of bottles and jars by the hour. He had a lot of manual dexterity in ability to spin cylinders. He would watch it and get severely excited and jump up and down in ecstasy. Now he is interested in reflecting light from mirrors and catching reflections. When he is interested in a thing, you cannot change it. He would pay no attention to me and show no recognition of me if I enter the room. . . .
>
> The most impressive thing is his detachment and his inaccessibility. He walks as if he is in a shadow, lives in a world of his own where he cannot be reached. No sense of relationship to persons.

He went through a period of quoting another person; never offers anything himself. His entire conversation is a replica of whatever has been said to him. He used to speak of himself in the second person, now he uses the third person at times; he would say, "He wants"—never "I want." . . .

He is destructive; the furniture in his room looks like it has hunks out of it. He will break a purple crayon into two parts and say, "*You* had a beautiful purple crayon and now it's two pieces. Look what *you* did."

He developed an obsession about feces, would hide it anywhere (for instance, in drawers), would tease me if I walked into the room: "You soiled your pants, now you can't have your crayons!"

As a result, he is still not toilet trained. He never soils himself in the nursery school, always does it when he comes home. The same is true of wetting. He is proud of wetting, jumps up and down with ecstasy, says, "Look at the big puddle *he* made."

When he is with other people, he doesn't look up at them. Last July, we had a group of people. When Charles came in, it was just like a foal who'd been let out of an enclosure. He did not pay attention to them but their presence was felt. He will mimic a voice and he sings and some people would not notice any abnormality in the child. At school, he never envelops himself in a group, he is detached from the rest of the children, except when he is in the assembly; if there is music, he will go to the front row and sing.

He has a wonderful memory for words. Vocabulary is good, except for pronouns. He never initiates conversation, and conversation is limited, extensive only as far as objects go.

Charles was born normally, a planned and wanted child. He sat up at 6 months and walked at less than 15 months—"just stood up and walked one day—no preliminary creeping." He has had none of the usual children's diseases.

Charles is the oldest of three children. The father, a high-school graduate and a clothing merchant, is described as a "self-made, gentle, calm, and placid person." The mother has "a successful business record, theatrical booking office in New York, of remarkable equanimity." The other two children were 28 and 14 months old at the time of Charles' visit to the Clinic. The maternal grandmother, "very dynamic, forceful, hyperactive, almost hypomanic," has done some writing and composing. A maternal aunt, "psychoneurotic, very brilliant, given to hysterics," has written poems and songs. Another aunt was referred to as "the amazon of the family." A maternal uncle, a psychiatrist, has considerable musical talent. The paternal relatives are described as "ordinary simple people."

Charles was a well developed, intelligent-looking boy, who was in good physical health. He wore glasses. When he entered the office, he paid not the slightest attention to the people present (three physicians, his mother, and his uncle). Without looking at anyone, he said, "Give me a pencil!" and took a piece of paper from the desk and wrote something resembling a figure 2 (a large desk calendar prominently displayed a figure 2; the day was February 2). He had brought with him a copy of *Readers Digest* and was fascinated by a picture of a baby. He said, "Look at the funny baby," innumerable times, occasionally adding, "Is he not funny? Is he not sweet?"

When the book was taken away from him, he struggled with the hand that held it, without looking at the *person* who had taken the book. When he was pricked with a pin, he said, "What's this?" and answered his own question: "It is a needle."

He looked timidly at the pin, shrank from further pricks, but at no time did he seem to connect the pricking with the *person* who held the pin. When the *Readers Digest* was taken from him and thrown on the floor and a foot placed over it, he tried to remove the foot as if it were another detached and interfering object, again with no concern for the *person* to whom the foot belonged. He once turned to his mother and excitedly said, "Give it to you!"

When confronted with the Seguin form board, he was mainly interested in the names of the forms, before putting them into their appropriate holes. He often spun the forms around, jumping up and down excitedly while they were in motion. The whole performance was very repetitions. He never used language as a means of communicating with people. He remembered names, such as "octagon," "diamond," "oblong block," but nevertheless kept asking, "What is this?"

He did not respond to being called and did not look at his mother when she spoke to him. When the blocks were removed, he screamed, stamped his feet, and cried, "I'll give it to you!" (meaning "You give it to me"). He was very skilful in his movements.

Charles was placed at the Devereux Schools.

Case 10. John F. was first seen on February 13, 1940, at 2 years, 4 months of age.

The father said: "The main thing that worries me is the difficulty in feeding. That is the essential thing, and secondly his slowness in development. During the first days of life he did not take the breast satisfactorily. After fifteen days he was changed from breast to bottle but did not take the bottle satisfactorily. There is a long story of trying to get food down. We have tried everything under the sun. He has been immature all along. At 20 months he first started to walk. He sucks his thumb and grinds his teeth quite frequently and rolls from side to side before sleeping. If we don't do what he wants, he will scream and yell."

John was born September 19, 1937; his birth weight was $7\frac{1}{2}$ pounds. There were frequent hospitalizations because of the feeding problem. No physical disorder was ever found, except that the anterior fontanelle did not close until he was $2\frac{1}{2}$ years of age. He suffered from repeated colds and otitis media, which necessitated bilateral myringotomy.

John was an only child until February, 1943. The father, a psychiatrist, is "a very calm, placid, emotionally stable person, who is the soothing element in the family." The mother, a high-school graduate, worked as secretary in a pathology laboratory before marriage—"a hypomanic type of person; sees everything as a pathological specimen rather than well; throughout the pregnancy she was very apprehensive, afraid she would not live through the labor." The maternal grandmother is "obsessive about religion and washes her hands every few minutes." The maternal grandfather was an accountant.

John was brought to the office by both parents. He wandered about the room constantly and aimlessly. Except for spontaneous scribbling, he never brought two objects into relation to each other. He did not respond to the simplest commands, except that his parents with much difficulty elicited bye-bye, pat-a-cake, and peek-a-boo gestures, performed clumsily. His typical attitude toward objects was to throw them on the floor.

Three months later, his vocabulary showed remarkable improvement, though his articulation was defective. Mild obsessive trends were reported, such as pushing aside the first spoonful of every dish. His excursions about the office were slightly more purposeful.

At the end of his fourth year, he was able to form a very limited kind of affective contact, and even that only with a very limited number of people. Once such a relationship had been established, it had to continue in exactly the same channels. He was capable of forming elaborate and grammatically correct sentences, but he used the pronoun of the second person when referring to himself. He used language not as a means of communication but mainly as a repetition of things he had heard, without alteration of the personal pronoun. There was very marked obsessiveness. Daily routine must be adhered to rigidly; any slightest change of the pattern called forth outbursts of panic. There was endless repetition of sentences. He had an excellent rote memory and could recite many prayers, nursery rhymes, and songs "in different languages"; the mother did a great deal of stuffing in this respect and was very proud of these "achievements": "He can tell victrola records by their color and if one side of the record is identified, he remembers what is on the other side."

At $4\frac{1}{2}$ years, he began gradually to use pronouns adequately. Even though his direct interest was in objects only, he took great pains in attracting the attention of the examiner (Dr. Hilde Bruch) and in gaining her praise. However, he never addressed her directly and spontaneously. He wanted to make sure of the sameness of the environment literally by keeping doors and windows closed. When his mother opened the door "to pierce

259

through his obsession," he became violent in closing it again and finally, when again interfered with, burst helplessly into tears, utterly frustrated.

He was extremely upset upon seeing anything broken or incomplete. He noticed two dolls to which he had paid no attention before. He saw that one of them had no hat and became very much agitated, wandering about the room to look for the hat. When the hat was retrieved from another room, he instantly lost all interest in the dolls.

At 5½ years, he had good mastery of the use of pronouns. He had begun to feed himself satisfactorily. He saw a group photograph in the office and asked his father, "When are they coming out of the picture and coming in here?"

He was very serious about this. His father said something about the pictures they have at home on the wall. This disturbed John somewhat. He corrected his father: "We have them *near* the wall" ("on" apparently meaning to him "above" or "on top").

When he saw a penny, he said, "Penny. That's where you play tenpins." He had been given pennies when he knocked over tenpins while playing with his father at home.

He saw a dictionary and said to his father, "That's where you left the money?"

Once his father had left some money in a dictionary and asked John to tell his mother about it.

His father whistled a tune and John instantly and correctly identified it as "Mendelssohn's violin concerto." Though he could speak of things as big or pretty, he was utterly incapable of making comparisons ("Which is the bigger line? Prettier face?" etc.).

In December, 1942, and January, 1943, he had two series of predominantly right-sided *convulsions*, with conjugate deviation of the eyes to the right and transient paresis of the right arm. Neurologic examination showed no abnormalities. His eyegrounds were normal. An electroencephalogram indicated "focal disturbance in the left occipital region," but "a good part of the record could not be read because of the continuous marked artefacts due to the child's lack of cooperation."

Case 11. Elaine C. was brought by her parents on April 12, 1939, at the age of 7 years, 2 months, because of "unusual development": "She doesn't adjust. She stops at all abstractions. She doesn't understand other children's games, doesn't retain interest in stories read to her, wanders off and walks by herself, is especially fond of animals of all kinds, occasionally mimics them by walking on all fours and making strange noises."

Elaine was born on February 3, 1932, at term. She appeared healthy, took feedings well, stood up at 7 months and walked at less than a year. She could say four words at the end of her first year but made no progress in linguistic development for the following four years. Deafness was suspected but ruled out. Because of a febrile illness at 13 months, her increasing difficulties were interpreted as possible postencephalitic behavior disorder. Others blamed the mother, who was accused of inadequate handing of the child. Feeblemindedness was another diagnosis. For eighteen months, she was given anterior pituitary and thyroid preparations. "Some doctors," struck by Elaine's intelligent physiognomy, "thought she was a normal child and said that the would outgrow this."

At 2 years, she was sent to a nursery school, where "she independently went her way, not doing what the others did. She, for instance, drank the water and ate the plant when they were being taught to handle flowers." She developed an early interest in pictures of animals. Though generally restless, she could for hours concentrate on looking at such pictures, "especially engravings."

When she began to speak at about 5 years, she started out with complete though simple sentences that were "mechanical phrases" not related to the situation of the moment or related to it in a peculiar metaphorical way. She had an excellent vocabulary, knew especially the names and "classifications" of animals. She did not use pronouns correctly, but used plurals and tenses well. She "could not use negatives but recognized their meaning when others used them."

There were many peculiarities in her relation to situations:

> She can count by rote. She can set the table for numbers of people if the names are given her or enumerated in any way, but she cannot set the table "for three." If sent for a specific object in a certain place, she cannot bring it if it is somewhere else but still visible.

She was "frightened" by noises and anything moving toward her. She was so afraid of the vacuum cleaner that she would not even go near the closet where it was kept, and when it was used, ran out into the garage, covering her ears with her hands.

Elaine was the older of two children. Her father, aged 36, studied law and the liberal arts in three universities (including the Sorbonne), was an advertising copy writer, "one of those chronically thin persons, nervous energy readily expended." He was at one time editor of a magazine. The mother, aged 32, a "self-controlled, placid, logical person," had done editorial work for a magazine before marriage. The maternal grandfather was a newspaper editor, the grandmother was "emotionally unstable."

Elaine had been examined by a Boston psychologist at nearly 7 years of age. The report stated among other things:

> Her attitude toward the examiner remained vague and detached. Even when annoyed by restraint, she might vigorously push aside a table or restraining hand with a scream, but she made no personal

appeal for help or sympathy. At favorable moments she was competent in handling her crayons or assembling pieces to form pictures of animals. She could name a wide variety of pictures, including elephants, alligators, and dinosaurs. She used language in simple sentence structure, but rarely answered a direct question. As she plays, she repeats over and over phrases which are irrelevant to the immediate situation.

Physically the child was in good health. Her electroencephalogram was normal.

When examined in April, 1939, she shook hands with the physician upon request, without looking at him, then ran to the window and looked out. She automatically heeded the invitation to sit down. Her reaction to questions—after several repetitions—was an echolalia type reproduction of the whole question or, if it was too lengthy, of the end portion. She had no real contact with the persons in the office. Her expression was blank, though not unintelligent, and there were no communicative gestures. At one time, without changing her physiognomy, she said suddenly: "Fishes don't cry." After a time, she got up and left the room without asking or showing fear.

She was placed at the Child Study Home of Maryland, where she remained for three weeks and was studied by Drs. Eugenia S. Cameron and George Frankl. While there, she soon learned the names of all the children, knew the color of their eyes, the bed in which each slept, and many other details about them, but never entered into any relationship with them. When taken to the playgrounds, she was extremely upset and ran back to her room. She was very restless but when allowed to look at pictures, play alone with blocks, draw, or string beads, she could entertain herself contentedly for hours. Any noise, any interruption disturbed her. Once, when on the toilet seat, she heard a knocking in the pipes; for several days thereafter, even when put on a chamber pot in her own room, she did not move her bowels, anxiously listening for the noise. She frequently ejaculated stereotyped phrases, such as, "Dinosaurs don't cry"; "Crayfish, sharks, fish, and rocks"; "Crayfish and forks live in children's tummies"; "Butterflies live in children's stomachs, and in their panties, too"; "Fish have sharp teeth and bite little children"; "There is war in the sky"; "Rocks and crags, I will kill" (grabbing her blanket and kicking it about the bed); "Gargoyles bite children and drink oil"; "I will crush old angle worm, he bites children" (gritting her teeth and spinning around in a circle, very excited); "Gargoyles have milk bags"; "Needle head. Pink wee-wee. Has a yellow leg. Cutting the dead deer. Poison deer. Poor Elaine. No tadpoles in the house. Men broke deer's leg" (while cutting the picture of a deer from a book); "Tigers and cats"; "Seals and salamanders"; "Bears and foxes."

A few excerpts from the observations follow:

Her language always has the same quality. Her speech is never accompanied by facial expression or gestures. She does not look into one's face. Her voice is peculiarly unmodulated, somewhat hoarse; she utters her words in an abrupt manner.

Her utterances are impersonal. She never uses the personal pronouns of the first and second persons correctly. She does not seem able to conceive the real meaning of these words.

Her grammar is inflexible. She uses sentences just as she has heard them, without adapting them grammatically to the situation of the moment. When she says, "Want me to draw a spider," she means, "I want you to draw a spider."

She affirms by repeating a question literally, and she negates by not complying.

Her speech is rarely communicative. She has no relation to children, has never talked to them, to be friendly with them, or to play with them. She moves among them like a strange being, as one moves between the pieces of furniture of a room.

She insists on the repetition of the same routine always. Interruption of the routine is one of the most frequent occasions for her outbursts. Her own activities are simple and repetitious. She is able to spend hours in some form of daydreaming and seems to be very happy with it. She is inclined to rhythmical movements which always are masturbatory. She masturbates more in periods of excitement than during calm happiness. . . . Her movements are quick and skilful.

Elaine was placed in a private school in Pennsylvania. In a recent letter, the father reported "rather amazing changes":

She is a tall, husky girl with clear eyes that have long since lost any trace of that animal wildness they periodically showed in the time you knew her. She speaks well on almost any subject, though with something of an odd intonation. Her conversation is still rambling talk, frequently with an amusing point, and it is only occasional, deliberate, and announced. She reads very well, but she reads fast, jumbling words, not pronouncing clearly, and not making proper emphases. Her range of information is really quite wide, and her memory almost infallible. It is obvious that Elaine is not "normal." Failure in anything leads to a feeling of defeat, of despair, and to a momentary fit of depression.

Discussion

The eleven children (eight boys and three girls) whose histories have been briefly presented offer, as is to be expected, individual differences in the degree of their disturbance, the manifestation of specific features, the family constellation, and the step-by-step development in the course of years. But even a quick review of the material makes the emergence of a number of essential common characteristics appear inevitable. These characteristics form a unique "syndrome," not heretofore reported, which seems to be rare enough, yet is probably more frequent than is indicated by the paucity of observed cases. It is quite possible that some such children have been viewed as feebleminded or schizophrenic. In fact, several children of our group were introduced to us as idiots or imbeciles, one still resides in a state school for the feebleminded, and two had been previously considered as schizophrenic.

The outstanding, "pathognomonic," fundamental disorder is the children's *inability to relate themselves* in the ordinary way to people and situations from the beginning of life. Their parents referred to them as having always been "self-sufficient"; "like in a shell"; "happiest when left alone"; "acting as if people weren't there"; "perfectly oblivious to everything about him"; "giving the impression of silent wisdom"; "failing to develop the usual amount of social awareness"; "acting almost as if hypnotized." This is not, as in schizophrenic children or adults, a departure from an initially present relationship; it is not a "withdrawal" from formerly existing participation. There is from the start an *extreme autistic aloneness* that, whenever possible, disregards, ignores, shuts out anything that comes to the child from the outside. Direct physical contact or such motion or noise as threatens to disrupt the aloneness is either treated "as if it weren't there" or, if this is no longer sufficient, resented painfully as distressing interference.

According to Gesell, the average child at 4 months of age makes an anticipatory motor adjustment by facial tension and shrugging attitude of the shoulders when lifted from a table or placed on a table. Gesell commented:

> It is possible that a less definite evidence of such adjustment may be found as low down as the neonatal period. Although a habit must be conditioned by experience, the opportunity for experience is almost universal and the response is sufficiently objective to merit further observation and record.

This universal experience is supplied by the frequency with which an infant is picked up by his mother and other persons. It is therefore highly significant that almost all mothers of our patients recalled their astonishment at the children's *failure to assume at any time an anticipatory posture* preparatory to being picked up. One father recalled that his daughter (Barbara) did not for years change her physiognomy or position in the least when the parents, upon coming home after a few hours' absence, approached her crib talking to her and making ready to pick her up.

The average infant learns during the first few months to adjust his body to the posture of the person who holds him. Our children were not able to do so for two or three years. We had an opportunity to observe 38-month-old Herbert in such a situation. His mother informed him in appropriate terms that she was going to lift him up, extending her arms in his direction. There was no response. She proceeded to take him up, and he allowed her to do so, remaining completely passive as if he were a sack of flour. It was the mother who had to do all the adjusting. Herbert was at that time capable of sitting, standing, and walking.

Eight of the eleven children acquired the *ability to speak* either at the usual age or after some delay. Three (Richard, Herbert, Virginia) have so far remained "mute." In none of the eight "speaking" children has language over a period of years served to convey meaning to others. They were, with the exception of John F., capable of clear articulation and phonation. Naming of objects presented no difficulty; even long and unusual words were learned and retained with remarkable facility. Almost all the parents reported, usually with much pride, that the children had learned at an early age to repeat an inordinate number of nursery rhymes, prayers, lists of animals, the roster of presidents, the alphabet forward and backward, even foreign-language (French) lullabies. Aside from the recital of sentences contained in the ready-made poems or other remembered pieces, it took a long time before they began to put words together. Other than that, "language" consisted mainly of "naming," of nouns identifying objects, adjectives indicating colors, and numbers indicating nothing specific.

Their *excellent rote memory*, coupled with the inability to use language in any other way, often led the parents to stuff them with more and more verses, zoologic and botanic names, titles and composers of victrola record pieces, and the like. Thus, from the start, language—which the children did not use for the purpose of communication—was deflected in a considerable measure to a self-sufficient, semantically and conversationally valueless or grossly distorted memory exercise. To a child 2 or 3 years old, all these words, numbers, and poems ("questions and answers of the Presbyterian Catechism"; "Mendelssohn's violin concerto"; the Twenty-third Psalm"; a French lullaby; an encyclopedia index page) could hardly have more meaning than sets of nonsense syllables to adults. It is difficult to know for certain whether the stuffing as such has contributed essentially to the course of the psychopathologic condition. But it is also difficult to imagine that it did not cut deeply into the development of language as a tool for receiving and imparting meaningful messages.

As far as the communicative functions of speech are concerned, there is no fundamental difference between the eight speaking and the three mute children. Richard was once overheard by his boarding mother to say distinctly, "Good night." Justified skepticism about this observation was later dispelled when this "mute" child was seen in the office shaping his mouth in silent repetition of words when asked to say certain things. "Mute" Virginia—so her cottage mates insisted—was heard repeatedly to say, "Chocolate"; "Marshmallow"; "Mama"; "Baby."

When sentences are finally formed, they are for a long time mostly parrot-like repetitions of heard word combinations. They are sometimes echoed immediately, but they are just as often "stored" by the child and uttered at a later date. One may, if one wishes, speak of *delayed echolalia*. Affirmation is indicated by literal repetition of a question. "Yes" is a concept that it takes the children many years to acquire. They are incapable of using it as a general symbol of assent. Donald learned to say "Yes" when his father told him that he would put him on his shoulders if he said "Yes." This word then came to "mean" only the desire to be put on his father's shoulders. It took many months before he could detach the word "yes" from this specific situation, and it took much longer before he was able to use it as a general term of affirmation.

The same type of *literalness* exists also with regard to prepositions. Alfred, when asked, "What is this picture about?" replied: "People are moving *about*."

John F. corrected his father's statement about pictures on the wall; the pictures were *"near* the wall." Donald T., requested to put something *down*, promptly put in on the floor. Apparently the meaning of a word becomes inflexible and cannot be used with any but the originally acquired connotation.

There is no difficulty with plurals and tenses. But the absence of spontaneous sentence formation and the echolalia type reproduction has, in every one of the eight speaking children, given rise to a peculiar grammatical phenomenon. *Personal pronouns are repeated just as heard*, with no change to suit the altered situation. The child, once told by his mother, "Now I will give you your milk," expresses the desire for milk in exactly the same words. Consequently, he comes to speak of himself always as "you," and of the person addressed as "I." Not only the words, but even the intonation is retained. If the mother's original remark has been made in form of a question, it is reproduced with the grammatical form and the inflection of a question. The repetition "Are you ready for your dessert?" means that the child is ready for his dessert. There is a set, not-to-be-changed phrase for every specific occasion. The pronominal fixation remains until about the sixth year of life, when the child gradually learns to speak of himself in the first person, and of the individual addressed in the second person. In the transitional period, he sometimes still reverts to the earlier form or at times refers to himself in the third person.

The fact that the children echo things heard does not signify that they "attend" when spoken to. It often takes numerous reiterations of a question or command before there is even so much as an echoed response. Not less than seven of the children were therefore considered as deaf or hard of hearing. There is an all-powerful need for being left undisturbed. Everything that is brought to the child from the outside, everything that changes his external or even internal environment, represents a dreaded intrusion.

Food is the earliest intrusion that is brought to the child from the outside. David Levy observed that affect-hungry children, when placed in foster homes where they are well treated, at first demand excessive quantities of food. Hilde Bruch, in her studies of obese children, found that overeating often resulted when affectionate offerings from the parents were lacking or considered unsatisfactory. Our patients, reversely, anxious to keep the outside world away, indicated this by the refusal of food. Donald, Paul ("vomited a great deal during the first year"), Barbara "had to be tube-fed until 1 year of age"), Herbert, Alfred, and John presented severe feeding difficulty from the beginning of life. Most of them, after an unsuccessful struggle, constantly interfered with, finally gave up the struggle and of a sudden began eating satisfactorily.

Another intrusion comes from *loud noises and moving objects*, which are therefore reacted to with horror. Tricycles, swings, elevators, vacuum cleaners, running water, gas burners, mechanical toys, egg beaters, even the wind could on occasions bring about a major panic. One of the children was even afraid to go near the closet in which the vacuum cleaner was kept. Injections and examinations with stethoscope or otoscope created a grave emotional crisis. Yet it is not the noise or motion itself that is dreaded. The disturbance comes from the noise or motion that intrudes itself, or threatens to intrude itself, upon the child's aloneness. The child himself can happily make as great a noise as any that he dreads and move objects about to his heart's desire.

But the child's noises and motions and all of his performances are as *monotonously repetitious* as are his verbal utterances. There is a marked limitation in the variety of his spontaneous activities. The child's behavior is governed by an *anxiously obsessive desire for the maintenance of sameness* that nobody but the child himself may disrupt on rare occasions. Changes of routine, of furniture arrangement, of a pattern, of the order in which everyday acts are carried out, can drive him to despair. When John's parents got ready to move to a new home, the child was frantic when he saw the moving men roll up the rug in his room. He was acutely upset until the moment when, in the new home, he saw his furniture arranged in the same manner as before. He looked pleased, all anxiety was suddenly gone, and he went around affectionately patting each piece. Once blocks, beads, sticks have been put together in a certain way, they are always regrouped in exactly the same way, even though there was no definite design. The children's memory was phenomenal in this respect. After the lapse of several days, a multitude of blocks could be rearranged in precisely the same unorganized pattern, with the same color of each block turned up, with each picture or letter on the upper surface of each block facing in the same direction as before. The absence of a block or the presence of a supernumerary block was noticed immediately, and there was an imperative demand for the restoration of the missing piece. If someone removed a block, the child struggled to get it back, going into a panic tantrum until he regained it, and then promptly and with sudden calm after the storm returned to the design and replaced the block.

This insistence on sameness led several of the children to become greatly disturbed upon the sight of anything broken or incomplete. A great part of the day was spent in demanding not only the sameness of the wording of a request but also the sameness of the sequence of events. Donald would not leave his bed after his nap until after he had said, "Boo, say 'Don, do you want to get down?'" and the mother had complied. But this was not all. The act was still not considered completed. Donald would continue, "Now say 'All right.'" Again the mother had to comply, or there was screaming until the performance was completed. All of this ritual was an indispensable part of the act of getting up after a nap. Every other activity had to be completed from beginning to end in the manner in which it had been started originally. It was impossible to return from a walk without having covered the same ground as had been covered before. The sight of a broken crossbar on a garage door on his regular daily tour so upset Charles that he kept talking and asking about it for weeks on end, even while spending a few days in a distant city. One of the children noticed a crack in the office ceiling and kept asking anxiously and repeatedly who had cracked the ceiling, not calmed by any answer given her. Another child, seeing one doll with a hat and another without a hat, could not be placated until the other hat was found and put on the doll's head. He then immediately lost interest in the two dolls; sameness and completeness had been restored, and all was well again.

The dread of change and incompleteness seems to be a major factor in the explanation of the monotonous repetitiousness and the resulting *limitation in the variety of spontaneous activity*. A situation, a performance, a sentence is not regarded as complete if it is not made up of exactly the same elements that were present at the time the child was first confronted with it. If the slightest ingredient is altered or removed, the total situation is no longer the same and therefore is not accepted as such, or it is resented with impatience or even with a reaction of profound frustration. The inability to experience wholes without full attention to the constituent parts is somewhat reminiscent of the plight of children with specific reading disability who do not respond to the modern system of configurational reading instruction but must be taught to build up words from their alphabetic elements. This is perhaps one of the reasons why those children of our group who were old enough to be instructed in reading immediately became excessively preoccupied with the "spelling" of words, or why Donald, for example, was so disturbed over the fact that "light" and bite," having the same phonetic quality, should be spelled differently.

Objects that do not change their appearance and position, that retain their sameness and never threaten to interfere with the child's aloneness, are readily accepted by the autistic child. He has a good *relation to objects*; he is interested in them, can play with them happily for hours. He can be very fond of them, or get angry at them if, for instance, he cannot fit them into a certain space. When with them, he has a gratifying sense of undisputed power and control. Donald and Charles began in the second year of life to exercise this power by spinning everything that could be possibly spun and jumping up and down in ecstasy when they watched the objects whirl about. Frederick "jumped up and down in great glee" when he bowled and saw the pins go down. The children sensed and exercised the same power over their own bodies by rolling and other rhythmic movements. These actions and the accompanying ecstatic fervor strongly indicate the presence of *masturbatory orgastic gratification*.

The children's *relation to people* is altogether different. Every one of the children, upon entering the office, immediately went after blocks, toys, or other objects, without paying the least attention to the persons present. It would be wrong to say that they were not aware of the presence of persons. But the people, so long as they left the child alone, figured in about the same manner as did the desk, the bookshelf, or the filing cabinet. When the child was addressed, he was not bothered. He had the choice between not responding at all or, if a question was repeated too insistently, "getting it over with" and continuing with whatever he had been doing. Comings and goings, even of the mother, did not seem to register. Conversation going on in the room elicited no interest. If the adults did not try to enter the child's domain, he would at times, while moving between them, gently touch a hand or a knee as on other occasions he patted the desk or the couch. But he never looked into anyone's face. If an adult forcibly intruded himself by taking a block away or stepping on an object that the child needed, the child struggled and became angry with the hand or the foot, which was dealt with per se and not as a part of a person. He never addressed a word or a look to the owner of the hand or foot. When the object was retrieved, the child's mood changed abruptly to one of placidity. When pricked, he showed fear of the *pin* but not of the person who pricked him.

The relation to the members of the household or to other children did not differ from that to the people at the office. Profound aloneness dominates all behavior. The father or mother or both may have been away for an hour or a month; at their homecoming, there is no indication that the child has been even aware of their absence. After many outbursts of frustration, he gradually and reluctantly learns to compromise when he finds no way out, obeys certain orders, complies in matters of daily routine, but always strictly insists on the observance of his rituals. When there is company, he moves among the people "like a stranger" or, as one mother put it, "like a foal who had been let out of an enclosure." When with other children, he does not play with them. He plays alone while they are around, maintaining no bodily, physiognomic, or verbal contact with them. He does not take part in competitive games. He just is there; and if sometimes he happens to stroll as far as the periphery of a group, he soon removes himself and remains alone. At the same time, he quickly becomes familiar with the names of all the children of the group, may know the color of each child's hair, and other details about each child.

There is a far better relationship with pictures of people than with people themselves. Pictures, after all, cannot interfere. Charles was affectionately interested in the picture of a child in a magazine advertisement. He remarked repeatedly about the child's sweetness and beauty. Elaine was fascinated by pictures of animals but would not go near a live animal. John made no distinction between real and depicted people. When he saw a group photograph, he asked seriously when the people would step out of the picture and come into the room.

Even though most of these children were at one time or another looked upon as feebleminded, they are all unquestionably endowed with good *cognitive potentialities*. They all have strikingly intelligent physiognomies. Their faces at the same time give the impression of *serious-mindedness* and, in the presence of others, an anxious *tenseness*, probably because of the uneasy anticipation of possible interference. When alone with objects, there is often a placid smile and an expression of beatitude, sometimes accompanied by happy though monotonous humming and singing. The astounding vocabulary of the speaking children, the excellent memory for events of several years before, the phenomenal rote memory for poems and names, and the precise recollection of complex patterns and sequences, bespeak good intelligence in the sense in which this word is commonly used. Binet or similar testing could not be carried out because of limited accessibility. But all the children did well with the Seguin form board.

Physically, the children were essentially normal. Five had relatively large heads. Several of the children were somewhat clumsy in gait and gross motor performances, but all were very skilful in terms of finer muscle coordination. Electroencephalograms were normal in the case of all but John, whose anterior fontanelle did not close until he was $2^1/_2$ years old, and who at $5^1/_4$ years had two series of predominantly right-sided convulsions. Frederick had a supernumerary nipple in the left axilla; there were no other instances of congenital anomalies.

There is one other very interesting common denominator in the backgrounds of these children. *They all come of highly intelligent families.* Four fathers are psychiatrists, one is a brilliant lawyer, one a chemist and law school graduate employed in the government Patent Office, one a plant pathologist, one a professor of forestry, one an advertising copy writer who has a degree in law and has studied in three universities, one is a mining engineer, and one a successful business man. Nine of the eleven mothers are

270

college graduates. Of the two who have only high-school education, one was secretary in a pathology laboratory, and the other ran a theatrical booking office in New York City before marriage. Among the others, there was a free-lance writer, a physician, a psychologist, a graduate nurse, and Frederick's mother was successively a purchasing agent, the director of secretarial studies in a girls' school, and a teacher of history. Among the grandparents and collaterals there are many physicians, scientists, writers, journalists, and students of art. All but three of the families are represented either in *Who's Who in America* or in *American Men of Science*, or in both.

Two of the children are Jewish, the others are all of Anglo-Saxon descent. Three are "only" children, five are the first-born of two children in their respective families, one is the oldest of three children, one is the younger of two, and one the youngest of three.

Comment

The combination of extreme autism, obsessiveness, stereotypy, and echolalia brings the total picture into relationship with some of the basic schizophrenic phenomena. Some of the children have indeed been diagnosed as of this type at one time or another. But in spite of the remarkable similarities, the condition differs in many respects from all other known instances of childhood schizophrenia.

First of all, even in cases with the earliest recorded onset of schizophrenia, including those of De Sanctis' dementia praecocissima and of Heller's dementia infantilis, the first observable manifestations were preceded by at least two years of essentially average development; the histories specifically emphasize a more or less gradual *change* in the patients' behavior. The children of our group have all shown their extreme aloneness from the very beginning of life, not responding to anything that comes to them from the outside world. This is most characteristically expressed in the recurrent report of failure of the child to assume an anticipatory posture upon being picked up, and of failure to adjust the body to that of the person holding him.

Second, our children are able to establish and maintain an excellent, purposeful, and "intelligent" relation to objects that do not threaten to interfere with their aloneness, but are from the start anxiously and tensely impervious to people, with whom for a long time they do not have any kind of direct affective contact. If dealing with another person becomes inevitable, then a temporary relationship is formed with the person's hand or foot as a definitely detached object, but not with the person himself.

All of the children's activities and utterances are governed rigidly and consistently by the powerful desire for aloneness and sameness. Their world must seem to them to be made up of elements that, once they have been experienced in a certain setting or sequence, cannot be tolerated in any other setting or sequence; nor can the setting or sequence be tolerated without all the original ingredients in the identical spatial or chronologic order. Hence the obsessive repetitiousness. Hence the reproduction of sentences without altering the pronouns to suit the occasion. Hence, perhaps, also the development of a truly phenomenal memory that enables the child to recall and reproduce complex "nonsense" patterns, no matter how unorganized they are, in exactly the same form as originally construed.

Five of our children have by now reached ages between 9 and 11 years. Except for Vivian S., who has been dumped in a school for the feebleminded, they show a very interesting course. The basic desire for aloneness and sameness has remained essentially unchanged, but there has been a varying degree of emergence from solitude, an acceptance of at least some people as being within the child's sphere of consideration, and a sufficient increase in the number of experienced patterns to refute the earlier impression of extreme limitation of the child's ideational content. One might perhaps put it this way: While the schizophrenic tries to solve his problem by stepping out of a world of which he has been a part and with which he has been in touch, our children gradually *compromise* by extending cautious feelers into a world in which they have been total strangers from the beginning. Between the ages of 5 and 6 years, they gradually abandon the echolalia and learn spontaneously to use personal pronouns with adequate reference. Language becomes more communicative, at first in the sense of a question-and-answer exercise, and then in the sense of greater spontaneity of sentence formation. Food is accepted without difficulty. Noises and motions are tolerated more than previously. The panic tantrums subside. The repetitiousness assumes the form of obsessive preoccupations. Contact with a limited number of people is established in a twofold way: people are included in the child's world to the extent to which they satisfy his needs, answer his obsessive questions, teach him how to read and to do things. Second, though people are still regarded as nuisances, their questions are answered and their commands are obeyed reluctantly, with the implication that it would be best to get these interferences over with, the sooner to be able to return to the still much desired aloneness. Between the ages of 6 and 8 years, the children begin to play in a group, still never *with* the other members of the play group, but at least on the periphery *alongside* the group. Reading skill is acquired quickly, but the children read monotonously, and a story or a moving picture is experienced in unrelated portions rather than in its coherent totality. All of this makes the family feel that, in spite of recognized "different" from other children, there is progress and improvement.

It is not easy to evaluate the fact that all of our patients have come of highly intelligent parents. This much is certain, that there is a great deal of obsessiveness in the family background. The very detailed diaries and reports and the frequent remembrance, after several years, that the children had learned to recite twenty-five questions and answers of the Presbyterian

Catechism, to sing thirty-seven nursery songs, or to discriminate between eighteen symphonies, furnish a telling illustration of parental obsessiveness.

One other fact stands out prominently. In the whole group, there are very few really warmhearted fathers and mothers. For the most part, the parents, grandparents, and collaterals are persons strongly preoccupied with abstractions of a scientific, literary, or artistic nature, and limited in genuine interest in people. Even some of the happiest marriages are rather cold and formal affiairs. Three of the marriages were dismal failures. The question arises whether or to what extent this fact has contributed to the condition of the children. The children's aloneness from the beginning of life makes it difficult to attribute the whole picture exclusively to the type of the early parental relations with our patients.

We must, then, assume that these children have come into the world with innate inability to form the usual, biologically provided affective contact with people, just as other children come into the world with innate physical or intellectual handcaps. If this assumption is correct, a further study of our children may help to furnish concrete criteria regarding the still diffuse notions about the constitutional components of emotional reactivity. For here we seem to have pure-culture examples of *inborn autistic disturbances of affective contact.**

Notes

From the Henry Phipps Psychiatric Clinic and the Harriet Lane Home for Invalid Children, the Johns Hopkins Hospital, and (cases 1 and 11) the Child Study Center of Maryland.

* Since the completion of this paper, 2 more cases of inborn autistic disturbance of affective contact have come under our observation.

117

ASPERGER'S SYNDROME: A CLINICAL ACCOUNT

Lorna Wing

Source: *Psychological Medicine*, 11, 1981: 115–129.

Synopsis

The clinical features, course, aetiology, epidemiology, differential diagnosis and management of Asperger's syndrome are described. Classification is discussed and reasons are given for including the syndrome, together with early childhood autism, in a wider group of conditions which have, in common, impairment of development of social interaction, communication and imagination.

Introduction

The many patterns of abnormal behaviour that cause diagnostic confusion include one originally described by the Austrian psychiatrist, Hans Asperger (1944, 1968, 1979). The name he chose for this pattern was *autistic psychopathy*, using the latter word in the technical sense of an abnormality of personality. This has led to misunderstanding because of the popular tendency to equate psychopathy with sociopathic behaviour. For this reason, the neutral term *Asperger's syndrome* is to be preferred and will be used here.

Not long before Asperger's original paper on this subject appeared in 1944, Kanner (1943) published his first account of the syndrome he called early infantile autism. The two conditions are, in many ways, similar, and the argument still continues as to whether they are varieties of the same underlying abnormality or are separate entities.

Whereas Kanner's work is widely known internationally, Asperger's contribution is considerably less familiar outside the German literature. The only published discussions of the subject in English known to the present author are by Van Krevelen (1971), Isaev & Kagan (1974), Mnukhin & Isaev (1975) (translation from Russian), Wing (1976), Chick *et al.* (1979),

Wolff & Barlow (1979) and Wolff & Chick (1980). In addition, a book by Bosch in which autism and Asperger's syndrome are compared, originally appearing in German in 1962, has been translated into English (Bosch, 1962). A paper given by Asperger in Switzerland in 1977 has appeared in an English version (Asperger, 1979). Robinson & Vitale (1954) and Adams (1973) gave clinical descriptions of children with behaviour resembling Asperger's syndrome, but without referring to this diagnosis.

In the present paper the syndrome will be described, illustrated with case histories, and the differential diagnosis and classification discussed. The account is based on Asperger's descriptions and on 34 cases, ranging in age from 5 to 35 years, personally examined and diagnosed by the author. Of these, 19 had the history and clinical picture of the syndrome in more or less typical form and 15 showed many of the features at the time they were seen, though they did not all have the characteristic early history (see below). Six of those in the series were identified as a result of an epidemiological study of early childhood psychoses in the Camberwell area of south-east London (Wing & Gould, 1979). The rest were referred to the author for diagnosis – 11 by their parents, through the family doctor, 2 by head teachers and 15 by other psychiatrists.

The following general description includes all the most typical features. But, as with any psychiatric syndrome identifiable only from a pattern of observable behaviour, there are difficulties in determining which are essential for diagnosis. Variations occur from person to person and it is rare to find, in any one case, all the details listed below.

The clinical picture

Illustrative case histories based on those of children and adults seen by the present author are to be found in the Appendix. Throughout the paper, the numbers in parentheses refer to these histories.

Asperger's description of the syndrome

Asperger noted that the syndrome was very much more common in boys than in girls. He believed that it was never recognized in infancy and usually not before the third year of life or later. The following description is based on Asperger's accounts.

Speech

The child usually begins to speak at the age expected in normal children, whereas walking may be delayed. A full command of grammar is sooner or later acquired, but there may be difficulty in using pronouns correctly, with the substitution of the second or third for the first person forms (No. 1). The content of speech is abnormal, tending to be pedantic and often consisting of lengthy disquisitions on favourite subjects (No. 2). Sometimes a word or phrase is repeated over and over again in a stereotyped fashion. The child or adult may invent some words. Subtle verbal jokes are not understood, though simple verbal humour may be appreciated.

Non-verbal communication

Non-verbal aspects of communication are also affected. There may be little facial expression except with strong emotions such as anger or misery. Vocal intonation tends to be monotonous and droning, or exaggerated. Gestures are limited, or else large and clumsy and inappropriate for the accompanying speech (No. 2). Comprehension of other people's expressions and gestures is poor and the person with Asperger's syndrome may misinterpret or ignore such non-verbal signs. At times he may earnestly gaze into another person's face, searching for the meaning that eludes him.

Social interaction

Perhaps the most obvious characteristic is impairment of two-way social interaction. This is not due primarily to a desire to withdraw from social contact. The problem arises from a lack of ability to understand and use the rules governing social behaviour. These rules are unwritten and unstated, complex, constantly changing, and effect speech, gesture, posture, movement, eye contact, choice of clothing, proximity to others, and many other aspects of behaviour. The degree of skill in this area varies among normal people, but those with Asperger's syndrome are outside the normal range. Their social behaviour is naïve and peculiar. They may be aware of their difficulties and even strive to overcome them, but in inappropriate ways and with signal lack of success. They do not have the intuitive knowledge of how to adapt their approaches and responses to fit in with the needs and personalities of others. Some are oversensitive to criticism and suspicious of other people. A small minority have a history of rather bizarre anti-social acts, perhaps because of their lack of empathy. This was true of 4 of the present series, one of whom injured another boy in the course of his experiments on the properties of chemicals.

Relations with the opposite sex provide a good example of the more general social ineptitude. A young man with Asperger's syndrome observes that most of his contemporaries have girl friends and eventually marry and have children. He wishes to be normal in this respect, but has no idea how to indicate his interest and attract a partner in a socially acceptable fashion. He may ask other people for a list of rules for talking to girls, or try to find the secret in books (No. 1). If he has a strong sex drive he may approach and touch or kiss a stranger, or someone much older or younger than himself, and, as a consequence, find himself in trouble with the police; or he may solve the problem by becoming solitary and withdrawn.

Repetitive activities and resistance to change

Children with this syndrome often enjoy spinning objects and watching them until the movement ceases, to a far greater extent than normal. They tend to become intensely attached to particular possessions and are very unhappy when away from familiar places.

Motor coordination

Gross motor movements are clumsy and ill-coordinated. Posture and gait appear odd (No. 1). Most people with this syndrome (90% of the 34 cases mentioned above) are poor at games involving motor skills, and sometimes the executive problems affect the ability to write or to draw. Stereotyped movements of the body and limbs are also mentioned by Asperger.

Skills and interest

Those with the syndrome in most typical form have certain skills as well as impairments. They have excellent rote memories and become intensely interested in one or two subjects, such as astronomy, geology, the history of the steam train, the genealogy of royalty, bus time-tables, prehistoric monsters, or the characters in a television serial, to the exclusion of all else. They absorb every available fact concerning their chosen field and talk about it at length, whether or not the listener is interested, but have little grasp of the meaning of the facts they learn. They may also excel at board games needing a good rote memory, such as chess (No. 2), and some have musical ability. Seventy-six per cent of the present author's series had special interests of this kind. However, some have specific learning problems, affecting arithmetical skills, reading, or, as mentioned above, writing.

Experiences at school

This combination of social and communication impairments and certain special skills gives an impression of marked eccentricity. The children may be mercilessly bullied at school, becoming, in consequence, anxious and afraid (Nos. 1 and 2). Those who are more fortunate in the schools they attend may be accepted as eccentric 'professors', and respected for their unusual abilities (No. 4). Asperger describes them as unsatisfactory students because they follow their own interests regardless of the teacher's instructions and the activities of the rest of the class (Nos. 3 and 4). Many eventually become aware that they are different from other people, especially as they approach adolescence, and, in consequence, become over-sensitive to criticism. They give the impression of fragile vulnerability and a pathetic childishness, which some find infinitely touching and others merely exasperating.

Modifications of Asperger's account

The present author has noted a number of additional items in the developmental history, not recorded by Asperger, which can sometimes be elicited by appropriate questioning of the parents. During the first year of life there may have been a lack of the normal interest and pleasure in human company that should be present from birth. Babbling may have been limited in quantity and quality. The child may not have drawn attention to things going on around him in order to share the interest with other people. He may not have brought his toys to show to his parents or visitors when he began to walk. In general, there is a lack of the intense urge to communicate in babble, gesture, movement, smiles, laughter and eventually speech that characterizes the normal baby and toddler (No. 3).

Imaginative pretend play does not occur at all in some of those with the syndrome, and in those who do have pretend play it is confined to one or two themes, enacted without variation, over and over again. These may be quite elaborate, but are pursued repetitively and do not involve other children unless the latter are willing to follow exactly the same pattern. It sometimes happens that the themes seen in this pseudo-pretend play continue as preoccupations in adult life, and form the main focus of an imaginary world (see the case history of Richard L. in Bosch, 1962).

There are also two points on which the present author would disagree with Asperger's observations. First, he states that speech develops before walking, and refers to 'an especially intimate relationship with language' and 'highly sophisticated linguistic skills'. Van Krevelen (1971) emphasized this as a point of differentiation from Kanner's early childhood autism, in which, usually, walking develops normally, or even earlier than average, whereas the onset of speech is markedly delayed or never occurs. However, slightly less than half of the present author's more typical cases of Asperger's syndrome were walking at the usual age, but were slow to talk. Half talked normally but were slow to walk, and one both walked and talked at the expected times. Despite the eventual good use of grammar and a large vocabulary, careful observation over a long enough period of time discloses that the content of speech is impoverished and much of it is copied inappropriately from other people or books (No. 3). The language used gives the impression of being learned by rote. The meanings of long and obscure words may be known, but not those of words used every day (No. 5). The peculiarities of non-verbal aspects of speech have already been mentioned.

Secondly, Asperger described people with his syndrome as capable of originality and creativity in their chosen field. It would be more true to say that their thought processes are confined to a narrow, pedantic, literal, but logical, chain of reasoning. The unusual quality of their approach arises from the tendency to select, as the starting point for the logical chain, some aspect of a subject that would be unlikely to occur to a normal person who has absorbed the attitudes current in his culture. Usually the result is inappropriate, but once in a while it gives new insight into a problem. Asperger also believed that people with his syndrome were of high intelligence, but he did not quote the results of standardized intellectual tests to support this. As will be seen from the case histories in the Appendix, the special abilities are based mainly on rote memory, while comprehension of the underlying meaning is poor. Those with the syndrome are conspicuously lacking in common sense.

It must be pointed out that the people described by the present author all had problems of adjustment or superimposed psychiatric illnesses severe enough to necessitate referral to a psychiatric clinic. Nine had left school or further education. Of these, 3 were employed, 3 had lost their jobs, and 3 had not obtained work. The author is also acquainted, through their parents who are members of the National Society for Autistic Children, with a few young adults reported to have some or all of the features of Asperger's syndrome, and who are using their special skills successfully in open employment. It would be inappropriate to give precise numbers or to include these in the series, because the author does not have access to case histories or assessment. For this reason, the series described here is probably biased towards those with more severe handicaps.

Course and prognosis

The published clinical descriptions are of children and young adults. No studies of the course and prognosis in later life are available.

Asperger emphasized the stability of the clinical picture throughout childhood, adolescence and at least into early adult life, apart from the increase in skills brought about by maturation. The major characteristics appear to be impervious to the effects of environment or education. He considered the social prognosis to be generally good, meaning that most developed far enough to be able to use their special skills to obtain employment. He also observed that some who had especially high levels of ability in the area of their special interests were able to follow careers in, for example, science and mathematics.

As Bosch (1962) pointed out, it is possible to find people with all the features characteristic of Asperger's syndrome other than normal or high intelligence. This applied to 20% of the series described here. If these are accepted as belonging to the same diagnostic category, then Asperger's rather hopeful view of the prognosis has to be modified to take such cases into account (see the case history of J. G., Appendix No. 5).

The prognosis is also affected by the occurrence of superimposed psychiatric illnesses. Clinically diagnosable anxiety and varying degrees of depression may be found, especially in late adolescence or early adult life, which seem to be related to a painful awareness of handicap and difference from other people (Nos. 2 and 3). Wolff & Chick (1980), in a follow-up study of 22 people with Asperger's syndrome, reported one who appeared to have a typical schizophrenic illness and another in whom this diagnosis was made, but less convincingly. Five of the 22 had attempted suicide by the time of early adult life.

The present author's series included 18 who were aged 16 and over at the time they were seen. Of these, 4 had an affective illness; 4 had become increasingly odd and withdrawn, probably with underlying depression; 1 had a psychosis with delusions and hallucinations that could not be classified; 1 had had an episode of catatonic stupor; 1 had bizarre behaviour and an unconfirmed diagnosis of schizophrenia; and 2 had bizarre behaviour, but no diagnosable psychiatric illness. Two of the foregoing had attempted suicide and 1 had talked of doing so. The rest were referred because of their problems in coping with the demands of adult life.

Though it appears that the risk of psychiatric illness in Asperger's syndrome is high, it is difficult to draw firm conclusions because of the nature of the samples that were studied. The 13 people mentioned above, before they were seen by the present author, had been referred to adult services because of superimposed psychiatric conditions, so the series was highly biased. Wolff's cases were somewhat less selective since they were referred as children and followed up into adult life, but, even so, they were clinic and not population based. Asperger (1944) noted that only 1 of his 200 cases developed schizophrenia. The true prevalence of psychiatric illnesses can be calculated only from an epidemiological study, including people with the syndrome not referred to psychiatric services.

Even in the absence of recognizable psychiatric disorder, adolescence may be a difficult time. The development of partial insight and increasing sexual awareness can cause much unhappiness (No. 1) and may lead to socially unacceptable behaviour. Peculiarities which may be ignored in a small child become very obvious in a young adult.

The degree of adjustment eventually achieved appears to be related to the level and variety of skills available and also to the temperament of the individual concerned. Good self-care, a special ability that can be used in paid employment, and a placid nature are needed if a person with Asperger's syndrome is to become socially independent.

Aetiology and pathology

Asperger (1944) considered his syndrome to be genetically transmitted. He reported that the characteristics tended to occur in the families, especially the fathers of those with the syndrome. Van Krevelen (1971) stated that, in many cases, the antecedents for generations back had been highly intellectual. In the present author's series, 55% had fathers who were in professional or managerial occupations, but the personalities of the parents were not studied systematically. In many cases, the mother alone was seen. The purpose of the interview was to discuss the problems of the child, not to investigate the parents. Including only those concerning whom some tentative conclusions could be drawn (from clinical impressions or evidence from other sources), it appeared that 5 out of 16 fathers and 2 out of 24 mothers had, to a marked degree, behaviour resembling that found in Asperger's syndrome. No features of the clinical picture appeared to be associated with higher or lower social class, level of education of the parents, or their personalities.

It is difficult to interpret the findings on social class, since the cases referred to clinics having a special interest in such problems are a selected group, with a strong bias towards higher social class and intellectual occupations in the parents. Schopler et al. (1979) and Wing (1980) noted a similar bias in the fathers of classically autistic children referred to clinics, which was not reflected in less selected groups with the same diagnosis. The findings concerning the parents' personalities have to be treated with caution because of the way they were obtained and the lack of any comparison group.

The syndrome can be found in children and adults with a history of pre-, peri- or post-natal conditions, such as anoxia at birth, that might have caused cerebral damage. This was true of nearly half of those seen by the present author (Nos. 3 and 4). Mnukhin & Isaev (1975) considered that the behaviour pattern was due to organic deficiency of brain function.

Emotional causes or abnormal child-rearing methods have been suggested, especially where the parents or siblings show similar peculiarities to the patient, but there is no evidence to support such theories.

Detailed epidemiological studies, based on total populations, are needed in order to establish which, if any, of these aetiological factors are relevant.

No specific organic pathology has been identified. No particular abnormalities of face or body have been reported. In childhood the physical appearance is usually, but by no means always, normal. In adolescence and adult life, the inappropriate gait, posture and facial expression produce an impression of oddness.

In general, on psychological assessment, tests requiring good rote memory are performed well, but deficits are shown with those depending on abstract concepts, or sequencing in time. Visuospatial abilities vary and the scores on testing may be markedly lower than those for expressive speech (No. 4). The results of psychological testing will be described in more detail elsewhere.

Epidemiology

As already mentioned, no detailed, large-scale epidemiological studies have been carried out, so that the exact prevalence of Asperger's syndrome is unknown. A major difficulty in designing such a study would be the establishment of criteria for distinguishing the syndrome from other similar conditions, as will be discussed later.

Wing & Gould (1979) carried out a study in which all the mentally and physically handicapped children aged under 15 in one area of London were screened in order to identify cases of early childhood psychosis and severe mental retardation. In this study, 2 children (0.6 per 10000 aged under 15) showed most of the characteristics of Asperger's syndrome, though they were in the mildly retarded range on intelligence tests, and 4 (1.1 per 10000) could have been diagnosed as autistic in early life, but came to resemble Asperger's syndrome later. There was a total of 35000 children aged under 15 in the area.

Wing & Gould did not use methods designed to identify mild cases of Asperger's syndrome, so that any children who were attending normal school and had not come to the attention of the educational, social or medical services would not have been discovered. The prevalence rate for the typical syndrome given above is almost certainly an under-estimate.

The syndrome appears to be considerably more common in boys than in girls. Asperger originally believed it to be confined to males, though he modified this view later (personal communication). Wolff & Barlow (1979) mentioned that the clinical picture could be seen in girls. In their series the male:female ratio was 9:1. In the present author's series there were 15 boys and 4 girls with the syndrome in fairly typical form, and 13 boys and 2 girls who had many of the features. The girls tended to appear superficially more sociable than the boys, but closer observation showed that they had the same problems of two-way social interaction.

Differential diagnosis

As with any condition identifiable only from a pattern of abnormal behaviour, each element of which can occur in varying degrees of severity, it is possible to find people on the borderlines of Asperger's syndrome in whom diagnosis is particularly difficult. Whereas the typical case can be recognized with ease by those with experience in the field, in practice it is found that the syndrome shades into eccentric normality, and into certain other clinical pictures. Until more is known of the underlying pathology, it must be accepted that no precise cut-off points can be defined. The diagnosis has to be based on the full developmental history and presenting clinical picture, and not on the presence or absence of any individual item.

Normal variant of personality

All the features that characterize Asperger's syndrome can be found in varying degrees in the normal population. People differ in their levels of skill in social interaction and in their ability to read non-verbal social cues. There is an equally wide distribution in motor skills. Many who are capable and independent as adults have special interests that they pursue with marked enthusiasm. Collecting objects such as stamps, old glass bottles, or railway engine numbers are socially accepted hobbies. Asperger (1979) pointed out that the capacity to withdraw into an inner world of one's own special interests is available in a greater or lesser measure to all human beings. He emphasized that this ability has to be present to a marked extent in those who are creative artists or scientists. The difference between someone with Asperger's syndrome and the normal person who has a complex inner world is that the latter does take part appropriately in two-way social interaction at times, while the former does not. Also, the normal person, however elaborate his inner world, is influenced by his social experiences, whereas the person with Asperger's syndrome seems cut off from the effects of outside contacts.

A number of normal adults have outstandingly good rote memories and even retain eidetic imagery into adult life. Pedantic speech and a tendency to take things literally can also be found in normal people.

It is possible that some people could be classified as suffering from Asperger's syndrome because they are at the extreme end of the normal continuum on all these features. In others, one particular aspect may be so marked that it affects the whole of their functioning. The man described by Luria (1965), whose visual memories of objects and events were so vivid and so permanent that they interfered with his comprehension of their significance, seemed to have behaved not unlike someone with Asperger's syndrome. Unfortunately, Luria did not give enough details to allow a diagnosis to be made.

Even though Asperger's syndrome does appear to merge into the normal continuum, there are many cases in whom the problems are so marked that the suggestion of a distinct pathology seems a more plausible explanation than a variant of normality.

Schizoid personality

The lack of empathy, single-mindedness, odd communication, social isolation and over-sensitivity of people with Asperger's syndrome are features that are also included in the definitions of schizoid personality (see review by Wolff & Chick, 1980). Kretschmer (1925) outlined some case histories of so-called schizoid adults, one or two of which were strongly reminiscent of this condition, although he did not provide sufficient detail to ensure the diagnosis. For example, one young man had no friends at school, was odd and awkward in social interaction, always had difficulty with speech, never took part in rough games, was oversensitive, and very unhappy when away from home. He thought out fantastic technical inventions and, together with his sister, invented a detailed imaginary world.

There is no question that Asperger's syndrome *can* be regarded as a form of schizoid personality. The question is whether this grouping is of any value. This will be discussed below in the section on classification.

Schizophrenia

Adults with Asperger's syndrome may be diagnosed as suffering from schizo-phrenia. The differential diagnosis of schizophrenia has been discussed elsewhere (J. K. Wing, 1978). The main difficulty arises from the fact that schizophrenia has been defined loosely by some and strictly by other workers.

If a loose definition of schizophrenia is accepted, based only on charac-teristics such as social withdrawal and speech disorder, then a case could perhaps be made for including Asperger's syndrome in this group. As with schizoid personality, the question is whether doing so has any advantages. Poverty of social interaction and abnormalities of speech can have many different causes, so the diagnosis of chronic or simple schizophrenia tends to cover a variety of conditions having little in common with each other.

Careful observation of speech in Asperger's syndrome discloses differ-ences from thought blocking and the 'knight's move' in thought described by Bleuler (1911). In Asperger's syndrome, speech may be slow, and there may be irrelevant or tangential replies to questions, but these problems are due partly to poor comprehension and partly to a tendency to become stuck in well-worn conversational grooves rather than to produce new ideas. Utterances are always logical, even if they are unrelated to the question, or originate from an unusual point of view. Thus one young man, when asked a general knowledge question about organized charities, said 'They do things for unfortunate people. They provide wheel-chairs, stilts and round shoes for people with no feet'. There is a marked contrast between the vague woolliness of schizophrenic thought and the concrete, pedantic approach found in Asperger's syndrome.

The term schizophrenia can be used more strictly. It can be confined to those who have, currently or in the past, shown the florid first-rank symptoms described by Schneider (1971). In this case, the differentiation of Asperger's syndrome rests on accurate definition of the clinical phenomena. Unless they have a superimposed schizophrenic illness, people with Asperger's syndrome do not experience thought echo, thought substitution or inser-tion, thought broadcast, voices commenting on their actions, voices talking to each other, or feelings that external forces are exerting control over their will, emotions or behaviour. The young man, L. P. (Appendix No. 2), when asked if he had such experiences, gave the matter long and careful thought and then said 'I believe such things to be impossible'.

During clinical examination it is necessary to be aware that comprehension of abstract or unfamiliar concepts is impaired in Asperger's syndrome. Those with the more severe form of the handicap may have a habit of answering 'yes' to any question they do not understand, this being the quickest way to cut short the conservation. Some may also pick up and repeat phrases used by other people, including other patients in a hospital ward, making diagnosis even more difficult.

Other psychotic syndromes

The tendency found in people with Asperger's syndrome to sensitivity and over-generalization of the fact that they are criticized and made fun of may, if present in marked form, be mistaken for a paranoid psychosis. Those who are preoccupied with abstract theories or their own imaginary world may be said to have delusions or hallucinations. One boy, for example, was convinced that Batman would arrive one day and take him away as his assistant. No rational argument could persuade him otherwise. This type of belief could be called a delusion, but is probably better termed an 'over-valued idea'. It does not have any specific diagnostic significance, since such intensely held ideas can be found in different psychiatric states.

Severe social withdrawal, echopraxia and odd postures may be noted. These may become more marked at times, and then they could be regarded as catatonic phenomena. Such catatonic symptoms can be associated with various conditions (including encephalitis) and, on their own, should not be considered as indicative of schizophrenia.

Obsessional neurosis

Repetitive interests and activities are part of Asperger's syndrome, but the awareness of their illogicality and the resistance to their performance characteristic of the classic case of obsessional neurosis are not found in the former. It would be of interest to investigate the relationship between Asperger's syndrome, obsessional personality, obsessional illness, and post-encephalitic obsessional conditions.

Affective conditions

The quietness, social withdrawal, and lack of facial expression in Asperger's syndrome might suggest a depressive illness. Shyness and distress when away from familiar surroundings could make an anxiety state a possible diagnosis, or excited talking about a rather fantastic grandiose, imaginary world might bring to mind hypomania. However, the full clinical picture and the early developmental history should clarify the diagnosis.

More difficult problems occur when affective illnesses are superimposed on Asperger's syndrome. Then a double diagnosis has to be made on the history and present state.

Early childhood autism

Asperger acknowledged that there were many similarities between his syndrome and Kanner's early infantile autism. Nevertheless, he considered they were different because he regarded autism as a psychotic process, and his own syndrome as a stable personality trait. Since neither psychotic process nor personality trait has been defined empirically, little more can be said about whether they can be distinguished from each other.

Van Krevelen (1971) and Wolff & Barlow (1979) agreed with Asperger that his syndrome should be differentiated from autism. They differ in their accounts of the distinguishing features and the impression gained from their papers is that, although there are some differences, the syndromes are more alike than unalike. The variations could be explained on the basis of the severity of the impairments, though the authors quoted above would not agree with this hypothesis. Thus the autistic child, at least when young, is aloof and indifferent to others, whereas the child with Asperger's syndrome is passive or makes inappropriate one-sided approaches. The former is mute or has delayed and abnormal speech, whereas the latter learns to speak with good grammar and vocabulary (though he may, when young, reverse pronouns), but the content of his speech is inappropriate for the social context and he has problems with understanding complex meanings. Nonverbal communication is severely impaired in both conditions. In autism, in the early years, there may be no use of gesture to communicate. In Asperger's syndrome there tends to be inappropriate use of gesture to accompany speech. In both conditions, monotonous or peculiar vocal intonation is characteristic. The autistic child develops stereotyped, repetitive routines involving objects or people (for example, arranging toys and household objects in specific abstract patterns, or insisting that everyone in a room should cross the right leg over the left), whereas the person with Asperger's syndrome becomes immersed in mathematical abstractions, or amassing facts on his special interests. Abnormal responses to sensory input – including indifference, distress and fascination – are characteristic of early childhood autism and form the basis of the theories of perceptual inconstancy put forward by Ornitz & Ritvo (1968) and of over-selectivity of attention suggested by Lovaas et al. (1971). These features are associated with greater severity of handicap, and lower mental age. They are not described as typical of Asperger's syndrome, and they are rarely seen in older autistic people with intelligence quotients in the normal range.

The one area in which this type of comparison does not seem to apply is in motor development. Typically, autistic children tend to be good at climbing and balancing when young. Those with Asperger's syndrome, on the other hand, are notably ill-coordinated in posture, gait and gestures. Even this may not be a particularly useful point of differentiation, since children who have typical autism when young tend to become clumsy in movement and much less attractive and graceful in appearance by the time of adolescence (see DeMyer, 1976, 1979 for a discussion of motor skills in autism and autistic-like conditions).

Bosch (1962) considered that Asperger's syndrome and autism were variants of the same condition. This author pointed out that, although Asperger and Van Krevelen (1971) listed features in the early history which they thought distinguished the 2 conditions, in practice these did not cluster into 2 groups often enough to justify the differentiation. The child in Appendix No. 6 illustrates this problem (see also Everard, 1980).

Classification

Asperger regarded the syndrome he described as a disorder of personality that could be distinguished from other types of personality abnormalities, although he recognized the similarities to early childhood autism. Wolff & Barlow (1979) argued that it should be classified under the heading of schizoid personality. In support of this view, Wolff & Chick (1980) reviewed the literature in which schizoid characteristics are described. As discussed above, the syndrome *can* be placed in this group, and further work in this field would be of interest, but, at the moment, classification under this heading has no useful practical implications. Although Wolff & Chick have listed 5 features, operationally defined, that they regard as core characteristics of schizoid personality, this term, as generally used, is so vague and ill-defined a concept that it covers a wide range of clinical pictures in addition to Asperger's syndrome. The aim should be not to enlarge, but to separate sub-groups from the broad category and thus to increase diagnostic precision. Furthermore, the word schizoid was originally chosen to underline the relationship of the abnormal personality to schizophrenia. The latter can occur in a person with Asperger's syndrome, but, as already discussed, there is no firm evidence of a special link between this syndrome and schizophrenia, strictly defined. To incorporate such an untested assumption into the name of the condition must give rise to confusion.

The reasons for personality variations are so obscure that classifying Asperger's syndrome under this heading does not lead to any testable hypotheses concerning cause, clinical phenomena, pathology or management. A more limited, but more productive, view of the problem is to consider it as a consequence of impairment of certain aspects of cognitive and social development.

As mentioned above, Wing & Gould (1979) carried out an epidemiological study of all mentally or physically handicapped children in one area of London, in an attempt to identify all those with autism or autistic-like conditions, whatever their level of intelligence. The results confirmed the following hypothesis. Certain problems affecting early child development tend to cluster together: namely, absence or impairment of two-way social interaction; absence or impairment of comprehension and use of language, non-verbal as well as verbal; and absence or impairment of true, flexible imaginative activities, with the substitution of a narrow range of repetitive, stereotyped pursuits. Each aspect of this triad can occur in varying degrees of severity, and in association with any level of intelligence as measured on standardized tests.

When all children with this cluster of impairments were examined, it was found that a very few resembled the description given by Asperger and some had typical Kanner's autism. A number could, tentatively, be classified as having syndromes described by authors such as De Sanctis (1906, 1908), Earl (1934), Heller (see Hulse, 1954) and Mahler (1952), although the definitions given by these writers were not precise enough for easy identification. The remainder had features of more than one of these so-called syndromes and could not be assigned to any single category. They could all be grouped under the general, but unsatisfactory, heading of early childhood psychosis. The justification for regarding them as related is that all the conditions in which the triad of language and social impairments occurs, whatever the level of severity, are accompanied by similar problems affecting social and intellectual skills. Furthermore, individuals with the triad of symptoms all require the same kind of structured, organized educational approach, although the aims and achievements of education will vary from minimal self-care up to a university degree, depending on the skills available to the person concerned.

This hypothesis does not suggest that there is a common gross aetiology. This is certainly not the case, since many different genetic or pre-, peri- or post-natal causes can lead to the same overt clinical picture (Wing & Gould, 1979). It is more likely that all the conditions in which the triad occurs have in common impairment of certain aspects of brain function that are presumably necessary for adequate social interaction, verbal and non-verbal communication and imaginative development. It is possible that these are all facets of one underlying in-built capacity – that is, the ability actively to seek out and make sense of experience (Ricks & Wing, 1975). Included in this would be the innate ability to recognize other human beings as distinct from the rest of the environment and of special importance. If this basic skill were diminished or absent, the effects on development would be profound, as is the case in all early childhood psychoses.

The full range of clinical material can be subdivided in many different ways, depending on the purpose of the exercise, but no aetiological classification is possible as yet. Sub-grouping on factors such as level of intelligence (Bartak & Rutter, 1976) or on degree of impairment of social interaction (DeMyer, 1976; Wing & Gould, 1979) has more useful practical implications for education and management than any based on the eponymous syndromes mentioned above.

In the light of this finding, is there any justification for identifying Asperger's syndrome as a separate entity? Until the aetiologies of such conditions are known, the term is helpful when explaining the problems of children and adults who have autistic features, but who talk grammatically and who are not socially aloof. Such people are perplexing to parents, teachers and work supervisors, who often cannot believe in a diagnosis of autism, which they equate with muteness and total social withdrawal. The use of a diagnostic term and reference to Asperger's clinical descriptions help to convince the people concerned that there is a real problem involving subtle, but important, intellectual impairments, and needing careful management and education.

Finally, the relationship to schizophrenia of Asperger's syndrome, autism and similar impairments can be reconsidered. Although they are dissimilar in family history, childhood development and clinical pictures, both groups of conditions affect language, social interaction and imaginative activities. The time of onset and the nature of the disturbances are different, but there are similarities in the eventual chronic defect states that either may produce. It is not surprising that autism and schizophrenia have, in the past, been confused. Progress has been made in separating them and it is important to continue to improve precision in diagnosis, despite the many difficulties met in clinical practice.

Management and education

There is no known treatment that has any effect on the basic impairments underlying Asperger's syndrome, but handicaps can be diminished by appropriate management and education.

Both children and adults with this syndrome, like all those with the triad of language and social impairments, respond best when there is a regular, organized routine. It is important for parents and teachers to recognize the subtle difficulties in comprehension of abstract language, so that they can communicate with the child in ways he can understand. The repetitive speech and motor habits cannot be extinguished, but, with time and patience, they can be modified to make them more useful and socially acceptable. Techniques of behaviour modification as used with autistic children can possibly be helpful if applied with sensitivity. However, Asperger (1979) expressed considerable reservations about using these methods with children with his syndrome who are bright enough to be aware of and, as Asperger put it, 'to value their freedom'.

Education is of particular importance because it may help to develop special interests and general competence sufficiently to allow independence in adult life. The teacher has to find a compromise between, on the one hand, letting the child follow his own bent completely, and, on the other, insisting that he conform. She also has to ensure that he is not teased and bullied by the rest of the class. There is no type of school that is particularly suitable for those with Asperger's syndrome. Some have performed well in schools for normal children, while others have managed better in schools for various kinds of handicaps. Educational progress depends on the severity of the child's impairments, but also on the understanding and skill of the teacher.

Most people with Asperger's syndrome who settle in open employment have jobs with a regular routine. They also have sympathetic employers and workmates who are willing to tolerate eccentricities. In many instances, work has been found by parents who persevere in approaching employers, despite all the difficulties.

Finding appropriate living accommodation also presents problems. Living with parents is the easiest solution, but cannot last for ever. Hostels or lodgings with a helpful landlady are the most usual answer. Tactful supervision may be needed to ensure that rooms are kept clean and tidy and clothes are changed regularly.

Superimposed psychiatric illnesses, if they occur, should be treated appropriately. Emotional distress in adolescents and young adults due to partial insight may be reduced to some extent by counselling from someone who has a full understanding of the syndrome. Such counselling consists mainly of explanation, reassurance and discussion of fears and worries. The counsellor has to adopt a simple and concrete approach in order to stay within the limits of the client's understanding. Psychoanalysis, which depends upon the interpretation of complex symbolic associations, is not useful in this condition.

Parents, in their child's early years, are usually confused and distressed by his strange behaviour. They need a detailed explanation of the nature of his problems if they are to understand and accept that he is handicapped.

Appendix

Case histories

As mentioned above, the following case histories are those of people who have been referred to psychiatric services. The high achievers mentioned by Asperger (1944) are not represented.

Case 1

This is a typical example of the syndrome.

Mr K. N. first presented as a psychiatric outpatient when he was aged 28, complaining of nervousness and shyness.

As a baby he was always placid and smiling and rarely cried. He used to lie in his pram for hours, laughing at the leaves on the trees. His mother remembered he did not point things out for her to look at, in contrast to his sister. He continued to be quiet and contented as a toddler. If other children took his toys he did not protest. Walking was somewhat delayed and he was slow in acquiring self-care skills, though not enough for his parents to worry.

He began to talk around 1 year of age. He had several words at this time, but, after seeing and hearing a car crash which startled him, he stopped talking and did not begin again until he was 3 years old. His parents thought his understanding of speech was normal. K. developed good grammar, though he referred to himself in the third person till 4–5 years old. He has never been communicative. Even as an adult he gives information only if questioned and then replies as briefly as possible. His facial expression and gestures are limited, and his voice is monotonous.

As a child he was attached to his mother, he never made any friends, and he was much teased at school. He remains a shy and socially isolated person though he would like to be able to make social contacts.

K. had no stereotyped movements, but has always been ill-coordinated and very poor at games. He does not swing his arms when he walks. He attended a private school and did well in subjects needing a good rote memory, such as history and Latin, but fell behind at the stage when comprehension of abstract ideas became necessary. He was in the army for a short time, but was not allowed to take part in marches and parades because of his clumsiness and inability to do the right thing at the right time. He was discharged because of these peculiarities.

K. did not object to changes imposed by others, but he was, and still is, orderly in his own daily routines and in arranging his own possessions.

From early in his life he liked toy buses, cars and trains. He amassed a large collection and would notice at once if a single item were missing. He would also make models with constructional kits. He played with such toys, on his own, for as long as he was allowed to continue. He had no other pretend play and never joined in with other children. The interest in means of transport has remained with him. In his spare time he reads factual books on the subject, watches cars and trains and goes on trips to see trains with fellow train-enthusiasts. He has no interest in fiction or any other type of non-fiction.

K. has been employed for many years in routine clerical work. He enjoys his job and his hobby, but is very sad and anxious because he is aware of his own social ineptness and would like to have friends and to marry. He writes many letters to advice columns in magazines, hoping for help with these problems. His concern over what he terms his 'shyness' finally made him ask for help from a psychiatrist.

The WAIS gave K. an IQ in the dull normal range, with similar verbal and non-verbal scores. He was particularly poor at sub-tests needing comprehension of a sequence of events.

Case 2

The second case history is also typical, but complicated by severe depression with onset in early adult life.

Mr L. P. was admitted to a psychiatric hospital at age 24 because of a suicidal attempt. He was born 4 weeks premature and had feeding problems in the first week or two. He was an easy, placid, rather unresponsive baby who rarely cried. He acquired motor and self-care skills, but his parents later realized that he passed these milestones more slowly than his sister, though they did not worry at the time. His father had a vague premonition that there was something odd about L. but not enough to seek advice.

He did not begin to speak until he was 3 years old, but this was attributed to the fact that the family was bilingual. However, by the time he went to school he was speaking in long, involved, pedantic sentences that sounded as if they had come from books. He tended to interpret words in odd ways. For example, when hearing someone described as 'independent' he thought this meant they always jumped in at the deep end of the swimming pool. He still takes jokes very seriously. He used to ask the same questions over and over again, regardless of the answers he was given. He did not initiate or join in conversations except by repetitive questioning.

L. remained placid and obedient throughout his childhood. He rarely initiated any activity, but waited to be told what to do. As a small child he used to rock himself when unoccupied. He had no imaginative play. He went to normal school, but did not join in with the other children and had no friends until he was about 14 years old. Then he did begin to mention one or two companions and referred to them as friends, but has lost touch since. He was bullied at school and remembers it as an unhappy time.

L. has always been concerned that his possessions should be orderly and that the daily routine should be followed exactly.

He is poor at games needing gross motor skills and at tasks requiring hand–eye coordination. His posture and gait are markedly odd. His face has a faintly bewildered expression that rarely changes. He uses large, jerky, inappropriate gestures to accompany speech. The odd impression he conveys is exacerbated by his old-fashioned choice of clothing.

L.'s memory is excellent and this enabled him to pass exams in subjects that can be learnt by rote. He is a very good chess player and enjoys taking part in matches. He can read well and enjoys books on physics and chemistry, concerning which he has memorized a large number of facts. He is particularly interested in time. He wears 2 watches, one set at Greenwich Mean Time and one at local time, even when these are the same.

His major problem is his social ineptitude. He will, for example, go on talking about his special subjects despite the most obvious signs of boredom in his audience. He makes inappropriate, often quite irrelevant, remarks in company and appears gauche and childish. He is painfully aware of his deficiencies, but is unable to acquire the skills necessary for social interaction. Nevertheless, he is kind and gentle and, if he realizes someone is ill or unhappy, he will be most sympathetic and do his best to help.

Since leaving school he has been employed as a filing clerk, and lives in a hostel.

L.'s parents did not seek psychiatric help when he was a child, but he has been in contact with psychiatric services since reaching adolescence. On the first occasion he had become agitated because of worries about sex. On the second, he was anxious and losing sleep because of a minor change in his routine at work. On the third he was admitted as an in-patient following attempted suicide, once again precipitated by the possibility of reorganization in the office where he works. He tried to drown himself, but failed because he is a good swimmer. He then tried to strangle himself, without success. Commenting on this he said 'The trouble is I am not a very practical person'. At admission he was dishevelled in appearance, deeply distressed and sad. His speech was painfully slow with long pauses between phrases. Its content was coherent, although, in his replies to questions, L. tended to add information that was correct, and related to the subject in hand, but not relevant in the context. For example, when asked about relations with his father L. said 'My father and I get on well. He is a man who likes gardening'.

L. blamed himself for all his problems, describing himself as an unpleasant person, whom no one could like and who could not manage his own life. He said he had heard people saying things about him such as 'L. is stupid', 'L. is a bad person', 'L. is a chemistry fanatic'. Careful questioning and subsequent observation showed that these were misinterpretation of overheard conversations and never occurred when L. was alone. For the first two admissions, the referring agency diagnosed an anxiety state, and, for the third, schizophrenia. The final diagnosis was Asperger's syndrome complicated by anxiety and depression (not schizophrenia).

L. scored in the average range on the WAIS, his verbal being rather higher than his performance score, mainly because of his large vocabulary.

Case 3

The third case history is that of a boy where abnormality was recognized from infancy.

B. H. is aged 10. He was delivered by forceps and had difficulty with breathing and cyanosis after birth, remaining in special care for 2 weeks. He was a large, placid baby, who would lie without moving for long periods. He was not eager to use gestures, to clap or to wave good-bye. His mother was worried about him from the beginning, partly because of the difficult birth and partly because of his behaviour.

His parents were certain that he replied 'Yes' appropriately to questions at 11 months. At around 14 months he began to speak in a fluent, but incomprehensible 'language' of his own.

He made no effort to crawl, but one day, aged 17 months, he stood up and walked. He learnt to crawl after this.

He retained his own language until aged 3 years, when he started to copy clearly words he heard, and then went on to develop understandable speech. His comprehension of language has always lagged behind his expression. By the age of 4 he could read. His parents said they did not teach him—he presumably learnt from the television. At the age of 5 he had a reading age of 9 years, but his comprehension was poor.

In his early years, B. remained quiet and passive, showing little emotion of any kind. He seemed to prefer a regular routine, but did not react at all to changes. He was not demanding and gave no trouble.

B. did not develop imaginative pretend play at the usual age. At the age of about 6 years he became fascinated with means of transport, read all about them and learnt all the technical terms. He enacts actions involving cars, aeroplanes and so on, but never with other children.

He appears clumsy and ill-coordinated, has problems with buttons and laces, and is afraid of climbing.

B. attends a special school. When first admitted he ignored the other children and carried on with his usual preoccupations. He appeared astounded when the teacher indicated that he should obey her instructions and follow the rest of the class. Gradually he began to fit in and to make active social approaches, though in a naïve and inappropriate fashion. He has difficulty in following the rules of any game.

He speaks in a pedantic style, in an accent quite unlike that of his local environment. For example, he referred to a hole in his sock as 'a temporary loss of knitting'. Many of his phrases are, like this one, inappropriately adapted quotations from television or books.

B. is now aware of and sensitive to other people's criticism, but appears unable to learn the rules of social interaction.

When tested at age 7 years he had a word recognition age of 12 years, scored at his age level on performance tasks, but was well below this on tests needing recall and comprehension of language.

Case 4

In the following example of the syndrome, the diagnosis is complicated by a history of illness and psychological stress in early life, and by visual impairment.

Miss F. G. is aged 26. Pregnancy and delivery were normal, but F. had a series of illnesses and operations, including a subdural haemorrhage of unknown aetiology and correction of strabismus before the age of 3 years. She has poor eyesight and has to peer very closely to see, but can read, write and type.

F. talked fluently at an early age, and had a large vocabulary. Her parents thought she was developing normally until the operation on her eyes at $2^1/_2$ years. Following this she was socially withdrawn for several months. No detailed description could be obtained, but her mother was quite certain that there was a marked change in behaviour. Despite the problems of social interaction, F.'s speech remained clear, with good vocabulary and grammar. She always had a remarkable memory for anything she had heard or read, including any statistical information. F. gradually became more friendly and, by about 3 years of age, she was making social approaches to her parents and others in the family. However, she did not interact much with other children. She copied her mother's activities a little, but did not develop normal pretend play or social play.

Her main interests as a young child were drawing and, later on, reading. She also collected costume dolls, which she arranged in rows that must not be disturbed.

F. went to a normal comprehensive school. She loved history and geography, and would memorize facts in these subjects with ease, but her teacher reported that she would do no work in any subject that did not interest her, such as mathematics.

She was accepted at school but recognized as odd. Her conversation contained many long quotations from books and she also often made irrelevant remarks.

F. was never good at practical tasks. Her parents tended to do things for her. They found that, if they asked her to do some task, she would begin, but soon stop and turn to her own preferred activity—usually reading a book.

After leaving school she obtained work as a typist. She proved an excellent copy typist and was outstandingly accurate at spelling. She made no friends with the other members of staff. After 4 years the pressure of work increased. F. became distressed and unable to cope. She left work and has been unemployed for 3 years. During this time she has been anxious and agitated and unable to do anything on her own. She spends her time reading and amassing facts. She tends to have childish temper tantrums if thwarted in any way.

The WAIS showed that F. had a verbal score in the average normal range, but performance was very much lower, being in the mildly retarded range. The verbal skills depended on her good vocabulary. She did poorly on any task where the elements have to be organized into a coherent whole.

Case 5

This is the history of a young man who showed the features of Asperger's syndrome, but who was mentally retarded and did not achieve independence as an adult.

Mr J. G. is aged 24 and attends a training centre for mentally retarded adults. J. was a quiet, unresponsive baby. He began to say a few words at the age of 2, but did not walk well until 2½ years old. At first he echoed, used phrases repetitively and had poor pronunciation. He learnt to read at the age of 5½ and always did well on reading tests, though his comprehension was poor. He knew many unusual or technical words, such as 'aeronautical' and 'pterodactyl' but would be puzzled by familiar ones such as 'yesterday'.

He was not aloof, but gentle and passive, tending to stand and watch other children, wanting to join in but not knowing how. He was very affectionate towards his own family. At age 24 he is still unable to interact socially, though is happy to be a passive member of a group.

He is clumsy in gait and posture and slow on tests of manual dexterity. J.'s special interests are music and cars. He can recognize any make of car, even if shown only a small part of the whole vehicle.

He attended a special school for mentally retarded children. He was described by his teacher as 'showing no initiative'. He was eventually placed in an adult training centre near his home, where he is happily settled.

His WAIS score at the age of 17 was on the borderline between mild and severe retardation, with the verbal level being very slightly better than the performance. His reading age was still well in advance of all other skills.

Case 6

The following case history is of a boy who at first was classically autistic and later developed the characteristics of Asperger's syndrome.

C. B. is aged 13. His mother dates C.'s problems from the age of 6 months when his head was accidentally bruised. From this time he became socially aloof and isolated, and spent most of his time gazing at his hands which he moved in complicated patterns in front of his face. At 1 year old he began to watch the passing traffic, but still ignored people. He continued to be remote, with poor eye contact, until 5 years of age. He passed his motor milestones at the usual ages and, as soon as he was physically able, he spent hours running in circles with an object in his hand, and would scream if attempts were made to stop him. At the age of 3 he began to be able to recognize letters of the alphabet and rapidly acquired skill at drawing. He then drew the salt and pepper pots, correctly copying the names written on them, over and over again. For a time this was his sole activity. Following this he became fascinated with pylons and tall buildings and would stare at them from all angles and draw them.

He did not speak till the age of 4, then for a long time used single words. After this, he acquired repetitive phrases and reversed pronouns. C. had many stereotyped movements as a young child, including jumping, flapping his arms and moving his hands in circles.

After the age of 5, C.'s speech and social contact markedly improved. He attended a special school until aged 11, where they tolerated a range of bizarre, repetitive routines. At one point, for example, he insisted that all his class and the teacher should wear watches that he had made from plasticine before lessons could begin. Despite all the problems, he proved to have excellent rote memory, absorbed all that he was taught, and could reproduce facts *verbatim* when asked. C. was transferred to a normal comprehensive school at the age of 11. He has good grammar and a large vocabulary, though his speech is naïve and immature and mainly concerned with his own special interests. He has learnt not to make embarrassing remarks about other people's appearances, but still tends to ask repetitive questions. He is not socially withdrawn, but he prefers the company of adults to that of children of his own age, finding it difficult to understand the unwritten rules of social interaction. He said of himself 'I am afraid I suffer from bad sportsmanship'. He enjoys simple jokes but cannot understand more subtle humour. He is often teased by his classmates.

His main interest is in maps and road signs. He has a prodigious memory for routes and can draw them rapidly and accurately. He also makes large, complicated abstract shapes out of any material that comes to hand, and shows much ingenuity in ensuring that they hold together. He has never had pretend play but is deeply attached to his toy panda to which he talks as if it were an adult when he needs comfort.

His finger dexterity is good, but he is clumsy and ill-coordinated in large movements and therefore is never chosen by the other children for sports and games teams.

C. is of average intelligence on the WISC, with better verbal than performance skills. He does well on tasks needing rote learning, but his teachers are deeply puzzled and concerned about his poor comprehension of abstract ideas and his social naïvety. They find him appealing but sadly vulnerable to the hazards of everyday life.

References

Adams, P. L. (1973). *Obsessive Children: a Sociopsychiatric Study.* Butterworths: London.
Asperger, H. (1944). Die 'autistischen Psychopathen' im Kindesalter. *Archiv für Psychiatrie und Nervenkrankheiten* **117**, 76–136.
Asperger, H. (1968). Zur differentialdiagnose des kindlichen Autismus. *Acta paedopsychiatrica* **35**, 136–145.
Asperger, H. (1979). Problems of infantile autism. *Communication* **13**, 45–52.
Bartak, L. & Rutter, M. (1976). Differences between mentally retarded and normally intelligent autistic children. *Journal of Autism and Childhood Schizophrenia* **6**, 109–120.
Bleuler, E. (1911). *Dementia Praecox or the Group of Schizophrenias* (trans. J. Zinkin). International University Press: New York, 1950.
Bosch, G. (1962). *Infantile Autism* (trans. D. Jordan and I. Jordan). Springer-Verlag: New York, 1970.
Chick, J., Waterhouse, L. & Wolff, S. (1979). Psychological construing in schizoid children grown up. *British Journal of Psychiatry* **135**, 425–430.
DeMyer, M. (1976). Motor, perceptual–motor and intellectual disabilities of autistic children. In *Early Childhood Autism* (ed. L. Wing), pp. 169–196. Pergamon: Oxford.
DeMeyer, M. (1979). *Parents and Children in Autism.* Winston: Washington.
De Sanctis, S. (1906). Sopra alcune varieta della demenza prococe. *Rivista Sperimentale de Freniatria e di Medicina Legale* **32**, 141–165.
De Sanctis, S. (1908). Dementia praecocissima catatonica oder Katatonie des früheren Kindesalters? *Folia Neurobiologica* **2**, 9–12.
Earl, C. J. C. (1934). The primitive catatonic psychosis of idiocy. *British Journal of Medical Psychology* **14**, 230–253.
Everard, P. (1980). *Involuntary Strangers.* John Clare Books: London.
Hulse, W. C. (1954). Dementia infantilis. *Journal of Nervous and Mental Disease* **119**, 471–477.
Isaev, D. N. & Kagan, V. E. (1974). Autistic syndromes in children and adolescents. *Acta paedopsychiatric* **40**, 182–190.
Kanner, L. (1943). Autistic disturbances of affective contact. *Nervous Child* **2**, 217–250.
Kretschmer, E. (1925). *Physique and Character.* Kegan Paul, Trench and Trubner: London.
Lovaas, O. I., Schreibman, L., Koegel, R. & Rehm, R. (1971). Selective responding by autistic children to multiple sensory input. *Journal of Abnormal Psychology* **77**, 211–222.
Luria, A. R. (1965). *The Mind of a Mnemonist* (trans. L. Solotaroff). Jonathan Cape: London, 1969.
Mahler, M. S. (1952). On child psychoses and schizophrenia: autistic and symbiotic infantile psychoses. *Psychoanalytic Study of the Child* **7**, 286–305.

Mnukhin, S. S. & Isaev, D. N. (1975). On the organic nature of some forms of schizoid or autistic psychopathy. *Journal of Autism and Childhood Schizophrenia* **5**, 99–108.

Ornitz, E. M. & Ritvo, E. R. (1968). Perceptual inconstancy in early infantile autism. *Archives of General Psychiatry* **18**, 76–98.

Ricks, D. M. & Wing, L. (1975). Language, communication and the use of symbols in normal and autistic children. *Journal of Autism and Childhood Schizophrenia* **5**, 191–221.

Robinson, J. F. & Vitale, L. J. (1954). Children with circumscribed interest patterns. *American Journal of Psychiatry* **24**, 755–767.

Schneider, K. (1971). *Klinische Psychopathologie* (9th edn). Thieme: Stuttgart.

Schopler, E., Andrews, C. E. & Strupp, K. (1979). Do autistic children come from upper middle class parents? *Journal of Autism and Developmental Disorders* **9**, 139–152.

Van Krevelen, D. A. (1971). Early infantile autism and autistic psychopathy. *Journal of Autism and Childhood Schizophrenia* **1**, 82–86.

Wing, J. K. (1978). Clinical concepts of schizophrenia. In *Schizophrenia: Towards a New Synthesis* (ed. J. K. Wing), pp. 1–30. Academic Press: London.

Wing, L. (1976). Diagnosis, clinical description and prognosis. In *Early Childhood Autism* (ed. L. Wing), pp. 15–48. Pergamon: Oxford.

Wing, L. (1980). Childhood autism and social class: a question of selection? *British Journal of Psychiatry* **137**, 410–417.

Wing, L. & Gould, J. (1979). Severe impairments of social interaction and associated abnormalities in children: epidemiology and classification. *Journal of Autism and Developmental Disorders* **9**, 11–29.

Wolff, S. & Barlow, A. (1979). Schizoid personality in childhood: a comparative study of schizoid, autistic and normal children. *Journal of Child Psychology and Psychiatry* **20**, 29–46.

Wolff, S. & Chick, J. (1980). Schizoid personality in childhood: a controlled follow-up study. *Psychological Medicine* **10**, 85–100.

118

INFANTILE AUTISM:
A GENETIC STUDY OF
21 TWIN PAIRS

Susan Folstein and Michael Rutter

Source: *Journal of Child Psychology and Psychiatry*, 18, 1977: 297–321.

Introduction

In his original description of the syndrome of infantile autism, Kanner (1943) noted that the condition was distinctive in that, in most cases, the children's behaviour had appeared abnormal right from early infancy. He suggested the presence of an inborn defect of presumably constitutional origin. Since then, there have been numerous hypotheses concerning the possible nature and origins of this defect (see Ornitz, 1973; Rutter, 1974). However, in spite of the supposition that the disorder is inborn, there have been surprisingly few attempts to investigate possible genetic influences.

The first set of evidence comes from family studies. There is no recorded case of an autistic child having an overtly autistic parent and it is decidedly unusual for a family to contain more than one autistic child, although such cases have been reported (Seidal and Graf, 1966; Verhees, 1976). The usually negative family history for autism seems to be out of keeping with genetic determination. However, this line of reasoning is fallacious. First, it is extremely rare for autistic persons to marry (Rutter, 1970) and there is only a single published report of one having given birth to a child (Kanner and Eisenberg, 1955). This fact alone invalidates the usual assumptions about the meaning of a family history. Second, autism is a very uncommon disorder, occurring in only about 2–4 children out of every 10,000 (Brask, 1967; Lotter, 1966; Wing *et al.*, 1976). If the population frequency is very low, the rate in relatives will also be low even in conditions with a high heritability (Smith, 1974; Curnow and Smith, 1975). On both these grounds a strong family history would *not* be expected even if autism was largely genetically determined.

Moreover, there are two positive findings from family history studies which *do* suggest possible hereditary influences. First, although the best available estimate indicates that only about 2 per cent of the siblings of autistic children suffer from the same condition (Rutter, 1967), this rate is 50 *times* that in the general population. Second, although a family history of autism is very rare, a family history of speech delay is much more common, being present in about a quarter of cases (Bartak *et al.*, 1975; Rutter *et al.*, 1971). This last observation raises the possibility that it is not autism as such which is inherited but rather that the genetic influence concerns some broader linguistic or cognitive impairment of which autism is but one part.

The second set of evidence comes from twin studies. These were reviewed 10 years ago (Rutter, 1967), with the conclusion that no valid inferences could be drawn. Since then, there have been several further reports (McQuaid, 1975; Kotsopoulos, 1976; Kean, 1975), but the conclusion remains the same (Hanson and Gottesman, 1976). The problems in interpretation are two-fold. First, the reports of monozygotic pairs far outnumber those of dizygotic pairs (22 compared with 10). As dizygotic pairs are twice as frequent in the general population, it is clear that there must have been serious selective biases in reporting.[1] This is sufficient in itself to disregard the findings. Second, excluding two pairs where the autism is associated with an overt physical disorder (Kallman *et al.*, 1940; Keeler, 1958) only five papers reporting same sexed pairs include both an adequate clinical description and evidence of zygosity (Bakwin, 1954; Kamp, 1964; McQuaid, 1975; Ward and Hoddinott, 1962; Vaillant, 1963). For what it is worth, these show two out of three concordance for monozygotic and one out of two concordance for dizygotic twin pairs. In addition, there are two opposite sexed pairs, one concordant (Kotsopoulos, 1976) and one discordant (Böök *et al.*, 1963). The great majority of the remainder report concordance in monozygotic pairs, but the papers lack either clinical details or evidence of zygosity and many are no more than passing references in publications on other topics (Chapman, 1957, 1960; Creak and Ini, 1960; Ornitz *et al.*, 1965; Polan and Spencer, 1959; Sherwin, 1953; Bruch, 1959; Keeler, 1957, 1960; Lovaas *et al.*, 1965; Lehman *et al.*, 1957; Brown, 1963; Weber, 1966; Stutte, 1960). The same problems apply to reports of twins with childhood schizophrenia (Havelkova, 1967; Cline, 1972). O'Gorman (1970) has described two monozygotic pairs concordant for "pseudo-schizophrenia" but the criteria for zygosity were not specified.

In studying genetic factors, it is necessary to bear in mind that autism is probably a behavioural syndrome with multiple aetiologies (Rutter, 1974). Certainly, it is known that the syndrome can develop in association with medical conditions as pathologically diverse as congenital rubella (Chess *et al.*, 1971) and infantile spasms (Taft and Cohen, 1971). Accordingly, the investigation of possible hereditary factors must take account of aetiological heterogeneity.

The need was apparent for a systematic and detailed study of a representative sample of twin pairs containing an autistic child. Because of the possibility that the genetic factor might apply to a broader range of disorders than autism *per se*, it would be essential to obtain detailed assessments of social, emotional, cognitive and linguistic functions in the non-autistic as well as the autistic twins. This demanded a personal study of the twins. Because twins are especially liable to suffer perinatal complications and because such complications have been thought to play a part in the aetiology of autism, it would also be necessary to obtain obstetric and neonatal data in order to check whether the concordance findings were a consequence of physical environmental factors rather than heredity. This is what we set out to do, and the present paper reports the findings.

Methods

(a) Subject selection

The first task was to obtain a complete and unbiased sample of same-sexed twin pairs which included an autistic child. Opposite-sexed pairs were excluded in view of the well-established finding that autism is very much commoner in boys. A list of autistic twin pairs collected over the years by the late Dr. M. Carter provided the start. Then we sought, using multiple sources of information, to obtain information on all school age autistic twin pairs in Great Britain. Letters and personal approaches were made to psychiatric and paediatric colleagues known to have a special interest in autism or who were consultants to special schools which catered for autistic children. A request for cases was also made to all members of the British Child Psychiatry Research Club. Through the Association of Head Teachers of Schools/Classes for autistic children, approaches were made to those running special schools or units for autistic children in Britain. Mrs. Monica White kindly searched the records of all children known to the National Society for Autistic Children, to identify all who were twins. A request for cases was also published in the Society Newsletter. Finally, a personal search was made, using the twin registers at the Maudsley Hospital and at the Hospital for Sick Children, London.

In this way, 33 possible pairs were identified and a detailed scrutiny was made of all available case notes and other clinical information. The sample was restricted to cases which might meet the clinical diagnostic criteria for autism outlined by Kanner (1943) and further delineated by Rutter (1971, 1977), namely, a serious *impairment in the development of social relationships* of the type characteristic of autism (that is with limited eye to eye gaze, poor social responsiveness, impaired selective bonding, a relative failure to go to parents for comfort, and, when older, a lack of empathy, a lack of personal friendships and little group interaction); together with *delayed and deviant language development* with some of the specific features associated with autism (namely poor language comprehension, little use of gesture, echolalia, pronominal reversal, limited social usage of language, repetitive utterances, flat or staccato speech and very restricted imaginative play); and also *stereotyped, repetitive or ritualistic play and interests* (as indicated by an abnormal attachment to objects, marked resistance to change, rituals, repetitive behaviour, unusual preoccupations and restricted interest patterns). Cases with an onset after age 5 years were excluded, but no further restriction was placed in terms of age of onset. Because this was a genetic study, children whose autism was associated with a known diagnosable neurological disorder (such as tuberose sclerosis or cerebral palsy) were also ruled out.

On the basis of information in case notes, eight twin pairs were excluded leaving a sample of 25 twin pairs to be studied in detail. After the children and parents had been seen and interviewed by one of us (SF), diagnoses were then made using all available data. At that final stage, a further four pairs were excluded, leaving a sample of 21 same-sexed pairs ranging in age from 5 to 23 years (six aged 5–9 years, eight aged 10–14 years and seven aged 15+ years). Table 1 gives the sources of selection for these 21 pairs, which constitute the basis of this paper. In a third of cases, the names were available from just one source, but most cases were notified by several different sources. It is clear that no one source would have been adequate.

(b) Zygosity

Zygosity was determined by physical appearance, fingerprints and blood grouping. Attention was paid to such detailed physical characteristics as eye colour and pattern of iris; hair colour, texture and curliness; and shape of nose, ears and hands as well as general appearance (Gedda, 1961). In eight of the pairs, the differences between the twins were sufficiently marked to be sure of dizygosity without the need for further testing. In two pairs, a designation of monozygosity was made on the basis of very close physical

Table 1 Source of cases.

	Sole source	Joint source
Dr. Carter's list	1	7
National Society	0	9
Schools	0	4
Maudsley Hospital Register	2	3
Hospital for Sick Children Register	0	3
Individual psychiatrists	3	12
Newsletter advert	1	0

similarity plus the results of fingerprint analysis using the ridge count method described by Holt (1961). Blood groups testing (Race and Sanger, 1975) was undertaken for 12 pairs,[2] nine of which proved to be monozygotic. Thus, the sample consists of 11 monozygotic and 10 dizygotic pairs.

(c) Data collection

In all cases, an attempt was made to interview the parents, using a standardized interview and also to interview and examine both twins. Complete information was obtained in 19 pairs. In one case, the parents and the autistic twin were interviewed but the normal twin was not seen, in a second no interview was undertaken. However, in both cases where personal interviewing was incomplete, the children had been previously studied very extensively and detailed descriptions, findings and photographs were made available to us.

Topics covered in detail by the parental interview included a systematic account of the children's social, emotional and behavioural development and present status; language development, competence and characteristics; early history and developmental milestones; account of pregnancy, labour and perinatal period; illnesses and separations; family characteristics and social circumstances; and family history of psychiatric and neurological disorder. Vineland Social Maturity scale (Doll, 1947) and Mecham Language Scale (Mecham, 1958) assessments were also undertaken.

The children were closely observed and interviewed at home or in hospital and all were given a detailed neuro-developmental examination. If systematic psychological test findings were not readily available, further testing of cognition and language was undertaken using the Wechsler (1949), Merrill–Palmer (Stutsman, 1948) and Reynell (1969) scales.

Paediatric and psychiatric case records were obtained and studied for all hospital admissions and attendance. Finally, hospital obstetric records were examined for all but one of the 17 twin pairs born in hospital.

(d) Diagnosis of autism

Systematic biases readily arise in twin research through the possibility of the psychiatric diagnosis of one twin being influenced by knowledge on his co-twin and on the zygosity of the pair. Accordingly, rigorous precautions were taken in the study to ensure that such diagnostic contamination could not occur. The procedure was as follows. First, one of us (S. F.) prepared a detailed separate summary of all available psychiatric and developmental information for each of the twin children included in the study. These summaries were then carefully scrutinized to ensure that all possible identifying information (such as family characteristics) were deleted. As a further precaution, the age of the child was given only in terms of a 5-year grouping.

The case histories were then put into random order and given a new case number so that it was no longer possible to sort by pairs. These randomized case histories without identifying information were then given to the other investigator (M. R.) for diagnosis, made "blind" both to pair and to zygosity. His diagnoses are those used for the purposes of all analyses.

Autism was diagnosed on the basis of the strict criteria already outlined. As noted, at this stage, the sample was reduced to 21 pairs including 25 autistic children as a result of these "blind" diagnoses. Fourteen children were diagnosed as showing typical and characteristic infantile autism.[3] A further 11 met the criteria for autism, but the clinical picture was somewhat atypical in some way. Thus, in one child the onset was not until the age of $3\frac{1}{2}$ years; in another child the course was unusual in that almost all autistic features were lost by the age of 6 years (interestingly, he was otherwise fairly typical except that an air encephalogram showed cortical atrophy); and other children were atypical in terms of more social responsiveness or less ritualistic activity than usual.

A separate diagnosis of cognitive/linguistic impairment was made on the basis of at least one of the following features: lack of phrase speech by 30 months, a verbal I.Q. or social quotient of 70 or below, grossly abnormal articulation persisting to age 5 years or older and scholastic differences of such severity as to require special schooling. All 25 autistic children met at least two of these criteria and a further six non-autistic children also did so.

Finally, a psychiatric assessment was made with respect to any non-autistic disorders which were present. In view of its possible connection with infantile autism, particular attention was paid to the possible presence of so-called "autistic psychopathy" meaning a condition characterized by gross social impairment, obsessive preoccupations or circumscribed interest patterns and poor coordination but normal general intelligence (van Krevelen and Kuipers, 1962; van Krevelen, 1963).

Description of sample

(a) Typical–atypical differentiation

In view of the uncertainty whether the typical–atypical differentiation had any validity or meaning, the clinical features of these two subgroups were systematically compared (see Table 2). Very few differences were found apart from the items which led to the group being classified as atypical. Thus, there were no marked differences in terms of sex, I.Q., language abnormalities or social class, and there were only marginally fewer repetitive and stereotyped symptoms. The main difference was that the atypical children showed less severe social abnormalities and four of them had an onset after 30 months (by definition none of the typical children had such a late onset). Also, biological hazards were slightly (but not significantly) less

Table 2 Comparison of typical and atypical cases.

	Typical (n = 14)	*Atypical (n = 11)*
% male	72	81
% social class I & II	43	55
% biological hazards	57	36
Mean I.Q.	52.9	61.4
Mean lang. abn. score*	5.0	4.3
Mean social abn. score†	4.6	3.0
Mean repetitive behav. score‡	3.7	3.0

* Based on six items: lack of use of gesture, echolalia, steteotyped speech, repetitive speech, lack of social use of speech, abnormal mode of delivery (nine non-speaking children omitted from this analysis).
† Based on five items: lack of social smiling in first year, lack of eye to eye gaze, lack of attachment to parents, abnormal relationship with peers, lack of empathy.
‡ Based on five items: abnormal attachment to objects, resistance to change, stereotyped play or interests, rituals, repetitive movements.

common in the atypical group. In view of the fact that, in most respects, the typical and atypical children were so similar, these two subgroupings are combined in presenting the results.

(b) Comparison with non-twin samples

The 21 twin pairs gave rise to 25 cases of autism. As is evident from Table 2 and from the case histories in the Appendix, the behavioural characteristics of the autistic twins were closely comparable to non-twin samples. Table 3 shows how other features compare with a study of singletons previously undertaken by one of us (Rutter *et al.*, 1967).

Of the 25 autistic children, 19 were male, giving a male: female ratio of 3.1 to 1 which is similar to most other studies. The parents came from all

Table 3 Sex, I.Q. and social class.

	Twins (this study)	*Singletons (Rutter et al., 1967)*
Sex ratio	3.2 : 1	4.25 : 1
I.Q.		
< 50	48.0%	43.0%
50–69	20.0%	28.5%
70+	32.0%	28.5%
Social class		
I and II	57.0%	55.5%
III	28.5%	41.3%
IV and V	14.5%	3.2%

social strata but were predominantly middle class, which is in line with most other series. Other family characteristics were also much as expected. Thus none of the parents suffered from schizophrenia and only one (case 19) of the 36 sibs was autistic (a rate of 2.8%). However, in three of the 21 families (14%) either a parent or sib had experienced a severe delay in the acquisition of spoken language (cases 2, 10 and 14).

About half the autistic children were severely retarded, but nearly a third had an I.Q. in the normal range on non-verbal tests, which again is closely comparable to other findings. By definition, none of the children had a diagnosable neurological condition. However, two-thirds showed impairment on developmental functions such as motor coordination or had isolated minor signs such as strabismus or choreiform movements. Four of the autistic children had developed epileptic fits during adolescence. In 11 cases, EEGs had been reported as abnormal, but, in most cases, the abnormalities were of a non-specific nature. Air encephalograms had been undertaken in three children; these showed left-sided cortical atrophy in one case, slight dilatation of the right lateral ventricle in a second case and no abnormality in a third. It may be concluded that, apart from the fact that they are twins, the 25 autistic children in the sample are closely similar to the autistic children described in non-twin populations.

Results

(a) Concordance for autism

Of the 10 dizygotic twin pairs, *none* was concordant for autism, whereas *four* of the 11 monozygotic pairs were concordant (Exact test; $P = 0.055$). This gives a 36% concordance rate by pair or a 53% concordance rate by proband for MZ pairs and in each case a zero per cent concordance for dizygotic pairs [see Gottesman and Shields (1976) for a discussion of concordance by pair or by proband].

Two of the concordant MZ pairs (1 and 3[4]) were closely similar in all respects. In each case, the twins were severely retarded and the autism was somewhat atypical in terms of the limited evidence of ritualistic features. However, in both the other two pairs, there were important differences between the twins in spite of concordance for autism. In one (2) there was an 18 point difference in non-verbal I.Q. and a 24 point difference in Peabody language quotient. The twin with a lower non-verbal I.Q. but higher verbal I.Q. made much more progress in both social relationships and use of language. In the fourth pair (4) there was a 39 point I.Q. difference; in this case, the more intelligent twin was less severely autistic, although the type of behaviour was closely similar in both. It is also notable that the more intelligent twin did not develop autism until 3 years of age, although apart from the late onset the clinical picture was typical of autism.

(b) Concordance for cognitive or social impairment

The next question is: what is inherited? Is it autism as such or is it some broader form of which autism is but one part? To answer this it is necessary to examine the pattern of disabilities in the non-autistic co-twins and to determine the concordance in MZ and DZ pairs for these disabilities.

In addition to the 25 autistic children, another six showed some form of cognitive impairment. In all cases, this involved some kind of speech or language deficit but the type of deficit varied. Three of the six children (cases 5, 8, and 12) had been markedly delayed in early speech development, not using phrase speech until 3 years or later. One of these (5) was also mildly retarded and attended a special school. A further child had markedly abnormal articulation to age 7 years, although she had not been delayed in early speech development. Another child (case 9) with SQ of 70 had been generally mildly retarded in development and did not use phrase speech until 28 months. The sixth child (case 6) had a verbal I.Q. 21 points below the non-verbal and attended an ESN school but there had been no speech delay.

Five of the six children with cognitive impairment were in MZ pairs. Thus, five of the seven non-autistic children in MZ pairs had cognitive abnormalities compared with only one of the 10 non-autistic children in DZ pairs (Exact test; $P = 0.0175$). As all the 25 autistic children also met the criteria for cognitive abnormality, the concordance rates may be recalculated for all forms of cognitive impairment, both autistic and non-autistic (see Table 4).

The results are striking. Nine of the 11 MZ pairs were concordant for some kind of cognitive disability, usually involving language, whereas this was so for only one out of the 10 DZ pairs (Exact test; $P = 0.0015$).

Only one child (case 8), included in the six just mentioned, had social or behavioural problems at all reminiscent of autism, and he was diagnosed as showing autistic psychopathy on the basis of little social usage of speech, circumscribed interest patterns and a lack of social relationships.

Three of the other children with cognitive impairments, however, also showed some kind of social or emotional disability. One child (7) was painfully sensitive and self-conscious, crying over imagined slights; another

Table 4 Pairwise concordance by zygosity.

	MZ pairs (n = 11)	DZ pairs (n = 10)	MZ–DZ difference (Exact test)
	(%)	(%)	
Concordance for autism	36	0	$P = 0.055$
Concordance for cognitive disorder (including autism)	82	10	$P = 0.0015$

(6) although friendly and sure of himself now, had had a severe and disabling dog phobia when younger, and a third (5) was rather shy, sensitive and lacking in confidence. A fourth child (13) without cognitive impairment developed a psychiatric disorder of uncertain nature at age 17 years. Because of the overlap with cognitive impairment, the concordance in terms of social/emotional difficulties (including autism) is similar: eight out of 11 MZ pairs compared with two out of 10 DZ pairs.

(c) Biological hazards and concordance

The major difference in concordance between MZ and DZ pairs strongly suggests the importance of hereditary influences in the aetiology of autism. However, before drawing that conclusion it is necessary first to check whether the concordance patterns are explicable in terms of biological hazards associated with the birth process. We identified five features known to be associated with brain damage (and hence likely to predispose to autism): severe haemolytic disease (Gerver and Day 1950), a delay in breathing of at least 5 minutes after birth (Drage and Berendes, 1966; Hunter, 1968), neonatal convulsions (Rose and Lombroso, 1970), a second birth which was delayed by at least 30 minutes following the birth of the first twin (Dunn, 1965; Kurtz et al., 1955) and multiple congenital anomalies. Such features were present in 11 out of the 42 children.

Table 5 shows the concordance for autism in terms of biological hazards. In only two pairs, did both children experience biological hazards and both these pairs were discordant for autism. It may be concluded that the concordance is likely to be due to genetic factors and certainly is not explicable in terms of the perinatal complications on which we had data, and the same applies to the concordance for cognitive impairment. In none of the six pairs concordant for cognitive impairment but not autism were biological hazards present in both twins.

(d) Biological hazards and discordance

The next question is why only some of the children with a cognitive impairment showed the syndrome of autism. The possible importance of biological

Table 5 Concordance/discordance for autism by presence of biological hazards.

	Biological hazards		
	Both twins	One twin only	Neither twin
Concordant	0	1	3
Discordant	2	6	9

hazards in this connection was re-examined by focusing on the 17 pairs discordant for autism. In six of these pairs one, but only one, of the twins had experienced one of the five specified biological hazards. In *all six* cases, it was the autistic twin who was affected (see left-hand side of Table 6). However, there were a further 11 cases (see right-hand side of Table 6) in which the biological hazards affected neither twin or both twins, and so did not account for the discordance.

In order to examine these 11 discordant cases further, a wider definition of biological hazard, in terms of a marked difference between the twins, was employed. This included a birth weight at least a pound less than the other twin (three cases) (Willerman and Churchill, 1967), a pathologically narrow umbilical cord (one case), a more severe haemolytic anaemia associated with neonatal apnoea (two cases), and a severe febrile illness possibly involving encephalitis (one case). This differentiated a further six cases (see Table 7), and again it identified the autistic one each time. It may be concluded that some form of biological impairment, usually in the perinatal period, strongly predisposed to the development of autism. The pattern of findings is summarized in Table 8.

Did the same biological hazards explain the presence of a cognitive deficit? To examine this question, we compared the six non-autistic twins who showed cognitive impairment with the 11 non-autistic twins without a cognitive deficit. The only two children (out of these 17) who had experienced a biological hazard were both *without* a cognitive disability. Clearly, biological hazards did *not* account for the presence of cognitive abnormalities.

Table 6 Biological hazards and discordance for autism.

	Biological hazards			
	Autistic twin only	*Other twin only*	*Both twins*	*Neither twins*
MZ pairs	2	0	0	5
DZ pairs	4	0	2	4

Table 7 Biological differences and discordance for autism.

	Biological differences		
	Autistic twin worse	*Other twin worse*	*No difference*
MZ pairs	2	0	3
DZ pairs	4	0	2

Table 8 Summary of biological hazards in discordant pairs.

Hazard	Autistic twin	Non-autistic twin
	MZ PAIRS	
Definite	Multiple congenital anomalies	—
	Neonatal convulsions	
Possible	Severe febrile illness	—
	Pathologically narrow cord	—
None	—	—
	—	—
	—	—
	DZ PAIRS	
Definite	Apnoea	—
	Delay second birth	—
	Delay second birth	—
	Delay second birth	—
Possible or	Severe haemolytic disease + apnoea	Delay second birth
Difference in severity	Severe haemolytic disease + apnoea	Mild haemolytic disease
	Birth weight 1¾ lb lower	—
	Birth weight 1¾ lb lower	—
None	—	—

(e) Psychosocial influences

The final issue was whether psychosocial environmental influences were associated with discordance in terms of either autism or cognitive impairment. Because both were evident from early life, it was necessary to focus on possible factors in the infancy period, which meant that our data were necessarily retrospective in large part and often crude. All pairs had been reared together during infancy, although in one case (11) the autistic child was often in hospital during the first year. In this case, the severe early lack of responsiveness was followed by maternal rejection. There were no differences between the autistic and non-autistic children in experiences other than those which were associated with the greater frequency of neonatal biological hazards. Thus, out of the nine cases in which there was a difference in time before discharge home after birth, in seven it was the autistic child who stayed in hospital longer. In some instances, this involved periods in an incubator or some kind of intensive care.

Discussion

(a) Sampling and selection

Before discussing the meaning of the findings it is necessary to consider the adequacy of our sampling, as the rest of the results hinge on that. In order to obtain as complete a sample as possible we used an unusually large number of sources of diverse kinds. As a result, most of the children were reported by several different agencies. This in itself provides some indication of the efficiency of our sampling techniques. However, two better checks are available. First, there is the monozygotic–dizygotic pair ratio. For same-sexed pairs surviving the first year, the ratio should be approximately 6 : 7 (Slater and Cowie, 1971), which is very close to our observed ratio of 11 : 10. Second, there is the number of autistic twins found. The Registrar-General figures for 1964 show that 6176 liveborn same-sexed twins were born that year (Slater and Cowie, 1971). Taking a 1-year survival rate of 88.1% (based on Gittelsohn and Milham's 1965 figures) that reduces to 5441. Our sampling was most thorough for the school years so if we multiply that by 13 to obtain the figure for the birth years 1958–1970 that makes 70,733 pairs and 141,466 children. The next step is to calculate the proportion of autistic children expected. We had to rely on information about children referred to clinics or special schools *and* diagnosed as autistic by them and later also by us. For this purpose, the administrative surveys probably provide the most appropriate initial guide. In Britain, the Department of Education figures showed a prevalence of 1.75 per 10,000 (Wing *et al.*, 1976) and in the U.S.A. Treffert's (1970) figure was 2.5 per 10,000. On this basis, we should have had between 24.8 and 35.4 children. However, as with other studies (Wing *et al.*, 1976), we found that not all the cases reported as autistic met our diagnostic criteria. In practice, we excluded about a quarter, which brings the expected number of twins in our final sample down to 18.6 to 26.6.[5] In fact (excluding the four children born before 1958 and the one living in Scotland) we obtained 20 autistic children who were part of a same-sexed pair—which is very close to the expected number. It may be concluded that there is every reason to believe that our sample of autistic twins was about as complete as it could be.

It is also necessary to consider whether the choice of a twin sample introduced any particular biases. The most obvious possibility concerns the frequency of perinatal complications. These tend to be rather commoner in multiple births than in single births (Dunn, 1965) and this may have increased the likelihood of our finding an association between birth hazards and autism. On the other hand, studies of singletons have also suggested that perinatal complications tend to be somewhat commoner in autistic children than in other children (see e.g. Lotter, 1967; Whittam *et al.*, 1966; Hinton, 1963; Moore, 1972; Knobloch and Pasamanick, 1974; Torrey *et al.*, 1975), although not usually to the extent found in this twin sample. It should be noted, however, that our sample did not have particularly low birth weights. Thirty of the 42 children had a birth weight of over 5 lb and none had a birth weight under 3 lb. We may conclude that our choice of a twin sample probably increased the likelihood of finding an association between perinatal complications and autism, but similar associations of lesser degree have been noted in singletons.

Similarly, it is well known that delayed acquisition of speech is commoner in twins than singletons. It might be suggested that this is why so many of the non-autistic twins showed impaired language. However, were this simply due to twinning, it would be expected to occur with equal frequency in the MZ and DZ pairs (Mittler, 1971). In fact, we found that abnormalities of language were much more frequent in the MZ than in the DZ twins. Moreover, the abnormalities we found did not consist of just speech delay but rather involved a wider range of cognitive functions.

Finally, there is the question of sample size. How much confidence can be placed on the MZ–DZ differences in concordance in view of the relatively small sample size of 21 pairs? Obviously, some caution is needed before drawing too sweeping conclusions, and clearly replication is required. Nevertheless, as already indicated, there are good reasons for supposing that this twin study has avoided the serious biases which plague twin research. Moreover, although the sample is small, the MZ–DZ differences were large and statistically significant. It seems likely that the concordance differences are true ones.

(b) Hereditary influences

The MZ–DZ difference in concordance for autism and the much larger difference in concordance for cognitive disorder clearly points strongly to the importance of genetic factors in the aetiology of autism. Indeed, the size of the MZ–DZ difference, together with the population frequency of autism indicate a very high heritability or coefficient of genetic determination (Smith, 1974; Curnow and Smith, 1975). The finding that concordance is strongly associated with the zygosity of the twin pairs and not at all with the presence of physical environmental hazards indicates that the concordance truly represents an hereditary influence rather than biological damage during the birth process. In this connection, it should be noted that there are *greater* intra-uterine environment differences in MZ than in DZ pairs, as reflected, for example, in the greater mean difference in birth weights in MZ pairs (Mittler, 1971).

(c) What is inherited?

The findings clearly point to the conclusion that the hereditary influences are concerned with a variety of cognitive abnormalities and not just with autism. In other words, autism is genetically linked with a broader range of cognitive disorders. The results also show that the cognitive deficits linked with autism usually involve delays or disorders in the acquisition of spoken language. Thus, of the six pairs concordant for cognitive impairment, in

313

three the non-autistic twin was not using phrase speech until after his third birthday. One of the remaining three showed a lesser degree of speech delay, a second had verbal skills much inferior to visuo-spatial, and the third had very abnormal articulation. It may be inferred that language difficulties of some kind are generally part of the problem. The conclusion is in keeping with the extensive evidence for the importance of abnormalities in language and symbolization in autism (Rutter, 1974).

One the other hand, in most of the non-autistic children, it was not usually a straightforward isolated developmental delay in language acquisition. First, two of the six children also had some general intellectual impairment. Second, in one case, the language delay involved echolalia, and in another it involved a lack of social usage comparable to that found in infantile autism. It seems that a language deficit may be a part of the cognitive impairment in most cases but it is not usually a "pure" or isolated delay in the acquisition of spoken language. Of course, it is not suggested that all forms of language impairment are genetically linked to autism. Indeed, in most respects, the language characteristics of autistic children are very different to those of children with a developmental language disorder (Bartak et al., 1975, 1977). However, it seems that some cases of language abnormality are generically linked with autism. Unfortunately, knowledge is lacking on how to tell which these are.

It is also necessary to ask whether the social and emotional difficulties which were present in most of the children with a cognitive deficit are also part of what is inherited. For several reasons, no firm conclusions are possible on this point. In the first place, social difficulties and emotional disturbance are quite common in any group of children with language delay (Rutter, 1972; Stevenson and Richman, 1977), and with a sample as small as ours it was not possible to determine whether difficulties were more common in this group. In the second place, only one of the six children with cognitive impairment had social difficulties of a kind at all similar to those shown by autistic children. It may be that the shyness, fears and sensitivity are part of what is inherited or it may be that, as in other children with language delay, they are merely temporary secondary emotional reactions to cognitive and communication difficulties. The present data do not allow a choice between these two possibilities.

A twin study could provide the opportunity to examine possible links between autism and schizophrenia. However, very few of the twins in this sample were old enough to determine whether autism and schizophrenia ever occur together in monozygotic pairs. None of the monozygotic twins had a disorder with any resemblance to schizophrenia. But there was one non-autistic dizygotic twin who showed social withdrawal at age 17 years. The possibility of schizophrenia clearly arises, but there was no evidence of thought disorder, delusions, hallucinations or any other first rank symptoms. Further follow-up is needed to make a diagnosis. Nevertheless, it should be added that, in spite of a large number of twin studies of schizo-phrenia, no case has ever been reported of infantile autism occurring in a non-schizophrenic co-twin.

(d) Mode of inheritance

It is obvious from the low rate of disorder in the sibs that autism is not a disease inherited in clear-cut Mendelian fashion. However, many factors (e.g. phenocopies, genetic heterogeneity, incomplete penetrance, high mutation rate, etc.) may distort the simple Mendelian ratios. In practice, it is extremely difficult on the basis of family data to differentiate between monogenic inheritance with incomplete penetrance and polygenic or multifactorial effects (Curnow and Smith, 1975). In the case of autism, the sorting out of mode of inheritance is much complicated by the fact that autistic children rarely marry and have children. One crucial piece of information which is needed is what happens to the offspring of non-autistic sibs or twins with cognitive impairment. Unfortunately, no information is available on that point and until this is known genetic model building seems premature.

(e) Environmental influences

Our findings clearly indicate that, in addition to hereditary factors, environ-mental hazards involving the risk of brain damage also play an important part in the aetiology of autism. Out of the 17 pairs discordant for autism, there were 12 in which autism was associated with some kind of biological hazard or difference which affected the autistic child and not his co-twin. In this series, with one exception, the biological features were all perinatal in origin. However, it is clear from studies of non-twin samples that autism may arise on the basis of quite diverse forms of brain pathology, including congenital rubella (Chess *et al.*, 1971) and infantile spasms (Taft and Cohen, 1971).

Although both hereditary and environmental influences play an import-ant part in the genesis of autism, the findings from this study suggest that they work in rather different ways. The MZ–DZ concordance differences showed that the hereditary factor(s) were concerned with the genesis of cognitive/linguistic abnormalities rather than with just autism as such. But this was not the case with the biological hazards at all. They were com-pletely *un*associated with non-autistic cognitive deficits in spite of a strong association with autism.

(f) Genetic–environmental interactions

That difference raises the question of how far hereditary and environmental influences cause different cases of autism and how far they act in conjunction as part of a multifactorial determination, Our data do not allow any firm conclusions on this point but they suggest that both occur.

The four MZ pairs concordant for autism suggest that, in some cases, genetic factors may be sufficient to cause autism. Only one of the eight autistic children in these four pairs suffered a hazard at all likely to lead to brain injury—his disorder was more severe than that of his co-twin.

On the other hand, it appears that brain injury alone may also be a sufficient cause of autism. This is suggested by the fact that biological hazards occurred with much the same frequency in MZ and DZ pairs. It is also indicated by the finding from other studies that the rate of autism in children with particular forms of brain pathology, such as caused by congenital rubella (Chess *et al.*, 1971) is considerably higher than that in the sibs of autistic children.

Nevertheless, many cases of autism appear to result from a combination of brain damage and an inherited cognitive abnormality. This is suggested by the finding that out of the seven MZ pairs discordant for autism, in four cases the autistic child but not his non-autistic co-twin had experienced some form of biological hazard liable to cause brain damage. In three of these four cases the non-autistic child had a cognitive deficit, suggesting that it may have been brain injury that converted the deficit into a full-blown autistic syndrome.

In this regard it is interesting that, over a decade ago, van Krevelen (1963) suggested that autism might result from the combination of an inherited personality deficit plus organic brain damage. The present results are in accord with that general hypothesis, but the deficit found involved cognitive/linguistic abnormalities rather than the "autistic psychopathy" syndrome postulated by van Krevelen.

In summary, we may conclude that this systematic study of 21 same-sexed twin pairs in which at least one twin showed the syndrome of infantile autism indicates the importance of a genetic factor which probably concerns a cognitive deficit involving language. It also indicates the importance of biological hazards in the perinatal period which may operate either on their own or in combination with a genetic predisposition. However, uncertainty remains on both the mode of inheritance and exactly what it is which is inherited.

Summary

A systematic study was made of a representative group of 21 same-sexed twin pairs (11 MZ and 10 DZ) in which at least one twin showed the syndrome of infantile autism. There was a 36 per cent pair-wise concordance rate for autism in MZ pairs compared with 0 per cent concordance in DZ pairs. The concordance for cognitive abnormalities was 82 per cent in MZ pairs and 10 per cent in DZ pairs. It was concluded that there were important hereditary influences concerning a cognitive deficit which included but was not restricted to autism. In 12 out of 17 pairs discordant for autism, the presence of autism was associated with a biological hazard liable to cause brain damage. It was concluded that brain injury in the infancy period may lead to autism on its own or in combination with a genetic predisposition. Uncertainty remains on both the mode of inheritance and exactly what is inherited.

Acknowledgements

We are deeply indebted to the many colleagues whose help made this study possible. We are particularly grateful to those who gave us access to their patients and who provided information about them: Mrs. L. Arendt, Dr. A. Bentovim, Dr. I. Berg, Dr. F. Bernard, Mrs. W. Brown, Dr. M. Crawford, Dr. M. Davies, Mr. C. Dyer, Dr. K. Fraser, Dr. E. Frommer, Professor P. Graham, Dr. J. Lisle, Dr. L. Minski, Dr. G. O'Gorman, Dr. M. Shepherd, Dr. G. Simon, Dr. F. Tomlinson, Dr. J. Towler, Miss D. Trowell, Dr. J. Varley and Dr. T. Weihs. Dr. J. Shields gave invaluable help in providing access to the Maudsley Hospital Twin Register, in advising us throughout the study, and in giving comments on an earlier draft of this paper. We are grateful to Professor C. Carter for allowing us access to the Hospital for Sick Children's Twin Register and for providing information on some cases; to Dr. R. Sanger who kindly undertook the blood grouping analysis for us and to Mr. Gregory Carey who undertook some of the dermatoglyphic analysis. We are also especially grateful to Dr. L. Bartak, Mrs. R. Hemsley and Mrs. P. Howlin who undertook psychological testing with a number of the twins and to Mrs. Monica White for searching the records of the National Society for Autistic Children to identify twins.

The study was supported in part by a grant from the MRC.

Appendix: Case summaries of cases
Monozygotic pairs

Case 1

Zygosity determined bld. grps. Pair concordant for (atypical) autism. Male. Age 22 yr.

Family. Fa. is industrial engineer. Mo. had one episode untrtd. depression. Three older sibs: two had single episodes of severe depression.

Pregn. Hyperemesis and fainting throughout. Gestation 36 weeks.

1st born twin. B. wt. 5 lb 2 oz. Normal neonatal course. Normal motor milestones. Severe eczema 4–9 months so that cd. not be picked up. Lack of responsiveness noted from 9 months. Lack of eye to eye gaze. Rejected comfort and cuddling. Lack of sympathy. No friendships. No babble, speech or gesture. Food fads and pica when younger. Strong attachment to skittle

317

up to 12 yr. Occ. repetitive brick play. No imaginative play. Finger-flicking mannerism and stereotyped gait. Head banging and wrist biting. Fits since 12 yr. Special school to 14 yr and the mental subn. hosp. EEG non-specific abn. Poor coordination, awkward gait. Language age < 1 yr. Social age 3 yr 7 months. Biochem. normal.

2nd born twin. B. wt. 5 lb 6 oz. Normal neonatal course. Normal motor milestones. Severe excema 4–9 months. Lack of responsiveness from 9 months. Lack of eye to eye gaze. Minimal parental attachment. No friendships. Rejected comfort and cuddling. Normal babble but no speech or gesture. V. Severe food fads. Upset by changes. Puts objects into rows. No imag. play. Finger-flicking mannerisms. Carried string and waved in front of eyes up to 12 yr. Wrist biting. Fits since 16 yr. Special school to 14 yr and then mental subn. hosp. EEG non-specific abn. Fair coordination, normal gait. Language age < 1 yr. Social age 3 yr 7 months. Biochem. normal.

Case 2

Zygosity determined bld. grps. Pair concordant for autism. Male. Age 12 yr.

Family. Fa. is plumber (born W. Indies), was late talking. Mo. anxious and recurrently depressed (untrtd.). Two sibs. (one older, one younger), one behav. diffs. at school.

Pregn. Anaemia, transfusion. Gestation 40 weeks.

1st born twin. B. wt. 6 lb 11 oz. Normal neonatal course. Normal motor milestones. Lack of responsiveness from 1 yr. Lack of eye to eye gaze, lack of attachments, avoids contact, no friendships. Single words 8 yr; phrases 10 yr. Echolalic, pronominal reversal, stereotyped sp. Poor articulation, lack of cadence and irregular rhythm. No gesture. Hands over ears. Fixed routines re walks and meals. Repetitive stereotyped drawings. Finger-flicking mannerisms, head banging. Attends special school. Myopia, poor gross motor coordination. EEG non-specific abn. WISG FS 56. VS 50. PS 75. S.Q. 44 Peabody L.Q. 33. Reynell language comprehension age 7 yr 10 mo. (At C.A. 12.1 yr). Neale Reading Age Acc 8 yr 4 months. Comprehension No score. Biochem. normal.

2nd born twin. B. wt. 6 lb 13 oz. Normal neonatal course. Normal motor milestones. Lack of responsiveness from 2nd yr. Lack of differentiation people to 5 yr. Minimal parental attachment. Solitary play, no friendships. No babble in lst 2 yr. Single words 2 yr, phrases 5 yr. Echolalia, stereotyped phrases, little social speech, lack of cadence up to last 2 yr. Head banging and pica when younger. Finger-flicking mannerism. Strong attachment to toy soldiers (takes to bed). Repetitive, stereotyped play and drawing. Upset by changes routine. Bath ritual. Marked improvment after age 10 yr so that now friendly with adults and using normal speech appropriately. Lack of friendships remain. Attends special school. Myopia, strabismus, poor coordination. EEG non-specific abn. Biochem. normal. WISG FS 57. VS 60.

PS 57. S.Q.59, Peabody, L.Q.57. Neale Reading Age (when C.A. 12.1 yr). Acc. 9 yr. 1 month. Comprehension 7 yr 3 months.

Case 3

Zygosity determined bld. grps. Pair concordant for (atypical) autism. Male. Age 14 yr.

Family. Fa. is porter, Mo. nurse. Four older sisters.

Pregn. normal, 34 weeks, gestation. 24 hr labour.

1st born twin. Breech. B. wt. 5 lb 10 oz. Normal neonatal course. Normal motor milestones. Severe crying and sleep dist. in infancy. Not cuddly, did not come for comfort, lack of differentiation people to 5 yr. Normal smiling and eye to eye gaze. No group play of friendships. Odd words only, occ. echoing. Upset by noise. No gesture. Whirls self and spins knives. Likes shiny objects. Various food fads. Pica (total lead intoxication). Wrist biting. Destructive. Restless. Special school to 11 yr and then mental subn. hosp. EEG sharp wave focus. Strabismus, wide-based gait, poor motor coordination. Mecham language age < 1 yr. Social age 18 months.

2nd born twin. Breech. B. wt 5 lb 4 oz. Normal neonatal course. Normal motor milestones. Severe crying and sleep dist. in infancy. Not cuddly, lack of differentiation people to 5 yr. Normal smiling and eye to eye gaze. No group play or friendship. Odd words only, occ. echoing. V. upset by noise, puts fingers in ears. No gesture. Age 3–5 yr severe screaming, aggression, and destruction. Breaks windows and furniture. Upset by changes. Attracted shiny objects. Likes to be swung around, likes spinning knives. Food fads. V. severe pica (total lead intoxication). Severe head banging, face slapping, pulled out hair. Occ. hand mannerisms. Toe walking when younger. Special school to 11 yr and then mental subn. hosp. One recent (major) fit with some social deterioration. EEG sharp wave focus. Strabismus. Poor coordination and wide-based gait. Planter responses equivocal. Mecham language < 1 yr. Social age 18 months.

Case 4

Zygosity determined bld. grps. Pair concordant for autism (one atypical). Male. Age 8 yr.

Family. Fa. univ. teacher. Mo. had one previous pregn.—terminated because hydramnios. Bilingual family.

Pregn. Vomiting early months. Pre-eclamptic toxaemia. Induced 39 weeks.

1st born twin. B. wt. 6 lb. 10 oz. Low forceps. Normal neonatal course. Normal motor milestones. Normal development apart from pronominal reversal until 3 yr when became anxious, tearful, upset. Speech deteriorated to poorly articulated monosyllables. After 6 months gradual improvement. Normal eye to eye gaze and normal relationship parents. Does not play peers and regarded as odd by them. Speech complex but stereotyped and echolalic: pronominal reversal, little appreciation of abstract. Upset by changes. Attached to cardboard buses which he carries around. Repetitive drawing buses and copying newspaper adverts. Limited imagination. Attends normal school. Leiter I.Q.90, S.Q.89. Mecham L.Q.113.

2nd born twin. B. wt. 5 1b. Born 30 min after twin, foetal distress and uterine inertia. Given positive pressure O^2, breathed 7 min. Urinary tract infection. Disch. hosp. after 4 weeks. Diffs. feeding. Lack of cuddling. Normal motor milestones. Absorbed twiddling cotton reel at 8 months. Blank facial expression and lack of eye to eye gaze. Not attached to parents until after 2 yr and then limited. No friendships, some beginning of limited grp. play. Normal babble. First words 58 months—still few words only, occ. echolalia. Waves bye-bye. Excellent memory spatial relationships. Dislikes new situations. Several attachments to odd objects (e.g. buttons), swings string in front of face. Hand twisting mannerism and odd gait. Repetit. stereotyped play. Pica. Attends special school. Biochem. normal. M.P. I.Q.51. S.Q.32. Mecham language age < 18 months.

Case 5

Zygosity determined bld. grps. Pair discordant for autism, concordant for cognitive and social/emotional disorder. Female. Age 15 yr.

Family. Fa. engineer (univ. grad.). One normal older sister. Mo. also had one still birth at 7 months.

Pregn. Bleeding at 2 months. 39 week gestation. Twins not diagn. and delivery at home.

1st born twin. B. wt. 5 1b 8 oz. Normal neonatal course. Sat 10 months. Walked 21 months. Normally cuddly responsive baby. Single words 20 months. Phrases 36 months. Normal usage speech. Became more passive when tormented by autistic sib. twin. Shy sensitive girl with low self-esteem but otherwise normal social relationships—affectionate, sympathetic and has a few friends. Behav. normal. Normal school until 11 yr and then special school (ESN). WISC I.Q. FS 51. VS 61. PS 48. Reading age 8 yr 10 months. S.Q. 115. Poor coordination.

2nd born twin. B. wt. 5 1b. Breech. Delay in breathing. Cord v. narrow and white. Haemorrhagic disease 2 days. Sat 10 months. Walked 23 months. Lack of responsiveness from infancy: not interested in people, distressed by noise, wd. crawl on wood but not carpet. No attachment to parents until after 5 yr and then minimal. Lack of eye to eye gaze, did not come for comfort. Approaches small children but no play with peers and no friendships. Some echoed words at 30 months but no phrases until 6 yr. Speech still stereotyped and repetitive with much delayed echoing. Marked resistance to all changes. Rigid stereotyped play with multiple routines and rituals. Various attachment to odd objects. Facial grimaces, hand flapping

320

and mannerism, bouncing gait. Pica in early childhood. Head banging and wrist biting age 3–6 yr. Strabismus. Clumsy. Awkward gait. Merrill–Palmer I.Q. 28. S.Q.40. Mecham I.Q.29.

Case 6

Zygosity determined bld. grps. Pair discordant for autism, concordant for cognitive and social/emotional disorder. Male. Age 10 yr.
Family. Fa. tradesman. One normal older sister. Mo. also had one still birth.
Pregn. Severe vomiting first trimester. Toxaemia last trimester; 2 admissions. 39 week gestation.
1st born twin. B. wt. 6 1b 7 oz. Normal neonatal course. Normal motor milestones. Severe excema in first year—mild since with occ. asthma. Responsive but difficult baby, often crying, v. poor sleeper. Did not come for comfort. Variable eye to eye gaze. Often rocks and appears detached. No group play, no friendships, some parallel play with twin. Some echoed words at 2 yr but diminished at 2½ yr. Now only echolalia and some spont. single words. No social usage sp. Slow to adapt to new situations. Lines up objects in rows. Good with constructional toys but no representational or imaginative play. Prefers routines. Severe dog phobia. Finger flicking mannerisms, rocks, grimaces. Pica. Head banging up to 5 yr. Attends special school. Pleasant temperament now but v. little reciprocity in social interaction. WISC Non-verbal I.Q.83. S.Q.34. Mecham language age 18 months.
2nd born twin. B. wt. 6 1b 4 oz. Normal neonatal course. Normal motor milestones. Excema and asthma for 4 months. Phrase speech before 2 yr. Now uses language normally but mild articulation defect. Sociable and friendly but rather immature and had severe dog phobia until a year ago. Behav. normal. Creative, imaginative play. Has won friends. Attends special school (ESN). WISC VS 79. PS 100. S.Q.97. Mecham L.Q.89. Poor fine motor coordination. Motor overflow.

Case 7

Zygosity determined bld. grps. Pair discordant for (atypical) autism, concordant for cognitive and social/emotional disorder. Female. Age 12 yr.
Family. Fa. Business manager. One normal older brother.
Pregn. Bleeding at 3 and 4 months. 35 week gestation.
1st born twin. B. wt. 4 1b. In hosp. 21 days for slow wt. gain. Normal neonatal course. Normal motor milestones. Cuddly responsive baby. Single words by 1 yr and phrases before 2 yr. Marked articulation defect to 7 yr. Talkative, sociable girl with many friends. V. sympathetic and emotionally concerned—befriends children with diffs. V. sensitive worrier; cries daily with imagined slights and failures at school. Apprehensive of new situations.

Reluctance to attend school (ordinary). Merrill–Palmer I.Q. above av. S.Q. 104. Mecham L.Q. 122.

2nd born twin. Breech. B. wt. 5 1b 4 oz. In hosp. 14 days. Normal neonatal course. Normal motor milestones. Single words 2 yr. Normal develop. apart from immature speech and poor articulation until $4^1/_2$ yr when had severe febrile illness and profound change in behav. Lost social responsiveness, marked reduction in speech, eating poor, appeared aimless, ceased to play. Until 6 yr lack of personal interaction, blank expression, lack of eye to eye gaze. Now somewhat more responsive but no friends. Stereotyped phrases, monotone, no social speech, echoes, poor articulation, excellent word memory. Eating rituals, repetitive drawing, rocking. No imag. play. Helps in house. Awkward gait. Attends special school. Merrill–Palmer I.Q. (non verbal) 98. S.Q. 41. Mecham I.Q. 29.

Case 8

Zygosity determined dermatoglyphics and appearance. Pair discordant for autism, concordant for cognitive and social/emotional disorder. Male. Age 10 yr.

Family. Fa. business manager. One younger sister (4 yr) with echoing and poor articulation. Lines up objects. Normal social relationships and normal social usage language. Having psychiat. trt. for encopresis. There are several eccentrics in mo.'s family.

Pregn. Bleeding at 3 months. Hydramnios. 35 week gestation. Both twins born with forceps for uterine inertia.

1st born twin. Face presentation. B. wt. 4 1b 11 oz. Normal Apgar score. In hosp. 50 days because of feeding diffs. from cleft palate. I.P. 1 wk pneumonia at 4 months. Several operations for congenital anomalies. Sat 9 months, walked 22 months. Not bowel trained until 9 yr. Lack of social smiling and responsiveness in first year. Stared at sun, refused to eat at 2 yr. Blank expression and lack of eye to eye gaze. No response to parents before 5 yr. No play with children. Echolalic speech 3 yr but no meaningful words until 6 yr. Now single words and stereotyped phrases. No social use sp. Marked resistance to change of routine or furniture. Carries string and flicks it. Various fixed routines. Likes to touch shiny objects. Used to rock and clap hands. No appropriate play. Severe pica. Attends special school. Rt. ptosis, fixed pupil and external palsy. Left strabismus and nystagmus. Repaired hare lip. Poor coordination. Merrill–Palmer I.Q. 24. S.Q. 17. Mecham L.Q. 18.

2nd born twin. Vertex. B. wt. 4 1b 12 oz. Normal Apgar score. In hospital 17 days. Normal neonatal course. Normal motor milestones. Cuddly, responsive baby. Single words 24 months, phrases after 3 yr. Stutters when excited, v. poor articulation. Vocab. adeq. but limited social speech. Normal relationships parents. Only recently started to play peers; does not initiate interaction. Anxious. No resistance to change. Series of circumscribed solitary interests (currently marbles). Also imag. play. Clumsy and socially gauche. Attends normal school but had special tutoring in reading and spelling. Slow fine motor movements. Shy but friendly boy. WISC VS 108. PS 122. S.Q. 95. Mecham L.Q. 70. Diagnosed as ? autistic psychopathy.

Case 9

Zygosity determined bld. grps. Pair discordant for autism, concordant for cognitive disorder. Female. Age 5 yr.

Family. Fa. street trader. Mo. I.P. 9 months for depression following misc. Nine older sibs and one younger. Mo. also had three misc.

Pregn. 34 wk gestation.

1st born twin. B. wt. 3 1b 6 oz. Normal neonatal course. In hosp. 3 weeks. Sat 13 months. Walked 21 months. Single words 2 yr, phrases soon after. Still wet at night. Not as cuddly or responsive as sibs in infancy. Normal relationship with parents but slightly less sympathetic and affectionate than sibs. Plays well with sibs but less with peers at school. Imag. play. Drawing immature. Normal usage of speech but articulation imperfect. Attends normal school. At interview appears friendly, responsive, inquisitive girl. Asymmetrical ears. S.Q. 70. Mecham L.Q. 82.

2nd born twin. B. wt. 4 1b 15 oz. Slow wt. gain. In hospital 1 month. Sat 15 months. Walked 24 months. Still wets and soils. During 1st year blank expression, wd. not be cuddled or consoled, sensitive to noise and did not respond to voice. Lack of eye to eye gaze, no parental attachment, no play with peers. In last year, became more responsive and cuddly. Some parallel play sibs. No speech; beginnings of babble. Likes set routines, will drink only from red cups. Routines. Twiddles things in front of her eyes. Finger twisting mannerisms and rocking. No imag. play. Attends special school. Right strabismus. D.Q. 40. S.Q. 32. Mecham language age < 1 yr.

Case 10

Zygosity determined bld. grps. Discordant pair (atypical autism). Male. 7 yr.

Family. Fa. accountant: late in speaking, said little before starting school. Odd personality. Mo. trtd. as I.P. for depression. Older bro. did not speak until 2½ yr. Socially awkward and no friends until 6 yr. Interested in maps and routes. Mo. also had one misc.

Pregn. Normal. 39 week gestation.

1st born twin. B. wt. 6 1b. Normal neonatal course. Normal motor milestones. Single words 18 months. Phrases 2 yr. Happy sociable infant. At 3 yr deterioration in speech, lack of emotional response, screaming, lack of response to sounds. Now blank facial expression, limited eye to eye gaze, no sympathy, no play with sibs or peers. Attached to mother. Stereotyped repetitive speech, echoing, monotone. Dislikes changes. Draws repetit. patterns. Puts toys in rows. Used to carry around odd objects (e.g. piece of linoleum). Strictly followed routines. Food fads. Hand and finger mannerisms. Rocks. Attends special school. Normal neurol. Merrill–Palmer I.Q. 68. S.Q. 44. Mecham L.Q. 37.

2nd born twin. B. wt. $5^1/_2$ lb. Tube fed 24 hr because would not suck but otherwise normal neonatal course. Normal motor milestones. Not a partic. cuddly baby but normally responsive and developed appropriate parental attachment. Sociable and enjoys his friendships. Good creative play. Single words 18 months. Phrases 20 months. Normal level and usage of language. Behav. normal. Attends normal school. Merrill–Palmer I.Q. 100. S.Q. 107. Mecham L.Q. 117.

Case 11

Zygosity determined by dermatoglypics. Discordant pair. Male 9 yr.

Family. Fa. business manager. Three older and one younger normal sibs. Parents divorced.

Pregn. 34 week gestation. Mo. ill in bed most of pregnancy.

1st born twin. B. wt. 5 lb. Tube fed several days. In incubator 1 week and left hospital 4 weeks after birth. Normal milestones. Phrase speech before 2 yr. Shy child in pre-school yrs. Now plenty of friends. No social, emotional or behav. problems. Apprehensive re dentist and medical attention. Attends normal school. WISC I.Q. FS 107. VS 109. PS 103. Normal language.

2nd born twin. B. wt. 4 lb 1 oz. One neonatal convulsion. In incubator 1 week. Thrived poorly and persistent feeding difficulties. Left hosp. 6 weeks after birth but readmitted twice during next 18 months. Unresponsive difficult baby, did not smile and did not want to be held. Lack of eye to eye gaze. Mother very distressed by difficulties and after a while could not bear to deal with child; no relationship with parents until after 6 yr. Lack of sympathy. Now beginning to play with peers. Good fine motor coordination but did not walk until $2^1/_2$ yr. Lack of babble. Single words after 2 yr; phrase speech 3 yr 10 months. Early echolalia and stereotyped phrases. Little social speech; poor abstraction and conceptualization. Counting rituals when younger. Follows routines. Repetitive stereotyped drawings. In psychiat hosp. age 2–5 yr. Since lived with father. Now attends normal school. I.Q. Biret 100. S.Q. 80. Mecham L.Q. 81. Manneristic gait; otherwise neurol. N.A.D.

Dizygotic pairs

Case 12

Zygosity on bld. grps. Pair discordant for autism, concordant for cognitive disorder. Male. 5 yr.

Family. Fa. accountant; rather obsessive personality, no social life. Two paternal uncles with definite social oddities; without friends, unusual circumscribed interests, unmarried, fastidious and precise. Normal older sister. Older bro. now normal but ? late in onset of speech, also head banging and resistance to change as baby.

Pregn. High B.P. Mo. I.P. × 3 for rest. 39 week gestation. Mo. is Rh neg. but no antibodies.

1st born twin. B. wt. 5 lb 12 oz. Dysmature appearance. Bilirubin rose to 10 mg. In special care unit. Lowest bld. sugar was 36 mg %. Motor milestones delayed. Walked 23 months. Lack of responsiveness and social smile in 1st yr. Does not want to be held or picked up. Variable eye to eye gaze. No interaction children. Sensitive to noise. Abn. babble. Single words 3 yr. Echolalia. Lack of social speech. Slow to adapt to new situations. Food fads. Various fixed routines (walks, meals, bedtimes). Puts toys in rows. No imag. play. Attends special school. Hand-flapping mannerism. Stiff-legged gait. Alternating strabismus. Poor gross motor coordination (fine O.K.). Merrill–Palmer I.Q. (non-verbal) 67. S.Q. 50. Mecham L.Q. 28.

2nd born twin. Breech. B. wt. 7 lb 9 oz. Normal neonatal course. Motor milestones delayed. Walked 21 months. Cuddly responsive baby. Single words 30 months. Phrases after 3 yr. Some echolalia. Occ. stereotyped repetitive phrases but also social speech. Behav. normal. Some imag. play. Friendly, sociable boy. Attends normal school. Merrill–Palmer I.Q. 74. S.Q. 82. Mecham L.Q. 60.

Case 13

Zygosity on marked diffs. appearance. Pair discordant for (atypical) autism, concordant for social/emotional disorder. Male. 18 yr.

Family. Fa. commercial artist (died when twins 13 yr). Had unusual personality and circumscribed interests. No sibs. Bilingual family.

Pregn. Severe vomiting. Mo. I.P. for 2/52 at 3 months. 41 week gestation. Obstructed labour 24 hr. Caesarian section after failed forceps delivery.

1st born twin. B. wt. 6 lb 4 oz. Normal neonatal course. Normal motor milestones. Played with faeces until 3½ yr. Cuddly but less responsive than sib. Sensitive to noise. Babble diff. from twin. Speech delayed but dates not recalled. Echolalia; repetition of phrases; stereotyped stilted speech; slow, ponderous way of talking; little social sp. Early lack of attachment to parents and continued lack of interaction with peers. First parental concern when did not settle at nursery school age 4 yr. Vague expression, limited eye to eye gaze. Slow to adapt to new situations. Markedly attached to rubber toy for several yr. Draws soldiers very repetitively. Collects epaulettes which he attaches to his clothes. Numerous hand and finger mannerisms. Attended special school to 16 yr. Rocking. Fits from 9 yr (only 4 in all). Uncertain variable EEG abn. Neurol. normal. WISC VS 62. PS 75. S.Q. S.Q. 43. Mecham L.Q. 30.

2nd born twin. B. wt. 8 1b. Rectal abscess at 6 weeks. Normal neonatal course. Normal motor milestones. Normal social and emotional develop. Did well at school. Passed 'O' levels at 16 yr. At 17 yr gradually stopped attending school, kept to his room, refused to get job. Surly and unpleasant to family. Held job for short while. Accepted at several colleges but attended courses for few days only. Spends time lying in bed reading about cybernetics and listening to music. WISC I.Q. VS 108. PS 131. Normal social maturity. Normal language. No thought disorder, delusions or hallucinations.

Case 14

Zygosity determined by bld. grps. Pair discordant. Male. 17 yr. Autistic twin and his caretakers seen. Mo. interviewed by phone. Normal twin not seen.

Family. Fa. farm owner. Anxious man prone to depression (not trtd.). Mo. slow to talk and reading diffs. until 10 yr. Two younger sisters, both of whom had exchange transfusions; one having psychiat. trt. (no details).

Pregn. Mo. Rhesus neg. with antibodies. Mo. had high B.P. and toxaemia —I.P. for 5 weeks before delivery. Caesarian section at term.

1st born twin. B. wt. 6 1b. 9 oz. Poor condition at birth with heavy meconium staining and severe jaundice—needed resuscitation. Cord bili-rubin 10.8. Three exchange transfusions. Sat 11–12 months. Walked 20–24 months. Toilet trained after 8 yr. Passive and unresponsive in first year. Lack of social smile, blank facial expression, lack of eye to eye gaze when young (now strange fixed stare), lack of attachments, ignores people. Lack of response to sounds (hearing normal). No speech. Takes hand to indicate needs. Food fads. Will not wear new clothes. Continuously flicks bits of paper in front of eyes. Attached to odd objects (boxes, bottles, bits of paper). Twists crinkly paper, jumps, pivots and leaps about room. No imag. play. Manneristic gait. In hosp. age 2 yr for 1 wk measles. Attended autistic unit for few years. In mental subn. hosp. since 9 yr. Normal EEG. Poor coordination. At age 6 yr his Merrill–Palmer I.Q. (non-verbal) was 76 but at age 14 yr his non-verbal I.Q. was only 30. S.Q. 13. Mecham language age < 1 yr.

2nd born twin. B. wt. 6 1b 15 oz. Good condition at birth. Cord bilirubin 4.2. Later had two exchange transfusions. Normal motor mile-stones. Phrase speech before 2½ yr. Normal relationships. No social, emotional or behav. problems. Attends normal school. Above av. attain-ment. Obtained six 'O' levels.

Case 15

Zygosity on basis of marked diffs. appearance. Discordant pair. Male. 16 yr.
Family. Fa. draughtsman. No sibs.

Pregn. Toxaemia. 36 week gestation.

1st born twin. B. wt. 4 1b. In incubator 10 days. In hosp. 30 days eye infection. Vomited and cried in first months. Slow feeder. Normal motor milestones. Lack of eye to eye gaze and failure to cuddle noted at 6 months. No parental attachment, did not come for comfort, no interaction other children. Blank or solemn facial expression. Single words $2^1/2$ yr, phrases 5 yr. Speaks little. Stereotyped phrases (echolalia when younger)— immature grammar, poor articulation. Some metaphorical lang. Singsong voice. Puts objects in rows. Refuses to go to new places. Various odd attachments (e.g. to hammers and then to soaps—all brands known by smell). At one time wd. only eat square things. Various quasi-obsessive interests. Hand and finger mannerisms. Rocks. Shakes string back and forth. Pica. No imag. play. Special school to 9 yr and then mental subn. hosp. Strabismus. Dysmorphic appearance. Poor coordination. Abn. gait. Normal EEG. Cystinuria. Merrill–Palmer I.Q. (non-verbal) 43. S.Q. 14. Mecham language age < 2 yr.

2nd born twin. B. wt. 5 1b 8 oz. Not in incubator. Normal neonatal course. Normal motor milestones. Single words 18 months, phrases $2^1/2$ yr. Normal usage lang. Normal social, emotional and behav. dvelop. Normal, responsive, sltly. shy adolescent. Attends academically selective school and has above av. attainments. S.Q. 103. Cystinuria. Optic atrophy left eye— otherwise neurol. normal.

Case 16

Zygosity on basis of marked physical diffs. Discordant pair. Male. 22 yr.

Family. Fa. teacher. Two older and one younger sib—all normal and above av. intelligence.

Pregn. 34 week gestation. Prolonged labour.

1st born twin. B. wt. 4 1b 6 oz. Normal neonatal course. One febrile convulsion. Normal motor milestones. Fully normal development in all respects. Sociable, friendly univ. graduate. Interviewed by' phone.

2nd born twin. B. wt. 4 1b 10 oz. Born 75 min after twin. Uterine inertia. Fed slowly. Normal motor milestones. Lack of social responsiveness after 1 yr. Detached expression. Lack of interest in people. No understanding emotion, no sympathy, still has no sense of socially appropriate. Single words 5 yr. Phrases $7^1/2$ yr. Early echoing and neologisms. Still little social speech, stereotyped lang., no understanding abstract, flat intonation, slow ponderous speech. Strict adherence to daily routines which rule family life. Always carries calendar and railway timetable. Plans journeys in excruciating detail. Draws very well but v. repetitively. Excellent spatial memory (able to make accurate models and floor plans from memory). Hand mannerisms when young, still has odd movements when excited. Attended special school. EEG non-specific abn. Air encephalogram basically normal but slight dilatation right lat. ventricle. Osteoma right arm. Biochemistry normal. WISC VS 50. PS 93. S.Q. 62. Mecham L.Q. 34.

Case 17

Zygosity on basis of marked physical diffs. Also probably diff. bld. grps. (because only one twin had erythrobtastosis foetalis). Discordant pair. Male. 13 yr.

Family. Fa. electrician (born West Indies). Three older children all normal and of above av. attainment (two passed 'O' levels and third not yet at that age). Mo. occ. depressed (not tretd.).

Pregn. Mo. Rhesus neg. with antibodies. 33 week gestation.

1st born twin. B. wt. 4 1b 2 oz. Bilirubin 19.5 mg % on day 3. Exchange transfusion. Apnoea and cyanosis day 5. Tube fed through day 7. In hosp. 33 days. Apparently normal motor milestones (dates not recalled). Would not be cuddled in early years. Blank expression. Lack of eye to eye gaze. Some attachment mother. Ignores other children. No speech. Hands over ears. No gesture. Resists changes in furniture and ornaments. Insists on same routes on walks. Mealtime ritual. Carried around bricks when younger. Compulsive touching of people's shoulders. Facial grimaces, rocks, finger-flicking mannerisms. Bites wrists and bangs head. No imag. play. In mental subn. hosp. Normal physical exam. except bilat. undescended testicles. Biochemistry normal. EEG low amplitude spikes right temporal region. Merrill–Palmer I.Q. (non-verbal) 43. S.Q. 36. Mecham language age < 1 yr.

2nd born twin. B. wt. 3 1b 7 oz. Born 1 hr after twin. Forty days in hospital for wt. gain but not jaundiced or transfused. Normal motor milestones. Well behaved social, friendly child without problems. Av. attainments at ordinary school. Excels in sports but poor fine motor coordination. S.Q. 90. Mecham L.Q. 80.

Case 18

Zygosity determined bld. grps. Discordant pair. Female, 12 yr.

Family. Fa. factory foreman. Two older bros. both psychiat. normal but one had tutoring for reading diffs.

Pregn. Normal 40 week gestation.

1st born twin. B. wt. 5 lb 13 oz. Vertex. Sucked poorly and fed slowly, otherwise normal neonatal course. Sat 10–11 months. Walked 30 months. Socially unresponsive infant. Screaming, rocking and inattention at 12 months. No smiling until 6–7 months. Not cuddly. Lack of eye to eye gaze, blank expression. Lack of parental attachment, never came for comfort. No interaction peers. Little babble, no speech, no gesture. Very upset by any changes. Puts objects in piles. Insists on set routines. Attachment to kitchen spoon 1–4 yr. Dextrous at spinning plates. Swings string in front of face.

Constant hand and finger mannerisms, rocking. No imag. play. Pica when younger. Age 4 yr stuck object up rectum causing peritonitis. Infectious hepatitus age 12 yr when develop. fits. In mental subn. hosp. Left strabismus. Good fine but poor gross motor coordination, awkward gait. Hypotonia. Normal EEG. Biochemistry normal. S.Q. 23. Mecham language age < 1 yr.

2nd born twin. B. wt. 6 lb 10 oz. Normal neonatal course. Normal motor milestones. Normal social, emotional and behav. develop. Interesting, enthusiastic and talkative adolescent. Attends ordinary school and attainments above average. S.Q. 111. Normal language.

Case 19

Zygosity on basis marked physical diffs. Pair discordant (atypical autism). Female. Age 14 yr.

Family. Fa. printer. Died when twins 10 yr. Two older bros.; one autistic and mentally retarded (not seen but no speech, lack of eye to eye contact, hand and finger mannerisms and attachment to unusual objects). Strong F. H. on father's side of severe myopia.

Pregn. Severe vomiting first trimester. 40 week gestation.

1st born twin. B. wt. 5 lb 9 oz. Vertex. Normal neonatal course. Normal motor milestones. Phrases by 12 months. Normal social, emotional and behav. develop. (although verbally precocious). Friendly, sociable, attractive adolescent. Attends ordinary school and is top of class. Gross myopia from early age. Severe bilat. uveitis age 7 yr requiring extensive hospitalization and trt. with steroids. Apart from eyes, normal on examination. S.Q. 125. Normal language.

2nd born twin. B. wt. 6 lb 6 oz. Born 45 min after twin. Delay in crying but otherwise normal neonatal course. Sat 9 months. Walked 26 months. Lack of eye to eye gaze, blank expression, gazed at hands in 1st yr. Came for comfort and fond of parents but detached and did not give affection. Approaches and joins in with other children but no friendships. No social sense, asks embarrassing Q of strangers. Very sensitive to noise but lack of response to voice when young. Single words 2 yr, phrases 4 yr. Early echolalia, pronominal reversal to 13 yr, stereotyped phrases, monotone, little social speech. Many rituals revolving around time. Repetitive stereotyped play. Attached to partic. hat for yrs. Collects bottles. Limited imag. play. Rocks. Attends special school. Left strabismus. Abn. right optic disc. Severe myopia. Poor coordination, choreiform movements. Non-verbal I.Q. 59. S.Q. 49. Mecham I.Q. 49.

Case 20

Zygosity on basis marked physical diffs. Pair discordant. Male. 6 yr.

Family. Fa. artist. Mo. had psychiat. trt. for emotional dist. One normal younger sib.

Pregn. Normal. 36 week gestation.

1st born twin. B. wt. 5 1b 15 oz. Normal neonatal course. Normal motor milestones. Normal social, emotional and behav. develop. Attends normal school. Serious, creative, talented and imag. child. WISC FS 142. VS 154. PS 121. S.Q. 102. Mecham I.Q. 122.

2nd born twin. Breech. B. wt. 5 1b 5 oz. Resuscitated. Apnoea 9 min. Poor sucking. Normal motor milestones. No social smile until after 9 months. Lack of cuddle, interest, response, and eye to eye gaze in first yr. Lack of parental attachment until 3 yr but now relates well to family and beginning to play with peers. Slightly socially disinhibited and asks personal questions of strangers. Impulsive. V. sensitive to noise. Speech began at 3 yr; at first stereotyped and repetitive but normal level of usage in last yr. Marked distress with new situations when younger but not now. Likes routines. Finger mannerisms when younger. Repetitive play and lack of imagination until last yr—now normal. Attends normal school. Left strabismus. Notched left earlobe. Poor fine motor coordination. Air encephelogram showed left cortical atrophy. EEG focal abn. on left. WISC FS 115. VS 125. PS 100. S.Q. 81. Mecham L.Q. 104.

Case 21

Zygosity on basis diffs. in appearance. Pair discordant. Female. 20 yr. Extensive info. from case notes and other reports but family not seen.

Family. Fa. salesman with recurrent manic–depressive illness.

Pregn. Severe vomiting first trimester. 34 week gestation.

1st born twin. B. wt. 5 1b 6 oz. Normal neonatal course. Shy and anxious at time of Fa.'s illness but otherwise a friendly sociable girl with many friends. No behaviour diffs. Above av. Attainment. Currently a univ. student.

2nd born twin. Breech. B. wt. 4 1b 13 oz. Born 30 min after twin. Slow feeder. Kept in hosp. 5 weeks. Normal motor milestones but enuretic to age 8 yr. Cried freq. Unaffectionate, unresponsive baby. Lack of eye to eye gaze, little interest in people, superficial relationships. Little interaction other children, no friendships. Late onset babble. Single words 36 months, phrases 10 yr. Persistent echolalia, pronominal reversal, stereotyped repetitions of phrases, poor articulation. Repetitive representational drawing. No imag. play. Tantrums on change of routine. Various compulsive activities. Early attachment to odd objects. Hand flapping. Bites arm. Drinks large quantities. Attended special school and then sheltered workshop. Normal EEG and air encephalogram. Hypotonia, high arched palate—otherwise neurol. normal. Biochemistry normal. WISC FS 45. VS 48. PS 50. Peabody I.Q. 55.

Notes

1 Unless MZ twins were peculiarly liable to autism, which seems implausible.
2 In two pairs, the blood tests showed that the parents' view of zygosity was wrong.
3 The original "blind" diagnoses gave only 12 cases, but further information made available later on one concordant pair caused them to be transferred from the atypical to the typical category. This change does not affect the concordance findings.
4 Numbers refer to case summaries in the Appendix.
5 However, using Lotter's (1966) true prevalence figures and also a broader definition of autism than we employed, there should be 63 autistic twins in the country who could be identified by means of a population survey.

References

BAKWIN, H. (1954) Early infantile autism. *J. Pediat.* **45**, 492–497.
BARTAK, L., RUTTER, M. and COX, A. (1975) A comparative study of infantile autism and specific developmental receptive language disorder. I. The children. *Br. J. Psychiat.* **126**, 127–145.
BARTAK, L., RUTTER, M. and COX, A. (1977) A comparative study of infantile autism and specific developmental receptive language disorders—III. Discriminant functions analysis. *J. Autism Childhood Schizophrenia* (in press).
BÖÖK, J. A., NICHTERN, S. and GRUENBERG, E. (1963) Cytogenetical investigations in childhood schizophrenia. *Acta psychiat. scand.* **39**, 309–323.
BRASK, B. H. (1967) The need for hospital beds for psychiatric children: an analysis based on a prevalence investigation in the County of Århus. *Ugeskr. Laeg.* **129**, 1559–1570.
BROWN, J. L. (1963) Follow-up of children with atypical development (infantile psychosis). *Am. J. Orthopsychiat.* **33**, 855–861.
BRUCH, H. (1959) Studies in schizophrenia. *Acta psychiat. neurol. scand.* Suppl. 130.
CHAPMAN, A. H. (1957) Early infantile autism in identical twins. *A.M.A. Archs Neurol. Psychiat.* **78**, 621–623.
CHAPMAN, A. H. (1960) Early infantile autism. *A.M.A. J. Dis. Child.* **99**, 783–786.
CHESS, S., KORN, S. J. and FERNANDEZ, P. B. (1971) *Psychiatric Disorders of Children with Congenital Rubella.* Brunner/Mazel, New York.
CLINE, D. W. (1972) Videotape documentation of behavioural change in children. *Am. J. Orthopsychiat.* **42**, 40–47.
CREAK, M. and INI, S. (1960) Families of psychotic children. *J. Child Psychol. Psychiat.* **1**, 156–175.
CURNOW, R. N. and MITH, C. (1975) Multifactorial models for familial diseases in man. *J. R. statist. Soc. Am.* **138**, (2), 131–169.
DOLL, E. A. (1947) *Vineland Social Maturity Scale.* Educational Test Bureau, Minneapolis.
DRAGE, J. S. and BERENDES, H. (1966) Apgar scores and outcome of the new born. *Pediat. Clin. N. Am.* **13**, 637–643.
DUNN, P. M. (1965) Some perinatal observations in twins. *Dev. Med. Child Neurol.* **7**, 121–134.
GEDDA, L. (1961) Twins. *History and Science.* C. C. Thomas, Springfield, IL.
GERVER, J. M. and DAY, R. (1950) Intelligence quotient of children who have recovered erythroblastosis fetalis. *J. Pediat.* **36**, 342–348.

GITTELSOHN, A. M. and MILHAM, S. (1965) Observations on twinning in New York State. *Br. J. prev. soc. Med.* **19**, 8–17.

GOTTESMAN, I. I. and SHIELDS, J. (1976) A critical review of recent adoption, twin, and family studies of school and family studies of schizophrenia: behavioural genetic perspectives. *Schizophrenia Bull.* **2**, 360–401.

HANSON, D. R. and GOTTESMAN, I. I. (1976) The genetics, if any, of infantile autism and childhood schizophrenia. *J. Autism Childhood Schizophrenia* **6**, 209–234.

HAVELKOVA, M. (1967) Abnormalities in siblings of schizophrenic children. *Can. psychiat. Ass. J.* **12**, 363–369.

HINTON, G. G. (1963) Childhood psychosis or mental retardation: a diagnostic dilemma—II. Pediatric and neurological aspects. *Can. med. Ass. J.* **89**, 1020–1024.

HOLT, S. (1961) The inheritance of dermal ridge patterns. In *Recent Advances in Genetics* (Edited by Penrose, L.), pp. 101–119. Little Brown, Boston.

HUNTER, J. A. (1968) Perinatal events and permanent neurological sequelae. *N.Z. med. J.* **68**, 108–113.

KALLMANN, F. J., BARRERA, S. E. and METZGER, H. (1940) The association of hereditary microphthalmia with mental deficiency. *Am. J. ment. Defic.* **45**, 25–36.

KAMP, L. N. J. (1964) Autistic syndrome in one of a pair of monozygotic twins. *Folia psychiat. neurol. neurochir. Neerlt.* **67**, 143–147.

KANNER, L. (1943) Autistic disturbances of affective contact. *Nerv. Child* **2**, 217–250.

KANNER, L. and EISENBERG (1955) Notes on the follow-up studies of autistic children. In *Psychopathology of Childhood* (Edited by HOCH, P. H. and ZUBIN, J.). Grune & Stratton, New York.

KEAN, J. M. (1975) The development of social skills in autistic twins. *N.Z. med. J.* **81**, 204–207.

KELLER, W. R. (1957) Stress, experimental psychology, child psychiatry. Discussion of paper presented by Leo Kanner. *APA Psychiatry Rep.* **7**, 66–76.

KEELER, W. R. (1958) Autistic patterns and defective communication in blind children with retrolental fibroplasia. In *Psychopathology of Communication* (Edited by HOCH, P. H. and ZUBIN, S.), pp. 64–83. Grune & Stratton, New York.

KEELER, W. R. (1960) Personal communication. Cited by RIMLAND (1964).

KNOBLOCH, H. and PASAMANICK, B. (eds.) (1974) *Gesell and Amatruda's Developmental Diagnosis*, third edition. Harper & Row, Hagerstown.

KOTSOPOULOS, S. (1976) Infantile autism in DZ twins: a case report. *J. Autism Childhood Schizophrenia* **6**, 133–138.

KURTZ, G. R., KEATING, W. J. and LOFTUS, J. B. (1955) Twin pregnancy and delivery. Analysis of 500 twin pregnancies. *Obstet. Gynec.* **6**, 370–378.

LEHMAN, E., HABER, K. and LESSER, S. R. (1957) The use of reserpine in autistic children. *J. nerv. ment. Dis.* **125**, 351–356.

LOTTER, V. (1966) Epidemiology of autistic conditions in young children—I. Prevalence. *Social Psychiat.* **1**, 124–137.

LOTTER, V. (1967) Epidemiology of autistic conditions in young children—II. Some characteristics of the parents and children. *Social Psychiat.* **1**, 163–173.

LOVAAS, O. O., SCHAEFFER, B. and SIMMONS, J. Q. (1965) Building social behaviour in autistic children by use of electric shock. *J. exp. Res. Personality* **1**, 99–109.

McQUAID, P. E. (1975) Infantile autism in twins. *Br. J. Psychiat.* **127**, 530–534.

MECHAM, M. J. (1958) *Verbal Language Development Scale*. Western Psychological Services, California.

MITTLER, P. (1971) *The Study of Twins*. Penguin, Harmondsworth.

MOORE, M. (1972) A study of the aetiology of autism from a study of birth and family characteristics. *J. Irish med. Ass.* **65**, 114–120.

O'GORMAN, G. (1970) *The Nature of Childhood Autism*, 2nd edition. Butterworths, London.

ORNITZ, E. M. (1973) Childhood autism: a review of the clinical and experimental literature. *Calif. Med.* **118**, 21–47.

ORNITZ, E. M., RITVO, E. R. and WALTER, R. D. (1965) Dreaming sleep in autistic twins. *Archs gen. Psychiat.* **12**, 73–79.

POLAN, C. G. and SPENCER, B. L. (1959) A checklist of symptoms of autism in early life. *W. Va. med. J.* **55**, 198–204.

POLLIN, W., STABENEAU, J. R., MOSHER, L. and TUPIN, J. (1966) Life history differences in identical twins discordant for schizophrenia. *Am. J. Orthopsychiat.* **36**, 492–509.

RACE, R. R. and SANGER, R. (1975) *Blood Groups in Man*, 6th edition. Blackwell, Oxford.

REYNELL, J. (1969) *Reynell Developmental Language Scales*. N.F.E.R., Slough.

RIMLAND, B. (1964) *Infantile Autism*. Appleton–Century–Crofts, New York.

ROSE, A. L. and LOMBROSO, C. T. (1970) Neonatal seizure states: a study of clinical, pathological and electroencephalographic features in 137 full-term babies with a long-term follow-up. *Paediatrics* **45**, 404–425.

RUTTER, M. (1967) Psychotic disorders in early childhood. In *Recent Developments in Schizophrenia* (Edited by COPPEN, A. and WALK, A.). *Br. J. Psychiat., Spec. Publ.* **1**,

RUTTER, M. (1970) Autistic children: infancy to adulthood. *Seminars in Psychiatry* **2**, 435–450.

RUTTER, M. (1971) The description and classification of infantile autism. In *Infantile Autism* (Edited by CHURCHILL, D. W., ALPERN, G. D. and DE MEYER, M. K.), pp. 8–28. C. C. Thomas, Springfield, IL.

RUTTER, M. (1972) The effects of language delay on development. In *The Child with Delayed Speech* (Edited by RUTTER, M. and MARTIN, J. A. M.), pp. 176–188. SIMP/Heinemann Medical, London.

RUTTER, M. (1974) The development of infantile autism. *Psychol. Med.* **4**, 147–163.

RUTTER, M. (1977) Infantile autism and other child psychoses. In *Child Psychiatry: Modern Approaches* (Edited by RUTTER, M. and HERSOV, L.). Blackwell Scientific, Oxford.

RUTTER, M., BARTAK, L. and NEWMAN, S. (1971) Autism—a central disorder of cognition and language? In *Infantile Autism: Concepts, Characteristics and Treatment* (Edited by RUTTER, M.), pp. 148–171. Churchill–Livingstone, Edinburgh.

RUTTER, M., GREENFELD, D. and LOCKYER, L. (1967) A five to fifteen year follow-up of infantile psychosis—II. Social and behavioural outcome. *Br. J. Psychiat.* **113**, 1183–1199.

SEIDAL, U. P. and GRAF, K. A. (1966) Autism in two brothers. *Med. Offr.* **115**, 227–229.

SHERWIN, A. C. (1953) Reactions to music of autistic (schizophrenic) children. *Am. J. Psychiat.* **109**, 823–831.

SLATER, E. and COWIE, V. (1971) *The Genetics of Mental Disorders*. Oxford University Press, Oxford.

SMITH, C. (1974) Concordance in twins: methods and interpretation. *Am. J. hum. Genet.* **26**, 454–466.

STEVENSON, J. and RICHMAN, N. (1977) Behaviour, language and development in three-year-old children. *J. Autism Childhood Schizophrenia*, in press.

STUTSMAN, R. (1948) *Guide for Administering the Merrill–Palmer Scale of Mental Tests.* World Books. New York.

STUTTE, H. (1960) Kinder und Jugend psychiatrie. In *Psychiatrie der Gegenwort*, Vol. II (Edited by GRUHLE, H. W. and MAYER-GROSS, W.). Springer, Berlin.

TAFT, L. T. and COHEN, H. J. (1971) Hypsarrhythmia and infantile autism: a clinical report. *J. Autism Childhood Schizophrenia* **1**, 327–336.

TORREY, E. F., HERSH, S. P. and McCABE, K. D. (1975) Early childhood psychosis and bleeding during pregnancy: a prospective study of gravid women and their offspring. *J. Autism Childhood Schizophrenia* **5**, 287–298.

TREFFERT, D. W. (1970) Epidemiology of infantile autism. *Archs gen. Psychiat.* **22**, 431–438.

VAILLANT, G. E. (1963) Twins discordant for early infantile autism. *Archs gen. Psychiat.* **9**, 163–167.

VAN KREVELEN, D. A. (1963) On the relationship between early infantile autism and autistic psychopathy. *Acta paedopsychiat.* **30**, 303–323.

VAN KREVELEN, D. A. and KUIPERS, C. (1962) The psychopathology of autistic psychopathy. *Acta paedopsychiat.* **29**, 22–31.

VERHEES, B. (1976) A pair of classically early infantile autistic siblings. *J. Autism Childhood Schizophrenia* **6**, 53–60.

WARD, T. F. and HODDINOTT, B. A. (1962) Early infantile autism in fraternal twins. *Can. Psychol. Ass. J.* **7**, 191–195.

WEBER, D. (1966) Zur Atiologie autistischer Syndrome des Kindesalters. *Praxis der kinder psychologie und kinder psychiatrie*, **15**, 12–18.

WECHSLER, D. (1949) *Wechsler Intelligence Scale for Children.* The Psychological Corporation, New York.

WHITTAM, H., SIMON, G. B. and MITTLER, P. J. (1966) The early development of psychotic children and their sibs. *Dev. Med. Child Neurol.* **8**, 552–560.

WILLERMAN, L. and CHURCHILL, J. A. (1967) Intelligence and birth weight in identical twins. *Child Dev.* **38**, 623–629.

WING, L., YEATES, S. R., BRIERLEY, L. M. and GOULD, J. (1976) The prevalence of early childhood autism: comparison of administrative and epidemiological studies. *Psychol. Med.* **6**, 89–100.

119

WHY DO AUTISTIC INDIVIDUALS SHOW SUPERIOR PERFORMANCE ON THE BLOCK DESIGN TASK?

Amitta Shah and Uta Frith

Source: *Journal of Child Psychology and Psychiatry*, 34, 1993: 1351–1364.

Abstract

Systematic variations of the block design task were given to 20 autistic, 33 normal and 12 mildly retarded subjects. Designs were contrasted which were either "whole" or segmented, rotated or unrotated, and which did or did not contain obliques. Only segmentation, but neither of the spatial orientation factors, revealed a significant group difference. Autistic subjects, regardless of age and ability, performed better than controls when presented with unsegmented designs. This result suggests that they need less of the normally required effort to segment a gestalt, and thus supports the hypothesis of weak central coherence as a characteristic of information processing in autism.

Introduction

One of the many puzzling aspects of autism is the marked dissociation between various cognitive abilities. This is reflected in an uneven level of performance on IQ subtests and appears to occur in autistic people of all ages and ability levels. Research on autism has, for the most part, concentrated on the performance impairments. The phenomenon of islets of ability has been regarded as something of a myth or else as merely an interesting but theoretically unimportant fact. There have been few attempts to elucidate why islets of ability occur so frequently in autism, or, more generally, how good performance is achieved on certain IQ subtests by individuals whose achievement on other subtests is so poor. The explanation of islets as intact areas of functioning is one possibility, but lacks predictive power. To overcome this impasse, Frith (1989) suggested that it might be possible to explain both positive and negative extremes of performance in terms of a single underlying cognitive dysfunction.

We previously reported on the superior ability of autistic adolescents to find embedded figures suggesting that autistic people have a special facility in seeing parts in wholes (Shah & Frith, 1983). A relative superiority has also been shown in autistic children's ability to learn and to recall random strings of words compared to meaningful prose, the opposite of normal children's pattern of performance (Hermelin & O'Connor, 1971). Similar results were found when the stimuli were either random or structured strings of words or colours (Frith, 1970a, b). Autistic subjects appear to process unconnected stimuli, outside a meaningful context, with remarkable efficiency. But tasks with this requirement are unusual. They are found more often in the laboratory than in real life. Information processing in real life almost always involves interpretation of individual stimuli in terms of overall context and meaning. Laboratory tasks and tests of academic skills are often difficult for normal children precisely because they do not involve global meaning. The opposite may be the case for autistic individuals, at least those who perform well on certain IQ tests, but fail markedly in real life situations. On the basis of these and other considerations, Frith (1989) proposed that the normal "effort after meaning" which appears to be a manifestation of an autonomous characteristic of human information processing, and which she terms central coherence, is abnormally weak in autism. This hypothesis relates the efficiency in processing unconnected stimuli to an unusual ease with which autistic individuals can resist the normal "pull" of strongly coalescing, i.e. meaningful wholes. One expectation from this postulated facility is a relative preference for processing local as opposed to global features. This idea fits well with superior performance on embedded figures. It might also go some way towards explaining superior performance on other tasks where a local rather than global processing strategy is adaptive, such as rote memory for unconnected stimuli.

The aim of the present study was to test the central coherence hypothesis by investigating strategies underlying performance on the block design task. We chose this task because it is the only subtest of the Wechsler intelligence scales (Wechsler, 1974, 1981) on which autistic subjects as a group have been consistently reported as showing superior performance relative to other subtests (Lockyer & Rutter, 1970; Tymchuk, Simmons & Neafsey, 1977; Ohta, 1987). Recent reports by Bowler (1992) and Venter, Lord and Schopler (1992) again confirmed this fact as a robust phenomenon. Block design superiority may well be an important marker for autism. It is hardly ever reported for non-autistic mentally handicapped persons.

The block-design task was invented by Kohs (1923). The task is to construct a design as fast as possible. Kohs considered his test to be an adequate measure of intelligence: "*It requires first the breaking up of each design presented into logical units, and second a reasoned manipulation of blocks to reconstruct the original design from separate parts. The results of this activity, it is presumed, yield a fair index of this analytic-synthetic power which we term 'intelligence'.*" This analysis suggests that the block design task, just like embedded figures, may favour weak central coherence. In both tasks designs with a strong Gestalt quality have to be segmented into constituent parts.

The block design test still constitutes an important part of currently popular batteries for measuring intelligence. For example, it features in the Wechsler intelligence scales for children (Wechsler, 1974), and for adults (Wechsler, 1981), and the British Ability Scales (Elliot, Murray & Pearson, 1979). In these tests the block design task is considered a useful tool for measuring non-verbal abstract conceptualisation and spatial visualisation (Sattler, 1974). Factor-analytic studies of the Wechsler Scales in normal populations showed that the block design subtest contributes substantially to the space-performance or perceptual organisation factor. They also found it to be the best estimate of "g" among the performance scale subtests, and the fourth-best measure of "g" among the 12 subtests (Maxwell, 1959; Cohen, 1959).

There has also been some interest in the clinical use of the block design test. In the past various authors (Bolles & Goldstein, 1938; Nadel, 1938; Reissenweber, 1953; Shapiro, 1952) have reported that psychiatric patients and patients suffering from certain cerebral lesions perform poorly on the test. Children with Williams syndrome are also substantially impaired on this task, and, interestingly, show difficulties when processing the global features of stimuli in a figure-copying task (Bihrle, Bellugi, Delis & Marks, 1989). It has been claimed that different types of errors on the block design task can be distinguished in adult patients with left-hemisphere and right-hemisphere lesions (Kaplan, 1983). Right-hemisphere-damaged patients in contrast to left-hemisphere patients were found to make errors which broke the overall pattern (Ben-Yishay, Diller, Mandelberg, Gordon & Gerstman, 1971). However, such errors are probably not specific to right hemisphere lesions; they are also shown by normal adults without lesions and by adults with a history of alcoholism (Kramer, Kaplan, Blusewicz & Preston, 1991).

Apart from the suggestion of intact visuo-spatial skills (e.g. Prior, 1979), little has been offered by way of explanation of superior block design performance in autism. Indeed it is difficult to understand why the block design task proves so difficult for people with diverse types of brain damage, yet is apparently easy for autistic people who, we must assume, also have brain abnormalities. A task analysis suggests that at least the following components are amenable to experimental manipulation: segmentation, obliqueness and rotation. These components may influence the adoption of particular strategies and crucially contribute to the superior performance of autistic individuals.

337

Segmentation

Gestalt psychologists (e.g. Wertheimer, 1923; Koffka, 1935) have ascribed great importance to the tendency to perceive *patterns as wholes* rather than as collections of details. However, when details of the whole need to be perceived, for example, the constituent elements in the block design task, this tendency has to be overcome and new structures (mapping onto the individual blocks) have to be mentally imposed. This step appears to require both time and effort, but in varying degrees for different individuals. Children appear to be less efficient at overcoming the tendency to see the whole than adults (Cramaussel, 1924; Witkin, 1950; Ames, Learner, Metraux & Walker, 1953; Meili-Dworetzki, 1956; Hemmendinger, 1953; Ghent, 1956). Furthermore, the ability to segment the gestalt may be particularly susceptible to the effects of brain injury (Teuber, Battersby & Bender, 1951; Teuber & Weinstein, 1956; Cobrinik, 1959).

Gestalt psychologists suggested that the balance between perception of parts and wholes is normally tilted towards wholes, and this has found recent experimental support in the global precedence effect (Navon, 1977, 1981). The bias in favour of wholes can be seen as a manifestation of central coherence. From the hypothesis that autistic individuals exhibit weak central coherence we would expect that for them the balance would be tipped towards parts. They should therefore show a special facility for the mental segmentation component of the block design task.

Obliqueness

The second factor concerns presence or absence of *oblique* lines, that is, lines which are at a 45° angle *relative to the square frame of the whole design*. Accurate perception and reproduction of obliqueness is thus an important factor for successful construction which involves correct positioning of diagonals. Diagonals present more difficulty than horizontals and verticals in tasks testing perception and reproduction (Burns, Mandel, Ogilvie & Taylor, 1958; Olson & Hildyard, 1977; Bryant, 1969). Furthermore, mastering the oblique in terms of memory for direction of slant is a relatively late development (Rudel & Teuber, 1963; Olson, 1970). Children with brain-damage have been reported to find obliques especially difficult (Rudel & Teuber, 1971), as do adult psychiatric patients (Shapiro, 1951, 1952, 1954).

Rotation

In addition to orienting the lines within a single block segment, the subject must construct the whole design in the correct *spatial orientation relative to the page*. One factor which is known to increase the task difficulty of the block design task is a 45° orientation of the whole design, so that a diamond shape is presented. Thus, in the Wechsler Scales all the most difficult designs of the task are presented at 45° rotation. Increased difficulty due to presenting square designs as diamonds has been reported by Shapiro (1952) for brain-damaged and schizophrenic patients.

Manipulating these three task components enables us to test two hypotheses: individual differences in speed and accuracy on the block design test may be due to differences solely in terms of general spatial ability. If superior general spatial ability in autistic subjects accounts for their superior performance, then this should be manifest in better ability to deal with all three components (segmentation, obliqueness and rotation) relative to controls. In contrast, the central coherence hypothesis proposes that the advantage of autistic subjects in the block design task is due specifically to their postulated facility for segmentation. If so, this advantage should be manifest only when designs with unsegmented shapes are presented, regardless of their spatial orientation. To test these alternatives we manipulated the block design task in such a way that we could compare performance on segmented and unsegmented patterns, and independently on oblique and non-oblique, rotated and unrotated patterns. We compared autistic subjects with normally developing children and, in order to evaluate the specificity of the findings to autism, we also compared them to mentally retarded children of the same age and non-verbal IQ.

Method

Subjects

Twenty autistic subjects aged between 16 and 25 years took part in this experiment. They were recruited through schools and training centres run by the National Autistic Society, and had all received a diagnosis of autism based on DSM-III or DSM-IIIR (American Psychiatric Association, 1983, 1987). IQ was tested with the WISC-R or the WAIS except for two subjects who were not able to comprehend task instructions for some of the subtests. These subjects were tested on the Leiter International Performance Scale (Leiter, 1980), Leiter IQ being comparable to the non-verbal IQ of the WISC-R in autistic children (Shah & Holmes, 1985). The non-verbal IQ of the autistic group ranged from 57 to 108. To achieve more homogeneous groups with regard to intellectual ability, the subjects were divided into two groups with a cut-off point of non-verbal IQ of 85 (one standard deviation from the mean on the Wechsler Scales). The High IQ autistic group consisted of autistic people with at least normal non-verbal IQ. The Low IQ autistic group consisted of autistic people with non-verbal IQs at the borderline or upper end of the mildly retarded range. The advantage of using homogeneous groups of autistic people is that each group can be matched to its own control group on stringent criteria. We therefore included three control groups.

The *old normal group* consisted of 17 children with normal non-verbal IQ, to be compared with the High IQ autistic group. Although they were, on average, a little younger than the autistic subjects, they were all over the age of 15 and likely to have reached an adult level of functioning. These subjects were tested only on the non-verbal scale of the WISC-R or the WAIS. The *young normal group* consisted of 16 normally intelligent children from a local primary school. They were younger than the low IQ autistic subjects, but their performance (in terms of raw scores) on the WISC-R non-verbal scale was of a similar level.

The *learning disabled group* consisted of 12 subjects with non-verbal IQ in the mildly retarded or borderline range, comparable to the Low IQ autistic group in terms of both non-verbal IQ and chronological age. Their verbal, and hence full-scale IQ is higher than that of the autistic group. This was inevitable because of the tendency for non-verbal IQ to be much higher than verbal IQ in the autistic group. These subjects were recruited from a College of Further Education which has a special course for school-leavers with mild learning difficulties. The subject characteristics of the five groups are given in Table 1.

Design and materials

The basic task modelled the classic Kohs' block paradigm. The subject was shown a two-dimensional pattern on a card and was required to construct a similar pattern always using four blocks. Four identical yellow and black

Table 1 Subject characteristics.

	High IQ autistic	Low IQ autistic	Old normal	Young normal	Mentally handicapped
Male : female ratio	9:1	8:2	15:2	15:1	11:1
n	10	10	17	16	12
Age (years)					
Mean	18.6	18.5	16.0	10.9	17.8
s.d.	1.7	3.0	0.6	0.3	2.5
Performance IQ					
Mean	96.7	71.0	100.6	105.6	76.3
s.d.	8.4	6.7	7.1	5.5	5.5
Verbal IQ					
Mean	73.3	56.8	N/A	N/A	74.5
s.d.	15.8	8.5			8.0
Full-scale IQ					
Mean	83.3	62.0	N/A	N/A	73.7
s.d.	11.0	7.4			5.9

one-inch cube blocks were used, as shown in Fig. 1. These blocks remained the same throughout, while task demands dictated by the type of design used, were varied. Figures 2 and 3 show the complete sets of designs. The designs were grouped into sets such that each of the three component factors, segmentation, obliqueness and rotation, were combined with each other equally. The designs were drawn individually on two-inch square white cards. There were five designs in each set, making a total of forty. There were three additional designs for demonstration. One example from each of the eight sets of designs used is shown in Fig. 4.

The effect of *segmentation* was investigated by presenting the same designs as wholes or as four separate blocks (see examples in Fig. 4). The effect of presence or absence of *oblique lines relative to the design contour*, was investigated by presenting designs containing at least one oblique compared with designs which contained only horizontal and vertical contours. The effect of *orientation of the whole shape* was investigated by presenting the same designs as either squares or diamonds, i.e. rotated by 45° relative to the page.

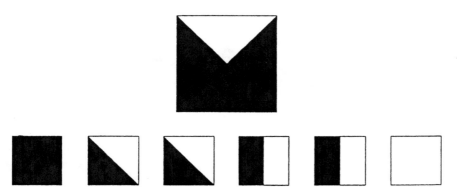

Figure 1 Example of the experimental block design task. The design is to be constructed from four blocks, each of which has the faces shown.

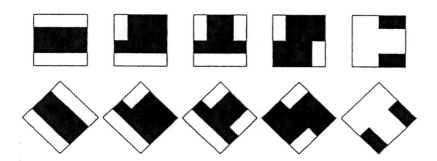

Figure 2 Complete set of "whole" designs, without obliques, rotated and unrotated.

341

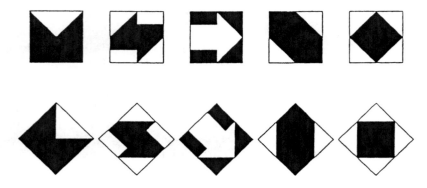

Figure 3 Complete set of "whole" designs, with obliques, rotated and unrotated.

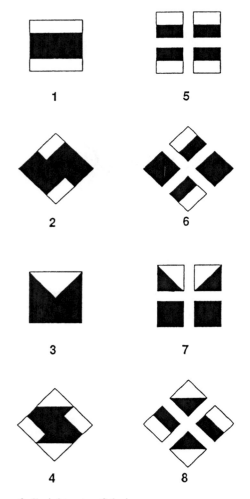

1	5
2	6
3	7
4	8

Figure 4 Examples of all eight sets of designs.

Procedure

The Wechsler tests, including the block design subtest, were given in the prescribed manner. The experimental block design tasks were carried out in a separate session. The subject was given a rectangular piece of cardboard to work on. The card with the design was also placed on a similar piece of card-board. Both were placed in a fixed position with their edges parallel to the table. First, the subject was shown the four blocks and was told that all four were the same; that is they all had one side that was yellow, one side that was black, two sides that were divided horizontally into yellow and black and two sides that were divided diagonally into yellow and black. The subject was then given three practice trials, with the request to work as fast as possible.

Each subject was tested on each of the eight sets, i.e. a total of forty designs. After each trial, the examiner picked up the four blocks and dropped them back randomly. The time taken (in seconds) was recorded with a maximum time limit of three minutes. The order of presentation of the sets was the same for all subjects (4,3,2,1,8,7,6,5) in an attempt to equalize practice effects. The segmented sets were all presented in the second half of the testing session after the unsegmented sets. This was done because of the strong possibility that subjects would be alerted to the facilitating effect of strategically segmenting the designs into individual blocks. We were not interested in the ability to improve performance by this sort of insight, but rather in the ability to solve the mental segmentation problem spontane-ously. Nevertheless, the fixed order is a weakness in the design which does not enable us to assess higher order interactions or main effects of conditions. For our specific predictions we were, however, only interested in three possible group interactions (group × segmentation; group × oblique; group × rotation) which we hoped would not be subject to systematically different effects of practice or fatigue.

Results

Wechsler block design performance

The block design score was the peak of performance relative to all given subtests for seven of the 10 high IQ autistic subjects (scaled scores 13–19), and for six of the 10 low IQ autistic subjects (scaled scores 9–15). In all cases where block design did not yield the highest score, object assembly did, or else both tests were equal. The single exception was subject TC in the high IQ autistic group. TC had a block design score of 9, which was as low as object assembly and lower than his scores on picture arrangement and coding subtests. He showed significantly poorer performance on block design than any of his peers, who all performed at least 1 sd above the mean. Only one subject in the low IQ autistic group, with a score of 6 on block design, performed below average relative to chronological age. However, his score for object assembly was 10. Figure 5 illustrates the group subtest profiles showing pronounced performance peaks in block design, and secondarily object assembly, for both autistic groups, but not for the controls.

Experimental block design performance

The accuracy level, that is, the percentage of designs constructed correctly within the time allocated, was extremely high for all the autistic and normal subjects, ranging from 96% to 100% with a mean of 99%. For the learning disabled subjects, however, the accuracy was significantly lower and ranged from 62% to 100%, with a mean of 90%. Four of the 12 individuals in this group performed below the level of any of the other subjects tested. Accuracy in this group was particularly poor for unsegmented sets.

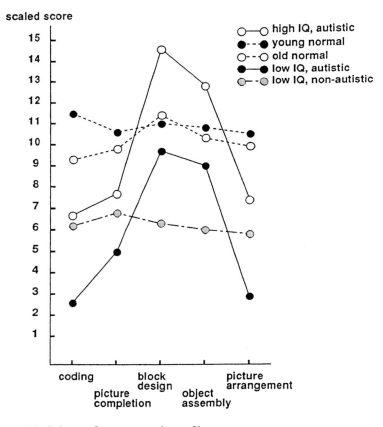

Figure 5 Wechsler performance scale profiles.

The following analyses are based on time scores. For each subject, the time taken for the five designs in each set was summed to give a total time (in seconds) for each set. The maximum time allowed for a single design was 180 sec whether or not the design was completed.

Table 2 gives the mean and standard deviations of the log time taken for each set by each group. The results were analysed by means of analysis of variance on logarithmic transformation of the raw data. This transformation was necessary in order to normalise the distribution of scores. The mean scores based on these transformations, comparing the three task factors, are illustrated for all 5 groups in Fig. 6. Inspection suggests that only the segmentation factor was interacting with diagnostic group and this was indeed borne out by the statistical analysis.

An overall ANOVA including all 5 groups was rejected because of inhomogeneity of variance. This was due to outliers in the learning-disabled group where time scores were distorted due to low accuracy levels. The analysis of normal and autistic groups using a $2 \times 2 \times 2 \times 2 \times 2$ factorial design (with two group factors, diagnosis and ability, and three task factors, segmentation, obliqueness and rotation) produced a single highly significant interaction of task and group factors, namely diagnosis × segmentation ($F = 16.61$, df 1,46, $p < .001$). This interaction was confirmed separately in three subsequent analyses comparing high IQ autistics and older normals ($F = 3,69$ df 1,24, $p < .06$), low IQ autistics and younger normals ($F = 12.58$, df 1,23, $p < .001$), and also low IQ autistic and learning disabled subjects

Table 2 Time taken to construct 8 sets of 5 designs in log seconds (see Fig. 4 for examples of each set).

Set		High IQ autistic	Low IQ autistic	Old normal	Young normal	Mentally handicapped
1	Mean	1.57	1.76	1.68	1.89	2.18
	s.d.	.16	.19	.15	.18	.36
2	Mean	1.62	1.78	1.70	1.89	2.13
	s.d.	.13	.18	.12	.12	.34
3	Mean	1.76	1.98	1.85	2.14	2.49
	s.d.	.24	.22	.18	.20	.32
4	Mean	1.93	2.13	1.95	2.30	2.52
	s.d.	2.8	2.3	.20	.20	.40
5	Mean	1.54	1.63	1.50	1.54	1.66
	s.d.	.15	.15	.13	.08	.12
6	Mean	1.56	1.69	1.58	1.70	1.78
	s.d.	.12	.16	.12	.13	.16
7	Mean	1.60	1.74	1.56	1.69	1.80
	s.d.	.15	.15	.09	.12	.21
8	Mean	1.66	1.77	1.65	1.82	2.07
	s.d.	.12	.19	.13	.10	.25

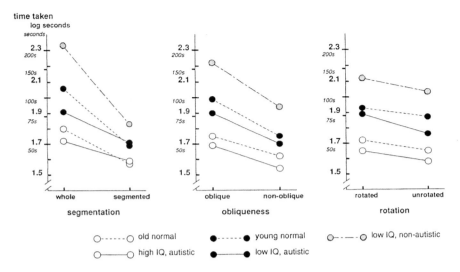

Figure 6 Performance on contrasted sets of the experimental task.

(F = 13.66, df = 1,19, p < .001). The interaction can be readily interpreted by reference to Fig. 6: autistic subjects performed better than their controls *only* when whole designs are presented, but not when they are pre-segmented. It is possible, but implausible, that this effect reflects differences in how the groups responded to the order of presentation: one would have to assume that the autistic subjects, compared to all the other subjects, were more alert in the first half of the session and showed less facilitation by practice in the second half. The effects of obliqueness and rotation were very similar in all groups; designs which contain obliques and designs which are rotated are more difficult for everybody. Finally, as expected, subjects of lower ability levels performed more poorly on the experimental tasks than those of higher ability, and younger children performed less well than older children.

Discussion

When explaining peaks rather than troughs in the performance of autistic individuals, we are in a position to rule out a host of factors which are sometimes claimed to confound the explanation of impairments in autism. We can rule out problems in motivation, pragmatic difficulties, or language problems which might compromise task understanding. This study again provided evidence for superior performance by autistic individuals on the block design subtest of the Wechsler Scales, superior relative to their performance on other subtests and superior relative to mildly retarded individuals of similar age and non-verbal IQ. One other subtest, object assembly, which is a type of jigsaw puzzle, also gave rise to high performance in autistic people. Block design and object assembly tasks are similar in that both require the construction of a whole from parts. While object assembly may be performed in a top-down fashion, guided by the meaningful whole or gestalt, it is also possible to construct the design in a bottom-up way on the basis of local connections (lines, contours) between the puzzle pieces. Indeed, since for the more difficult test items the subject is not told the identity of the final whole shape, a local, bottom-up, strategy may be more adaptive. In this way it is possible to explain the relatively good performance seen in the autistic group on object assembly and block design in terms of the same processing characteristics.

We hypothesised that a facility to segment parts in wholes is a consequence of weak central coherence in autistic individuals. We proposed that this facility alone could explain their performance superiority on the block design task. Using eight variants of the target task we found that subjects with autism, regardless of overall ability, performed significantly better than controls precisely in those conditions where whole designs had to be mentally segmented. This superiority disappeared when the patterns were presented in pre-segmented form. For the control groups the difference between the time taken to construct whole versus pre-segmented designs was considerable. This suggests that the task component of mental segmentation is a major cause of difficulty with the block design test for most subjects. We also found that obliques and rotated shapes contribute to task difficulty. However, segmentation was the only task component which discriminated subjects with autism from controls. They were affected by the two visuo-spatial orientation components to the same extent as their normal and learning-disabled peers. This suggests that the autistic islet of ability on the Wechsler block design subtest cannot be explained in terms of superior general spatial ability. It does not follow, however, that good block design performance in other populations is necessarily to do with segmentation skill rather than general spatial ability. Likewise, poor block design performance will usually indicate an impairment in general spatial processing. This may be the case, for example, in Williams Syndrome and some cases of right-hemisphere damage.

In the high IQ autistic group one subject (TC) did not show a performance peak on either block design or object assembly subtests. We cannot extrapolate from our small numbers as to how frequently this pattern might occur. When this subject was removed the average time difference between segmented and unsegmented patterns for the able autistic group was further reduced (1.61 and 1.54 log time, compared to 1.72 and 1.54). Thus the speed advantage of the autistic group over the normal controls on unsegmented patterns became even more pronounced. While we are confident that the results of the experimental block design task relate to Wechsler block design performance and accurately reflect group trends, we clearly cannot attribute performance superiority and a facility for mental segmentation to every individual autistic subject.

The present study confirms that there is an islet of ability in block design performance in autism, which appears to be independent of other aspects of IQ. It also strengthens the hypothesis that this islet is a consequence of weak central coherence here manifested in an enhanced ability to segment a gestalt. A useful contrast is provided by the mentally handicapped individuals. For this group, the task component of segmentation was a major source of difficulty even with the simplest designs of the task. Normally strong, rather than abnormally weak, coherence would have to be presumed in this group.

Although the present task and the embedded figures task (Shah & Frith, 1983) differ, one particular cognitive requirement is the same: in both tasks, the tendency to see the whole has to be resisted in favour of seeing the constituent elements. Clearly there can be many different reasons for showing this type of local over global preference. For instance, a difference in cognitive style or in consciously adopted strategy may result in a preference for parts over wholes. Witkin and his colleagues (Witkin *et al.*, 1954; Witkin, Dyk, Faterson, Goodenough & Karp, 1962) have hypothesised that performance on embedded figures reflects the cognitive style of field dependence/independence. Individuals who have particular difficulty in overcoming a preference for wholes, for example, mentally retarded children, show a field-dependent mode of perceiving. They do not readily separate an item from its context (Witkin & Goodenough, 1981). On academic tasks in particular this could be a disadvantage. Here field independence aids performance. Conversely, on many real-life tasks where overall context needs to be taken into account, field independence may have detrimental effects. It remains to be seen whether the hypothesis of weak central coherence in autism relates to cognitive style and context sensitivity in normal individuals. It also remains to be seen just what aspects of the syndrome of autism weak central coherence is capable of explaining. Before a systematic attempt is made, it will be essential that further empirical tests of the hypothesis are carried out. Such tests are currently in progress.

Acknowledgements

The experiments included in this paper were carried out while the first author held a research post at the MRC Social Psychiatry Unit and were reported in her doctoral thesis (Shah, 1988).

The authors would like to thank Francesca Happé and Chris Frith for their help in preparing this paper. They are grateful to the staff and pupils of the following establishments for their participation and co-operation in the study: Helen Allison School for Autistic Children and Jubilee Workshop, Gravesend; the Sybil Elgar School for Autistic Children, Ealing; Overcliffe House, Gravesend; South East London College of Further Education, Lewisham; Woodmansterne School, Streatham.

References

American Psychiatric Association (1983). *Diagnostic and statistical manual of mental disorders* (3rd Edn). Washington, DC: American Psychiatric Association.

American Psychiatric Association (1987). *Diagnostic and statistical manual of mental disorders* (3rd Edn, rev.). Washington, DC: American Psychiatric Association.

Ames, L. B., Leamer, J., Metraux, R. & Walker, R. (1953). Development of perception in the young child as observed in response to the Rorschach Test Blots. *Journal of Genetic Psychology*, **82**, 183–204.

Ben-Yishay, Y., Diller, L., Mandelberg, I., Gordon, W. & Gerstman, L. J. (1971). Similarities and differences in block design performance between older normal and brain-injured persons: a task analysis. *Journal of Abnormal Psychology*, **78**, 17–25.

Bihrle, A. M., Bellugi, U., Delis, D. C. & Marks, S. (1989). Seeing either the forest or the trees: dissociation in visuospatial processing. *Brain and Cognition*, **11**, 37–49.

Bolles, M. & Goldstein, K. (1938). A study of impairment of abstract behaviour in schizophrenic patients. *Psychiatric Quarterly*, **12**, 42–65.

Bowler, D. M. (1992). "Theory of mind" in Asperger's syndrome. *Journal of Child Psychology and Psychiatry*, **33**, 877–893.

Bryant, P. E. (1969). Perception and memory of the orientation of visually presented lines by children. *Nature*, **224**, 1331–1332.

Burns, B. D., Mandel, G., Pritchard, R. & Webb, C. (1969). The perception of briefly exposed point sources of light. *Quarterly Journal of Experimental Psychology*, **21**, 299–311.

Cobrinik, L. (1959). Unusual reading ability in severely disturbed children: clinical observation and retrospective inquiry. *Journal of Autism and Childhood Schizoophrenia*, **4**, 163–175.

Cohen, J. (1959). The factorial structure of the WISC at ages 7:6, 10:6 and 13:6. *Journal of Consulting Psychology*, **23**, 285–299.

Cramaussel, E. (1924). Ce que voient des yeux d'enfants. *Journal of Psychology*, **21**, 161–170.

Elliot, C. D., Murray, D. J. & Pearson, L. S. (1979). *The British ability scales*. Windsor: NFER-Nelson Publishing Co. Ltd.

Frith, U. (1970a). Studies in pattern detection in normal and autistic children: I. Immediate recall of auditory sequences. *Journal of Abnormal Psychology*, **69**, 413–420.

Frith, U. (1970b). Studies in pattern detection in normal and autistic children: II. Reproduction and production of color sequences. *Journal of Experimental Child Psychology*, **10**, 120–135.

Frith, U. (1989). *Autism: explaining the enigma*. Oxford: Basil Blackwell.

Ghent, L. (1956). Perception of overlapping and embedded figures by children of different ages. *American Journal of Psychology*, **69**, 575–587.

Hemmendinger, L. (1953). Perceptual organization and development as reflected in the structure of Rorschach test responses. *Journal of Projective Techniques*, **17**, 162–170.

Hermelin, B. & O'Connor, N. (1971). *Psychological experiments with autistic children*. Oxford: Pergamon Press.

349

Kaplan, E. (1983). A process approach to neuropsychological assessment. In: T. K. Boll & B. K. Bryant (Eds), *Clinical neuropsychological brain function: research measurement and practice* (pp. 129–167). Washington, DC: APA.

Koffka, K. (1935). *Principles of gestalt psychology*. New York: Harcourt.

Kohs, S. C. (1923). *Intelligence measurement*. New York: Macmillan.

Kramer, J. H., Kaplan, E., Blusewicz, M. J. & Preston, K. A. (1991). Visual hierarchical analysis of block design configural errors. *Journal of Clinical and Experimental Neuropsychology*, **13**, 455–465.

Leiter, R. G. (1980). *The Leiter international performance scale*. Chicago: Stoelting.

Lockyer, L. & Rutter, M. (1970). A five to fifteen year follow-up study of infantile psychosis: IV. Patterns of cognitive ability. *British Journal of Social and Clinical Psychology*, **9**, 152–163.

Maxwell, A. E. (1959). A factorial analysis of the Wechsler intelligence scale for children. *British Journal of Educational Psychology*, **29**, 237–241.

Meili-Dworetzki, G. (1956). The development of perception in the Rorschach. In B. Klopfer (Ed.), *Developments in the Rorschach technique* (pp. 108–176). World Book.

Nadel, A. B. (1938). A qualitative analysis of behaviour following cerebral lesions diagnosed as primarily affecting the frontal lobes. *Archives of Psychology*, Whole No. 224.

Navon, D. (1977). Forest before trees: the precedence of global features in visual perception. *Cognitive Psychology*, **9**, 353–383.

Navon, D. (1981). The forest revisited: more on global precedence. *Psychological Research*, **43**, 1–32.

Ogilvie, J. C. & Taylor, M. M. (1958). Effect of orientation on the visibility of fine wires. *Journal of the Optical Society of America*, **48**, 628–629.

Ohta, M. (1987). Cognitive disorders of infantile autism: a study employing the WISC, spatial relation conceptualization and gesture imitations. *Journal of Autism and Developmental Disorders*, **17**, 45–62.

Olson, D. R. (1970). *Cognitive development: the child's acquisition of diagonality*. New York and London: Academic Press.

Olson, D. & Hildyard, A. (1977). On the mental representation of oblique orientation. *Canadian Journal of Psychology*, **31**, 3–13.

Prior, M. R. (1979). Cognitive abilities and disabilities in infantile autism: a review. *Journal of Abnormal Child Psychology*, **7**, 357–380.

Reissenweber, M. (1953). The use of modified block designs in the evaluation and training of the brain injured. *Psychological Monographs: General and Applied*, **67**, Whole No. 371, 1–28.

Rudel, R. G. & Teuber, H. L. (1963). Discrimination of direction of lines in children. *Journal of Comparative and Physiological Psychology*, **56**, 892–898.

Rudel, R. G. & Teuber, H. L. (1971). Spatial orientation in normal children and in children with early brain injury. *Neuropsychologia*, **9**, 401–407.

Sattler, J. M. (1974). *Assessment of children's intelligence*. Philadelphia: Saunders.

Shah, A. (1988). *Visuo-spatial islets of abilities and intellectual functioning in autism*. Unpublished PhD thesis. University of London.

Shah, A. & Frith, U. (1983). An islet of ability in autistic children: a research note. *Journal of Child Psychology and Psychiatry*, **24**, 613–620.

Shah, A. & Holmes, N. (1985). Brief report: the use of the Leiter International Performance Scale with autistic children. *Journal of Autism and Developmental Disorders*, **15**, 195–203.

Shapiro, M. B. (1951). Experimental studies of a perceptual anomaly: 1. Initial experiments. *Journal of Mental Science*, **97**, 91–100.

Shapiro, M. B. (1952). Experimental studies of perceptual anomaly: 2 Confirmatory and explanatory experiments. *Journal of Mental Science*, **98**, 605–617.

Shapiro, M. B. (1954). An experimental investigation of the block design rotation effect: an analysis of a psychological effect of brain damage. *British Journal of Mental Psychology*, **27**, 84–88.

Teuber, H. L., Battersby, W. S. & Bender, M. B. (1951). Performance of complex visual tasks after cerebral lesions. *Journal of Nervous and Mental Diseases*, **114**, 413–429.

Teuber, H. L. & Weinstein, S. (1956). Ability to discover hidden figures after cerebral lesions. *Archives of Neurological Psychiatry*, **76**, 369–379.

Tymchuk, A. J., Simmons, J. Q. & Neafsey, S. (1977). Intellectual characteristics of adolescent childhood psychotics with high verbal ability. *Journal of Mental Deficiency Research*, **21**, 133–138.

Venter, A., Lord, C. & Schopler, E. (1992). A follow-up study of high-functioning autistic children. *Journal of Child Psychology and Psychiatry*, **33**, 489–507.

Wechsler, D. (1974). *Wechsler intelligence scale for children—revised*. NY: The Psychological Corporation.

Wechsler, D. (1981). *Wechsler adult intelligence scales—revised*. NY: The Psychological Corporation.

Wertheimer, R. M. (1923). Untersuchungen zur Lehre von der Gestalt: II. *Psychologische Forschung*, **4**, 301–350.

Witkin, H. A. (1950). Individual differences in ease of perception of embedded figures. *Journal of Personality*, **19**, 1–15.

Witkin, H. A., Dyk, R., Faterson, H. F., Goodenough, D. R. & Karp, S. A. (1962). *Psychological differentiation*. New York: Wiley.

Witkin, H. A. & Goodenough, D. R. (1981). *Cognitive styles: essence and origins*. New York: International University Press.

Witkin, H. A., Lewis, H. B., Herzman, M., Machover, K., Meissner, P. B. & Wapner, S. (1954). *Personality through perception*. New York: Harper.

120

STUDYING WEAK CENTRAL COHERENCE AT LOW LEVELS: CHILDREN WITH AUTISM DO NOT SUCCUMB TO VISUAL ILLUSIONS

A research note

Francesca G. E. Happé

Source: *Journal of Child Psychology and Psychiatry*, 37, 1996: 873–877.

While anecdotal reports of abnormal perceptual experiences in autism abound, there have been to date no experimental studies showing fundamental perceptual peculiarities. The present paper reports results from a first study of low-level visual integration in autism. Twenty-five subjects with autism, 21 normal 7- and 8-year-olds, and 26 children with learning difficulties were asked to make simple judgements about six well-known visual illusions. Two conditions were used, in an attempt to explore group differences; standard two-dimensional black and white line drawings, and the same figures augmented with raised coloured lines. The subjects with autism were less likely to succumb to the two-dimensional illusions than were the other groups, and were less aided by the three-dimensional 'disembedded' condition. These striking results are discussed with reference to the 'central coherence' account of autism.

Introduction

Perceptual abnormalities are a common feature of the autobiographical accounts of individuals with autism (Grandin, 1984; Williams, 1992; White & White, 1987). Hypo- and hyper-sensitivity to sound, touch or vision are described, as well as fragmented perception and intense experience of normally unnoticed aspects of the environment. To date, however, these possible peculiarities have not been systematically explored. Frith and

Baron-Cohen (1987), reviewing research in this area, concluded that there was no empirical evidence against the hypothesis that low-level perceptual processes are intact in autism.

Current psychological theories of autism (reviewed in Happé, 1994a, b) focus mainly on the social impairments, and have relatively little to say about the non-social deficits and assets seen in autism. Non-social features which are clinically prominent include the restricted repertoire of interests (necessary for diagnosis in the third revised version of the Diagnostic and Statistical Manual, DSM-III-R, of the APA, 1987), the obsessive desire for sameness (one of two cardinal features for Kanner & Eisenberg, 1956), the islets of ability (an essential criterion in Kanner, 1943), the idiot savant abilities (striking in one in 10 individuals with autism; Rimland & Hill, 1984), the excellent rote memory (emphasized by Kanner, 1943) and the preoccupation with parts of objects (a diagnostic feature in DSM-IV, APA, 1994).

The 'central coherence' theory presented by Frith (1989) and further developed by Frith and Happé (1994) and Happé (1994a, c) is one exception to this general trend. These authors suggest that the non-social features of autism, both assets and deficits, may follow from a tendency to process local vs global information, and a failure to process incoming stimuli in context. One question concerns the level at which coherence is hypothesized to be lacking. Findings that subjects with autism are better than controls at spotting embedded figures (Shah & Frith, 1983), and that they are better able to reproduce unsegmented block designs (Happé, 1994c; Shah & Frith, 1993) suggest problems in coherence at a relatively early perceptual or attentional stage. By contrast, demonstrations of failure to process information in context during sentence reading (Frith & Snowling, 1983; Happé, in press) point to deficits in coherence at higher levels of meaning extraction.

The present study represents a first attempt to establish the level at which central coherence is weak in subjects with autism. Visual illusions were chosen as figures devoid of 'higher level' meaning, which nonetheless appear to require the integration of perceptual features. Gregory (1967) has pointed out that in many illusions 'induced' and 'inducing' parts can be easily distinguished. Taking this suggestion of a figure-ground separation, illusions appear to present examples of the effects of context on perception at very low levels. For example, the central circles in the Titchener illusion (Fig. 1) are easily perceived as the same size when seen in isolation (as in the control figure, Fig. 1), but when placed in the inducing context (of surrounding small or large circles) are judged to be of different sizes. In this illusion the central circles presumably become part of a whole figure gestalt which changes subjects' perception of these parts.

If subjects with autism are able to process the induced parts separately from the inducing context—that is, if they fail to integrate all elements of the illusions—then it might be predicted that they will make more accurate

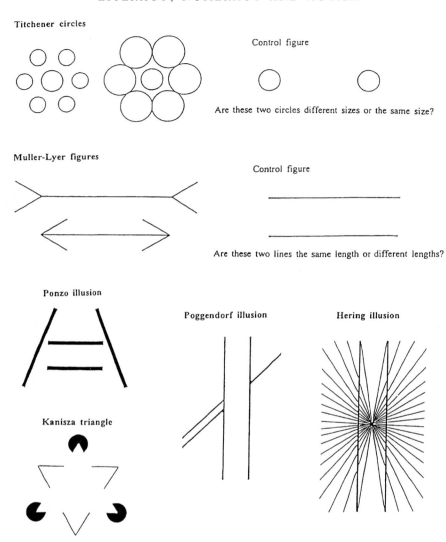

Figure 1 Two-dimensional stimuli for visual illusions study and examples of control stimuli.

judgements, and fail to succumb to the common illusory effects. If their better performance on the illusions *is* due to this weak coherence, then a manipulation which artificially segments out the parts to be judged (through colour and depth) should help the controls to perform as accurately as the subjects with autism, who should themselves be little aided by this pre-segmentation.

Method

Subjects

Twenty-five children with autism took part in the study. All were attending special schools for autism, and all had received a diagnosis of autism by experienced clinicians using the guidelines of standard criteria such as DSM-III, DSM-III-R (APA, 1987). Control subjects of two types were also tested. Twenty-one young normal children approximately matched as a group to the mean verbal mental age (VMA) of the autism group were tested. Twenty-six children with moderate (non-specific) learning difficulties (MLD), but without autism, were also tested. This group was of mixed aetiology and attended special schools in London.

Most subjects were assessed with the British Picture Vocabulary Scale (BPVS; Dunn, Dunn, Whetton, & Pintilie, 1982) to establish a receptive vocabulary age equivalent. For six subjects with autism and eight subjects in the MLD group, however, verbal IQ and VMA were calculated from the Wechsler Intelligence Scale for Children—Revised (WISC-R; Wechsler, 1974). Subject characteristics are shown in Table 1. The autism and MLD groups did not differ in any subject variable.

Materials

A selection of six well-known illusions was used, taken from illustrations in standard psychology textbooks. These comprised the Ponzo illusion, Titchener circles, Kanisza triangle, Muller-Lyer figures, Hering illusion and the Poggendorf illusion (see Fig. 1). The illusions varied in size from approximately 6 × 6cm to 10 × 7cm. Each illusion was presented in two

Table 1 Subject Characteristics.

Group	N		Age (y:m)	VMA	BPVS standardized score/WISC-R VIQ
Autism	25	Mean	13:1	7:1	58.7
		SD	2:4	2:3	14.2
		Range	(8:1–16:8)	(3:7–13:0)	(40–92)
MLD	26	Mean	12:0	7:9	67.3
		SD	2:2	2:0	11.0
		Range	(6:6–14:9)	(4:8–11:1)	(46–85)
Normal	21	Mean	7:9*	8:6	106.0*
		SD	0:4	1:6	13.3
		Range	(7:5–8:4)	(5:7–11:6)	(78–132)

* $p < .001$.

conditions. In the two-dimensional condition the illusions were shown in black and white on a laminated card. In addition, control figures were presented for each illusion (see examples in Fig. 1). These were used to ensure that each subject had sufficient language to comprehend and answer the test questions, and was motivated and able to make simple line length and orientation judgements with non-illusory figures. Subjects who were unable to answer questions about the control stimuli were excluded from the sample.

The three-dimensional illusions were created by adding brightly coloured plastic strips/shapes over the original black and white line drawings. In each case the raised forms highlighted those parts of the figure about which the subject was asked to make a judgement. So, for example, in the Muller-Lyer illusion, the two straight line segments were overlaid with raised plastic lines of the same dimensions as the original lines. The coloured plastic forms, which were blue, red or yellow, stood up approximately 4mm from the surface of the card.

Procedure

Each subject was tested in a quiet place in his/her school. The standard two-dimensional illusions, with their control figures, were shown to the subject first. The experimenter shuffled the cards, presenting illusions and control stimuli interspersed in random order. The three-dimensional illusions were shown to the subject on a second visit, between 1 and 3 weeks later. Subjects were asked the following questions, as appropriate to the illusion: 'Are these two lines the same length or different lengths?' (Ponzo and Muller-Lyer illusions), 'Are these two circles different sizes or the same size?' (Titchener circles), 'How many triangles can you see here?' (Kanisza), 'Does line A join up with line B or line C?' (Poggendorf), 'Are these two lines straight or curvy?' (Hering illusion). Order of alternatives in the test question was counterbalanced, and where subjects answered 'Different', they were asked to point out the longer line/larger circle.

Results

The mean number of illusions by which subjects were 'fooled' (i.e. gave typical incorrect judgements) is shown in Table 2. As can be seen, the autism group succumbed to fewer illusions in the standard two-dimensional form than did the control groups. Control subjects, as predicted, made significantly more accurate judgements in the three-dimensional condition than with the two-dimensional illusions. In the autism group, however, the difference between two- and three-dimensional illusion performance was not significant. Interestingly, in the three-dimensional condition the autism and control groups did not differ ($F(2,69) = .40$, $p = .67$). On multiple

356

Table 2 Group Results. Number of Illusions to Which Subjects 'Succumbed' (max = 6).

Group	N		Two-dimensional illusions	Three-dimensional illusions
Autism	25	Mean	2.24*	1.80
		Range	1–5	0–3
		SD	.93	.91
MLD	26	Mean	3.42	2.00
		Range	2–5	0–5
		SD	1.03	1.20
Normal	21	Mean	4.09	2.09
		Range	2–6	0–5
		SD	1.09	1.34

* $F(2, 69) = 20.08$, $p < .000$; Tukey test, autism group < MLD and normal, $p < .001$.

regression ANOVA there was a significant group by condition interaction ($F(2,69) = 9.95$, $p = .000$).

In terms of frequency data, only seven of the 25 subjects with autism (i.e. 28%) succumbed to three or more of the six two-dimensional illusions, compared with 20 (77%) of the MLD and 20 (95.2%) of the young normal controls. For the three-dimensional illusions, the comparable frequencies were seven subjects with autism (28%), eight (31%) subjects with MLD and nine (42.9%) young normal subjects succumbing to half or more of the illusions. Most subjects in the control groups were aided by the disembedded three-dimensional condition in making accurate judgements, i.e. most subjects succumbed to fewer illusions in the three-dimensional form than in the two-dimensional form. This was not true for the subjects with autism. While less than half (44%) of the autism group was aided by the three-dimensional disembedded condition, almost all (95%) the normal controls and most (73%) of the MLD group were more accurate in the three-dimensional than the two-dimensional condition. Chi-sqaure analysis showed that the autism group differed significantly in this respect from both control groups (autism vs normal, $\chi^2 = 13.67$, $p < .001$; autism vs MLD, $\chi^2 = 4.44$, $p < .05$).

The pattern of results for the individual illusions is shown in Table 3. Of the six illusions, two showed somewhat different results. The Muller-Lyer figure stood out from the other illusions as the most 'persuasive' to all groups. Eighty-one per cent of the normal children, 88% of MLD subjects and, interestingly, 88% of the autism group succumbed to this illusion, erroneously judging the lines to be of different lengths. This was the only illusion which 'tricked' a significant proportion of the autism group. The other illusion which did not follow the pattern of result reported above, was

357

Table 3 Frequency Data for Individual Illusions, Percentage of Subjects who Succumbed to Each Illusion.

Group	Ponzo	Kanisza	Titchener	Muller-Lyer	Hering	Poggendorf
Autism						
Two-dimensional	28.0	8.0	32.0	88.0	40.0	28.0
Three-dimensional	24.0	12.0	28.0	60.0	24.0	36.0
MLD						
Two-dimensional	34.6	42.3	61.5	88.5	69.2	57.7
Three-dimensional	19.2	42.3	34.6	30.8	46.2	26.9
Normal						
Two-dimensional	52.4	57.1	71.4	80.9	76.2	61.9
Three-dimensional	28.6	61.9	23.8	28.6	33.3	38.1

the Kanisza triangle which differed in being relatively unaffected by the three-dimensional 'disembedded' condition (i.e. as many errors were made on the three-dimensional version of the triangle as on the two-dimensional version).

Discussion

The present study was a first exploration of illusory figure perception in autism. The results are striking and somewhat surprising; subjects with autism made more accurate judgements of illusory figures and less often succumbed to the typical mis-judgements. That their success on this task was due to failure to integrate the induced lines and the inducing context, is indicated by the results from the three-dimensional condition. Where the induced lines were artificially disembedded from the inducing context, through colour and depth, control subjects performed like subjects with autism, and the group differences disappeared. This effect is akin to Shah and Frith's (1993) finding with the block design task, where pre-segmenting the designs brought control, performance to the level of the autism group's success, but did not aid the subjects with autism. The theory that people with autism have weak central coherence predicts and explains the present finding, and it is not apparent that any other current theory of the disorder (e.g. deficits in executive function, theory of mind) can readily account for these results.

Differences between the visual illusions used also suggest that weak coherence may provide a good explanation for the success of the autism group. The only illusion to which a significant proportion of the autism group succumbed was the Muller-Lyer. This illusion cannot easily be split into induced figure and inducing context, since the arrow heads in the version used are connected to the judged lines and form part of the same 'object'. It is not clear exactly why perception of the Kanisza triangle was so little affected by the three-dimensional condition, but it is worth noting that this illusion is unlike the others used in that it induces perception of illusory contours.

The present findings are surprising in so far as the visual illusions appear to require integration at very low levels, and it seemed unlikely a priori that subjects would show weak coherence at this level. It will, of course, be necessary to replicate these results with other samples of subjects and different stimuli. More sophisticated techniques are available for estimating the magnitude of illusory effects (e.g. asking subjects to adjust lines to match lengths), but it is impressive that even using quite gross judgements and very simple methods, significant group differences could be found. If subjects with autism do fail to integrate visual information at this low level, it may be necessary to think again about perceptual abnormalities, reports of fragmented perception, and how people with autism 'see the world'.

Acknowledgements

The data reported in this paper were collected with the help of the following schools, to whom I am extremely grateful: Helen Allison School, Sybil Elgar School, Springhallow School, Chalgrove School, Fairway School, Dollis School and Northway School. I would also like to thank Nicole Berenson and Melanie Bernitz for their help with collecting the data, and Uta Frith, and other colleagues at the CDU, for invaluable advice and discussion.

Abbreviations

BPVS, British Picture Vocabulary Scale; DSM, Diagnostic and Statistical Manual of the American Psychiatric Association; MLD, moderate learning difficulties; VMA, verbal mental age; WISC-R, Wechsler Intelligence Scale for Children—Revised.

References

American Psychiatric Association (1987). *Diagnostic and statistical manual of mental disorders (DSM-III-R)* (3rd ed., rev.). Washington, DC: American Psychiatric Association.

American Psychiatric Association (1994). *Diagnostic and statistical manual of mental disorders (DSM-IV)* (4th ed.). Washington, DC: American Psychiatric Association.

Dunn, L. M., Dunn, L. M., Whetton, C., & Pintilie, D. (1982). *British Picture Vocabulary Scale*. Windsor, U.K.: NFER-Nelson.

Frith, U. (1989). *Autism: explaining the enigma*. Oxford: Blackwell Scientific Publications.

Frith, U., & Baron-Cohen, S. (1987). Perception in autistic children. In D. J. Cohen, A. Donnellan, & R. Paul (Eds.), *Handbook of autism and pervasive developmental disorders* (pp. 85–102). New York: John Wiley.

Frith, U. & Happé, F. (1994). Autism: beyond 'theory of mind'. *Cognition, 50,* 115–132.

Frith, U. & Snowling, M. (1983). Reading for meaning and reading for sound in autistic and dyslexic children. *Journal of Developmental Psychology, 1,* 329–342

Grandin, T. (1984). My experiences as an autistic child and review of selected literature. *Journal of Orthomolecular Psychiatry, 13,* 144–175

Gregory, R. L. (1967). *Eye and brain.* New York: World University Library.

Happé, F. G. E. (1994a). Annotation: Psychological theories of autism. *Journal of Child Psychology and Psychiatry, 35,* 215–229.

Happé, F. (1994b). *Autism: an introduction to psychological theory.* London: UCL Press.

Happé, F. G. E. (1994c). Wechsler IQ profile and theory of mind in autism: a research note. *Journal of Child Psychology and Psychiatry, 35,* 1461–1471.

Happé, F. (in press). Central coherence and theory of mind in autism: reading homographs in context. *British Journal of Developmental Psychology.*

Kanner, L. (1943). Autistic disturbances of affective contact. *Nervous Child, 2,* 217–250.

Kanner, L. & Eisenberg, L. (1956). Early infantile autism 1943–1955. *American Journal of Orthopsychiatry, 26,* 55–65

Rimland, B., & Hill, A. L. (1984). Idiot savants. In Wortis, J. (Ed.), *Mental retardation and developmental disabilities,* Vol. 1 (pp. 155–169). New York: Plenum Press.

Shah, A. & Frith, U. (1983). An islet of ability in autistic children: a research note. *Journal of Child Psychology and Psychiatry, 24,* 613–620.

Shah, A. & Frith, U. (1993). Why do autistic individuals show superior performance on the Block Design task? *Journal of Child Psychology and Psychiatry, 34,* 1351–1364.

Wechsler, D. (1974). *Wechsler Intelligence Scale for Children—Revised.* New York: The Psychological Corporation.

Williams, D. (1992). *Nobody nowhere.* London: Doubleday.

White, B. B. & White, M. S. (1987). Autism from the inside. *Medical Hypotheses, 24,* 223–229.

121

BRIEF REPORT: SPECIFIC EXECUTIVE FUNCTION PROFILES IN THREE NEURODEVELOPMENTAL DISORDERS

Sally Ozonoff and Jenise Jensen

Source: *Journal of Autism and Developmental Disorders*, 29, 1999: 171–177.

Introduction

It has been proposed that deficient executive functions, such as flexibility, set maintenance, organization, planning, and working memory, may be primary cognitive deficits of autism (Hughes, Russell, & Robbins, 1994; Ozonoff, Pennington, & Rogers, 1991). Executive deficits may also play a part in several other developmental and neurological disorders, however (Ozonoff, 1997; Pennington & Ozonoff, 1996), including attention-deficit hyperactivity disorder (ADHD; Chelune, Ferguson, Koon, & Dickey, 1986) and Tourette syndrome (TS; Bornstein, 1990; Gladstone *et al.*, 1993). This finding has raised the so-called "discriminant validity question" (Pennington, 1994; Pennington & Ozonoff, 1996): That is, how can disorders differing in behavioral phenotype share the same cognitive underpinnings? One answer to this question is that specific types of executive impairment may be associated with specific neurodevelopmental disorders. Since the class of executive behaviors is large and diverse, it is important to clarify precisely which functions are impaired in each disorder. We hypothesized that when the broad domain of executive function was parsed into specific components (e.g., planning, flexibility, inhibition), different disorders would demonstrate different executive profiles.

Three measures, the Wisconsin Card Sorting Task (WCST), the Tower of Hanoi (TOH), and the Stroop Color-Word Test, have traditionally been used to measure executive function deficits in neurodevelopmental

361

disorders. The WCST (Grant & Berg, 1948; Heaton, Chelune, Talley, Kay, & Curtiss, 1993) was designed primarily to test flexibility, the TOH (Borys, Spitz, & Dorans, 1982) to measure planning ability and working memory, and the Stroop (1935) to assess inhibition of prepotent behavior.

Using these measures, most studies of autism have found evidence of executive dysfunction. For example, on the WCST, autistic subjects are highly perseverative in their responses compared to controls (Bennetto, Pennington, & Rogers, 1996; Ozonoff, 1995; Prior & Hoffman, 1990; Ozonoff & McEvoy, 1994; Ozonoff et al., 1991; Rumsey, 1985; Rumsey & Hamburger, 1988, 1990; Szatmari, Tuff, Finlayson, & Bartolucci, 1990). Similarly, every study using the TOH or related Tower of London has found highly deficient performance in autistic samples relative to controls (Bennetto et al., 1996; Hughes et al., 1994; Ozonoff & McEvoy, 1994; Ozonoff et al., 1991). In contrast, the only studies administering the Stroop to autistic samples both failed to find any group differences (Bryson, 1983; Eskes, Bryson, & McCormick, 1990). This suggests that inhibition may be a relatively more spared component of executive function in autism (Ozonoff & Strayer, 1997).

Executive function impairment in ADHD, the most prevalent of developmental disorders, has been investigated aggressively recently, using all three measures. Although a few studies have demonstrated deficits on the WCST in ADHD (Boucugnani & Jones, 1989; Chelune et al., 1986; Gorenstein, Mammato, & Sandy, 1989; Shue & Douglas, 1992), more than half of the investigations have shown no statistically significant differences from controls (Barkley, Grodzinsky, & DuPaul, 1992; Fischer, Barkley, Edelbrock, & Smallish, 1990; Grodzinsky & Diamond, 1992; Loge, Staton, & Beatty, 1990; McGee, Williams, Moffitt, & Anderson, 1989; Pennington, Groisser, & Welch, 1993; Weyandt & Willis, 1994). In contrast, all but one study (Cohen, Weiss, & Minde, 1972) found deficient performance on both the TOH (Aman, Roberts, & Pennington, 1998; Pennington et al., 1993; Weyandt & Willis, 1994) and Stroop in children with ADHD, relative to controls (Barkley et al., 1992; Boucugnani & Jones, 1989; Gorenstein et al., 1989; Grodzinsky & Diamond, 1992; Hopkins, Perlman, Hechtman, & Weiss, 1979; LaVoie & Charlebois, 1994; Lufi, Cohen, & Parish-Plass, 1990; Reardon & Naglieri, 1992). This raises the possibility that the executive impairments of ADHD may differ from those of autism.

The involuntary movements and vocalizations that characterize TS have been theorized to be due to an inability to suppress unintended behavior, thus reflecting a failure of inhibition. Research attempting to tap this impairment using both the Stroop and the WCST has been ambiguous, however. Although Gladstone et al. (1993) found significant differences between TS subjects and a comparison group with OCD on the WCST, most studies have failed to find any differences between TS and controls on this measure (Bornstein, 1990, 1991a; Bornstein & Yang, 1991; Harris *et al.*, 1995; Randolph, Hyde, Gold, Goldberg, & Weinberger, 1993; Sutherland, Kolb, Schoel, Whishaw, & Davies, 1982; Yeates & Bornstein, 1994). Surprisingly, since the Stroop is generally considered to measure inhibition, only one of three studies utilizing this measure with TS subjects found any differences relative to control groups (Channon, Flynn, & Robertson, 1992; Georgiou, Bradshaw, Phillips, Bradshaw, & Chiu, 1995; Silverstein, Como, Palumbo, West, & Osborn, 1995).

Although previous studies have examined executive dysfunction in autism, ADHD, and TS separately, none has directly compared all three disorders simultaneously. If the domain of executive function is central to all of these disorders, it is important to determine which specific executive deficits characterize each disorder and distinguish it from the others. Specifically, it has been proposed that autistic subjects are primarily deficient in flexibility and planning, those with ADHD have difficulty sustaining attention and inhibiting behavior, and individuals with TS have difficulty with inhibition, particularly controlling prepotent impulses (Pennington & Ozonoff, 1996). In the present study, an executive battery tapping each of these functions was administered to children with autism, TS, and ADHD. The most convincing evidence of our hypothesis would be a group by task interaction effect, with autistic subjects demonstrating deficiency on the WCST and TOH, but not the Stroop, while TS and ADHD subjects demonstrate the opposite pattern.

Method

Subjects

Autistic Group. Fifty-five children with autism were recruited for participation through the Autism Society of Utah and other agencies serving people with autism. Diagnosis was verified using the Autism Diagnostic Interview-Revised (ADI-R; Lord, Rutter, & LeCouteur, 1994) and the Autism Diagnostic Observation Schedule (ADOS; Lord *et al.*, 1989). Fifteen subjects were excluded because they did not meet either ADI-R, ADOS, or DSM-IV (American Psychiatric Association, 1994) criteria for Autistic Disorder, leaving a final autistic sample of 40. Subjects ranged in age from 6 to 18 years and all had Full-scale IQ (FSIQ) scores of 70 or above. See Table I for descriptive characteristics of the sample.

Tourette Syndrome Group. Thirty-one children with TS were recruited through the Departments of Child Psychiatry and Neurology at a large local children's hospital and through mental health professionals. Diagnosis was confirmed using the Diagnostic Interview Scale for Children-Revised (DISC-R; Shaffer *et al.*, 1993) and the Tourette Syndrome Symptom List

Table I Descriptive Characteristics of the Samples [M(SD)].

	Autistic (n = 40)	TS (n = 30)	ADHD (n = 24)	Controls (n = 29)
Age	12.6 (3.4)	12.6 (2.5)	11.1 (2.0)	12.1 (3.0)
VIQ	93.3 (20.0)[b]	98.5 (11.5)[b]	105.5 (12.6)	107.8 (12.3)
PIQ	98.6 (19.8)[a]	103.7 (13.0)	108.3 (9.9)	106.8 (12.5)
FSIQ	95.2 (18.8)[b]	100.8 (10.0)[a]	107.2 (10.8)	107.8 (10.8)

[a] $p < .05$ from controls.
[b] $p < .01$ from controls.

(TSSL; Cohen, Leckman, & Shaywitz, 1985) administered to one parent during testing. Five children were excluded from participation due to failure to demonstrate at least two motor or one vocal tic, as required by DSM-IV. Four subjects diagnosed with Chronic Tic Disorders were also included in the group, since recent research suggests these disorders are on the same continuum and share the same genetic basis as TS (Spencer, Biederman, Harding, Wilens, & Faraone, 1995), bringing the total TS sample to 30. Subjects were examined for comorbid ADHD and obsessive-compulsive disorder (OCD) using the DISC-R, the IOWA Conners Rating Scale (Loney & Milich, 1982), and the Leyton Obsessional Inventory (LOI; Berg, Rappoport, & Flament, 1986). Ten TS subjects met criteria for comorbid ADHD, one for comorbid OCD, and three for both ADHD and OCD. TS subjects ranged in age from 8 to 17 years and had FSIQ scores of 70 or above (see Table I).

Attention-Deficit Hyperactivity Disorder Group. Thirty-one children diagnosed with ADHD were recruited through the Department of Child Psychiatry at a large children's hospital and through local mental health professionals. Diagnosis was verified with the DISC-R and the IOWA Conners administered to one parent. Nine children were dropped from the study for failing to meet criteria for ADHD on one of the two diagnostic measures, leaving a final sample of 24 subjects in this group. ADHD subjects ranged in age from 8 to 18 years and all had FSIQ score above 70 (see Table I).

Controls. Thirty-three subjects were recruited by word of mouth through research personnel. Subjects were screened for symptoms of autism, TS, ADHD, and OCD using the DISC-R, the IOWA Conners Rating Scale, the TSSL, and the LOI. Four children were excluded for showing signs of disorder on the screening measures (1 with undiagnosed tics and 3 with undiagnosed ADHD), resulting in a final control sample of 29. Control subjects ranged in age from 8 to 17 years and all had FSIQ scores above 70 (see Table I).

Measures

Diagnostic measures

Tourette Syndrome Symptom List (TSSL; Cohen *et al.*, 1985). This parent report questionnaire measures the number, type, and severity of current and past tics. It was used to document the presence (in TS subjects) or absence (in other groups) of two motor and one vocal tic, as required by DSM-IV criteria.

IOWA Conners Rating Scale (Loney & Milich, 1982). This measure is a modified version of the Conners Rating Scale (Conners, 1990) that was administered to parents to assess the presence and severity of their children's ADHD symptoms while off medication. Two separate subscales are used on the IOWA Conners, an Inattention-Overactivity (IO) subscale and an Aggression (A) subscale, to measure these two distinct facets of ADHD (Loney & Milich, 1982). A score of 11 or above on the IO subscale indicated that a subject met criteria for ADHD (Loney & Milich, 1982).

Leyton Obsessional Inventory–Child Version (LOI; Berg *et al.*, 1986). This measures the presence and severity of self-reported obsessive-compulsive behavior. It was administered to subjects in interview format. A cutoff score of 25 (Flament *et al.*, 1988) was used to diagnose OCD.

Experimental measures

Three tasks of executive function were administered to all subjects.

Wisconsin Card Sorting Task (WCST; Grant & Berg, 1948). This task is thought to measure flexibility, since it requires subjects to shift cognitive set up to six times during the task. The primary index of executive dysfunction on the WCST used in the present study was the number of perseverative responses, in which the subject continued to sort by a previously correct category despite feedback that it was incorrect (Heaton *et al.*, 1993).

Tower of Hanoi (TOH; Borys *et al.*, 1982). This task is thought to measure planning capacities since successful performance requires mental anticipation of potential disk moves and their consequences. Following several specific rules, subjects must move disks from a prearranged sequence on three different pegs to match a goal state determined by the examiner in as few moves as possible.

Stroop Color-Word Test (Stroop, 1935). This task is used to measure inhibition, since it requires subjects to suppress an automatic, prepotent response in order to perform a less automatic one. In the critical inhibition condition, a color word is printed in a different color ink (e.g., the word BLUE is printed in green ink) and the subject is required to inhibit the urge to read the word, instead naming the color of ink.

Testing procedure

All subjects were tested at the Psychology Department of the University of Utah within the context of a larger study. Complete participation required two 2-hour sessions, with the order of the three experimental measures counterbalanced across groups. Subjects were also administered the Wechsler Intelligence Scale for Children—Third Edition (WISC-III), diagnostic measures, and tests used in a different study (Ozonoff & Strayer, 1997). Subjects were paid $5 an hour for participating.

Results

There were no significant group differences in age. However, controls demonstrated significantly higher VIQ, PIQ, and FSIQ than autistic subjects [VIQ: $t(67) = -3.45$, $p < .01$; PIQ: $t(67) = -1.95$, $p < .05$; FSIQ: $t(67) = -3.23$, $p < .01$] and significantly higher VIQ and FSIQ than TS subjects [VIQ: $t(57) = -3.00$, $p < .01$; FSIQ: $t(57) = -2.57$, $p < .05$]. See Table I. Thus, FSIQ was covaried in all subsequent analyses involving these groups.

A repeated-measures analysis of variance (ANOVA) was conducted, with group membership as the between-subjects factor, test (WCST, TOH, Stroop) as the within-subjects factor, and FSIQ as the covariate. Significant main effects of group, $F(3, 97) = 4.01$, $p < .05$, and test, $F(2, 196) = 26.35$, $p < .001$, were found. As predicted, a significant group by test interaction effect, $F(6, 196) = 8.46$, $p < .001$, was also evident.

Analyses of simple effects were then performed to examine the source of these findings. See Table II for group mean performance on the three measures. On the Wisconsin Card Sorting Test, a significant effect of group was found after covarying FSIQ, $F(3, 109) = 5.06$, $p < .01$. Planned contrasts of the cell means indicated that the group effect was due to significantly more perseverative performance by the autistic than the control group, $F(1, 60) = 4.38$, $p < .05$; the TS group, $t(58) = 2.72$, $p < .01$; and the ADHD group, $t(51) = 3.09$, $p < .01$. Neither the TS nor ADHD groups differed significantly from controls ($ps > .4$). On the Tower of Hanoi, a significant group effect was also found after covarying FSIQ, $F(3, 117) = 2.92$, $p < .05$.

Table II Group Mean Performance on Executive Measures [$M(SD)$].

	Autistic (n = 40)	TS (n = 30)	ADHD (n = 24)	Controls (n = 29)
WCST	40.3 (38.3)[a]	19.1 (16.2)	13.9 (9.3)	16.1 (11.8)
TOH	33.0 (12.5)[b]	39.3 (8.9)	38.0 (5.4)	40.1 (5.3)
Stroop	27.7 (11.4)	31.6 (11.9)	27.4 (7.0)[c]	32.0 (9.6)

[a] $p < .01$ from controls, TS, and ADHD.
[b] $p < .01$ from controls, $p < .05$ from TS and ADHD.
[c] $p < .05$ from controls.

Contrasts revealed the source of this effect to be significantly deficient planning strategies on the part of the autistic group relative to the control group, $F(1, 63) = 4.58$, $p < .05$; the TS group, $t(63) = -2.32$, $p < .05$; and the ADHD group, $t(57) = -1.87$, $p < .05$. Again, neither ADHD nor TS subjects differed significantly from controls ($p > .1$ and .9, respectively). Finally, on the Stroop Color-Word Test, a significant ADHD–control group difference was found, $t(50) = 1.94$, $p < .05$, indicating inhibitory dysfunction in this group. Neither autistic nor TS subjects differed from controls in inhibitory function ($ps > .3$ and .7, respectively).

Individual differences in executive profiles within the autistic group were also examined. Only 1 of 40 subjects performed above respective control group means on all three executive tests. Twenty percent performed above the control mean on two executive tests, 36% on just one of the dependent measures, and half the sample performed below the control group means on all three executive function tasks. Thus, executive deficits appeared to be quite pervasive within the autistic group and group differences were not accounted for by the very poor performance of just a few subjects. What distinguished subjects with better executive performance from those with more deficits? An ANOVA on the four subgroups (subjects deficient on zero, one, two, and three measures, respectively) revealed that they differed significantly in age $F(3, 39) = 3.55$, $p < .05$, but not VIQ, PIQ, or FSIQ (all $ps > .25$). Contrasts further demonstrated that the autistic subgroup deficient on only one measure was significantly older than the subgroups deficient on two, $t(17) = 2.60$, $p < .05$, and three, $t(26) = 3.01$, $p < .01$, measures [who did not differ from each other; $t(29) = 0.06$, $p = .95$]. Furthermore, the 1 subject with intact performance on all three tests was the oldest in the sample (18 years 7 months).

Since previous research has indicated that the neuropsychological characteristics of TS may vary as a function of comorbidity (Bornstein, 1991a; Harris et al., 1995; Ozonoff, Strayer, McMahon, & Filloux, 1998; Silverstein et al., 1995), additional analyses comparing the subgroup of TS subjects with comorbid ADHD and/or OCD ($n = 14$) to those with no evidence of comorbidity ($n = 16$) and to controls were carried out. There were, however, no significant main or interaction effects with comorbidity.

Discussion

Executive function deficits have been reported in a wide variety of developmental, psychiatric, and neurological disorders, including autism, ADHD, and TS. The so-called discriminant validity question asks how different disorders displaying distinct phenotypes can share the same underlying cognitive pattern. One answer to this question has been put forth: that a more fine-grained analysis will demonstrate that the particular type of dysfunction differs across conditions (Ozonoff, 1997). For example, autism may be primarily a disorder of flexibility and planning, while TS and ADHD may share inhibitory dysfunction. While previous studies have examined parts of this hypothesis in isolation, the contribution of the present investigation is that it directly compares three neurodevelopmental disorders on three tasks measuring different dimensions of executive function. The strongest evidence for our general hypothesis would be a group by task interaction effect, which in fact was found. Analyses of simple effects demonstrated that, in large part, the specific aspects of this hypothesis were borne out as well. As predicted, the autistic group demonstrated difficulties on the WCST and TOH, thought to indicate flexibility and planning problems, while performing normally on a test of inhibition, the Stroop. Impairment on at least one executive test was found in 39 of 40 autistic subjects, so the pattern was quite pervasive among the sample. Their deficits on the WCST and TOH were significant relative not only to controls but also to children with other neurodevelopmental disorders, namely, TS and ADHD. Conversely, the ADHD group demonstrated difficulty on the Stroop, but not the WCST or TOH. This crossover effect indicates that the profiles of executive dysfunction differ in the groups.

There was some suggestion that there may be age-related changes in performance on executive tests in autistic children, with younger subjects deficient on more tests than older subjects. However, cross-sectional investigations such as this one cannot definitively address this issue. Previous longitudinal studies have not found age-related improvements in executive function (Ozonoff & McEvoy, 1994), so the present study's results must be independently replicated.

Contrary to our hypothesis, the TS group demonstrated no deficits relative to controls. While this was not predicted a priori, this finding does replicate previous studies that also failed to find evidence of dysfunction on the Stroop in TS (Channon et al., 1992; Silverstein et al., 1995). Unfortunately, these results do little to clarify the already murky picture of executive abilities in TS. Even within a single research group, results can be contradictory. For example, Bornstein's group found deficits on the WCST in one TS sample (Bornstein, 1991a) but not another (Bornstein, 1991b) and deficits on the Category test in adults with TS (Bornstein, 1991b), but not children (Bornstein, Baker, Bazylewich, & Douglass, 1991). Similarly, we have found executive impairments using a different inhibitory measure, a negative priming task, in a previous investigation of TS (Ozonoff et al., 1998), but not in the present one, using the Stroop. Thus, evidence of executive dysfunction in TS remains uncertain.

These results indicate that the "discriminant validity problem" may only be a problem at a superficial level of analysis. That is, several disorders *do* share executive function problems with autism. At a more microanalytic level of analysis, however, the disorders can be differentiated on the basis of their executive profiles. Administration of a more extensive battery of executive function measures to these three neurodevelopmental disorders may permit identification of unique executive profiles, with disorder-specific patterns of strength and weakness. Such executive "fingerprints" may be useful aids in identification of the conditions, as well as in designing best practices for their remediation.

Acknowledgment

This study was supported by a grant to the first author (R29-MH52229).

References

Aman C. J., Roberts, R. J., & Pennington, B. F. (1988). A neuropsychological examination of the underlying deficit in ADHD: The frontal lobe vs. right parietal lobe theories. *Developmental Psychology, 34*, 956–969.

American Psychiatric Association. (1994). *Diagnostic and statistical manual of mental disorders.* (4th ed.). Washington, DC. Author.

Barkley, R. A., Grodzinsky, G., & DuPaul, G. J. (1992). Frontal lobe functions in attention deficit disorder with and without hyperactivity: A review and research report. *Journal of Abnormal Child Psychological, 20*, 163–188.

Bennetto, L., Pennington, B. F., & Rogers, S. J. (1996). Intact and impaired memory functions in autism. *Child Development, 67*, 1816–1835.

Berg, C. J., Rapoport, J. L., & Flament, M. (1986). The Leyton Obsessional Inventory—Child Version. *Journal of the American Academy of Child Psychiatry, 25*, 84–91.

Bornstein, R. A. (1990). Neuropsychological performance in children with Tourette's syndrome. *Psychiatry Research, 33*, 73–81.

Bornstein, R. A. (1991a). Neuropsychological correlates of obsessive characteristics in Tourette syndrome. *Journal of Neuropsychiatry and Clinical Neurosciences, 3*, 157–162.

Bornstein, R. A. (1991b). Neuropsychological performance in adults with Tourette's syndrome. *Psychiatry Research, 37*, 229–236.

Bornstein, R. A., Baker, G. B., Bazylewich, T., & Douglass, A. B. (1991). Tourette syndrome and neuropsychological performance. *Acta Psychiatrica Scandinavica, 84*, 212–216.

Bornstein, R. A., & Yang, V. (1991). Neuropsychological performance in medicated and unmedicated patients with Tourette's disorder. *American Journal of Psychiatry, 148*, 468–471.

Borys, S. V., Spitz, H. H., & Dorans, B. A. (1982). Tower of Hanoi performance of retarded young adults and nonretarded children as a function of solution length and goal state. *Journal of Experimental Child Psychology, 33*, 87–110.

Boucugnani, L. L., & Jones, R. W. (1989). Behaviors analogous to frontal lobe dysfunction in children with attention deficit hyperactivity disorder. *Archives of Clinical Neuropsychology, 4*, 161–173.

Bryson, S. E. (1983). Interference effects in autistic children: Evidence for the comprehension of single stimuli. *Journal of Abnormal Psychology, 92*, 250–254.

Channon, S., Flynn, D., & Robertson, M. M. (1992). Attentional deficits in Gilles de la Tourette syndrome. *Neuropsychiatry, Neuropsychology, and Behavioral Neurology, 5,* 170–177.

Chelune, G. J., Ferguson, W., Koon, R., & Dickey, T. O. (1986). Frontal lobe disinhibition in Attention Deficit Disorder. *Child Psychiatry and Human Development, 16,* 221–234.

Cohen, D. J., Leckman, J. F., & Shaywitz, B. A. (1985). The Tourette syndrome and other tics. In D. Scaffer, A. A. Ehrhardt, & L. L. Greenhill (Eds.), *The clinical guide to child psychiatry* (pp. 3–28). New York: Free Press.

Cohen, N. J., Weiss, G., & Minde, K. (1972). Cognitive styles in adolescents previously diagnosed as hyperactive. *Journal of Child Psychology and Psychiatry, 13,* 203–209.

Conners, C. K. (1990). *Manual for Conners' Rating Scale.* North Tonawanda, NY: Multi-Health Systems.

Eskes, G. A., Bryson, S. E., & McCormick, T. A. (1990). Comprehension of concrete and abstract words in autistic children. *Journal of Autism and Developmental Disorders, 20,* 61–73.

Fischer, M., Barkley, R. A., Edelbrock, C. S., & Smallish, L. (1990). The adolescent outcome of hyperactive children diagnosed by research criteria: II. Academic, attentional, and neuropsychological status. *Journal of Consulting and Clinical Psychology, 58,* 580–588.

Flament, M. F., Whitaker, A., Rapoport, J. L., Davies, M., Berg, C. Z., Kalikow, K., Sceery, W., & Shaffer, D. (1988). Obsessive compulsive disorder in adolescence: An epidemiological study. *Journal of the American Academy of Child and Adolescent Psychiatry, 27,* 764–771.

Georgiou, N., Bradshaw, J. L., Phillips, J. G., Bradshaw, J. A., & Chiu, E. (1995). Advance information and movement sequencing in Gilles de la Tourette's syndrome. *Journal of Neurology, Neurosurgery and Psychiatry, 58,* 184–191.

Gladstone, M., Carter, A. S., Schultz, R. T., Riddle, M., Schahill, L., & Pauls, D. L. (1993). *Neuropsychological functioning of children affected with Tourette's Syndrome and obsessive-compulsive disorder.* Paper presented at the meeting of the International Neuropsychological Society, Galveston, TX.

Gorenstein, E. E., Mammato, C. A., & Sandy, J. M. (1989). Performance of inattentive–overactive children on selected measures of prefrontal-type function. *Journal of Clinical Psychology, 45,* 619–632.

Grant, D. A., & Berg, E. A. (1948). A behavioral analysis of degree of reinforcement and ease of shifting to new responses in a Weigle-type card sorting problem. *Journal of Experimental Psychology, 32,* 404–411.

Grodzinsky, G. M., & Diamond, R. (1992). Frontal lobe functioning in boys with attention-deficit hyperactivity disorder. *Developmental Neuropsychology, 8,* 427–445.

Harris, E. L., Schuerholz, L. J., Singer, H. S., Reader, M. J., Brown, J. E., Cox, C., Mohr, J., Chase, G. A., & Denckla, M. B. (1995). Executive function in children with Tourette Syndrome and/or Attention Deficit Hyperactivity Disorder. *Journal of the International Neuropsychological Society, 1,* 511–516.

Heaton, R. K., Chelune, G. J., Talley, J. L., Kay, G. G., & Curtiss, G. (1993). *Wisconsin Card Sorting Test manual: Revised and expanded.* Odessa, FL: Psychological Assessment Resources.

Hopkins, J., Perlman, T., Hechtman, L., & Weiss, G. (1979). Cognitive style in adults originally diagnosed as hyperactives. *Journal of Child Psychology and Psychiatry and Allied Disciplines, 20*, 209–216.

Hughes, C., Russell, J., & Robbins, T. W. (1994). Evidence for executive dysfunction in autism. *Neuropsychologia, 32*, 477–492.

Lavoie, M. E., & Charlebois, P. (1994). The discriminant validity of the Stroop Color and Word Test: Toward a cost-effective strategy to distinguish subgroups of disruptive preadolescents. *Psychology in the Schools, 31*, 98–107.

Loge, D. V., Staton, R. D., & Beatty, W. W. (1990). Performance of children with ADHD on tests sensitive to frontal lobe dysfunction. *Journal of the American Academy of Child and Adolescent Psychiatry, 29*, 540–545.

Loney, J., & Milich, R. (1982). Hyperactivity, inattention, and aggression in clinical practice. *Developmental and Behavioral Pediatrics, 3*, 113–147.

Lord, C., Rutter, M., & Le Couteur, A. (1994). Autism Diagnostic Interview— Revised: A revised version of a diagnostic interview for caregivers of individuals with possible pervasive developmental disorders. *Journal of Autism and Developmental Disorders, 24*, 659–685.

Lord, C., Rutter, M. L., Goode, S., Heemsbergen, J., Jordan, H., Mawhood, L., & Schopler, E. (1989). Autism Diagnostic Observation Schedule: A standardized observation of communicative and social behavior. *Journal of Autism and Developmental Disorders, 19*, 185–212.

Lufi, D., Cohen, A., & Parish-Plass, J. (1990). Identifying Attention Deficit Hyperactive Disorder with the WISC—R and the Stroop Color and Word Test. *Psychology in the Schools, 27*, 28–34.

McGee, R., Williams, S., Moffitt, T., & Anderson, J. (1989). A comparison of 13-year-old boys with attention deficit and/or reading disorder on neuropsychological measures. *Journal of Abnormal Child Psychology, 17*, 37–53.

Ozonoff, S. (1995). Reliability and validity of the Wisconsin Card Sorting Test in studies of autism. *Neuropsychology, 9*, 491–500.

Ozonoff, S. (1997). Components of executive function in autism and other disorders. In J. Russell (Ed.), *Autism as an executive disorder*. New York: Oxford University Press.

Ozonoff, S., & McEvoy, R. E. (1994). A longitudinal study of executive function and theory of mind development in autism. *Development and Psychopathology, 6*, 415–431.

Ozonoff, S., Pennington, B. F., & Rogers, S. J. (1991). Executive function deficits in high-functioning autistic individuals: Relationship to theory of mind. *Journal of Child Psychology and Psychiatry and Allied Disciplines, 32*, 1081–1105.

Ozonoff, S., & Strayer, D. L. (1997). Inhibitory function in nonretarded children with autism. *Journal of Autism and Developmental Disorders, 27*, 59–77.

Ozonoff, S., Strayer, D. L., McMahon, W. M., & Filloux, F. (1998). Inhibitory deficits in Tourette syndrome: A function of comorbidity and symptom severity. *Journal of Child Psychology and Psychiatry, 39*, 1109–1118.

Pennington, B. F. (1994). The working memory function of the prefrontal cortices: Implications for the developmental and individual differences in cognition. In M. M. Haith, J. Benson, R. Roberts, & B. F. Pennington (Eds.), *Future-oriented processes in development* (pp. 243–289). Chicago: University of Chicago Press.

Pennington, B. F., Groisser, D., & Welsh, M. C. (1993). Contrasting cognitive deficits in attention deficit hyperactivity disorder versus reading disability. *Developmental Psychology*, *29*, 511–523.

Pennington, B. F., & Ozonoff, S. (1996). Executive functions and developmental psychopathologies. *Journal of Child Psychology and Psychiatry Annual Research Review*, *37*, 51–87.

Prior, M. R., & Hoffmann, W. (1990). Brief report: Neuropsychological testing of autistic children through an exploration with frontal lobe tests. *Journal of Autism and Developmental Disorders*, *20*, 581–590.

Randolph, C., Hyde, T. M., Gold, J. M., Goldberg, T. E., & Weinberger, D. R. (1993). Tourette syndrome in monozygotic twins: Relationship of tic severity to neuropsychological function. *Archives of Neurology*, *50*, 725–728.

Reardon, S. M., & Naglieri, J. A. (1992). PASS cognitive processing characteristics of normal and ADHD males. *Journal of School Psychology*, *30*, 151–163.

Rumsey, J. M. (1985). Conceptual problem-solving in highly verbal, nonretarded autistic men. *Journal of Autism and Developmental Disorders*, *15*, 23–36.

Rumsey, J. M., & Hamburger, S. D. (1988). Neuropsychological findings in high-functioning men with infantile autism, residual state. *Journal of Clinical and Experimental Neuropsychology*, *10*, 201–221.

Rumsey, J. M., & Hamburger, S. D. (1990). Neuropsychological divergence of high-level autism and severe dyslexia. *Journal of Autism and Developmental Disorders*, *20*, 155–168.

Shaffer, D., Schwab-Stone, M., Fisher, P., Cohen, P., Piacentini, J., Davies, M., Conners, C. K., & Regier, D. (1993). The Diagnostic Interview Schedule for Children—Revised version (DISC—R): I. Preparation, field testing, interrater reliability, and acceptability. *Journal of the American Academy of Child and Adolescent Psychiatry*, *32*, 643–650.

Shue, K. L., & Douglas, V. I. (1992). Attention deficit hyperactivity disorder and the frontal lobe syndrome. Special Issue: The role of frontal lobe maturation in cognitive and social development. *Brain and Cognition*, *20*, 104–124.

Silverstein, S. M., Como, P. G., Palumbo, D. R., West, L. L., & Osborn,. (1995). Multiple sources of attentional dysfunction in adults with Tourette's syndrome: Comparison with attention deficit-hyperactivity disorder. *Neuropsychology*, *9*, 157–164.

Spencer, T., Biederman, J., Harding, M., Wilens, T., & Faraone, S. (1995). The relationship between tic disorders and Tourette's syndrome revisited. *Journal of the American Academy of Child and Adolescent Psychiatry*, *34*, 1133–1139.

Stroop, J. R. (1935). Studies of interference in serial verbal reactions. *Journal of Experimental Psychology*, *18*, 643–662.

Sutherland, R. J., Kolb, B., Schoel, W. M., Whishaw, I. Q., & Davies, D. (1982). Neuropsychological assessment of children and adults with Tourette Syndrome: A comparison with learning disabilities and schizophrenia. In A. J. Friedhoff & T. N. Chase (Eds.), *Advances in Neurology* (Vol. 35, pp. 311–322). New York: Raven.

Szatmari, P., Tuff, L., Finlayson, A. J., & Bartolucci, G. (1990). Asperger's Syndrome and autism: Neurocognitive aspects. *Journal of the American Academy of Child and Adolescent Psychiatry*, *29*, 130–136.

Weyandt, L. L., & Willis, W. G. (1994). Executive functions in school-aged children: Potential efficacy of tasks in discriminating clinical groups. *Developmental Neuropsychology, 10,* 27–38.

Yeates, K. O., & Bornstein, R. A. (1994). Attention deficit disorder and neuro-psychological functioning in children with Tourette's syndrome. *Neuropsychology, 8,* 65–74.

122

DIFFICULTIES IN AUDITORY ORGANISATION AS A POSSIBLE CAUSE OF READING BACKWARDNESS

L. Bradley and P. E. Bryant

Source: *Nature*, 271, 1978: 746–747.

Learning to read and write involves auditory perception, for the child must learn how different kinds of sounds are written. It might seem, however, that although auditory perception is essential to reading, it would not be a significant source of difficulty, for, apart from a few exceptional cases, most children who have difficulties with reading can hear perfectly well, and can discriminate and understand the words which they signally fail to read[1]. But discriminating words is not the only aspect of audition involved in reading. The child must also be able to group together words which are different but which have sounds in common. If he is to learn the rules of reading and writing he must understand that 'hat', 'cat' and 'mat', though different, nevertheless have a sound in common. We report here results which suggest that difficulties in this kind of grouping may be a significant source of difficulty in learning to read.

We compared a large group of children of normal intelligence, but 18 months or more behind the average reading skill for their age, with a group of younger children also of normal intelligence, whose reading skills were normal for their age and were the same as those of the backward readers. Details of the two groups are given in Table 1. Although the two groups were approximately equal in reading ability and were both of normal intelligence for their age, the backward readers were on average over three years older than the other group.

This is a novel kind of comparison and our reason for making it was to distinguish between cause and effect. The vast majority of studies of reading backwardness and all the studies of auditory perception in backward

Table 1 Details of the two groups.

	N	Age		IQ (WISC)		Reading age (Neale)		Spelling age (Schonell)	
		Mean	Range	Mean	Range	Mean	Range	Mean	Range
Backward readers	60	10 yr 4 mth	8 yr 4 mth–13 yr 5 mth	108.7	93–137	7 yr 7 mth	6 yr–9 yr 4 mth	6 yr 10 mth	5 yr–8 yr 9 mth
Normal readers	30	6 yr 10 mth	5 yr 8 mth–8 yr 7 mth	107.9	93–119	7 yr 6 mth	6 yr–9 yr 2 mth	7 yr 2 mth	5 yr 1 mth–10 yr 2 mth

readers[2-4] compare backward with normal readers of the same age and intellectual level, the only difference between the groups being in how far they have learned to read. The trouble with this traditional design is that any difference which is found between backward and normal readers might just as well be the result of the former group's limited experience in reading. But if, as in our design, the two groups have reached the same reading level, and yet the backward readers are worse on a perceptual task, the fact that the two groups have the same reading ability as one another rules out the possibility that the backward readers' perceptual failure is merely the result of a lack of reading experience.

The method which we used in experiment 1 to test the grouping of sounds was to say four monosyllabic words to them. Three of the words had a sound in common which the fourth did not share. The child had to say which was the odd word out. There were three series, each with six trials (18 trials in all). In one series, all four words always had the same middle phoneme, but the last two phonemes were the same in three of the words while the odd one word had a different final phoneme (for example, weed, peel, need, deed). Another series was the same except that the middle phoneme was different in the odd word (for example, nod, red, fed, bed). In the third series, three words had the same opening phoneme while the odd one did not (for example, sun, see, sock, rag). The position of the odd word varied systematically in all three series.

We ensured that all the children understood and could perform the oddity task in practice trials, and we also eliminated forgetting words as a cause of failure, by preliminary trials in which children were given four words at a time and asked to recall them. We discarded two backward readers who consistently failed in these trials; all the others made virtually no memory errors. We took great care to pronounce each word with the same emphasis in order not to give the child any additional cue to the correct word. The experimenter also always hid her mouth from the child's view with a card, so that the shape of her mouth would not provide any additional cue for any of the children.

This experiment (Table 2) produced a startling difference between the two groups, the backward readers being markedly worse than the normal

Table 2 Mean error scores (out of 6) in experiment 1.

Series	Odd word	Backward readers		Normal readers	
		N	60	N	30
		Mean	s.d.	Mean	s.d.
1	Last letter different	1.15	1.43	0.17	1.11
2	Middle letter different	1.49	1.58	0.37	0.99
3	First letter different	2.62	2.26	0.67	1.188

group in all three series. Putting the series together, 91.66% of the 60 backward readers made errors and 85% made more than one error. Only 53.33% of the 30 normal readers made any errors and only 26.66% more than one. This difference is all the more remarkable, given that the backward reading group, being older by an average of $3^1/_2$ years, was actually of a considerably higher intellectual level than the normal reading group. We suggest that many backward readers may be held back by a particular difficulty with organising sounds.

Although the backward readers were worse on all three series (F: 32.499; $d.f.$ 1,88; $P < 0.001$ in an analysis of variance), they were at a particular disadvantage to the normal readers with the series in which three of the four words had the same opening phoneme (F: 4.28; $d.f.$ 2,176; $P < 0.05$). The relationship of this difficulty with the first phoneme to these children's problems with reading and writing should be investigated.

The large size of our groups enabled us to distinguish between those children who made more than one error over the three series and those who made only one error or none at all (Table 3). A clear developmental trend was found among the normal readers, as those who made one or no errors were significantly older and had significantly higher intelligence quotient (IQ) scores, and reading and spelling ages. However no such trend was found among the backward readers; here the only significant difference was that the few children who made one or no errors had a significantly higher spelling age than the rest. This suggests that difficulties in organising sounds may have particularly harmful effects on spelling among backward readers.

We needed further evidence to demonstrate that the large difference between backward and normal readers in categorising sounds was not due to the fact that we sometimes unconsciously emphasised one word more than another, despite our attempts not to do so. This evidence came from experiment 2, with the same children. They were given 10 words spoken successively (dish, car, boat, train, ball, mouse, dog, rake, truck, tent), and asked each time to produce a word which rhymed with each of these words. Here no extraneous cues of emphasis could possibly provide the correct answer.

Again, despite their superior age and overall intellectual ability, the backward readers were by far the worse of the two groups (Table 4), 38.33% of the former group and only 6.66% of the latter failing to produce a rhyming word in one or more trials. This task was probably easier than the earlier oddity test, since in both groups more children succeeded on every trial. But the relative failure of the backward readers in the second experiment is striking confirmation of their difficulty with categorising sounds. Overall, our results strongly suggest that this difficulty could be an important cause of reading failure.

We thank the Oxford Area Health Authority, the Human Development Research Unit at the Park Hospital, and the SSRC for support for this

Table 3 Division of the two groups into those making one or no errors and those making more than one error in experiment 1.

	Backward readers			Normal readers		
	One or no errors	More than one error	t test of the difference	One or no errors	More than one error	t test of the difference
N	9	51		22	8	
Mean age	10 yr 6 mth	10 yr 3 mth	0.59 NS	7 yr 1 mth	6 yr 4 mth	2.25*
Mean IQ	112.55	108.06	1.26 NS	109.73	102.87	2.63*
Mean reading age	7 yr 11 mth	7 yr 6 mth	1.51	7 yr 9 mth	6 yr 8 mth	2.91†
Mean spelling age	7 yr 4 mth	6 yr 9 mth	2.05*	7 yr 6 mth	6 yr 4 mth	2.41*

* $P < 0.05$ † $P < 0.01$

Table 4 Number in each group producing failures in experiment 2.

	Total N	No. of failures										
		0	1	2	3	4	5	6	7	8	9	10
Backward readers	60	37	4	4	4	2	2	2	2	0	0	3
Normal readers	30	28	1	0	0	0	1	0	0	0	0	0

research. and the Oxfordshire, Berkshire, and Buckinghamshire Education Authorities for their cooperation.

References

1. Wallach, L., Wallach, M. A., Donier. M. & Kaplan, N. F. *J. educ. Psychol.* **69**, 36 (1977).
2. Audley, R. J., *Presidential address to British Association.* Lancaster (1976).
3. Liberman, I. Y. *Bull. Orton. Soc.* **23**, 65–77 (1973).
4. Venezky. R. L., Shiloah, Y. & Calfee, R. *Wisconsin Research and Development Center for Cognitive Learning, Technical Report No.* 277 (1972).

123

THE IDENTIFICATION AND PREVALENCE OF SPECIFIC READING RETARDATION

B. Rodgers

Source: *British Journal of Educational Psychology*, 53, 1983: 369–373.

Summary

The existence of a hump at the tail of the distribution of under-/over-achievement in reading is generally accepted, yet the evidence in support of this is far from conclusive. In a national sample of 8,836 10-year-olds, part of the Child Health and Education study, the over-representation of children with severe under-achievement, i.e. specific reading retardation, could not be confirmed. The implications are that specific reading retardation is the extreme of a continuum of under-achievement and that any cut-off point on this continuum used for its definition is arbitrary. Estimates of the prevalence of specific reading retardation must therefore be accompanied by the precise criteria used for its identification.

Introduction

Early studies of under-achievement have been criticised because of short-comings in the definition of this concept (Crane, 1959; Thorndike, 1963). In particular, the uses of the accomplishment quotient (the ratio of achievement age to mental age) and of percentile discrepancy between general ability and achievement are suspect on statistical grounds, in that both these indices necessarily identify groups of under-achievers who have higher mean ability scores than over-achievers. In order to avoid this undesirable consequence it has been recommended that the index of under-/over-achievement is computed as the discrepancy between predicted and observed attainment, when predicted values are obtained from the regression equation of attainment scores on ability scores for the appropriate population, i.e., the regression residual (Thorndike, 1963; Lavin, 1965).

This technique was adopted by Yule *et al.* (1974) who used regression equations of reading score on non-verbal intelligence score to identify over- and under-achievers in five populations of schoolchildren. The scores utilised to establish the regression equations were obtained by the administration of group tests to all children in these populations. Because performance on a group intelligence test is typically influenced by reading skill, severe under-achievers in reading were also identified by the administration of individual tests to sub-samples of three of the five groups. Two main findings emerged from these studies. First, the distribution of residual scores was reported to be approximately normal with equal numbers of over- and under-achievers. This is an inevitable consequence if the two test scores are themselves normally distributed and linearly related (Glossop *et al.*, 1979). Second, the prevalence of severe under-achievement (or specific reading retardation) was reported to be greater than that predicted from the assumption of normally distributed residuals. The expected percentage of children falling at least two residual standard deviations below predicted reading score was 2.28, but a significantly greater percentage was observed in three of the five populations assessed using group tests and in all three sub-samples assessed using individual tests. The existence of this so-called 'hump' at the lower end of the distribution of under-/over-achievement was taken to imply "that there is a group of children with severe and specific reading retardation which is *not* just the lower end of a normal continuum" (Yule *et al.*, 1974, p. 10).

The existence of this 'hump', corresponding to specific reading retardation, is now generally accepted (Sampson, 1975; Spreen, 1976; Glossop *et al.*, 1979; Tansley and Panckhurst, 1981) and yet there are a number of reasons why one should express caution about the finding:

(*a*) The acknowledged ceiling effect of the group reading tests and the resultant deviation from linearity of the regression functions could have influenced the outcomes of analysis.

(*b*) The histogram plots of residuals presented in Yule *et al.*'s Figure 1 could more accurately be described as negatively skewed distributions rather than as Gaussian distributions with humps at the extreme lower end.

(*c*) The prevalence of specific reading retardation for the same group of children was found to vary considerably according to which tests were used. Table 1 presents figures derived from Yule *et al.*'s Tables 4 and 7 which show the prevalence obtained for three groups of children using (i) group non-verbal and reading test scores, (ii) individual WISC and Neale Analysis reading accuracy scores and (iii) individual WISC and Neale Analysis comprehension scores. For Isle of Wight 10-year-olds the figures are 5.38, 3.09 and 3.61 per cent respectively, for London 10-year-olds 2.75, 6.32, and 9.26 per cent and for Isle of Wight

Table 1 Rates of Specific Reading Retardation Obtained using different Tests.

| | Observed (%) | | | |
	(i) Group Tests	(ii) Reading Accuracy	(iii) Reading Comprehension	Predicted (%)
Isle of Wight 10-year-olds	5.38	3.09	3.61	2.28
London 10-year-olds	2.75	6.32	9.26	2.28
Isle of Wight 14-year-olds	3.64	4.35	4.40	2.28

14-year-olds 3.64, 4.35 and 4.40 per cent. The only apparent explanation of such variation is the influence of floor and ceiling effects, particularly for the group tests.

(d) The likelihood of a 'hump' having resulted from incorrect or inappropriate standardisation of tests was ruled out by the statement that "the test was standardised on precisely the same population as that which showed the hump" (Yule *et al.*, 1974, p. 10). There is still a possibility, however, that test score distributions deviated from the normal to an extent sufficient to distort the outcomes of analysis. There was certainly a greater proportion of children than expected with raw reading scores falling more than two standard deviations below the mean in the Isle of Wight 9-year-old and 10-year-old populations (Yule and Rutter, 1970). Table 3.3 of *Education, Health and Behaviour* indicates that 57 9-year-olds and 70 10-year-olds had low reading scores, corresponding to 4.99 and 6.17 per cent of these age groups respectively. The expected proportion is 2.28 per cent.

In view of these difficulties it was thought appropriate to attempt a similar analysis with a large, national sample of children, who had been assessed using individual reading and ability tests which were relatively free of floor and ceiling effects and for which the resultant scores had been normalised on the sample itself. Such a sample was provided by the Child Health and Education Study (CHES)—the 1970 British birth cohort.

Method

Child health and education study

The 1970 birth survey was a study of all births occurring in Great Britain and Northern Ireland during the week 5th–11th April, 1970 (Chamberlain *et al.*, 1975; Chamberlain *et al.*, 1978). Two subsequent attempts—in 1975 and 1980—were made to contact all the children who had been born in the study week and were living in England, Scotland or Wales. The majority of children included in the 5-year-old and 10-year-old follow-ups had also been included in the original survey but additional children, for example those who had moved into the country in the intervening period, were also studied. The data for the second of these follow-ups were obtained in an interview with parents, a questionnaire completed by each study-child's mother, a medical examination of the child, a questionnaire completed by the child's teacher and headteacher, a short questionnaire filled in by the child him/herself and a battery of tests administered to the child by his/her teacher. Included in these tests were a shortened version of the Edinburgh Reading Test—constructed from items used in Stages 2, 3 and 4 of the Edinburgh Reading Tests (Godfrey Thomson Unit for Educational Research, 1977, 1980; Moray House College of Education, 1980)—and four individual ability scales—Word Definitions, Recall of Digits, Similarities and Matrices —that were taken from the British Ability Scales (BAS) (Elliott *et al.*, 1979a) with some modification appropriate for teacher administration.

The sample used for the analysis presented in this paper consisted of 8,836 children out of a total of approximately 13,000 contacted in the CHES ten-year study. Efforts were made to obtain a sample representative of the total population and an indication that these were successful was given by the observation that scores on individual BAS scales corresponded closely with published national norms (Elliott *et al.*, 1979b). The variables used in the analysis were derived from the raw scores obtained on the Shortened Edinburgh Reading Test and BAS by a normalisation procedure. The distributions of scores for the reading test and individual ability scales were standardised to have a mean score of 100 and a standard deviation of 15. A total BAS score was computed from the four standardised scale scores and this total was then re-standardised to give a mean of 100 and standard deviation of 15. As a consequence of the normalisation procedure adopted the distributions of resultant standardised scores were found to suffer minimal skewness and kurtosis.

Of the 8,836 children 8,659 (98 per cent) had complete test score information. Of these, 198 children (2.3 per cent) had a total BAS score falling below 70. Although the floor of the reading test was sufficiently low to allow the inclusion of many of this group in subsequent analysis, it was decided to follow the convention adopted by Yule *et al.* (1974) and exclude them. The final analysis was therefore carried out for 8,461 children.

Results

The standardised reading scores and BAS scores were submitted to a regression analysis with BAS score as the independent variable and reading score as the dependent variable. The conditions of linearity and homoscedasticity were satisfied by the data, permitting this type of analysis. The use of child's age as an additional independent variable was found not to be necessary. This was partly due to the facts that the study children were of similar age and were tested within a short time of one another (91 per cent in four months), but also it reflected the lack of a seasonal trend over the period of testing. A similar phenomenon was observed in the National Child Development Study (1958 British birth cohort) when children were tested at 11 years of age (Goldstein and Fogelman, 1974).

The correlation of reading score with BAS score was found to be 0.730. The regression equation was:

$$\text{Reading score} = 25.0 + 0.751 \times \text{BAS score}$$

and the residual standard deviation 9.8. Residuals were calculated and their distribution is shown in histogram form in Figure 1 on a scale marked in

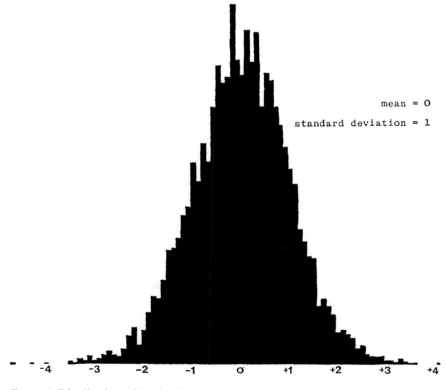

Figure 1 Distribution of Under-/Over-Achievement.

residual standard deviations. This can be compared with Yule *et al.*'s Figure 1. On the assumption of a normal distribution of residuals one would expect to find 192 children (2.28 per cent) with scores falling more than two standard deviations below the mean. The actual number was 194 (2.29 per cent). The very small difference between observed and predicted numbers does not approach statistical significance.

Discussion

These results fail to support the hypothesis that the prevalence of specific reading retardation is greater than that predicted from the assumption of a normally distributed index of under-/over-achievement. Figure 1 demonstrates that there is no discontinuity in the distribution of differences between obtained and predicted reading scores and indeed there is no suggestion of any bimodality which could be taken to indicate the presence of two underlying populations.

These findings have two particular implications. First, the inference that a 'hump' in the distribution represents severe under-achievement due to pathological conditions can no longer be made. Rutter and Yule (1975) have been careful to point out that the 'hump' did "not necessarily imply any kind of pathological or biological entity" (p. 185). Although this warning has not gone completely unheeded (Sampson, 1975) some authors do appear to have overlooked it (Spreen, 1976; Glossop *et al.*, 1979). Second, any decision as to which cut-off point to use to identify severe underachievement in reading is arbitrary and therefore the issue of prevalence of specific reading retardation is inextricably bound up with its definition. Estimates of prevalence which are unaccompanied by the precise criteria used for identification (e.g., Tansley and Panckhurst, 1981) are of little value. In addition this study has provided a means of identifying children with specific reading retardation which could be of use to those wishing to carry out smaller but more detailed studies. The area of further research which would have the most immediate practical implications is the invest-igation of the effects of treatment. It could prove important to ascertain whether children with different categories of reading difficulty benefit from different forms of remedial help.

Of course, the findings described here in no way detract from the usefulness of the concept of specific reading retardation, as distinct from that of reading backwardness as defined by Yule and Rutter (1970). The large data set collected by CHES will permit a detailed study of the different characteristics of children falling into these two categories which would considerably add to existing knowledge (Rutter and Yule, 1973) and, in the event of future follow-ups, further studies of prognosis will be possible (Yule, 1973).

Acknowledgments

The selection of items for the Shortened Edinburgh Reading Test was carried out by Dr. Philip Gammage and Mr. Walter Barker in conjunction with the Godfrey Thomson Unit for Educational Research, University of Edinburgh. The use of the British Ability Scales was by kind permission of the test authors and publisher and the advice of Dr. Colin Elliott throughout the scoring of the scales was most appreciated. The author wishes to acknowledge the many individuals who have contributed to the Child Health and Education Study and is grateful to colleagues who made helpful comments on an earlier draft of this paper, especially Mr. Albert Osborn, Principal Research Officer of the study. Financial support for this work was provided by the Department of Education and Science.

References

CHAMBERLAIN, R., CHAMBERLAIN, G., HOWLETT, B., and CLAIREAUX, A. (1975). *British Births 1970 Volume 1: The First Week of Life*. London: Heinemann.

CHAMBERLAIN, G., PHILLIPP, E., HOWLETT, B., and CLAIREAUX, A. (1978). *British Births 1970 Volume 2: Obstetric Care*. London: Heinemann.

CRANE, A. R. (1959). An historical account of the accomplishment quotient idea. *Br. J. educ. Psychol.*, 29, 252–259.

ELLIOTT, C. D., MURRAY, D. J., and PEARSON, L. S. (1979a). *British Ability Scales Manual 3: Directions for Administration and Scoring*. Windsor: NFER.

ELLIOTT, C. D., MURRAY, D. J., and PEARSON, L. S. (1979b). *British Ability Scales Manual 4: Tables of Abilities and Norms*. Windsor: NFER.

GLOSSOP, J. A., APPLEYARD, R., and ROBERTS, C. (1979). Achievement relative to a measure of general intelligence. *Br. J. educ. Psychol.*, 49, 249–257.

GODFREY THOMSON UNIT FOR EDUCATIONAL RESEARCH (1977). *Manual of Instructions for the Edinburgh Reading Test Stage 4*. Sevenoaks: Hodder and Stoughton Educational.

GODFREY THOMSON UNIT FOR EDUCATIONAL RESEARCH (1980). *Manual of Instructions for the Edinburgh Reading Test Stage 2 (2nd ed)*. Sevenoaks: Hodder and Stoughton Educational.

GOLDSTEIN, H., and FOGELMAN, K. (1974). Age standardisation and seasonal effects in mental testing. *Br. J. educ. Psychol.*, 44, 109–115.

LAVIN, D. E. (1965). *The Prediction of Academic Performance: A Theoretical Analysis and Review of Research*. New York: Russell Sage Foundation.

MORAY HOUSE COLLEGE OF EDUCATION (1980). *Manual of Instructions for the Edinburgh Reading Test Stage 3 (2nd ed)*. Sevenoaks: Hodder and Stoughton Educational.

RUTTER, M., and YULE, W. (1973). Specific reading retardation. In MANN, L., and SABATINO, D. A. (Eds.), *The First Review of Special Education Volume 2*. Philadelphia: Buttonwood Farms.

RUTTER, M., and YULE, W. (1975). The concept of specific reading retardation. *J. child Psychol. Psychiat.*, 16, 181–197.

SAMPSON, O. C. (1975). Fifty years of dyslexia. A review of the literature, 1925–1975. I. Theory. *Res. in Educ.*, 14, 15–32.

SPREEN, O. (1976). Neuropsychology of learning disorders: post-conference review. In KNIGHTS, R. M., and BAKKER, D. J. (Eds.), *The Neuropsychology of Learning Disorders: Theoretical Approaches*. Baltimore: University Park Press.

TANSLEY, P., and PANCKHURST, J. (1981). *Children with Specific Learning Difficulties*. Windsor: NFER-Nelson.

THORNDIKE, R. L. (1963). *The Concepts of Over- and Under-Achievement*. New York: Teachers College, Columbia University.

YULE, W. (1973). Differential prognosis of reading backwardness and specific reading retardation. *Br. J. educ. Psychol.*, 43, 244–248.

YULE, W., and RUTTER, M. (1970). Selection of children with intellectual or educational retardation. In RUTTER, M., TIZARD, J., and WHITMORE, K. (Eds.), *Education, Health and Behaviour*. London: Longman.

YULE, W., RUTTER, M., BERGER, M., and THOMPSON, J. (1974). Over- and underachievement in reading: distribution in the general population. *Br. J. educ. Psychol.*, 44, 1–12.

124

VERY EARLY LANGUAGE DEFICITS IN DYSLEXIC CHILDREN

Hollis S. Scarborough

Source: *Child Development*, 61, 1990: 1728–1743.

At 2$\frac{1}{2}$ years of age, children who later developed reading disabilities were deficient in the length, syntactic complexity, and pronunciation accuracy of their spoken language, but not in lexical or speech discrimination skills. As 3-year-olds, these children began to show deficits in receptive vocabulary and object-naming abilities, and as 5-year-olds they exhibited weaknesses in object-naming, phonemic awareness, and letter-sound knowledge that have characterized kindergartners who became poor readers in other studies. These late preschool differences were related to subsequent reading status as well as to prior language skills, but early syntactic proficiency nevertheless accounted for some unique variance in grade 2 achievement when differences at age 5 were statistically controlled. The language deficits of dyslexic children were unrelated to maternal reading ability and were not observed in children from dyslexic families who became normal readers. The implications of the results for etiological issues are discussed.

"Dyslexia," or "reading disability," refers to severe reading problems that cannot be attributed to sensory, intellectual, emotional, or socioeconomic handicaps or to other known impediments to learning to read. By definition, therefore, dyslexics are not identified until they have tried and failed to learn to read in school. By that time, it is difficult to determine whether observed differences between reading-disabled children and their classmates reflect direct causes, or merely consequences, of reading failure. To circumvent this problem, one can take a prospective approach, whereby children are examined before they try to learn to read. In the study to be reported, the role of language-processing deficits in the etiology of dyslexia was investigated in a long-term prospective study of 2-year-olds who later were identified as disabled readers.

By studying such young children it was possible to look for early precursors to dyslexia that would be relatively unconfounded by the effects of preschool reading instruction and consequent differences in "preliteracy" achievement. Most prior prospective studies of reading disability have been conducted with children who are initially between the ages of $4^{1}/_{2}$ and 6 years, when they are about to begin formal schooling or are in the first year of school. One consistent finding of those studies has been that many of the best predictors of later reading achievement are measures of skills very similar to those involved in reading itself: recognizing and naming letters, matching sounds to letters, writing one's name, and so forth (e.g., Jansky & deHirsch, 1972; Mann, 1984; Share, Jorm, Maclean, & Matthews, 1984). Because differences in the preliteracy skills of normal and disabled readers are already established by the late preschool years, to discover more fundamental antecedents of dyslexia required the examination of even younger children.

Early language development was chosen as the focus of the present investigation because prospective and retrospective studies have consistently found that language-processing abilities are deficient in kindergartners and older children with poor literacy skills, while most nonverbal cognitive abilities of disabled readers are unimpaired. Accordingly, virtually every recent review has judged that a language-based origin for reading disabilities is most consistent with available findings (e.g., Kamhi & Catts, 1989; Kavanagh & Yeni-Komshian, 1985; Perfetti, 1985; Stanovich, 1988; Vellutino, 1979).

A broad range of linguistic impairments has been observed in prior prospective studies of reading disability. Kindergartners and prekindergartners who later exhibit low reading achievement exhibit weaknesses in receptive vocabulary (e.g., Share et al., 1984; Stanovich, Cunningham, & Feeman, 1984), object naming (e.g., Share et al., 1984; Wolf & Goodglass, 1986), syntax comprehension (e.g., Share et al., 1984), syntax production (e.g., Butler, Marsh, Sheppard, & Sheppard, 1985), phonological production (e.g., Butler et al., 1985; Silva, McGee, & Williams, 1985), syntactic awareness (e.g., Tunmer, Herriman, & Nesdale, 1988), and phonemic awareness (e.g., Lundberg, Olofsson, & Wall, 1980; Mann, 1984; Mann & Ditunno, 1990; Stanovich, Cunningham, & Cramer, 1984; Stuart & Coltheart, 1988).

Some or all of these linguistic deficits may also be evident in dyslexic children at even younger ages. Very recently, for instance, Bryant, Bradley, Maclean, and Crossland (1989) showed that the ability of 40-month-olds to recite nursery rhymes was predictive of their emerging phonological awareness skills and letter knowledge (and thereby, indirectly, of grade 1 reading). The early emergence of differences between dyslexic and nondyslexic children is also suggested by retrospective parental reports of early language deficits in children who became disabled readers (e.g., Ingram, Mason, & Blackburn, 1970; Rutter & Yule, 1975) and by follow-up studies showing a high incidence of later reading problems in samples of preschoolers who were treated for language impairment (Weiner, 1985).

Although many linguistic weaknesses have been shown to antedate reading disabilities, it is not clear whether a specific aspect of language ability (e.g., impaired phonological processing) or a more general linguistic deficiency is most directly responsible for reading failure (Bowey & Patel, 1988; Kamhi & Catts, 1989; Stanovich, 1988; Vellutino, 1979). Among the language measures associated with dyslexia, the strongest predictors of subsequent reading achievement are usually those that require the representation, retrieval, or metalinguistic analysis of phonological information (e.g., Share et al., 1984; Stanovich, Cunningham, & Cramer, 1984; Stuart & Coltheart, 1988; Wagner & Torgesen 1987). Furthermore, some have argued that purported measures of lexical and syntactic proficiency may actually reflect a child's difficulties with phonological or memory processing aspects of the task (e.g., Fowler, 1988; Shankweiler & Crain, 1986). On the other hand, a specific deficit in phonological processing does not account well for the findings of some recent studies, in which reading was more successfully predicted by more general language assessments (e.g., Bowey & Patel, 1988; Butler et al., 1985). The issue of specificity is further clouded by the possibility that the scope of impairment is likely to vary according to the criteria used to classify reading disabilities and is likely to broaden over time as a consequence of the cognitive, instructional, and motivational changes brought about by the child's reading difficulties (Stanovich, 1988). In the present study, assessments of syntactic and lexical as well as phonological skills were made at a very early age so that the nature and breadth of the dyslexic children's presumed early language deficits could be evaluated with respect to this etiological issue.

Method

Subjects

Three groups of 30-month-old children were studied: 20 children from "dyslexic families" (see below) who subsequently became disabled readers, 12 children from dyslexic families who became normal readers, and 20 other normal children selected so as to resemble the dyslexic group closely in IQ, socioeconomic status, and sex (see Table 1). All 52 subjects were from lower- to upper-middle-class (Hollingshead & Redlich, 1958) monolingual families residing in central New Jersey, and none had any gross visual, audiological, or neurological deficits. The subjects were all participants in a larger investigation of the relations between preschool development and

390

Table 1 Comparability of Contrasted Groups.

	Disabled Readers from Dyslexic Families	Normal Readers from Control Families	Normal Readers from Dyslexic Families
Number of children	20	20	12
Boys:girls	11:9	9:11	5:7
Cases with dyslexic mothers (%)	55	0	50
Cases with dyslexic fathers (%)	45	0	50
Family members dyslexic (%)	55.3 (21.9)	0	53.3 (26.1)
Socioeconomic status[a]	2.95 (.89)	2.95 (.89)	2.50 (.85)
IQ at 36 months[b]	107.0 (13.5)	110.5 (11.5)	113.9 (12.0)
IQ at 60 months[c]	112.1 (11.9)	115.7 (11.2)	116.0 (10.4)
IQ at grade 2[d]	110.0 (10.2)	114.4 (10.4)	117.4 (10.5)
Grade 2 reading[e]	479.2 (7.9)	502.0 (7.3)	501.8 (6.4)
Grade 2 math[f]	75.5 (19.5)	82.4 (24.9)	74.0 (22.2)

Note: Standard deviations are shown in parentheses.
[a] On a 5-point scale based on parental education and occupational prestige (Hollingshead & Redlich, 1958); lower values represent higher status.
[b] Short form of the McCarthy Scales (Kaufman, 1977).
[c] McCarthy Scales of Preschool Abilities (McCarthy, 1972).
[d] Wechsler Intelligence Scale for Children—revised (Wechsler, 1974).
[e] Reading Cluster of the Woodcock-Johnson Psychoeducational Battery (Woodcock & Johnson, 1977).
[f] Percentile on a school-administered nationally standardized test.

later reading achievement; pursuant to the goals of that study, the reading abilities of members of the children's immediate families were evaluated, and the children's reading status at grade 2 (age 8.0 years) was assessed.

Family incidence of dyslexia.—Dyslexia tends to run strongly in families (e.g., DeFries, Vogler, & LaBuda, 1985). Therefore, preschoolers with dyslexic relatives are more likely than other youngsters to develop reading problems, and the sample for the study was selected so as to overrepresent such children. Subjects were recruited in 1979–1981 through advertisements and referrals that encouraged families with 2-year-old children, "especially those families in which someone has experienced a severe childhood reading problem," to make confidential inquiries. All willing respondents who reported cases of dyslexia in the family, plus a subset of the many other respondents, were included in an original sample of 88 children; 10 families subsequently withdrew due to geographic relocation or loss of interest.

Of the 78 subjects remaining in the study, 34 were from dyslexic families. These children each had at least one parent or older sibling who exhibited low reading achievement despite normal IQ. The immediate families of the other 44 participants had no reading-disabled members. The criteria used to classify family members have been described in detail previously (Scarborough, 1984, 1989a).

Outcome reading status.—The Reading Cluster of the Woodcock-Johnson Psychoeducational Battery (Woodcock & Johnson, 1977) and the Wechsler Intelligence Scale for Children—Revised (Wechsler, 1974) were administered to 66 of the 78 subjects (31 from dyslexic families and 35 from nondyslexic families) at the end of grade 2. The reading status of the other 12 children was estimated from scores earned on school-administered nationally standardized tests of reading achievement and scholastic aptitude.

As previously described (Scarborough, 1989a), expected reading levels for this suburban New Jersey sample were based on analyses of the achievement scores of subjects from *non*dyslexic families. A cutoff of 1.5 SD below the mean of this group was used, and any child in the entire sample whose achievement score was more than 1.5 SD below the control mean was designated as reading disabled. There were 24 such cases in the entire sample; their z scores ranged from -1.5 to -5.8 ($M = -2.68$).[1]

Outcomes were strongly determined by family type. Of the 34 children from dyslexic families, 22 (65%) developed reading problems. This incidence level is considerably higher than that of Finucci, Gottfredson, and Childs (1985), who found that 36% of alumni of a school for dyslexic adolescents reported (in a follow-up questionnaire) having at least one reading-disabled offspring. This disagreement between studies may result from differences in recruitment or diagnostic methods, or simply from sampling variation. For the present analyses of linguistic differences at age 30 months, two of the 22 reading-disabled subjects had to be excluded for lack of preschool data at that age, resulting in a sample size of 20 for the dyslexic group.

In contrast, all but two (95%) of the other 44 children became normal readers. From these 42, 20 normal readers from normal families were selected to form a comparison group that would be as similar as possible to the reading-disabled group with regard to sex, SES, and IQ. This was done by first making all possible one-to-one matches between dyslexic children and those in the pool of possible controls (which could be done for 11 of the 20 cases) and then selecting nine others who were dissimilar to a dyslexic child only in sex (two cases), SES (four cases, in two of which the SES was higher for the reading-disabled child), or IQ (three cases, in all of which IQ was more than 7 points higher for the control child). Choices among potential control subjects who were equally well matched to a dyslexic case were made by random drawing.[2] As shown in Table 1, the resulting groups were very similar in the distribution of sex,[3] SES, and IQ but could not be analyzed as matched pairs of individuals.

One-way analyses of variance with planned pairwise contrasts between groups revealed no differences in grade 2 math achievement, SES, or IQ, although the IQ difference between the two groups from dyslexic families approached statistical significance at age 36 months, $F(1,49) = 2.976$, $p = .091$. IQ was thus controlled for in all analyses.

392

Procedures

In the larger project of which this study is a part, six evaluations of pre-school development were conducted between the ages of 2 and 5 years. Language proficiency at age 30 months was the major focus of the present analyses, but some test scores obtained at other ages were also analyzed for this report so as to clarify the interpretation of the findings at 30 months.

At age 30 months (± 2 weeks), each child was seen at home, in the presence of one or both parents, for a single session lasting about 2 hours. Seven measures of early language skill were analyzed for this study, including three test scores and four measures of natural language production during a 30-min mother-child play session.

Language tests.—Vocabulary recognition, naming vocabulary, and speech discrimination were assessed using the Peabody Picture Vocabulary Test (PPVT; Dunn, 1965), Boston Naming Test (BNT; Kaplan, Goodglass, & Weintraub, 1978), and Phoneme Discrimination Series (PDS), respectively. On each PPVT trial, the child must indicate which of four line drawings corresponds to a spoken word. On successive trials of the BNT, the child must name pictured objects of increasing difficulty. On each of 24 PDS trials, the child must indicate which of two similarly named objects (e.g., bear/pear) is the one whose name has been spoken. Two children from the dyslexic group would not cooperate on the BNT, and one of them also refused to take the PDS, as did one child from each of the other two groups. Analyses involving these measures were carried out using available scores only.

The PDS was readministered at age 36 months, and the PPVT and BNT at age 42 months. A third administration of the BNT was also included in a readiness assessment (see below) at age 60 months.

Natural language production.—Language samples were drawn from videorecorded mother-child play sessions with age-appropriate materials supplied by the examiners. All maternal and child utterances during play were transcribed along with contextual notes, and every transcript was reviewed for accuracy by a second transcriber prior to analysis. Four language production measures were derived from each child's transcript.

Two measures of productive syntax were coded for each child from a corpus of 100 successive intelligible child utterances within each transcript, excluding imitations, self-repetitions, and routines (such as counting or singing). Mean length of utterance (MLU) was computed according to conventional guidelines for counting morphemes (Brown, 1973). MLU is widely used to estimate a young child's general syntactic performance level, but the validity and interpretation of this measure have sometimes been questioned (Crystal, 1974; Klee & Fitzgerald, 1985). Thus, the Index of Productive Syntax (IPSyn; Scarborough, 1990) was also used as a measure of grammatical complexity. IPSyn scores are derived by crediting the occurrence of up to two unique tokens of 56 types of constructions, including noun phrase elaborations, verb phrase constructions, inflectional morphemes, interrogative and negative forms, and simple and complex sentence structures. IPSyn scores thus reflect the diversity of syntactic and morphological forms produced by the child.

As an index of phonological production ability, the child's consonant pronunciation error rate was based on the accuracy of the child's pronunciation of the first 100 identifiable words in the corpus, excluding determiners, pronouns, auxiliary verbs, proper nouns, and yes/no responses.[4] The number of omissions, additions, substitutions, and transpositions of consonant phonemes in those words was tallied for each child.

Last, lexical diversity was scored as the number of distinct lexical types (i.e., the number of different words) produced among the first 250 identifiable words (tokens) in the transcript. Richards (1987) has argued that this approach to scoring productive vocabulary is more stable and less confounded by syntactic proficiency than more traditional type-token scores based on a fixed number of utterances or a smaller number of lexical tokens.[5]

For each language-production measure, 10% to 25% of the corpora were coded independently by two scorers, and at least 92% of coding judgments were found to be in agreement in each case.

Assessment of readiness skills at age 60 months.—The subjects were evaluated at age 60 months (when most had not yet begun kindergarten) with respect to some known precursors to reading achievement. As reported previously (Scarborough, 1989a), only the BNT and the Sounds and Letters Test (which includes eight letter-identification items, 16 letter-sound correspondence items, and 20 phonological awareness items requiring rhyme matching or first-sound matching of spoken words) of the Stanford Early School Achievement Test, Level 1 (Madden, Gardner, & Collins, 1981) were predictive of grade 2 reading achievement (with IQ controlled). Hence just these scores were included in the present analyses.

Feedback to parents.—Parents who requested it were given information about their child's performance on standardized instruments only and were advised to interpret these scores cautiously in light of the questionable predictive validity of preschool instruments. In only one case was a child's productive language deficit at age 30 months noticed by the examiners who made the in-home recording; when this was brought to the parents' attention, their response was to disregard it.

Results

Group differences in early language proficiency

The mean scores of the three groups on language measures at age 30 months are provided in Table 2, and intercorrelations among the seven measures in

Table 2 Language Proficiency of Groups at Age 30 Months.

Measure	Disabled Readers from Dyslexic Families		Normal Readers from Control Families		Normal Readers from Dyslexic Families	
	M	SD	M	SD	M	SD
Language tests:						
PPVT	25.2	11.1	31.2	12.9	33.1	6.1
BNT	8.6	2.8	9.1	3.2	10.2	3.4
PDS	19.9	2.3	20.3	3.6	21.7	2.1
Natural production:						
MLU	2.35	.58	2.89	.48	2.97	.66
IPSyn	46.6	13.4	61.7	11.7	58.8	11.9
Consonant errors	43.0	17.9	27.5	16.0	26.3	14.2
Lexical diversity	83.5	10.8	84.1	11.0	86.3	9.7

Table 3. Substantial correlations among the three test scores were obtained even when shared variance with IQ was partialed out. However, with IQ controlled, the test scores were not significantly related to the natural production measures other than MLU. Lexical diversity was weakly correlated with IPSyn, and not with other aspects of productive language. Pronunciation error rate was moderately correlated with both syntax measures, which were very closely related. A principal components factor analysis of MLU and IPSyn was thus used to derive a single factor score for syntactic production.

To test the main hypothesis that early language deficits would be exhibited by children who become disabled readers, multivariate analyses of covariance (MANCOVA), with IQ at 36 months as the covariate, were

Table 3 Correlations among Language Measures at Age 30 Months.

Measures	1	2	3	4	5	6	7
1. PPVT		.48***	.66***	.54***	.39**	−.24	.31*
2. BNT	.44**		.54***	.37**	.32*	−.31*	.34*
3. PDS	.60***	.50***		.39**	.27	−.22	.20
4. MLU	.36**	.39**	.32*		.85***	−.44**	.23
5. IPSyn	.22	.25	.16	.83***		−.56***	.39*
6. Consonant errors	−.09	−.28	−.15	−.38**	−.50***		−.13
7. Lexical diversity	.23	.27	.15	.15	.31*	−.05	

Note: Simple correlations among measures are shown above the diagonal, and partial correlations with IQ at age 36 months controlled are below the diagonal.
* *p* < .05.
** *p* < .01.
*** *p* < .001.

carried out. Because they appeared to tap relatively independent facets of early language proficiency, test scores and natural language production measures were analyzed separately with respect to group differences. A MANCOVA with PPVT, BNT, and PDS test scores as the predictors revealed no significant group effect: Wilks's lambda = .907, $F(6,84) = 0.704$, $p = 0.65$; this analysis included only the 48 children for whom all three test scores were available.

A second MANCOVA, with consonant error rate, lexical diversity, and the syntax factor as predictors, yielded a significant group effect, Wilks's lambda = .730, $F(6,92) = 2.618$, $p = .022$. Planned pairwise contrasts between groups indicated that there was no difference at age 30 months between the two groups who became normal readers, Wilks's lambda = .990, $F(3,46) = 0.160$, $p = .922$. The dyslexic group, however, differed from the normal readers from nondyslexic families, Wilks's lambda = .753, $F(3,46) = 4.229$, $p = .004$, and from the normal readers from dyslexic families, Wilks's lambda = .836, $F(3,46) = 2.795$, $p = .050$. Univariate results indicated that the syntax factor, $F(2,48) = 6.421$, $p = .003$, and consonant error rate, $F(2,48) = 4.620$, $p = .015$, differed among groups, but that lexical diversity did not, $F(2,48) = 0.065$, $p = .937$.

These results established, as hypothesized, that early language skills of the dyslexic group were poorer than those of the other two groups, which did not differ from each other. The inclusion of two equivalent groups would necessarily make subsequent variance analyses of the relation of preschool differences to reading outcomes less meaningful and less powerful. Thus, the two groups of children who became normal readers were collapsed into a single group in the remaining analyses.

Three analyses of covariance were carried out to determine which aspect(s) of language production—syntax, phonology, or vocabulary— contributed uniquely to the difference between children who became disabled readers and children who became normal readers. In successive analyses, each language-production measure in turn served as the predictor, and the other two measures served as covariates in addition to IQ. Not surprisingly, in view of the univariate results of the MANOVA described above, there was no difference between dyslexic and normal groups in lexical diversity after variance due to IQ, the syntax factor, and consonant error rate was removed, $F(1,47) = 0.528$, $p = .471$. Likewise, when IQ, the syntax factor, and lexical diversity were controlled, consonant error rate accounted for no significant additional variance in outcomes, $F(1,47) = 2.818$, $p = .100$. The syntax score, however, did significantly differentiate the groups even with IQ, consonant errors, and lexical diversity controlled, $F(1,47) = 6.450$, $p = .014$. Thus the phonological differences between groups, revealed in the univariate MANOVA results, accounted for no unique variability in outcomes beyond that accounted for by syntactic differences.

Family incidence of reading disability

The finding that children from dyslexic families who did not develop reading disabilities resembled the other normal readers, rather than the other children from dyslexic families, suggests that the early language deficits of reading-disabled children did not stem only from being reared in a family with dyslexic members. This suggestion was supported by other analyses of the data.

The 32 children from dyslexic families had an average of 1.63 older family members (55% of household) with reading disability. If verbal communication patterns within such families are unusual, preschoolers from dyslexic families might be exposed to qualitatively or quantitatively different language input. Of particular importance to language development might be the input provided by the child's mother, who was the child's primary caretaker—and hence probably the major language model—in nearly all of the families in the present sample.

One might thus expect that children who became disabled readers would be more likely to have reading-disabled mothers or to have a higher incidence of reading disability in their immediate families than the children from dyslexic families who became normal readers. As shown in Table 1, this was not the case in the present sample. It might also be hypothesized that the severity—rather than the incidence—of a child's weaknesses might be influenced by the mother's status. That is, even if genetic transmission (or some other nonenvironmental factor) was responsible for the language and reading problems observed in the children who became disabled readers, environmental differences might ameliorate or exacerbate a child's predisposition to have difficulty acquiring language and reading. If so, one would expect that, within the dyslexic group, the 11 children with dyslexic mothers might have more severe deficits than the nine children whose mothers are normal readers. However, no large or significant differences between these two subgroups in IQ, in language scores at age 30 months, or in reading ability at grade 2 were observed (all p's > .10). Ongoing analyses of maternal language will potentially yield direct evidence of whether the linguistic input to dyslexic children is atypical, but until those results are available, no firm conclusions can be drawn. Thus the present results are consistent with, but do not provide a clear test of, the hypothesis that dyslexia is a genetically transmitted disorder. Considerable evidence for the heritability of dyslexia has been found in recent studies in behavioral genetics (e.g., DeFries, Fulker, & LaBuda, 1987; Olson, Wise, Conners, Rack, & Fulker, 1989; Smith, Kimberling, Pennington, & Lubs, 1983).

Language and readiness skills in the later preschool years

Analyses of covariance, with IQ as the covariate, were carried out to examine differences between the dyslexic and normal groups on subsequent scores on the three language tests that had been given at 30 months. Table 4 shows group means (separately for the two normal groups) on these follow-up tests and provides partial correlations with the prior administration of each test, with IQ controlled. Scores for one normal reader on the PDS at age 36 months and for two normal readers on the BNT and PPVT at 42 months were not available.

The PDS, when readministered at age 36 months, again failed to differentiate the children who became disabled readers from the children who became normal readers, $F(1,48) = 0.571$, $p = .454$. However, language test scores obtained 6 months earlier were strongly correlated with PDS scores at 36 months, and consonant pronunciation was the only language-production measure related to subsequent phoneme discrimination ability. Thus, although PDS scores were unrelated to outcomes at either age, this test was apparently sensitive to individual differences that were also tapped by other measures.

In contrast, both of the vocabulary test scores at age 42 months were significantly lower for the reading-disabled group: PPVT, $F(1,47) = 4.038$, $p = .050$; BNT, $F(1,47) = 5.770$, $p = .020$. These two measures were again

Table 4 Performance on Readministrations of the Phoneme Discrimination Series (PDS), Peabody Picture Vocabulary Test (PPVT), and Boston Naming Test (BNT).

	PDS, 36 Months	PPVT, 42 Months	BNT, 42 Months
Comparison of groups (means):			
Disabled readers from dyslexic families	20.6	39.1	13.9
	(2.5)	(10.4)	(5.3)
Normal readers from control families	21.3	46.6	17.4
	(2.3)	(8.8)	(4.4)
Normal readers from dyslexic families	22.0	45.0	18.5
	(2.0)	(12.7)	(4.8)
Partial correlations[a] with earlier language measures:			
30-month language tests:			
PPVT	.42**	.48***	.44**
BNT	.50***	.72***	.58***
PDS	.63***	.38**	.21
30-month natural production:			
MLU	.22	.40**	.30*
IPSyn	.17	.33*	.38**
Consonant errors	−.36*	−.35*	−.36**
Lexical diversity	.11	.31*	.14

Note: Standard deviations are in parentheses.
[a] Controlling for IQ at 36 months.
* $p < .05$.   ** $p < .01$.   *** $p < .001$.

Table 5 Language and Preliteracy Skills at Age 60 Months.

| | Boston Naming Test | Sounds and Letters Test | | | |
		Letter-Recognition Items	Phoneme Awareness Items	Letter-Sound Items	Total Score
Comparison of groups (means):					
Disabled readers from	24.8	6.3	10.8	6.5	23.5
dyslexic families	(6.8)	(1.7)	(4.0)	(3.8)	(8.6
Normal readers from	29.7	7.4	13.7	8.5	29.6
control families	(7.0)	(1.0)	(3.7)	(4.9)	(7.8)
Normal readers from	30.9	7.2	14.3	11.5	32.9
dyslexic families	(8.4)	(.8)	(3.0)	(4.5)	(5.2)
Partial correlations[a] with early language measures:					
30-month language tests:					
PPVT	.37**	.19	.32*	.05	.13
BNT	.70***	.18	.36*	.08	.20
PDS	.29*	−.07	.19	.06	.10
30-month natural production:					
MLU	.27	.43**	.40**	.22	.38**
IPSyn	.32*	.51***	.36**	.23	.40**
Consonant errors	−.50***	−.49***	−.34*	−.37**	−.44**
Lexical diversity	.26	.08	.15	.19	.19

Note: Standard deviations are in parentheses.
[a] Controlling for IQ at 36 months.
* $p < .05$.   ** $p < .01$.   *** $p < .001$.

strongly intercorrelated ($r = .62$, $p < .001$). Moreover, BNT and PPVT scores were related not only to vocabulary test scores obtained 1 year earlier but also to earlier syntactic and phonological production abilities.

As Table 5 shows, the children who became disabled readers also did more poorly as 5-year-olds. Analyses of covariance, with IQ at 60 months serving as the covariate, were carried out for the language and preliteracy tests administered at age 60 months. Group differences on the BNT were again found, $F(1,47) = 5.139$, $p = .028$, and scores on this test were correlated with language tests, IPSyn scores, and consonant error rates of the children 3 years earlier. As expected, the Sounds and Letters Test also revealed substantial differences in favor of the children who became normal readers, $F(1,47) = 9,383$, $p = .004$. Moreover, each of the readiness skills assessed in subsections of this test was weaker for the dyslexic group: letter identification, despite an apparent ceiling effect in the normal group, $F(1,47) = 6.936$, $p = .011$; phonemic awareness, $F(1,47) = 7.231$, $p = .010$; and knowledge about letter-sound correspondences, $F(1,47) = 4.072$, $p = .049$. MLU, IPSyn, and consonant errors at age 30 months all predicted letter recognition, phonemic awareness, and total Sounds and Letters scores at age 5, but only early consonant production skill was also related to subsequent abilities on items requiring knowledge of letter-sound correspondences. In contrast, early vocabulary test scores were correlated solely with the phonemic awareness subtest.

As described above, early syntactic and phonological production abilities were strongly predictive of outcome reading status in the sample. To see whether these differences at age 30 months were directly related to grade 2 classifications, or only indirectly through intervening differences in readiness skills at age 60 months (which were also strongly related to outcomes), analyses of covariance were carried out with IQ, BNT, and Sounds and Letters scores at age 60 months as the covariates. A significant effect of group was still obtained for the syntax factor score, $F(1,45) = 5.103$, $p = .029$, but not for consonant error rate, $F(1,45) = 2.336$, $p = .133$. These results suggest that the relation of early syntactic deficits to reading disabilities was not simply mediated by problems with language and preliteracy in the late preschool years.

Discussion

Precursors of reading disabilities

Because dyslexia is usually defined in terms of reading achievement, the condition cannot be diagnosed until a child's difficulties in reading become apparent during the school years. As reviewed earlier, prospective research studies have often shown that such children often have poor *pre*literacy skills even before they begin kindergarten. Preliteracy weaknesses were also a precursor of subsequent reading disability in the present sample at age 60 months, suggesting that these children resembled those in other prospective studies despite differences in recruitment methods. Having learned less about letters and letter-sound correspondences as preschoolers, the children were already exhibiting problems with learning to read.

Previous prospective studies have further demonstrated that these children's preliteracy deficits are accompanied by oral language difficulties that are also related to subsequent progress in reading. This, too, was seen in the present sample; as 5-year-olds, the children with poor letter-sound knowledge and who later became poor readers were also deficient in object-naming and phonemic awareness skills. Very recent work (Bryant *et al.*, 1989) has revealed that some oral vocabulary and phonological processing differences among children as young as 40 months are related to future reading achievement, although those effects appear to be mediated by late preschool metaphonological skills. The present study identifies even earlier characteristics that distinguish children who become disabled readers from those who become normal readers and confirms prior findings that weakness in language skill is a precursor to reading disability.

The main focus of the study was oral language proficiency at 30 months of age. At that time, normal language development typically undergoes rapid improvements in syntactic complexity, pronunciation accuracy, and vocabulary size (e.g., Dale, 1976). In the present sample, syntactic differences among 2-year-olds corresponded most closely with the children's eventual outcomes, but phonological production was also substantially impaired in the children who were later identified as poor readers. Not surprisingly, these productive language skills are often deficient in kindergartners who later develop reading problems (Butler *et al.*, 1985; Silva *et al.*, 1985) and in dyslexic schoolchildren (Catts, 1986; Donahue, Pearl, & Bryan, 1982; Feagans & Short, 1984; Siegel & Ryan, 1984; Taylor, Lean, & Schwartz, 1989). Syntactic complexity and speech accuracy are correlated in young normal children (e.g., Dobrich & Scarborough, 1984) and in children with expressive language impairments (e.g., Wolfus, Moscovitch, & Kinsbourne, 1980). The interdependence of these two facets of language development is further suggested by Panagos, Quine, and Klich's (1979) demonstration that more speech errors tend to be made during a child's production of complex than simple syntactic forms.

On the other hand, some early linguistic abilities were apparently intact in the children who became disabled readers. For example, there was no evidence of early receptive phonological impairment, a result that is consistent with Mann and Ditunno's (1990) recent finding that kindergartners' speech discrimination abilities were not predictive of reading achievement. It is thus unlikely that the early syntactic and phonological production problems of the children who became dyslexic can be explained simply on the basis of incomplete or distorted perception of language input.

There was also little evidence for very early problems in vocabulary development among the children who later developed reading disabilities. At age 30 months, diversity of words in natural conversation, elicited object-naming abilities (on the BNT), and recognition of spoken words (on the PPVT) were not closely related either to concurrent productive syntactic and phonological deficits or to future reading abilities in the sample. Vocabulary deficits, of course, *have* often been associated with reading problems in prior prospective studies (e.g., Bryant *et al.*, 1989; Share *et al.*, 1984; Stanovich, Cunningham, & Feeman, 1984; Wolf & Goodglass, 1986), and this result was also observed in the present sample—but not until the children were 42 months old.

This observed change in the relation of vocabulary skill to later reading achievement was probably not due merely to the methods of assessment used. Floor effects were not apparent for either the BNT or PPVT at 30 months, and moderate across-age and concurrent correlations were observed among these scores, so it is unlikely that the vocabulary tests were just insensitive to early lexical differences among the groups. On the other hand, lexical diversity during natural conversation was not strongly related to any concurrent or subsequent measures in the study, and it is not yet known whether this measure will, like tested vocabulary skills, also emerge as a predictor of reading disability at older ages. Although the type-token ratio has long been used as a clinical tool and has been associated with reading achievement differences among schoolchildren (Fry, Johnson, & Muehl, 1970; Idol-Maestas, 1980), little is actually known about what such scores tell us about individual differences in productive vocabulary development (Richards, 1987). When more longitudinal data on natural language development become available for the sample, the validity of this measure will be examined closely.

Nevertheless, the BNT and PPVT test results indicate that vocabulary deficits may not emerge as precursors to reading disabilities at as early an age as do syntactic and phonological production deficits. Conceivably, vocabulary problems could be consequences of earlier structural language deficiencies. Even if syntactic and phonological production problems are initially quite specific and compartmentalized, this disruption of the normal interdependence among developing components of the language faculty might impede the further progress of other components, including vocabulary growth. Such a diffusion in the scope of language impairment over time might also occur if conversational partners adjusted their speech to the perceived ability level of the child, thus providing less enriching input. For whatever reason, by age 42 months some vocabulary deficits of children who become disabled readers appear to predict their later reading problems.

In sum, the picture that emerges from research on the precursors of dyslexia is one of a child who not only has difficulty with reading and language during the school years but who also typically experiences problems with preliteracy skills during the late preschool period; exhibits vocabulary deficiencies, poor rhyme recitation skills, and phonemic awareness deficits from the age of 3 or 4 years; and produces shorter, syntactically simpler sentences and less accurate pronunciations of words than other 2-year-olds.

The etiology of reading disability

Although early deficits in syntactic and phonological processing appear to be precursors to reading disabilities many years later, and although even broader language deficits are associated with inadequate literacy skills from the time children usually start learning letter names and letter-sound correspondences, these findings do not mean that a dyslexic child's difficulty in learning to read is necessarily brought about by these linguistic weaknesses.

Several approaches to explaining dyslexia will be considered in light of the present findings.

Explaining reading failure.—What causes dyslexia? When dyslexia is defined as primarily a reading failure, then the central etiological goal is to explain what goes awry during the process of learning to read, and to determine to what extent the deficient language skills a child brings to the learning situation may impede that process. It is generally agreed that the major task facing the beginning reader is to decode grapheme strings into recognizable phonemic sequences. To do this, an appreciation of the fact that *spoken* words are composed of sequences of phonemes (which often correspond in regular ways to letter sequences) is of great help to the learner, much more so perhaps than sophisticated syntactic and vocabulary skills. Phonological processing abilities at the time that formal instruction in decoding begins may thus play an important role in the acquisition of reading (Liberman, Shankweiler, Fischer, & Carter, 1974).

In contrast, the syntactic and lexical skills of kindergartners who become disabled readers are probably not so impaired as to impede their understanding of the relatively simple words and sentences found in primers. The children's poor performance in tasks that purportedly assess lexical and syntactic skills may often instead primarily reflect their phonological limitations, including difficulties with verbal coding for short-term memory and with retrieval of stored phonological information (Fowler, 1988; Shankweiler & Crain, 1986). Although poor oral language skills could adversely affect teacher-student communication, and thereby reduce the effectiveness of instruction, the fact that the reading-disabled children's achievement problems do not extend to math suggests that the source of their reading problems is probably not merely a failure to understand and be understood by their teachers.

Consequently, most contemporary views reject the notion that general language deficits are directly responsible for reading difficulties in favor of the hypothesis that a more specific deficit in phonological—or, more narrowly, in *meta*phonological—skill is the more likely proximal cause of poor reading achievement, at least in the early school years (e.g., Kamhi & Catts, 1989; Stanovich, 1988; Wagner & Torgesen, 1987). In support of this hypothesis, correlations between phonological skills and future reading achievement have been demonstrated in many prior prospective studies of preschoolers, as noted earlier. Moreover, training in phonemic awareness skills has been shown to be effective, although not dramatically so, in improving reading acquisition (e.g., Blachman, 1989; Bradley & Bryant, 1983; Williams, 1980). The present findings of impaired phonemic awareness and name-retrieval skills in 5-year-olds who became disabled readers are consistent with the conclusion that phonological processing is the aspect of language skill most closely related to outcomes, with only secondary contributions, if any, from more general language deficiencies.

403

Plausible though this hypothesis might be, it may not provide a complete explanation of reading failure. There is abundant evidence that the reading difficulties of dyslexic children begin to emerge from the time that they start learning to recognize letters and to appreciate letter-sound correspondences. Moreover, the relation between metaphonological and literacy skills is apparently one of reciprocal causation, such that phonological proficiency facilitates the learning of letter-sound correspondences, which in turn enhances phonological skill and awareness (e.g., Ehri, 1985; Morais, Carey, Alegria, & Bertelson, 1979; Stuart & Coltheart, 1988). To explain reading failure in terms of these phonological skills, therefore, may say little more than that a child's success in early literacy achievement is predictive of subsequent progress in reading, and raises the question of what underlies the early deficits in literacy and phonological processing to begin with (Kamhi, 1989; Tunmer *et al.*, 1988).

The relevance of syntactic and lexical deficits to reading acquisition also cannot be ruled out entirely, despite the greater weight of evidence for strong correlations between phonological performance and subsequent reading scores. Bowey and Patel (1988), for instance, have shown that when general language abilities are carefully assessed, metaphonological abilities do *not* account for any unique variance in reading achievement. Also, several follow-up studies of samples of clinically identified language-impaired preschoolers, reviewed by Weiner (1985), have shown that children with broad deficit profiles are at much greater risk for reading disabilities than children with only phonological impairments. Finally, the present finding that some additional variance in outcomes was predicted by very early syntactic abilities, above and beyond the contributions of phonemic awareness and early literacy skills at age 60 months, suggests that the prevailing explanation of reading disability may be overly narrow, and that it might be fruitful to consider a different etiological approach.

Explaining developmental dyslexia.—The answer to the question, "What causes dyslexia?" may depend on whether one takes the traditional view of dyslexia as fundamentally a reading problem, or instead defines it as a broader condition of which reading problems are merely the most evident —and most debilitating—symptom. Dyslexia, that is, may be a disorder (or an extreme of natural variation) that emerges even before any literacy demands are made on the child (Catts, 1989; Kamhi & Catts, 1989). If so, the sentence-production and pronunciation deficits at age 30 months in the present study would be early symptoms of dyslexia, as would many of the preschool characteristics that have so far been called "precursors" to dyslexia. Reading failure itself would also be a symptom of the disorder. The observed relations among early and late symptoms would thus arise, at least in part, because each reflected persisting individual differences along the more fundamental underlying dimension. Of course, the earlier symptoms could also contribute to the development or expression of the later ones.

What might this hypothesized underlying condition be? The possibilities are many, given that so little is yet known about early symptoms. Possible exogenous conditions would include child-rearing patterns that could adversely affect early language development and that might occur more often in dyslexic families than in others, such as infrequent verbal interchanges in the household, low parental expectations regarding progress in language development, or decreased emphasis on language-related activities, including reading. This possibility cannot be entirely ruled out, especially since the early deficits identified in this study all involved measures of performance during mother-child interaction, but is counterindicated by the present findings that the children from dyslexic families who did not develop reading problems exhibited normal early language proficiency, and that equally severe language deficits occurred in children whose mothers were dyslexic as in children with normal mothers. Furthermore, any differences in child-rearing patterns cannot be so broad as to affect *all* aspects of the child's future development, since most of the affected subjects in this study and others have exhibited normal nonverbal processing and adequate math achievement.

Possible endogenous conditions would include a variety of cognitive or personal characteristics (and associated neurological substrates). A genetically transmitted trait, of course, would most readily account for the extent to which dyslexia runs in families. Differences in temperament, health, sociability, attention, and the like might conceivably lead to the symptoms observed in dyslexic children, but the normal nonverbal development of these children might not as easily be explained. A more plausible hypothesis is that the underlying dimension of difference involves an intrinsic limitation in some verbal-cognitive capacity that constrains language processing to a greater extent than other aspects of development.

Along these lines, Kamhi and Catts (1989) have argued that the process of representing or retrieving phonological information may be the fundamental source of difficulty. This notion would account particularly well for name-retrieval, verbal memory, and phonological deficits associated with reading disabilities but would not as readily explain the present findings of syntactic deficits and unimpaired lexical skills (including name retrieval) at age 30 months.

Instead, the nature of syntactic and phonological rule systems may make them particularly difficult for dyslexic children to acquire and use efficiently. For both of these "structural" components of a language (and arguably for few, if any, other human faculties), the child must discover rules that govern the order-dependent combination of abstract formal elements (phonemic and syntactic categories) into higher-order structures of which only the surface features are uttered and perceived. Moreover, the generation and comprehension of these multiple levels of abstract structural relations go on simultaneously during speaking and listening, making the acquisition problem even more difficult. A limitation in dealing with any of various aspects (abstractness, low redundancy, order sensitivity, duality of structure, etc.) of acquiring and using such a system might conceivably later impede the acquisition of letter-sound correspondence rules as well. There is indeed some evidence that the decoding problems of dyslexic school-children are attributable, in part, to such rule-learning difficulties (Manis *et al.*, 1987; Morrison, 1987).

In addition, early structural language deficits themselves might affect the quality of linguistic models provided by conversational partners, or alter the child's tendency to engage in language-dependent preschool activities. These or other imaginable consequences of early structural language problems could in turn produce short- and long-term developmental effects (on vocabulary acquisition, memory processing strategies, and metalinguistic awareness) above and beyond the initial underlying problem. Some such consequences might be preventable, even if the intrinsic underlying limitation and early symptoms are not.

In conclusion, the present results reveal that potentially important differences between children who do and do not become disabled readers are evident by the third year of life. The causal relations between these early symptoms and eventual reading problems are probably complex and often indirect. A clearer etiological picture may emerge when more is learned about the preschool development of the present sample from ongoing analyses of their productive language skills at other ages, of the maternal language input they receive, of their emerging attitudes toward literacy, and of their attentional and motivational characteristics.

Notes

This research was supported in part by grants from the National Institute of Child Health and Human Development and the March of Dimes Birth Defects Foundation. Maria Hager, Janet Wyckoff, and Wanda Dobrich assisted with data collection and analysis, and Martin Braine, Virginia Mann, Adele Abrahamsen, Bruce Pennington, Guy Van Orden, and two anonymous reviewers provided helpful comments on the paper. Thanks are also extended to the families who participated in this study for their patience and goodwill.

1 On average, the reading scores of these 24 cases were 2.64 SE below levels defined by a regression of reading on IQ within the subsample from nondyslexic families (Scarborough, 1989a).
2 The 22 other normal readers from nondyslexic families were 15 girls and seven boys whose mean SES was 1.91 (SD 0.31). Their mean reading score was 502.5 (SD 5.4), and mean IQs were 114.6 (SD 11.4) at age 36 months, 118.8 (SD 10.1) at 60 months, and 125.7 (SD 9.9) at grade 2.
3 Although the ratio of dyslexic boys to girls is often less than 2:1 when classifications are based on test scores rather than school placement (Finucci & Childs, 1981; Naiden, 1976), the ratio obtained in the present project was nevertheless lower than expected. Perhaps this is due to other differences in ascertainment bias

from study to study or is a consequence of the mode of familial transmission (DeFries, in press). Sex differences in adult reading ability have been discussed previously (Scarborough, 1984).
4 This was done so that highly frequent words (like *Mommy, no, this, there,* and *what*) would not be the predominant productions scored for pronunciation, and so that words used primarily by more syntactically advanced 2-year-olds (like *the* and auxiliary verbs) would not confound the assessment of phonological production. Vowel pronunciation was not scored because of possible dialect differences and anticipated difficulties in achieving reliable transcription and coding.
5 A more traditional lexical diversity measure was used in previous analyses of this sample (Scarborough, 1989b, 1989c).

References

Blachman, B. A. (1989). Phonological awareness and word recognition: Assessment and intervention. In A. G. Kamhi & H. W. Catts (Eds.), *Reading disabilities: A developmental language perspective* (pp. 133–158). Boston: Little, Brown.
Bowey, J. A., & Patel, R. K. (1988). Metalinguistic ability and early reading achievement. *Applied Psycholinguistics,* **9**, 367–383.
Bradley, L., & Bryant, P. E. (1983). Categorizing sounds and learning to read—a causal connection. *Nature,* **301**, 415–421.
Brown, R. (1973). *A first language: The early stages.* Cambridge, MA: Cambridge University Press.
Bryant, P. E., Bradley, L., Maclean, M., & Cross-land, J. (1989). Nursery rhymes, phonological skills and reading. *Journal of Child Language,* **16**, 407–428.
Butler, S. R., Marsh, H. W., Sheppard, M. J., & Sheppard, J. L. (1985). Seven-year longitudinal study of the early prediction of reading achievement. *Journal of Educational Psychology,* **77**, 349–361.
Catts, H. W. (1986). Speech production/phonological deficits in reading-disordered children. *Journal of Learning Disabilities,* **19**, 504–508.
Catts, H. W. (1989). Defining dyslexia as a developmental language disorder. *Annals of Dyslexia,* **39**, 50–64.
Crystal, D. (1974). A review of Brown's *A first language. Journal of Child Language,* **1**, 289–307.
Dale, P. (1976). *Language development.* New York: Holt, Rinehart & Winston.
DeFries, J. C. (in press). Gender ratios in reading-disabled children and their affected relatives: A commentary. *Journal of Learning Disabilities.*
DeFries, J. C., Fulker, D. W., & LaBuda, M. C. (1987). Evidence for a genetic etiology in reading disability in twins. *Nature,* **329**, 537–539.
DeFries, J. C., Vogler, G. P., & LaBuda, M. C. (1985). Colorado family reading study: An overview. In J. L. Fuller & E. C. Simmel (Eds.), *Behavior genetics: Principles and applications* (Vol. **2**, pp. 357–368). Hillsdale, NJ: Erlbaum.
Dobrich, W., & Scarborough, H. S. (1984). Form and function in early communication: Language and pointing gestures. *Journal of Experimental Child Psychology,* **38**, 475–490.
Donahue, M., Pearl, R., & Bryan, T. (1982). Learning disabled children's syntactic proficiency on a communicative task. *Journal of Speech and Hearing Disorders,* **47**, 397–403.

Dunn, L. M. (1965). *Peabody Picture Vocabulary Test.* Circle Pines, MN: American Guidance Service.

Ehri, L. C. (1985). Effects of printed language acquisition on speech. In D. R. Olson, N. Torrance, & A. Hildyard (Eds.), *Literacy, language, and learning* (pp. 333–367). Cambridge: Cambridge University Press.

Feagans, L., & Short, E. J. (1984). Developmental differences in the comprehension and production of narratives by reading-disabled and normally achieving children. *Child Development*, **55**, 1727–1736.

Finucci, J. M., & Childs, B. (1981). Are there really more dyslexic boys than girls? In A. Ansara, N. Geschwind, A. Galaburda, M. Albert, & N. Gartrell (Eds.), *Sex differences in dyslexia* (pp. 1–9). Towson, MD: Orton Dyslexia Society.

Finucci, J. M., Gottfredson, L. S., & Childs, B. (1985). A follow-up study of dyslexic boys. *Annals of Dyslexia*, **35**, 117–136.

Fowler, A. E. (1988). Grammaticality judgments and reading skill in grade 2. *Annals of Dyslexia*, **38**, 73–94.

Fry, M. A., Johnson, C. S., & Muehl, S. (1970). Oral language production in relation to reading achievement among selected second graders. In D. J. Bakker & P. Satz (Eds.), *Specific reading disability: Advances in theory and method* (pp. 123–146). Rotterdam: Rotterdam University Press.

Hollingshead, A. B., & Redlich, F. C. (1958). *Social class and mental illness.* New York: Wiley.

Idol-Maestas, L. (1980). Oral language responses of children with reading difficulties. *Journal of Special Education*, **14**, 385–404.

Ingram, T. T. S., Mason, A. W., & Blackburn, I. (1970). A retrospective study of 82 children with reading disability. *Developmental Medicine and Child Neurology*, **12**, 271–281.

Jansky, J., & deHirsch, K. (1972). *Preventing reading failure.* New York: Harper.

Kamhi, A. G. (1989). Causes and consequences of reading disabilities. In A. G. Kamhi & H. W. Catts (Eds.), *Reading disabilities: A developmental language perspective* (pp. 67–99). Boston: Little, Brown.

Kamhi, A. G., & Catts, H. W. (1989). *Reading disabilities: A developmental language perspective.* Boston: Little, Brown.

Kaplan, E., Goodglass, H., & Weintraub, S. (1978). *Boston Naming Test.* Boston: published by the authors.

Kaufman, A. S. (1977). A McCarthy short form for rapid screening of preschool, kindergarten, and first-grade children. *Contemporary Educational Psychology*, **2**, 149–157.

Kavanagh, J. F., & Yeni-Komshian, G. (1985). *Developmental dyslexia and related reading disorders.* Bethesda, MD: National Institute of Child Health and Human Development.

Klee, T., & Fitzgerald, M. D. (1985). The relation between grammatical development and mean length of utterance in morphemes. *Journal of Child Language*, **12**, 251–269.

Liberman, I., Shankweiler, D., Fischer, F., & Carter, B. (1974). Explicit syllable and phoneme segmentation in young children. *Journal of Experimental Child Psychology*, **18**, 201–212.

Lundberg, I., Olofsson, A., & Wall, S. (1980). Reading and spelling skills in the first school years predicted from phonemic awareness skills in kindergarten. *Scandinavian Journal of Psychology*, **21**, 159–173.

Madden, R., Gardner, E. F., & Collins, C. S. (1981). *Stanford Early School Achievement Test*. New York: Psychological Corp.

Manis, F. R., Savage, P. L., Morrison, F. J., Horn, C. C., Howell, J. J., Szeszulski, P. A., & Holt, L. K. (1987). Paired associate learning in reading-disabled children: Evidence for a rule-learning deficiency. *Journal of Experimental Child Psychology*, **43**, 25–43.

Mann, V. A. (1984). Longitudinal prediction and prevention of early reading difficulty. *Annals of Dyslexia*, **34**, 117–136.

Mann, V. A., & Ditunno, P. (1990). Phonological deficiencies: Effective predictors of future reading problems. In G. Pavlides (Ed.), *Perspectives on dyslexia* (Vol. **2**, pp. 105–131). New York: Wiley.

McCarthy, D. (1972). *McCarthy Scales of Children's Abilities*. New York: Psychological Corp.

Morais, J., Carey, L., Alegria, J., & Bertelson, P. (1979). Does awareness of speech as a sequence of phonemes arise spontaneously? *Cognition*, **7**, 323–331.

Morrison, F. J. (1987). The nature of reading disability: Toward an integrative framework. In S. J. Ceci (Ed.), *Handbook of cognitive, social, and neuropsychological aspects of learning disabilities* (pp. 33–62). Hillsdale, NJ: Erlbaum.

Naiden, N. (1976, February). Ratio of boys to girls among disabled readers. *Reading Teacher*, 439–442.

Olson, R., Wise, B., Conners, F., Rack, J., & Fulker, D. (1989). Specific deficits in component reading and language skills: Genetic and environmental influences. *Journal of Learning Disabilities*, **22**, 339–348.

Panagos, J. M., Quine, M. E., & Klich, R. J. (1979). Syntactic and phonological influences on children's articulation. *Journal of Speech and Hearing Research*, **22**, 841–848.

Perfetti, C. A. (1985). *Reading ability*. New York: Oxford University Press.

Richards, B. (1987). Type/token ratios: What do they really tell us? *Journal of Child Language*, **14**, 201–209.

Rutter, M., & Yule, W. (1975). The concept of specific reading retardation. *Journal of Child Psychology and Psychiatry*, **16**, 181–197.

Scarborough, H. S. (1984). Continuity between childhood dyslexia and adult reading. *British Journal of Psychology*, **75**, 329–348.

Scarborough, H. S. (1989a). Prediction of reading disability from familial and individual differences. *Journal of Educational Psychology*, **81**, 101–108.

Scarborough, H. S. (1989b, June). *Reading disabilities and early language deficits: A longitudinal study*. Paper presented at the meeting of the American Psychological Society, Alexandria, VA.

Scarborough, H. S. (1989c, June). *Early language deficits of two-year-olds who became disabled readers*. Paper presented to the Joint Conference on Learning Disabilities, Ann Arbor, MI.

Scarborough, H. S. (1990). Index of productive syntax. *Applied Psycholinguistics*, **11**, 1–22.

Shankweiler, D., & Crain, S. (1986). Language mechanisms and reading disorder: A modular approach. *Cognition*, **24**, 139–168.

Share, D. L., Jorm, A. F., Maclean, R., & Matthews, R. (1984). Sources of individual differences in reading acquisition. *Journal of Educational Psychology*, **76**, 1309–1324.

Siegel, L. S., & Ryan, E. B. (1984). Reading disability as a language disorder. *Remedial and Special Education*, **5**, 28–33.

Silva, P. A., McGee, R., & Williams, S. (1985). Some characteristics of 9-year-old boys with general reading backwardness or specific reading retardation. *Journal of Child Psychology and Psychiatry*, **26**, 407–421.

Smith, S. D., Kimberling, W. J., Pennington, B. F., & Lubs, H. A. (1983). Specific reading disability: Identification of an inherited form through linkage analyses. *Science*, **219**, 1345–1347.

Stanovich, K. E. (1988). The right and wrong places to look for the cognitive locus of reading disability. *Annals of Dyslexia*, **38**, 154–177.

Stanovich, K. E., Cunningham, A. E., & Cramer, B. B. (1984). Assessing phonological awareness in kindergarten children: Issues of task comparability. *Journal of Experimental Child Psychology*, **38**, 175–190.

Stanovich, K. E., Cunningham, A. E., & Feeman, D. J. (1984). Intelligence, cognitive skills, and early reading progress. *Reading Research Quarterly*, **19**, 278–303.

Stuart, M., & Coltheart, M. (1988). Does reading develop in a sequence of stages? *Cognition*, **30**, 139–181.

Taylor, H. G., Lean, D., & Schwartz, S. (1989). Pseudoword repetition ability in learning-disabled children. *Applied Psycholinguistics*, **10**, 203–219.

Tunmer, W. E., Herriman, M. L., & Nesdale, A. R. (1988). Metalinguistic abilities and beginning reading. *Reading Research Quarterly*, **23**, 134–158.

Vellutino, F. R. (1979). *Dyslexia: Theory and research*. Cambridge, MA: MIT Press.

Wagner, R. K., & Torgesen, J. K. (1987). The nature of phonological processing and its causal role in the acquisition of reading skills. *Psychological Bulletin*, **101**, 192–212.

Wechsler, D. (1974). *Wechsler Intelligence Scale for Children—revised*. New York: Psychological Corp.

Weiner, P. (1985). The value of follow-up studies. *Topics in Language Disorders*, **5**, 78–92.

Williams, J. P. (1980). Teaching decoding with an emphasis on phoneme analysis and phoneme blending. *Journal of Educational Psychology*, **72**, 1–15.

Wolf, M., & Goodglass, H. (1986). Dyslexia, dysnomia, and lexical retrieval: A longitudinal study. *Brain and Language*, **28**, 154–168.

Wolfus, B., Moscovitch, M., & Kinsbourne, M. (1980). Subgroups of developmental language impairment. *Brain and Language*, **10**, 152–171.

Woodcock, R. W., & Johnson, M. B. (1977). *Woodcock-Johnson Psychoeducational Battery*. Boston: Teaching Resources Corp.

125

THE DEVELOPMENT OF GRAPHEME–PHONEME CORRESPONDENCE IN NORMAL AND DYSLEXIC READERS

Margaret J. Snowling

Source: *Journal of Experimental Child Psychology*, 29, 1980: 294–305.

The present experiment was concerned with the development of grapheme–phoneme conversion ability in normal and reading-age matched dyslexic readers. The use of grapheme–phoneme correspondences was observed in a recognition memory task for pronounceable nonwords. The nonwords were presented in either the visual or auditory modality and had to be recognized immediately from the converse modality, thus necessitating decoding of stimuli across modalities. The use of grapheme–phoneme correspondences increased with reading age in the normal readers but not in the dyslexics. It was postulated that dyslexics have a specific difficulty in grapheme–phoneme conversion. For them an increase in reading age is attributable mainly to an increase in size of sight vocabulary.

Since the first description of the syndrome of congenital word blindness (Pringle Morgan, 1896), the precise nature and even the very existence of developmental dyslexia has been under discussion. More recent epidemiological studies have, however, made it possible to arrive at a clearly defined description of the population of children who might justifiably be described as dyslexic.

Rutter and his associates (Rutter & Yule, 1973; Rutter, Tizard, Yule, Graham & Whitmore, 1976) tested the reading and spelling of the total 9- and 10-year population of the Isle of Wight and, using regression equations, they were able to predict the reading achievement expected of each child on the basis of his or her age and W.I.S.C. IQ (Yule, 1967). In this way, they separated children whose reading could not be accounted for by low intelligence from those whose reading was in line with a generally lower level of cognitive functioning. The former group was specifically retarded in reading whereas the latter group was generally backward, including being backward in reading. Important differences between these two groups emerged. Specific reading retardation was associated primarily with speech and language difficulties, while general reading backwardness was related to developmental delay in a much wider range of functions.

Other independent studies suggest that dyslexics may have considerable difficulties in the sphere of language (Vellutino, Steger, Harding, & Phillips, 1975; Vellutino, Pruzek, Steger, & Meshoulam, 1973). In particular, Vellutino (1977) has argued that most of the characteristic "dyslexic" difficulties may be due to perplexities in verbal labeling, verbal learning, and other modes of verbal processing.

Despite the influence these studies have had in arguing for the separation of children with specific reading problems from other poor readers, there is as yet little evidence that the performance of the two groups is in any way qualitatively different. Further, although reference is often made to the distinctive nature of dyslexic reading behavior, few empirical studies have shown it to be different from that of normal readers.

Reading can refer to many things. It could for instance be described as a "psycholinguistic guessing game" (Goodman, 1967; Smith, 1971) in which the meaning is gained from contextual cues with the minimum of phonemic mediation. This process relies heavily on semantic and syntactic abilities and if dyslexics have difficulties in these spheres, then the process will necessarily suffer. Reading can also refer to "decoding," or the translation of written words into some speech-like form before they can be understood. Hence, we are able to "read" aloud words in a foreign language with which we are totally unfamiliar. This type of reading relies heavily on phonological skills and so, once again, if dyslexics have language difficulties, they would be expected to be poor at reading.

Even when single words without context must be read, there is evidence that there are at least two alternative routes to meaning, the graphemic–semantic (or semantic) route and the graphemic–phonemic (or phonemic) route. The use of the semantic route implies that the meaning of a word is arrived at directly from its visual appearance, while using a phonemic route necessitates converting the word first into a sound before it is interpreted. Studies of adult aphasic patients with acquired dyslexia have shown that selective impairment of one or other of these routes is possible (Marshall & Newcombe, 1973; Shallice & Warrington, 1975; Patterson & Marcel, 1977). The faulty operation of the phonemic route is seen in patients with what has been described as phonemic dyslexia or deep dyslexia. Patterson and Marcel

(1977) and Saffran and Marin (1977) have clearly demonstrated that these patients have difficulty in using the phonemic route as they are almost totally unable to read aloud orthographically regular nonsense words.

The present experiment thus aims to control for reading levels between experimental (dyslexic) and normal-reader control groups in order to isolate the specific reading characteristics of the dyslexic subjects. Matching according to Reading Age ensures that all subjects are reading at the same quantitative level, although they may use qualitatively different decoding strategies. Reading Ages can be derived from standardized reading tests of various types. They may involve reading single words, sentences, or passages. One thing which they all have in common is the requirement to read real words. It is possible that, just like patients with acquired dyslexia, developmental dyslexics have selective impairment of either the semantic or phonemic route to reading, even though such impairments are masked when they are required to read real words with which they are very familiar.

If there was any difficulty in grapheme–phoneme translation (i.e., use of the phonemic route), it would be evident when S were required to read words outside their sight vocabulary. Such words could not be pronounced on the basis of previous learning experience from their visual appearance. To this end, pronounceable nonsense words which would be unfamiliar to both dyslexic and normal readers were used in the present experiment. One seemingly direct way of comparing the two groups in the use of grapheme–phoneme conversion rules is to compare their ability to read aloud these nonsense words. However, poorer performance may be due to an inability to articulate the correct response just as much as to a deficit in grapheme–phoneme translation. A recognition test was used so that, if poorer performance were to be observed in either group, it could not be attributed to a failure at the articulation stage. Hence, the response was provided and the subject only had to indicate whether or not it was correct. Recognition was tested immediately following presentation of each nonsense word stimulus in order to rule out any difference in memory functions between the two groups.

To clarify what Reading Age means in terms of the level of grapheme–phoneme skills achieved, it was decided to examine the performance of normal readers with different reading ages. It seems reasonable to assume that the higher the Reading Age (R.A.), the more proficient would be the use of grapheme–phoneme conversion rules and hence the better the performance at the experimental task. If this were the case, then there would be empirical evidence that, as often assumed, "decoding" increases with increasing R.A. On the other hand, if no development were seen in these abilities, it would have to be concluded that R.A. is no more than a measure of size of sight vocabulary.

To pursue the argument further, if dyslexic children have a deficit manifested in a difficulty in translating graphemes into phonemes, their performance on the experimental task would not be expected to increase with reading age in the same way as the normal reader's performance. If this were the case, one would have to conclude that they have developed alternative strategies for reading real words. For them, a given R.A. could not prescribe a given level of achievement of grapheme–phoneme conversion skills.

When nonsense words are presented in one modality (either auditory or visual) and have to be recognized in the other modality (visual or auditory), "decoding" or grapheme–phoneme conversion of one of the stimuli is required. Thus the present experiment compared dyslexic and normal children, matched for R.A., for the auditory and visual recognition of nonsense words after visual or auditory presentation.

Method

The method chosen was to present a nonsense word either visually or auditorily and then to ask the subject to say whether it was the same as or different from an auditorily or visually presented recognition stimulus. To ensure that there were no problems in the functioning of visual or auditory modalities themselves, it was necessary to include two within-modality conditions: Auditory presentation–Auditory recognition test (A–A) and Visual presentation–Visual recognition test (V–V).

The two conditions of central importance were those in which the stimulus was presented in one modality and tested in another. In a Visual presentation–Auditory recognition test condition (V-A), a grapheme–phoneme conversion is required. In the converse, Auditory presentation–Visual recognition test condition (A-V) there are two possible strategies. Either the auditory stimulus could be translated into a visual representation via phoneme–grapheme rules and the visual representation could be compared with the visually presented recognition stimulus, or, alternatively, the auditory stimulus could be held in some short-term store while the visually presented recognition stimulus was translated into a phonemic representation via grapheme–phoneme rules, so that the two stimuli could be compared in phonemic form.

Thus, there were four conditions, two within modalities and two between modalities. Each S was administered all four conditions with order of presentation randomized.

Subjects

A group of 36 normal readers (15 boys and 21 girls) and a group of 18 children diagnosed dyslexic (14 boys and 4 girls) took part in the experiment. The mean C.A. of the normal readers was 9 years 5 months (range 6:6 to 10:9) while the dyslexics, although of similar reading ability, were older, mean C.A. 12 years 1 month (range 9:2 to 15). The verbal IQ of the two groups were within the same range; normal readers had a mean verbal IQ of 105 (range 72 to 127) while dyslexic children had a mean verbal IQ of 106 (range 81 to 130). Each group was divided into four subgroups according to R.A. In the 7-year R. A. group there were 9 normal and 5 dyslexic S. The 8-year R.A. group and the 9-year R.A. group each contained 9 normal and 4 dyslexic S while there were 9 normal and 5 dyslexic S in the 10-year R.A. group.

The normal readers were selected at random from different classes within the same school, so as to provide representatives from the various age groups at the primary-school level. The dyslexic children were all attending a special "Dyslexia Unit" at a London teaching hospital. They had been diagnosed dyslexic following extensive psychometric testing, on the grounds that their reading and spelling abilities were significantly poorer than their C.A. and W.I.S.C. IQ would predict.

Materials

Stimuli were all four-letter pronounceable nonsense words. Those selected all had one essential feature: if the middle two letters in the word were transposed, the word remained pronounceable. These pronounceable modifications of the original items then served as distractors in the recognition tests for the original presentation stimuli (e.g., sond–snod, dron–dorn, brap–barp, sint–snit).

Twelve recognition stimuli were presented in each condition (A–A, V–V, V–A, and A–V). Six of these were identical with the initial stimulus word and required the response "same" and six were modifications of the original item for which the correct response was "different." Two parallel sets of stimuli were made up so that different stimuli could be presented to alternate subjects. This procedure allowed an assessment of the generalizability of results across both subjects and stimuli to be made. Thus, for the same presentation item in each condition, in one form an original item was given in test phase and in the other form, a distractor item was given. These alternative forms were labeled forms A and B.

A set of stimulus cards was compiled for use in the Visual presentation and Visual test conditions. Each consisted of a white card (150 × 100 mm) on which one of the nonsense words was presented centrally. The word was printed in lower case with black ink, each letter being approximately 5 × 5 mm plus ascenders and descenders. The stimuli were thus large and clear, making them easily read. The auditory items were read from prepared lists.

Procedure

Clear instructions about the experimental task were given to each child and they were "talked through" a few trials to ensure that they fully understood what was required of them. Instructions specific to each condition were given prior to that condition only and not all together at the beginning, as that would have confused especially the youngest children. It was emphasized that words would be only slightly changed if at all, so it was necessary to be extremely careful when deciding whether the recognition stimuli were the same as or different from the presentation stimuli.

The instructions given prior to the within-modal conditions were as follows.

> "You are about to see (hear) some nonsense words. Nonsense words are words which I have made up and no one has seen (heard) them before. The nonsense words will be presented in pairs one after another. Sometimes the two nonsense words will be the same. If they are the same, you should put a tick on your response sheet. If they are different, you should put a cross."

The procedure was similar for the cross-modal conditions and in all conditions the recognition test followed immediately after the presentation of the stimuli. In addition the following instructions were given.

> "This task is quite difficult as I am trying to trick you. I will sometimes give you two nonsense words which are only very slightly different. There is a way to stop me from tricking you. That is, if you think that the two nonsense words are the same but are not sure, put a tick and a question mark (✓) on your response sheet. If you think they are different, put a cross and a question mark (✗?). Wherever there is a question mark on your sheet, you cannot be marked wrong."

Each child was given extensive practice in the use of this confidence rating scale.

Scoring

In recognition tests it is possible for subjects to give correct responses by guessing. Guessing is a particular problem when working with children. Therefore, d' scores from signal detection analysis were used, Banks (1970). Such scores describe the level of correct recognition excluding the probability that such correct responses would have occurred by chance.

The first d' score was based upon the probability of saying "same" when it was the same. This was taken as:

$$\frac{\text{the No. of } \checkmark \text{ responses}}{\text{the No. of } \checkmark\text{?, } \times\text{, } \times\text{? responses combined}} \tag{1a}$$

for 'same' stimuli and the probability of saying "same" when it was different; taken as:

$$\frac{\text{the No. of} \checkmark \text{ responses}}{\text{the No. of} \checkmark?, \times, \times? \text{ responses combined}} \tag{1b}$$

again, but this time for "different" stimuli.
The computations require to derive the other d' values were:

$$\frac{\text{the No. of} \checkmark \text{ and } \checkmark? \text{ responses}}{\text{the No. of} \times \text{ and } \times? \text{ responses combined}} \tag{2}$$

$$\frac{\text{The No. of} \checkmark, \checkmark?, \text{ and } \times? \text{ responses}}{\text{The No. of} \times \text{ responses}} \tag{3}$$

The mean of these three values was taken as a measure of recognition for each S on each condition. The scores thus derived were used in subsequent analyses.

Results

Inspection of individual scores for dyslexic and normal readers indicated that there was no difference between performance on the two forms, A and B, of the experimental task. Indeed an ANOVA confirmed that although there was a significant difference between conditions (A–A, V–V, V–A, A–V), $F(3, 156) = 54.53$, $p < .001$, there was no significant difference between forms (A and B), $F(1, 52) = 0.10$, $p < .7$. Thus the combination of data from both forms of the experimental task was justified.

An ANOVA was carried out upon the complete data for the dyslexic and normal readers, collapsed across reading age. There was a significant difference between conditions, $F(3, 156) = 61.3$, $p < .001$, but no overall difference between the normal and dyslexic readers. There was, however, a significant interaction between conditions and groups, $F(3, 156) = 5.1$, $p < .01$ (see Table 1). Multiple t tests indicated that this interaction was due to the differential performance of the dyslexic and normal reader groups on the Visual presentation–Auditory recognition test (V–A) condition (t (52) = −2.79, $p < .01$). The normal readers performed better than the dyslexics. The reader groups performed at a similar level on the other three conditions (A–A, V–V, and A–V).

Two further analyses were carried out taking reading age into account. The question asked was whether performance in any of the conditions would change with an increase in R.A. in either of the groups.

Table 1 Mean d' Scores for Dyslexic and Normal Readers over Conditions.

Group	Conditions			
	A–A	V–V	A–V	V–A
Normal readers (N = 36)	3.68	2.04	1.63	1.85
Dyslexics (N = 18)	4.07	2.04	1.24	0.63

Taking the normal readers first, the data were grouped according to R.A. and subjected to a mixed design ANOVA (see Table 2). There was a large and highly significant difference between reading age groups. $F(3, 32) = 11.9$, $p < .001$, and also between conditions, $F(3, 96) = 26.7$, $p < .001$. Subsequent Newman–Keuls analyses showed that the 9- and 10-year R.A. groups performed significantly better than the 7- and 8-year R.A. groups.

Testing for simple effects on the condition term showed that Auditory presentation–Auditory recognition test (A–A) resulted in better performance than any of the other conditions which did not differ from one another. Moreover, there was a correlation between R.A. and performance on the V–V condition, $r (34) = .72$, $p < .001$. Further, performance on V–V was correlated with performance on both A–V ($r = .53$) and V–A ($r = 0.42$).

Turning to the dyslexics, an ANOVA indicated that there was a significant difference between conditions, $F(3, 42) = 50$, $p < .001$, as there was for normal readers. Again A–A was the easiest of all the conditions, but this time it was significantly easier than A–V which in turn was significantly easier than V–A (see Table 3). Unlike the normal readers, there was no significant difference between the reading age groups. None of the correlations between R.A. and performance on any of the experimental conditions reached significance. Furthermore, the correlation between R.A. and performance on the V–V condition for the dyslexics ($r = .26$) was significantly different from that for the normal readers, $z = 2.07$, $p < .05$.

Table 2 Mean d' Scores for Normal Readers, Grouped according to R.A. over Conditions.

Reading age in years	Conditions			
	A–A	V–V	A–V	V–A
7	3.16	0.76	0.40	0.69
8	3.52	1.67	1.38	0.88
9	4.03	2.16	2.21	2.32
10	3.99	3.54	2.54	3.53

Table 3 Mean *d'* Scores for Dyslexic Readers, Grouped according to R.A. over Conditions.

Reading age in years	Conditions			
	A–A	*V–V*	*A–V*	*V–A*
7	4.55	1.46	0.68	0.17
8	3.83	2.29	1.11	−0.29
9	3.84	1.83	1.34	1.58
10	3.99	2.58	1.83	1.06

Discussion

The results show interesting similarities and differences between the dyslexic and the normal reader groups. Moreover, they indicate that the relationship between performance and reading age is much stronger in the normal than in the dyslexic group.

The closest similarity between the groups was in the Auditory presentation–Auditory recognition condition which was easiest for all subjects. There was no improvement in performance with increasing Reading Age, suggesting a ceiling effect. As the task was made as difficult as possible, the distinctions between presentation and recognition test items, e.g., sond–snod, being very subtle, one can infer that this task is mastered at an early age. We can certainly conclude that any problems posed by the other conditions cannot simply be attributed to auditory discrimination problems.

A group difference emerged in the Visual presentation–Visual recognition test condition. The normal readers showed improved performance on this condition with increasing reading age, but the dyslexics did not. Performance on V–V was in fact correlated with R.A. in the normal, but not in the dyslexic group. Since this was a significant difference, it is possible that some ability which develops together with R.A. in normal readers but not in dyslexics is used in the V–V condition. It is hypothesized that the more advanced normal readers may have used a phonemic or "speech-based" code in order to match the stimuli although presentation and recognition stimuli were both visual in character. In contrast, the dyslexic readers, despite increasing R.A., may have continued to match the stimuli visually without resorting to conversion into a phonemic code. However, an alternative interpretation would be that both groups invoked visual matching, the more advanced normal readers simply being better at this than the dyslexics.

The A–V and V–A or "cross-modality" conditions are those which definitely must be based on a grapheme–phoneme conversion. In these conditions, it is necessary to decode both stimuli into the same modality in order to recognize them at above chance level. If the normal readers, as hypothesized, implicitly used grapheme–phoneme conversions in the V–V condition, their level of performance on that condition should be related to their level of performance on these cross-modal conditions. This was indeed the case, as performance on V–V was in fact at the same level as performance on both A–V and V–A in the normal reader group although it was not in the dyslexic group. The dyslexics, unlike the normals, were significantly better with Visual presentation–Visual recognition tests than with the cross-modality conditions. This suggests that the dyslexics treated both the A–A and the V–V material in terms of the modality in which the stimuli were presented. In other words, probably no decoding of the visual material into phonemic form occurred. Where such coding was required, as in the cross-modality conditions, the performance of the dyslexic subjects was poor.

The most important significant difference between the groups was in the V–A condition. This is the condition which is most like real reading, and it seems that the normal readers immediately decoded the visual presentation stimulus into an auditory form for comparison with the auditory recognition stimulus. Thus, the visual presentation was already decoded (implicity "read") when the recognition stimulus was presented.

The A–V condition is less similar to reading—an additional step is necessary. The hypothetical sequence of processes carried out by the normal readers in the condition is to hold the auditory stimulus in store while the visual recognition stimulus is decoded into auditory form. Comparison then occurs between two auditory representations. Hence, in the A–V condition, it is the recognition stimulus which needs recoding while the initial item is held in store. This process seems more difficult for normal readers than the process required in the V–A condition. In fact, in the overall ANOVA (collapsing across R.A.), it appears that the dyslexics performed at a similar level to normals under the A–V condition. However, closer inspection of the data showed this apparent similarity arose because, at the lowest reading level, the dyslexic's performance was superior to that of the normals. However, at all other reading levels, the dyslexics were worse than the normal readers.

Thus, the results of the present experiment suggest that dyslexic children defined by Yule's (1967) criteria perform in a qualitatively different manner from other poor readers. Dyslexic children identified in this way are not just like readers at the lower end of the normal distribution of reading skill, for they do not perform similarly to a group of reading age-matched younger normal readers. Although they can develop strategies to read whole words and hence build a considerable sight vocabulary, they find it difficult to decode unfamiliar words into sound.

The dyslexics' difficulty in grapheme–phoneme conversions may be the manifestation of a more general verbal deficit as contended by Vellutino (1977). This would be in line with the preponderance of children with speech and language difficulties noted by Rutter *et al.* (1976) among specifically retarded readers. The translation of graphemes into phonemes is indeed a complex task requiring many subskills. Orthographic awareness, phonemic segmentation, verbal labelling, and perhaps verbal memory are just some of the subprocesses involved.

It is highly relevant that the developmental dyslexics in this study behaved in a way similar to the phonemic dyslexics described by Patterson and Marcel (1977). Like them, although matched for their ability to read real words, ensuring a given level of reading via the semantic route, they seem impaired at recognizing nonsense words. This implies a selective impairment of the grapheme–phoneme route.

This leads to the second important question to which the present study was directed, namely the relationship between reading age as measured by a standardized reading test and level of grapheme–phoneme translation. Grapheme–phoneme translation was seen (as often assumed) to increase with reading age in normal readers. This was not so for the dyslexic readers. Grapheme–phoneme conversion or the "decoding" process does not seem to become increasingly efficient in spite of an increase in reading age. For these subjects, the increase in reading age is therefore most likely due to an increase in sight vocabulary, or reading via a semantic route.

In summary, normal development of reading is characterized by a developmental increase in decoding ability together with an increase in the size of sight vocabulary. However, developmental dyslexics form one group of readers for whom this is not the case. Development of reading skill for them is also characterized by an increasing sight vocabulary, but seemingly with no corresponding increase in grapheme–phoneme conversion ability. Such children seem to lack the "decoding" skills which normally accompany a given reading level. Thus they cannot readily read words which they do not know. They exhibit a selective impairment in the phonological route to reading: an impairment which is analogous to that shown by adult aphasic patients with an acquired dyslexia. This finding in particular renders more plausible the interpetation of the dyslexics' reading difficulties as the manifestation of an underlying language deficit.

Note

This experiment was carried out as part of a Ph.D. at University College London, and supported by a Medical Research Council Studentship. The author is indebted to her supervisor Dr. Uta Frith for invaluable advice throughout the course of the research. She is also grateful to Dr. B. Hermelin for helpful comments on an earlier draft of this paper and to Dr. C. D. Frith for statistical advice.

References

Banks, W. P. Signal detection theory and human memory. *Psychological Bulletin*, 1970, **74**, 81–99.

Goodman, K. S. Reading: A psycholinguistic guessing game. *Journal of the Reading Specialist*, 1967, **4**, 126–135.

Marshall, J. C., & Newcombe, F. Patterns of paralexia: A psycholinguistic approach. *Journal of Psycholinguistic Research*, 1973, **2**, 175–199.

Patterson, K. E., & Marcel, A. J. Aphasia, dyslexia and the phonological coding of written words. *Quarterly Journal of Experimental Psychology*, 1977, **29**, 307–318.

Pringle Morgan, W. A case of congenital word blindness. *British Medical Journal*, 1896, **2**, 1378.

Rutter, M., Tizard, J., Yule, W., Graham, P., & Whitmore, K. Research report. Isle of Wight studies 1964–1974. *Psychological Medicine*, 1976, **6**, 313–332.

Rutter, M., & Yule, W. Specific reading retardation. In L. Mann & D. Sabatino (Eds.), *The First Review of Special Education*. Philadelphia: Buttonwood Farms, 1973.

Saffran, E. M., & Marin, O. S. M. Reading without phonology: Evidence from aphasia. *Quarterly Journal of Experimental Psychology*, 1977, **29**, 515–525.

Shallice, T., & Warrington, E. K. Word recognition in a phonemic dyslexic patient. *Quarterly Journal of Experimental Psychology*, 1975, **27**, 187–199.

Smith, F. *Understanding reading*. New York: Holt, Rinehart & Winston, 1971.

Vellutino, F. R. Alternative conceptualizations of dyslexia: Evidence in support of a verbal deficit hypothesis. *Harvard Educational Review*, Special Issue on Reading and Language, Summer, 1977.

Vellutino, F. R., Pruzek, R. M., Steger, J. A., & Meshoulam, U. Immediate visual recall in poor and normal readers as a function of orthographic–linguistic familiarity. *Cortex*, 1973, **9**, 368–385.

Vellutino, F. R., Steger, J. A., Harding, C. J., & Phillips, F. Verbal vs nonverbal paired–associate learning in poor and normal readers. *Neuropsychologia*, 1975, **13**, 75–82.

Yule, W. Predicting reading ages on Neale's Analysis of Reading Ability. *British Journal of Educational Psychology*, 1967, **37**, 252–255.

126

PERSISTENCE OF DYSLEXICS' PHONOLOGICAL AWARENESS DEFICITS

Maggie Bruck

Source: *Developmental Psychology*, 28, 1992: 874–886.

This study examined the phonological awareness skills of dyslexic children, adults with childhood diagnoses of dyslexia, and good readers at various age levels. Comparisons of the dyslexics to good readers of the same age or the same reading level indicated that dyslexics do not acquire appropriate levels of phoneme awareness, regardless of their age or reading levels, although they eventually acquire appropriate levels of onset-rime awareness. Even adults with fairly high levels of word recognition skill show phoneme awareness deficits. For normal readers reliable increases in phoneme awareness were associated with age and reading level, whereas for dyslexic subjects these associations were not reliable.

The relationship between explicit awareness of the phonological structure of words (phonological awareness) and the acquisition of literacy skills has received much attention over the past 10 years. Measures of phonological awareness (such as counting the number of syllables or phonemes, deleting segments, or judging the similarity of sounds for orally presented words or nonwords) are highly correlated with children's ability to read and spell words as well as with their knowledge of the correspondences between spellings and sounds (see Adams, 1990; Wagner & Torgesen, 1987, for recent reviews). Phonological awareness skills also consistently differentiate good and poor readers. These differences are most dramatic in the case of dyslexic children, whose phonological awareness skills are not only poorer than those of normal readers of the same age but also than those of younger normal readers of the same reading level (e.g., Bradley & Bryant, 1978; Bruck & Treiman, 1990; Manis, Szeszulski, Holt, & Graves, 1988; Olson, Wise, Connors, & Rack, 1990).

Most researchers agree that poor phonological awareness is one of the core deficits that accounts for dyslexics' initial word recognition deficits and for their poor ability to learn the relationships between spelling and sounds, a critical component of word recognition (e.g., Bradley & Bryant, 1978, 1983; Lundberg, 1987; Share, Jorm, Maclean, & Matthews, 1984; Stanovich, 1992; Stanovich, Cunningham, & Cramer, 1984). However, there is little research on the degree to which phonological awareness skills improve as dyslexics become older and acquire some reading skill. Existing data merely indicate that phonological awareness skills of dyslexics (aggregating over a wide range of ages and reading levels) are not appropriate for their age or reading levels; they do not indicate whether, like normal readers (e.g., Bowey & Francis, 1991; Calfee, Lindamood, & Lindamood, 1973; Liberman, Shankweiler, Fischer, & Carter, 1974), dyslexics' phonological awareness skills improve as they become older and better readers or, if at certain ages or reading levels, dyslexics eventually acquire appropriate levels of phonological awareness skills. The present study examines the association of reading level and age with the phonological awareness skills of dyslexics.

There are a number of possible outcomes. One possibility is that regardless of age or reading level, dyslexics show deficits in phonological awareness and, unlike normal readers, dyslexics' phonological awareness skills do not improve with age or reading skill. This outcome would extend the findings of follow-up studies that dyslexics continue to show word recognition difficulties at all ages (Bruck, 1985, 1990; Forell & Hood, 1986; Labuda & DeFries, 1988; Manis & Custodio, 1991) and that at all ages, dyslexics' word recognition deficits are associated with an inadequate grasp of the associations between spellings and sound of words (see Olson et al., 1990, for a review). Failure to develop phonological awareness skills could therefore account for deficient word recognition skills at all ages.

A second possible outcome is that dyslexics' phonological awareness skills will improve as their word recognition skills increase and that, with sufficient experience with print and at some critical level of word recognition skills, some dyslexics will eventually develop normal phonological awareness skills. This outcome is consistent with the view that there is a bidirectional relationship between phonological awareness and reading acquisition (e.g., Morais, 1987). According to this position, the child must have some basic level of phonological awareness in order to learn to read. However, in the process of learning to read an alphabetic language, the information that the child has learned about the orthographic structures of words facilitates further development of phonological awareness skills, which in turn promote further development of word recognition skills. Thus, Perfetti, Beck, Bell, and Hughes (1987) found that prereaders' existing phonological skills were greatly enhanced once they had received reading instruction, and this enhancement was related to further development of word recognition skills. The bidirectional model can be restated to make the following predictions about the development of dyslexics' phonological awareness skills. Dyslexics' initial failure to acquire normal word recognition skills reflects poor phonological awareness skills. However, as is the case for normal readers, the development of word recognition skills promotes the growth of phonological awareness, although at a slower rate. Because dyslexics' word recognition skills do improve with age (Bruck, 1988, 1990; Forell & Hood, 1986; Labuda & DeFries, 1988; Manis & Custodio, 1991), with some older dyslexics achieving fairly high levels of word recognition skill (Bruck, 1990; Lefy & Pennington, 1991; Scarborough, 1984), dyslexics' phonological awareness skills will improve and higher functioning dyslexics will show normal levels of phonological awareness skill despite initial phonological awareness deficits.

A third possible outcome is that dyslexic's phonological awareness skills increase as word recognition skills improve, although they never achieve normal levels of phonological awareness skill. This outcome would be predicted by the bidirectional model with the following codicil: Dyslexics' failure to develop adequate levels of critical components of word recognition skill, such as knowledge of spelling–sound correspondences (see Olson et al., 1990), inhibits the emergence of full metacognitive insights concerning the phonological structures of words.

There are few studies that directly test these hypotheses concerning the development of dyslexics' phonological awareness skill. Some studies show that although the phonological awareness skills of poor readers develop as a function of age and reading ability, their performance remains consistently below that of normal readers (Calfee et al., 1973; Juel, 1988). However, it is not clear whether the subjects in these studies are dyslexic. In Juel's study (1988), the children came from minority low socioeconomic backgrounds, and thus their patterns of development may reflect home background factors that are not causal determinants of reading failure for dyslexics. Calfee et al. (1973) classified poor and good readers on the basis of a median split of standardized reading test scores; therefore, many of these poor readers would not be classified as dyslexic, because their reading skills were not severely retarded. One study by Fox and Routh (1983) is more relevant, because their subjects met the traditional criteria of dyslexia. These researchers identified a group of very disabled Grade 1 readers with poor phonological awareness skills. When retested 3 years later, the children performed at ceiling on the same phonological awareness test, suggesting that dyslexic children may eventually acquire age-appropriate phonological awareness skills. However, these data are inconsistent with those from other studies that show that dyslexic children above the age of 9 years (the age of the retested subjects in the Fox & Routh study) perform more poorly than normal readers on phonological awareness tasks (Bruck & Treiman, 1990; Pratt & Brady, 1988). It appears that because of ceiling effects, Fox and Routh's task may not have been an adequate measure of phonological awareness.

Other studies show that adults with severe reading problems perform poorly on phonological awareness tasks (Byrne & Ledez, 1983; Liberman, Rubin, Duques, & Carlisle, 1985; Pratt & Brady, 1988; Read & Ruyter, 1985), suggesting that phonological awareness skills do not reach normal levels simply as a function of age. However, based on the information that is presented about these adult subjects' backgrounds, it seems that their poor performance may be associated with factors other than dyslexia, such as lack of education, emotional problems, or motivational problems.

Thus, because of issues regarding subject selection and measurement procedures, the existing data do not indicate if dyslexics' phonological awareness skills develop as a function of age and reading skill. The present study examines this issue. In doing so, it incorporates two elements into its design that allow a more elaborate interpretation of its results.

The first element involves a specification of the types of phonological awareness skills to be assessed. Most studies that compare dyslexics and normal readers treat phonological awareness as a unified skill; little attention is given to the linguistic structures of the items included in the phonological awareness tasks. In contrast, current linguistic descriptions of the subunits of words include three hierarchical levels—the largest is the syllable and the smallest is the phoneme. At an intermediate level, syllables are divided into onset-rime units.[1] The developmental findings that children first develop awareness of syllables, then onsets and rimes and, finally, phonemes support the psycholinguistic validity of these distinctions for English speakers (e.g., Bruck & Treiman, 1990; Treiman & Zukowski, 1991). Furthermore, other studies show that these sublexical units are differentially influenced by the acquisition of word recognition skills. Thus, prereaders have good awareness of larger sublexical units such as the syllable and the onset or rime but poor awareness of the smaller phoneme unit. Phoneme awareness skills are most influenced by the introduction of literacy skills (e.g., Bowey & Francis, 1991; Goswami & Bryant, 1990; Morais, 1987; Perfetti et al., 1987; Treiman & Zukowski, 1991). Thus, awareness of larger sublexical skills may be prerequisites of initial reading acquisition, with phoneme awareness becoming important only later (see Goswami & Bryant, 1990). Existing comparisons of dyslexic and normal children do not indicate whether dyslexics are deficient in all areas of phonological awareness; it is not known if dyslexics differ from normal children in terms of syllable, onset, rime, and phoneme awareness or if they only differ on certain types of sublexical units. The present study not only makes these comparisons but also examines the development of awareness of each type of sublexical unit.

The second element of this study involves the use of measures to assess the degree to which orthographic information is used when making phonological judgments. As reviewed earlier, some researchers claim that, in the process of learning to read an alphabetic language, the information that the child has learned about the orthographic structures of words facilitates further development of phonological awareness skills, which in turn promote further development of word recognition skills. Examples of how orthographic information facilitates phonological judgments are provided in the two following studies. Children, with some reading skills, report that they hear four sounds in *pitch* but only three sounds in *rich*; they report hearing the "*t*" in *pitch* (Ehri & Wilce, 1980). In a similar vein, when asked if auditorally presented pairs of words rhyme, adults take longer to accept rhyming pairs that do not share orthographic units, like *tree–key*, than rhyming pairs that do share common orthographic units, like *tree–knee* (Seidenberg & Tanenhaus, 1979). Young normal readers also show an orthographic interference effect (Pearson & Barron, 1989; Waters & Seidenberg, 1983), which increases as word recognition skills improve (Zecker, 1991).

Two studies examined orthographic interference effects in dyslexics. Zecker (1991) examined the effect of orthographic structure on the rhyme judgments of dyslexic children between the ages of 7.0 and 11.5 years. In contrast to normal subjects of all ages who showed reliable orthographic interference effects, only dyslexics older than 10 years showed an orthographic interference effect. These data suggest that dyslexic children are delayed in their use of orthographic information when making phonological judgments. The data do not indicate whether this delay reflects an inadequate knowledge base to effectively use orthographic information (i.e., poor knowledge of the spellings of words) or a delay in dyslexic children's ability to automatically activate orthographic information regardless of the size of the knowledge base. The second study is a case study of a highly literate university student with a probable childhood history of dyslexia (Campbell & Butterworth, 1985). Despite her good reading skills, this woman had poor knowledge of the correspondences between spellings and sounds and poor phonological awareness skills. Further testing suggested that she performed phonological awareness tasks on the basis of the letters in the words (she used orthographic information), rather than on the basis of their sounds. This effect was much greater than that obtained for normal subjects. These two studies suggest that, with increased reading skills, dyslexics do use orthographic information when making phonological judgments, and that perhaps with high levels of reading skill, dyslexics rely on orthographic information to a greater extent than normal readers. Of course, this conclusion is highly tentative in that the two studies used different tasks, and also because it is not clear how typical Campbell and Butterworth's subject is compared with other adults with childhood diagnoses of dyslexia. To better understand the pattern of development of phonological awareness skills of dyslexics, the present study examines the degree to which dyslexics of various ages and reading levels use orthographic information when making phonological judgments.

Method

Design

Two different samples of dyslexics were tested. The first sample included school-age children who met common definitions of dyslexia; their word recognition skills were substantially below age-expected levels despite normal intelligence, adequate school and home environments, and absence of physical or sensorial deficits. At the time of testing, these children were between the ages of 8 and 16 years, and their scores on a standardized word recognition test ranged from a Grade 1 to a Grade 6 level. The second sample included adults who were diagnosed in childhood as dyslexic; they were selected because of poor word recognition skills during childhood, not at the time of testing. At the time of follow-up, these adults were between the ages of 19 and 27 years, and their scores on a standardized word recognition test ranged from a Grade 1 to a Grade 12 level.

Four control groups of good readers were also tested: Grade 1, Grade 2, Grade 3, and college students. For the elementary school-aged children, the range of word recognition scores was similar to that found in the dyslexic child sample.

To examine if dyslexics ever acquire "appropriate" levels of phonological awareness skills, two types of analyses were carried out separately on the child and adult samples. First, to determine if dyslexics acquire normal levels of word recognition skills for their age, their performance was compared to that of the control subjects of the same age. It is possible, however, that any between-group differences on phonological awareness skills might reflect differences in word recognition skills. That is, the normal readers may perform better on the phonological awareness tasks because they have better word recognition skills than the dyslexics. Thus, a second standard for evaluating the degree to which dyslexics attain appropriate levels of phonological awareness skills involved a "reading-level match" in which dyslexics were compared with normal readers of the same word recognition level (see Backman, Mamen, & Ferguson, 1984, for a discussion of these designs). If dyslexics perform more poorly than normal but younger readers, then this suggests that dyslexics show a deficit in phonological awareness skills. On the other hand, if dyslexics perform similarly to normal readers of the same reading level, then this reflects a developmental delay; dyslexics are progressing as expected, given their levels of word recognition skills. In the present study, dyslexic children were compared with elementary school children with similar levels of word recognition ability. For the dyslexic adult sample, a stricter test of this hypothesis was set up. The phonological awareness skills of the best functioning adults—those reading above a Grade 7 level—were compared with those of the Grade 3 children who were 13 years younger and whose levels of word recognition skills were substantially lower than those of the adult dyslexics.

To examine the association between reading skill and phonological awareness skills, separate analyses of variance (ANOVAs), in which level of word recognition skill served as the independent variable and phonological awareness test scores served as the dependent variable, were carried out on the dyslexic child, dyslexic adult, and normal child samples. (This procedure was not carried out on the normal college students who showed little variability in word recognition scores, because most performed near ceiling levels.) Next, within the normal sample, children were compared with adults to determine if phonological awareness skills change from childhood to adulthood. Before carrying out this analysis on the dyslexic data, preliminary analyses were run that indicated that the children and adults were drawn from the same population. This hypothesis was raised by the fact that, unlike the normal children and adults, different criteria were used to select the dyslexic child and dyslexic adult samples. Specifically, although word recognition scores were a criterion for selection of the children at the time of testing, this was not a criterion for the selection of the adults.

The battery of phonological awareness tasks included separate measures of syllable, onset, rime, and phoneme awareness. The inclusion of these separate measures allows a more precise specification than has previously been provided of the types of phonological awareness deficits that characterize dyslexics at different levels of development. The use of discrete measures also allows a more detailed examination of the relationship of reading level with phonological awareness. Based on the literature review, reading level should correlate more highly with phoneme than with syllable or onset-rime awareness tasks, at least in the normal samples (e.g., Bowey & Francis, 1991; Goswami & Bryant, 1990).

The battery also included tasks that assess the use of orthographic information in phonological awareness judgments. These results clarify any developmental trends obtained for the analyses of the phonological awareness measures. Thus if dyslexics' phonological awareness skills improve, the orthographic tasks allow the assessment of the degree to which this development is associated with the use of orthographic information. Based on the literature review, increases in phonological awareness should be paralleled by increases in the use of orthographic information, at least for normal readers (e.g., Zecker, 1991).

Subjects

Dyslexic children. Thirty-six dyslexic children were selected from the patient population of a clinic that specializes in the assessment and treatment of specific reading disorders. The average age of initial assessment at the clinic was 9 years and 8 months. When tested for this study, subjects were between 8 and 16 years old and were attending elementary or secondary school. They had IQ scores of 90 or higher on either the Verbal or Performance subscale of the Wechsler Intelligence Scale for Children—Revised (Wechsler, 1974). Mean Verbal, Performance, and Full Scale IQ scores were 99, 107, and 103, respectively. In addition, all children scored below the 30th percentile on the word recognition subtest of the Wide Range Achievement Test—Revised, Level 1 (WRAT–R; Jastak & Wilkinson, 1984). Detailed clinical assessments revealed that these children's reading difficulties were not associated with social, emotional, cultural, pedagogical, or medical factors.

Dyslexic adults. Thirty-nine adults with childhood diagnoses of dyslexia were identified from the patient files of the same clinic from which the dyslexic children were chosen. Childhood file information was used to identify patients who met the following exclusionary definition of dyslexia: (a) The child experienced difficulty learning to read despite at least average intelligence; (b) reading problems were not associated with social, emotional, cultural, pedagogical, or medical factors, as evidenced by detailed clinical assessments; and (c) childhood reading difficulties were associated with word recognition problems, as evidenced by performance on the Word Recognition and Oral Reading subtests of the Durrell Analysis of Reading Difficulty (Durrell, 1955). On the Durrell test, all subjects scored at least 1.5 grades below level on one subtest, and all scored below grade level on both subtests. (Average performance on the Word Recognition subtest was a low Grade 3 level when average placement was Grade 5.) Mean childhood Verbal, Performance, and Full Scale IQ scores on the WISC or WISC–R (Wechsler, 1949, 1974) were 99, 109, and 105, respectively. The average age at which the children were first assessed at the clinic was 9 years and 3 months.

At follow-up testing, the adults were between 19 and 27 years of age. Nineteen subjects were in college programs, and the remaining 20 subjects had no further educational training after leaving high school. At follow-up, in addition to the phonological awareness tests, the adult subjects were given standardized reading and spelling tests, which included word recognition and spelling subtests of the WRAT–R, Level II (Jastak & Wilkinson, 1984) as well as an extensive battery of tests to assess components of word recognition skills. The experimental tasks revealed that the dyslexics had weak single-word recognition skills: They read single words very slowly and they had poor knowledge of spelling–sound correspondences. Although most subjects performed poorly on the follow-up standardized tests, it is important to note that admission to the study was not contingent on this performance but rather on their childhood reading tests; at follow-up, one third of the subjects scored above the 30% on the WRAT–R, Level II.

Normal readers. Four groups of good readers and spellers were tested. There were 13 Grade 1, 15 Grade 2, 15 Grade 3, and 20 college students. Subjects were included if they scored at or above their grade level on both the reading and spelling subtests of the WRAT–R (Level I for the school-aged children and Level II for the adults).

The grade school children were sampled from two suburban schools in the Montreal area. The college students were recruited by advertising at local universities and junior colleges.

Test battery

Six measures were obtained from three different untimed phonological awareness tasks. All stimuli were nonwords. For each task, there were four practice trials for which the subject was given feedback and correction. No feedback was given for the test trials. At the beginning of all practice and test trials, the subject heard a nonword stimulus and then repeated the nonword. If an item was mispronounced (a rare occurrence), it was repeated by the examiner until a correct repetition was obtained. The subject then carried out the manipulation required for that task.

Syllable counting. Five blocks were placed in front of the subject. The subject heard a nonword on a tape recorder and then used the blocks as counters to indicate the number of syllables in the nonword. There were 30 trials consisting of 10 two-syllable, 10 three-syllable, and 10 four-syllable nonwords. The items were randomly ordered in one list.

Phoneme counting. The format and procedures of this task were identical to the syllable counting task. The stimuli consisted of 30 monosyllabic nonwords ranging from two to four phonemes, with 10 items of each phoneme length. Half of the items (nondigraph items) contained the same number of letters as phonemes (e.g., *tisk*). The remaining items contained one digraph, and thus these items contained more letters than phonemes (e.g., *leem* contains four letters but only three phonemes). Items were randomly ordered.

Nondigraph and digraph items were analyzed separately. Following the suggestions of Tunmer and Nesdale (1982), nondigraph items served as a "pure" measure of phoneme awareness. Because digraph errors are of interest only to the degree that subjects erroneously report orthographic rather than phonological information, the types of digraph errors were examined. Errors were classified as overshoots or as undershoots. For example, if the subject incorrectly replied that the three-phoneme nonword *leem* contained four sounds, this was coded as an overshoot error; the subject's response reflected attention to the number of letters rather than to the phonemes in the nonword. If the subject incorrectly replied that the nonword *leem* contained two phonemes, then this was coded as an undershoot error, which probably reflects attention to the sound properties of the nonword and thus is more similar in nature to errors on nondigraph items. If orthographic information is used when making phonological judgments, then there should be a significant proportion of overshoot responses on digraph errors.

Deletion. The experimenter told the subject to say what was left of the nonword item after removing either the first or the last sound. To ensure that the subject understood which sound (initial or final) to delete, the experimenter placed in front of the subject a paper strip with "first" written on the left and "last" written on the right. On each trial, the examiner pointed to the appropriate place on the strip to indicate which sound was to be removed.

There were 24 randomly ordered trials. For 4 of the trials, subjects were told to delete the first sound of a consonant–vowel–consonant (CVC) nonword (e.g., *voot*) in which the first phoneme could only be represented by one grapheme. Successful performance on these items requires an initial segmentation of the nonword into onset and rime units, and then deletion of the onset. These are called *deletion onset items*. For 12 of the items, successful performance required segmentation into phonemes, and then deletion of one phoneme: For 4 items, the subject was told to delete the first phoneme of a CCVC nonword (e.g., *snup* becomes *nup*), for 4 items the subject was told to delete the last phoneme of a CVC nonword (e.g., *tal* becomes *ta*), and for 4 items the subject was told to delete the last phoneme of a CVCC nonword (e.g., *lusk* becomes *luss*). For these 12 deletion phoneme items, the deleted phoneme could be represented by only one letter. The remaining 8 items required deletion of the first or last sound of a nonword, but unlike all other 16 items, the phoneme to be removed was a digraph (e.g., *thoace* becomes *oace* or *poash* becomes *poa*). As was the case in the phoneme counting task, errors on the digraph items are of interest because they reflect the degree to which subjects use orthographic information when making phonological judgments. Errors on the digraph deletion items were examined to determine how frequently subjects removed the first letter (e.g., *thoace* becomes *hoace*) or the last letter (*poash* becomes *poas*). If subjects use orthographic information on phonological awareness tasks, then there should be a significant proportion of letter deletion responses on digraph errors.

Procedures

Subjects were tested individually. The dyslexic children, the dyslexic adults, and the normal college students were tested in a laboratory at the clinic. The normal children were tested in their home schools; the Grade 2 and 3 children were tested in January, and the Grade 1 children were tested in April. The phonological awareness tasks were administered in two sessions separated by at least 24 hr. Half of the subjects received two tests on the first day and one test on the second day. The other subjects received the opposite order.

Results

The results are presented in the following four sections.

Do dyslexics acquire phonological awareness skills that are appropriate for their age level?

Dyslexic children were compared with normal children of the same age. Given the wide age range of the dyslexic children (7.9 to 16.5 years) and the constricted age range of the normal children (6.6 to 9.2 years), sub-samples of each group were selected to make the required comparisons. Normal and dyslexic children were not matched on an individual basis, rather, the ranges of ages that overlapped between the normal and dyslexic samples were used as cutoff points, and all children who fell between these points were included in the subsequent analyses. There were 9 dyslexic and 19 normal children between 7.9 and 9.0 years of age. By virtue of the restricted age range of the normal sample, the subsample of age-matched dyslexic children were the youngest and the poorest readers in the dyslexic sample.

In a separate analysis, adult dyslexics were compared with the normal college students. The two groups were not perfectly matched for age; the dyslexics were approximately 18 months older than the normal subjects. This difference works in favor of the hypothesis that, with age, dyslexics eventually show age-appropriate phonological awareness skills.

Table 1 shows the mean ages, WRAT–R reading scores, and phonological awareness test scores for dyslexic and age-matched control children as well as for the dyslexic adults and control college students.[2]

Dyslexic children made more errors than normal children on all four phonological awareness measures. Dyslexic children made more syllable counting errors, $F(1, 26) = 9.41$, $p < .005$, nondigraph "pure" phoneme counting errors, $F(1, 26) = 15.69$, $p < .01$, deletion onset errors, $F(1, 26) = 15.21$, $p < .01$, and deletion phoneme errors, $F(1, 26) = 9.91$, $p < .01$, than normal children of the same age. There were also between-group differences on the two measures that reflected the degree to which the children used orthographic information when making phonological judgments. Compared with the normal readers of the same age, dyslexic children made fewer overshoot responses on digraph errors in the phoneme counting task, $F(1, 26) = 13.94$, $p < .01$, and they made fewer single-letter deletion responses on digraph errors in the deletion task, $F(1, 13) = 6.71$, $p < .05$.[3]

Comparisons of the adult dyslexics and normal college students produced similar results. Dyslexic adults made more errors on the syllable counting, $F(1, 57) = 16.41$, $p < .01$, deletion phoneme, $F(1, 57) = 28.52$, $p < .01$, and phoneme counting nondigraph items, $F(1, 57) = 24.70$, $p < .01$, than normal college students. Adult dyslexics were similar to college students on onset deletion items; both groups made few if any errors, reflecting mastery of this skill. When making phonological judgments, adult dyslexics did not use

Table 1 Age Comparisons of Normal and Dyslexic Subjects.

| | Children | | | | Adults | | | |
| | Normal (n = 19) | | Dyslexic (n = 9) | | Normal (n = 20) | | Dyslexic (n = 39) | |
Variable	M	SD	M	SD	M	SD	M	SD
Age	8.4	0.3	8.5	0.4	20.8	1.9	22.3	1.9
WRAT–R Reading								
Raw score	71	9	47	3	112	5	82	14
Grade level	5B		2B		12+		8B	
Percentile	88		8		90		21	
Syllable counting errors (%)	11	10	26	15	2	6	18	17
Deletion: onset errors (%)	0	0	28	32	0	0	6	18
Deletion: Phoneme errors (%)	23	16	50	29	12	16	39	19
Phoneme counting: nondigraph errors (%)	9	12	27	14	2	4	18	14
Orthographic errors								
Phoneme counting: overshoot responses (%)	94	18	58	31	90	19	71	32
Deletion: letter deletion (%)	52	47	5	13	67	44	12	28

Note: WRAT–R = Wide Range Achievement Test—Revised (Level I for children and Level II for adults); B = beginning. Orthographic error scores represent the proportion of orthographic responses for errors on these items.

orthographic information to the same extent as normal readers of the same age. Adult dyslexics made fewer overshoot responses on digraph errors in the phoneme counting task, $F(1, 54) = 5.73$, $p < .05$, and they made fewer single-letter deletion responses on digraph errors in the deletion task, $F(1, 24) = 15.02$, $p < .01$.

To summarize, for most comparisons, dyslexic children and adults performed below age-expected levels, suggesting that dyslexics never attain age-appropriate levels of phonological awareness. The one exception was that adult dyslexics performed at age-expected levels on awareness of onsets. Performance on the orthographic items suggests that dyslexics of all ages do not use orthographic information to the same extent as normal readers when performing phonological awareness tasks.

Dyslexics may have performed more poorly than age-matched control subjects because their word recognition skills are lower than those of the normal readers. To examine this possibility, the next analyses compare the phonological awareness skills of dyslexics to normal readers of the same reading level or of a lower reading level.

Do dyslexics acquire phonological awareness skills that are appropriate for their reading level?

Two sets of analyses were carried out. First, a subsample of dyslexic children were compared with a subsample of the normal children of the same reading level. These matches were not made on an individual basis, rather, the reading scores that overlapped between the normal and dyslexic samples were used as cutoff points, and all children who fell between these points were included in the subsequent analyses. There were 31 dyslexic children and 37 normal children with WRAT–R reading raw scores between 46 and 77. This eliminated 5 of the poorest dyslexics and 8 of the best control children from this analysis.

In the second analysis, the 26 best adult dyslexic subjects, all of whom read above the Grade 7 level, were compared with the Grade 3 children. These comparisons reflect the degree to which dyslexic adults' phonological awareness skills are similar to those of children who are at least 13 years younger. In addition, it should be noted that the Grade 3 children had lower reading and spelling levels than the dyslexic adults (the average spelling grades for the adults and children on the WRAT–R were end of Grade 6 and beginning of Grade 5, respectively). Thus the comparison is set up in such a way as to bias the results toward superior performance by the older and better reading and spelling adult dyslexics. Table 2 shows the mean ages, WRAT–R scores, and phonological awareness test scores for dyslexic and level-matched control children as well as for the dyslexic adults and the Grade 3 children.

For the child comparisons, dyslexics compared more poorly than normal readers of the same reading level on all four measures of phonological awareness: syllable counting, $F(1, 66) = 5.67$, $p < .05$; deletion onset items, $F(1, 66) = 18.42$, $p < .01$; deletion phoneme items, $F(1, 66) = 22.98$, $p < .01$; and phoneme counting task, $F(1, 66) = 6.72$, $p < .01$. The two measures of use of orthographic information also yielded significant group differences. Compared with normal children, dyslexic children had lower rates of over-shoot responses on digraph errors, $F(1, 66) = 6.24$, $p < .01$, and they made fewer single-letter deletion responses on digraph errors in the deletion task, $F(1, 37) = 4.37$, $p < .05$.

Dyslexic adults and Grade 3 children performed similarly on the syllable counting task and on the onset deletion items. However, on the two pho-neme segmentation tasks, the Grade 3 children performed better than the adult dyslexics. Grade 3 children made fewer deletion phoneme errors, $F(1, 39) = 11.78$, $p < .01$, and fewer phoneme counting errors on nondigraph items, $F(1, 39) = 5.93$, $p < .05$, than adult dyslexics. Also, the Grade 3 children made more orthographic type errors than did the dyslexics. On the phoneme counting task, they had proportionately more overshoot responses on digraph errors, $F(1, 36) = 7.61$, $p < .01$, and when they made errors on

Table 2 Dyslexics Compared With Normal Readers of Similar or Lower Reading Levels.

	Children				Adults			
	Normal (n = 37)		Dyslexic (n = 31)		Normal (n = 15)		Dyslexic (n = 26)	
Variable	M	SD	M	SD	M	SD	M	SD
Age	7.8	0.7	11.6	2.5	8.7	0.3	22.4	2.3
WRAT–R Reading								
Raw score	62	9	59	9	75	5	90	8
Grade level	2M		2M		5E		10E	
Percentile	63		6		83		30	
Syllable count errors (%)	15	15	25	19	13	10	16	15
Deletion: onset errors (%)	1	4	15	19	0	0	5	10
Deletion: phoneme errors (%)	28	18	53	25	18	14	35	17
Phoneme counting:								
nondigraph errors (%)	16	18	28	17	6	7	16	13
Orthographic errors								
Phoneme counting:								
overshoot responses (%)	79	33	59	34	99	4	77	30
Deletion: letter deletion (%)	42	47	16	32	53	51	10	24

Note: WRAT–R = Wide Range Achievement Test—Revised (Level I for children and Level II for adults); M = middle; E = end. Orthographic error scores represent the proportion of orthographic responses for errors on these items.

deletion digraph items, these were more likely than those of the adult dyslexics to involve deleting one of the letters of the digraph, $F(1, 15) = 6.50$, $p < .05$.

In summary, the results of the child and adult comparisons reveal that, in the case of larger sublexical units such as the syllable or the onset-rime distinction, adult dyslexics may eventually perform similarly to normal children. However, on phoneme awareness tasks, dyslexics never approximate levels of performance that are appropriate for their reading levels. Finally, both dyslexic children and dyslexic adults do not use orthographic information when performing phonological tasks to the same extent as normal children with equivalent or lower levels of word recognition skill.

Do dyslexics' phonological awareness skills change as a function of age and reading level?

Separate ANOVAs in which level of word recognition skill served as the independent variable were first carried out on the child and on the adult data. Separate analyses were carried out because of some overlap between word recognition scores of children and adults that would obscure or confound relationships among reading level, age, and phonological awareness scores. In each sample, the subjects were divided into three equal groups (low, middle, and high) on the basis of their WRAT–R reading scores. Table 3 presents the mean ages, WRAT–R scores, and phonological test scores for each of the six groups. Because reading group membership was highly correlated with age for the dyslexic children ($r = .69$), the results of the child analysis reflect the associations between age and reading level with phonological awareness. The results of the adult analyses reflect the association between reading level and phonological awareness only, because there was no significant correlation between group membership and age for the adults.

There were no significant effects of reading level for any of the phonological measures for both the children and the adults. Thus analyses of within-group variability reveal that phonological awareness skills do not change as a function of reading level or age for dyslexic children, or as a function of reading level for dyslexic adults. The results also suggest that, contrary to initial predictions, dyslexics' use of orthographic information when making phonological judgments does not increase as a function of word recognition skills.

The strongest evidence for an association between phonological awareness with age or reading skill involves direct comparisons between the dyslexic children and adults. However, because word recognition scores at the time of phonological awareness testing was a selection criterion for the children but not for the adults, it is possible that the two samples were not drawn from the same population. The following analyses of the childhood characteristics of the two samples were carried out to test this hypothesis.

The two groups were first diagnosed at the same clinic at the same ages (9 years and 8 months for the child sample and 9 years and 4 months for the adult sample). The IQ scores for the two groups as measured in childhood were also the same. The Verbal, Performance, and Full Scale WISC IQs of the dyslexic children were 99, 107, and 103, respectively. When tested in childhood, the scores for the adult dyslexics were 99, 109, and 103.

Of course, the best measure to assess comparability of the two groups involves a test of word recognition that was given to the two groups at approximately the same age. The adult sample was assessed in the early 1970s when the most common test given to all patients was the Durrell Analysis of Reading Difficulty (Durrell, 1955). However, this test was rarely given to the subjects in the child sample who were assessed in the late 1980s. Even when the test was given, the scores of the two groups cannot be compared because of a major revision of the Durrell test in the early 1980s. There were, however, 9 dyslexic adults who as children were given the WRAT–R Word Recognition subtest. Although this test has been renormed, the items have not changed over the time period. The average WRAT–R childhood raw score for these 9 subjects was 58, which was also the average score for the 36 subjects in the child sample. Furthermore, the range of scores was similar for these two groups. Thus a subsample (approximately

Table 3 Dyslexics' Phonological Awareness Performance as a Function of Reading Level.

| | Child dyslexics | | | | | | Adult dyslexics | | | | | |
| | Low (n = 12) | | Middle (n = 12) | | High (n = 12) | | Low (n = 13) | | Middle (n = 13) | | High (n = 13) | |
Variable	M	SD	M	SD	M	SD	M	SD	M	SD	M	SD
Age	9.5	1.8	10.8	1.1	13.7	2.3	22.0	1.1	22.0	2.2	22.8	2.4
WRAT–R Reading												
Raw score	47		56		68		66		83		96	
Range	41–51		52–59		61–77		40–77		78–90		91–108	
Grade level	2B		2E		4B		3E		8B		12	
Percentile	5		6		12		2		15		46	
Syllable count errors (%)	26	16	19	14	28	25	23	19	15	17	16	14
Deletion: onset errors (%)	29	37	21	24	8	16	10	28	4	9	6	11
Deletion: phoneme errors (%)	44	28	63	19	45	23	47	22	40	18	31	14
Phoneme counting: nondigraph errors (%)	31	16	33	14	22	18	22	14	17	14	14	14
Orthographic errors												
Phoneme counting: overshoot responses (%)	58	30	51	34	66	37	61	35	73	33	80	29
Deletion: letter deletion (%)	4	12	26	41	7	19	17	36	7	15	11	28

Note: WRAT–R = Wide Range Achievement Test—Revised (Level I for children and Level II for adults); B = beginning; E = end. Orthographic error scores represent the proportion of orthographic responses for errors on these items.

25%) of the adult dyslexic subjects in fact had the same reading scores as children as the total sample of the child dyslexic subjects. This finding, in addition to the results that the two groups had similar childhood IQ scores and similar ages at clinic entry, suggests that the adults and children were drawn from the same population.

Based on the assumption of sample comparability, two analyses were carried out to compare some of the subjects from the adult and child samples. The first analysis involved a comparison of the phonological awareness measures of the 9 adult dyslexics with childhood WRAT–R scores to 9 child dyslexics who were matched on the basis of these scores and the age at which the scores were obtained. Thus, in this analysis, children and adults were selected using the same criteria, both scored below the 30% on the WRAT–R when all subjects were of the same age. These data are presented in Table 4.

Although there were changes in reading scores from childhood to adulthood for the adult sample, $F(1, 17) = 51.14$, $p < .01$, and although at time of testing the adults' word recognition scores were superior to those of the children, $F(1, 17) = 21.59$, $p < .01$, there were no statistically significant differences between the two groups' performance on the phonological awareness measures (all $ps > .23$). This comparison between a subset of the child

Table 4 Comparison of Subset of Child and Adult Dyslexics.

Variable	Children (n = 9)		Adults (n = 9)	
	M	SD	M	SD
WRAT–R Reading (childhood scores)				
Raw score	58	11	58	11
Percentile	9		11	
Age of child WRAT–R Test	11.3		11.1	
WRAT–R Reading (adult scores)				
Raw score			81	10
Percentile			17	
Age of adult WRAT–R Test			21.4	
Syllable count errors (%)	22	11	13	19
Deletion: onset errors (%)	22	29	14	33
Deletion: phoneme errors (%)	46	25	46	26
Phoneme counting:				
nondigraph errors (%)	22	18	19	15
Orthographic errors				
Phoneme counting:				
overshoot responses (%)	69	35	75	35
Deletion: letter deletion (%)	15	22	15	33

Note: WRAT–R = Wide Range Achievement Test—Revised (Level I for children and Level II for adults).

dyslexics and a subset of the adult dyslexics (whose reading skills were equivalent to those of the child subset when they were the same age as the child subset but who, at the time of phonological awareness testing, were older and better readers than the children) reinforces the claim that phonological awareness skills do not show reliable developmental changes in dyslexics.

However, inspection of Table 3 suggests that there might be differences between some of the child and adult subsamples. To test this hypothesis, the scores of the two groups of best functioning adults (those who read above a Grade 7 level) were pooled (see Table 2 for means) and compared with those of the three groups of children by means of Dunnet t tests. To briefly summarize these comparisons, all groups of children performed similarly to the adults on the syllable counting task and on the orthographic measures. The highest functioning children performed similarly to the adults on all measures. The two lowest functioning groups of dyslexic children made more deletion onset errors and more phoneme counting errors than the adults. The latter result is the first and only piece of evidence that dyslexics' phoneme awareness skills may change as a function of reading skill and age.

Do normal readers' phonological awareness skills change as a function of age and reading level?

Analyses of variance were carried out on the phonological test battery using grade (Grade 1, Grade 2 vs. Grade 3) as the independent variable.[4] Planned comparisons were carried out to examine significant effects. Table 5 presents the mean ages, WRAT–R scores, and phonological test scores for each grade of normal readers. (Because of ceiling effects on the word recognition measures, the variability within the normal college sample was not examined, as it was for the adult dyslexics.) As can be seen, grade level is highly correlated with age ($r = .83$) and with WRAT–R reading scores ($r = .83$).

There were no significant effects of grade for syllable counting and for onset deletion items, both measures of large sublexical units. There were significant effects of grade for the phoneme items on the deletion task, $F(2, 40) = 3.63$, $p < .05$, with the Grade 3 children performing better than the Grade 2 and Grade 1 children. There was also a significant grade effect for the nondigraph items on the phoneme counting task, $F(2, 40) = 12.98$, $p < .01$; the Grade 1 children made significantly more errors than the Grade 2 and Grade 3 children. The children's use of orthographic information when performing phonological judgment tasks also increased as a function of grade, as shown by the increase in the number of overshoot responses made on digraph items in the phoneme counting task, $F(2, 40) = 6.47$, $p < .01$. Grade 1 children made fewer overshoot errors than Grade 2 and Grade 3 children, who did not differ. Although there was not a significant effect of grade for letter-deletion error responses on the deletion task,

Table 5 Normal Children's Phonological Awareness Performance as a Function of Grade Level.

Variable	Grade 1		Grade 2		Grade 3	
	M	SD	M	SD	M	SD
Age	7.2	0.3	7.8	0.5	8.7	0.3
WRAT–R Reading						
Raw score	54		65		75	
Range	46–74		54–73		65–85	
Grade level	2M		3E		5E	
Percentile	67		76		83	
Syllable count errors (%)	19	12	11	19	13	10
Deletion: onset errors (%)	2	7	0	0	0	0
Deletion: phoneme errors (%)	30	18	34	19	18	14
Phoneme counting:						
nondigraph errors (%)	31	20	10	13	6	7
Orthographic errors						
Phoneme counting:						
overshoot responses (%)	61	37	83	32	99	4
Deletion: letter deletion (%)	0	0	52	47	53	51

Note: WRAT–R = Wide Range Achievement Test—Revised (Level I for children and Level II for adults); M = middle; E = end. Orthographic error scores represent the proportion of orthographic responses for errors on these items.

$F(2, 17) = 2.86$, $p < .09$, planned comparisons revealed that Grade 1 children made fewer of these errors than Grade 2 and Grade 3 children, who did not differ.

Finally, the scores of the Grade 1, Grade 2, and Grade 3 children were compared to those of the normal college readers (shown in Table 1) to determine whether and at what point adult proficiency is attained in the early grade levels. Analyses of variance with the independent factor of grade (Grade 1, Grade 2, Grade 3, and college), were followed up by Dunnett *t* tests to compare each grade with the adults. To briefly summarize these results: (a) All groups performed similarly on the deletion onset items; (b) Grade 1 children differed from the adults on all other measures; (c) Grade 2 children differed from the adults on syllable counting and on deletion phoneme items; and (d) Grade 3 differed from the adults only on syllable counting. The fact that syllable counting differentiated the children from the adults may reflect a larger than anticipated memory component that is sensitive to age effects in normal readers.

In summary, for all tasks, except syllable counting and onset deletion, normal children's performance on phonological awareness tasks improved as a function of grade level. These increases occurred on the phoneme awareness tasks. By Grade 3, the children performed at the same level as normal college students.

Discussion

There are two major findings of this study. First, the results of the age-matched and reading-matched comparisons show that dyslexics do not acquire appropriate levels of phoneme awareness, regardless of their age or their reading levels, although some adults do eventually acquire appropriate levels of onset-rime awareness. Second, analyses of within-group variability indicate that dyslexics' phoneme awareness skills show little development as a function of age or reading level; however, dyslexics' awareness of onsets and rimes develops with reading skill. In contrast, good readers' phoneme awareness does increase as a function of reading skill, whereas onset awareness does not. The latter result reflects the fact that even the youngest children have mastered this skill.

According to some theoretical models, onset-rime awareness is a prerequisite reading skill, presumably one that dyslexics initially lack (e.g., Bradley & Bryant, 1983; Goswami & Bryant, 1990). In the present study, dyslexic children show poorer awareness of the onset-rime distinction than reading- or age-matched subjects. Consistent with some models that posit a bidirectional relationship between phonological awareness and reading skill (e.g., Morais, 1987), as reading skills improve, dyslexics eventually acquire appropriate levels of onset-rime awareness; dyslexic adults show ceiling effects (reflecting mastery) on onset items, similar to those shown by normal college readers. Also, in one dyslexic child–adult comparison, adults performed better than the poorest child readers on the onset measure.

Very different patterns of results are obtained for the two phoneme awareness tasks (phoneme counting–nondigraph items and deletion–phoneme items) in which dyslexics perform consistently more poorly than normal readers of the same age or reading levels. Even the best functioning adult dyslexics (who read above a Grade 7 level) perform more poorly than Grade 3 children, who were poorer readers and spellers than the adult dyslexics. These results are consistent with those of previous studies that have documented the failure of dyslexic children to achieve age- or reading-appropriate levels of phonological awareness (e.g., Bradley & Bryant, 1978; Bruck & Treiman, 1990; Pratt & Brady, 1988). The present study extends these findings; it demonstrates that as word recognition improves, dyslexics acquire appropriate levels of onset-rime awareness but show persisting phoneme awareness deficits. Furthermore, poor phoneme awareness does not reflect a developmental delay. That is, dyslexics do not acquire phoneme awareness at a slower rate than normal readers; at no point do they achieve appropriate age or reading levels of skill. Phoneme awareness deficits characterize dyslexics at all ages.

Within-group analyses suggest that phoneme awareness does not develop as a function of age or reading level for dyslexic children. There also seems to be little development of this skill between childhood and adulthood.

A subset of 9 adult dyslexics and 9 child dyslexics performed comparably on the phoneme awareness tasks. This analysis is conceptually powerful in that it equates for childhood severity of reading problems by matching the adults and children on childhood reading scores and age at which the scores were obtained. These results suggest that were the child dyslexics to be tested some 10 years later, their performance would be similar to that of the adults and essentially unchanged from their current performance. A second analysis that compared all of the child dyslexics with the 26 adults with reading levels above the Grade 7 level showed that on one of the two phoneme awareness tasks, the two lowest functioning groups of dyslexic children (all reading below a Grade 3 level) performed more poorly than the adults. Thus, this last result offers some suggestion of increase of phoneme awareness from childhood to adulthood.

This pattern of development is quite different from that seen in normal children. Not only do good readers' phoneme awareness skills increase as a function of reading skill, but also, after 2 and at the most 3 years of instruction, control children perform similarly to skilled adults. Although it is also true that the most skilled dyslexic children performed similarly to the most skilled dyslexic adults, all these dyslexics performed substantially below age or reading expected levels on the phonological awareness tasks.

What factors might account for these dramatic between-group differences in rates of development? One obvious factor is IQ. In the present study, the degree to which IQ underlies differences between normal and dyslexic readers' performance on the phonological awareness tasks cannot be assessed, because IQ data were not collected for the normal children. It is highly probable, given the results of many previous studies (see Wolford & Fowler, 1984, for a review), that there are IQ differences between the normals and dyslexics, and therefore the results of the present study may be confounded by between-group IQ differences. However, there are several reasons to question this assumption. First, IQ scores of dyslexic children may be the consequences of reading disabilities and not the causes of phonological awareness deficits (see Stanovich, 1988). Second, results of previous studies show that IQ does not significantly correlate with the phonological measures (see Stanovich, 1988, for a review). In the case of the present study, the full-scale IQ scores of the dyslexic children did not correlate significantly with any of the dependent variables. Thus even if the normal and dyslexic readers in this study do differ in terms of IQ, it appears that this measure is unrelated to performance on the phonological awareness tests and would not account for dyslexics' persistent phonological awareness deficits.

More plausible explanations for dyslexics' persisting phonological awareness deficits are suggested by a consideration of their performance on the two measures of overshoot errors and letter deletion errors, which reflected the extent to which orthographic information is used when making phonological awareness judgments. First, for all analyses, dyslexics did not use orthographic information to the same extent as normal readers. Even Grade 3 children used orthographic information to a greater extent than high-functioning adult dyslexics. Second, although the use of orthographic information increased in good readers as a function of word recognition skill, this association was not obtained for the dyslexics.

These results suggest that dyslexics do not appropriately use orthographic information when making phonological awareness judgments. This poor strategy may be one factor contributing to dyslexics' poor performance on phonological awareness tasks. As noted earlier, some researchers argue that the relationship between phonological awareness and the acquisition of literacy in an alphabetic language is bidirectional (e.g., Goswami & Bryant, 1990; Perfetti *et al.*, 1987). In the case of normal development, children must have critical levels of awareness of certain sublexical components of words (e.g., onset rime) in order to learn an alphabetic script. As a result of learning the alphabetic principle (i.e., the learning of spelling–sound correspondences), children's awareness of phonemes develops, and this further promotes the growth of reading skills. The data from the orthographic tasks show that in fact good readers do use their knowledge of the correspondences between spellings and sounds when making phonological awareness judgments, and this strategy increases with word recognition skills. For example, they incorrectly report that the orally presented nonword *deem* has four sounds, presumably because the spoken stimulus automatically invokes an abstract orthographic representation that reflects the child's knowledge of the associations between phonemes and graphemes. This suggests that in most circumstances, when the number of phonemes equals the number of letters (as in the nondigraph phoneme counting items), normal readers' phoneme awareness is facilitated by the automatic activation of orthographic information. Dyslexics' poor use of orthographic information thus limits their insights into the phonemic structure of the language.

The issue that now arises concerns the basis for dyslexics' poor use of orthographic information. Does it reflect a knowledge deficit or a process deficit? According to the knowledge deficit position, dyslexics do not use orthographic information when making phonological judgments because they have poor knowledge of the associations between sounds and spellings. For example, when asked to say what is left when the first sound of *thoace* is removed, because of poor knowledge of the correspondences between the phoneme /θ/ and the grapheme /th/, dyslexics rarely give the response of *hoace*. That is, inadequate spelling–sound knowledge impedes the activation of appropriate orthographic information. This hypothesis is consistent with the findings that at all ages and reading levels, dyslexics show deficits in knowledge of spelling–sound correspondences (see Olson *et al.*, 1990, for a review). According to the processdeficit explanation, dyslexics have the requisite knowledge about sound–spelling information, but they do not automatically use this information when making phonological awareness judgments. That is, there is an independence between orthographic and phonological codes.

Some evidence is presented to address these arguments. However, it should be noted that the evidence is indirect and is most pertinent to the interpretation of the performance of the dyslexic adults. Because the adult dyslexics performed better than the Grade 3 children on a test of written spelling (WRAT–R), which is a reflection of the quality of orthographic representations (e.g., Perfetti, 1992), it might be argued that the prominent differences between dyslexic adults and normal children on overshoot responses and letter deletion responses cannot reflect these adults' poorer orthographic representations.[5] If use of orthographic information on phonological tasks reflected spelling skill, one would expect that these two measures would be highly correlated. In fact, this was the case for the normal children ($r = .50$ and $r = .44$ for spelling score with percentage overshoot errors and percentage deleted letter errors, respectively), but these correlations were not significant for the adult dyslexics.

Perhaps the WRAT–R spelling test was not a good measure of knowledge, and a more direct measure of spelling–sound correspondences would correlate with use of orthographic information. As part of another study on the word recognition skills of adult dyslexics, these same adults were given a nonword reading test, which is a measure of knowledge of spelling–sound correspondences (see Bruck, 1990). Relative to agematched and reading-matched control subjects, these adult dyslexics performed very poorly on a nonword task (see Bruck, 1990). Nevertheless, there was much variation in their error rates (15%–75%). For the purposes of this article, the correlation between nonword performance and performance on the orthographic tasks was computed to determine if dyslexics with better knowledge of spelling–sound correspondences were more likely to use orthographic information when making phonological awareness judgments. None of these correlations were significant. Although it could still be argued that no relationships were detected because spelling–sound knowledge was so poor for all subjects that it failed to activate orthographic information, the process deficit position provides an alternative hypothesis. Even when adult dyslexics have the requisite knowledge, they do not automatically activate available orthographic codes for phonological tasks.

Even if one accepts a process-deficit explanation for the adult dyslexics, it is still possible that the dyslexic children's poor performance on orthographic measures reflected a knowledge deficit. That is, even though the poorest functioning dyslexic children and the highest functioning dyslexic adults showed similar levels of performance on the orthographic measures, different mechanisms may underlie the performance of each group. Given the lack of spelling and nonword data on the children, this claim cannot be verified.

Whatever the final outcome of this debate, the data concerning the relationship of the use of orthographic and phonological codes in dyslexics are inconsistent with Campbell and Butterworth's (1985) results, which are based on an examination of one subject who showed an interesting but perhaps atypical constellation of component reading skills. Their measure was similar to "overshoot responses on digraph errors" used in the present study. Certainly, on this measure, none of the dyslexics in this study showed greater than expected reliance on orthographic information. The present results are similar in some respects to those reported by Zecker (1991), who found that younger dyslexics did not use orthographic information to the same extent as normal readers. However, with age, dyslexics showed age-appropriate patterns of performance. The different results may reflect the use of different types of tasks. The rhyme judgment task, used by Zecker, may involve more automatic forms of information activation, whereas the tasks used in the present study may require more deliberate use of available information. If this is correct, then it does suggest that differences between older dyslexics and normals on the orthographic tasks do reflect process deficits.

In summary, dyslexic children between the ages of 8 and 16 years not only show deficits in phoneme awareness when compared with good readers of the same age and reading level, but they also show little if any development of phoneme awareness as their reading skills increase. Similar patterns of results are found for adult dyslexics. Further analyses of the data suggested that this arrest in development is associated with the failure to use orthographic information when making phonological judgments. Although the exact explanation for this result requires further study, it is clear that current theoretical models that posit a bidirectional relationship between word recognition and phoneme awareness do not account for the performance of dyslexics, although they do account for the performance of good readers. That is, for the normal children, it is clear that awareness of onset-rime units are acquired very early; however, phoneme awareness develops as a function of word recognition skills. Furthermore, the development of phoneme awareness is associated with increases in the use of orthographic information when making phonological judgments. For the dyslexics, it appears that word recognition skill facilitates awareness of onset-rime units, but it has much less if any impact on the development of phoneme awareness and on the use of orthographic information. However, these data may be consistent with a more general model of the relationship between phonological awareness and word recognition by suggesting that initially dyslexic children encounter much difficulty in learning to read because of pervasively deficient phonological awareness skills. When they eventually acquire word recognition skills, there is little interaction between orthographic and phonological codes. As a result, phoneme awareness skills are not promoted and thus word recognition skills remain relatively weak.

These data contribute to an increasing literature on the phonological deficits of dyslexics and show that persisting phonological awareness deficits of dyslexics remain a crucial stumbling block for the acquisition of fluent word recognition skills throughout their life span.

Notes

This research was supported by a National Health and Welfare Scholar Award, by Grant 0GP000A1181 from the Natural Sciences and Engineering Research Council, and by Grant EQ4245 from Fonds pour la Formation de Chercheurs et l'Aide a la Recherche. Melanie Barwick, Alison Phinney, Alison Kulak, and Donna Higham assisted with the collection of these data.

1 The rime is obligatory and consists of the vowel and any consonant(s) that comes after it. The onset consists of any consonant(s) preceding the vowel. For example, for the one-syllable word *clasp*, the onset is *cl* and the rime is *asp*. The onset consists of two phonemes and the rime consists of three phonemes.
2 Adults received Level II of the WRAT–R, whereas all the children received Level I. According to the manual, the scores of the two forms can be directly compared by subtracting 31 from the Level II Reading scores (Jastak & Wilkinson, 1984). These adjusted means are presented in the tables of the article.
3 The analyses of the orthographic errors only include subjects who made errors on these items. Thus the degrees of freedom for these analyses may differ from those of the analyses of the phonological awareness tests.
4 The analyses were repeated by using reading level as the dependent variable. Based on their WRAT–R reading scores, the children were divided into three groups. These results were identical to those based on grade. Therefore, only those based on grade—the more natural grouping that reflected subject selection procedures—are reported.
5 It is possible that adult dyslexics did not know the conventional spellings of the nonwords. In this case, one could argue that they did not show use of orthographic information, because they did not have the information. Because the subjects were not asked to spell the stimuli used in the phonological awareness tests, one cannot directly test this hypothesis. However, given the fact that they were spelling at the Grade 6 level, one assumes that they knew the spelling patterns of these very simple words.

References

Adams, M. J. (1990). *Beginning to read: Thinking and learning about print.* Cambridge, MA: MIT Press.
Backman, J., Mamen, M., & Ferguson, H. B. (1984). Reading level design: Conceptual and methodological issues in reading research. *Psychological Bulletin, 96*, 560–568.
Bowey, J., & Francis, J. (1991). Phonological analysis as a function of age and exposure to reading instruction. *Applied Psycholinguistics, 12*, 91–122.
Bradley, L., & Bryant, P. (1978). Difficulties in auditory organization as a possible cause of reading backwardness. *Nature, 271*, 746–747.
Bradley, L., & Bryant, P. (1983). Categorizing sounds and learning to read—A causal connection. *Nature, 310*, 419–421.

Bruck, M. (1985). The adult functioning of children with specific learning disabilities. In I. Sigel (Ed.), *Advances in applied developmental psychology* (pp. 91–129). Norwood, NJ: Ablex.

Bruck, M. (1988). The word recognition and spelling of dyslexic children. *Reading Research Quarterly, 23*, 51–69.

Bruck, M. (1990). Word recognition skills of adults with childhood diagnoses of dyslexia. *Developmental Psychology, 26*, 439–454.

Bruck, M., & Treiman, R. (1990). Phonological awareness and spelling in normal children and dyslexics: The case of initial consonant clusters. *Journal of Experimental Child Psychology, 50*, 156–178.

Byrne, B., & Ledez, J. (1983). Phonological awareness in reading-disabled adults. *Australian Journal of Psychology, 35*, 185–197.

Calfee, R., Lindamood, P., & Lindamood, C. (1973). Acoustic–phonetic skills and reading: Kindergarten through twelfth grade. *Journal of Educational Psychology, 64*, 293–298.

Campbell, R., & Butterworth, B. (1985). Phonological dyslexia and dysgraphia in a highly literate subject: A developmental case with associated deficits of phonemic processing and awareness. *The Quarterly Journal of Experimental Psychology, 37A*, 435–475.

Durrell, D. (1955). *The Durrell Analysis of Reading Difficulty*. New York: Harcourt, Brace & World.

Ehri, L. C., & Wilce, L. S. (1980). The influence of orthography on reader's conceptualization of the phonemic structure of words. *Applied Psycholinguistics, 1*, 371–385.

Forell, E., & Hood, J. (1986). A longitudinal study of two groups of children with early reading problems. *Annals of Dyslexia, 35*, 97–116.

Fox, B., & Routh, D. (1983). Reading disability, phonemic analysis, and dysphonetic spelling: A follow-up study. *Journal of Clinical Child Psychology, 12*, 28–32.

Goswami, U., & Bryant, P. (1990). *Phonological skills and learning to read*. Hillsdale, NJ: Erlbaum.

Jastak, S., & Wilkinson, G. (1984). *The Wide Range Achievement Test—Revised*. Wilmington, DE: Jastak Associates.

Juel, C. (1988). Learning to read and write: A longitudinal study of 54 children from first through fourth grades. *Journal of Educational Psychology, 80*, 437–447.

Labuda, M., & DeFries, J. C. (1988). Cognitive abilities in children with reading disabilities and controls: A follow-up study. *Journal of Learning Disabilities, 21*, 562–566.

Lefy, D., & Pennington, B. (1991). Spelling errors and reading fluency in compensated adult dyslexics. *Annals of Dyslexia, 41*, 143–162.

Liberman, I. Y., Rubin, H., Duques, S., & Carlisle, J. (1985). Linguistic abilities and spelling proficiency in kindergarten and adult poor spellers. In D. Gray & J. Kavanagh (Eds.), *Biobehavioral measures of dyslexia* (pp. 163–176). Parkton, MD: York Press.

Liberman, I. Y., Shankweiler, D., Fischer, F. W., & Carter, B. (1974). Explicit syllable and phoneme segmentation in the young child. *Journal of Experimental Child Psychology, 18*, 201–202.

Lundberg, I. (1987). Are letters necessary for the development of phonemic awareness? *European Bulletin of Cognitive Psychology, 5*, 472–475.

Manis, F., & Custodio, R. (1991, April). *Development of spelling–sound and ortho-graphic knowledge: A two-year follow-up of dyslexic children.* Paper presented at the meeting of the Society for Research on Child Development, Seattle, WA.

Manis, F. R., Szeszulski, P., Holt, L., & Graves, K. (1988). A developmental perspective on dyslexic subtypes. *Annals of Dyslexia, 37*, 139–153.

Morais, J. (1987). Segmental analysis of speech and its relation to reading ability. *Annals of Dyslexia, 37*, 126–141.

Olson, R., Wise, B., Connors, F., & Rack, J. (1990). Organization, heritability, and remediation of component word recognition and language skills in disabled readers. In T. Carr & B. A. Levy (Eds.), *Reading and its development: Component skills approaches* (pp. 261–322). San Diego, CA: Academic Press.

Pearson, L., & Barron, R. (1989, March). *Orthography influences beginning readers' auditory rhyme judgments.* Paper presented at the American Education Research Association meeting, San Francisco.

Perfetti, C. A. (1992). The representation problem in reading acquisition. In P. Gough, L. Ehrl, & R. Treiman (Eds.), *Reading acquisition* (pp. 145–174). Hillsdale, NJ: Erlbaum.

Perfetti, C. A., Beck, L., Bell, L., & Hughes, C. (1987). Phonemic knowledge and learning to read are reciprocal: A longitudinal study of first grade children. *Merrill-Palmer Quarterly, 33*, 283–319.

Pratt, A. C., & Brady, S. (1988). Relation of phonological awareness to reading disability in children and adults. *Journal of Educational Psychology, 80*, 319–323.

Read, R., & Ruyter, L. (1985). Reading and spelling skills in adults of low literacy. *Remedial and Special Education, 6*, 43–52.

Scarborough, H. (1984). Continuity between childhood dyslexia and adult reading. *British Journal of Psychology, 75*, 329–348.

Seidenberg, M. S., & Tanenhaus, M. K. (1979). Orthographic effects on rhyme monitoring. *Journal of Experimental Psychology: Human Learning and Memory, 5*, 546–554.

Share, D. L., Jorm, A. F., Maclean, R., & Matthews, R. (1984). Sources of individual differences in reading acquisition. *Journal of Educational Psychology, 76*, 1309–1324.

Stanovich, K. E. (1988). The right and wrong places to look for the cognitive locus of reading disability. *Annals of Dyslexia, 38*, 154–177.

Stanovich, K. (1992). Speculations on the causes and consequences of individual differences in early reading acquisition. In P. Gough, L. Ehri, & R. Treiman (Eds.), *Reading acquisition* (pp. 307–342). Hillsdale, NJ: Erlbaum.

Stanovich, K. E., Cunningham, A. E., & Cramer, B. (1984). Assessing phonological awareness in kindergarten children: Issues of task comparability. *Journal of Experimental Child Psychology, 38*, 175–190.

Treiman, R., & Zukowski, A. (1991). Children's awareness of syllables, onsets, rimes, and phonemes. In S. Brady & D. Shankweiler (Eds.), *Phonological processes in literacy* (pp. 67–83). Hillsdale, NJ: Erlbaum.

Tunmer, W. E., & Nesdale, A. R. (1982). The effects of digraphs and pseudowords on phonemic segmentation in young children. *Applied Psycholinguistics, 3*, 299–311.

Wagner, R., & Torgesen, J. (1987). The nature of phonological processing and its causal role in the acquisition of reading skills. *Psychological Bulletin, 101*, 192–212.

Waters, G., & Seidenberg, M. (1983, April). *Orthographic and phonological code activation in auditory and visual word recognition in good and poor readers.* Paper presented at the meeting of the American Educational Research Association, Montreal, Quebec, Canada.

Wechsler, D. (1949). *Wechsler Intelligence Scale for Children.* New York: Psychological Corporation.

Wechsler, D. (1974). *Wechsler Intelligence Scale for Children—Revised.* New York: Psychological Corporation.

Wolford, G., & Fowler, C. (1984). Differential use of partial information by good and poor readers. *Developmental Review, 4,* 16–35.

Zecker, S. (1991). The orthographic code: Developmental trends in reading-disabled and normally achieving children. *Annals of Dyslexia, 41,* 178–192.

127

DOES DYSLEXIA EXIST?

Keith E. Stanovich

Source: *Journal of Child Psychology and Psychiatry*, 35, 1994: 579–595.

Introduction

Obviously, in order to answer the question posed in the title, we must specify what we mean by the term dyslexia. And, in doing so, we immediately encounter the crux of the problem. This problem is a recurring one in the field of developmental disabilities, and it arises because the field has repeatedly displayed a preference for terminology that connotes unverified theories about causation. For example, in this journal Bishop (1992) has recently noted how the terms developmental dysphasia and developmental aphasia have "fallen into disfavour in the U.K. and U.S.A., largely because they misleadingly imply that we are dealing with a single condition with a known neurological basis" (p. 3). Likewise, the term dyslexia is out of favor in many educational and research communities within North America—and for similar reasons. As we shall see, "dyslexia" carries with it so many empirically unverified connotations and assumptions that many researchers and practitioners prefer to avoid the term.

Indeed, it does seem that reading research could benefit from adopting more neutral terms for the phenomena that it studies. Terminology that is less likely to carry with it a speculative theory is to be preferred in the early stages of scientific investigation. The reading field seems unnaturally prone to popularizing terminology that carries with it unproven theory. For example, publications in early literacy research in North America are currently littered with the terms "emergent literacy" and "invented spelling". But, just as with "dyslexia", these are not neutral terms. They are not descriptions of certain operationally-defined performance patterns in early literacy. These terms convey a theory of early literacy acquisition (e.g. that it is natural and will normally progress without much formal tuition) that is without empirical support (Adams, 1990; Liberman & Liberman, 1990; Perfetti, 1991). The theory carried with the term "dyslexia" seems similarly to have outrun the evidence.

451

With these strictures in mind, we will begin our discussion at the beginning. Whether or not there is such a thing as "dyslexia", there most certainly
are children who read markedly below their peers on appropriately comprehensive and standardized tests. In this most prosaic sense, poor readers
obviously exist. Controversy begins only when we address the question of
whether, within this group of poor readers, there are groups of children who
are "different". Terms like congenital word-blindness and dyslexia were
coined to describe groups of children who were thought to be different from
other poor readers in their etiology, neurological makeup, and cognitive
characteristics. From the very beginning of research on reading disability,
it was assumed that poor readers who were of high intelligence formed a
cognitively and neurologically different group. Investigators who pioneered
the study of the condition then known as congenital word-blindness were at
pains to differentiate children with this condition from other poor readers.
Hinshelwood (1917) stated clearly that he intended the term congenital
word-blindness not for all poor readers but instead for those who were high
functioning in other cognitive domains:

> When I see it stated that congenital word-blindness may be com-
> bined with any amount of other mental defects from mere dullness
> to low-grade mental defects, imbecility or idiocy, I can understand
> how confusion has arisen from the loose application of the term
> congenital word-blindness to all conditions in which there is defec-
> tive development of the visual memory center, quite independently
> of any consideration as to whether it is a strictly local defect or
> only a symptom of a general cerebral degeneration. It is a great
> injustice to the children affected with the pure type of congenital
> word-blindness, a strictly local affection, to be placed in the
> same category as others suffering from generalized cerebral defects,
> as the former can be successfully dealt with, while the latter are
> practically irremediable.
>
> (pp. 93–94)

Similarly, the term dyslexia has often been reserved for children displaying discrepancies between intelligence and reading ability. In the 1970s and
1980s, proponents of the generic term learning disabilities—coined largely
as a school service-delivery category (Kirk, 1963; Lerner, 1985)—continued
the tradition of assuming that there were important etiological, neurological and cognitive differences between high-IQ and low-IQ poor readers,
despite the fact that there existed no more evidence for this assumption in
1970 than there was in Hinshelwood's day.
    One might have thought that researchers would have begun with the
broadest and most theoretically neutral definition of reading disability—
reading performance below some specified level on some well-known and

psychometrically sound test—and then proceeded to investigate whether there were poor readers with differing cognitive profiles *within* this broader group. Unfortunately, the history of reading disabilities research does not resemble this logical sequence. Instead, early definitions of reading disability *assumed* knowledge of differential cognitive profile (and causation) within the larger sample of poor readers and defined the condition of reading disability in a way that actually served to preclude empirical investigation of the unproven theoretical assumptions that guided the formulation of these definitions!

This remarkable sleight-of-hand was achieved by tying the definition of reading disability to the notion of aptitude/achievement discrepancy (Reynolds, 1985; Shepard, 1980; Siegel, 1989; Stanovich, 1991). That is, it was assumed that poor readers of high aptitude—as indicated by IQ test performance—were cognitively different from poor readers of low aptitude and that they had a different etiology. The term dyslexia, or reading disability, was reserved for those children showing significant discrepancies between reading ability and intelligence test performance. Such discrepancy definitions have become embedded in the legal statutes governing special education practice in many states of the United States (Frankenberger & Fronzaglio, 1991; Frankenberger & Harper, 1987) and they also determine the subject election procedures in most research investigations (Stanovich, 1991). The critical assumption that was reified in these definitions—in almost total absence of empirical evidence—was that degree of discrepancy from IQ was meaningful: that the reading difficulties of the reading-disabled child with reading-IQ discrepancy (termed specific reading retardation in the classic investigation of Rutter & Yule, 1975) were etiologically and neurologically distinct from those characterizing the reading-disabled child without IQ discrepancy (termed general reading backwardness in the Rutter & Yule, 1975 study).

Quite early in the history of research on dyslexia, researchers adopted a strong theoretical bias by tying an intuition about differential causation so closely to the notion aptitude/achievement discrepancy (see Pennington, Gilger, Olson & DeFries, 1992; Taylor & Schatschneider, 1992). It was simply assumed that reading difficulty unaccompanied by low IQ was a distinct entity from other reading problems. It was not until the mid-1970s that we had the data from the ground-breaking epidemiological comparison of poor readers with and without reading-IQ discrepancy conducted by Rutter and Yule (1975), and only in the past decade has their data been supplemented by that from other investigations of a similar type.

From a total sample of 2300 9-year-old children, Rutter and Yule (1975; Rutter, 1978) defined two groups of poor readers who were equal in reading achievement (each approximately 33 months below the general population mean). However, the mean IQ of the specific reading retardation group (102.5) was significantly higher than that of the reading backwardness group (80). Rutter and Yule (1975) reported some significant differences between the two groups, but also several similarities. The specific reading retardation group was less likely to have organic brain damage or to display various neurological abnormalities. The backward group was more likely to display a variety of motor abnormalities and to show left/right confusion. The groups had similar proportions of family members with histories of reading difficulties and similar histories of delays in language development. Rutter and Yule were careful to point to the fact that many aspects of the classic "dyslexic syndrome" were *not* found disproportionately in their specific reading retardation group (e.g. left/right confusion, neurological signs, directional confusion and familial linkage, see also Taylor, Satz & Friel, 1979).

Some of the differences that were uncovered in the Isle of Wight studies have been difficult to replicate. For example, the data on differential prognosis for reading are contradictory. Rutter and Yule (1975) found differential growth curves for the specifically disabled and the general retardation groups. The latter displayed greater growth in reading but less growth in arithmetic ability than the specifically disabled children. However, this finding of differential reading growth rates has failed to be replicated in some other studies (Bruck, 1988; Labuda & DeFries, 1989; McKinney, 1987; Share, McGee, McKenzie, Williams & Silva, 1987; van der Wissel & Zegers, 1985).

Are there distinct etiologies for some cases of reading disability?

Nevertheless, as Pennington *et al.* (1992) argue, the issue of "whether RD is just the lower tail of the multifactorially determined, normal distribution of reading skill, or whether some cases of RD represent an etiologically distinct disorder" (p. 562) is separable from the issue of whether there are differences between poor readers with and without reading-IQ discrepancy. We must ask first whether there is evidence that some children within the entire group of poor readers display evidence for a distinct etiology. At that point, we are in a position to address the question of whether poor readers *with* reading-IQ discrepancy children happen to *be* those with a distinct etiology. As Pennington *et al.* (1992) note, "If no cases of RD represent an etiologically distinct disorder or syndrome, then it is pointless to argue about how to define a syndrome that does not exist!" (pp. 562–563).

The issue of a distinct etiology for some cases of reading difficulty is, in fact, a confusing one. Much attention has focused on the issue of whether there is a statistically discernible "hump" in the lower tail of the distribution of reading ability. Some studies have found evidence for such a hump (Rutter & Yule, 1975; Stevenson, 1988), but others have not (Rodgers, 1983; Shaywitz, Escobar, Shaywitz, Fletcher & Makugh, 1992). Resolving the "hump issue", however, will not give the definitive answer to the distinct etiology question because, even if such a hump is not found "a few etiologically distinct factors, plus noise, can give rise to a normal phenotypic distribution" (Pennington *et al.*, 1992, p. 563).

Genetic epidemiology provides a sounder basis for establishing distinct causation for some cases of reading disability. Here the evidence is more definitive. In several examples, Pennington *et al.* (1991) found evidence for sex limited, autosomal additive or dominant transmission of reading disability, although there is evidence for genetic heterogeneity (see Pennington, 1990; Smith, Kimberling & Pennington, 1991; Stevenson, 1992a). Twin studies have also consistently indicated a moderate heritability for the group deficit in reading ability displayed by the twin probands—as well as significant genetic covariance between the group deficit and phonological coding and awareness skills (DeFries, Fulker & LaBuda, 1987; Olson, Wise, Conners, Rack & Fulker, 1989; Pennington *et al.* 1992; Stevenson, 1992a, 1992b). Pennington, Van Orden, Kirson and Haith (1991) summarize the evidence: "These behavior genetic analyses are consistent with the view that the heritable component in dyslexia at the written language level is in phonological coding and the heritable precursor to this deficit in phonological coding is a deficit in phoneme awareness" (p. 183).

Further evidence that reading disability might have distinct etiology comes from neuroanatomical studies (see Hynd, Marshall & Gonzalez, 1991, and Hynd, Marshall & Semrud-Clikeman, 1991 for reviews). For example, both post mortem and *in vivo* studies have indicated that atypical symmetry in the planum temporale is associated with reading disability (Galaburda, 1991; Galaburda, Sherman, Rosen, Aboitz & Geschwind, 1985; Larsen, Hoien, Lundberg & Odegaard, 1990; Steinmetz & Galaburda, 1991). Larsen *et al.* (1990) found that the atypical symmetry was directly associated with the phonological coding deficit that is the primary phenotypic indicator of reading disability (see below). Additional cortical anomalies have been identified in other studies (see Hynd, Marshall & Gonzalez, 1991; Semrud-Clikeman, Hynd, Novey & Eliopulos, 1991).

Does discrepancy measurement identify poor readers with a distinct etiology?

Thus, there is some support for a distinct etiology for at least some cases of reading disability. Reading difficulty appears to be moderately heritable. At least some cases of reading difficulty appear to be genetically transmitted in an autosomal dominant pattern. Some cases also appear to be associated with distinct neuroanatomical anomalies. All of these findings provide a foundation for a principled concept of dyslexia, but they are not—in and of themselves—enough to justify current definitional practice. There is still one critical link missing in the chain of evidence. The phenotypic performance pattern that defines the concept of dyslexia must be reliably and specifically linked with these indicators of distinct etiology. As discussed in the introduction, both research and educationally-based definitions of dyslexia have incorporated the notion of reading-IQ discrepancy (Stanovich, 1991). This practice arose because of the intuition that children with reading-IQ discrepancies would be more likely to display a distinct etiology. Thus, identifying reading-IQ discrepancies was viewed as an easy way of selecting those children characterized by this distinct etiology. The basic assumption was that there were fundamental etiological, neurological and (reading-related) cognitive differences between poor readers with and without IQ-reading discrepancy. It is this assumption that is presently without empirical support.

Reading disabled children display a characteristic profile of cognitive skills (to be discussed below); reading disability displays moderate heritability; evidence of a number of different modes of genetic transmission has been found (Pennington, 1990; Stevenson, 1992a); and some reading disabled children display atypical neuroanatomical features. However, the problem is that there is not one bit of evidence indicating that these characteristics are more true of poor readers with IQ-reading discrepancy than of poor readers without such discrepancies.

For example, genetic linkage studies have usually employed a discrepancy criterion in defining cases of reading disability. However, we have no knowledge of whether similar evidence of genetic linkage would be found if reading disability were defined without reference to discrepancy in such studies. Likewise, no extant study has systematically related the neuroanatomical correlates of reading disability to degree of reading-IQ discrepancy. There is again no evidence in the literature indicating that similar relationships between neuroanatomical features such as symmetry of the planum temporale and reading disability would not be found if reading disability were defined without reference to IQ-reading discrepancy. For instance, the Larsen *et al.* (1990) study of planum temporale symmetry defined reading-IQ discrepancy in their sample using the Raven Matrices test. The use of a nonverbal test which displays very low correlations with reading and other verbal skills (Stanovich, Cunningham & Feeman, 1984) might well have resulted in a sample containing several subjects with depressed verbal IQs and/or below average full scale IQs (Stanovich, 1991; Stanovich, Nathan & Vala-Rossi, 1986). Such subjects might well have been classified as nondiscrepant, or "garden-variety" poor readers (see Gough & Tunmer, 1986, and Stanovich, 1988, 1991) had other verbally-loaded aptitude measures been used in discrepancy assessment (see Stanovich, 1991, for an extensive discussion of the implications of using different aptitude benchmarks). Thus, this particular study might well be providing indirect evidence *against* the hypothesis that these atypical symmetries are unique to poor readers with reading-IQ discrepancy and would not be found in poor readers without such discrepancies. Further negative evidence comes from the finding that neurological disorders are no more common among poor readers with reading-IQ discrepancies. If anything, the opposite appears to be the case (Ingram, Mason & Blackburn, 1970; Ruter & Yule, 1975; Silva, McGee, Williams, 1985).

The issue of differential etiology for children with reading delays that are, or are not, discrepant with IQ has been directly addressed in twin studies of genetic influence. Olson, Rack, Conners, DeFries and Fulker (1991) did find that the heritability of the group deficit of high-IQ (full scale) reading disabled twins (.67) was higher than the heritability of the group deficit for low-IQ reading disabled twins (.40), but this difference was not statistically significant. A parallel analysis based on verbal IQ rather than full-scale IQ revealed heritability values of .59 and .49, a difference that was again not statistically significant. Pennington *et al.* (1992) defined two groups of reading disabled children: one using a reading/IQ regression equation and the other using an age-only discrepancy. The group heritability for low scores on the IQ-discrepancy criterion was .46 and the group heritability for low scores on the age-discrepancy criterion was .49. The authors concluded that "These values indicate that approximately 50% of the deficit in scores for both diagnostic continua is due to heritable factors. The similarity in values suggests that the estimated proportion of genetic variance contributing to RD is essentially the same, regardless of the manner in which RD is identified. Thus, there is no evidence here for differential external validity of the two phenotypes" (p. 567). Pennington *et al.* (1992) also found that the genetic covariance between phonological coding ability and the IQ-discrepancy diagnosis (.60) was slightly higher than the corresponding covariance for phonological coding and the age-discrepancy criterion (.47), but this difference was not significant. The investigators concluded that "The heritability analyses are primarily consistent with the hypothesis that the same genes influence each diagnostic phenotype" (Pennington *et al.*, 1992, p. 570).

Other investigations have also failed to provide strong evidence for markedly different heritability of deficits among high- and low-IQ reading-disabled children who are reading at the same level (Stevenson, 1991, 1992b; Stevenson, Graham, Fredman & McLoughlin, 1987). Stevenson (1991) did find that the heritability of a group deficit in spelling ability tended to be greater for spelling scores residualized on IQ than for raw spelling scores, but this tendency was not present in most of his measures of reading ability. Taken collectively, the findings from all of these studies "do not refute a possible biological basis for reading disability—only the hypothesis that the biological basis is different for children who meet IQ-based discrepancies" (Fletcher, 1992, p. 547).

IQ-discrepancy and the reading disability phenotype

In summary, although genetic and neuroanatomical studies may be narrowing in on a syndrome of dyslexia, that syndrome does not seem to be strongly correlated with degree of IQ-discrepancy in the reading-disabled population.

It is really not so surprising that genetic and neuroanatomical correlates have not been found to be differentially associated with the presence or absence of a reading-IQ discrepancy. This is because IQ-discrepancy appears to be at best weakly correlated with the primary phenotypic indicators of reading disability. What are those indicators?

Although there may be small groups of children who have specific comprehension difficulties (Oakhill & Garnham, 1988), there is a great deal of converging evidence indicating that most cases of reading disability arise because of difficulties in the process of word recognition (e.g. Bruck, 1988, 1990; Morrison, 1991; Perfetti, 1985; Siegel, 1985; Siegel & Faux, 1989; Siegel & Ryan, 1989; Snowling, 1991; Stanovich, 1981, 1986, 1988). These difficulties are, in turn, due to deficiencies in processes of phonological coding whereby letter patterns are transformed into phonological codes. Problems with phonological coding lead to the most diagnostic symptom of reading disability: difficulty in pronouncing pseudowords (e.g. Bruck, 1988, 1990; Felton & Wood, 1992; Manis, Custodio & Szeszulski, 1993; Olson et al. 1989; Siegel, 1989; Siegel & Ryan, 1988; Snowling, 1981, 1991). In contrast to phonological coding, processes of orthographic coding—where words are recognized via direct visual access—appear to be relatively less impaired in disabled readers (Frith & Snowling, 1983; Holligan & Johnston, 1988; Olson, Kliegl, Davidson & Foltz, 1985; Olson et al. 1989; Pennington et al. 1986; Rack, 1985; Siegel, 1993; Stanovich & Siegel, 1994; Snowling, 1980).

The precursor to the phonological coding difficulty appears to be a deficit in segmental language skills sometimes termed phonological awareness or phonological sensitivity (e.g. Bentin, 1992; Bowey, Cain & Ryan, 1992; Bradley & Bryant, 1978, 1985; Bruck, 1990, 1992; Bruck & Treiman, 1990; Bryant, Maclean, Bradley & Crossland, 1990; Goswami & Bryant 1990; Olson et al., 1989; Stanovich, 1982, 1992; Stanovich, Cunningham & Cramer, 1984; Vellutino & Scanlon, 1987; Wagner & Torgesen, 1987). Becoming aware of the segmental structure of language appears to be a prerequisite to rapid reading acquisition in an alphabetic orthography. Lack of phonological awareness inhibits the learning of the alphabetic coding patterns that underlie fluent word recognition (Bryant et al., 1990; Goswami & Bryant, 1990; Stanovich et al., 1984; Tunmer & Hoover, 1992; Tunmer & Nesdale, 1985).

As previously indicated, the most distinctive indicator of the phonological coding deficits that are characteristic of reading disability is difficulty in naming pseudowords (Rack, Snowling & Olson, 1992). Reading-disabled children not only perform worse than chronological age peers on pseudoword tasks, but they also underperform reading-level controls, i.e. younger nondisabled children equated on word recognition skill. This pseudoword deficit in a reading-level match is one of the most distinctive indicators of the reading-disabled phenotype (Olson et al., 1989; Rack et al. 1992; Stanovich & Siegel, 1994). However, several studies that have compared the performance of poor readers with and without reading-IQ discrepancy have found that they display equivalent pseudoword deficits (Felton & Wood, 1992; Fredman & Stevenson, 1988; Share *et al.* 1990; Siegel, 1988, 1989, 1992; Stanovich & Siegel, 1994). This primary indicator of reading disability does not distinguish disabled readers with IQ-discrepancy from those without such discrepancies (see also, Fletcher *et al.*, 1994).

Likewise, measures of orthographic processing, on which reading-disabled children are less impaired, show no differences between poor readers with and without reading-IQ discrepancy (Fredman & Stevenson, 1988; Siegel, 1992; Stanovich & Siegel, 1994). Finally, the spelling-sound regularty effect, often interpreted as an indicator of the relative reliance (although not necessarily of relative skill, see Rack *et al.*, 1992) on phonological and orthographic coding processes appears to be of a similar magnitude in reading-disabled children and younger reading-level controls. This also appears to be true for both poor readers without (Beech & Harding, 1984; Stanovich, Nathan & Zolman, 1988; Treiman & Hirsh-Pasek, 1985) and for poor readers with reading-IQ discrepancy (Baddeley, Logie & Ellis, 1988; Ben-Dror, Pollatsek & Scarpati, 1991; Brown & Watson, 1991; Bruck, 1990; Holligan & Johnston, 1988; Olson, Kliegl, Davidson & Foltz, 1985; Siegel & Ryan, 1988; Watson & Brown, 1992).

Thus, there is no indication that the nature of processing within the word recognition module differs at all for poor readers with and without IQ-discrepancy. Their relative strengths in phonological and orthographic coding processes, and their relative reliance on these subskills, appears to be nearly the same. The relative tradeoff between phonological and orthographic subskills—one of the most reliable phenotypic behavior patterns associated with reading disability—does not distinguish poor readers with and without reading-IQ discrepancy. This finding is consistent with the lack of evidence for a difference between these two groups in genetic and neuroanatomical studies.

Not surprisingly, there *are* cognitive differences between poor readers with and without reading-IQ discrepancy outside of the word recognition module (Ellis & Large, 1987; Siegel, 1992; Stanovich, 1988; Stanovich & Siegel, 1994), because these children differ in intelligence. Some of these cognitive differences may be related to comprehension processes. Thus, there may well be reading comprehension differences between the two groups when they are equated on word recognition ability (Bloom, Wagner, Reskin & Bergman, 1980; Ellis & Large, 1987; Jorm, Share, Maclean & Matthews, 1986; Silva, McGee & Williams, 1985), although even this expectation has not always been borne out (Siegel, 1988, 1989; Felton & Wood, 1992). These differences might well relate to certain educational issues such as the reading level to be expected of a student subsequent to remediation of their primary word recognition problem (Stanovich, 1991). However, it is important to note that any such differences are not indicators of the core processing problem that caused the word recognition deficit that triggered the diagnosis of reading disability: Phonological coding difficulties probably resulting from deficient phonological awareness. Thus, such differences outside of the word recognition model provide no rationale for a definition of reading disability based on IQ-discrepancy. Such definitions would only give the mistaken impression that children with reading-IQ discrepancy have distinctive genetic/neurological etiology. Indirect validation of the idea of differentiating poor readers on the basis of reading-IQ discrepancies would come from data showing that high- and low-IQ poor readers are differentially sensitive to specific educational interventions. There is, however, no body of evidence indicating that poor readers with reading-IQ discrepancy respond differently to various educational treatments than do poor readers without such discrepancies.

Whither dyslexia?

Thus, the research literature provides no support for the notion that we need a scientific concept of dyslexia separate from other, more neutral, theoretical terms such as reading disabled, poor reader, less-skilled, etc. Yes, there is such a thing as dyslexia if by dyslexia we mean poor reading. But if this is what we mean, it appears that the term dyslexia no longer does the conceptual work that we thought it did. Indeed, whatever conceptual work the term is doing appears to be misleading. The concept of dyslexia is inextricably linked with the idea of an etiologically distinct type of reading disability associated with moderate to high IQ. Certainly an extreme form of this belief can be seen in the promotional activities of many advocacy groups and in media portrayals of "dyslexia". The typical "media dyslexic" is almost always a very bright child. Indeed, this media portrayal has now entered the realm of folk belief, for there exists a popular myth that dyslexia is the "affliction of geniuses" (Adelman & Adelman, 1987; Coles, 1987), if anything, *more* likely to occur in very bright people. This folk belief has even subtly affected the thinking of researchers who, without much thought, appear to have embraced the unverified assumptions about the meaning of reading-IQ discrepancy promulgated in school and clinic-based definitions and often derived from pragmatic considerations rather than scientific ones.

In fact, it appears that: (1) reading-IQ discrepancy measurement fails to identify a distinct phenotypic pattern of word recognition subskills; (2) reading-IQ discrepancy measurement does not identify a group of children with significantly different heritability values for core information processing deficits; (3) there are as yet no indications that neuroanatomical anomalies that are associated with reading disability are more characteristic of high-IQ than of low-IQ poor readers. As Taylor and Schatschneider (1992) argue, "IQ criteria were imposed primarily as a means of ruling out confounding variables and for assisting in the search for specific cognitive antecedents" (p. 630). It appears that the intuition that IQ discrepancy measurement would provide such assistance is mistaken. IQ discrepancy does not carve out a unique information processing pattern in the word recognition module that is the critical locus of reading disability. If there is a special group of reading disabled children who are behaviorally/ cognitively/genetically "different" it is becoming increasingly unlikely that they can be quickly picked out using reading-IQ discrepancy as a proxy for the genetic and neurological differences themselves.

Rather than becoming further distracted by the IQ issue, it may well be more fruitful for the field to explore the implications of conceptualizing reading disability as residing on a continuum of developmental language disorder (see Bishop & Adams, 1990; Catts, 1991; Gathercole & Baddeley, 1987; Kamhi, 1992; Kamhi & Catts, 1989; Scarborough, 1990). For example, Gathercole and Baddeley (1987) argue that "although language problems are typically detected prior to the children receiving reading instruction . . . it is possible that the alphabetic literacy skills required in reading may be more sensitive to the adequacy of speech analytic skills than other aspects of normal linguistic development, such that a mild deficit may only be detectable in reading performance. More severe subjects may result in the more generalized symptom complex associated with developmental language disorder . . . This is also clearly consistent with the notion that the two populations may quantitatively differ rather than qualitatively" (p. 464).

In light of these attempts to conceptualize reading disability as a milder form of language disability, it is interesting to note that the question of whether a discrepancy-defined disability is different from a disability defined purely in terms of chronological age occurs in analogous form in the area of developmental language disorder (Aram, Morris & Hall, 1992; Cole, Dale & Mills, 1990). Cole *et al.* (1990) describe how prior to more recent concerns about the relation between cognition and language "Any child who demonstrated a discrepancy between chronological age and language age would generally have been considered a candidate for language intervention by speech-language pathologists" (p. 291). However, an assumed tight link between language and cognition has recently led to what is called the Cognitive Referencing model, which has the implication that "Children who have developed language skills at a level equal to their cognitive skills are not considered to be language delayed, even if their language skills are significantly below chronological age" (p. 292). However, just as in the area of reading disability, Cole *et al.* point out that "it is surprising that there is little or no empirical evidence for evaluating the Cognitive Referencing model" (p. 292).

In summary, the search for neurological and genetic correlates of reading disability is being conducted with vigor in research laboratories around the world. The moral of the tale told in this Annotation is that there appears to be no reason for such investigations to restrict their research samples in advance based on reading-IQ discrepancy. Indeed, our ability to map the multidimensional space of reading-related cognitive skills would be impaired by such a procedure. Likewise, the argument put forth here should not be read as an argument for eliminating the inclusion of IQ measures in research studies of reading disability. Researchers may well want to investigate whether relationships with genetic or environmental variables are differentially related to reading raw scores and reading scores residualised on IQ (Stevenson, 1991; Stevenson & Fredman, 1990). For example, in a previously mentioned study, Stevenson (1991) found that the heritability of a group deficit in spelling ability tended to be greater for spelling scores residualised on IQ than for raw spelling scores. Such findings are often *not* primarily viewed as establishing a separate genetic etiology for one group of poor readers (or spellers). Instead, they may be viewed as establishing that the genetic factors influencing spelling are not the same as those influencing IQ.

To conclude, no one disputes the logical possibility of distinct etiologies within the population of poor readers. Obviously, if a group of children were not taught to read and not exposed to print, their reading disability would have a distinct causation different from that in the general disabled population. The point, instead, is that it has yet to be demonstrated that whatever distinct causes actually exist are correlated with the degree of reading-IQ discrepancy. Because the term dyslexia mistakenly implies that there is such evidence, the reading disabilities field must seriously consider whether the term is not best dispensed with.

Acknowledgement

The preparation of this paper was supported by a grant from the Natural Sciences and Engineering Research Council of Canada to Keith E. Stanovich.

References

Adams, M. J. (1990). *Beginning to read: thinking and learning about print.* Cambridge, MA: MIT Press.

Adelman, K. A. & Adelman, H. S. (1987). Rodin, Patton, Edison, Wilson, Einstein: were they really learning disabled? *Journal of Learning Disabilities,* **20**, 270–279.

Aram, D., Morris, R. & Hall, N. (1992). The validity of discrepancy criteria for identifying children with developmental language disorders. *Journal of Learning Disabilities,* **25**, 549–554.

Baddeley, A. D., Logie, R. H. & Ellis, N. C. (1988). Characteristics of developmental dyslexia. *Cognition,* **30**, 198–227.

Beech, J. & Harding, L. (1984). Phonemic processing and the poor reader from a developmental lag viewpoint. *Reading Research Quarterly,* **19**, 357–366.

462

Ben-Dror, I., Pollatsek, A. & Scarpati, S. (1991). Word identification in isolation and in context by college dyslexic students. *Brain and Language*, **40**, 471–490.

Bentin, S. (1992). Phonological awareness, reading, and reading acquisition. In R. Frost & L. Katz (Eds), *Orthography, phonology, morphology, and meaning* (pp. 193–210). Amsterdam: North-Holland.

Bishop, D. (1992). The underlying nature of specific language impairment. *Journal of Child Psychology and Psychiatry*, **33**, 3–66.

Bishop, D. & Adams, C. (1990). A prospective study of the relationship between specific language impairment, phonological disorders and reading retardation. *Journal of Child Psychology and Psychiatry*, **31**, 1027–1050.

Bloom, A., Wagner, M., Reskin, L. & Bergman, A. (1980). A comparison of intellectually delayed and primary reading disabled children on measures of intelligence and achievement. *Journal of Clinical Psychology*, **36**, 788–790.

Bowey, J. A., Cain, M. T. & Ryan, S. M. (1992). A reading-level design study of phonological skills underlying fourth-grade children's word reading difficulties. *Child Development*, **63**, 999–1011.

Bradley, L. & Bryant, P. E. (1978). Difficulties in auditory organization as a possible cause of reading backwardness. *Nature*, **271**, 746–747.

Bradley, L. & Bryant, P. E. (1985). *Rhyme and reason in reading and spelling*. Ann Arbor: University of Michigan Press.

Brown, G. D. A. & Watson, F. L. (1991). Reading development in dyslexia: a connectionist approach. In M. Snowling & M. Thomson (Eds), *Dyslexia: Integrating theory & practice* (pp. 165–182). London: Whurr Publishers.

Bruck, M. (1988). The word recognition and spelling of dyslexic children. *Reading Research Quarterly*, **23**, 51–69.

Bruck, M. (1990). Word-recognition skills of adults with childhood diagnoses of dyslexia. *Developmental Psychology*, **26**, 439–454.

Bruck, M. (1992). Persistence of dyslexics' phonological awareness deficits. *Developmental Psychology*, **28**, 874–886.

Bruck, M. & Treiman, R. (1990). Phonological awareness and spelling in normal children and dyslexics: the case of initial consonant clusters. *Journal of Experimental Child Psychology*, **50**, 156–178.

Bryant, P. E., Maclean, M., Bradley, L. & Crossland, J. (1990). Rhyme and alliteration, phoneme detection, and learning to read. *Developmental Psychology*, **26**, 429–438.

Catts, H. W. (1991). Early identification of reading disabilities. *Topics in Language Disorders*, **12**, 1–16.

Cole, K. N., Dale, P. S. & Mills, P. E. (1990). Defining language delay in young children by cognitive referencing: Are we saying more than we know? *Applied Psycholinguistics*, **11**, 291–302.

Coles, G. S. (1987). *The learning mystique*. New York: Pantheon.

DeFries, J. C., Fulker, D. & Labuda, M. (1987). Evidence for a genetic etiology in reading disability in twins. *Nature*, **329**, 537–539.

Ellis, N. & Large, B. (1987). The development of reading: as you seek so shall you find. *British Journal of Psychology*, **78**, 1–28.

Felton, R. H. & Wood, F. R. (1992). A reading level match study of nonword reading skills in poor readers with varying IQs. *Journal of Learning Disabilities*, **25**, 318–326.

Fletcher, J. M. (1992). The validity of distinguishing children with language and learning disabilities according to discrepancies with IQ: introduction to the special series. *Journal of Learning Disabilities*, **25**, 546–548.

Fletcher, J. M., Shaywitz, S. E., Shankweiler, D., Katz, L., Liberman, I., Francis, D. J., Stuebing, K. & Shaywitz, B. A. (1994). Cognitive profiles of reading disability: comparisons of discrepancy and low achievement definitions. *Journal of Educational Psychology*, **86**, 31–48.

Frankenberger, W. & Fronzaglio, K. (1991). A review of states' criteria and procedures for identifying children with learning disabilities. *Journal of Learning Disabilities*, **24**, 495–500.

Frankenberger, W. & Harper, J. (1987). States' criteria and procedures for identifying learning disabled children: a comparison of 1981/82 and 1985/86 guidelines. *Journal of Learning Disabilities*, **20**, 118–121.

Fredman, G. & Stevenson, J. (1988). Reading processes in specific reading retarded and reading backward 13-year-olds. *British Journal of Developmental Psychology*, **6**, 97–108.

Frith, U. & Snowling, M. (1983). Reading for meaning and reading for sound in autistic and dyslexic children. *British Journal of Developmental Psychology*, **1**, 329–342.

Galaburda, A. (1991). Anatomy of dyslexia: argument against phrenology. In D. Duane & D. Gray (Eds), *The reading brain: the biological basis of dyslexia* (pp. 119–131). Parkton, MD: York Press.

Galaburda, A. M., Sherman, G., Rosen, G., Aboitz, F. & Geschwind, N. (1985). Developmental dyslexia: four consecutive patients with cortical anomalies. *Annals of Neurology*, **18**, 222–233.

Gathercole, S. E. & Baddeley, A. D. (1987). The processes underlying segmental analysis. *European Bulletin of Cognitive Psychology*, **7**, 462–464.

Goswami, U. & Bryant, P. (1990). *Phonological skills and learning to read*. Hove, England: Lawrence Erlbaum.

Gough, P. B. & Tunmer, W. E. (1986). Decoding, reading, and reading disability. *Remedial and Special Education*, **7**, 6–10.

Hinshelwood, J. (1917). *Congenital word-blindness*. London: Lewis.

Holligan, C. & Johnston, R. S. (1988). The use of phonological information by good and poor readers in memory and reading tasks. *Memory & Cognition*, **16**, 522–532.

Hynd, G. S., Marshall, R. & Gonzalez, J. (1991). Learning disabilities and presumed central nervous system dysfunction. *Learning Disability Quarterly*, **14**, 283–296.

Hynd, G. S., Marshall, R. & Semrud-Clikeman, M. (1991). Developmental dyslexia, neurolinguistic theory and deviations in brain morphology. *Reading and Writing: An Interdisciplinary Journal*, **3**, 345–362.

Ingram, T., Mason, A. & Blackburn, I. (1970). A retrospective study of 82 children with reading disability. *Developmental Medicine and Child Neurology*, **12**, 271–281.

Jorm, A., Share, D., Maclean, R. & Matthews, R. (1986). Cognitive factors at school entry predictive of specific reading retardation and general reading backwardness: a research note. *Journal of Child Psychology and Psychiatry*, **27**, 45–54.

Kamhi, A. & Catts, H. (1989). *Reading disabilities: a developmental language perspective*. Austin: PRO-ED.

Kamhi, A. G. (1992). Response to historical perspective: a developmental language perspective. *Journal of Learning Disabilities*, **25**, 48–52.

Kirk, S. (1963). *Behavioral diagnosis and remediation of learning disabilities*. Paper presented at the Conference on the Exploration into the Problems of the Perceptually Handicapped Child. Evanston, IL: Fund for the Perceptually Handicapped Child.

Labuda, M. & DeFries, J. C. (1989). Differential prognosis of reading-disabled children as a function of gender, socioeconomic status, IQ and severity: a longitudinal study. *Reading and Writing: An Interdisciplinary Journal*, **1**, 25–36.

Larsen, P. J., Hoien, T., Lundberg, I. & Odegaard, H. (1990). MRI evaluation of the size and symmetry of the planum temporale in adolescents with developmental dyslexia. *Brain and Language*, **39**, 289–300.

Lerner, J. (1985). *Learning disabilities* (4th edn.). Boston, MA: Houghton Mifflin Company.

Liberman, I. Y. & Liberman, A. M. (1990). Whole language vs. code emphasis: underlying assumptions and their implications for reading instruction. *Annals of Dyslexia*, **40**, 51–77.

Manis, F. R., Custodio, R. & Szeszulski, P. A. (1993). Development of phonological and orthographic skill: a 2-year longitudinal study of dyslexic children. *Journal of Experimental Child Psychology*, **56**, 64–86.

McKinney, J. D. (1987). Research on the identification of learning-disabled children: perspectives on changes in educational policy. In S. Vaughn & C. Bos (Eds), *Research in learning disabilities* (pp. 215–233). Boston: College-Hill.

Morrison, F.J. (1991). Learning (and not learning) to read: a developmental framework. In L. Rieben & C. Perfetti (Eds), *Learning to read: basic research and its implications* (pp. 163–174). Hillsdale, NJ: Lawrence Erlbaum Associates.

Oakhill, J. & Garnham, A. (1988). *Becoming a skilled reader*. Oxford: Basil Blackwell.

Olson, R., Kliegl, R., Davidson, B. & Foltz, G. (1985). Individual and developmental differences in reading disability. In G. E. Mackinnon & T. Waller (Eds), *Reading research: advances in theory and practice* (Vol. 4, pp. 1–64). London: Academic Press.

Olson, R. K., Rack, J., Conners, F., DeFries, J. & Fulker, D. (1991). Genetic etiology of individual differences in reading disability. In L. Feagans, E. Short & L. Meltzer (Eds), *Subtypes of learning disabilities* (pp. 113–135). Hillsdale, NJ: Erlbaum.

Olson, R. K., Wise, B., Conners, F., Rack, J. & Fulker, D. (1989). Specific deficits in component reading and language skills: genetic and environmental influences. *Journal of Learning Disabilities*, **22**, 339–348.

Pennington, B. F. (1990). The genetics of dyslexia. *Journal of Child Psychology and Psychiatry*, **31**, 193–201.

Pennington, B. F., Gilger, J., Olson, R. K. & DeFries, J. C. (1992). The external validity of age-versus IQ-discrepancy definitions of reading disability: lessons from a twin study. *Journal of Learning Disabilities*, **25**, 562–573.

Pennington, B. F., Gilger, J., Pauls, D., Smith, S. A., Smith, S. D. & DeFries, J. (1991). Genetic and neurological influences on reading disability: an overview. *Journal of the American Medical Association*, **266**, 1527–1534.

Pennington, B. F., McCabe, L. L., Smith, S., Lefly, D., Bookman, M., Kimberling, W. & Lubs, H. (1986). Spelling errors in adults with a form of familial dyslexia. *Child Development*, **57**, 1001–1013.

Pennington, B. F., Van Orden, G., Kirson, D. & Haith, M. (1991). What is the causal relation between verbal STM problems and dyslexia? In S. A. Brady & D. P. Shankweiler (Eds), *Phonological processes in literacy* (pp. 173–186). Hillsdale, NJ: Erlbaum.

Perfetti, C. A. (1985). *Reading ability*. New York: Oxford University Press.

Perfetti, C. A. (1991). The psychology, pedagogy, and politics of reading. *Psychological Science*, **2**, 70–76.

Rack, J. (1985). Orthographic and phonetic coding in developmental dyslexia. *British Journal of Psychology*, **76**, 325–340.

Rack, J. P., Snowling, M. J. & Olson, R. K. (1992). The nonword reading deficit in developmental dyslexia: a review. *Reading Research Quarterly*, **27**, 28–53.

Reynolds, C. R. (1985). Measuring the aptitude-achievement discrepancy in learning disability diagnosis. *Remedial and Special Education*, **6**, 37–55.

Rodgers, B. (1983). The identification and prevalence of specific reading retardation. *British Journal of Educational Psychology*, **53**, 369–373.

Rutter, M. (1978). Prevalence and types of dyslexia. In A. Benton & D. Pearl (Eds), *Dyslexia: an appraisal of current knowledge* (pp. 5–28). New York: Oxford University Press.

Rutter, M. & Yule, W. (1975). The concept of specific reading retardation. *Journal of Child Psychology and Psychiatry*, **16**, 181–197.

Scarborough, H. S. (1990). Very early language deficits in dyslexic children. *Child Development*, **61**, 1728–1743.

Semrud-Clikeman, M., Hynd, G. S., Novey, E. & Eliopulos, D. (1991). Dyslexia and brain morphology: relationships between neuroanatomical variation and neurolinguistic tasks. *Learning and Individual Differences*, **3**, 225–242.

Share, D. L., Jorm, A., McGee, R., Silva, P., Maclean, R., Matthews, R. & Williams, S. (1990). Word recognition and spelling processes in specific reading disabled and garden-variety poor readers. Unpublished manuscript.

Share, D. L., McGee, R., McKenzie, D., Williams, S. & Silva, P. A. (1987). Further evidence relating to the distinction between specific reading retardation and general reading backwardness. *British Journal of Developmental Psychology*, **5**, 35–44.

Shaywitz, S. E., Escobar, M. D., Shaywitz, B. A., Fletcher, J. M. & Makugh, R. (1992). Evidence that dyslexia may represent the lower tail of a normal distribution of reading ability. *The New England Journal of Medicine*, **326**, 145–150.

Shepard, L. (1980). An evaluation of the regression discrepancy method for identifying children with learning disabilities. *The Journal of Special Education*, **14**, 79–91.

Siegel, L. S. (1985). Psycholinguistic aspects of reading disabilities. In L. Siegel & F. Morrison (Eds), *Cognitive development in atypical children* (pp. 45–65). New York: Springer.

Siegel, L. S. (1988). Evidence that IQ scores are irrelevant to the definition and analysis of reading disability. *Canadian Journal of Psychology*, **42**, 201–215.

Siegel, L. S. (1989). IQ is irrelevant to the definition of learning disabilities. *Journal of Learning Disabilities*, **22**, 469–479.

Siegel, L. S. (1992). An evaluation of the discrepancy definition of dyslexia. *Journal of Learning Disabilities*, **25**, 618–629.

Siegel, L. S. (1993). The development of reading. In H. Reese (Ed.), *Advances in child development and behavior* (Vol. 24, pp. 63–97). San Diego, CA: Academic Press.

Siegel, L. S. & Faux, D. (1989). Acquisition of certain grapheme-phoneme correspondences in normally achieving and disabled readers. *Reading and Writing: an Interdisciplinary Journal*, **1**, 37–52.

Siegel, L. S. & Ryan, E. B. (1988). Development of grammatical-sensitivity, phonological, and short-term memory skills in normally achieving and learning disabled children. *Developmental Psychology*, **24**, 28–37.

Siegel, L. S. & Ryan, E. B. (1989). Subtypes of developmental dyslexia: the influence of definitional variables. *Reading and Writing: An Interdisciplinary Journal*, **1**, 257–287.

Silva, P. A., McGee, R. & Williams, S. (1985). Some characteristics of 9-year-old boys with general reading backwardness or specific reading retardation. *Journal of Child Psychology and Psychiatry*, **26**, 407–421.

Smith, S. D., Kimberling, W. J. & Pennington, B. F. (1991). Screening for multiple genes influencing dyslexia. *Reading and Writing: An Interdisciplinary Journal*, **3**, 285–298.

Snowling, M. (1980). The development of grapheme–phoneme correspondence in normal and dyslexic readers. *Journal of Experimental Child Psychology*, **29**, 294–305.

Snowling, M. (1981). Phonemic deficits in developmental dyslexia. *Psychological Research*, **43**, 219–234.

Snowling, M. (1991). Developmental reading disorders. *Journal of Child Psychology and Psychiatry*, **32**, 49–77.

Stanovich, K. E. (1981). Relationships between word decoding speed, general name-retrieval ability, and reading progress in first-grade children. *Journal of Educational Psychology*, **73**, 809–815.

Stanovich, K. E. (1982). Individual differences in the cognitive processes of reading I: word decoding. *Journal of Learning Disabilities*, **15**, 485–493.

Stanovich, K. E. (1986). Matthew effects in reading: some consequences of individual differences in the acquisition of literacy. *Reading Research Quarterly*, **21**, 360–407.

Stanovich, K. E. (1988). Explaining the differences between the dyslexic and the garden-variety poor reader: The phonological-core variable-difference model. *Journal of Learning Disabilities*, **21**, 590–612.

Stanovich, K. E. (1991). Discrepancy definitions of reading disability: has intelligence led us astray? *Reading Research Quarterly*, **26**, 7–29.

Stanovich, K. E. (1992). Speculations on the causes and consequences of individual differences in early reading acquisition. In P. Gough, L. Ehri & R. Treiman (Eds), *Reading acquisition* (pp. 307–342). Hillsdale, NJ: Erlbaum Associates.

Stanovich, K. E., Cunningham, A. E. & Cramer, B. (1984). Assessing phonological awareness in kindergarten children: issues of task comparability. *Journal of Experimental Child Psychology*, **38**, 175–190.

Stanovich, K. E., Cunningham, A. E. & Feeman, D. J. (1984). Intelligence, cognitive skills, and early reading progress. *Reading Research Quarterly*, **19**, 278–303.

Stanovich, K. E., Nathan, R. & Vala-Rossi, M. (1986). Developmental changes in the cognitive correlates of reading ability and the developmental lag hypothesis. *Reading Research Quarterly*, **21**, 267–283.

Stanovich, K. E., Nathan, R. G. & Zolman, J. E. (1988). The developmental lag hypothesis in reading: longitudinal and matched reading-level comparisons. *Child Development*, **59**, 71–86.

Stanovich, K. E. & Siegel, L. S. (1994). The phenotypic performance profile of reading-disabled children: a regression-based test of the phonological-core variable-difference model. *Journal of Educational Psychology*, **86**, 1–30.

Steinmetz, H. & Galaburda, A. M. (1991). Planum temporale asymmetry: in-vivo morphometry affords a new perspective for neuro-behavioral research. *Reading and Writing: An Interdisciplinary Journal*, **3**, 331–343.

Stevenson, J. (1988). Which aspects of reading ability show a "hump" in their distribution? *Applied Cognitive Psychology*, **2**, 77–85.

Stevenson, J. (1991). Which aspects of processing text mediate genetic effects? *Reading and Writing: An Interdisciplinary Journal*, **3**, 249–269.

Stevenson, J. (1992a). Genetics. In N. Singh & I. Beale (Eds), *Learning disabilities: nature, theory, and treatment* (pp. 327–351). New York: Springer.

Stevenson, J. (1992b). Identifying sex differences in reading disability: lessons from a twin study. *Reading and Writing: An Interdisciplinary Journal*, **4**, 307–326.

Stevenson, J. & Fredman, G. (1990). The social environmental correlates of reading ability. *Journal of Child Psychology and Psychiatry*, **31**, 681–698.

Stevenson, J. Graham, P., Fredman, G. & McLoughlin, V. (1987). A twin study of genetic influences on reading and spelling ability and disability. *Journal of Child Psychology and Psychiatry*, **28**, 229–247.

Taylor, H. G., Satz, P. & Friel, J. (1979). Developmental dyslexia in relation to other childhood reading disorders: significance and clinical utility. *Reading Research Quarterly*, **15**, 84–101.

Taylor, H. G. & Schatschneider, C. (1992). Academic achievement following childhood brain disease: implications for the concept of learning disabilities. *Journal of Learning Disabilities*, **25**, 630–638.

Treiman, R. & Hirsh-Pasek, K. (1985). Are there qualitative differences in reading behavior between dyslexics and normal readers? *Memory and Cognition*, **13**, 357–364.

Tunmer, W. E. & Hoover, W. (1992). Cognitive and linguistic factors in learning to read. In P. B. Gough, L. C. Ehri & R. Treiman (Eds), *Reading Acquisition* (pp. 175–214). Hillsdale, NJ: Erlbaum.

Tunmer, W. E. & Nesdale, A. R. (1985). Phonemic segmentation skill and beginning reading. *Journal of Educational Psychology*, **77**, 417–427.

Vellutino, F. & Scanlon, D. (1987). Phonological coding, phonological awareness, and reading ability: evidence from a longitudinal and experimental study. *Merrill-Palmer Quarterly*, **33**, 321–363.

Wagner, R. K. & Torgesen, J. K. (1987). The nature of phonological processing and its causal role in the acquisition of reading skills. *Psychological Bulletin*, **101**, 192–212.

Watson, F. & Brown, G. (1992). Single-word reading in college dyslexics. *Applied Cognitive Psychology*, **6**, 263–272.

Wissel, A., van der & Zegers, F. E. (1985). Reading retardation revisited. *British Journal of Developmental Psychology*, **3**, 3–9.

Yule, W., Rutter, M., Berger, M. & Thompson, J. (1974). Over- and underachievement in reading: distribution in the general population. *British Journal of Educational Psychology*, **44**, 1–12.

128

GENETIC ANALYSIS OF DYSLEXIA AND OTHER COMPLEX BEHAVIORAL PHENOTYPES

Bruce F. Pennington and Shelley D. Smith

Source: *Current Opinion in Pediatrics*, 9, 1997: 636–641.

In this review, we discuss recent data on the genetics of developmental dyslexia and consider broader issues involved in the search for genes influencing complex behavioral phenotypes. These issues include 1) the need for a sophisticated analysis of the phenotype and the need for interdisciplinary collaboration between geneticists and cognitive neuroscientists, 2) the likelihood of genetic heterogeneity and non-Mendelian inheritance and the necessity for linkage methods to deal with these issues, and 3) how association analyses complement linkage analyses.

There have been only a few publications on the genetics of dyslexia in the period covered by this review. In this review, we discuss that new data and consider broader issues in the genetic analysis of complex behavioral phenotypes.

New data on the genetics of dyslexia

One major new publication on the genetics of dyslexia is that by Grigorenko *et al.* [1••], the results of which are discussed by Pennington [2•]. Grigorenko *et al.* [1••] studied extended families of dyslexic probands originally diagnosed and treated by June Orton, who incidentally was the wife of Samuel T. Orton [3,4], an early pioneer in dyslexia research (for whom the Orton

469

Dyslexia Society is named). They used several reading-related phenotypes derived from the cognitive analysis of reading development as well as both parametric and nonparametric methods of linkage analysis, which is discussed later in this review. In short, both the phenotypic and genotypic methods were state of the art, and it is this kind of interdisciplinary collaboration that is needed to identify genes that influence complex behavior. They found that their single-word reading phenotype was significantly linked to a marker near the centromere on chromosome 15 and that their phoneme awareness phenotype was very significantly linked to markers on the short arm of chromosome 6. Because the single-word phenotype was not linked to the markers on chromosome 6 and the phoneme awareness phenotype was not linked to the marker on 15, they argue that different genes influence different components of reading. However, they did not find a significant difference between the results for each measure at each genetic location, so the evidence for these differential genetic influences is preliminary. Most importantly, these results provide one of the first independent replications of genetic linkage results for a complex human behavior. Smith et al. [5] first reported linkage between dyslexia and a centromeric marker on chromosome 15 and then linkage between dyslexia and markers on the short arm of chromosome 6 in two separate samples [6].

One of the most provocative conclusions of Grigorenko et al. [1••] is that cognitively dissociable components of the reading process are linked to separate genes and that the mapping from genes to aspects of cognition may be quite close indeed. This conclusion merits further discussion, for both methodological and theoretical reasons. The methodological point is that finding significant evidence for linkage with one measure but not another does not imply that the results for the two measures are significantly different form each other, just as two correlations may not be significantly different from each other, even though one is statistically significant and the other is not. Both the variance and reliability of the behavioral phenotypes and differences in the informativeness of markers may lead to seemingly different linkage results for two correlated phenotypes, especially in small samples. However, Grigorenko et al.'s [1••] interpretation of their findings implies a genetic "double dissociation" between the genes influencing the two phenotypes, in much the same way cognitive neuroscientists use contrasting cognitive profiles across two groups with different brain lesions, or contrasting patterns of cerebral blood flow across two tasks in a neuroimaging study to dissect cognition. But this implied double dissociation does not fit the cognitive science understanding of reading. Single-word reading is not cognitively separate from phoneme awareness, since phoneme awareness is essential for the development of single-word reading; thus, their genetic influences should overlap, at least to some extent. In sum, any conclusion about their genetic independence is premature until there is significant difference in linkage at each location, and even then it would be important to rule out problems related to the variation in phenotypes and markers. Nonetheless, the strategy of combining a detailed cognitive analysis of a complex behavioral trait with linkage is a very productive one, which has wide applicability to other behaviorally defined disorders.

The search for genes influencing complex behavioral phenotypes

The search for genes influencing a complex trait such as dyslexia must allow for the strong probability of genetic heterogeneity and non-Mendelian inheritance. A number of genes may influence the phenotype, and influence of any one of the genes can range through a continuum from a fully penetrant dominant or recessive Mendelian gene, to a gene with reduced penetrance such that other genetic or environmental factors reduce the probability of expression; to a quantitative trait locus that influences a measurable part of the overall phenotypic variation produced by a number of separate loci; or to a susceptibility locus, which contributes to the variation but in itself is neither necessary nor sufficient to the expression of the phenotype [7–9]. Lander and Schork [7] have recommended the use of linkage analysis, including nonparametric allele-sharing methods such as sib-pair analysis when penetrance and mode of inheritance are problematic, along with association analysis and linkage disequilibrium to identify the genomic regions that may contain genes influencing complex traits. Recently, these methods have been successful in identifying genes or genomic regions influencing several complex traits that have frustrated researchers for years.

Like dyslexia, insulin-dependent diabetes mellitus has been known to be familial, but no single gene could be identified as causal. Association with human leukocyte antigen-DR and -DQ subtypes were known, and now, careful molecular analysis has been able to show that this is due at least in part to specific mutations in these two loci, some of which confer susceptibility while others are protective [10]. These loci appear to be the primary genetic influences on insulin-dependent diabetes mellitus, but automated full genome searches and sib-pair linkage analysis have identified at least 10 other loci [11–15]. Association analysis of the identified regions (ie, linkage disequilibrium testing) has further narrowed these regions and pointed to potential candidate genes. For example, linkage analysis localized a susceptibility gene, IDDM7, to a region of chromosome 2 containing the human homologue to the mouse iddm5 gene. Subsequent association analysis identified linkage disequilibrium between diabetes and the iddm5 locus, making it very likely that IDDM7 is the human equivalent to iddm5 [14]. In addition to pointing out the capabilities of automated screening and sib-pair analyses to localize regions containing genes for complex traits, these studies also demonstrate that association analysis can be used to identify candidate genes in these regions, even in outbred populations.

Similar studies have been useful in elucidating four genes that contribute to liability for Alzheimer syndrome [16], five loci contributing to non-syndromic cleft lip and palate [17], one gene influencing attention deficit hyperactivity disorder [18], a gene (*LIMK1*) that influences visuospatial cognition in Williams syndrome [19], and the *minibrain* gene as one gene contributing to learning deficits in Down syndrome [20]. In addition, association studies are underway to identify genes influencing IQ [21]. Thus, while this is a relatively new area of research, gene identification in complex disorders has already been successful. In what follows, we discuss linkage methods, heterogeneity, and association analysis in more detail.

Linkage methods

In classical, family-based linkage analysis, the transmission of marker alleles through at least two generations of a family is compared with the transmission of the phenotype being studied (the trait phenotype) to determine if the marker locus and the trait locus assort independently (free recombination of parental haplotypes) or if they show decreased recombination, indicating that the two loci are close together on the same chromosome. Maximum likelihood methods are used to compute the likelihood of linkage at a given level of recombination, and this is compared in an odds ratio with the likelihood of the data given free recombination. Because individual families are generally too small to determine if an apparent decrease in recombination is statistically significant, the $\log_{10}$ of the ratio is taken so that the results of different families can be added together. This statistic is termed *the lod score* (the log of the odds of linkage). A lod score over 3 is generally accepted as showing evidence of linkage, while a lod score less than -2 rejects linkage [22]. This method of linkage analysis is powerful in that linkage can be determined in a single large family, and the best estimate of the distance between genes can be determined. However, this is a parametric method, meaning that the parameters such as genotype-specific penetrances (reflecting mode of inheritance and penetrance) and gene frequency must be specified for the trait locus; this phenotype being studied must also be reliably assessed across generations and ages. If the parameters are unknown, the analyses can be rerun over a range of parameters, although this would increase the risk that significant results could be obtained by chance as more tests are run. Curtis and Sham [23] pointed out that this risk can be reduced if the parameters tested are limited to those that fit the observed population prevalence of the disorder.

Nonparametric, allele-sharing forms of linkage analysis require larger populations, but do not require that penetrance and mode of inheritance are known; thus, they may be much more appropriate for complex disorders such as dyslexia [24, 25]. In these methods, the proportion of marker alleles identical by descent (*ie*, the same allele inherited from the same parent) in sets of relatives (usually pairs of siblings, although other combinations of pedigree members may be used) is compared with the phenotypic similarity between the relatives. For example, full siblings will have 0, 0.5, or 1.0 alleles identical by descent at a particular locus. If the trait locus is closely linked to a marker, similarity between siblings for the marker alleles should correspond to similarity for the trait phenotype, regardless of penetrance or mode of inheritance. The identical by decent value for the genotypes of a pair of siblings at a given locus is estimated from the parental genotypes, which may not be fully informative. If parental genotypes are unknown, allele frequencies can be used to determine the probability that the alleles are identical by descent.

Often, only affected siblings are used to avoid problems of nonpenetrance. Conversely, use of discordant sibling pairs may be valuable in detecting genes with higher penetrances. Selection for extreme values of the phenotype at both ends of the spectrum also makes detection of a gene effect more efficient [26,27].

Haseman and Elston [28] described the regression analysis method of sibling pair analysis in which the square of the phenotypic difference between siblings is regressed upon the proportion of alleles identical by decent for the marker. This has been revised by a number of groups, most recently by Fulker *et al.* [29], and expanded to include interval analysis by Cardon and Fulker [27] and multipoint analysis [30,31]. These approaches have led to the apparent localization of a quantitative trait locus (QTL) for reading disability to chromosome 6p21.3 [6,32].

For complex traits, the "positional cloning" method of gene localization is not effective in narrowing the region beyond a 1–2 cM without very large populations. Haplotyping and exclusion of regions by mapping of crossovers cannot be done because of the ambiguities of diagnosis produced by reduced penetrance and heterogeneity in complex traits. Therefore, once the region is narrowed as much as possible by linkage methods, the search for the gene itself must focus on evaluation of candidate genes within the critical region. This has been termed the *positional candidate approach* [33]. As detailed below, there are a number of methods for identifying and evaluating candidates.

Heterogeneity

We are assuming that dyslexia can be caused by a number of different genes. This genetic heterogeneity makes identification of each gene more difficult. Particularly in the lod score method; if heterogeneity is not taken into account, a gene that is linked in some families may be excluded by other unlinked families. There are several methods that test for homogeneity of the lod scores, estimating the most likely proportion of linked families and testing for significance of linkage in those families. One commonly used method is the admixture method implemented by the HOMOG program by Ott [34]. The two alternate hypotheses of linkage with homogeneity and linkage with heterogeneity are both compared with the null hypothesis of no linkage; if the null hypothesis is rejected, the two alternate hypotheses are compared to see which best explains the data. Faraway [35] has elaborated on the distribution of the admixture test statistic and has demonstrated that this modification increases the power to detect linkage in disorders that are known to be heterogeneous. This modification has been included in the LODLINK program of the S.A.G.E. computer software package (LSU Medical Center, New Orleans, 1994).

Heterogeneity has somewhat less of an effect on sibling pair analysis, since linkage will not actually be excluded by heterogeneity, but larger sample sizes will be required to detect genes when heterogeneity is present. The number of pairs of siblings required to reach significance can be estimated based on the number and spacing of marker loci and the increased relative risk conferred by the locus. Weeks and Lathrop [36] have shown that if the equivalent to a lod score of 3.0 is required, which would fit the criteria set by Lander and Kruglyak [37], a population of 200 sibling pairs would have 90% power to detect any locus with a λ (relative risk) exceeding approximately 2.25.

The addition of multipoint mapping and selection for severity of the phenotype (when measured as a quantitative trait) further increases the ability of sibling-pair analysis to detect QTLs. For example, Cardon and Fulker [27] examined the power of their interval mapping technique for different levels of selection of probands. Heritability of the QTL, additivity, and dominance were also examined in a series of simulations. The power was figured as the proportion of simulations that correctly detected the QTL at $\alpha = 0.05$. The more stringent the selection of probands, the greater the power; interval mapping further increased the power in most cases, particularly for recessive conditions and rare alleles. They concluded that a gene could be detected even in the presence of a second gene influencing the same trait (genetic heterogeneity), with reliable power in a sample of about 250 sibling pairs even when the susceptibility alleles were very common and heritabilities were low.

The ability to screen a large number of markers for linkage makes the traditional criteria for linkage analysis (lod score > 3.0) too low; however, heterogeneity and decreased penetrance may make it difficult for the analyses of complex disorders to reach more stringent criteria without large and expensive studies. Although a consensus has not formally been reached, criteria have been suggested for considering linkages at increasing levels of significance. In this way, studies obtaining lower levels of significance can still be reported so that replications can be attempted, but localization cannot formally be claimed until more stringent criteria are met. For example, Thomson [38] suggested three levels of significance and the requirements for replication: 1) weak linkage or association (< 0.05) obtained in at least three independent data sets, 2) moderate (< 0.01) obtained in at least two data sets, or 3) strong linkage (< 0.001) in one, or in the overall, data set. She stated, "Some may argue that these criteria are too permissive, but with complex diseases it is surely preferable to err on the side of false linkage which can later be refuted, than to pass over a genuine linkage" and "Even if a region is not initially confirmed with other data sets, it should not be excluded from further considerations, although given limited resources, more promising regions will usually warrant immediate attention." Kruglyak and Lander [30] pointed out that the significance levels cited by Thomson do not actually refer to genome-wide searches. They contended that when a genome search is done, the appropriate significance level for suggestive linkage would be $< 7 \times 10^{-4}$, for significant linkage would be $< 2 \times 10^{-5}$, and highly significant linkage would be $< 3 \times 10^{-7}$, corresponding to lods of 2.2, 3.6, and 5.4, respectively. Confirmation of a significant linkage in a separate population should require $P < 0.01$. These standards have been set quite recently, and some geneticists have expressed the opinion that they are overly stringent, but they should serve to distinguish "provisional" from proven linkages. They also noted, however, that complex traits may never reach statistical significance, and that other methods, such as association analysis to identify linkage disequilibrium, may be needed to establish linkage.

Association analysis

When two genes are linked within a family, specific alleles for both loci will be inherited together because they are close together on the same parental chromosome. Between families, however, the specific alleles that are linked should be different. Conversely, association between two loci refers to the nonrandom co-occurrence of specific alleles; for example, the association between a certain HLA type with a disease, such that one HLA allele is significantly more frequent in individuals with the disease than in the general population.

Association can reflect several situations, including 1) linkage disequilibrium between the marker allele and a susceptibility locus, 2) a direct relation between the marker allele and the phenotype, or 3) an artifact. First, the marker allele may be very closely linked to the allele influencing the disorder, such that linkage disequilibrium exists. Given that the mutation influencing the disorder occurred on a given ancestral chromosome, alleles at loci that were tightly linked on that chromosome will stay with it through a number of generations until there has been enough recombination to separate them. Thus, the persistence of association through linkage disequilibrium is dependent upon the distance between the loci, the number of generations since the mutation, and the number of independent mutations in the population. If association is caused by linkage disequilibrium, the marker locus should show both linkage and association (given that the appropriate linkage model is used).

As an example, an association analysis with dyslexia has been reported [39] using a form of the *C4B* gene, which is located within the region of 6p covered by the Cardon *et al.* [6,32] and Grigorenko *et al.* [1] studies. (The C4 protein is involved in activating the complement cascade in response to pathogens, so that the pathogens can be attacked and lysed by the immune system.) In this study, dyslexia was broadly defined, using DSM-IIIR criteria. Typing of the C4B protein, rather than DNA typing, was used to define a null allele (one which does not produce a protein). Twelve subjects with dyslexia were typed, and the null allele was found in eight of the 12, compared with 16 of 79 control subjects. This represented a significant increase in the dyslexic subjects ($P < 0.001$) and would be supportive of the linkage results of Cardon *et al.* [6,32] and Grigorenko *et al.* [1]. However, the sample size is quite small, and the method for choosing control subjects is not described. Also, because typing was at the protein rather than gene level, more than one allele may be represented if there is more than one mutation, which can result in lack of a gene product. Second, it is also possible that the associated marker allele is actually responsible for liability for the phenotype. Because the associated allele is usually not present in all of the individuals with the disorder, it could be a QTL or a susceptibility locus.

Finally, an apparent association can also be an artifact of population stratification. For example, if the individuals with a disorder are drawn from a separate ethnic population from the individuals without the disorder and if the allele frequencies for the marker allele are different for the two ethnic groups, a specific allele could be more frequent in the affected population than the unaffected population simply because it is more frequent in that ethnic group as a whole. This phenomenon may be responsible for a number of the failures to replicate associations [40].

The problem of stratification between affected and unaffected populations can be alleviated by using within-family control subjects, *ie*, the "control population" becomes the parental alleles that are not transmitted to affected offspring. This is the basis of the haplotypebased haplotype relative risk method [41,42]. The frequency with which a given allele is transmitted by each parent to an affected child is compared with the frequency of that same allele in the parental homolog that was not transmitted to the child. Terwilliger [43] has developed a maximum likelihood method of association analysis that can consider multiple alleles and closely linked loci.

Association analysis can be an important tool for identifying QTLs, since it is even less sensitive to misdiagnosis, decreased penetrance, and genetic heterogeneity than allele-sharing analyses [44–46], and it has been able to detect loci that linkage is unable to identify. However, it requires a large sample size. In addition, it is not generally considered to be a good screening tool for linkage in an outbred population since it is likely that linkage will have to be quite close in order for disequilibrium to exist, meaning that many closely spaced markers would need to be typed [7]. However, as laboratory procedures are increasingly automated and if costs decrease, genome screens with association analysis may become more common. It can be applicable when there are a reasonable number of candidate loci, which have already been identified. Ultimately, association can identify causal mutations within a gene.

Linkage and association analysis can be used to identify a small region containing a gene influencing the phenotype, but this region will likely contain many genes, and any one of them may contain the causal mutation. To be efficient, the researcher will need to prioritize the search for mutations to candidates that are thought to be involved in the pathogenesis of the trait. Sometimes candidates are quite clear—a gene that influences a similar trait in an animal model, for example, or is known to be involved in a metabolic pathway that is critical to the trait. A gene known to affect neural migration in fetal brain would be a good candidate for a reading disability gene, however, there can be surprises. The same gene may have different effects in an animal model, or a protein may not be known to have a functional relationship to a trait until the linkage is established, so once the plausible candidates have been exhausted, the remaining candidate genes may need to be screened.

Ultimately, association can identify alleles that are actually the causal mutations within a candidate gene. The challenge is to determine whether a particular DNA change in a gene is a benign polymorphism linked to the causal mutation or if it is the mutation itself. It can be difficult to determine if it is causal, particularly if the mutation only confers susceptibility, such that it is not present in all affected individuals. To be considered a candidate mutation, DNA sequencing of the gene and the mutation must demonstrate that the mutation is likely to have functional significance, such as production of a frameshift mutation or stop codon, alteration of an intron or exon splice junction, presence in highly conserved region of the gene, or alteration of a critical amino acid in a possible binding site. Finally, the association of the mutation with the phenotype must be replicated in an independent population.

Once a gene influencing a trait is identified, the fascinating work begins to delineate the pathogenesis. "Knockout" animal models can be used, and detailed studies of individuals who can be demonstrated to carry the mutation can be done. In this way, the effects of the gene on development can be determined, and hopefully this will lead to the most appropriate therapies.

Acknowledgments

This research was supported by two NICHD Center grants: Learning Disability Research Center grant P50 HD27802 and Mental Retardation Research Center grant P30 HD04024, and by two NIMH grants: K02 MH00419 (RSA) and R37 MH38820 (MERIT).

Abbreviation

QTL   quantitative trait locus

References and recommended reading

Papers of particular interest, published within the annual period of review, have been highlighted as:

- •   Of special interest
- ••   Of outstanding interest

1. Grigorenko EL, Wood FB, Meyer MS, Hart LA, Speed WC, Shuster A,
•• Pauls DL: **Susceptibility loci for distinct components of developmental dyslexia on chromosomes 6 and 15**. *Am J Hum Genet* 1997, **60**:27–39.
   Uses measures of different cognitive components of reading to test for differential linkage in a sample of dyslexic families. Found that deficits in phoneme awareness were linked to markers on the short arm of chromosome 6, whereas deficits in single word reading were linked to a marker near the centromere of chromosome 15. Exemplifies the interdisciplinary interaction between cognitive neuroscience and genetics needed to identify genes which influence complex behaviors.

2. Pennington BF: **Using genetics to dissect cognition [invited editorial]**.
• *A Hum Genet* 1997, **60**:13–16.
   A discussion of Grigorenko *et al.* [1••] that also summarizes previous work on the cognitive phenotype and genetics of developmental dyslexia.

3. Orton ST: **Word-blindness in school children**. *Arch Neurol Psychiatr* 1925, **14**:582–615.

4. Orton ST: *Reading, Writing, and Speech Problems in Children*. New York: Norton; 1937.

5. Smith SD, Kimberling WJ, Pennington BF, Lubs HA: **Specific reading disability: identification of an inherited form through linkage and analysis**. *Science* 1983, **219**:1345–1347.

6. Cardon LR, Smith SD, Fulker DW, Kimberling WJ, Pennington BF, DeFries JC: **Quantitative trait locus for reading disability on chromosome 6**. *Science* 1994, **266**:276–279.

7. Lander ES, Schork NJ: **Genetic dissection of complex traits**. *Science* 1994, **265**:2037–2048.

8. Plomin, R, Owen JM, McGuffin P: **The genetic basis of complex human behaviors**. *Science* 1994, **264(5166)**:1733–1739.

9. Greenberg DA: **Linkage analysis of "necessary" disease loci versus "susceptibility" loci**. *Am J Hum Genet* 1993, **52**:135–143.

10. Erlich HA, Zeidler A, Chang J, Shaw S, Raffel LJ, Klitz W, Beshkov Y, Costin G, Pressman S, Bugawan T, Rotter J: **HLA class II alleles and susceptibility and resistance to insulin dependent diabetes mellitus In Mexican-American families.** *Nature Genet* 1993, **3**:358–364.

11. Davies JL, Dawaguchi Y, Bennett ST, Copeman JB, Cordell HJ, Pritchard LE, Reed P, Gough S, Jenkins S, Palmer S, *et al.*: **A genome-wide search for human type 1 diabetes susceptibility genes.** *Nature* 1994, **371**:130–136.

12. Field LL, Tobias R, Magnus T: **A locus on chromosome 15q26 (IDDM3) produces susceptibility ot insulin-dependent diabetes mellitus.** *Nature Genet* 1994, **8**:189–194.

13. Hashimoto L, Habita C, Beressi JP, Delepine M, Besse C, Cambon-Thomsen A, Deschamps I, Rotter J, Djoulah S, James M, *et al.*: **Genetic mapping of a susceptibility locus for insulin-dependent diabetes mellitus on chromosome 11q.** *Nature* 1994, **371**:161–164.

14. Cordell HJ, Todd JA: **Multifactorial inheritance in type 1 diabetes.** *Trends Genet* 1995, **11**:499–504.

15. Luo DF, Jui MM, Muir A, Maclaren NK, Thomson G, She JX: **Affected sib-pair mapping of a novel susceptibility gene to insulin-dependent diabetes mellitus (IDDM8) on chromosome 6q25–q27.** *Am J Hum Genet* 1995, **57**:991–919.

16. Pericek-Vance MA, Haines JL: **Genetic susceptibility to Alzheimer disease.** *Trends Genet* 1995, **11**: 504–508.

17. Murray JC: **Face facts: genes, environment, and clefts.** *Am J Hum Genet* 1995, **57**:227–232.

18. Cook EH, Stein MA, Kraswoski MD, Cox JN, Kieffer JE, Leventhal BL: **Association of attention-deficit disorder and the dopamine transporter gene.** *Am J Hum Genet* 1995, **56**:993–998.

19. Frangiakalds JM, Ewart AK, Morris CA, Mervis CB, Bertrand J, Robinson BF, Klein B, Ensing G, Everett L, Green E, *et al.*: **LIM-kinase1 hemizygosity implicated in impaired visuospatial constructive cognition.** *Cell* 1996, **86**: 59–69.

20. Smith DJ, Stevens ME, Sudanagunta SP, Bronson RT, Makhinson M, Watabe AM, O'Dell T, Fung T, Weir H-u, *et al.*: **Functional screening of 2Mb of human chromosome 21q22.2 in transgenic mice implicates *minibrain* in learning defects associated with Down syndrome.** *Nat Genet* 1997, **16**:28–36.

21. Plomin R, McClearn GE, Smith DL, Vignetti S, Chorney MJ, Chorney K, Venditti CP, Kasarda S, Thompson L, Detterman D, Daniels J, *et al.*: **DNA markers associated with high versus low IO: the IQ quantitative trait loci (QTL) project.** *Behav Genet* 1994, **24**:107–118.

22. Morton NE: **Sequential tests for the detection of linkage.** *Am J Hum Genet* 1955, **7**:227–318.

23. Curtis D, Sham PC: **Model-free linkage analysis using likelihoods.** *Am J Hum Genet* 1995, **57**:703–715.

24. Pauls DL: **Behavioral disorders: lessons in linkage.** *Nature Genet* 1993, **3**:4–5.

25. Rutter M: **Psychiatric genetics: research challenges and pathways forward.** *Am J Med Genet (Neuropsychiat Genet)* 1994, **54**:185–198.

26. Risch N, Zhang H: **Extreme discordant sib pairs for mapping quantitative trait loci in humans.** *Science* 1995, **268**:1584–1589.

27. Cardon LR, Fulker DW: **The power of interval mapping of quantitative trail loci, using selected sib pairs.** *Am J Hum Gen* 1994, **55**:825–833.

28. Haseman JK, Elston RC: **The investigation of linkage between a quantitative trait and a marker locus.** *Behav Genet* 1972, **2**:3–19.
29. Fulker DW, Cardon LR, DeFries JC, Kimberling WJ, Pennington BF, Smith SD: **Multiple regression analysis of sib pair data on reading to detect quantitative trait loci.** *Reading and Writing: An Interdisciplinary Journal* 1991, **3**:299–313.
30. Kruglyak L, Lander ES: **Complete multipoint sib-pair analysis of qualitative and quantitative traits.** *Am J Hum Genet* 1995, **57**:439–454.
31. Fulker DW, Cherry SS, Cardon LR: **Multipoint interval mapping of quantitative trait loci using sib pairs.** *Am J Hum Genet* 1995, **56**:1224–1233.
32. Cardon LR, Smith SD, Fulker DW, Kimberling WJ, Pennington BF, DeFries JC: **Quantitative trait locus for reading disability: a correction.** *Science* 1995, **68**:5217.
33. Collins FS: **Positional cloning moves from perditional to traditional.** *Nature Genet* 1995, **9**:347–350.
34. Ott J: *Analysis of Human Genetic Linkage.* Baltimore: The Johns Hopkins University Press; 1985.
35. Faraway JJ: **Distribution of the admixture test for the detection of linkage under heterogeneity.** *Gen Epidem* 1993, **10**:75–83.
36. Weeks DE, Lathrop GM: **Polygenic disease: methods for mapping complex disease traits.** *Trends in Genetics* 1995, **11**:513–519.
37. Lander E, Kruglyak L: **Genetic dissection of complex traits: guidelines for interpreting and reporting linkage results.** *Nat Genet* 1995, **11**:241–247.
38. Thomson G: **Identifying complex disease genes: progress and paradigms.** *Nature Genet* 1994, **8**:108–110.
39. Warren RP. Singh VK, Averett RE, Odell JD, Maciulis A, Burger RA, Daniels WW, Warren WL: **Immunogenetic studies in autism and related disorders.** *Molec Chem Neuropath* 1996, **28**:77–81.
40. Kidd KK: **Associations of disease with genetic markers: Déjà vu all over again.** *Am J Med Gen (Neuropsychiatric Genetics)* 1993, **48**:71–73.
41. Falk CT, Rubenstein P: **Haplotype relative risks: an easy reliable way to construct a proper control sample for risk calculations.** *Ann Hum Gen* 1987, **51**:227–233.
42. Terwilliger JD, Ott J: **A haplotype-based "haplotype relative risk" approach to detecting allelic associations.** *Hum Heredity* 1992, **42**:337–346.
43. Terwilliger JD: **A powerful likelihood method for the analysis of linkage disequilibrium between trait loci and one or more polymorphic marker loci.** *Am J Hum Genet* 1995, **56**:777–787.
44. Crowe RR: **Candidate genes in psychiatry: an epidemiological perspective.** *Am J Med Genet (Neuropsychiatric Genetics)* 1993, **48**:74–77.
45. Hodge SE: **Linkage analysis versus association analysis: distinguishing between two models that explain disease-marker associations.** *Am J Hum Genet* 1993, **53**:367–384.
46. Spielman RS, McGinnis RE, Ewens WJ: **Transmission test for linkage disequilibrium: the insulin gene region and insulin-dependent diabetes mellitus (IDDM).** *Am J Hum Genet* 1993, **52**:506–516.

129

DEVELOPMENTAL
DYSCALCULIA

Ruth S. Shalev, Raaya Weirtman and Naomi Amir

Source: *Cortex*, 24, 1988: 555–561.

Abstract

We conducted a neurobehavioral evaluation on eleven children with developmental dyscalculia in order to determine which aspects of arithmetic processes are affected in this disorder. Our results indicate that memorization of numerical facts in these children was poor or virtually non-existent and the ability to solve simple arithmetic exercises impaired. By contrast, comprehension and production of number functions were intact. Although all children had been referred for evaluation of selective deficits in arithmetic skills, they also displayed a mild degree of dyslexia, dysgraphia, anomia, and grapho-motor dysfunction. We conclude that cognitive mechanisms underlying arithmetic ability can be dissociated developmentally and suggest that remediation programs be designed only after detailed analyses of arithmetic and associated cognitive skills.

Developmental dyscalculia (DD) is a primary cognitive disorder of childhood manifested by a disturbance in arithmetic ability (Slade and Russell, 1971). Dyscalculia has been used as a general term, encompassing all aspects of arithmetic difficulty. However, it is unclear which specific parameters of arithmetic function are impaired in DD. The literature on adults with acquired dyscalculia distinguishes between dyscalculia due to aphasic deficit, to visuo-spatial disorders and to impairment of calculation per se (Hecaen, Angelergues and Houilliers, 1961; Grewel, 1952; Benson and Weir, 1972). For children with DD this classification has been modified to include alexia and agraphia for numbers, spatial dyscalculia, anarithmetia, attentional-sequential dyscalculia and mixed type (Badian, 1983).

More recently, cognitive scientists (McCloskey, Caramazza and Basili, 1985) studying acquired dyscalculia in adults, have departed from the approach of ascribing deficits to a single area of neuropsychological dysfunction. A model was devised based on their definition of normal number processing and calculation. McCloskey *et al.* (1985) define normal arithmetic function in terms of three subskills: number comprehension, number production and calculation processing. The comprehension category includes comprehension of quantities, the symbolic nature of numbers (lexical processing), and digit order (syntactic processing). The number production subsystems are counting, reading, and writing numbers. Calculation is subdivided into comprehending operational symbols (eg. +, −), executing arithmetic exercises and memorizing numerical fact. We applied this model to eleven children with DD.

Materials and methods

Subjects

Eleven children referred to the Neuropediatric Diagnostic Unit of the Bikur Cholim Hospital for a selective deficit in learning arithmetic participated in this study. Criteria for inclusion were normal perinatal history, neurological development, hearing and vision in addition to normal intelligence (see Table I) and attendance in the regular school system. None of the children had any major psychiatric or emotional difficulties. There were 4 boys and 7 girls, 9.8–15 years old at time of testing. The youngest child was in fifth

Table I Data in Dyscalculic Children.

Subjects	Age	Sex	Handedness	Grade	IQ	WISC-R VIQ	WISC-R PIQ
1	15.3	M	R	10	94	90	101
2	14.8	M	R	9	112	106	118
3	12.4	M	R	7	115	109	118
4	10.3	M	R	5	105	98	112
5	11.9	F	R	6	92	87	100
6	11.9	F	R	6	109	101	115
7	11.8	F	R	6	91	84	102
8	11.2	F	R	5	84	80	91
9	10.0	F	R	5	119	95	142
10	10.0	F	R	5	102	100	107
11	9.8	F	R	5	105	99	112

grade. Children younger than this were excluded to eliminate those with relative inexperience with arithmetic.

Ten normal children ages 9.7–11.3 served as controls. They were chosen by their teachers who considered them to be normal achievers in arithmetic.

Test and procedure

Diagnostic battery

The following tests were administered to all children with DD: WISC-R, reading and reading comprehension of age appropriate material, dictation and written description of the cookie-theft picture of the Boston Diagnostic Aphasia Examination (Goodglass and Kaplan, 1972), and a comprehensive battery of arithmetic tests (see below). Depending on the specific complaints, additional testing was administered, including the Boston naming test (40 items) (Kaplan, Goodglass and Weintraub, 1983), sentence repetition (Wechsler, 1974), Raven's colored progressive matrices (Raven, 1965), and three dimensional house drawing (Goodglass and Kaplan, 1972).

Arithmetic battery

This battery of tests was constructed to evaluate number comprehension, number production and calculation processing, and was administered to both subjects and controls.

Tests devised primarily for number comprehension included:

(1) *Matching Written Arabic Numbers to Quantities*: In a multiple choice task, the children matched the appropriate quantity of drawn stimuli (dots or dashes) to a single written arabic number. There were 6 such tasks.

(2) *Appreciation of Relative Quantities*: Two groups of identically shaped non-numerical stimuli were drawn on each of 4 cards. The children were asked to indicate the group with more, less or equivalent number of stimuli.

(3) *Comprehension of Quantities*: On a multiple choice task, the children had to choose 2 equal quantities of stimuli which were composed of different shapes and in different spatial orientations. The number of stimuli ranged from 2 to 9; there were 6 tasks in this group.

(4) *Comprehension of Numerical Values*: The children, presented with 9 pairs of written arabic numbers (e.g. 15, 21) were required to identify the larger or smaller member of each pair. The same task was repeated orally.

(5) *Serial Order*: Children were presented with 2 groups of written numbers (e.g. 111, 11, 101, 1011) which were to be ordered by quantity, from smaller to greater and vice-versa.

Tests devised for number production included:

(1) *Counting Task*: The children were asked to count aloud numbers of stimuli (dots, dashes, etc) appearing in rows or groups. The number of stimuli ranged from 4 to 13; there where 6 such tasks.
(2) *Production (Writing) of Numbers*: Writing and reading 4 single and 8 multidigit arabic and verbal numbers to dictation and copy.

Tests of calculation processing included:

(1) *Comprehension of Operation symbols*: The children were shown the symbol, asked to name and give example of appropriate arithmetic operation for +, −, ×, /.
(2) *Fact Retrieval*: The children were required to do 10 oral computation of simple, presumably memorized addition, subtraction, multiplication and division exercises, e.g. 12 − 9, 6 × 3, 21/7.
(3) *Calculation*: Written arithmetic exercises in addition, subtraction, multiplication and division were presented. The children had first to copy and compute the arithmetic problems. There were 8 items in each operation. The exercises became progressively more complex beginning from single numerical units, e.g. 3 − 2, 9/3, 16 × 14, 192/3. Some of the exercises required "carrying over". A similar task where the children had to write the exercises from dictation was also done.

Results

Arithmetic errors were subdivided into categories of number comprehension, number production and calculation; the mean scores of the dyscalculic children and controls are listed in Table II. The 10 control children made no errors on tests of number comprehension and production. On the calculation subset, 3 children made errors on double digit multiplication (e.g. 16 × 14) and multidigit division (124/4) which they could not correct. The remaining children performed correctly on all problems.

Arithmetic errors were similarly subdivided for the dyscalculic children. Ten DD children performed without error on all tasks assessing number comprehension and no differences were found between the two groups (Table II). Concepts of quantities were present in 10 children. One child (case 8) had difficulties in comprehending verbal concepts of "greater" and "less" and made a considerable number of errors on the comprehension of relative quantities task.

In the number production category mild difficulties were seen in syntactical processing in 2 children and counting in 1 child. The syntactical errors seen (cases 6, 8) were, for example, writing 15 instead of 51. Counting was impaired in 1 child (case 7), who could not synchronize oral counting to the

Table II Mean Scores for Arithmetic Battery.

Arithmetic Battery Subtests	Dyscalculic Ss Mean ± S.D.	Controls Mean ± S.D.	chi-square
Number comprehension			
1. Matching Numbers to quantity	9.4 ± 2.0	10.0 ± 0.0	
2. Appreciation of relative quantity	9.5 ± 1.5	10.0 ± 0.0	
3. Comprehension of quantity	10.0 ± 0	10.0 ± 0.0	
4. Comprehension of numerical rulers	10.0 ± 0	10.0 ± 0.0	
5. Serial order	10.0 ± 0	10.0 ± 0.0	
Number production			
1. Counting	9.5 ± 1.5	10.0 ± 0.0	
2. Reading Numbers	10.0 ± 0	10.0 ± 0.0	
3. Writing Numbers	9.4 ± 1.4	10.0 ± 0.0	
Calculation			
1. Comprehension of operat symbols	9.5 ± 1.0	10.0 ± 0.0	
2. Fact retreival	5.5 ± 2.3	9.5 ± 0.9	14.12*
3. Addition	7.5 ± 1.9	10.0 ± 0.0	14.50*
4. Subtraction	6.0 ± 2.3	10.0 ± 0.0	14.48*
5. Multiplication	6.0 ± 1.9	9.5 ± 0.9	13.23*
6. Division	3.2 ± 1.4	9.3 ± 1.2	15.67*

* These tasks were significant at the .001 level according to chi-square approximation.

movement of her finger. The scores of the dyscalculic children were essentially similar to those of the controls.

The calculation category was the area of primary difficulty and the scores of the DD children are listed in Table III. In 5 of 6 subtests in this category, their scores were significantly lower than those of the controls. All 11 DD children understood calculation symbols of addition, subtraction and multiplication while only 9 comprehended the division symbol. The more severely impaired children demonstrated difficulties in addition, subtraction and multiplication as well as division. All DD subjects failed on division.

Table III Calculation Processing Scores for 11 Dyscalculic Children.

	Subjects										
Calculation tasks	1	2	3	4	5	6	7	8	9	10	11
Fact Retrieval	4.0	7.0	8.0	4.0	6.0	8.0	5.0	3.0	8.0	1.0	6.0
Addition	8.0	8.0	9.0	7.5	7.0	8.5	7.5	3.0	10.0	5.5	9.0
Subtraction	6.0	8.0	9.0	5.5	7.5	10.0	3.5	3.0	7.5	4.5	8.0
Multiplication	3.5	5.5	8.0	5.0	6.0	9.0	6.5	3.5	7.0	4.0	8.0
Division	3.5	4.0	3.0	4.5	4.5	3.5	0.0	1.5	4.5	3.0	3.0

Two children were unable to add past "10" although the remaining 9 could do more complex addition. Only 1 child (case 9) could subtract at near-age appropriate level. Three had difficulties in single digit subtraction exercises (e.g. 7 – 2) and 2 others in 2 digit number exercise (e.g. 15 – 6). They used strategies such as finger counting or counting other visible concrete objects to arrive at the correct answer.

Three children could not perform single digit multiplication exercises e.g. 5 × 6, but could solve problems if the answer was 10 or below, e.g. 2 × 5. Three other children could do overlearned multiplication table exercises but if the exercise was not routine e.g. 13 × 3 or more complex, e.g. 142 × 3, they would err. The children were unable to use the knowledge learned from one exercise to solve a similar problem presented immediately afterward. For example, although the child could solve 10 × 2, he could not then solve 11 × 2.

Division was impaired in all children. Two (cases 7, 8) could not solve exercises which involved numbers lower than 10 (e.g. 9/3), the remainder failing with exercises such as 21/7, 24/6. The children were also unable to explain or demonstrate the division process conceptually or technically. For example, 24/6 would be approached, unsuccessfully, as an addition problem: 6 + 6 + 6 = 24 (sic). Faulty technique was seen then children would attempt to solve a task such as 72/3 backwards from right to left.

The DD children who were more proficient in calculation also had the more readily accessible and extensive fact inventories. Those who did have some fact inventory were the best calculators. However, no such factual memory for division could be elicited. For exercises such as 6 × 3 the child could retrieve the answer, yet not for 18/6.

There were additional cognitive deficits. All of the DD children had some reading disability (1–2 years below class level), 10 had evidence of dysgraphia; and anomia was present in 9. Five of 6 children were impaired on sentence repetition, a test of attention and short term verbal memory. Grapho-motor skills, as assessed by copy of 3-dimensional house, were impaired in 8 children. By contrast, Raven's matrices, administered to 6 children, was normal in 5. Performance IQ (7) was considerably higher than verbal IQ in all children and for the group there was a 16 point difference between the two (Table I). The total IQ of the children ranged from 84–119.

Discussion

In this group of adolescent and pre-adolescent dyscalculic children memorization and retrieval of calculation facts was severely impaired, as was the ability to calculate, particularly divide. In contrast number compehension and number production was virtually intact in 10 of the 11 children.

Typically the children had difficulty in fact retrieval but could show that they knew how to calculate by using finger counting and other appropriate strategies. Each exercise was approached as if for the first time ever, even when the child had just solved an essentially similar exercise. Though a few children had considerable memory and fact retrieval for the calculation procedures they could perform, for division none of the children understood the operation nor had they any division fact memory at their disposal. The combined deficits preclude easy categorization into the Badian (1983) classification of DD. The difficulties these children have is not just an anarithmetia where there is confusion carrying out arithmetic operations coexisting with adequate knowledge of number facts and tables. The sequential-attentional category is also not applicable; in that category forgetting to remember and difficulty learning tables are the focus of the arithmetic problems. In another seven part classification scheme, the number fact memory issue is not addressed (Kosc, 1971).

Investigators studying arithmetic disabilities in children have proposed that DD children have short term memory systems which develop at a slower rate than normals (Siegel and Linder, 1984), and that their inability to carry and recall number tables is the result of memory deficits (Cohen, 1971). Their incompetency in arithmetic has been attributed to a failure to memorize and automatize basic number facts rather than a problem in comprehension of the arithmetic operations (Ackerman, Anhalt and Dykman, 1986). In fact, the failure to automatize is considered relevant to learning disabilities in general (Garnett and Fleishner, 1983). However, the direct relationship between fact memorization and the ability to calculate seen in this study suggest that in some developing children the memory aspect of arithmetic may be dependent upon a prior understanding of the calculation procedure. By contrast, in adults with the acquired form of the disorder, fact retrieval can still exist in persons who have lost their previously normal ability to calculate (McCloskey et al., 1985).

Memory was not the only difficulty handicapping these children. They displayed varying degrees, of dyslexia, dysgraphia, anomia and graphomotor impairment. In this group DD is the most severe manifestation of a wider range of cognitive disorders. Thus in children with DD, the approach we recommend is to define which area of arithmetic processing is impaired and test for contributory cognitive impairment.

Acknowledgements

We thank Drs. L. Obler, M. Kinsbourne, M. L. Albert for their useful comments and Dr. H. Brownell for statistical advice.

References

ACKERMAN, P. T., ANHALT, J. M., and DYKMAN, R. A. Arithmetic automatisation failure in children with attention and reading disorders: associations and sequela. *Journal of Learning Disabilities, 19*: 222–232, 1986.

BADIAN, N. A. Dyscalculia and nonverbal disorders of learning. In H. R. Miklebust (Ed.), *Progress in Learning Disabilities*, 5. New York: Grune and Stratton, Inc., 1983, pp. 235–264.

BENSON, D. F., and WEIR, W. F. Acalculia: acquired anarithmetia. *Cortex*, 8: 465–472, 1972.

BOLLER, F., and GRAFMAN, J. Acalculia: Historical development and current significance. *Brain and Cognition*, 2: 205–223, 1983.

COHEN, R. Dyscalculia. *Archives of Neurology*, 4: 301–307, 1961.

GARNETT, K., and FLEISCHNER, J. Automatization and basic fact performance of normal and learning disabled children. *Learning Disability Quarterly*, 6: 223–230, 1983.

GOODGLASS, H., and KAPLAN, E. The Assessment of Aphasia and Related Disorders. Philadelphia: Lea and Febiger, 1972.

GREWEL, F. Acalculia. *Brain*, 75: 397–407, 1952.

HÉCAEN, H., ANGELERGUES, R., and HOUILLIERS, S. Les variétés cliniques des acalculies au cours des lésions retrorolandiques: approche statistique du problème. *Revue Neurologique*, 105: 85–103, 1961.

KAPLAN, E., GOODGLASS, H., and WEINTRAUB, S. *Boston Naming Test*. Philadelphia: Lea and Febiger, 1983.

KOSC, L. Developmental dyscalculia. *Journal of Learning Disabilities*, 7: 164–177, 1974.

McCLOSKEY, J., CARAMAZZA, A., and BASILI, A. Cognitive mechanisms in number processing and calculation: evidence from dyscalculia. *Brain and Cognition*, 4: 171–196, 1985.

RAVEN, J. C. *Guide to Using the Coloured Progressive Matrices*. London: H.K. Lewis; New York: Psychological Corporation, 1965.

SLADE, P. D., and RUSSELL, G. F. M. Developmental dyscalculia: a brief report on four cases. *Psychological Medicine*, 1: 292–298, 1971.

WECHSLER, D. *Wechsler Preschool and Primary Scale of Intelligence*. New York: Psychological Corporation, 1967.

130

CHILDREN WITH DEVELOPMENTAL DYSCALCULIA

Neil Gordon

Source: *Developmental Medicine and Child Neurology*, 34, 1992: 459–463.

Some children present with learning difficulties which impede their progress in school, in spite of satisfactory spoken and written language-skills. For example about 6 or 7 per cent of seven- and eight-year-old children have difficulties of co-ordination sufficient to affect their acquisition of motor skills[1]. some of these children may also have impairments of speech and language, but often they do not. Although such disorders are not always recognised as specific disabilities, they should be if an adequate assessment is carried out. However, it can be very difficult to identify certain disabilities if they affect an aspect of learning of a particularly subtle kind.

There is no doubt that some children do have considerable difficulties in acquiring the expected skill in numeracy for their age. Sometimes this not due to a specific learning disorder, but to factors such as missing the relevant lessons, emotional disorders, below-average intelligence, and lack of interest and motivation; the last is sometimes related to socio-economic factors[2]. If the disability is due to a specific developmental dyscalculia, the child may well not be referred for assessment because such a disability is much more socially acceptable than an inability to read or write, and is not thought to be a serious educational problem. Often people will say, with a degree of pride, 'I was never any good at maths'.

It has been estimated that 6 per cent of the school population has serious problems with arithmetic and, especially if they have behaviour difficulties, there may be little provision for helping these children[3]. There is no doubt that this disability is particularly complex, and that no single cause can explain all the different types of dyscalculia; and this may well account for the number of theories which try to do this. Dyscalculic children seem to omit facial features in their drawings, especially the nose, and BADIAN[4] suggests that this may be due to lack of visual attention to exact details. Certainly there seems to be evidence that a child's drawing can predict later numerical ability. It has been suggested that children with a severe disability of this kind, but with normal reading ability, have not advanced to the Piagetian stage of concrete operations needed for numerical but not reading skills[5]. In addition, memory may play an important part, being often related to attainment, especially if it is difficult for a child to recall ways of tackling problems.

Links between dyscalculia and right cerebral hemisphere dysfunction

Of particular importance is a link between right cerebral function and dyscalculia, and therefore between spatial and mathematical abilities. This could be due to an inability to point accurately to objects being counted, resulting in errors—a trend which may develop into poor calculation. If inco-ordination resulting from visual spatial dysfunction is particularly severe, various other aspects of learning motor skills will be affected, such as speech articulation, and the acquisition of reasonably neat writing; with all the effects this will have on social behaviour[6]. Abnormal behaviour may be a factor, but it is the link between these two disabilities which is of fundamental importance; there can be no doubt about the spatial quality of mathematics, with figures set out in rows, diagrams having crossing lines, and equations having figures with functions dependent on their position in space[2]. General intelligence, verbal and spatial ability, and specific numerical skills are all involved in the attainment of mathematics, but verbal ability may have only an indirect relationship with the latter; those with specific mathematical difficulties usually do better on performance than on verbal tasks. Children with treated phenylketonuria tend to show deficits in conceptual and visual spatial skills, which may explain their reported difficulty with mathematics[7]. BERRY et al.[8] also found that treated phenylketonuric children had no apparent reading and spelling disability, but their arithmetic scores were significantly low. Boys tend to be better than girls at mathematics and also spatial tasks, but this could be due to cultural influences[9].

ROURKE and FINLAYSON[10] studied 45 nine- to 14-year-old children with learning disabilities. They were divided into three groups: those who were deficient in reading, spelling and arithmetic; those who were good at arithmetic, compared with their standard in reading and spelling; and those whose reading and spelling were good, but who had difficulties with arithmetic. The performance of the first two groups was better than that of the third on measures of visuo-perceptual and visuo-spatial abilities; the third group was better on measures of verbal and auditory-perceptual abilities, as might be expected. The findings indicate that the first two groups performed in a way which suggests left cerebral dysfunction, and the third group in a way suggesting right cerebral dysfunction. This is compatible with a right cerebral superiority for certain types of calculation, involving visuo-spatial organisation and integration. As will be discussed later, some functions of the left cerebral hemisphere play a part in numeracy skills, and obviously it is dangerous to localise cerebral functions too specifically. Certainly the educational approach to the children in the three groups will be different, and the pattern of abilities and deficits exhibited by the various types of learning-disabled children must be carefully specified before remedial education is planned. The results of psychometric tests in Turner's syndrome show that affected girls do relatively well on verbal tests, but poorly on performance and numerical ones. It is suggested that in this syndrome there is involvement of the right parietal lobe, possibly related to the basic chromosome defects[11]. All this strongly supports the association between perceptual motor disabilities and dyscalculia, both being evidence of right cerebral hemisphere dysfunction.

The role of the left cerebral hemisphere is acquiring numeracy skills

This association between numeracy skills and right-hemisphere dysfunction is also recognised in acquired dyscalculia among adults, although the left cerebral hemisphere does contribute to certain aspects of this disability. Gerstmann syndrome, caused by lesions in the left parieto-occipital region, consists of finger agnosia, right-left disorientation, agraphia and acalculia. However, the last may be more of a manifestation of aphasia than a true disorder of numeracy; for example a difficulty in reading and writing numbers. Also there may be difficulties for the older child in solving arithmetical problems when there is evidence of left cerebral involvement, when instead of using the analytic abilities of this hemisphere, the child relies on more immature cognitive strategies of the right cerebral hemisphere. This hypothesis is compatible with a lag in the development of hemisphere specialisation[12].

Particularly in the early stages of development, the left cerebral hemisphere may play a signficant role in acquiring numeracy skills. COHN[6] points out that when a child learns the correspondence of quantities of things with particular sounds he is equipped for arithmetic operations, at least at the phonetic level. At the time that correspondence between number sounds and quantity occurs, the child appears ready to learn graphic number symbols, and because the number can be kept indelibly on paper while new correspondences are made, and also during the process of relational operations, graphic forms of calculations are capable of high accuracy and rapidity of execution.

A developmental type of Gerstmann syndrome has been described, consisting of constructional apraxia, spelling deficits and reading disabilities[13].

A possible cause of the reading and writing retardation could be a difficulty in the correct differentiation or arrangement of parts that constitute a whole, but this is open to doubt. The localising significance of congenital Gerstmann syndrome has still to be established.

Emotional and behavioural disorders and the right cerebral hemisphere

There are definite correlations between defective visuo-spatial organisation due to right-hemisphere dysfunction and disorders of behaviour. WEINTRAUB and MESULAM[14] have described the syndrome of right cerebral hemisphere dysfunction. Affected children suffer from emotional and interpersonal difficulties, shyness, visuo-spatial disturbances and problems with mathematics, as well as impairment of certain aspects of communication, such as poor eye-contact, absence of gesture and lack of speech prosody. In addition, there may be right-left confusion, poor sense of direction, and difficulty with tasks such as riding a bicycle. Social maturity is low.

Emotional and behavioural disorders are therefore likely to affect children with developmental dyscalculia, who tend to be maladjusted and asocial. In contrast, it has been shown that those who are good at mathematics are more secure, assertive, sociable and well adjusted. Those with right cerebral hemisphere dysfunction and learning disorders have difficulty understanding the affective state of others, and have a poor comprehension of non-verbal communication; there seems to be no doubt that there are differences in social behaviour associated with high and low verbal and numerical ability[4].

Emotional sensitivity involves the right cerebral hemisphere, and those with impaired function of this hemisphere, apart from having a low level of perception and imagery, often have impaired relationships with other children and few friends. When difficulties with arithmetic are found among such children with adequate performance on reading and writing, the learning disability can be considered a result of socio-economic disturbances. However, this is not always so, and if the dyscalculia is a specific entity an opportunity for successful remedial teaching can be lost[15]. It has been claimed that socio-emotional disturbances among learning-disabled children are due to central processing deficiencies[16].

Different types of developmental dyscalculia

Various types of developmental dyscalculia have been identified by BADIAN[4].

(1) Alexia and agraphia for numbers and words, which may be uncommon compared with other types of developmental dyscalculia and be obscured by the many different problems of children with dyslexia. However, these children may well have difficulties with the syntactical

properties of numbers, being apt to reverse the position of numbers and add additional zeros which impairs their mathematical skills.

(2) Spatial dyscalculia; for which there is considerable evidence. In written addition and subtraction this is exhibited by both horizontal and vertical confusion, and there can be considerable disorganisation when arranging rows and columns of figures. Telling the time proves difficult, with confusion of the hands of the clock and reversal of the hours and minutes when writing times. Oral mathematics and numerical reasoning is often superior to written calculation skills. The fact that numbering digits backwards is particularly difficult for these children may depend on the visuo-spatial component in this task.

(3) Anarithmetia, with a mix-up of the procedures involved in addition, subtraction and multiplication. There may also be extreme confusion in carrying out the tasks of written arithmetic. There are problems of memory, but the important defect is the muddle between one mathematical task and another.

(4) Attention-sequential dyscalculia, in which addition and subtraction are inaccurate, and there are difficulties in learning and recalling multiplication tables and the decimal point is often forgotten. This type is found among children with attention deficit syndrome.

(5) Mixed types of dyscalculia, as in Gerstmann syndrome, comparable to the mixed types of dyslexia in BODER's classification of this disability[17]. Although developmental dyscalculia reflects a congenital cerebral dysfunction, mixed types can simulate acquired dyscalculia in adults.

KOSC[18] uses a different classification of developmental dyscalculia: verbal, with difficulties in naming mathematical terms and relations; practognostic, with a disturbance of mathematical manipulation of real or pictured objects; lexical, with a disability in reading mathematical symbols; graphical, with a similar disability in manipulating mathematical symbols in writing; ideognostical, with an inability to understand mathematical ideas and relations in doing mental calculations; and operational, with the skill for carrying out mathematical operations directly disturbed. This type is also called anarithmetia, as in BADIAN's classification, and a typical example is an interchange of operations: addition instead of multiplication, subtraction instead of division, or the substitution of complex operations by simple ones.

Conclusions

Developmental dyscalculia, a developmental lag in the acquisition of numerical skills, can be manifested in a number of ways, including: inability to recognise number symbols; stephosymbolia or mirror writing: failure to recognise the basic mathematical operations or use of operator or separator symbols; inability to recall tables and 'carry' numbers in multiplication; and failure to maintain the proper order of numbers in calculation[6].

Some children seem to be born with a defective ability to discriminate and manipulate spatial and numerical relationships, and lack the basic tools of mathematics. Such children can make progress at first using learning by rote, but as they grow older they will find mathematics increasingly difficult; and this is likely to cause anxiety[2]. If teaching is inappropriate and there are adverse socio-economic conditions, there is a strong possibility that depression and anxiety will occur, with poor self-image, failure to reach full potential and a variety of behaviour disorders; common findings among children with learning difficulties. However, many children with learning disorders are not held in low esteem by their teachers, parents and peers, and can be popular, although they are always at risk of acquiring low social status[19]. Developmental dyscalculia may not have the stigma of some of the other learning disorders, but it is important that it is recognised when it occurs as a specific entity, and that the child is referred for a full assessment. Only then can management and educational help be logically planned.

SEMRUD-CLIKERMAN and HYND[20] have reviewed recent research on non-verbal learning disabilities and make recommendations for the future. There are inconsistencies among studies on children with learning disabilities and their social perception and interaction skills, but considering the great variation in methodology perhaps this is not surprising; and more studies are needed. Both cerebral hemispheres seem to contribute to mathematical skills in different ways, and it may be that only very specific deficits in arithmetic are manifested in children with learning disabilities of right cerebral origin. It is of special interest that experiments show that the thalamus on both sides is also involved. Dysfunction at this level may impede allocation of hemisphereic attentional resources implicated in developmental dyslexia, and deficits in sensory processing may involve subcortical structures, especially in right-hemisphere learning disorders related to visual-spatial input, and expression of emotion.

The delineation of subgroups is important for research, as is the link between dyscalculia and social perception, where both are manifestations of right cerebral hemisphere dysfunction. More may be learned from the study of acquired dyscalculia and the way this affects cerebral function, and the results applied to the developmental type. New remedial techniques can then be formulated.

References

1. Rutter, M., Tizard, J., Whitmore, K. (1970) *Education, Health and Behaviour.* London: Longman.
2. Lansdown, R. (1978) 'Retardation in mathematics: consideration of multifactorial determination.' *Journal of Child Psychology and Psychiatry,* **19**, 181–185.

3. Badian, N. A., Ghublikan, M. (1982) 'The personal-social characteristics of children with poor mathematical computation skills.' *Journal of Learning Disabilities*, **16**, 154–157.
4. Badian, N. A. (1983) 'Developmental dyscalculia.' *In* Mykelbust, H. R. (Ed.) *Progress in Learning Disabilities.* New York: Grune & Stratton.
5. Saxe, G., Shaheen, S. (1981) 'Piagetian theory and the atypical case: an analysis of the developmental Gerstmann's syndrome.' *Journal of Learning Disabilities*, **14**, 131–135.
6. Cohn, R. (1968) 'Developmental dyscalculia.' *Pediatric Clinics of North America*, **15**, 651–668.
7. Pennington, B. F., van Doorninck, W. J., McCabe, L. L., McCabe, E. R. B. (1985) 'Neurophysiological deficits in early treated phenylketonuric children.' *American Journal of Mental Deficiency*, **89**, 467–474.
8. Berry, H. K., O'Grady, D. J., Perlmutter, L. J., Bofinger, M. K. (1979) 'Intellectual development and academic achievement of children treated early for phenylketonuria.' *Developmental Medicine and Child Neurology*, **21**, 311–320.
9. Maccoby, E. M., Jacklin, C. N. (1974) *The Psychology of Sex Differences.* Stanford: Stanford University Press.
10. Rourke, B. P., Finlayson, M. A. J. (1978) 'Neurophysiological significance of variations in patterns of academic performance: verbal and visual-spatial abilities.' *Journal of Abnormal Child Psychology*, **6**, 121–133.
11. Money, J. (1973) 'Turner's syndrome and parietal lobe functions.' *Cortex*, **9**, 387–393.
12. Weinstein, M. A. (1980) 'A neurophysiological approach to math disability.' *New York University Education Quarterly*, **11**, 22–28.
13. Kinsbourne, M., Warrington, E. K. (1968) 'The developmental Gerstmann's syndrome.' *Archives of Neurology*, **8**, 490–501.
14. Weintraub, S., Mesulam, M. M. (1983) 'Developmental learning disabilities of the right hemisphere.' *Archives of Neurology*, **40**, 464–468.
15. Rourke, B. P., Strang, J. (1978) 'Neurophysiological significance of vairations in patterns of academic performance: motor, psychomotor and tactile-perceptual abilities.' *Journal of Pediatric Psychology*, **3**, 62–66.
16. Rourke, B. P., Fisk, J. L. (1981) 'Socio-emotional disturbances of learning disabled children: the role of central processing deficits.' *Bulletin of the Orton Society*, **31**, 77.
17. Boder, E. (1973) 'Developmental dyslexia: a diagnostic approach based on three atypical reading-spelling patterns.' *Developmental Medicine and Child Neurology*, **15**, 663–687.
18. Kosc, L. (1974) 'Developmental dyscalculia.' *Journal of Learning Disabilities*, **7**, 164–177.
19. Dudley-Marling, C. C., Edmiaston, R. (1985) 'Social status of learning-disabled children and adolescents: a review.' *Learning Disability Quarterly*, **8**, 189–204.
20. Semrud-Clikeman, M., Hynd, G. W. (1990) 'Right hemispheric dysfunction in non-verbal learning disabilities: social, academic and adaptive functioning in adults and children.' *Psychological Bulletin*, **107**, 196–209.

INDEX

Marcel, A. J. **IV** 412, 421
marginal babbling **II** 87
Marin, O. **IV** 412
Markman, A. B. **II** 3
Markman, E. M. **III** 291
Marsh, *et al.* **IV** 29–30
Marsh, G. **IV** 35
Marvin, R. S. **II** 534
maternal speech **II** 60
mathematics **IV** 143–54; calculations in informal circumstances **IV** 143; pedagogical assumption of educators **IV** 150; reasoning **I** 479
Mazzie, C. **II** 2
Mead, G. H. **III** 534
mean length of utterance (MLU) **IV** 393
Meaney, M. J. **I** 483
meaning: language **III** 204; speaker **III** 199; utterance **III** 199
mechanism: animal defense **III** 41–2; causal **III** 52; conception of **III** 152; of development **III** 148–55
Mehler, J. **II** 38, 49
memory **II** 396, 455, 479, 497, 523, **III** 207–12; accuracy of recognition **III** 434–5; and autism **II** 588; autobiographical **III** 426–40; Delayed Recall (DR) **III** 392–3; difficulties **I** 68; Immediate Recall (IR) **III** 392; influence of **I** 63; meta *see also:* metamemory; perceptual **III** 426–7, 439; Point and Name (PN) **III** 392–3; recall **II** 449; recognition **III** 375, 426–7; recognition in children **III** 376; retrospective **III** 516; short-term **III** 339–56, 454–64; system **II** 495; time-monitoring **III** 516–35; traces **II** 357; visual **III** 465; working **III** 302, 310, 313–14, 316, 318
mental: capacity **III** 48; contents **II** 534; representation **II** 522; retardation **II** 585
Mervis, C. **I** 166, 174, 221, 243–4
Messer, D. J. **II** 60, 143
Mesulam, M. **IV** 492
metacognition **III** 139, 153–4; awareness **III** 153–4; difficulties **III** 48; understanding **III** 152
metamemory **III** 491–515; condition **III** 505; free recall **III** 509

metaphor **III** 73; child-as-scientist **III** 124–57; computer **III** 261
metareasoning **III** 156
metric data qualities **IV** 55–6
metrical segmentation strategy **II** 51–2
microgenetic research **III** 150, 154
microinformation **III** 231–2
Mierkiewicz, **IV** 205, 207
Millar, W. **I** 98, 324
Miller, D. **I** 309, **II** 565, **IV** 14
Miller, G. A. **II** 275
Miller, R. **IV** 14
mimicry **III** 41
Minnesota **III** 539; and interracial adoption **III** 539
Miura, I. **IV** 220
mnemonic strategy **III** 405–25
Mnukhin, S. **IV** 281
monosyllables **II** 134
Montague, W. E. **I** 128, **III** 476
Montgomery, K. **I** 313
Morais, J. **IV** 14, 84
Mori, I. **I** 497
morphological marker **III** 247
morphological rules; the child's use of **II** 235
Morton, J. **III** 454, 463
Moskowitz, B. **IV** 25
Mossler, D. G. **II** 516, 534
mother-child free play **II** 119
mother-infant bonding **II** 6
motherese **II** 58–9, 168; as language teaching strategy **II** 79–80
mothers' speech **II** 61, 67, 168; verb uses **II** 219–28, 220, 222, 224–7
motion: c-shaped-tube problem **III** 96–7, 107; falling object problem **III** 97–102; knowledge about **III** 95–107; moving reference frame illusion **III** 98–9, 107; persistence theory **III** 127; problem **III** 96–9
motion verbs **II** 212
motor movement: measure of **I** 136–7; research in **I** 132–8; sequences **I** 177
movement **II** 363; distinction between passive and active **I** 313
Munsinger, H. **III** 552, 560
Murphy, C. M. **II** 143

naive: biology **I** 1; physics **I** 1
naming explosion **II** 172, 173–4, 182
naming game **II** 182